IN THE RING
WITH
BOB FITZSIMMONS

Adam J. Pollack

Win By KO Publications
Iowa City

In the Ring With Bob Fitzsimmons

Adam J. Pollack

(ISBN-13): 978-0-9799822-0-0

(ISBN-10): 0-9799822-0-0

(hardcover: 55# acid-free alkaline paper)

Library of Congress Control Number: 2007939210

Includes bibliographical references and index.

Cover design by Daniel Middleton ©

Manufactured in the United States of America.

Win By KO Publications

Iowa City, Iowa 52246

winbykopublications.com

Contents

Preface: The Series Continues

Welcome to the world of the fight to the finish, where championship bouts continued until someone was knocked out, where there were no mouthpieces, no handwraps, no protective foul cups, no training headgear, where floors and ring posts were often hard, when gloves were only five ounces and the eight-ounce glove was considered a big pillow to only be used in friendly exhibitions, when fights were never stopped on cuts, when a fight was rarely stopped just because a guy was a little wobbly or because he went down a number of times, where even decisions were based on who did the most damage and was the more aggressive, not just based on who knew how to tap, run, grab and survive. This was a time when your pay depended on success, when the phrase 'winner take all' was not just a bluff. These were some tough guys.

This is the third book in my heavyweight champion series, *Reigns of Fame and Shame*. The first two were *John L. Sullivan: The Career of the First Gloved Heavyweight Champion,* and *In the Ring With James J. Corbett.* My goal has been to answer the questions that no other book answered. I wanted history based not on speculation, hearsay, and legend, but based on what local reports said at the time.

I have found that achieving the richest and most complete understanding of these fighters' careers is accomplished by reference to multiple local primary source accountings. These accounts enliven the opponents and the fights, offer new facts, discuss issues that secondary sources failed to consider, and give fresh perspective on matters previously only discussed in a limited or incomplete way. Greater than ever before, this book offers a much stronger understanding of Bob Fitzsimmons' career, skills, and ability, and the era's fight scene, including top contenders and the legal, political, and social issues which affected the fight game.

Using mostly local contemporary newspaper reports, this book provides a more thorough analysis and detailed discussion of:

Bob Fitzsimmons' many Australian bouts. Local Australian primary sources shed new light on Fitz's early career, and show the long road he took to stardom. Because so many of the era's great fighters were produced in Australia, to understand the world's fight scene one must be familiar with Australian boxing.

Fitz's alleged fixed fight with Jim Hall. Find out whether Bob took a dive.

The legal and political fallout from the deaths of Con Riordan and Andy Bowen.

The alleged fixed fight with Tom Sharkey. The behind the scenes story is itself worth the price of admission. The court battle and all the sensational testimony are fully covered. Was it a grand conspiracy?

The complete back and forth verbal jousting, taunting, and confident exclamations between Fitzsimmons and Jim Corbett. No other fight ever had as much free advertising and hot discussion as a result of its mouthy combatants. They were the kings of smack talk, the inventors of building up fights with verbal and even physical confrontation.

The unbelievable legal and political battles the boxers and promoter Dan Stuart had to go through in order to bring fights off. This story has governors, armed militiamen, and judges threatening violence and lengthy prison sentences, following, chasing, and arresting these men, and generally impeding the sport's progress in any way that they could.

All of Fitzsimmons' American fights and most of his exhibitions (up to the heavyweight championship), including lesser known and previously unknown bouts, and massive pre- and post-fight coverage of his most significant bouts. This also includes Fitz and Corbett's daily training regimen leading up to their big fight. Even new controversial facts about the Corbett fight are revealed.

I hope you enjoy learning about Bob Fitzsimmons as much as I did!

CHAPTER 1

Australian Boxing

No discussion of boxing's magical 1880s to 1890s era is complete without talking about Australian boxing, where the true foundation of Bob Fitzsimmons' greatness was laid. During those decades, Australia produced a deep field of talented boxers that would become boxing's staple fighters. Most of them trained, fought, and exhibited at Larry Foley's Hall in Sydney, New South Wales, Australia. Foley was a fighter in his 30s who ran a fistic academy in the gymnasium at the rear of his White Horse Hotel on George Street. At some point, England's legendary former London Prize Ring Rules world bareknuckle champion Jem Mace came to live there, and both Foley and Mace provided young pupils valuable boxing instruction.

While boxing was tackling many legal obstacles in England and America, Australian law was a bit more lenient, especially during the rise of Queensberry rules boxing in the 1880s, which gave the sport a more civilized image. Without the constant need to worry about the law, boxing flourished in Australia. At his hall, Larry Foley legally hosted weekly gloved boxing bouts, which mostly included 4-round exhibitions, but sometimes lengthier fights to the finish.

Throughout the 1880s, the fraternity of talented boxers who sparred, trained, and exhibited with each other at Foley's included men such as Peter Jackson, Frank "Paddy" Slavin, Tom Lees, Jim Hall, Dan Creedon, Joe Goddard, Steve O'Donnell, Mick Dooley, Billy Smith, Billy McCarthy, Young Griffo, and Bob Fitzsimmons, but there were many others. Having in one city such a strong crop of boxers who were consistently legally able to spar, train, and fight provided them with the experience required to become excellent world-class boxers.

During the early 1880s, heavyweight champion John L. Sullivan of the U.S.A. made gloved boxing an extremely popular money-making sport. This caused a vast increase in the sport's participants. Although boxing was popular in Australia, the big money was in the United States. The sizable purses available in the U.S. eventually led to an infusion of highly skilled and talented Australian fighters into the world of American boxing. It was in America that Bob Fitzsimmons would earn his most significant victories and gain respect, fame, and fortune. Yet, it was in Australia that

Fitzsimmons developed the skills that would later enable him to become world-renowned.

The story of Bob Fitzsimmons is mostly the tale of a small but great middleweight who eventually defeated heavyweights. Fitzsimmons was almost five years younger than John L. Sullivan, but over three years older than James J. Corbett. While Sullivan and Corbett were making their marks as heavyweights, Fitzsimmons was a middleweight. He actually boxed the majority of his career as a middleweight.

Listed between 5'11 ½" and 5'11 ¾", "Ruby Robert" (as he was later called because he was a freckled red-head) began his career at around 145-150 pounds and usually weighed no more than that in Australia. At that time, the middleweight limit was 154 pounds (today's junior middleweight limit), only later changing to 158 pounds. What makes his story all the more amazing is that if a young Bob Fitzsimmons were fighting today, he would probably fight as a 147-pound welterweight, a division which did not even exist until the late 1880s.

What few realize is that Bob Fitzsimmons had a difficult and long journey to the top, that his greatness and eventual recognition as a superior pugilist came through years of experience and hard work. Although a respected middleweight, Bob toiled in relative obscurity in Australia, at least in comparison to the star status that he later achieved in America. Because he was not a participant in the more prestigious heavyweight division, which had a deep field of local talent, the smaller Fitzsimmons mostly remained in the shadows during the early part of his career.

Fitzsimmons' story is a reflection of the reality that few boxers achieve greatness overnight. Bob's early career had its ups and downs, but ultimately his hard work and determination led to great success. A close examination of Fitzsimmons' Australian career is important, because it was that experience that allowed him to develop into a fighter known as amongst the best boxers of all time. Fitzsimmons' Australian career proves that the hard road to glory sometimes yields the most lasting and significant results.

The mature Bob Fitzsimmons could do it all. Regardless of his size, Fitzsimmons became renowned for his crushing two-fisted power, even against much larger men, making him pound for pound one of history's hardest punchers. However, he was also a skilled boxer. He could fight at long range or on the inside, as a middleweight or a heavyweight, with or without gloves. He had solid skills, good conditioning, and an ability to recover quickly after being hurt. Although he was more of a puncher than a boxer, he had a good jab and could utilize elusive defensive and offensive footwork, head movement, and feints. He had an excellent sense of timing and distance. He was able to effectively set up his punches, find and create openings even in times of adversity, and land a devastating punch. His trickiness also made it difficult for his opponents to get a read on his offense or defense.

Bob Fitzsimmons is a fighter who defies classification. He was a bareknuckle and gloved fighter; a middleweight, a heavyweight, and a light heavyweight; a puncher and a boxer; an Englishman, a New Zealander, an Australian, and an American. He was a hybrid, a chameleon, a model of adaptation and versatility. Like his fighting style, Fitzsimmons was a man of many shapes. Over the course of his lengthy career, he was a champion at three different weights, winning middleweight, heavyweight, and then light heavyweight world titles. Bob Fitzsimmons was one of those special fighters that only seemed to improve over time and upon whom age had little adverse effect. This was a product of his experience, skill, activity level, and good habits, as much as talent.

To this day, Fitzsimmons is revered as one of the greatest pound for pound boxers who ever lived. Yet, a thoroughly detailed accounting of his championship rise and reign based on local primary source accountings has never been written, until now.

CHAPTER 2

The Underappreciated Middleweight

Historians and fans often like to categorize fighters, but Bob Fitzsimmons fits a lot of identities. He was actually born in Helston, Cornwall, England, and therefore many claim him as an English fighter. Like Sullivan and Corbett, Fitzsimmons was of Irish descent. Fitz claimed that he was half Irish. One report said, "The father was a very powerful, raw-boned Irishman." So the Irish could claim him as well. Another report said that Fitz was "Scotch-bred," which might have been his mother's ancestry. Although a young Fitz boxed a bit as an amateur in New Zealand, he obtained most of his skills and formative experience in Australia, so he really was an Australian-bred fighter. However, Fitzsimmons actually had more fights and boxed the longest in America, and he claimed U.S. citizenship during his career there, so he was an American fighter as well.

Like most things in boxing, there is some discrepancy as to Fitzsimmons' birth date. During most of his boxing career, primary sources usually listed Bob as being born on June 4, 1862, and sometimes June 14, 1862. However, while he was still heavyweight champion, in 1899, his original birth certificate was found, and it said that he was actually born on May 26, 1863, making him one year younger than what had previously been represented.[1]

Bob had some tough brothers who could fight bareknuckle, and he possibly learned a bit about boxing from them while they lived in England and New Zealand. One writer said that as a lad in school, "it was a word and blow with him. I think from what I know of the family all round that it would take a heavyweight to knock Bob out."

---

[1] *San Francisco Examiner*, May 30, 1899. The birth certificate was reprinted in Gilbert Odd, *The Fighting Blacksmith* (London: Pelham Books Ltd., 1976), Appendix III. This book will use the 1863 birth date to calculate Fitzsimmons' age. Secondary sources usually report his birth date as May 26, 1863. *National Police Gazette*, February 22, 1894, February 18, 1899; See an album called "Fight of the Century," published by H.S. Crocker Co., San Francisco in 1897; Cyberboxingzone.com.

In England, Bob's father was the Cornish borough's policeman, and upon his forced retirement as a result of local political issues, when Bob was about 10 years of age, the family migrated to Timaru, New Zealand.[2]

Like Corbett, a scholastic career was not for Fitzsimmons. As an 11- or 12-year-old boy in New Zealand, Bob gained some notoriety for being a good schoolyard fighter. He was often truant, and eventually dropped out.

Instead of attending school, Bob worked as a striker in a foundry for three years, swinging a heavy sledge-hammer. After leaving the foundry, he worked as a painter, then paperhanger, and finally settled on being a horse-shoer for his brother, a trade by which he earned a living throughout his years in New Zealand and Australia. Physically challenging work helped form his powerful muscles. Because he was such a good blacksmith, one of his later nicknames was "The Fighting Blacksmith." Throughout his career, Bob often liked to impress boxing fans with how quickly he could make horseshoes, which were one of his favorite gifts to give.

What Fitzsimmons claimed really motivated him to learn to fight was being the victim of a brutal assault. At about age 11, as he was walking by a football field, Bob encountered a football that had been kicked over a fence. He kicked it back as hard as he could. One of the team captains jumped over the fence, ran at Bob, and struck him on the nose, smashing and cutting a severe gash into it. Bob was senseless and bloody for quite some time. Fitz claimed that when the boys teased him about his broken nose, he decided not to return to school.

After his encounter with the bully, Fitzsimmons was determined to learn to box and defend himself, hoping to one day get revenge (which never came, because after he learned to fight he never again saw the boy). He sewed some gloves out of aprons, filled them with shavings, leather clippings, and cotton, and began boxing with his pals. As a young lad, Fitzsimmons boxed often with the neighborhood boys. "In a couple of years I could outbox any of them easily and I was growing tall." Bob sometimes took lessons at a local saloon from Dan Lea, a former champion of south-west England.

Fitzsimmons claimed to have fought his first bareknuckle fights under London Prize Ring Rules at around the age of 15, and he said that he won them all. Some report that Bob's first opponent was a burly blacksmith named Tom Baines, whom he knocked out in the 1st round. One source reports that this fight actually took place when Bob was a bit older.[3]

---

[2] *Sydney Referee* (hereinafter *"Referee"*), March 4, 1891, January 21, 1891; *Times-Democrat*, March 17, 1892; Christopher Tobin, *Fitzsimmons: Boxing's first triple world champion* (Timaru, NZ: David A. Jack and C.P. Tobin, 1983, 2000), 6.
[3] Odd at 27-29, 34; Tobin at 8-9; Mike Attree,

Most of what is known about Fitz's early career comes from what secondary and semi-primary sources report, which are likely based on Fitzsimmons' claims, not primary source newspaper accounts. Like most boxers, Bob's memory might have been incorrect on a number of points.

Most report that Fitzsimmons was first noticed at Timaru, New Zealand's Theatre Royal when he boxed in an amateur tournament hosted by Jem Mace, the former great English world bareknuckle champion who was making a tour of the colonies. The 140-pound Fitzsimmons entered the lightweight division and knocked out four men in one night to win New Zealand's amateur championship and a gold watch. Reported dates for this tournament vary from 1880 (when Bob was 17 years old) to 1882 (when Bob was 19 years old).[4]

The story told is that about one year later, Bob knocked out five men to win the amateur tournament for the second year in a row. Some sources allege that present at the tournament was Jem Mace's star pupil, Herbert "The Maori" Slade, a 200-pounder billed as Australia's heavyweight champion. That same evening, a 148-pound Fitzsimmons boxed Slade and so clearly bested him that Mace stopped the bout after only 2 or 3 rounds, not wanting to allow Fitz to knock him out.[5] Mace then put on the gloves to box with Bob, but the audience, thinking that Mace would try to knock him out, hissed and hooted until the boxers desisted.[6] This is the story that most American newspapers reported after Bob immigrated there.

One source says that Fitz was mistaken in believing that he had boxed Herbert Slade, when in fact he had defeated Slade's brother.[7] Early American reports of Herbert Slade's career listed him as undefeated.[8]

It has also been claimed that Jem Mace advised Bob to travel to Australia to join Larry Foley's famed boxing school. However, given that Fitz did not move to Australia for another three years, it is questionable as to how impressive he really was or whether Mace actually encouraged him. If he really was that good, Mace probably would have taken Bob along with him. Furthermore, Foley's school was not open at that time. Still, some said that Bob remained in New Zealand because of his love interest, Alice

http://www.fitzsimmons.co.nz/html/facts.html.

[4] Odd at 34-35; Tobin at 9-10; Mike Attree, Id.; *Times-Democrat*, January 11, 1891; *Philadelphia Press*, March 4, 1892; *New York Clipper*, March 12, 1892; *El Paso Daily Herald*, February 17, 1896.

[5] Rex Lardner, *The Legendary Champions* (N.Y.: American Heritage Press, 1972), 102; Nat Fleischer, *The Heavyweight Championship* (N.Y.: G.P. Putnam's Sons, 1949, 1961), 118; Odd at 37; *Philadelphia Press*, March 4, 1892; *Daily Picayune*, January 12, 1891. The *Philadelphia Press*, April 12, 1893, agreed. John L. Sullivan would stop Slade in 3 rounds in August 1883, and Slade subsequently became a Sullivan sparring partner on his national tour.

[6] *Times-Democrat*, January 11, 1891.

[7] Mike Attree, http://www.fitzsimmons.co.nz/html/facts.html.

[8] Odd at 37-38.

Jones, whom he eventually married, as well as his family ties and obligations in the forging business.

Years later, when speaking of his early experiences, Fitz said, "Goodness me, when Jem Mace came to Australia he promised a watch to the winner of his tournament, and after I had knocked out five men he gave me his bloomin' photograph."[9]

Jem Mace

Primary source accounts may alter the previous understanding about Fitzsimmons' alleged amateur "tournament" victories. From March to December 1882, Jem Mace toured New Zealand making money by giving boxing exhibitions with an entertainment company. Mace was traveling with world wrestling champion Professor William Miller, who was described as almost a giant, with superb muscular development. On Tuesday June 13, 1882, the *Timaru Herald* informed, "We remind those of our readers who take an interest in matters pugilistic, that the Mace Combination Company are to make their first appearance in Timaru this evening at the Theatre Royal."

On the evening of the 13th, a full house was in attendance to see the Mace-Miller Combination Company. It was not an amateur tournament, but rather an exhibition show which included boxing and wrestling, exhibitions of strength, and even singing. Miller exhibited his strength with a 182-pound dumbbell. Mace sparred a man named Edmonds 3 rounds.

A couple amateurs then took the stage in a friendly bout, one of them showing "a very creditable degree of skill and coolness." It is quite possible that the better amateur was a 19-year-old Fitzsimmons, but no names were provided. Miller and Edmonds then exhibited statuesque wrestling poses, after which Miller and Mace concluded with a boxing exhibition.[10]

The next evening, on June 14, 1882, the Mace and Miller combination gave their second and final entertainment at the theatre. The house was full below, and half-full above. Mace gave boxing exhibitions with Edmonds and Miller.

Gloved boxing contests between three amateurs were watched with a good deal of interest. "Two of these appeared the first night, and now one

9 *San Francisco Chronicle*, April 6, 1891.
10 *Timaru Herald*, June 13, 14, 1882.

of them beat a new-comer, and then his former antagonist." Mace acted as the judge and presented the winner with a meerschaum pipe. Again, this was likely Fitzsimmons defeating two men – a man previously not seen, and then the same opponent as on the previous night, defeating him once again. If this was Fitz, clearly he boxed twice that evening, not three or four times as has been claimed. Unfortunately, no names were provided.

Following these exhibitions was a scheduled 25-minute wrestling match between Professor Miller and the local man, Herbert Slade. Near the end of time, both went down on their faces, and Miller rolled Slade over and gained a fall to win the match.[11] Nothing was mentioned about Slade doing any boxing.

Mace returned to Timaru to exhibit there again on September 13, 1882, only three months later, not the one year that Fitzsimmons alleged.

> Mr. James Mace opens the Theatre Royal tonight with a miscellaneous athletic entertainment, in which he will 'set-to' with H.A. Slade, the well-known South Canterbury wrestler, and who under Mace's tuition is becoming an accomplished boxer.

Mace was also set to exhibit with G. Belcher, "and local amateurs are invited to compete for money prizes."

That evening, Mace boxed with Slade, who "has already acquired a great degree of skill with the gloves, and it is plain that he can already hold his own against even first-rate boxers."

Following the Mace-Slade exhibition, four couples of amateurs put on the gloves to box, "but their performances were more amusing than interesting as exhibitions of skill, one or two good boxers among them being matched with poor players. Among these was a younger brother of Slade." It was said that the winners were to box off with one another the following evening, and fresh local competitors were invited to come forward to box as well. Thus, if one of these amateurs was Fitzsimmons, the impression given from this article is that he likely only had one bout that evening; because otherwise the article would not have said that the winners were to box off on the following night. This also confirms that if Fitzsimmons boxed a Slade, it was most likely Herbert's younger brother, not the much bigger Herbert Slade. After the amateurs boxed, Mace boxed with Belcher.[12]

---

[11] *Timaru Herald*, June 15, 1882.
[12] *Timaru Herald*, September 13, 14, 1882.

The following evening, on September 14, 1882, there was a very small house at the Theatre Royal. Jem Mace and Herbert Slade gave a set-to that received applause, "Slade being considered by good judges to be a most promising adept with the gloves." Slade then gave a short exhibition of wrestling with a younger cousin.

"Some contests between amateurs filled up the programme of the evening, which was cut rather short on account of the poor attendance." Fitzsimmons was likely one of those boxing that night against one or more of the winners from the previous night's bouts. He probably only boxed once, possibly twice. None of these reports ever mentioned Bob's name. He most certainly did not box Herbert Slade on that night and likely not ever. In December 1882, Mace and Slade traveled to the United States.[13]

Despite reports that he received some instruction, in 1897, Fitzsimmons claimed to have been self taught and a natural fighter. "Most people seem to think that I was a pupil of Jim Mace in New Zealand, but such is not the case. I won trophies in tournaments that were arranged by Mace, but I never had a lesson in boxing in my life."[14]

At the beginning of Bob's career, John L. Sullivan was making the gloved bout popular in America, but it was still a new thing, and the rest of the western world saw bareknuckle London rules fighting as the real deal. During Sullivan's reign, Fitzsimmons occasionally fought as a small middleweight bareknuckler in New Zealand.

London rules bouts gave Fitzsimmons some valuable experience. He learned how to wrestle and fight in clinches, because above the waist holding, hitting, and wrestling moves were legal in such fights. He learned that conditioning and hitting hard to vital areas was important, because the only way to win was by incapacitating an opponent for just over 30 seconds, and rounds only ended when someone was knocked or thrown down. He also likely learned the importance of accuracy; punch selection and placement, because landing on the skull could break the bare hands.

According to Fitzsimmons, after winning the amateur tournament for the second year in a row (which in reality may have been the same year - 1882), he turned professional as a bareknuckle fighter in New Zealand. Bob was 19 years old. He said that his first opponent was Arthur Cooper. Fighting under bareknuckle London Prize Ring rules (LPR) in Timaru, he defeated Cooper in 3 rounds. Next up was Jack Murphy, who was taken out in 4 LPR rounds. Jim Crawford followed, whom Bob knocked out in 3

13 *Timaru Herald*, September 15, 1882.
14 *Rocky Mountain News*, March 1, 1897.

LPR rounds. Some say that Bob also defeated a Pat McCarney.[15] Much of Fitzsimmons' early career is difficult to confirm.

As gloved boxing became popular, and more importantly, legal, increasingly Bob's bouts were gloved. In the mid- to late-1880s, probably all of his bouts were with gloves. After moving to Sydney, New South Wales, Australia (some say 1883, others 1885), a 148-pound Fitzsimmons defeated a 170-pound heavyweight named Brawsmead (sometimes called Alf Brinsmead) in 2 rounds. A middleweight named Jack Greentree was stopped in 3 rounds, allegedly at Foley's. Bob defeated Dick Sandal or Sandall, who became an amateur champion after Fitz had left New Zealand, in 4 rounds.

Some say that Bob won a 4-rounder against Joe or Jack Riddle, which may have been a gloved points decision or just an exhibition. Riddle was years later listed as standing 5'8" and weighing 168 pounds. Bob supposedly also stopped a black fighter named Pablo Fanque or Frank in the 2nd round (some say February 1886).[16]

In Sydney, likely in about 1886, a 22-year-old Fitzsimmons obtained instruction from Larry Foley. Foley's gym, where weekly 4-round gloved exhibition bouts and gloved fights to the finish were commonplace, was producing what were or would become some of the world's best fighters. *The Police Gazette* years later said, "Jem Mace…started a boxing school in Australia, where he taught Larry Foley all he knew; Foley became a teacher, and numbered among his pupils Peter Jackson, Jim Hall, Bob Fitzsimmons, Dan Creedon and Young Griffo."[17] Foley's also produced and featured Frank "Paddy" Slavin, Joe Goddard, and Steve O'Donnell, amongst others.

Little known is the fact that at some point, the middleweight Fitzsimmons received boxing instruction from heavyweight Peter Jackson, up until the time Jackson left for America in late April 1888. In 1890, the *Sydney Referee* said, "Bob is a pupil of Jackson."[18] It also later said that Fitz did little boxing in New Zealand, but "took a liking to it after being under the skilful hands of Peter Jackson for a while."[19] This provides insight into Fitz's later high opinion of Professor Jackson's abilities, and is partly

---

[15] *National Police Gazette*, February 22, 1896, February 18, 1899; Cyberboxingzone.com; Odd at 38, 41; Fleischer, *The Heavyweight Championship*, at 118. Some secondary source records indicate that Murphy was stopped in 8 rounds. A later secondary source claims that Crawford defeated Fitz, not the other way around, and that the bout took place in Sydney. Crawford has been reported to have weighed 170 pounds to Fitz's 148. These claims are unproven.

[16] *National Police Gazette*, February 22, 1896, February 18, 1899; Attree; Tobin at 50; Odd at 41; *Brooklyn Daily Eagle*, June 9, 1899; *Referee*, September 30, 1891.

[17] *Police Gazette*, July 15, 1905.

[18] *Referee*, February 5, 1890.

[19] *Referee*, January 21, 1891.

informative as to how Fitzsimmons had developed so many skills. Jackson became the Australian heavyweight champion in September 1886.

Peter Jackson

It is clear that the hot local boxers of the time were heavyweights Peter Jackson and Frank Slavin, both of whom weighed around 190-200 pounds. As Bob was only a small middleweight, he did not gain significant recognition until much later. As a result, there was not enough money in boxing for him to make it his primary source of income. Fitz continued working the forge as a smith to support himself and his wife, Alice Jones.[20]

Local papers usually issued weekly reports of Foley's boxing events, but one possible reason why the dates of Fitzsimmons' Sydney bouts prior to 1886 have not been located is that Foley's hall had not yet opened. A local source reporting as of January 3, 1887 said that Foley's had been "open for upwards of a year," thus placing its opening sometime in late 1885 or early 1886.[21]

Previously, much of Fitzsimmons' early boxing history has been a mystery, but herein, local primary sources will reveal some of the secrets of his career.

The Sydney Daily Telegraph and *Sydney Tribune*, which printed identical follow-up reports, said that on Saturday, May 8, 1886, a boxing exhibition show was held at Foley's Athletic-hall before a large crowd. "Brinsley and Simmons were first to engage attention with a very lively set-to." Simmons was likely the almost 23-year-old Bob Fitzsimmons. Also exhibiting that evening were Jim Mace, Pablo Fanque, Jim Hall (a future Fitz opponent),

---

[20] Odd at 39-40.
[21] *Sydney Daily Telegraph* (hereinafter *"Daily Telegraph"*), January 3, 1887.

and Jim Fogarty. The spectators were well-pleased by the excellence of the bouts, and the applause was almost deafening.[22]

A week later, on May 15, 1886, beginning at 8 p.m., Foley's hosted another exhibition. The show usually concluded at 10:30 p.m. (2 ½ hours), although this one ended at 10:00 p.m. (a boxer failed to appear). On that night, the middleweight Fitzsimmons (who likely weighed around 150 pounds) faced off with the larger heavyweight Mick Dooley (who likely weighed around 170-175 pounds). A few months earlier, in March 1886, 24-year-old heavyweight Peter Jackson had stopped Dooley in the 3rd round.

Mick Dooley

According to the *Daily Telegraph*, after some preceding exhibitions,

> Dooley was then opposed by Fitzsimmons, and for the first two rounds, during which the play was only light, there was nothing to boast of on either side, but Dooley went to work in earnest in the third, and was so busy all over his opponent that the latter, after being knocked down, wisely declined to continue.[23]

Thus, the much larger Dooley stopped Fitzsimmons, who retired after being decked in the 3rd round. Years later, Dooley claimed that he once knocked Fitz out. Fitzsimmons said the claim was untrue, that he had never boxed with Dooley, and that he "never has been defeated in his life." Clearly, Fitzsimmons has some credibility problems. Most American sources did not mention Fitzsimmons' boxing with Dooley because they relied on Bob for an accounting of his career.[24] However, in 1894, Billy

---

[22] *Daily Telegraph*, May 10, 1886; *Sydney Tribune* (hereinafter "*Tribune*"), May 14, 1886. Hereinafter, usually only the *Telegraph* will be provided, because the two issued identical reports.
[23] *Daily Telegraph*, May 17, 1886.
[24] *National Police Gazette*, February 20, 1897.

Murphy said that he had seen Fitzsimmons pull off the gloves publicly at Larry Foley's eight years earlier, in the 3rd round of a bout with Mick Dooley.[25]

Fitzsimmons always claimed to have been undefeated. Technically, he was correct, because it was only an exhibition, not an official fight to the finish. Thus, he had no obligation or financial incentive to continue. However, it was clear that he had quit after being dropped, albeit by a much larger man. This likely adversely affected the local opinion of Fitzsimmons. Dooley was a well-respected Australian fighter who would continue to make a name for himself in the succeeding years.

Some secondary sources claim that Fitz boxed 4 rounds with Steve O'Donnell on May 22, but the local report does not confirm it. On that night, Jim Fogarty caused Brinsley to retire after the 1st round. Mick Dooley then caused Fogarty to quit after 2 rounds. After another bout, Peter Jackson boxed 4 rounds with Pablo Fanque, the latter acting purely on the defensive because Jackson had contracted to knock him out. Other exhibitions followed, including one between Larry Foley and an amateur.[26]

It is possible that Fitz boxed O'Donnell, but the bout was not mentioned, or it took place on another night. O'Donnell was a regular Foley exhibitor who would eventually travel to America and become a contender and favorite James J. Corbett sparring partner.

Steve O'Donnell

---

[25] *Boston Post,* June 20, 1894.
[26] *Daily Telegraph,* May 21, 24, 1886. Fitz was not advertised to box, nor does the post-exhibition report mention him.

While he was in the U.S., Fitz said that back in Australia he and O'Donnell had only once engaged in a private friendly sparring session in the gymnasium when no one else was around.

> The only time we ever had the gloves on together in Australia was one evening in the gymnasium after the pupils were all gone. I proposed it and if I remember rightly, there was no one present but ourselves. We sparred for a short time in the lightest manner possible, neither attempting to gain any advantage or thinking of such a thing... There was not a blow struck that would hurt a ten-year-old boy.[27]

Bob was also quoted as saying, "I only met him in a practice bout of three rounds, on an evening when I had got through work, and then he did not best me."[28]

About 800 people paid admission to see the exhibition show which took place on Wednesday, June 2, 1886. The 23-year-old Fitzsimmons again boxed Mick Dooley. Bob lasted the 4 rounds this time, but was inferior to Dooley. "[T]he much-improved Dooley did as he liked with Fitzsimmons."[29]

Fitz and Dooley boxed a third time three days later, on Saturday, June 5, 1886, again before a large attendance at Foley's. "Dooley had more to say than Fitzsimmons in a light spar."[30]

Local primary sources do not support some secondary source allegations that Fitz knocked out Dooley in the 2nd round on July 10. According to both the *Daily Telegraph* and the *Sydney Morning Herald*, on that evening, Dooley stopped Jim Fogarty in the 2nd round.[31]

In 1891, the *Sydney Referee* said, "Fitzsimmons has proven that he is a good fighter, and, though never able to cope with Dooley, he is undoubtedly a good man."[32] It also a couple months later said, "Well, Dooley downed him once in three rounds, and could do the trick again tomorrow." Clearly, the local press held Mick Dooley in higher regard than Fitzsimmons, and it is unlikely that Bob ever defeated him.[33]

---

[27] *Times-Democrat*, September 28, 1894.
[28] *Times-Democrat*, September 30, 1894.
[29] *Daily Telegraph*, June 3, 1886. Foley boxed 4 rounds with Fanque.
[30] *Daily Telegraph*, June 7, 1886; *Sydney Bulletin*, June 12, 1886.
[31] Odd at 41-42; Tobin at 11; *Daily Telegraph*, *Sydney Morning Herald*, July 12, 1886.
[32] *Referee*, January 14, 1891.
[33] *Referee*, March 25, 1891. On March 24, 1887, hard punching heavyweight Frank Slavin would stop fellow heavyweight Dooley in the 10th round. *Sydney Bulletin*, March 26, 1887.

It was in July 1886 in Salt Lake City, Utah that a 180-pound 19-year-old James J. Corbett, having had just over one year of training at San Francisco's Olympic Athletic Club, engaged in his first professional matches, boxing against Frank Smith and Duncan McDonald. These fights might have been hippodromes (fakes, or pursuant to some type of covert agreements). Corbett had been a California amateur heavyweight champion.

The older Fitzsimmons had engaged in serious professional bouts before Corbett did so, but in some respects, they were similar in their development at this point. Both men would continue to engage in regular local 4-round gloved exhibitions, which provided them with excellent experience. However, Fitzsimmons would eventually have many more serious bouts than Corbett did. Their paths would eventually cross.

Fitz was advertised to box on August 7, 1886 against a boxer named "McArdell" or "M'Ardill." "Fitzsimmons and M'Ardill opened with an interesting encounter extending over four rounds, all of which were in the former's favor." Another report said that Fitz and "Ardel" boxed a "fair four rounds."

Also that evening, Steve O'Donnell got the better of Jack Molloy (who would later that year box Fitz), and Bill McCarthy was superior to Jack Hickey (both future Fitz opponents), these exhibitions lasting 3 rounds each. Tom Lees, Larry Foley, and Professor Peter Jackson also boxed that night in separate exhibitions.[34]

Tom Lees

On Wednesday, August 25, 1886 at Foley's, Fitzsimmons boxed against then Australian heavyweight champion Tom Lees (who probably weighed around 180 pounds). Lees had won the championship with an 1885 KO12 over Bill Farnan, who held an 1884 KO4 over Peter Jackson, Peter's only loss. Lees and Farnan had fought an April 1886 rematch, but the police stopped the bout after 19 rounds. However, they finished the fight the next day, and Lees again defeated Farnan, via a 4th round knockout. Lees was another regular exhibitor at Foley's Athletic-hall.

[34] *Daily Telegraph*, August 7, 9, 1886; *Sydney Morning Herald*, August 9, 1886.

The middleweight-sized Fitzsimmons boxed 4 rounds against the heavyweight champion Lees, though not impressively, mostly attempting to survive and not get hurt. "Fitzsimmons essayed to stand before the Victorian heavyweight, Lees, during four rounds, but he is evidently more given to running away than boxing and his exhibition was a very tame one." Earlier that evening, Professor Jackson exhibited with Bill McCarthy.[35] The following week, Lees bested Mick Dooley in a 4-round exhibition.

In America on September 18, 1886, after heavyweight champion John L. Sullivan dropped Frank Herald in the 2nd round, the police stopped the bout. Sullivan was still dealing with the sport's legal limitations.[36]

In Australia on September 25, 1886 before a crowd of 1,100 at Foley's, for a bet of 200 pounds per side ($1,000 U.S.), 25-year-old Peter Jackson won the Australian heavyweight championship under gloved Queensberry rules when Tom Lees retired during the 30th round.[37]

Weekly boxing at Foley's was an extremely popular attraction. In the local newspaper, a cartoon depicted the huge and muscular Larry Foley standing next to a diminutive minister. Foley's gym was called "Larry Foley's Chapel." The minister lamented that his Sunday morning sermons drew only 8 pounds, whereas Foley's Saturday night prize-fight drew 800 pounds. The minister asked Foley how it was that his sermon against gambling raised so little while the prize-fight (Jackson-Lees) raised so much. Foley responded, "Your reverence, it's just this way. My show is for the young men, your show is for the old women."[38]

Primary and semi-primary sources do not confirm claims that Fitz possibly had an October 7, 1886 4-round bout against fellow middleweight William Smith, later known as "Australian" Billy Smith.[39] In July 1886, Billy McCarthy had knocked out Smith in the 12th round.[40]

On October 9, 1886 at Foley's, Fitzsimmons again boxed M'Cardell/McCardell (both spellings used by the locals) at a Peter Jackson sparring benefit. The show's sparring was good, but not as heavy or exciting as on some previous occasions. Fitz and M'Cardell boxed 4

[35] *Daily Telegraph, Sydney Morning Herald,* August 26, 1886.
[36] For further detail on John L. Sullivan's fights, see Adam J. Pollack, *John L. Sullivan: The Career of the First Gloved Heavyweight Champion* (North Carolina: McFarland & Co., 2006).
[37] *Sydney Bulletin,* October 2, 1886. Jackson was said to weigh 24 pounds more than Lees (which probably put Tom's weight somewhere around 170-175 pounds).
[38] *Sydney Bulletin,* October 9, 1886.
[39] Boxrec.com; Cyberboxingzone.com; Mike Attree.
[40] *Morning Oregonian,* December 12, 1889. For further detail on Corbett's bouts, See Adam J. Pollack, *In the Ring With James J. Corbett* (Iowa City: WIN BY KO Publications, 2007). Billy Smith would go on to box James J. Corbett in December 1889, losing two 6-round decisions.

"harmless" and "lightly-tested" rounds. Jim Hall boxed M'Carty/M'Carthy (likely Billy) and Peter Jackson boxed Steve O'Donnell.[41]

In the U.S., on November 13, 1886, a huge San Francisco crowd watched John L. Sullivan knock out Paddy Ryan in 3 rounds.

In Sydney, 200 spectators watched Foley's exhibition show on December 4, 1886. Jim Hall and Pat Kiely/Kiley gave separate exhibitions. Fitzsimmons boxed Jack Molloy/Malloy, another Foley regular who in 1886 had boxed 4-round exhibitions with the likes of Mick Dooley, Steve O'Donnell, Larry Foley, Billy McCarthy, Peter Jackson, and Dick Sandall. In July 1886, Tom Lees had scored a KO2 over Molloy. "Molloy and Fitzsimmons provided the cleverest spar of the evening, and sent the spectators away well satisfied." Another local source said, "Fitzsimmons and Molloy had a light quick, set-to."[42]

The Daily Telegraph as of January 1887 said that the patronage accorded to Foley's had not fallen off, "notwithstanding that it has been open for upwards of a year, and the crowds that gather nightly fully testify to the popularity of it and the proprietor." Boxing was no novelty; it had legitimate ongoing support.

Amongst the exhibition bouts held before a full house at Foley's on January 1, 1887, Fitzsimmons boxed with Frank Slaven (later called Slavin). Frank Patrick/Paddy Slaven was a hot heavyweight prospect who was to become a top world contender. The much larger Slaven (likely weighing in the mid-180-pound range) impressed observers much more than the smaller Fitzsimmons did. *The Daily Telegraph* reported, "Slaven and Fitzsimmons wound up the evening with a set-to that the latter had decidedly the worst of." *The Sydney Bulletin* said that Slaven "played with Fitzsimmons for four rounds."[43] According to the *Sydney Referee*,

> Fitzsimmon and Slaven, the latter claiming the Queensland championship, closed proceedings with a friendly set-to. The latter is a remarkably fine young fellow, and when he gets a little "Foley Polish" on him, will, if appearances and style, combined with his apparent ability, go for anything, hold his own with the first rank.[44]

---

[41] *Daily Telegraph*, October 11, 1886; *Sydney Morning Herald*, October 12, 1886.

[42] *Daily Telegraph*, December 6, 1886; *Sydney Bulletin*, December 11, 1886; Boxrec.com.

[43] *Daily Telegraph*, January 3, 1887; *Sydney Bulletin*, January 8, 1887. Slavin likely weighed 180-190 pounds to Fitz's 150-154 pounds.

[44] *Referee*, January 6, 1887. *The Referee* is only available beginning in late 1886, but is useful because it was quite a popular newspaper and frequently reported on boxing.

The press considered heavyweight Frank Slaven the coming man. "Great things are expected of Slaven, a splendid specimen of humanity, standing over six feet high."

Although the middleweight-sized Fitzsimmons was generally having the worst of it in exhibitions against heavyweights, he was usually spotting them 20-40 pounds. Such experience prepared him for a later time when he would face big punchers and larger men in serious bouts, and likely helped him develop survival techniques. Receiving instruction from and probably sparring with the much larger 190-200-pound Peter Jackson also provided Bob with excellent experience against a big man.

Frank Slavin

Unfortunately, Fitzsimmons was not often making the more significant money that could be won in serious fights to the finish. Apparently, either he was not ready or was not sufficiently backed with money to obtain such matches. So, Bob was primarily a 4-round exhibitor.

In addition to some of his underwhelming exhibition performances (particularly against the heavyweights), one possible reason why Bob never had a lot of financial backers is because of his somewhat odd appearance. He simply did not look like a winner. One of the common themes for Fitzsimmons was the rather denigrating descriptions of his appearance. He had thin legs, a strangely built torso, long arms, and a relatively small balding head. He simply did not emit a pleasing appearance or sense of proportion to evoke a feeling of confidence in backers or the press. Not only did men such as Sullivan, Corbett, Jackson, Slavin, and later Jim Hall have impressive looking bodies, but they were also somewhat handsome. They all had the look of a champion. Fitzsimmons was not the most attractive. For whatever reason, when it came to assessing athletic qualities, appearance sometimes counted.

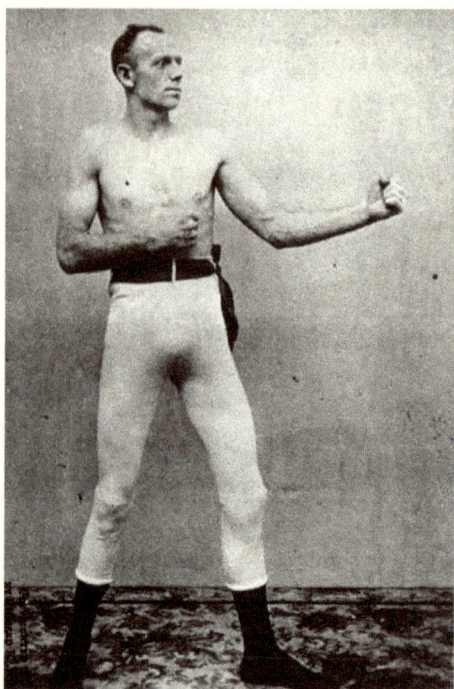

Bob Fitzsimmons

Another potential reason Fitzsimmons did not obtain a great deal of backing is because some considered his style ungainly and awkward. Some even called it funny. Few realized its efficacy. However, there were those who later appreciated Bob's skill.

Perhaps because Fitzsimmons was also devoting his time to being a blacksmith and was not making much money in boxing, he did not take the sport quite as seriously as he might otherwise. Maybe he simply did not feel the need to be impressive in exhibitions because there was no prize money or decision on the line, and he just worked with his opponents in a friendly way in order to keep them willing to box with him, so he could make a little money. Or maybe he was just not that good, but improved over time. The locals might have unfairly judged him based on his performances against men with big size advantages. Perhaps being from New Zealand hurt him. Regardless of the reason, Bob Fitzsimmons was not a local star.

The following week after Bob exhibited with Slaven, Foley announced that he would back Slaven against anyone. "Professor" Jackson, an instructor at Foley's, said that he would take up the challenge. Within a month, Frank Slavin's photo (the spelling now changed) was illustrated on the front cover of the *Referee* as "The Coming Man."[45]

---

[45] *Referee*, February 3, 1887.

On January 8, 1887, there were again a large number of spectators at Foley's hall for the weekly exhibitions. *The Daily Telegraph* said, "Fitzsimmons and 'a friend' commenced proceedings with four harmless rounds."[46] *The Referee* criticized,

> The first to don the mittens were Fitzsimmons and a friend, for four rounds, but the event caused very little enthusiasm, as they did not attempt legitimate business. Whether the former tried or not, it is hard to say, but the fact remains that if he did, he has fallen away in no small degree, as the friend showed by far the most points at the latter end.[47]

Apparently, the exhibition was so friendly that Fitz allowed his unknown opponent to get the better of him.

In January 1887 in Minnesota, U.S.A., after breaking his left arm early in the bout, John L. Sullivan fought Patsy Cardiff to a 6-round draw. On February 2 in San Francisco, Professor Jim Corbett boxed a 3-round exhibition with professional heavyweight Mike Brennan.

Fitz again took part in Foley's exhibition program on February 12, 1887. The hall was crowded to its fullest extent, and at least another 200 persons were content with standing room positions. According to the *Daily Telegraph*, "Bonnar and Fitzsimmons set the ball rolling with a four rounds encounter, but the play was only light and neither attempted to beat his opponent." *The Referee* said that the 1st round was very tame. The 2nd was just slightly better, but the 3rd and 4th rounds were quite lively. "Here and there some good countering ensued, but Fitzsimmons' reach was too long for his sable companion, and, altogether, their show can be written off in the one word 'friendly.'" Like Corbett, Fitzsimmons knew how to work with his opponents in a relatively tame fashion, for these were mostly just friendly exhibitions for either no money or just a small amount of money. No official decisions were rendered.

Bonnar was apparently Jack Bonnar, but he was not Philadelphia's Jack Bonner. Calling him "sable" seems to be an indication that he was a black fighter. Also exhibiting that evening was Frank Slaven, Frank's brother Bill Slaven (a future Fitz opponent), and some others.[48]

Although secondary sources say that Fitz exhibited 4 rounds with George Seale three days later, on February 15, the local sources do not

---

[46] *Daily Telegraph*, February 14, 1887. Later, Slaven boxed 4 rounds with Jack Molloy.
[47] *Referee*, January 13, 1887.
[48] *Daily Telegraph*, January 10, 1887; *Referee*, February 17, 1887.

definitively confirm it. *The Daily Telegraph* mentioned Bill Slaven boxing Jim Fogarty, Professor Jackson boxing Pat Kiely, and Jack Molloy boxing Frank Slaven, amongst others, but did not mention Fitzsimmons. *The Sydney Morning Herald* advertised Fitz, "the New Zealand champion," as set to meet Seale, "champion amateur," but even its post-exhibition report did not mention their having boxed.[49]

On Thursday, February 24, 1887, 300 people watched exhibitions which included Jack Molloy against Bill Slaven, Peter Jackson against Pat Kiley, as well as Mick Dooley and the American Martin "Buffalo" Costello in separate bouts. Fitzsimmons boxed someone who was only called "a friend."[50]

Australian primary sources do not mention or confirm later claims of the following Fitzsimmons bouts: March 1 W4 Dick Sandall (another Foley regular); March 20 KO5or7 Bill Slavin (most likely inaccurate); and April 4 KO2or3 George Enger or Eager (who had fought Edward "Starlight" Rollins, the Australian colored middleweight champion, as he was then called, to a draw). Unfortunately, reports back then are at times inconsistent, and some bouts may have been left out of the follow-up reports that were issued.[51]

Secondary sources report that on May 28, 1887 at Foley's, Fitz boxed a 4-round exhibition against Jim Hall. *The Referee* reported,

> Something funny was in store when Jim Hall and Fitzzimmons, a German, put up their hands and the roars of laughter and funnyisms which they produced were really beyond description. Hall, however, had the best of the bout, and although several "come downs" eventuated, Hall knew most about when and where to land.[52]

This was an odd description. Was this Bob Fitzsimmons or another man? Why was Fitz called a German? He was typically listed as a New Zealander. What was so funny? Were they faking or clowning around? Was Fitz's style

---

[49] *Daily Telegraph*, February 16, 1887; *Sydney Morning Herald*, February 14, 16, 1887.
[50] *Daily Telegraph*, February 25, 1887.
[51] Cyberboxingzone.com; *Daily Picayune*, January 12, 1891; *Times-Democrat*, January 11, 1891; *National Police Gazette*, January 24, 1891, February 18, 1899; Cyberboxingzone.com; *Philadelphia Press*, March 4, 1892. The Sandall and Enger/Eager bouts were reported by American semi-primary sources. As for the Bill Slavin bout, March 20 was a Sunday, and boxing was not allowed to take place on Sunday, so it is unlikely that this alleged Slavin bout took place on that date, if at all. Fitz and Bill Slavin did box one year later, so perhaps these later sources were off by a year. One source claimed that Fitz fought Enger with 8-ounce gloves, while Enger wore 3-ounce gloves.
[52] *Referee*, June 2, 1887.

funny somehow? His name was spelled with two "z"s instead of one "z" and an "s." Was this the usual spelling error as seen so often in these reports, or was it another boxer? Was Bob play-acting as if he was a German?

The Tribune report did not mention Fitzsimmons' name. It said that Hall boxed against a "foreigner." Fitz may have been considered a foreigner, but it would be odd to call him that given that he was a regular at these shows and his proper name had usually been used in its reports. Was this was another Fitz? Maybe it was a new reporter unfamiliar with him.

Regarding Hall's boxing with the "foreigner," the *Tribune* said, "The latter's tactics were of the most peculiar nature, his ideas of boxing being decidedly primitive, and the figure he cut kept the audience in roars of laughter throughout." This does not sound like Fitzsimmons, so it might have been someone else, or it could have been Bob hippodroming (faking or acting), but this is speculation.[53]

On July 16, 1887, Peter Jackson sparred 3 scientific rounds with future Corbett sparring partner Steve O'Donnell. Champion Jackson "had all the best."[54] As for Corbett, at that time he was a 20-year-old boxing professor at San Francisco's Olympic Club, and in August 1887 he boxed an 8-round no decision bout with former Sullivan opponent Jack Burke.

On September 24, 1887, the 24-year-old Fitzsimmons boxed in a serious bout against a fellow named Travers, later called Dave Travers. Fitz was a semi-regular 4-round exhibitor, but this time it was for real – a fight to the finish. "Fitzsimmons and a boxer rejoicing in the appellation of Travers opened with a fight 'to a finish,' but it was not of long duration and the latter cried a go in the third round." During his career, when it was for real, in a fight to the finish, Bob Fitzsimmons usually won by knockout.[55]

Secondary sources report that Fitz boxed Dan Hickey on January 23, 1888. The local paper advertised Hickey as set to box Fitz on January 26, but as was often the case, the advertisement turned out to be incorrect and the bout did not take place. Instead, on Thursday January 26, 1888, "Another good meeting was that between T. Taylor and Fitzsimmons, and as neither spared the other throughout a set-to of similar length [4 rounds], they were well received."[56] Hickey did years later become a favorite Fitz sparring partner.

---

[53] *Tribune*, June 3, 1887. Also boxing that night were Pat Kiely and Steve O'Donnell; Professor McCarthy; and Foley against Dooley.
[54] *Referee*, July 21, 1887.
[55] *Daily Telegraph*, September 26, 1887. Also boxing that night in separate exhibitions were Jem Mace and Peter Jackson.
[56] *Daily Telegraph*, January 27, 1888. Years later, Hickey became a favorite Fitz sparring partner.

On February 11, 1888, the "long-legged and long-armed" Fitzsimmons boxed a 4-round exhibition bout with the "astute and tricky Professor McCarty." This was Billy McCarthy, a highly respected and very experienced top middleweight who was a teacher and regular exhibitor. McCarthy had scored an 1886 KO12 over Billy Smith for what was called the Australian middleweight title, and fought Martin "Buffalo" Costello to an 1887 35-round draw, but also in 1887 lost the middleweight title when Jim Fogarty stopped him in the 28th or 29th round ("After M'Carthy had made all the fighting, and had Fogarty apparently in trouble, the latter took advantage of a reckless opening offered, and dropped his right on Mac's jaw with such force, that poor Billy was unable to come to time, and Fogarty won."). Subsequent 1887 results included D20 Paddy Gorman, KO12 Jim Nolan, KO17 Bill Burgess, and D17 Frank Slavin. McCarthy was no slouch.

According to the *Referee*, against Fitzsimmons,

> McCarty...tried all he knew...during the four rounds.... He did not succeed in landing a fair blow all through the first two rounds, his lightning deliveries, which usually get on to the best of his opponents were taken on the guard as coolly and neatly as if Mac was only teaching the hits and stops, while nothing but the Professor's slipperiness saved him from a severe grueling. He evidently had a great respect for his opponent's prowess as a hitter, for he exerted himself to an enormous extent, and ducked and dodged and ran like a deer to avoid Fitz's vicious hits.[57]

At that point, for the first time, the 24-year-old Fitzsimmons began receiving some recognition, especially because he did so well against such a highly regarded opponent. Fitz was called "without a doubt, the best science man, bar Jackson, in Sydney." That was a very high compliment indeed. Clearly, Bob had developed into a fine fighter. He suddenly went from a boxer who received little recognition to one who received a glowing compliment.

Of this encounter, the *Tribune* was much more reserved, but gave Fitz some recognition. It said,

---

[57] *Referee*, July 7, 1887 (said Fogarty stopped McCarthy in the 28th round), February 16, 1888, April 24, 1889; Boxrec.com. The newspapers sometimes called him McCarty, and at other times called him McCarthy.

It became whispered about that there was very little love between this latter pair and they rattled through four clinking good rounds. Fitzsimmons shaped better than is his wont and by no means had the worst of the encounter when time was called.

Apparently, a motivated Fitzsimmons did not hold back this time, and as a result looked better than he had in the past. Fitz and McCarthy would meet again a couple years later in America, in a professional fight to the finish.[58]

The exhibition performance against McCarthy catapulted Bob into a legitimate, serious bout. On Monday March 5, 1888, Fitzsimmons took on fellow middleweight and regular Foley exhibitor William Slavin, Frank Slavin's brother. In late July 1887, Bill Slavin had weighed 162 pounds in a losing effort against Billy Smith, who easily stopped him in the 6th round. However, a few weeks prior to the Fitzsimmons match, Slavin had stopped Paddy Gorman in 5 rounds. Gorman had fought McCarthy to a 20-round draw.[59]

The Referee said that Bill Slavin had a "nasty left hand that, to a boxer who does not go in for science, is a terror. He is moreover six feet high and very strong."

On Monday night he never got one of these left-hand stabs fair home, the spidery Fitz stopping them as simply as could be and jumping back from the right with a pitying smile each time it was sent out by the brawny Slavin.

During the first round Fitz led frequently with his left, and whenever he did so he got there sure, and the sound thereof was convincing proof that these wiry, long arms had nothing but good stuff in them.

As a result of an accidental head butt in the 2nd round, Slavin was severely cut on his forehead, which bled profusely and affected his vision. Slavin made it through the 3rd round and caught his second wind. However, he could not hit the active Fitzsimmons.

In the 5th round, Slavin suddenly rushed Bob, who moved about and laughed. Fitz eventually turned and slugged with him and they both gave it their all. Fitzsimmons was not hit as often, and he kept snapping Slavin's

---

[58] *Tribune*, February 17, 1888.
[59] *Referee*, August 4, 1887; Boxrec.com.

nose around to his ear, until Bill finally fell against the ropes, helpless. However, the call of "corners" gave Slavin a respite to recuperate.

In the 6th round, Slavin's mouth and nose were bleeding, while Fitz was unmarked.

> [Fitzsimmons] went in for a finish, and had Slavin quite done, and no doubt…would have succeeded in making this the finale, but a person in the audience, more humane than discreet, called, "That'll do, shake hands," and Slavin held out his hand and shook. Fitz thought he was giving in, and pulled off his gloves with a happy smile, and after Slavin had been ungloved they first heard the voice of the referee telling them to fight on. As, however, both were satisfied, they agreed to allow proceedings to be stayed. Thus ended one of the gamest and most stubborn contest seen for many a day.

Summarizing, another *Referee* writer also said,

> In the Fitzsimmons-Slavin go the contest was perfect science against a little skill and great strength and reach, and, as usual, science held a strong lead all through. Fitz is a New Zealander, as thin as a broom handle, but very wiry, and there is no more finished sparer, after Jackson, ever steps into the square ring. He got all over Slavin, and escaped that cruel left, that banged away so merrily on Paddy Gorman.[60]

However, the *Daily Telegraph* had a slightly different take on the result of this fight. It said,

> Another interesting and particularly exciting engagement was that between Fitzsimmons and W. Slavin. Each punched the other so heartily from the commencement of hostilities that they were fought almost to a standstill, and at the end of the fifth round Slavin very wisely declined to continue and he acknowledged his opponent's superiority.[61]

---

[60] *Referee*, March 8, 1888.
[61] *Daily Telegraph,* March 6, 1888.

Regardless of whether it was a 5th or 6th round retirement, Fitzsimmons was the better fighter, and once again had impressed the local press.

Five days later, on March 10, 1888 in France, John L. Sullivan fought Charles Mitchell to a 39-round bareknuckle London Prize Ring rules draw that lasted over three hours.

Bill Slavin and Fitzsimmons were billed to box again on March 17 in a 4-round exhibition, but the follow-up *Daily Telegraph* report made no mention of them having boxed.[62]

Fitzsimmons did box a 4-round exhibition with Bill Slavin on Tuesday April 17, 1888, as advertised. The existing *Referee* report is difficult to read and is blackened out, but from what can be read it said that they boxed an "interesting and amusing" 4 rounds. It appears to say that they were agile and exhibited cleverness in dodging, but there is also a reference to "roars of laughter."

Was Bob engaging in antics and horseplay in these tame exhibitions? Perhaps that is what he did when nothing serious was on the line. After all, he had stopped Slavin the previous month, so perhaps he felt that he had nothing to prove and agreed to work with Bill, making it obvious that it was just for fun. Perhaps Bob's less than serious attitude in some of his exhibition bouts was why the press did not catch onto him sooner as a really good fighter. Or, was his awkward style simply unappreciated by some and perceived as amusing or funny? This has to be counterpointed with the more recent observations that Fitz was the best, most finished scientific sparrer around other than Peter Jackson.

As for Peter Jackson, he left for America the following day.[63] When Professor Jackson arrived in San Francisco, he was an instant success, for experts were very impressed with his skills. Before 1888 was over, he would score a KO19 over George Godfrey and a KO24 against Joe McAuliffe.

---

[62] *Daily Telegraph*, March 17, 19, 1888.
[63] *Daily Telegraph*, April 18, 1888; *Referee*, April 12, 19, 1888. Also boxing on the 17th were Mick Dooley against Steve O'Donnell, Billy Smith in another exhibition, and Professor Peter Jackson against Laurence Foley.

CHAPTER 3

Fixing a Loss or Losing in a Fix?

One of the most significant opponents of Bob Fitzsimmons' Australian career was Jim Hall, whom Bob boxed a number of times between 1888 and 1890. What happened in these bouts is significant, because years later in America, the two would meet again in a mega-fight grudge match, in part because of what happened in at least one of their Australian fights.

On November 10, 1888 at Foley's Gymnasium, 25-year-old Bob Fitzsimmons boxed a 4-round exhibition with then 20-year-old Australian Jim Hall, another Foley regular who had boxed exhibitions with the likes of Mick Dooley, Tom Meadows, and possibly Fitzsimmons. In late March 1888, Hall stopped Jack Molloy in the 6th round. A later description of Hall said that he stood about 6'1", had long arms, and was a full fledged middleweight.[64]

Jim Hall

Over the course of the 4 rounds, Fitz was clearly better than Hall. According to the *Daily Telegraph* and the *Tribune*, Fitzsimmons "was quicker than his opponent and might have claimed a big call had he chosen at the finish." *The Referee* gave a more difficult to understand description, but also gave the impression that Fitz was better, saying, "That agile and lathy 'take in,' Fitzsimmons, set to with Tim Hall [sic], and though he did not put it all up 'he got there just the same.'"[65] Thus, the initial impression at this time, although in just a limited rounds exhibition, was that Fitz was superior.

[64] *Referee,* August 13, 1890; Boxrec.com. Some secondary sources report that on October 17, 1887, Hall stopped Jim Fogarty in the 20th round to win the Australian middleweight crown, but this has not been confirmed (and may be false).
[65] *Daily Telegraph,* November 12, 1888; *Tribune,* November 16, 1888; *Referee,* November 14, 1888; Boxrec.com.

A couple weeks later, on November 24, 1888, Fitzsimmons again sparred Jim Hall "a very nice four rounds" before the main event.[66]

On December 1, 1888, Fitzsimmons boxed a 3-round bout against a fighter named M'Ewen. *The Sydney Bulletin* described Fitz as tall and thin, while M'Ewen was short and thick, "with an aspect of comic ferocity on his face, and he fought with his mouth open."

> [M'Ewen's] strategy consisted in charging wildly at Fitzsimmons from the beginning of the round to the end, and he fought after the fashion of a cat on a hot stove. Now and then, thanks to his unwonted excitement, the men got tangled up in hard-knots and had to be untied by their seconds, and at other times M'Ewen seemed to have violent fits in four corners at once. Occasionally, too, he would rush into Fitzsimmons when the latter wasn't there, and then he would lose his balance and twirl round like a top, and Fitz would give him a friendly smack on the back as he revolved. Towards the close of the third round, however, M'Ewen seemed to get his legs hitched in his antagonist's hair, and the wildest comedy that the house had ever seen was brought to a sudden termination amid howls of inextinguishable mirth from the one-pound seats and shrieks of fiendish glee from the ten-shilling department and the gallery.[67]

It is unclear as to how matters ended. It could have been that the bout simply ended, or that Fitz suddenly stopped him with a blow, or that it was somewhat of a disqualification. Obviously, this writer found M'Ewen's style comical.

Without mentioning the opponent's name, the *Daily Telegraph* said of this exhibition attended by 700 people, "Fitzsimmons and another followed with three, and the latter engagement, if it lacked skill, made up fully by the amount of laughter it evoked, and was truly a side-splitting scene owing to the antics of the unknown."[68]

Probably as a result of their two prior exhibition bouts, folks wanted to see Fitzsimmons and Jim Hall in the ring together in a serious fight. On January 19, 1889 at Foley's, 25-year-old Bob Fitzsimmons and 20-year-old Jim Hall fought each other in what was billed as a fight for the Australian Middleweight Championship (154 pounds), although it was only scheduled for 8 rounds. *The Daily Telegraph* said,

---

[66] *Referee*, November 27, 1888.
[67] *Sydney Bulletin*, December 8, 1888.
[68] *Daily Telegraph*, December 3, 1888.

Jim Hall

It is only after much wrangling that the pair have been got together, and from the genuine character of the engagement, a scientific and interesting encounter may confidently be anticipated. As the advertisement announces, the match is for the middleweight championship and a trophy value 25 guineas.[69]

The Referee said that they met "to decide the question of supremacy (so advertised) for the middleweight championship and the house." The fact that both papers noted that the bout was "advertised" as being for the middleweight championship was likely their way of suggesting that there might be some dispute as to whether it truly was a championship fight. Jim Fogarty had generally been called the Australian champion, so this was likely not a true title fight, but rather for local recognition.

According to the *Referee*, Fitzsimmons dressed in black tights, while Hall wore white pants. In the 1st round, Fitz forced matters, landing his heavy right to the face and neck. Hall clinched and hugged quite often, and it was evident even at this stage that Fitz would win. Good fighting took place at the end of the round, and Fitz had the better of it, planting his left three times on Hall's cheek with good effect.

---

[69] *Daily Telegraph*, January 19, 1889.

In the 2nd round, Fitz eagerly engaged Hall, landing well to the face, neck, and ribs. Fitz forced the fighting and drove his left to the cheek a number of times. A right to the cheek dropped Hall. The call of "corners" saved Jim from the 10-count.

In the 3rd round, Fitz landed his right to the face and ribs, causing Hall to clinch quite often during the round. Fitz still forced matters and once staggered Hall with a punch to the mouth.

Hall came up groggy for the 4th round, and was quite defensive as Bob attacked. It appeared that Hall was trying to make a draw of it by surviving.

The 5th round saw fast fighting, with Fitz scoring more often and effectively. Bob did most of the work, with Hall clinching every few seconds. A right to the ribs made Jim grunt. Bob landed a good punch to the ear, and then as Hall was coming off the ropes to clinch, Fitz landed a right uppercut on the nose, causing it to bleed. Hall then gave up the fight.

The local paper summarized:

> From first to last Fitzsimmons forced the fighting and held a decided lead, and it was apparent that unless Hall got a chance knockout blow before six rounds went by; he must go out before the eighth. Fitzsimmons' right swings were his most formidable blows, and it was with one of these that he downed Hall in the second round. The blow that bested him was a heavy right uppercut, but he might have lasted a round or two more had he not bent down and tried to hug the wily Bill. This was the only bad feature of the mill, viz., hugging and clinching, and Hall (for Fitzsimmons exhibited no inclination to clinch) had to be cautioned by the referee on several occasions. Taken altogether, I think the best man won, and I am sure Hall will admit that he was fairly beaten.

However, another writer from the same newspaper was more critical of both men, saying, "though Fitz is a wonderfully clever boxer neither is up to 'star' form, and should not pose as stars till they have earned a name in the lower rank."[70] Once again, Fitz had underwhelmed a critic despite his cleverness and domination in a knockout victory.

The Daily Telegraph presented its version of matters:

---

[70] *Referee*, January 23, 1889.

The fight of the evening – Fitzsimmons v. Jim Hall, for eight rounds – followed, and from the call of time it was apparent that both meant business. Each displayed slight nervousness at commencing, and a lot of wild hitting was indulged in, though Fitzsimmons "got there" pretty often. In the second round the work was very merry, both fighting well till Hall was sent down, and but for the call of "time" the affairs would probably have ended there and then. Both men tired a good deal in the third innings, which was responsible for a lot of clinching, Hall showing signs that the finish of the eighth round would have been acceptable, and Fitzsimmons was none too strong. After sparring for wind at the commencement of the fourth round the principals closed, and for hugging too repeatedly the referee had continually to warn them. Up to this Fitzsimmons had a decided lead, and handled Hall so unsparingly in the fifth round that after two minutes' hostilities the latter retired, quite satisfied that in Fitzsimmons he had met his master. It was a "good go," and those who were present were well pleased.[71]

Immediately after Fitz defeated Hall, according to one writer, Billy M'Carty (McCarthy) challenged Bob for 50 to 25 pounds, saying that Bob could set his own date for the fight, "which I fear will be never." The writer argued that Fitz would not be able to claim the championship in the face of the challenge. Apparently, nothing came of it, but it is not clear why. Before heading to America, McCarthy last fought in Australia on April 22, 1889, boxing Jim Fogarty to an 8-round draw. "From first to last the battle was all in M'Carthy's favour."[72]

Despite his loss to Fitzsimmons, the younger Jim Hall was still touted as a hot prospect, and he earned a number of good wins over the next year. Not only did Hall fight often, but he also sparred almost every week in Foley's exhibition shows.

Bob Fitzsimmons' inactive career over the next year lies in stark contrast to Jim Hall's consistent activity. Sources do not report any bouts for Bob from January until November 1889. This seems strange. Just when he had secured his biggest victory, Fitz disappeared from the scene for almost a year, while the man whom he had conquered was obtaining many bouts and gaining recognition. Was this a coincidence? Was Bob's disappearance from the scene punishment for having defeated Hall, or was no one willing to fight him after that? Was Hall simply a well-managed and favored fighter, thought to have more potential than the older Fitz? Was Bob unable to find backers? Maybe there was not enough money in boxing

---

[71] *Daily Telegraph*, January 21, 1889.
[72] *Referee*, January 23, 1889, April 24, 1889.

for Bob, so he focused on his blacksmith business instead. Perhaps Fitz's bouts simply have not been located, or were not reported. However, this seems unlikely, given that Hall's bouts were consistently reported.

In America, in April 1889, Peter Jackson scored a KO10 over Patsy Cardiff. In a June 1889 professional fight to the finish, 22-year-old heavyweight James J. Corbett defeated 20-year-old Joe Choynski via KO27. In July, 30-year-old world heavyweight champion John L. Sullivan scored a KO75 against Jake Kilrain in an over 2-hour bareknuckle London rules battle. For engaging in this illegal prizefight, John L. was tried, convicted, and sentenced to a year in prison, although the verdict was later overturned. Sullivan became inactive during the next three years, having no serious bouts, only engaging in some short and friendly exhibitions.

In Australia, other than the loss to Fitzsimmons, 1889 was Jim Hall's year. On June 24, Hall scored a KO22 over Starlight. On July 6, Hall boxed Jack Slavin in an odd fight that merits some description, given what was later said about Hall's career and its relation to Fitzsimmons. The "fight" was described as "tame" and the men fought like "old women." Slavin's blows mostly hit the air, evoking laughter. Hall began heavy hitting in the 5th and 6th rounds and had Jack groggy and hurt.

> Slavin started posturing so peculiarly in the seventh that screams of laughter were heard. ... The eighth round was a disgrace to the ring. It became patent to everyone that it was a farce which the boxers thought had lasted quite long enough, and Hall followed Slavin round the ring asking him to quit guarding with his left and let him hit him on the cheek so that he could pretend to go out. Slavin was afraid to, apparently dreading a bona-fide one on the chin. Seeing how open the thing was Molloy called out to Slavin to come out of the ring, and threw up the towel. ... Mr. Laurence Foley...asked what they meant. "Go on," he said to the boxers; "do you think I'm going to have this large and respectable audience robbed? Fight on, and fight d-d hard or you won't get a cent between you.

They resumed without anything being done. The 9th was also very tame and uneventful. Hall chased Slavin around in the 10th, until a right to Jack's jaw knocked him down and out. "His seconds dragged him to his chair and the 'fight' was all over, ending a farce with quite a thrilling tragedy."[73] The article more than implied that the fight was a hippodrome/fix.

On July 20, Hall scored an impressive KO6 over Jack Molloy.

---

[73] *Referee*, June 26, July 10, 1889.

Hall is a pupil of Professor Peter Jackson, the champion, and is a credit to his mentor. He is wonderfully cool, boxes with consummate skill, and hits where it will do most good, and thundering hard then. This is the third aspirant he has laid out inside of about five weeks.[74]

In early August, Hall scored a KO8 over heavyweight Jim Nolan.

From first to last Nolan never had the ghost of a show with Hall, who is an undoubtedly clever boxer, a terribly hard hitter, and like nearly all of Jackson's pupils, smart on his feet and cool in the ring. There are mighty few could beat Jim Hall at his weight.[75]

On August 24, the very active Hall knocked out Herb Goddard (not Joe) in the 4th round. "From the commencement of the fight Hall had all his own way, hitting his man when and where he liked, and getting away from Goddard's right like a true artist."[76]

On September 14, an almost 168-pound Hall pounded on Jim Burge over 10 rounds, but was unable to knock him out.[77]

At that time, Hall and Jim Fogarty signed to fight in a 15-round bout. "As Fogarty is middle-weight champion, that title is also included in the articles." However, another opined, "The limit is too short to be satisfactory, and can have nothing to do with any championship." This writer wanted a fight to the finish.[78]

Another writer said of the time's championship confusion,

"For the middle-weight championship of Australia." I'm sick of seeing those words, which are tacked on to every announcement of a slogging match between every pair who are too big to call themselves light-weights. The Fogarty-Hall fight won't stand as for that title for the simple reason that Fogarty couldn't bring himself down to 11st., 4 lb. [158 pounds] in six, let alone four weeks. He'll fight about 12 st. [168 pounds] probably. ... Mr. Foley's tournament, which will go on

---

[74] *Referee*, July 24, 1889.
[75] *Referee*, August 10, 1889. Some later sources said that Nolan was a 196-pound heavyweight.
[76] *Referee*, August 28, 1889.
[77] *Referee*, September 18, 1889.
[78] *Referee*, September 18, 1889.

even if only eight enter, will be the only way to decide who really has the right to be called champion of the middle-weights.[79]

This makes it clear that although the Hall-Fitzsimmons fight earlier in the year had been advertised as being for the middleweight championship, it most certainly did not earn Bob universal recognition.

Many considered the Fogarty-Hall bout as being for the middleweight championship, despite the fact that Fogarty had become a heavyweight.

> Fogarty holds the title of middle-weight champion of Australia, and has hitherto been able to keep his title against all who have endeavoured to rob him of it. He is a terribly hard hitter, and wins all his battles by a knock-out hit, patiently waited for, on the jaw. …
>
> Hall is, on the other hand, an upstanding, straight, pegging fighter. He has splendid feet, and they help him a lot by taking him out of danger and enabling him to constantly attack with his long, far-reaching left, and get back in time to avoid the cross counter so fatal to many. He uses both hands very effectively, but knows the value of a straight strong left, and uses it principally till he is sure, or pretty sure, where his right will drop. …
>
> Hall has taken great care of himself, training for a month past at Mortlake under Jack Fuller, who has paid him every attention.
>
> The battle is bound to be willing, as, should Hall succeed in defeating Fogarty he will be undoubted champion of Australia. Should he win, Hall will leave for America in the Alameda, and throw down the gauntlet to all comers at middle-weight there.[80]

The October 16, 1889 Hall-Fogarty championship battle was called a 15-round fizzle, but Hall was superior. "Fogarty never trained at all. … It was a poor fight and a patent job." Fogarty vomited after the 5th round, and Hall's mouth bled freely. In the 13th round, Hall dropped Fogarty. "He came up vomiting and totally unable to fight," but was saved by the call of time. Hall dropped "the flabby mass" five times in the 14th round. In the 15th round, Hall knocked down the "champion" three times, but Fogarty lasted the distance, technically forcing it to be called a draw, which was the case when a championship fight did not end in a knockout.[81]

---

[79] *Referee*, September 25, 1889.
[80] *Referee*, October 16, 1889.
[81] *Referee*, October 23, 1889.

Although Hall had not officially defeated Fogarty, his performance essentially earned Jim recognition as Australia's best middleweight, and the press gradually began calling him the champion.

Hall's booming recognition probably made Fitzsimmons' victory over him even more creditable, and likely motivated or helped Bob's return. Back on the scene again, at a November 26, 1889 benefit, Fitzsimmons sparred Pat Kiely (likely 4 rounds). Listed as a Peter Jackson pupil, Kiely had boxed in many 4-round exhibitions with Jackson. Mick Dooley had knocked out Kiely in 5 rounds, in either 1888 or 1889. Also at this benefit, Jim Hall sparred Professor West 4 pretty rounds.[82]

Four days later, on November 30, 1889, Fitzsimmons undertook to knock out Professor West within 8 rounds for a wager of 10 pounds a side. In January 1888, Mick Dooley had stopped West in 2 rounds. For this fight, Jim Hall, who had sparred with him that same week, seconded West.

According to the *Referee*, in the 1st round, Fitz landed two good left-right combinations to the head. As the Professor tried to clinch, a left uppercut dropped West for the first time. West was dropped again, and failed to beat the count. *The Daily Telegraph* said that Fitzsimmons stopped him in two minutes of the 1st round. It criticized that neither man had a big enough reputation to draw a big crowd.[83]

On December 14, 1889, Jim Hall scored a KO4 over black heavyweight Pablo Fanque. Hall was "now pretty freely acknowledged to be our best middleweight."[84]

On December 16, 1889, Bob Fitzsimmons fought Dick Ellis in a scheduled 20-round bout. According to the *Referee*, "after boxing three feeble rounds Ellis gave in. He was in no condition to fight, anyway, being very weak from a prolonged attack of dysentery." *The Daily Telegraph*'s version said,

A glove contest between Dick Ellis of NZ and Fitzsimmons of Sydney came off in the Standard Theatre last evening. The first round was indecisive, but in the second the local man took a decided lead, and in the third had all the best of it. On the call of "corners," Ellis intimated that he was satisfied, and the match was awarded to Fitzsimmons.[85]

---

[82] *Referee*, July 3, 1889; November 27, 1889.
[83] *Referee*, December 4, 1889. The existing original is so decomposed that it is difficult to read and part of it is missing. Therefore, it is unclear how the second knockdown occurred; *Daily Telegraph*, December 2, 1889.
[84] *Referee*, December 26, 1889.
[85] *Referee*, December 18, 1889; *Daily Telegraph*, December 17, 1889; Odd at 43 incorrectly said

Some later sources said that Ellis weighed 176 pounds to Fitz's 148 pounds.[86] Only about 50 people witnessed the fight, once again showing that Bob did not command big drawing powers, for whatever reason.

In Portland, Oregon, U.S.A. in December 1889, James Corbett won two 6-round decision bouts against Australian Billy Smith, no knockouts or slugging being allowed there. In late December in Portland, Corbett fought Dave Campbell (who middleweight champion Jack Dempsey had knocked out in 3 rounds) to a 10-round draw that might have been a hippodrome, the fighters agreeing to work with one another to keep it even.

Peter Boland, Champion Middleweight of Victoria, challenged Jim Hall to a fight, because "I understand that he is now through recent performances and failure of any to accept his repeated challenges Champion Middle-weight of New South Wales, if not Australia."[87]

On January 18, 1890, on the night of the Hall-Boland fight, with the combatants in the ring, Fitzsimmons entered the ring and challenged the winner to fight for any part of 50 pounds. "Foley told him to put up a deposit, and Fuller hauled out a fiver to place in my hands for a forfeit, but Fitz could not come. He, however, said he would procure the money and make a match on Monday."

Jim Hall stopped Peter Boland in the 16th round, when Boland's second decided to retire him.

[Hall] fought a most manly, even chivalrous battle, and proved beyond a question that he has a right to the title he has earned – that of middle-weight champion of Australia. It is more than probable that Jim Hall will accompany Mr. L. Foley on his trip to America.[88]

On February 1, 1890 at Foley's hall, Fitzsimmons took on Dave Conway, who called himself the middleweight champion of Ballarat, Victoria. *The Daily Telegraph* said that Fitz "clean beat Conway, of Ballarat, in four rounds." Speaking of Fitzsimmons in this bout, the *Referee* said,

This slippery cuss never showed his unique dodging powers to such advantage as when on Saturday night he met Conway…. In this four-round go…Fitz simply played with him, and the rusher might just as

the bout never took place.
[86] *Times-Democrat*, January 11, 1891; *Philadelphia Press*, March 4, 1892.
[87] *Referee*, January 1, 1890.
[88] *Referee*, January 22, 1890.

well have tried to punch a wriggling snake as Fitz, who was all too merciful in view of Conway's pretensions.[89]

This gave the impression that Fitz allowed him to last the 4 rounds. Bob later claimed that he stopped him in 3 rounds.

Fitzsimmons and Jim Hall had scheduled a rematch for early February 1890, just over a year after Bob had defeated him. The very experienced Hall was coming off his January 18, 1890 KO16 over Peter Boland, and since losing to Fitzsimmons the previous year, had racked up about a dozen good victories, mostly via knockout.

The week before the Fitz-Hall rematch, the *Referee* gave its assessment of Fitzsimmons:

> There is not perhaps in Australia a man more likely to try out our middleweight champion and test his true merits to the utmost than the young New Zealander, Bob Fitzsimmons. Scaling about 11st. [154 pounds], and every inch as hard as nails, he is a hard hitter, rarely misses when he lets go, and is the most agile man I ever saw in a ring. In appearance Fitz is a consumptive streak, but a judge can see that he is all bone and muscle, and in reality very strong. He stands nearly or quite as tall as the champion, and is the hardest man to get on to who ever came under my notice.[90]

Bob had impressed some sportsmen and writers, but the *Referee* was acting as if it had no knowledge about the fact that Fitz had previously defeated Hall in early 1889. No one mentioned that prior fight.

The Referee also said, "Like Hall, Bob is a pupil of Jackson, and the champion heavyweight said, ere he left Australia on his all-conquering tour [in April 1888], that he should not be surprised to find Fitzsimmons champion when he returned." If both Fitz and Hall had received instruction from Jackson, then it is understandable how Bob and Jim might have sparred or fought in private before, something Fitz later claimed. Both were students at the Foley School where Jackson was a professor, and Fitz and Hall had sparred there in the weekly shows. Obviously, Jackson thought more of Fitzsimmons than Hall.[91]

---

[89] *Daily Telegraph*, February 3, 1890; *Referee*, February 5, 1890.
[90] *Referee*, February 5, 1890. 11 stone meant that Fitz weighed 154 pounds. A stone is 14 U.S. pounds.
[91] *Referee*, February 5, 1890.

Fitz and the now Australian middleweight champion Hall were set to box to a finish for the championship and 50 pounds a side (100 pounds total) at Foley's. The battle was predicted to be "the hardest of the champion's career so far" and would require Hall "to have every ounce up to defeat the dodgy Robert."

The day before their championship fight, on February 10, 1890 at Foley's, Fitz boxed Edward "Starlight" Rollins, known as the colored middleweight champion, in a 4-round exhibition. That same evening, Jim Hall exhibited 1 round with a black fighter named Sally Day.[92]

The Fitzsimmons-Hall fight took place the next evening, on February 11, 1890. Fitzsimmons was 26 years old at that point, and the *Referee* said that he looked to be in better condition than the 21-year-old Hall. Bob was described as a "clever and agile New Zealander, who has been looked upon as one of our smartest middle-weights for two years now. They fought for 100 pounds and the gate money."

After some preliminary bouts before a large crowd at Foley's, Jim and Bob stepped into the ring at 8:30 p.m. Mr. A.J. Hales, also known as "Smiler" Hales, a *Referee* writer, was the referee.

According to the *Referee*, the notable aspects of the 1st round were that Hall threw long and effective left leads and heavy rights to the ribs, one of which almost dropped Fitzsimmons. Fitz engaged in clever countering and made determined attempts with his right for the jaw, but Hall evaded them with quick in-stepping and neat guarding. Fitz lifted his shoulder to guard against Hall's attempts to the land on the point of the chin.

The 2nd round was similar, though Hall did the more effective work and discolored Bob's left eye with a hard right. Hall "stabbed" Bob's mouth heavily and hit the ribs with hard straight rights.

Hall fought furiously in the 3rd round, but Fitz's cleverness with head movements caused Jim to miss, hitting the air or shoulders. Neither man did much damage, but Hall grew fatigued. Jim used his intelligence to remain unharmed by jabbing or coming in with his forearm across Bob's throat. He also recovered by walking around. At the conclusion of the round, Hall sent in a left to the mouth and a hard right on the jaw that shook Fitz up.

Fitzsimmons looked confident to begin the 4th round, and advanced with a smile.

---

[92] *Referee*, February 12, 1890. Secondary sources generally say the Fitz-Starlight bout took place on February 4, but they might have been slightly off. The Wednesday February 12, 1890 edition of the *Referee* said there was a boxing exhibition on Monday night, which would have been February 10. If it meant the previous Monday, it would have been February 3.

He feinted with his left to draw Hall, and laid his jaw bare for one second. Rising on his toes Hall brought the right smashing across, hissing through his teeth like a blacksmith welting hot iron. It dropped with all his weight and strength on Fitz's jaw, just above the point, and Bob fell in a heap under his conqueror's legs as the impetus carried him on. Right on his back he rolled, and lay screwing up his face and looking very cronk.

Fitzsimmons was counted out. His "seconds dragged Fitz to his corner, but he slid off the chair again, and even when taken to the dressing room did not seem to know where he was." It was said that champion Hall was scheduled to leave for America the following Wednesday.[93]

The Daily Telegraph also provided its account, which differed from the *Referee*'s story, giving the impression of a more even bout.

The two men set to work, both getting home several heavy body hits and fighting hard, the first round ending without either party having any advantage. Rounds 2 and 3 were give and take, the fight being fast and furious and the men retired to their corners rather exhausted. At the call of time for round 4 Hall went straight for his man and letting out both left and right simultaneously floored him with a lucky hit on the point of the jaw. Fitzsimmons not coming up at the call of time the fight was awarded to Hall who was loudly cheered. The fight was one of the fastest seen at Foley's for a long time.[94]

So, in the 4th round, a hard right to the jaw knocked out Fitzsimmons…or did it? A year later, Fitzsimmons claimed to have thrown the fight in an agreement with gamblers for what translated to $75, and he always held firm to that claim.[95] There has been some question as to whether Fitz really threw it or just made the claim to avoid having to admit defeat. $75 was a paltry amount to have accepted to throw a middleweight championship, especially since the purse for winning was 100 pounds ($500) plus the gate money, which was a whole lot more than $75. Also,

---

[93] *Referee*, February 12, 1890. *The Daily Telegraph* confirmed that they fought on the 11th. "Jim Hall and Fitzsimmons meet at Foley's Hall this evening to decide which is to be middleweight Champion of Australia, 50 pounds being staked on the result." *Daily Telegraph*, February 11, 1890.
[94] *Daily Telegraph*, February 12, 1890.
[95] *San Francisco Chronicle*, April 6, 1891; *New York Clipper*, March 12, 1892; *Daily Picayune*, September 4, 1892; *National Police Gazette*, February 18, 1899; Fleischer, *The Heavyweight Championship* at 119.

one would think that Bob's subsequent purses as Australian middleweight champion would have been more after a win than a loss.

However, it is also possible that Fitz would not have even been granted the fight unless he had agreed to throw it, which would have meant no money at all. If he had double-crossed them, they might not have paid him, and he could have been blackballed from use in future shows (or worse). Perhaps his inability to secure fights after defeating Hall had demonstrated to Bob that a win over the favored/well liked fighter was not that lucrative after all. Maybe he was promised more fights if he did Hall's people a favor. Possibly, he threw it for more money than what he claimed, or maybe he was simply in dire financial straits at that time, and $75 was a lot for a man who had not made very much in his bouts and exhibitions.

Fitzsimmons said that economics dictated his actions in throwing the fight. He said that he had made just 10 shillings from his 5th round victory over Hall, which was only about $2.50. He was not making much from the fight game. A San Francisco newspaper reporting Fitz's claims in 1891 said,

> Shortly afterward Hall, who seems to have had command of some little money and was willing to part with it for pugilistic glory, offered Bob $75 to let him lick him in six rounds. Fitz accepted the offer, for he was in dire need of money, but he says he had hard work keeping his end of the bargain, as Hall was so tired at the end of three rounds that Bob had to fairly throw himself out in the fourth to get the money.[96]

Years later, Joe Goddard, a top heavyweight who saw the fight, corroborated Bob's version.[97]

The initial fight descriptions did not hint at a possible fix and they certainly do not have the sound of a fixed fight. They gave the impression of a legitimate competitive fight in which Fitz got caught by a good knockout puncher. Simply from reading these reports, it would seem that if Fitz threw it, he did an excellent acting job.

That said, Fitzsimmons had defeated Hall fairly easily in their January 1889 fight just one year earlier, and it was quite clear that he was the better fighter. This rematch seemed to be a complete roll reversal, at least if you read the *Referee* account. Still, the young and respected Hall had gained a great deal of experience and had many good knockout victories since losing to Fitzsimmons, and was fight-sharp.

---

[96] *San Francisco Chronicle,* April 6, 1891.
[97] *Times-Democrat,* March 9, 1893.

However, there is support even in the local primary sources fairly soon after the bout that there was more than a hint of crookedness about this fight. Almost two weeks after the bout, the *Sydney Bulletin* said,

> Jem Hall's last "fight," previous to his departure for the States, that with Fitzsimmons, proved another of those contests which knock spots off the anti-pugilist preachers in crying the death-knell of pugilism. No one thought Fitz had a ghost of a show with the clever middle-weight, but they at least expected a genuine set-to for their money. This they didn't get. The usually cool Hall obviously "gammoned," blowing like a grampus the while, until the fourth round, when Fitzsimmons received a feather-weight tap on the jaw, and fell all of a heap.[98]

The Bulletin wasn't buying it, feeling that Fitz had thrown the fight. And this was an article printed soon after the fight.

While in America in 1892, Fitzsimmons offered some further insight into his relationship with Hall. "Out in Australia I used to fight for $5, and glad to get the chance. Hall was a big card there and I used to follow the show, boxing him when the bill didn't fill. Of course I was not allowed to let out or I would have got fired."[99] Perhaps this explains why a number of Fitz's exhibition bouts were described as tame. His continued pay depended on his working with the more favored local opponents, the ones who filled the seats and brought in the money. Bob was just a strange looking foreigner, and not necessarily all that popular with the fans.

Also in 1892, Fitzsimmons claimed that while in Australia, he had defeated Hall in an additional, private bout. He said,

> Is Jack Fuller still alive? Just ask him about a private trial I gave Jim Hall at Mortlake. I think he was present and kept time or refereed the fight. He will tell you how I knocked the stuffing out of Hall... I tell you, my friends, Hall will remember the punching I gave him at Mortlake to the end of his days.[100]

An 1893 newspaper also reported that Fitz claimed to have twice defeated Hall in Australia and to have once laid down to him.[101] Another

---

[98] *Sydney Bulletin,* February 22, 1890.
[99] *Newark Evening News,* April 27, 1892.
[100] *Referee,* October 19, 1892.
[101] *Chicago Herald,* March 26, 1893.

American newspaper said that "there was an air of hippodroming about their other fights." This meant that they may have had prearranged/fixed results, and also indicated that Fitz and Hall had fought multiple times.[102] It is unclear as to what the basis of knowledge was for that newspaper's claim.

In subsequent years, there was some debate regarding who was the better fighter, whether their bouts were legitimate, and how many times they had fought. An 1893 American report said, "Hall claims that Bob was whipped on the level, and many Australian sportsmen are inclined to the belief. Fitzsimmons also claims that he afterward thrashed Hall in private in five rounds, but that statement also lacks verification."[103] The 5-rounder alluded to may have been their prior 5-round bout which Fitz won. Perhaps Bob was alluding to one of their earlier exhibition bouts. However, it is possible that they fought once more in a private bout.

If they did have another unreported bout, it most likely took place after their January 1889 fight, but before their February 1890 rematch. In an 1891 report after Fitz had already left Australia, Bob claimed that he and Hall had *not* fought again in Australia after the alleged fixed loss, so if Bob had defeated him twice before, it had to have been earlier.

> He declared that he had whipped Hall twice in Australia, and made no bones of stating that when he was beaten by Hall it was a pre-arranged affair, as he was to receive so much money for going out. Further, he stated that after he had faithfully performed his part of the contract (the going out business) the money was not forthcoming, and he never could draw Hall into a fight subsequently. He wound up by calling Hall a cur, and saying that Jim only wanted to advertise himself at his (Fitzsimmons') expense.[104]

In the weeks and months following the 4th round knockout loss, there were some strong hints and suggestions even by the *Referee* that Fitz indeed threw the fight against Hall. After his next fight, in late February 1890, one writer commented, "As for Fitzsimmons, he is simply a fool to throw away his reputation as he has been doing lately, and unless he is desirous of being known as champion faker of Australasia he had better fight square and clean, as I know he can if on the job."[105]

A couple months later, in April 1890, the same newspaper called Fitzsimmons "the best middleweight boxer we have yet raised, and, I firmly

---

[102] *Daily Picayune*, March 9, 1893.
[103] *Brooklyn Daily Eagle*, March 9, 1893.
[104] *Referee*, April 29, 1891.
[105] *Referee*, February 26, 1890.

believe, the best at the weight that lives…. He has not been able to get on many square fights here because all the boys were frightened of the New Zealander."[106] Certainly, this discounted the recent Hall loss and gave the impression that it was not on the square. Perhaps this also explains why Fitzsimmons did not fight for ten months after knocking out Hall in January 1889. No one would fight him. Perhaps needing the money, he might have agreed to throw the fight for the cash and the opportunity to obtain bouts and earn.

Obviously, for whatever reason, the handsome and younger native Hall was seen as more marketable than the odd looking foreigner Fitzsimmons. After Bob had defeated Hall for very little money, he encountered a drought. Yet, Hall was set up with a number of fights and became middleweight champion, despite the fact that Fitz had defeated him. Maybe losing did not look all that bad to Bob.

Finally, in August 1890, when discussing Hall's victory over Fitz, the same local paper again mentioned that it might not have been legitimate. Hall "[b]eat Bob Fitzsimmons in three and a half rounds, but there was a strong flavor of crookedness about this last encounter." Still, that same paper also said that Hall was looking good recently, and, "I fancy that if he ever meets Fitzsimmons as well as he is at the present time he will whip him."[107]

Interestingly enough, on August 25, 1890, Hall was in the process of beating up and finishing heavyweight Owen Sullivan, but was hit by a straight right that knocked him out in the 11th round.[108] Making things even more intriguing is the fact that bookmaker and former Hall backer Joe Harris a year later claimed that Hall admitted to him that he threw the Sullivan fight for $1,000.[109]

Some secondary sources later claimed that Hall needed a good win to help catapult him into a fight with then world middleweight champion Jack Dempsey. This claim does not make sense, given that Americans had no idea who Fitzsimmons was, Hall had racked up quite a few significant victories that would have legitimized him as a contender anyway, and his travel to the U.S. was already scheduled even before the Fitz fight took place. Regardless, Hall's people probably wanted to erase the one stain on his record, and agreed to split the purse with Bob on a 60/40 basis if Bob threw the fight. Fitz consented because it would still be his biggest payday.

One secondary source even claimed that the two went through a "rehearsal" together shortly before the fight, where Fitz "knocked out"

[106] *Referee,* April 16, 1890.
[107] *Referee,* August 13, 1890.
[108] *Referee,* August 27, 1890.
[109] *Referee,* June 24, 1891.

Hall in the 1st round. However, few knew that the result of the rehearsal was prearranged. Word of their impromptu fight caused the betting odds to shift sharply in Bob's favor, which meant that a bet on Hall in their upcoming fight would yield an even bigger return. However, neither primary nor semi-primary source accounts told this story. Hall always denied that the fight had been fixed, claiming that he had hit Fitz with one of the best rights that he ever threw.[110]

The question was whether Fitz preferred to be considered a cheater and a faker rather than a loser, and claimed to throw the fight so he could say that Hall had not defeated him when he really had, or whether he indeed told the truth when he said that he had essentially lied to the public (and deceived gamblers) by putting on a fake performance. He certainly never admitted to being bested by Mick Dooley, which he had, so he definitely had a lot of pride. However, even the Australian newsmen made more than one allusion to the belief that Fitz had thrown the Hall fight, so he really may have done so. Either way, throwing the fight or claiming to throw the fight was a bad mark on his integrity.

Despite the loss, or perhaps because of it, Fitzsimmons was back in the ring again just eleven days after the Hall fight. Certainly, it seemed pretty quick for a man to be fighting again so soon after being badly knocked out, if he really was, as the initial *Referee* report would have led one to believe. The fact that he was boxing in a fight to the finish so soon afterwards is one indication that Bob probably was not legitimately concussed.

Fitzsimmons and colored middleweight champion Edward "Starlight" Rollins fought on February 22, 1890 in a finish fight for 20 pounds a side and the gate money. Bob had boxed the experienced Rollins in a 4-round exhibition before the Hall fight. Some records indicate that in 1889, Jim Hall had twice stopped Starlight, in 22 rounds and in 5 rounds. That same year, the local *Referee* called Starlight the "blackest nigger from this to the back of beyond" who was "open for a match with any of the second-class middle-weights, such as Fitzsimmons." It also said, "Starlight has decidedly improved in his style, standing into his man more and not depending so much on acrobatic back springs as he used to do. ... Starlight is a decidedly hard hitter."[111] Regarding the prospective Rollins-Fitz fight, the local paper reported that it "should be a hot one, but the white man ought to win."[112]

---

[110] Odd at 45-48; Tobin at 12. They also claimed that Hall later got drunk and in a bar brawl received a knife gash to his hand, so he was unable to leave for America, which placed Bob in the perfect position to be the Australian representative sent overseas.

[111] *Referee,* March 20, 1889, January 1, 1890.

[112] *Referee,* February 19, 1890.

It is difficult to get a read on exactly what happened from the *Referee's* account, because its author fashioned a somewhat odd comedic take on the fight, with a strong twinge of racial prejudice. Apparently, he was trying to suggest that the fight was funny in some way, and potentially a hippodrome. The article was entitled, "A Comedy in Nine Acts."

The fighters were described: "Starlight, the black boxer whose smile resembles a schoolboy's first bite out of a ripe watermelon.... I could smell his rank strongly as the fight wore on." And Bob: "Fitzy is a man who was built by his parents for the purpose of getting through the world in a hurry. I have heard that he does most of his training gliding up and down a water-spout, and I believe it, for

Edward "Starlight" Rollins

he's slippery enough to glide anywhere." The fight was to a finish, "or until one got hit, which was all the same under the circumstances." Apparently, the bout was somewhat tame.

Round 1 – "The darkie looked serious, Fitzy smiled encouragingly…. Fitzy led short with his left, the nigger dancing to the nor'-east corner, executing an Irish jig as he went. Fitzy tried to look cross, and went after him." Bob punched and Starlight "ducked with the rapidity and grace of a hearse horse shying at a week-old corpse."

Round 2 – They sparred and feinted, "the spectators begging them not to get too far away from each other for the fear of getting lost. Starlight pretended to get the needle and went for gore, and got gruel as Fitzy tried to stab over his shoulder with a red hot left, but the 'nig' ducked his thick lips fair into it as he came, and sat down looking like a black boil on a white background." The suggestion was that Starlight ran into a left that dropped him.

Round 3 – "Fitzy went right along to make the pace, and the 'nig' did an even-time sprint from corner to corner, finishing up a quick spin on his off ear under the ropes. When he got on to the two planks which, in his case, do duty for feet, he made a snorting sort of noise, swung his dreadful right, and got it beautifully round Fitzy's neck." Starlight threw his right multiple times, but each time missed around the neck, "with the unerring precision of a blind boy."

Round 4 – "Starlight did a Zulu war dance and then mixed it with a Scotch reel. Fitzy, not to be wiped out by the nigger, wobbled round the ring, doing a Maori marriage jig. The thing got quite exciting."

Round 5 – "All this round fierce fighting was the order of the day, and once Fitzy nearly hit the nigger, who looked up and made a mouth, as to say that that sort of thing was not in the agreement." The suggestion here is that they were hippodroming. Eventually, after some clinching, "Starlight went down and put his thumb in his mouth to prevent himself from crying."

Round 6 – "Fitzy rushed and let go his right. The nig tied himself up in a knot and refused to be comforted. A wail of sympathy from the crowd, however, put him on his feet again, and once more the dreadful carnage went on. Fitzy poked Starlight in the lower regions and laughed, the darkie slipped down and tried to make out he was hurt." After rising, "The nig stamped the floor with his foot, and emitted an odour that nearly drove everyone from the ring side, and no wonder Fitz wanted to spar at long range." It appears that Starlight went down twice in the round.

Round 7 – "Fitz hit the dark cloud in the ribs, and he squealed and fell snorting to the floor." After rising, Starlight missed a punch and fell over the ropes on his head. "Fitz seized him by the feet and dragged him into the ring."

Round 8 – "Considering the fierce nature of the preceding round this one was a bit tame, and Starlight still kept displaying a tendency to go home and turn the mangle."

Round 9 – "More quit on the part of the nig, Fitzy trying to look fierce, but looking very funny. The white feather was sticking out all over Starlight. Heaps of antics on both sides, but no fight…. The nigger gathered his knees together, closed his eyes, opened his sawmill of a mouth, and went out."

The writer suspected that Fitzsimmons took part in fake fights/hippodromes, this one included. Of the poor fight, the author said, "A few more like it and the black flag will wave over the sport of boxing in this city." Starlight had not been impressive and it was suggested that he take up another profession. "As for Fitzsimmons, he is simply a fool to throw away his reputation as he has been doing lately, and unless he is desirous of being known as champion faker of Australasia he had better fight square and clean, as I know he can if on the job. I tell both boys this, as I wish them well."[113]

---

[113] *Referee*, February 26, 1890. Odd at 49 suggested that Starlight retired with a broken hand, but this appears to be incorrect.

The Daily Telegraph described this bout at Foley's as "a bit out of the common," but "a treat."

> Fitzsimmons and Starlight were matched to a finish, and for the seven rounds that Starlight lasted it was nothing but one continued screech. Very little damage was done on either side, but the show was almost as funny as could be until Starlight considered he had had enough and threw up the sponge in the seventh round.

Thus, this account says it only lasted 7 rounds, as opposed to the *Referee's* claim that it went 9 rounds. It too felt that the bout was tame and funny. Again, it was yet another Fitz bout that led to some laughter.[114]

An 1891 American source said that Bob knocked Starlight out with rights to the face. It quoted Fitz as saying, "Well, you're a hard nigger for sure, though I did get you."[115]

In March 1890, Fitzsimmons, "the long, lean, serpentine youth, with the wriggling shoulders and queer grin," made offers to undertake to knock out Dick Sandall or Jim Burge in 8 rounds, but nothing came of the proposals.[116] In early April, Fitz offered to fight any middleweight in Australia for 50 or 100 pounds per side.[117] Although his offers were not accepted, Fitz's life was about to change.

In 1892, recalling his Sydney days, Fitz said, "What sport we used to see on Saturday nights in that old shed at the rear, and so cheap too. Why, champions of the present day used to spar four willing rounds – and go all the way – for a caser, and under the artful supervision of Mr. Foley, too."[118] Robert Fitzsimmons was about to enter a world where top fighters could earn big bucks.

---

[114] *Daily Telegraph,* February 24, 1890. In America a couple years later, this was reported as a KO9 for Fitzsimmons. *New York Clipper,* March 12, 1892.

[115] *Daily Picayune,* January 12, 1891. Another American source incorrectly claimed that Fitz was dropped in the 9th, but that Rollins broke his hand and had to give up. *National Police Gazette,* January 24, 1891, February 22, 1896.

[116] *Referee,* March 6, 1890, March 19, 1890. Although American sources report that Fitz stopped Professor West on March 1, 1890 in 2 minutes of the 1st round, the locals did not mention the fight. This may have been an allusion Bob's November 1889 KO1 over West. *Times-Democrat,* January 11, 1891; *Brooklyn Daily Eagle,* March 9, 1893; Odd at 49; *Philadelphia Press,* March 4, 1892; *New York Clipper,* March 12, 1892; *Daily Telegraph,* March 1, 3, 1890.

[117] *Referee,* April 9, 1890.

[118] *Referee,* October 19, 1892.

CHAPTER 4

American Appreciation

On April 16, 1890, called by a local writer the best middleweight alive and the best middleweight Australia ever produced, 26-year-old Bob Fitzsimmons set sail for San Francisco, California, in the United States. Speaking of Bob, the Australian press said,

He is one of the queerest-looking pieces of pugilistic furniture that ever pulled off a shirt when he is fighting, and the great 'Frisco club men may smile when they see him perform in the first round or two, but they won't when the feeling is over, and the fight begins in earnest if their money is on the other man. He has not been able to get on many square fights here because all the boys were frightened of the New Zealander. I can earnestly and honestly recommend him…. He is a blacksmith by trade, and his frame is like a long pole bound with whipcord. He is 6 ft. high, and fights 10st. 8 lb. He will go direct to the California Club, and meet his old chum, Peter Jackson…and he will be ready to take on any man they like to pit him against – English, American, or Australian.[119]

Calling the 148-pound Fitzsimmons the best middleweight in the world and the best middleweight that Australia ever produced, and alluding to the fact that Fitz was unable to get many square fights, certainly was more than a hint that Fitzsimmons was not only better than Jim Hall, but that the Hall rematch was fixed.

Fitzsimmons used this *Referee* article about him as a way to introduce and sell himself to San Francisco's California Athletic Club, where his former teacher Peter Jackson had trained and fought. In fact, portions of the article were printed in San Francisco's *Daily Alta California*.[120] After arriving in America, one New York report said that Bob was brought over

---

[119] *Referee*, April 16, 1890. 10 stone, 8 pounds converts to 148 U.S. pounds.
[120] *Referee*, January 21, 1891; *Daily Alta California*, May 19, 1890.

by a man "who has the reputation of being an excellent judge of the right article."[121]

Some secondary sources have reported that Fitz was a replacement for Jim Hall, who was injured in a bar brawl and could not go to America. However, on the same date that Fitz left, the *Referee* reported that *both* Hall and Fitzsimmons were scheduled to leave that day for America.

> I am no judge of the game if Jim Hall does not soon attach the middle weight championship of the world to his belt and as soon as he has accomplished that feat of arms Fitz will be after him with that red head and wriggling shoulder blade of his, and I fancy I know who'll get the rough end of the dog then.[122]

The following week's report simply said that Fitz had left, and that Hall, "who was to have sailed in the same boat, did not go." Hall did not travel to America for another year.[123]

In early 1891, a *Referee* writer said that he had interviewed Fitz on the day that he left for America, and Bob told him this story of his life, including how he came to travel to the United States:

> He landed with his parents at Auckland when very young, and stayed in New Zealand until he had learnt his trade as a blacksmith. He did very little boxing in that country, but took a liking to it after being under the skilful hands of Peter Jackson for a while, and he then determined to follow up the game more as a means of amusement than as a livelihood, as he was always a hard-working young fellow, and stuck close to his trade as shoeing smith until a short time prior to his departure from our shores. He entered into an engagement with Jim Hall and several others to tour this country and America, but owing to some misunderstanding the show fell through, and Fitzy was about to resume his avocation as a smith. He had 5 pounds up in my hands at this time to fight any middle-weight in Australia, and he called to take it down, and while chatting over the situation I advised him to try his luck on American soil. He stated that he had a friend who would find him money enough to go if I thought he had good

---

[121] *New York Clipper*, May 24, 1890.
[122] *Referee*, April 16, 1890.
[123] *Referee*, April 23, 1890.

prospects. He made up his mind in a few hours, and was soon on board the Zealandia.[124]

It is clear from this article that Fitzsimmons did not earn enough from boxing to make it his primary profession. He was a blacksmith by trade, boxed for fun, and to pick up what little extra money that he could, which apparently was not much. He was about to travel and exhibit with Hall, but when the show fell through, it appeared that he was about to give up on the sport for a while and resume his smith business. However, when the local press gave him its stamp of approval, Bob was able to obtain the backing that he needed to travel to America.

A few months prior to Bob's arrival in the U.S., in February 1890, San Francisco's own heavyweight, James J. Corbett, had won a 6-round decision over Jake Kilrain. In April, Corbett easily bested Dominick McCaffrey in less than 4 rounds. The easterners were very high on Corbett and began discussing him as a man who might one day be able to dethrone John L. Sullivan. Corbett resumed his professorship at San Francisco's Olympic Athletic Club.

Peter Jackson had already established himself as a top world heavyweight contender, having fought a few fights to the finish at San Francisco's California Athletic Club. Jackson then toured America and also had some overseas victories as well. In May 1890 in Chicago, Jackson would defeat "Denver" Ed Smith in a 5-round decision bout.

Almost eight years after Bob began his boxing career, just shy of his 27th birthday, on May 10, 1890, Fitzsimmons arrived in San Francisco. The local paper said that Fitz was "yet another Australian bruiser" who was "spoken of as a really good middle-weight."[125] Bob had been brought over on the Zealandia by Tom James, "who has the reputation of being an excellent judge of the right article in the pugilistic line when he sees it perform. We will soon find out what sort of stuff the newcomer is made of."[126]

Four days later, on May 14, 1890, a fortuity befell Fitzsimmons. Due to an attack of malaria, Reddy Gallagher had to pull out of his scheduled late May fight with Australia's Billy McCarthy. That night, the California Club board of directors discussed the possibility of having Fitzsimmons serve as a substitute. Club president Lem Fulda suggested that Fitz submit to a try-out with the club's middleweight professor, Frank Allen, to see if he would do. Fitzsimmons, who was there at Fulda's invitation, consented.

[124] *Referee*, January 21, 1891.
[125] *San Francisco Chronicle*, May 12, 1890.
[126] *New York Clipper*, May 24, 1890.

The New Zealander was nothing loth, and in a three-round bout he proved himself to be a boxer of rare merit. Fitzsimmons is close on six feet in height, but only weighs 145 pounds. He has thin legs, but well-developed chest, arms and shoulders. ... He is a pupil of Peter Jackson, and his style is very similar to the colored champion's. He boxes in an easy, confident attitude and can use his right hand on his opponent's head and body with great precision and effect. He impressed the directors very favorably, and President Fulda remarked in a low, sweet voice at the end of the trial, "He's a corker."[127]

Bob had an odd appearance, and did not look like a fighter. Because the Americans were not sure about him, they tested him out in private to see what he could do, to see if he was the genuine article. Back home it was said, "Fitzsimmons is somewhat of a pugilistic puzzle to San Francisco sports. They are loath to believe that such an elongated specimen of humanity can be much of a slugger, but the stories of his cleverness have set them guessing." *The Referee* said that California Club middleweight trial horse Frank Allen was selected to spar 3 rounds with Fitz in private, and its correspondent viewed it. "It will suffice to say that Fitzy covered himself with glory and the other fellow with blows."[128]

As a result, Fitzsimmons was asked to take Gallagher's place against McCarthy in a fight to the finish, giving him only about two weeks to train, but he accepted. The fact that Fitz was willing to engage in a finish fight so soon after his arrival in America showed the type of confidence that he had, as well as the good condition in which he kept himself. Plus, it was simply too much money to turn down. The winner was to receive $1,000 and the loser $250. For the time, that was serious money, more than Bob had ever seen.[129]

That week, Fitzsimmons also sparred with some local fighters; including Joe Choynski, a Jewish fighter of some note. The 165-175-pound Choynski had fought exclusively as a heavyweight, and had a number of knockout victories to his credit. He had sparred Peter Jackson 4 rounds in June 1888. In June 1889, in a brutal war, James J. Corbett knocked out Choynski in the

---

[127] *San Francisco Chronicle, San Francisco Examiner*, May 15, 1890. Secondary source claims that this bout took place on the 10th or the 17th are wrong. Although the impression from the local account was that Fitz boxed Allen 3 rounds, some secondary sources claim that Bob knocked out Frank Allen in the 1st round. An 1895 source said that it had to be stopped because Allen broke his wrist in a fall after being dropped by a punch to the jaw. The impression given by the local next day account is that these later sources are incorrect. Cyberbozingzone.com; *Brooklyn Daily Eagle*, June 9, 1895; Odd at 52.
[128] *Referee,* July 2, 1890.
[129] *San Francisco Bulletin,* May 15, 1890.

27th round. In March 1890, Choynski scored a KO2 over Billy Wilson, a respected black fighter.

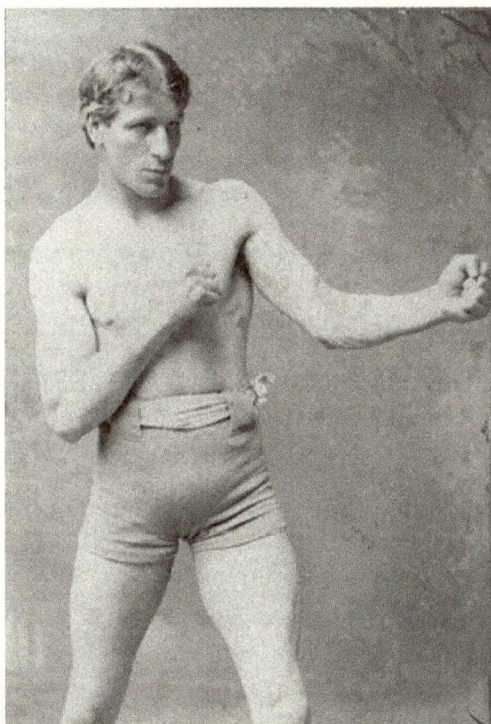

Joe Choynski

Choynski was training for a late May bout with Jack "Bubbles" Davis (which he would win via KO9), so Bob and Joe sparred with each other in preparation for their respective upcoming fights. Fitz and Choynski became friends and occasional sparring partners, but years later would engage in a serious contest against one another.

Future Fitz manager Jimmy Carroll later said of Bob, "When he got to 'Frisco he had a friendly set-to with Joe Choynski, a decent, honest fellow and a good fighter. I did not see it, and when I asked Joe about the long fellow he said: 'Jimmy, look out for him. He's a wonder; and don't think he can't hit hard, for he kept me busy.'"[130]

Many years later, Choynski said that Fitz had arrived in America poorly dressed, almost friendless, and carrying all his belongings in a single carpet-bag. "Fitzsimmons was about as unimpressive looking a fighter as I had ever seen. He was cheaply attired and looked hardly more than a welterweight, lanky and knock-kneed." However, when boxing with him,

---

[130] *Times-Democrat,* January 16, 1891.

Joe changed his mind. "I discovered quickly that he was a finished boxer even then; in fact much more of a boxer than in later years, when he completely changed his style and went in for slugging in order to make the most of his terrific hitting power."[131]

As of May 19, the *San Francisco Chronicle* described Fitzsimmons as a "tall, wiry individual who sets about fighting the same as if he loved it. He is a clever sparrer and a pretty hard man to down."[132] The following week Bob was called tall and lanky, and a "pugilistic conundrum."

> If there were anything in looks Fitzsimmons could be backed at 1000 to 1 as a sure loser...for he sports about the worst pair of shanks that ever upheld a gladiator.... When in action the tall antipodean hops like an overgrown tarantular.... Still it is whispered in sporting circles that Fitzsimmons is a regular "corker."

Fitz had relatively thin legs and a large upper body, leading to such comments as "in the shoulders and arms the New Zealander is a fighting Hercules, but below the waist he is a crane."[133]

Fitzsimmons trained at Barney Farley's, being looked after by Martin Murphy. Bob had been taking long walks and runs ever since arriving in America. He was described as "hard as flint" and "if he turns out to be half as good a man as his Australian friends rate him as being, Billy will be kept on the move while the battle is in progress."[134]

Fitzsimmons and McCarthy were quite familiar with one another. Both had trained at Foley's and were regular weekly exhibitors there. They were "old chums and both pupils of Peter Jackson."[135] Like Fitz, McCarthy had sparred with Jackson. In Australia, McCarthy had fought many lengthy fights to the finish, for a time was the Australian middleweight champion, and eventually earned status as a boxing professor.

What the San Francisco sports probably did not realize was that Fitzsimmons and McCarthy had boxed a 4-round exhibition in February 1888, and Bob had the advantage. Still, even if they had known, a couple years of time had passed; McCarthy had gained a great deal of experience, and had impressed the local San Francisco sportsmen. Subsequent to Bob and Billy's sparring, McCarthy had boxed 1888 8-, 15-, and 17-round draws

---

[131] *Winnipeg Free Press*, January 8, 1927. Special thanks to Chris LaForce for this information.
[132] *San Francisco Chronicle*, May 19, 1890.
[133] *San Francisco Chronicle*, May 26, 1890.
[134] *San Francisco Morning Call*, May 18, 1890; *Daily Alta California*, May 19, 1890.
[135] *Referee*, July 2, 1890.

with Billy Smith, had lost an 1888 8-rounder to Mick Dooley, and fought Jim Fogarty to an 1889 8-round draw, but was the superior fighter. [136]

McCarthy had been living in San Francisco since mid-1889 and had demonstrated his ability to the locals. In November 1889 at San Francisco's California Athletic Club, McCarthy scored a KO21 or 23 over Denny Kelliher. Most importantly, on February 18, 1890 at the same location, McCarthy valiantly fought world middleweight champion Jack "The Nonpareil" Dempsey for the title, but was stopped in the 28th round. McCarthy's solid performance against Dempsey made the upcoming bout significant for Fitzsimmons, because it would be a good way to gauge his ability. Americans were impressed with McCarthy, and he was initially the slight betting favorite against Fitzsimmons.[137]

In assessing the match-up, the *San Francisco Morning Call* said,

---

[136] Boxrec.com.
[137] *Referee*, July 2, 1890.

McCarthy would be an exceedingly hard man to defeat were it not for his short arms. To land his favorite punches he has to resort to numerous artful moves; but once within range, he sends the mittens home with such good effect that his opponent oftentimes wonders how he gets there so often in the few moments of attack.

Fitzsimmons is comparatively a stranger here. The only estimate of his qualities as a fighter is in the reports taken from Australian exchanges, which give him an exalted standing in the class he represents. Fitz is a pupil of Professor Peter Jackson, who predicted a brilliant future for the New Zealander before taking his departure from the Antipodes.

McCarthy's opponent is a peculiarly shaped fellow. He would not be picked out of a crowd of ordinary citizens as a man who had defeated formidable opponents. His arms and legs are extremely long, and Australians who have seen him in battle say that apart from his cleverness he can reach his opponent's nose at phenomenal range. Some predict that he is the coming champion middle-weight of the world.[138]

Another paper said that Fitz had "a most curious style…that at first is apt to prove puzzling and misleading. McCarthy will be a hard man to defeat, however."[139]

Nineteen days after arriving in America, on May 29, 1890 at San Francisco's California Athletic Club, 27-year-old Bob Fitzsimmons took on Billy McCarthy in a fight to the finish wearing five-ounce gloves. McCarthy weighed 160 pounds to Fitzsimmons' 154 pounds.

When McCarthy entered the ring, the crowd howled with delight, showing that he was the favorite over the unknown. Bob entered the ring a few seconds later at 8:55 p.m., seconded by Joe Choynski and Martin Murphy. Bob bowed as he was introduced. Hiram Cook was the referee. Present to watch the fight was Professor James Corbett.

After the men shook hands and stood bare-chested, the crowd expressed its surprise, saying "Ugh!" when they saw Bob's abnormal chest and arm development. That combined with his approximate 6'0" height compared to McCarthy's 5'7" height changed the minds of many as to whom the favorite should be.

---

[138] *San Francisco Morning Call*, May 25, 1890.
[139] *Daily Alta California*, May 26, 1890.

Robt. Fitzsimmons
AUSTRALIA

The following account of the fight is an amalgamation of multiple local sources, including the *San Francisco Examiner*, *San Francisco Chronicle*, *San Francisco Evening Post*, *Daily Alta California*, and *San Francisco Evening Bulletin*.

1st round

McCarthy led first and landed to the neck, "which caused the slouchy-looking fellow to hump himself together and show his speed. He replied with a left and right hand lead as quick as a flash, and, stepping back, was out of reach of a return." Billy forced the fighting; ducking low, but fell short with his punches. He tried clinching, but broke fairly.

2nd round

When McCarthy led, Fitz ducked the blow so it only hit the neck, but Bill followed up with an uppercut that landed. Fitz then broke away and repaid him with a left jab on the jaw and a right smash to McCarthy's left temple that brought blood. "After this Fitzsimmons began a regular tattoo on McCarthy's heart, the shorter man being absolutely smothered." By the end of the round, McCarthy had a swollen and bleeding eye. "It was good, gory fighting...but the gore was all Billy's."

3rd round

McCarthy could not do anything on the outside. "From the first to the fifth round Fitzsimmons toyed with McCarthy, stabbing him when and where he pleased with his long arms, McCarthy being unable to reach back with his short arms." Long lefts caused both of Billy's eyes to bleed. Fitz's punches were like "human piston rods flying in and out with wonderful precision and force."

After breaking from a clinch, Fitz landed a left to the chin so hard that "the teeth ground together with a sound like a shoe scraped on a rosined floor." Two local papers agreed that Bob rushed in and dropped the groggy McCarthy with a right-hand smash in the face. Billy got up dazed, but the bell saved him.

Another local newspaper presented a slightly different version of the round's events. "Fitz turned his right loose, and his arm coiled about McCarthy's neck like a long white serpent. He quietly waited for McCarthy to disentangle himself. This done and Fitz with great deliberation knocked him down with his left." Bob walked to his corner. After Billy rose, "he went for Bob with a vim, and was doing some good infighting when the gong sounded."

Most local sources agreed that McCarthy was dropped once, although one said that he was knocked down twice in the round.

4th round

Both came up fresh to begin the round and went for infighting. "Bob tried to put Billy to sleep this time, and came very near slaughtering him. He smashed him on both cheeks at his pleasure and nearly blinded Mac with his own blood." Billy was still quite plucky, and although defeat seemed inevitable, he fought hard throughout. After all, "He was fighting for coin."

Fitz staggered McCarthy with a left, and a right to the ear sent McCarthy through the ropes, "flying as if to dash his brains out by a dive off the high platform." Mac almost fell out of the ring. Bob "gallantly saved Billy, however, by grabbing him by the toes and pulling him back again for more medicine."

Upon rising after 8 seconds, McCarthy fought very hard, contesting every inch of ground and holding Fitz to a standstill. However, Mac "got it again and again."

5th round

Fitz landed both his left and right, while McCarthy failed to land. Bill gamely sacrificed his body to Bob's left leads so that he might get close enough for a hard return, but it was to no avail. It was all Fitzsimmons. McCarthy was "almost completely blinded by little rills of blood flowing into his strabismatic eyes." After Bill struck Bob below the belt, Fitz momentarily stopped fighting and "his tightly drawn face showed that he suffered considerable pain."

6th through 8th rounds

Although McCarthy kept rushing and struggling, he was "only a sandbag for punishment." During these rounds, "Fitzsimmons punished McCarthy badly about the face, causing the blood to flow freely."

The crowd admired Fitzsimmons' fair method of fighting. When there was a clinch, Bob would simply lift his arms, break and allow McCarthy to free himself, and "never during the fight did he take an undue advantage."

9th round

Most of the local sources agreed that McCarthy was dropped three times in the round, although one claimed that he went down four times.

At the start of the round, Fitz's blood was up and he drove in smashing heart blows by the score, "turning his plucky adversary purple with punishment." Bob then shifted his focus up to the head, landing a terrific left on the jaw which dropped Bill for an eight-count. McCarthy was bleeding so badly that he left a bloody imprint of his body upon the ring floor. Upon rising, Bill was met by a right to the jaw that dropped him for nine seconds. He continued fighting, but Fitz again knocked him down, this time sending him through the ropes. Billy would have fallen off the stage, but Bob in sportsmanlike fashion caught him by the arm and pulled him back.

As the time-keepers were counting for the third knockdown in the round, the electric bell rang. "McCarthy had been terribly punished in the last round, and was knocked down three times, going to his corner in a bloody and weak condition."

Responding to the crowd's cries for the sponge to be thrown up, Police Captain Douglass wisely mounted the platform and ordered the fight stopped.

> [McCarthy's] goose was cooked. He wanted to fight yet another, but he could not. His seconds threw up the sponge by order of the police. Plucky Billy was a badly whipped man. He was unable to knock an imaginary fly off the nose of Fitzsimmons all night.

Referee Hiram Cook declared Fitzsimmons the winner.

The fight was described as a mismatch.

> The tall man proved a very cool, clever boxer, and with his long, clean left-handers on the face and punishing rights on the body he stopped all of McCarthy's rushes and fairly slaughtered his stocky, short-armed opponent, who seemed almost wholly unable to hit him.[140]

Much later descriptions of the bout said that after he teased Fitzsimmons by calling him a "bald headed kangaroo," Bob battered McCarthy, dropping him several times en route to a 9th round knockout victory, far surpassing champion Jack Dempsey's 28th round accomplishment.[141]

---

[140] *San Francisco Examiner, San Francisco Chronicle, San Francisco Evening Post, Daily Alta California, San Francisco Evening Bulletin*, all May 30, 1890. The account rendered herein is an amalgamation of these sources.
[141] Fleischer at 121; *National Police Gazette*, August 23, 1890, January 24, 1891, February 18, 1899.

Already, Fitzsimmons had demonstrated that he was one of the world's best middleweights, and he quickly became a hot commodity. "Now Bob is in the swim as a prize for any club. Whereas he was impecunious, an unknown a few weeks ago, he is now opulent and famous."[142] It was said that he should and probably would be matched to fight champion Dempsey. Prestigious boxing clubs wanted to see Bob in action.[143] How ironic. For years, Bob had been a relative nobody in Australia. In less than a month in America, he was a big hit.

On July 9, 1890 in an exhibition before 250 members of the California Athletic Club, Fitzsimmons and Joe Choynski boxed "four lively but friendly rounds." The exhibitions had to be relatively tame because the police had lately been clamping down on boxing, and the police captain was present. Later that evening, after intervening boxing, club swinging, and wrestling exhibitions, Fitzsimmons threw Neil Merritt in a catch-as-can wrestling exhibition.[144]

The next day, Fitzsimmons left for New Orleans, Louisiana, in company with Jimmy Carroll, the lightweight who was then acting as his manager and trainer, and Joe Choynski. Carroll had been a member of John L. Sullivan's late 1886 exhibition tour and had sparred with Steve Taylor and George LaBlanche. In a March 1890 championship fight in San Francisco, undefeated world lightweight champion Jack McAuliffe stopped Carroll in the 47th round. Carroll came back with an April 1890 KO14 over Australian Billy Smith, also in San Francisco.

Bob was scheduled to fight Arthur Upham in New Orleans at the end of July. A San Francisco paper predicted, "Fitzsimmons is a tough member and is so long in the reach, besides being a good in-fighter, that if Upham cannot make the pace a hot one from the start he will find himself badly left."[145]

On July 28, 1890 at the New Orleans Audubon Athletic Club, Bob Fitzsimmons fought Arthur Upham for either a $1,500 or a $1,850 purse (depending on the source). The crowd paid $3 and $4 for tickets. 27-year-old Fitzsimmons was listed as 6-feet in height and weighing either 153 or 155 pounds. 26-year-old Upham was said to stand 5'8" or 5'8 ¾" and weigh 153 ½ pounds. They fought to the finish with five-ounce gloves.

The men stepped into the ring at 9:03 p.m. Bob was seconded by Carroll and Tommy Danforth. The room was hot, so the men wore nothing but shoes and small trunks. They began boxing at 9:15 p.m.

---

[142] Id.
[143] *Referee*, July 2, 1890.
[144] *San Francisco Chronicle*, July 8, 10, 1890.
[145] *Daily Alta California*, July 28, 1890.

The local *Daily Picayune* said Upham looked strong and carried his guard in regulation style. Although Fitz "seemed to have no particular use for his hands," he nevertheless appeared on the alert. The local *Times-Democrat* said,

> As they commenced sparring…the New Zealander did not stand with shoulders squared in the orthodox position, but with a loose and almost slouching attitude of the shoulders, he presented only his left side to his antagonist with his lead only slightly extended and often resting quietly by his side, while his right was swinging in the loosest possible manner, with a pendulum motion…. Upham looked rather nervous, though his face wore a decidedly mechanical smile, while Fitz was laughing good naturedly and heartily as they sparred around the ring, apparently taking each other's measure.

They boxed lightly for a while, and Upham was unable to reach the long-armed Fitzsimmons. Bob did little more than show him that it was hopeless to try to land. Even at this early stage, the disparity in ability was "painfully evident."

> Toward the close of the round Fitzsimmons appeared for a moment to forget himself and landed a swinging counter on Upham's neck. The blow did not appear to be at all a heavy one, but the New Englander went down almost as suddenly as though he had been struck with a sledge hammer. Upham was on his feet again within the required limit and from that to the end of the round the Australian merely tapped him on head, neck, and chest with open hands and with no intention of inflicting anything like punishment. When the gong sounded for the close of the round the universal verdict was that Upham "was not in it."

The Daily Picayune's version of the knockdown said that when Upham turned to move away from his "seemingly awkward pursuer," Fitz fired his right and caught Upham in the back of the neck, sending him down. For the remainder of the round, Fitz seemed to be playing with him.

2nd round

It seemed as if Fitzsimmons could put Upham out any time he wanted. Bob struck him all over the head and body whenever he chose to, and Upham was unable to land any returns.

Fitz was more aggressive in this round, swelling Upham's mouth with a straight left. A left uppercut straightened up Upham. Art fought back hard, but Fitz was able to elude his blows. A right to the nose staggered Upham.

The Times-Democrat said Upham was knocked down twice, requiring almost the full ten seconds to rise each time, appearing unsteady on his legs when he did.

The Daily Picayune described three knockdowns. In a clinch, after Bob struck him with a right uppercut to the neck, Arthur voluntarily went down. A chopping blow to the back of the neck sent Upham down again. A right on the ducking Upham dropped him on his face for the third time in the round. Upham's mouth and nose were swollen, his ribs sore, and there were lumps on his left temple.

From that point on, Upham did not try to fight, but would close in and clinch as soon as he could. Bob did not do anything while they were clinched.

Neither man heard the gong ending the round. The referee seized and pulled Bob away, although Fitz "was merely tapping Upham, as though in play."

3rd round

Daily Picayune: (DP): Upham continued trying, but he absorbed more punishment to the body and head. Four rights in succession dropped Arthur again, but he was saved by the bell.

Times-Democrat (TD): After some clinches, Fitz landed a solid right swing that landed around the left eye and dropped Upham. It also caused a gash and raised an unsightly lump. Again, it appeared that Fitz backed off; simply cuffing Arthur, even though it seemed as if one solid blow would have ended it. Still, "Upham went down several times, sometimes with very good cause, and at others on the shallowest of pretexts, but the Australian made no complaint." Upham was going down to survive and get a rest.

It seemed brutal to allow Upham to continue the utterly hopeless contest, "and Fitzsimmons in an undertone intimated as much." However, Arthur's second refused to throw in the towel.

For a while, Bob only tapped him lightly, in the manner that would be expected in a friendly exhibition bout, and the audience laughed. Bob's seconds urged him to finish matters, and responding to them, he walked up to Upham, and with a volley of punches to the body and head, finishing with the left uppercut, knocked Arthur down. Fitz suggested to Upham that he remain down, but Upham rose. A right quickly dropped him again.

According to the *Times-Democrat*, while Arthur was on the floor, Bob walked over to the referee and asked,

> Don't you think you had better give me this fight? That man can't fight any more, and I dislike giving him any more punishment when he is in that condition. I don't want to be brutal, and I am not going to commit murder.

The referee agreed, but Upham's second argued and protested furiously. Perhaps Upham's cornerman had a bet on how long the fight would last. Meanwhile, Upham was carried to his corner by his other cornerman, before the round had ended. Since it was a finish fight, the referee felt that he had to allow it to continue into the next round.

The Daily Picayune simply said that after the knockdown, Upham was saved by the bell, and did not mention anything about Arthur's seconds debating with the referee or prematurely entering the ring to assist Upham.

5th round

DP: At the beginning of the round, Fitz twice hit Upham's neck with his right, and down Arthur went. He rose, but another right sent him back down. Again he rose, but a left uppercut dropped him. Upham still got up, until a right to the jaw sent him down for the fourth and final time in the round, ending the fight. Upham slid down against the ring post, and Fitz caught him and laid him down gently. He was out cold.

TD: Upham staggered up, but was unable to defend himself. After cuffing him for a few seconds, Fitz landed a blow to the throat that sent Arthur's head backwards, and the back of his neck struck one of the ring posts. He fell limp and helpless, but Fitzsimmons caught him by the wrists as he was going down and gently lowered him to the floor. There was no doubt this time that he was knocked out. Bob picked him up and passed Arthur to his seconds. He remained unconscious for some seconds after being carried back to his corner, but eventually came to and shook Bob's hand.[146]

The Times-Democrat was very impressed with Fitzsimmons in every way. It said that Bob had proven himself to be scientific, shifty, and humane. He had played with his opponent, but put him out under compulsion, trying to administer as little punishment as possible. "The most striking feature of this fight was the extraordinary humanity exercised by Fitzsimmons from the very outset."

Fitzsimmons promises to be the coming middleweight now before the public. His extraordinary reach and phenomenal quickness give him a tremendous advantage over almost any fighter who can come within the middleweight limit. Besides all this, he is shifty, scientific, very quick, and cool headed. He is a man of steady habits and robust health, and in short, he seems to have everything in his favor for a brilliant future.[147]

In Australia, it was reported that nearly every club in America and England were bidding for Fitz's services. Bob Fitzsimmons was well on his way towards the championship.[148]

---

[146] *Daily Picayune, Times-Democrat,* July 29, 1890; *National Police Gazette,* August 23, 1890, January 24, 1891, February 18, 1899; Fleischer at 121.
[147] *Times-Democrat,* July 29, 1890; *Referee,* September 24, 1890.
[148] *Referee,* September 3, 1890.

CHAPTER 5

World Middleweight Champion

Bob Fitzsimmons had been so impressive in his two American fights to the finish that the experts wanted to see him pitted against the highly respected very experienced world middleweight champion Jack Dempsey. Dempsey was then considered one of the world's best fighters, regardless of weight - hence his nickname, "The Nonpareil," meaning having no equal. Eventually, the big match was made, set to be held in New Orleans, Louisiana in January 1891 for a $12,000 purse, an amount that very few fighters in the world could command, including heavyweights.[149]

The 28-year-old Dempsey's career had begun back in 1883, and the significant battles of his career included: 1883 WDQ34 Ed McDonald, KO23 and KO6 Jack Boylan; 1884 KO22 George Fulljames; 1885 KO3 Dave Campbell (who later had an 1889 D10 with Jim Corbett); 1886 KO27 Jim Fogarty, W6 Pete McCoy, KO13 George LaBlanche, D10 Jack Burke (Dempsey better)(Burke had an 1885 L5 to John L. Sullivan and later had an 1887 ND8 against Corbett); 1887 KO45 Johnny Reagan; and 1888 W10 Dominick McCaffrey (who had an 1885 L7 to Sullivan, and later had an 1890 LKOby4 to Corbett) and D6 Mike Donovan. Back in 1885, Dempsey privately sparred a then 18-year-old James J. Corbett, who was just embarking on his amateur career. Corbett was later called a heavyweight version of Dempsey.

In an August 1889 over-the-weight-limit non-title bout, Dempsey suffered a rematch KOby32 loss to George LaBlanche. Dempsey appeared

---

to be the better fighter and was winning throughout, but was said to have been knocked out by a chance blow. Dempsey was still considered the superior pugilist overall, and was still the champion because it was a non-title fight. The middleweight limit was then 154 pounds, and Dempsey weighed 151 pounds to LaBlanche's 161 pounds (technically a heavyweight). Thus, Dempsey was still undefeated as a middleweight. Apparently, attempts by Dempsey to secure a rubber match were unsuccessful. In February 1890, Jack came back with a title defense KO28 over Billy McCarthy.[150]

In August 1890, the *Referee* reported that Dempsey had won 50 out of 51 ring battles, "and was only beaten once by a fluke hit." It had a high regard for Dempsey, but felt that he would have a tough task to defeat Fitzsimmons at this stage in his career.

> Jack is not the man he was; the terrible thumpings he has had during his long and glorious career must have shattered his constitution, and it is hardly fair to ask him now to meet a young and vigourous fighter, taller and longer in the reach, clever and tricky, and sound in his physical structure.[151]

Regardless, it was an exciting matchup that evoked a great deal of interest and discussion, particularly in the U.S. According to the *National Police Gazette*, Fitzsimmons was taller, heavier, had a longer reach, and was called a scientific pugilist who "possesses wonderful stamina, and he is said to be a very shifty prize ring tactician and a tremendous hitter."[152] Still, Dempsey was a highly respected, skilled veteran fighter who was beloved by the entire boxing world. "Dempsey has a reputation which extends to the utmost parts of the earth." Most Americans favored Dempsey to win, feeling that no man weighing less than 154 pounds could defeat him.[153]

However, the general feeling was that Fitz had a good chance, which made the match intriguing. "Many believe the Nonpareil invincible, but on the other hand it is known that Fitzsimmons is not only well scienced, but displays generalship of a first-rate order. Furthermore, he is a steady man in

---

[150] *Times-Democrat*, January 11, 1891; Boxrec.com. LaBlanche went on in late 1889 to be stopped in the 13th round by George Kessler. A few years later, in 1893, Billy McCarthy would stop LaBlanche in the 16th round.
[151] *Referee*, August 6, 1890.
[152] *Referee*, December 24, 1890, quoting *National Police Gazette*.
[153] *Referee*, January 14, 1891; November 10, 1890.

his habits." It was said that the match would be the heaviest betting affair in years.[154]

Dempsey trained in Galveston, Texas and New Orleans. Fitzsimmons trained at nearby Bay St. Louis, Mississippi for some months prior to the fight.[155]

When asked his opinion regarding who would win, James J. Corbett said that it would be in bad taste to express an opinion, because they were both friends of his and good men. "The man who gets away with that fight will unquestionably be the best middleweight living today." Dempsey had been high on Jim after sparring with him. Apparently, Corbett had written a letter of recommendation for Fitz when Bob came to New Orleans the previous year, and Fitz was pleased with the cordial reception which Jim had helped secure for him. Obviously, at this stage, Jim and Bob had gotten along well, but that would later change in a big way.[156]

The local New Orleans papers had their usual big-fight pre-fight analysis. *The Times-Democrat* reported that the greater part of the talent believed that Dempsey would win, but that the Australian's backers gave good reasons for their faith in him.

> The followers of Dempsey point to his long and brilliant series of victories as a proof that he is absolutely unbeatable in his class. ... His friends also say that his defeat by LaBlanche was the result of a mere accident... Those who are betting their money on Dempsey say that he is a quick, hard hitter, an all-day stayer and a man who can, if necessary, endure the severest punishment without weakening or becoming "rattled."
>
> Those who pin their faith to Fitzsimmons' chances set out with the proposition that a good big man is better than a good little one, and that their man has, as far as he has been tried, shown himself an unquestionably good one, they see no reason for believing he is Dempsey's inferior in speed, science, pluck or staying power. A majority of those who saw him defeat Arthur Upham concluded that Upham made such a poor showing that he could not with propriety be rated as a "trial horse" for anybody, but when they saw Upham "do up" Tom Casey without being very severely tested they concluded that the Zealander must have been a pretty fair boxer after all, and that the reason why he had made such a poor showing against

[154] *Daily Alta California,* December 15, 1890; *San Francisco Chronicle,* December 16, 1890.
[155] *New York Clipper,* December 20, 1890; *Times-Democrat,* January 10, 1891.
[156] *Times-Democrat,* January 8, 9, 1891.

Bob Fitzsimmons was that he had been sent against a middleweight of extraordinary quality.[157]

Jack Dempsey

It listed Dempsey as only having lost once in 45 battles, and said that he had long been considered a pugilistic model in science, pluck, endurance, judgment and ready resources of strategy. One said that if Bob was victorious, "he will certainly be a wonder." John L. Sullivan's backers, Jim Wakely and Charles Johnson, both picked Dempsey.

Still, well-respected experts like Mike Donovan and Billy Edwards picked Fitzsimmons. Bob had easily dispatched McCarthy, who had given Dempsey a good fight, and that left an impression on Fitz's followers. Bob was called a tremendously hard hitter, and although Dempsey was a shrewd and cunning general, he did not have the punch that Fitzsimmons had.[158]

A few days before the bout, the local *Daily Picayune* described Fitz as weighing 152 pounds, and as being "wiry and muscular, agile and wonderfully supple, and has a seeming awkwardness that makes his movements the more puzzling."[159]

It was said that this was the first fight since Sullivan-Kilrain that aroused such a great deal of interest. Dempsey was called the most formidable middleweight the world had ever seen. Fitzsimmons was a called the "New Zealand Wonder." The general opinion was that the contest would be a test of endurance and skill such as had never before been witnessed.[160]

Although the purse was a whopping $12,000 (of which $1,000 was to go to the loser), the New Orleans Olympic Club would still make a handsome profit. "In view of this no one can doubt that pugilism under Queensberry rules has grown to be immensely popular in this country." Economics proved it. "Of all the actors, poets, painters, philosophers, statesmen, jurists

---

[157] *Times-Democrat*, January 9, 1891. In 1892, Upham, would defeat Bill Johnson, "the terrible Swede," in 18 punishing rounds, when the Swede broke his right hand. *Chicago Daily News*, April 18, 1892.
[158] *Times-Democrat*, January 9, 13, 1891.
[159] *Daily Picayune*, January 11, 1891.
[160] *Times-Democrat*, January 10, 15, 1891.

and divines that ever lived, no one nor no three of them could have earned anything like that sum through long days and nights of the most exhaustive and fruitful work."[161]

The Nonpareil

Dempsey told a gambler that he was in better condition than he had been at any time since he fought Fogarty. He expected to weigh between 147 and 150 pounds the day of the fight. His daily training routine had included a 15-mile walk and run, four hours of bag punching, and exercise with dumb bells. He had also been sparring with heavyweight Mike Conley, "The Ithaca Giant." On the night before the fight (the 13th), Dempsey sparred 4 rounds with undefeated world lightweight champion Jack McAuliffe at a benefit, both men showing their quickness and cleverness.[162]

---

[161] *Times-Democrat,* January 14, 15, 1891; *Referee,* January 21, 1891.
[162] *Times-Democrat,* January 11-14, 1891.

The bookmakers were firm believers in Dempsey, and there was heavy wagering on the fight. "The fight will break or make a good many New Orleans people, who have been backing the New Zealander."[163]

On January 14, 1891 in New Orleans, at age 27, Bob Fitzsimmons fought his first world title bout, for the middleweight championship against the 28-year-old champion, the original "Nonpareil" Jack Dempsey. Fitz and Dempsey fought to a finish with 5-ounce gloves before a crowd of 4,000 – 4,500. The crowd paid $10 for seats on the benches; $17 for single chairs in the boxes, while others paid $100 for a lodge of six chairs. The receipts were over $35,000. One woman dressed like a man was discovered, arrested and booked for violating the ordinance against appearing in men's attire.

[163] *Times-Democrat,* January 11-14, 1891.

Pursuant to Dempsey's demand, it was stipulated in the contract that both men were to weigh-in no more than 154 pounds (the middleweight limit) five minutes before entering the ring, and that each man had to post $1,000 as a guaranty that he would be on weight.

There will be no weighing in at 154 in the afternoon and fighting at 160 at night. Dempsey's friends claim that their man will win on account of "Fitz" giving out in the legs. "Fitz" on this point says: "Let them talk. No man I ever fought had a word to say about my legs after I got through with him."

Fitz manager/trainer Jimmy Carroll said that Bob's legs were good, and was willing to bet up to $1,000 that Fitz could outrun any pugilist in the world from one to ten miles.

Just imagine fighters today having to weigh-in on weight right before entering the ring. Heck, now they do not even weigh in on the day of the fight, a huge mistake, fraud, and insult to boxing's history. Fighters call themselves "middleweight" champions, but that is not what they are when they enter the ring. What do you think Fitz could get down to if he could weigh-in the day before, as fighters do today?

For the fight, most sources agreed that Dempsey only weighed 147 ½ pounds to Fitzsimmons' 150 ½ pounds.[164] And this was their weights as taken just before they entered the ring! Thus, Dempsey and Fitzsimmons were really actually welterweights in today's terms, more so than middleweights. And Bob was in his late 20s, not a growing young man. This makes it all the more amazing that he would one day win the world heavyweight championship.

Fitzsimmons was listed as standing about 6' ¼", while another said he was 6'1" in his shoes. Dempsey was listed as standing 5'8 ¾". The ring was 24-square-feet, with padded ropes and posts. Outside the ring was a seven-foot-wide space for the seconds, which was enclosed by an outer ring of barbed wire. Eight electric arc lights, in addition to a large number of coal-oil lamps, illuminated the arena.

Fitzsimmons entered the ring at 9:02 p.m., attended by Jimmy Carroll and Doc O'Connell. Dempsey entered a minute later, seconded by Gus Tuthill and Jack McAuliffe. In Jack's corner were drinks of tea, rum, and

---

[164] *Times-Democrat, Brooklyn Daily Eagle, San Francisco Examiner*, all January 15, 1891; *National Police Gazette*, January 24, 1891; Lardner at 104; *Referee*, November 10, 1890, March 25, 1891; *Daily Alta California*, December 29, 1890. The only significant weight discrepancy was whether Fitz was 150 ¼ pounds or 150 ½ pounds.

ale. Both men wore trousers and shoes, but were bare-chested. *The Brooklyn Daily Eagle* said that Dempsey wore blue, while Fitz's apparel was crimson with a band of white at the top. The gloves were weighed at 5 ounces and the men made their selections. At 9:28 p.m., the boxers advanced to the scratch and shook hands.

Unless otherwise noted, the round by round account is taken primarily from the local New Orleans *Times-Democrat*.

1st round

Both were smiling, but Fitzsimmons forced the fight. Bob feinted at the stomach and then landed a punch to the neck that sounded all over the house. Dempsey broke ground and Fitz followed. When Bob drew close he would unload a series of rapid punches to the head, some landing, some missing, while Dempsey guarded with his gloves, demonstrating marvelous cleverness.

At the end of the round, Bob's supporters cheered, but Dempsey's followers still felt confident. One man said, "That's the way Jack always fights. Wait till the sixth round. Jack is just fooling and drawing that fellow out till he gets onto his style, then you'll see how nice and pretty he'll do him." Dempsey was a finish fighter who knew how to take his time. In between rounds, Bob smiled and spoke with Jimmy Carroll in the corner.

2nd round

The aggressive Fitz cornered Dempsey. Jack fought his way out, but received two hard body shots. Bob pressed and Jack moved about rapidly, occasionally landing a body blow on Bob. Dempsey mostly focused on the body, and it appeared that he was also looking to land his famous uppercut. Fitz mainly played for the head and neck, countering there when Dempsey landed to the ribs.

After a sharp rally, Dempsey clinched. After breaking, Fitz landed a terrific right to the side of Dempsey's body that caused him to break ground rapidly. It was later said that this punch weakened him. Fitz followed up but Dempsey clinched repeatedly, trying to save himself from the punches that he was receiving to the head and body. Just before the gong sounded, Bob rushed Dempsey to the ropes and almost knocked him through them with a blow to the neck.

Fitz had the best of it throughout the round. Dempsey's forehead had a deep red mark on it. "The Nonpareil's friends began to have some doubt of his ability to defeat the agile and shifty Australian, but insisted that the relative merits of the men would not be known until after the sixth or seventh round."

3rd round

Fitzsimmons went after Dempsey, keeping him ducking and dodging. Dempsey threw a long right, but Bob swayed back and countered with a left uppercut to the chin. "The blow did not look to be a heavy one, but Dempsey staggered back and looked a trifle 'rattled' from the effects of it." Fitz followed up and landed a right to the mouth that sent Jack to the ropes. Dempsey clinched, but after breaking, it was observed that he was bleeding slightly from the mouth.

Jack danced about, still looking strong and active. "Dempsey lashed out with right and left, but both blows were easily dashed aside, and then Fitz let go a stunning right-hander which appeared to catch his man between the eyes on the bridge of the nose, and Dempsey fell backward heavily. This was the first knockdown." It was later said that his nose was broken. Although Jack rose bleeding from the nose, he was still strong, fresh, and collected. When Bob threw a left hook, Jack stepped in for a clinch, but Fitz was too quick in stepping back, uppercutting Dempsey on the mouth or nose region, perceptibly staggering Jack and bringing a freer flow of blood. Dempsey clinched to survive and missed a vicious right uppercut.

4th round

Fitz again forced matters, ducking or blocking Dempsey's blows. Bob worked him to the ropes, landed a right and left to the breast and neck, but received a couple in return. A heavy right caused Dempsey to stagger away. They mixed it up a bit, but Dempsey started running around the ring to escape. However, Jack could not escape the reach of the long-armed, quick-footed Fitzsimmons. Bob landed a couple solid body shots, and then followed with a shower of blows until time was called. It was Fitz's round from beginning to end, and Dempsey's distress was marked.

5th round

"Fitz continued to follow his man around the ring, using right and left with apparently equal skill and effect, but Dempsey kept clinching to gain time and the punishment was not severe till near the end of the round." Towards the end, Dempsey rushed in for a clinch, but Fitz landed a right and left on the neck in rapid succession, sending Jack to the ropes dazed and bleeding. Fitz appeared to have him at his mercy, but the bell rang.

6th round

After a hot rally, Bob rushed Dempsey around the ring, but both gave and received some stinging punches. Fitz kept pressing, and Jack clinched. They fought savagely again, but Bob did most of the forcing. Fitz had the best of the round and gave more than he received, although Dempsey landed some telling blows.

7th round

Dempsey was growing weaker and groggier, but was still a game and skillful ring general. He would move and clinch, but punch whenever it appeared that he could land. Bob landed a left and right, and Jack landed a good counter right, but it had no effect, as Fitz only laughed and kept forcing the fight, landing solid blows and working Jack back.

After receiving a right and left, Dempsey fell against the ropes in a sitting posture, his hands hanging helplessly at his side. Fitz declined to hit him in that position. After standing again, Dempsey hit the body, but the blows had no effect. The round ended in a clinch, with Dempsey barely able to keep his feet.

Brooklyn Daily Eagle (BDE) and *San Francisco Examiner* (SFE): Dempsey's mouth and nose were bleeding. Bob dropped Jack into the ropes with an uppercut.

8th round

The blood was flowing from Dempsey's nose and cuts in his face, running down his cheeks. Fitz was fresh and light on his feet, without a mark. Jack was still plucky, but he could not move Fitzsimmons. Bob landed a heavy right to the ear and another on the ribs which drove Dempsey against the ropes. Fitz laughed while Jack clinched at every opportunity. Bob struck him repeatedly to the body and head, all of which rendered Dempsey somewhat groggy. The body blows seemed to have the most effect. Jack still showed his ring intelligence and took every opportunity afforded him to land, but it looked as if he would lose. Dempsey's strength and agility had disappeared.

9th round

Dempsey dodged around, but was groggy as Fitz rained blows upon him. Jack's only escape was to fall in and clinch. Bob landed everywhere multiple times, but the most damaging blow was a right uppercut to the body.

Bob fought Dempsey down to the ground several times. Jack would occasionally strike out at his opponent, but Bob was fresh and strong on his legs, and had no difficulty stopping or dodging the blows. Dempsey was down again at the end of the round, and the gong saved him.

10th round

Fitzsimmons forced Dempsey around the ring, administering telling blows, including a good uppercut. Jack clinched firmly and often. Bob landed frequently, and after a rally, forced Dempsey to the ropes. Jack again clinched to save himself. After breaking, Bob hit Dempsey with two rights to the jaw. Dempsey closed in and hugged, but fell to the ground from weakness. Dempsey required two attempts to be able to rise to his feet. A savage right to the face lifted Jack completely off his feet, falling full length on his back, his head striking the lower rope. The gong sounded a second after the blow landed, saving Dempsey.

BDE/SFE: After knocking Dempsey down three times with uppercuts, Fitz picked him up and said, "Jack, you are whipped. I can't hit you." Bob asked Jack to give up, but the game Dempsey insisted continuing, telling Bob that he would have to knock him out. The bell saved him.

11th round

Dempsey tried to run away, but "with one bound the Australian was in range again, and striking him heavily on the jaw with his right dashed him to the ground limp and helpless." Jack appeared out, but dazed and bleeding, showed his championship courage and determination by rising. Fitz easily beat down his guard, and another right to the side of the head dropped him again. He rose again, and Fitz seemed loath to give him more punishment, first appealing to Dempsey to retire, then to his seconds, but

Dempsey insisted on continuing. Another right sent Jack down in a heap for the third time in the round.

One of Dempsey's seconds made a motion with the towel, which nearly everyone took to mean that he was retiring him. Most were later of the opinion that the referee should have terminated the fight at this point, because such a signal was the commonly accepted way of retiring one's fighter. However, when Dempsey rose again, the referee cautioned Fitz that the fight was not over.

Twice Jack clinched and pulled Bob forward as Dempsey leaned back towards the ground, but Fitz was too strong to be pulled down and he let Jack down to the ground gently, as if he were a friend.

12th round

Fitz immediately rushed Dempsey about the ring, landing to the body and head until Jack was knocked down. Dempsey rose quickly, but after a couple Fitz feints, a terrific blow on the neck again dropped Jack. Despite struggling to do so, Dempsey managed to rise. Again, Bob looked appealingly at Jack's corner, but there was no response. Fitz decked him again. After rising and backing away, Jack was dropped for the fourth time in the round by a relatively light uppercut to the chin.

Dempsey's seconds, McAuliffe and Tuthill, both threw their fans and towels into the air, signaling that they were giving up the fight. Fitz went over to Dempsey and lifted him up. Dempsey's seconds entered the ring and took charge of him, bringing him to his corner. Bob retired to his own corner.

It seemed that the fight was over, but Dempsey protested against his seconds giving up. Jack appealed to the referee, and Tuthill then denied giving up the fight. The referee decided that the bout must go on. As they came together again, the gong sounded.

The decision to allow the fight to continue was later met with much criticism. It cost many gamblers their bets on the fight's duration.

BDE: "The twelfth round was sickening to the most bloodthirsty of the audience."

SFE: Fitz dropped Dempsey four times, mostly with rights. After the last knockdown, Fitz went to his corner, thinking the fight was over. Dempsey rose again though, and the bell rang.

Fitz gave Dempsey a "sharp little tap on the jaw and he fell forward on his face." Jack rose. Fitz was in no hurry to finish his staggering, bloody foe, seeming to pity him. A right just below and back of the ear sent Dempsey down for the last time. The fight was over at 10:17 p.m., having lasted 49 minutes. Bob Fitzsimmons had won the world middleweight championship.

The police held back the crowd of admirers who were trying to get past the barbed wire fence to shake Bob's hand.

It was said that it was only Dempsey's second loss in 50 bouts. The bridge of his nose was broken, his lips puffy, mouth bloody, cheek bruised and swollen, and left eye discolored and slightly swollen. Conversely, Fitzsimmons seemed fresh, and did not have a mark on his body.

The Times-Democrat wrote, "It was the almost universal opinion that the Australian was by far the greatest middleweight in the world, and one of the fairest fighters ever seen in the ring."

The Daily Picayune said that the fight "had been all one way." The general verdict was that "Fitzsimmons is a wonder and a class all by himself, and that Jack Dempsey is the cleverest and gamest man of his inches who ever entered a ring." The local writer further opined, "Neither Sullivan nor Jackson had ever met a really great fighter. Fitzsimmons met one in Dempsey." Bob was paid his $11,000 purse.

The San Francisco Examiner's fight summary said that Dempsey landed some good blows, but they had little effect on the shifty Fitzsimmons. The "long, knock-kneed angular Australian" chased Jack around the ring and dominated the fight.

The Brooklyn Daily Eagle summarized that Fitz was the aggressor and showed his superiority from the start. As the battle proceeded, there was no doubt as to what the result would be. Dempsey fought long and well, but was an outclassed and defeated man before it was halfway through. Dempsey knew this, but forged on anyway.

According to the *Times-Democrat*, Fitzsimmons said that he asked Dempsey to give up in the 10th round, not wanting to inflict any more punishment. He told Dempsey, "I am as strong as a bull, Dempsey, and you are weak." Jack replied, "I can't help it; you'll have to knock me out."

According to the other local paper, the *Daily Picayune*, regarding his discussion with Dempsey during the fight, Fitz said,

I asked him to quit when I saw that he had no more chance. I told him that I was strong enough to last all night and that he had better give up. "You fight," answered Dempsey, "I'm not gone yet," and I had to keep it up, much to my regret. His gameness cost me $5,000, which had been promised me in case I won in ten rounds.

Bob thought that he had won the fight when Jack's seconds threw up the towel and were in the ring. He felt that the last two rounds were unnecessary and more than Dempsey should have undertaken. "He's a game fighter, and as all know, I was as clever and kind to him as was possible under the circumstances."

Of the fight, the *Times-Democrat* quoted Fitzsimmons as saying that he did not wish to discuss it, that it was not proper for a winner to try and run down his defeated adversary. "I was not raised that way." However, the *Daily Picayune* said that the less than humble Fitzsimmons said, "It was not a hard one.... I did not work any harder than when punching the bag. I said before the fight that I would reach him, and that whenever I caught him with my right he would go down." That said, Bob also graciously said of Dempsey, "I think he is the gamest and best man I ever met. He can whip any other man of his weight in the country." The newspapers and experts agreed that no middleweight could defeat Dempsey but Fitzsimmons.

Afterwards, Bob said that he did not want Richard K. Fox's championship belt and would not accept it. Fox was the owner of the *National Police Gazette*.[165]

The victory gained Fitzsimmons an immense amount of respect from the boxing community. Although he did not witness the bout, John L. Sullivan, who was a Dempsey admirer, commented,

Fitzsimmons must be a whirlwind. He has the reputation of being a hard hitter and a fast fighter, but Dempsey is one of the most perfect men on his legs that ever lived.... The Australian must have weakened him from the start. If he did he is a good one. In fact any man is a good one that can whip Dempsey in any way, and he must be a phenomenal fighter that can whip him after the tenth round.

James J. Corbett, who had witnessed the fight, said that he had bet money on Bob. "Since I saw Fitzsimmons fight McCarthy I placed him as the greatest middleweight of the world. He is strong, long in the reach,

[165] *Times-Democrat*, January 15, 16, 1891; *Brooklyn Daily Eagle, San Francisco Examiner*, January 15, 1891; *National Police Gazette*, January 24, 1891.

clever, in fact very clever, and his wind is first class. Dempsey was overmatched." Corbett's sparring partner, Professor John Donaldson said, "Cleverness, a good cool head and a good temper is what a man needs in the ring, and Fitzsimmons has all that." Dempsey showed his old-time generalship, but was outclassed. Fitzsimmons showed great skill and surprising strength and agility.

Dempsey called Fitz the greatest fighter in the world. A Dempsey friend said, "I cannot imagine how any man with such height, such immense shoulders and body, and such large bones and muscles can only weigh 154 pounds." Because he looked so big, observers often thought Fitzsimmons weighed more than what was reported.[166]

Fitzsimmons many years later said of Dempsey that he was "one of the greatest fighters that ever lived…. He was an Irishman, wonderfully game, crafty, a superb ring general and lightning fast."[167]

Gus Tuthill said that Fitz was big and clever enough to go against John L. Sullivan. One newspaper called Bob "a phenomenon and the more sanguine look on him as the coming heavy weight champion. Their reason for this assertion is the easy manner in which he whipped the winner of fifty battles and the acknowledged king of the middleweight class." Already, Bob was being considered as a potential heavyweight champion!

Those who championed Fitzsimmons did so with objectivity. Even Dempsey's lone prior loss to LaBlanche was considered a late rounds fluke (LKOby32) in a fight which Jack had been winning, not to mention spotting his opponent 10 pounds (and the fact that he had previously defeated LaBlanche). Bob Fitzsimmons had thoroughly dominated a great fighter, demonstrating skill, punching power, endurance, defense, and the ability to track down and accurately hit a very experienced and tricky fighter.

The night after the fight, on January 15, Bob watched Jim Corbett give an exhibition with Professor John Donaldson. The local paper said, "Corbett showed great science, skill and activity, and the opinion of the audience was that he was the quickest big man on his feet they had ever seen." Regarding his future, when Fitz was asked about a possible fight with the heavyweight contender Corbett, Bob responded, "Corbett is too clever and too big. Middle weights are good enough for me."[168]

When asked what he thought about fighting Australia's Mick Dooley, Fitz said, "He's a heavy weight, and has never fought as a middle

[166] *Times-Democrat*, January 15-17, 1891; *Daily Picayune*, January 16, 1891.
[167] *Louisville Courier-Journal*, March 26, 1905.
[168] *Times-Democrat*, January 16, 1891; *Daily Picayune*, January 16, 1891.

weight."[169] This was Fitz's clever way of saying that Dooley could not get down in weight to fight him, and that he would not fight him unless he could. Unbeknownst to the American press was the fact that while in Australia, the larger Dooley had bested Fitz. Bob was not going to spot him the weight again. In late May, Joe Choynski would knock out the 169-pound Dooley in 2 rounds. Fitz would eventually fight Choynski.[170]

Fitzsimmons and trainer Jimmy Carroll returned to Bay St. Louis, Mississippi, where they had trained during the previous months. Bob signed a contract to make a sparring tour of the country.[171]

A month after the fight, on February 16, 1891, Fitzsimmons arrived in New York traveling with heavyweight Billy Woods. They were set to spar nightly and at the matinees during that week at the Miner's Bowery and Eighth Avenue variety theatres. Fitz said that he would not fight again for six months, feeling that he needed a rest.[172] That essentially meant that Bob would not box in serious bouts, but would travel around with Woods giving money-making exhibitions.

Billy Woods

Billy Woods' experience included: 1890 KO5 Jack Ryan, LKOby3 Billy Hennessey; and January 1891 KO2 Mike "the Ithaca Giant" Conley. In April, Woods would become a Jim Hall sparring partner. In September, he would score a KO13 over Jack Davis, but in December, Joe Choynski would stop Woods in the 34th round. Years later, Woods became a Corbett sparring partner.[173]

Jim Hall had arrived in America in February 1891, subsequent to Bob's victory over Dempsey, which was probably no coincidence. Hall immediately began claiming that he could defeat Fitzsimmons, and informed the press about how he had knocked out Bob in Australia. He showed them the *Referee* article which gave the impression of a legitimate

[169] *Daily Picayune*, January 16, 1891.

[170] *Referee*, October 14, 1891; Boxrec.com.

[171] *New York Clipper*, January 24, 1891.

[172] *New York Clipper*, February 21, 1891; *Chicago Herald*, February 18, 1891.

[173] Boxrec.com. Woods was later listed as weighing almost 200 pounds, but he likely weighed less at this time.

knockout victory for Hall over Fitzsimmons. This made the American press really want to see Fitzsimmons vs. Hall. Despite Fitz's claims that he had thrown the fight, some had their doubts, particularly because most observers were impressed with Hall's cleverness and punching power.

Although Hall had lost an 8-round decision to Billy McCarthy on January 20, 1891 in Australia, when he arrived in San Francisco in February 1891, he scored an impressive KO1 over Alec Greggains. Hall looked like a winner. Therefore, a fight to the finish between Hall and Fitzsimmons was made, eventually set to be held on July 22, 1891 in St. Paul, Minnesota.

During the week starting April 5, 1891 at Chicago's People's Theater, pursuant to his eight-week contract, Fitzsimmons exhibited in the third act of "Fashions," a clever farce comedy play. For 3 rounds, Fitz and Woods would "pound each other within the limits of the city ordinances. Ominous-looking eight-ounce gloves are used, as Billy Woods explained, 'just to soothe the Humane Society in case they got gay.'"[174]

On April 13, 1891, Fitz arrived in Pittsburg, performing with the "Fashions" comedy company there for a week. In the third act, Fitzsimmons and Billy Woods gave their 3-round set-to. "They made a fine appearance on the stage, and did some really strong work, although careful not to hurt each other. Their performance delighted the galleries, and they were compelled to come out again for a short round." [175]

In mid-April 1891, because their eight-week contract had not met with the hoped-for success, Fitz and the Fashion Dramatic Company parted ways. "Fitzsimmons has not been so much of an attraction on the road as has been represented." At that point, Billy Woods withdrew as Fitz's sparring partner and began working with Jim Hall, who at that time was scheduled to be Bob's next opponent. Still, Fitz continued exhibiting occasionally on his own.[176]

On April 27, 1891 at Chicago's Battery D before a crowd of 3,000-4,000, both Fitzsimmons and Hall gave separate exhibitions as part of a variety show which included boxing, wrestling, and club juggling. These exhibitions gave fans and the press an opportunity to size up the two future combatants.

First up was Hall, who stood 6'2" in his boxing pumps, and was weighing 164 pounds, 4 more than the 160-pound contract weight at which he had agreed to meet Fitzsimmons. Hall could not make middleweight, but the two had compromised. Bob was already weighing 160 pounds.

[174] *Chicago Tribune*, April 6, 1891.
[175] *Pittsburg Press*, April 14, 1891; *Pittsburgh Post*, April 9, 13, 14, 1891.
[176] *Daily Inter Ocean*, April 27, 1891; *San Francisco Chronicle*, April 27, 1891.

Hall boxed Billy Woods 2 rounds in such a tame and friendly fashion that the crowd hissed. "Hall has that distinctive Australian guard- the same as Fitzsimmons, Bill McCarthy and Slavin. His hands, for the most part, are on a line with his belt and only leave this position when thrown up to parry a blow or deliver one." Hall's feet were positioned in a way that allowed for universal movement.

Next up was Fitz and Abe Cougle, the local heavyweight described as a soft and flabby novice who "owes what little pugilistic reputation he possesses to having about a year ago fought a draw with Jimmy Dahoney." He was big and strong, but too slow and good-natured to be a good fighter.

1st round

They were supposed to spar 2 light rounds with 8-ounce gloves, so that Cougle could finish up with Hall for 2 more. This was the case in the 1st round, as they merely exchanged light taps. Fitz landed six light but clean blows. It was so tame that the crowd hissed a bit. Cougle only landed once, but it brought blood from Bob's chapped lips (or a cold sore), "and it was very evident from the glitter of the champion's eye that he did not like it." Some of the locals then grew excited and encouraged Abe to sail in, which nettled Fitz.

2nd round

Cougle began the round swinging heavily for Bob's head. One punch landed and upset Fitzsimmons. Bob blocked a swing and then staggered Cougle with a straight punch to the stomach and right and left to the jaw, sending him reeling across the ring. Cougle was too dazed to defend himself from Bob's vicious finishing punches. Amongst the shower of blows, a right to the jaw dropped him.

Cougle rose dazed and groggy. Bob mercilessly attacked him, "planting nothing but swings, and what swings they were! The dull sock of the big eight-ounce gloves as they came in contact with Cougle's face sounded like the breaking of inch pine." Bob crowded him to a corner and four blows sent him down again, "like an ox felled with a mallet."

The police lieutenant rushed into the ring and ordered that the bout be terminated, but it was unnecessary, for Cougle was knocked out, lying face down on the stage. He was carried to the corner.

Cougle was unable to box Hall, so Fitzsimmons and Billy Woods closed the show with their tame and "well-rehearsed three-round exhibition."

Later, Cougle said that he would "larrup" Fitz for his treachery in violating their understanding for a friendly bout.[177]

Four days later, on May 1, 1891 in Minneapolis, Minnesota, Fitz boxed Harris Martin, a local black fighter generally known as the "Black Pearl." He stood about 5'6" and generally weighed in the 145-150-pound range. He had about 21 victories to his credit, including a 38-round knockout over Black Frank. Secondary sources say he had an 1887 and 1888 W8 and D8 against Professor Charles Hadley, another experienced black fighter.

Harris Martin, The Black Pearl

According to the *Minneapolis Tribune*, the Pearl agreed to go 4 rounds with Bob, and if he lasted the distance, he would be paid $500. It was however, a tame and friendly sparring match for points.

Except three or four pretty hard breast and stomach punches, the Australian attempted to do no punching. He had every advantage over the Pearl and the spectators were satisfied to see him demonstrate his superiority without punishment. The Pearl simply kept matters easy by staying away the greater part of the time.[178]

Fitzsimmons won a 4-round decision.

---

[177] *Daily Inter Ocean, Chicago Times, Chicago Tribune*, all April 28, 1891; *Chicago Herald*, April 26, 27, 1891.

[178] *Minneapolis Tribune*, May 1, 2, 1891, July 19, 1891; Boxrec.com. On February 29, 1892 in a 154-pound bout, another black fighter named Charlie Turner would defeat Martin in 19 rounds. *Times-Democrat*, March 1, 1892.

Another semi-local paper described Bob as a 6'2", awkward-looking kangaroo, "as handy with his feet as with his hands, and the easy manner in which he gets away is remarkable. He uses both hands with equal cleverness and force…. There was no time last night when he could not land at will on the Pearl." Martin attempted a few counters, but could not harm Bob. "The Pearl is a good, clever and nervy fighter, but he is certainly not in it when pitted against so phenomenal a fellow as Fitzsimmons." Bob's reputation made Martin cautious and apprehensive. They boxed with six-ounce gloves, but "it is the opinion that even with gloves of that size Fitzsimmons could stop the Pearl about whenever he pleased." The referee had no trouble in awarding the 4-round decision to Fitzsimmons.

Oddly enough, despite the high praise given to Fitzsimmons, this article also opined that the bout had not been earnest enough to sustain the previously high opinion of him. Although Fitzsimmons was the superior man, the crowd, numbering about 800, was not satisfied by the exhibition because it was too mild for their tastes.[179]

On May 21, 1891 at San Francisco's California Athletic Club, in a fight to the finish, 182-186-pound 24-year-old James J. Corbett fought 197-199-pound 29-year-old Peter Jackson 61 rounds over four hours, until the referee stopped the bout and declared it no contest when it appeared that both men were too tired to obtain a knockout.[180]

On May 25, 1891 in Melbourne, Australia, Joe Choynski scored a KO2 over Mick Dooley.

One bookmaker predicted that the upcoming Fitzsimmons-Hall fight would be fixed. He claimed that both men had participated in fixes.

> Now, as to the coming fight between Hall and Fitzsimmons, I can assure you that it will be one of the biggest fakes ever fought in America…. It is a known fact that Hall and Fitzsimmons fought a fake in Australia, and I am therefore, surprised that any club should give them a purse here.

He also claimed that Hall had thrown his fight with Owen Sullivan.[181]
Fitzsimmons and Jim Hall were set to fight in St. Paul, Minnesota on July 22, 1891 for a $12,000 purse, with $11,000 going to the winner and $1,000 to the loser. Fitz trained for the fight with Jimmy Carroll. Bob said,

---

[179] *St. Paul Pioneer Press,* May 2, 1891. It was also reported that world welterweight champion Tommy Ryan was traveling with Fitzsimmons. They may have sparred.
[180] *Minneapolis Tribune,* May 1, 1891. It is possible that Fitz witnessed the Corbett-Jackson bout, for it was reported beforehand that he would do so.
[181] *Referee,* June 24, 1891.

Do I expect to win the fight? I never felt more confident of anything in my life. I have met Hall and know him thoroughly, and, although he is a clever man, I don't expect him to last more than a dozen rounds. He is clever on his feet and has a great reach, but his blows lack force. He is no tactician and wears himself out easily. He is a bit taller than I am, but his development of body and limb above the waist is light. The fight will be of the whirlwind order.

Billy Woods, who had previously sparred with Fitz and who was currently sparring with Hall, disagreed with Bob's assessment of Hall's punching power. He said that Hall could hit harder than most heavyweights. The betting favored Fitzsimmons.[182]

Jim Corbett, who was in town to witness the fight, sized them up. "I am not at all certain as to which one will win. Fitz is a wonderful middleweight. We all know that, for we have seen him fight, and we know that he is no common man. Hall...is certainly a clever fighter." He also said that both men were hard hitters and well scienced. Corbett was suggested as a possible referee for the fight, but Fitzsimmons objected to him, possibly because he had heard that Corbett was friends with Hall. This is unclear. Perhaps it was because of the Corbett-Jackson bout.[183]

Unfortunately, politics and the law proved to be a barrier to the fight, a common theme for many big fights during this era. Ministers and church-goers protested the fight and sought legal means to prevent it. They felt that prize fighting was brutal and attracted to the city only gamblers and toughs. Minnesota governor William Merriam backed them up, insisting that he would see to it that the fight would not take place, even if he had to call out the state militia.

Two days before the bout, arrest warrants were issued for Fitzsimmons and his trainers Jimmy Carroll and Barney Smith. The St. Paul police placed them under arrest on July 21. They went before a judge, who made Bob pay $500, and each of the two trainers pay $200 for bonds to keep the peace.

Since 1877, prizefighting was illegal in Minnesota. However, most took this to mean traditional bareknuckle fighting, and got around the law by boxing with gloves. In 1889, the law was amended to include sparring matches with or without gloves. Violation was a misdemeanor punishable by not less than thirty or more than ninety days incarceration. Despite this, gloved boxing had continued to take place in Minnesota. Quite often, politicians and police let the smaller bouts slide. However, the Fitz-Hall fight was high profile, and the attention it received caused the anti-boxing

---

[182] *Minneapolis Tribune*, July 12, 22, 1891.
[183] *St. Paul Pioneer Press*, July 18, 22, 23, 1891; *Minneapolis Tribune*, July 22, 1891.

folks to come out of the woodwork in force. When it came to big publicity fights, politicians were usually quite eager to get their names in the paper.

Governor Merriam had four companies of soldiers ready to prevent the fight. Under these circumstances, the Minnesota Athletic Club decided to declare the fight off. It had to pay each fighter a $1,500 forfeit it had deposited in case it failed to bring off the fight for any reason. It had also lost thousands in promoting the bout and in constructing the fight pavilion.

St. Paul's mayor, Robert A. Smith, was upset at the governor's actions, calling it an "outrageous interference with the municipal government." Mayor Smith also said, "Were the offense under our laws a felony, it might be excusable, but to order out the militia to prevent a misdemeanor, what criticism is too strong!" Quite frankly, it was not all that surprising. John L. Sullivan had to deal with the same type of political opposition during his career. Politics is a funny thing, and many politicians saw attacking boxing as a good way to earn brownie points with a certain segment of the population. This would not be the last time that Fitzsimmons encountered this type of adversity. Hall and Fitz would have to meet at another time.[184]

Just over a week later in Chicago, the 160-pound Hall sparred 200-pound Jim Corbett 4 rounds. Corbett later said, "Jim Hall is a wonder, I tell you. I boxed with him in Chicago the other night, and I have sparred with some clever men in my career, but by long odds Jim Hall is the cleverest boxer I ever tackled. I think he would have whipped Bob Fitzsimmons if they had fought."[185] Such comments helped to further build interest in what would later become a mega-fight between Hall and Fitzsimmons.

Following the Hall debacle, Fitz found it difficult to make a match. Negotiations with Ted Pritchard, Martin Costello, and others fell though.[186] Thus, Bob was relatively inactive for the rest of the year.

While in San Francisco on November 25, 1891, Fitzsimmons observed John L. Sullivan spar Paddy Ryan 3 rounds.[187]

Fitzsimmons then returned to his training quarters in Bay St. Louis, Mississippi, this time as a trainer. Fitz sparred with his trainer, lightweight Jimmy Carroll, helping to prepare Jimmy for his bout with Billy Myer, set for late December in New Orleans. Bob also sparred with lightweight Austin Gibbons, who was preparing for a bout with Andy Bowen.[188]

---

[184] *St. Paul Pioneer Press, Daily Inter Ocean,* July 22, 23, 1891; *Minneapolis Tribune,* July 20, 22, 1891.
[185] *Referee,* December 23, 1891.
[186] *Times-Democrat,* March 9, 1893.
[187] *San Francisco Chronicle,* November 26, 1891.
[188] Boxrec.com. In September 1890, Carroll had scored a KO21 over Andy Bowen, but in May 1891, Jimmy Dime knocked out Carroll in the 3rd round.

Jimmy Carroll

On December 12, 1891 in Bay St. Louis, Mississippi, Carroll sparred with Fitzsimmons, James Robertson, and Johnnie Griffin.[189]

The following day, on December 13, 1891, Fitz sparred 4 rounds with Austin Gibbons. Lightweight Gibbons' career included respective 1889 and 1890 KO24 and KO19 victories over Mike Cushing, and he was coming off a September 1891 bout with Jack McAuliffe that the police stopped in the 6th round and awarded to McAuliffe.[190]

Against Gibbons, Bob was attired in black tights, while Gibbons wore dark blue. Wearing 8-ounce gloves, "Gibbons showed science and quickness, and won much applause for his plucky aggressiveness against the giant." Another paper said that despite his weight and reach handicap, Gibbons made an interesting contest during their 4 rounds of sparring. Master of ceremonies James Robertson, who was in the ring with them, took a punch from Gibbons when Bob ducked it.

Fitzsimmons worked with his smaller opponent, but still impressed observers:

Fitz's tremendous legs and arms worked like a thrashing machine, and he has not lost one iota of his old-time cleverness. Fitz is too well known to make comments upon further than to say his every movement was the personification of ease, grace and agility.

---

[189] *Daily Picayune,* December 13, 1891.
[190] Boxrec.com.

The crowd enjoyed the exhibition. "Scientific sparring is evidently in favor at Bay St. Louis, to judge from the immense social and financial success scored by these pugilists."[191]

Austin Gibbons

On December 15, 1891, Fitzsimmons, Robertson, and Griffin each sparred 5 rounds with Carroll.[192]

On the 22nd, Jimmy Carroll knocked out Billy Myer in the 43rd round.

On the 29th, Austin Gibbons stopped Andy Bowen in the 48th round.

---

[191] *Daily Picayune, Times-Democrat*, December 14, 1891.
[192] *Daily Picayune*, December 16, 1891.

CHAPTER 6

Testing the Heavyweight Waters

In early January 1892, it was reported that Bob Fitzsimmons had been "so long out of a job, which of course, means that the exchequer is running low, that he now expresses himself willing to go outside of his class, and says he would like to try on either Charley Mitchell or Peter Maher."[193] By the end of the month, Fitz made a match to fight the heavyweight Maher to a finish with five-ounce gloves for a $10,000 purse ($9,000 winner, $1,000 loser) on March 2nd before the New Orleans Olympic Club.[194]

22-year-old 5'11 ½" Peter Maher was born in Ireland and had been boxing since the late 1880s. Amongst his many fights, the hard-punching Maher's career included: 1889 LKOby2or3 Peter Jackson (young Maher retired)(the American primary sources did not list this on his record); 1891 KO1 Gus Lambert (a 200+-pound heavyweight who had given Jackson a tough time of it in a 4-round bout), KO1 Jim Daly (who had lasted 6 rounds against the 220-pound Joe McAuliffe, and was a Corbett sparring partner), KO2 Jack Fallon (whose career included 1888 and 1889 KO10 and KO8 Tom Lees, and 1890 LKOby2 Jackson – bout stopped by police), and KO1 Sailor Charles Brown; and January 1892 KO1or2 Joe Godfrey. Maher had impressed experts with his skill, and more significantly, very big punching power, so this was considered a dangerous test for Bob.[195]

Fitz trained for the Maher fight at Bay St. Louis, Mississippi. He generally took six- to ten-mile walks and jogs, did some sprints, swung dumbbells, punched the bag for an hour and a half, and sparred with his trainers, which included Joe Choynski and Alec Greggains.[196]

Choynski and Greggains were excellent sparring partners for Fitzsimmons to have, because both were top fighters. The approximately 165-170-pound Choynski's recent results included: 1890 W10 Jim Fogarty;

---

[193] *New York Clipper,* January 9, 1892. Attempts to make matches with England's Mitchell or Ted Pritchard, as well as others, proved unsuccessful.
[194] *Philadelphia Public Ledger,* January 22, 1892.
[195] *New York Clipper,* March 12, 1892; Boxrec.com. Special thanks to historian Matt Donnellon, who has informed this author that local Irish reports confirm that Maher was scheduled to box 4 rounds against Peter Jackson, but retired after the 2nd or during the 3rd round. *Freeman's Journal* (Dublin), December 26, 1889 (Bout took place December 24).
[196] *New York Clipper,* March 5, 1892.

1891 LKOby4 Joe Goddard, KO2 Mick Dooley, KO2 Owen Sullivan (who held a victory over Hall), rematch LKOby4 Joe Goddard, and KO34 Billy Woods. Although Choynski had lost to Joe Goddard, both fights were all-out nonstop wars that saw both men hit the deck several times throughout.

Despite his 1891 KOby1 loss to Jim Hall, middleweight Alec Greggains had that year come back with a July KO26 Billy McCarthy and December KO18 George LaBlanche (the only man to defeat Dempsey prior to Fitz).[197]

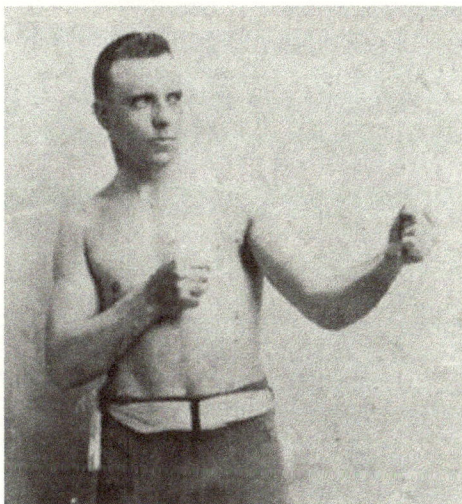

Alec Greggains

On February 13, Fitz ran eight miles before going through his athletic exercises. Bob was said to be putting on weight at a steady rate, sufficient to enable him to meet a heavyweight. Responding to John L. Sullivan's prediction that Maher would win, Fitz said that Sullivan had also incorrectly predicted that Dempsey would defeat him.

On February 14, 1892 in Bay St. Louis, Fitz sparred with Felix Vanquelin (also called Vaquelin), the South's heavyweight champion. In February 1890, Jake Kilrain had stopped Vanquelin in the 3rd round. Against Fitzsimmons, Vanquelin, "although rather short of wind, did very well. It will take a week at least before the big fellow is fit to give Fitz a good go." Apparently, Vanquelin was going to be one of Bob's sparring partners.[198]

On February 27, 1892 at the New Orleans Olympic Club, an exhibition of sparring matches included Fitzsimmons against Vanquelin, and Choynski against Greggains. In sparring Vanquelin, Fitz "kept himself in reserve and made no attempt at display, but his form was pronounced excellent."[199]

The betting had been fairly even, but turned slightly in Bob's favor.[200] Still, one paper opined, "The chances for Maher to defeat the long fellow of middleweights are good, and he should be a great favorite with the

---

[197] Boxrec.com.
[198] *New York Sun,* February 15, 1892.
[199] *New York Sun,* February 28, 29, 1892.
[200] *New York Sun,* February 28, 29, 1892.

betting fraternity throughout the country, with the possible exception of the New Orleans people, who believe that Fitzsimmons is a wonder." In New York, Maher was the favorite. One Maher supporter said,

I never saw a harder hitter in all my life. ... I saw Peter Jackson and Sailor Brown fight...and it took Jackson three rounds to stop the Sailor. It took Maher only thirty seconds to lick Brown, and Brown told me that Maher had hit him so hard that he couldn't hear for two weeks. ... If he hits Fitzsimmons he'll knock him down sure. He is an all round good man, and if he loses, which I never for an instant think he will, Fitz will be the greatest man the world ever produced.

Peter Maher

One criticized that Bob's hands were not as good as they should be. He had hurt his knuckles against both Upham and Cougle, and, "to make matters still worse, some days ago, while boxing all comers at his training quarters he hurt a hand on a big, ambitious black, who was in search of a set-to with the champion."

Regardless, Fitzsimmons was not intimidated or concerned. He said, "If the Irishman comes at me in a hurry, I'll thump the head off him; and if he tries to box with me, I'll fool him handily."[201]

On February 28, it was said that Fitz was wearing the additional weight well. No one could tell where he had added it. Bob said that he never felt better or stronger. "I expect to enter the ring weighing about 170 pounds. I may be a little over, but will not go under. I have heard that Maher is a big, strong fellow, a hard hitter, and a rushing fighter. I have never seen him."

That day, Fitz ran 4 miles, hit the ball for 4 hard rounds in different styles, then sparred 4 rounds with Joe Choynski, and 4 more with Alec Greggains. After their sparring was completed, Fitz weighed 168 pounds. A writer opined,

> Fitz is as clever as boxers are made, and he gets around as if he was on springs. No fighter was ever abler on his feet than Fitzsimmons, and no one more cleverer in getting out of the way of a blow. He can hit as hard as any man in the middleweight class, and as to wind, he can stand a whole night if needed. He too, has speed as well as the good-looking Irishman.[202]

At that time, Maher was said to be weighing about 177 pounds.[203]

On February 29, a couple days before the fight, Fitz went for a 7-mile walk and had "rattling bouts with Choynski and Greggains," his last sparring before the fight. Fitz said that science would not amount to much when a man got a good stiff punch on the jaw. It was said that Maher would likely weigh 180-185 pounds, while Bob would weigh 170-175 pounds. An unconcerned Jimmy Carroll said, "I have seen them all for the past fourteen years, and am convinced that Fitzsimmons is the master in his weight, and away above it, for that matter."[204]

Many of the top fighters felt that Maher would win. Jim Hall said that Maher should lick Bob in less than 6 rounds, although he also said that

---

[201] *Times-Democrat*, February 28, 1892.
[202] *New York Sun*, February 29, 1892; Boxrec.com.
[203] *Times-Democrat*, February 29, 1892.
[204] *New York Sun*, March 1, 1892.

weight did not matter with Fitz, for he was strong at 140 pounds, and strong at 170 pounds. "He must be a freak, indeed; that is all there is of it." Jim Corbett also favored Maher, but felt that Peter would have to do some fighting to win, feeling that it would be a long one. Frank Slavin, who had sparred with and knew Bob in Australia, said that Maher ought to win the fight, "unless Fitzsimmons has strengthened and improved wonderfully in the last few years. I saw him perform several times in the old country, and I think Hall can whip him." Still, Slavin felt that if Maher did not win within 6 rounds, he would not win. Carroll told Slavin that Bob had improved wonderfully. The New York betting favored Maher right up to the fight, although the New Orleans betting still favored Fitzsimmons.[205]

One San Francisco-based expert said, "Fitzsimmons will whip him sure…. He has more science, and has an awful reach, and the ability to hit a hard blow. … He can whip most of those heavyweights."[206] According to the *San Francisco Examiner*, as was the case for Fitz-Dempsey, there was an immense amount of interest in the fight, and a quarter of a million dollars in wagers changed hands.

On March 1, the day before the fight, Fitz weighed 170 pounds in the morning, and got up to 176 pounds during the day. Carroll said that Bob had no superfluous flesh, and was "one of those wonderful men upon whom twenty pounds or so do not show."[207]

Just over a year after weighing a mere 150 pounds to win the world middleweight championship, on March 2, 1892 in New Orleans, testing the heavyweight waters, a 165-170-pound 28-year-old Fitzsimmons took on the bigger, 178-185-pound almost 23-year-old Peter Maher.[208] *The New York Clipper* said that just before the bout, Fitz weighed 167 ¼ pounds. Maher owned up to 178 pounds, but looked bigger. *The Times-Democrat* said that Maher weighed about 185 pounds when he entered the ring. However, the announced weights were 165 pounds Fitzsimmons, 178 pounds Maher. Despite the extra weight, Fitz looked long, lean, and hard.

Bob's seconds were Carroll, Greggains, Choynski, and Professor Robertson. Billy Madden, Gus Tuthill, and Jack Fallon seconded Maher. The fight to the finish with 5-ounce gloves began at 9:10 p.m.

[205] *Times-Democrat,* March 1, 2, 1892; *New York Sun,* March 2, 1892.
[206] *Referee,* April 20, 1892.
[207] *New York Sun,* March 2, 1892.
[208] *Philadelphia Public Ledger, Philadelphia Inquirer, San Francisco Examiner,* all March 3, 1892; *New York Clipper,* March 12, 1892; Boxrec.com.

1ˢᵗ round

Daily Picayune (DP): During the round, a Fitz right to the neck that was a partial push sent Maher down. An angered Maher rose and rushed after Fitz, who danced away. As Bob moved, he would stop and attack, once landing hard on the nose. A left to the mouth cut Maher's lip, drawing blood. Maher viciously chased after him. Eventually, near the end of the round, Maher got Fitz to the ropes and hit him with a left to the ribs and right to the temple that left Bob groggy, causing him to fall partially through the ropes. The bell rang, and the dazed Fitz was carried to his corner. His seconds revived him with brandy, of all things.

Times-Democrat (TD): Early on, the men exchanged hard blows, Bob's getting there with better effect. Maher rushed to close quarters, but as he came in, Fitzsimmons smashed him on the ear with his terrific right, and Maher stumbled over Bob's knee and went down. Because he went over the knee and rolled partially off it as he fell, it looked as if the fall might have been due to a trip or stumble, but it may have been an actual knockdown. When he rose, Maher was somewhat groggy and fought wildly, indicating that he had received a terrible jar.

Fitzsimmons imprudently tried to force matters against a bigger man whose measure he had not yet fully taken, although it was understandable that he would try to seize the moment when he had his man hurt. However, Maher fought back hard, and amidst Peter's wild hitting and mad rushes, Maher landed a sharp left to the ear. Fitz ducked to get away from the follow up, but he either tripped or slipped, and Maher landed a tremendous uppercut to the jaw.

> Fitz's head flew up as though it would fly off his shoulders, and then, almost collapsed, he fell against the back of his neck, just catching the top rope, while he partially sat upon the lower one. Just then the gong sounded, but nobody heard it, and Maher, dazed and half blind from the heavy punishment he had already received, rushed wildly at him like an infuriated bull. Though looking to be at his antagonist's mercy through the awkward position in which he was caught, Fitzsimmons still dodged and parried with surprising cleverness, and as Maher was as wild as he was furious, he failed to do any more damage till the referee heard the gong and sent the men to their corners. They were both very groggy as they walked to their seats, and it was no wonder, for the fighting had been terrific. ... The uppercut he received, though largely a chance one, would in all probability have knocked him down had he not fallen against the ropes, but the wonderfully clever work he did with both head and hands when Maher wildly tried to follow up his advantage proved beyond doubt that his brain was perfectly clear ... It may be truthfully said that in this round each man narrowly escaped defeat.

Bob later told reporters that he badly injured his right hand when he decked Maher in this round.

2nd round

Maher's mouth was continually bleeding. They exchanged some solid body shots. Peter's rights reddened and marked Bob's ribs. After an exchange of some light punches, Fitz countered Maher with a terrific blow on the jaw and a straight punch to the chest which staggered him. Bob landed a left but received a chest blow in return. After some sparring, a blow to Maher's ear was countered by a punch to Bob's jaw, which made him stop to think.

Fitz repeatedly jabbed his left to the mouth. They exchanged hard blows, but Fitz was elusive. "Fitzsimmons, as he danced away, stopped, stepped forward quickly when he saw an opening, always bringing his powerful left with him." Bob ended the round with three rattling punches to the nose, which was now bleeding profusely. Maher's bloody face was a sickening spectacle.

3rd round

Bob was fresh, prancing about, jabbing the bloody Maher on the mouth and nose, the blood trickling down Peter's chin and chest in a tiny stream. Fitz landed a number of blows to the face and body. One jab sent Peter's head back. They exchanged again, with Fitz dodging several drives and countering with both hands to the nose. By the end of the round, Maher was bleeding profusely and showed unmistakable signs of weariness.

4th round

Maher focused on hitting the ribs, but Bob demonstrated his agility and made most of Peter's power shots fall short. Fitz kept away at long range and cleverly landed repeated stiff left jabs to the jaw, mouth, nose, and eye. "It was becoming very clear that should Maher win it would be an accident."

Peter's mouth and nose were full of blood, and the blood partially obscured his vision. Returning to his corner slightly staggering, Maher had a confused and half discouraged expression.

> Though evidently a man of phenomenal strength and endurance Maher was unmistakably groggy at the end of this round. He had been fighting rather wildly from the beginning of it, but it seemed as if the wonderful ducking and dodging of the swift and supple Australian was helping to wear him out as well as the oft-repeated and very stiff left-hand punches that were visiting his nose, mouth and chin. Fitzsimmons would again and again draw him into a savage rush, and then ducking under his lead dance away and laugh at him. Maher would swing wildly, and with tremendous force, and it looked as though he would in time defeat himself in pounding the empty air.

5th round

DP: A left nearly staggered Maher. Fitz became more aggressive. However, coming in, Bob was met with a right to the body that nearly doubled him up. Maher seized the moment and attacked as Bob moved away. Fitz caught him with a right, but was met with a right to the ribs. Bob displayed great science, but was still caught a number of times.

TD: Fitzsimmons kept landing his jab. Maher landed some to the head and body, but was bleeding badly. Fitz neatly dodged the big blows and smiled. Maher landed some swinging lefts to the body, but his face "caught the same old left-hand jabbing blow."

6th round

It remained competitive, but Bob's left jab repeatedly snapped Maher's head back. After Fitz landed two hard rights that hurt Peter, an angry Maher became wild and rushed. Fitz was clever in ducking, but a Maher left landed on the jaw and slightly staggered Bob for a moment. Peter missed the follow up blow. Bob landed a jab and Peter landed a body shot. Fitz kept dodging as Maher attacked the ribs.

> The men were disposed to rush things somewhat, but Maher proved the more aggressive of the two, though he received the most punishment. He continued to play on Fitzsimmons' ribs and stomach, while the Australian contented himself with jabbing him in the face. Maher was bleeding freely. The round had done him no good at all.

7th round

Appearing to be almost at his mercy, Bob hit Peter heavily on the stomach and bleeding mouth. The round featured Bob's continual lefts to the sore mouth.

At close quarters, there were stiff exchanges, and Fitz swung around and hit Peter with a pivot blow that almost took him out. Another local paper said that Maher rushed in, and Fitz, running away, dealt him a pivot blow on the ear. A non-local source said, "Suddenly Fitzsimmons swung around, extended and stiffened his right arm and dealt the astonished Maher a pivot blow that nearly knocked his head off."

Maher's seconds protested vigorously and some in the crowd cried foul. However, the pivot blow was not barred in the agreement, so the referee told them to fight on. Bob continued hitting the mouth with his savage left, drawing blood, landing four times without return. Despite the hammering, Maher was still strong. At the end of the round, by request, the pivot blow was barred.

8th round

Fitzsimmons forced the fighting this round. Bob in usual fashion ducked Maher's swinging lefts, and contented himself with using left jabs. Fitz sprang backward from Maher's hard body shots. He continued pumping in lefts, and Peter continued losing blood.

Maher's face was almost purple and he breathed with difficulty, having swallowed blood. Some blood was already clotted in his moustache and on his face. The blood flowed from his cut lip. His legs were still strong, but the condition of his face led one to believe that he was weak and groggy. Late in the round, when Maher's mouth and nose were hit, it sounded like hitting a sponge filled with blood. Bob hit him with a hard right at the bell.

9th round

The men began the round with renewed vigor. "Maher showed himself a trifle the harder hitter of the two, but was much slower than Fitzsimmons. The Antipodean smashed away for the face, landing nearly every blow and escaping many savage leads." Maher received repeated jabs, and the blood streamed down. Halfway through the round, Maher seemed a bit groggy, for the stiff half-arm jabs had done considerable damage.

Bob had mapped out a very good plan of attack. He had the reach advantage and ability to get away. Therefore, he took his time. "He would approach his man boldly, and after feinting with hand, elbow and shoulder, would shoot out his long left arm and jab Maher on the nose and mouth." Maher took it gamely, but could not prevent Bob from landing at will.

Peter tried time and again to land his right to the jaw, but Bob was too clever at ducking and too quick on his feet, eluding the blows. The one good blow Peter occasionally landed was a right to the ribs or heart, and it landed with good effect. One right uppercut to the ribs made Bob grunt.

Fitz appreciated Maher's strength, and although he did not run away, he was astute enough to keep Peter at arm's length and use his cleverness as a boxer. A non-local source said that the admirably cool Fitz was observed chatting and laughing between landing blows to Maher's mouth and avoiding most blows with good judgment.

Maher began talking to Bob, but what he said could not be heard. It was later reported that he was asking Bob not to knock him out, as he intended to give up the fight. Others said the opposite, that Maher asked Bob to finish him. Perhaps he was hoping to sucker Bob into an opening. At the end of the round, Fitz looked fresh, as if he had only been engaging in a friendly set-to. It appeared that he would be the winner.

10th round

Maher appeared surprisingly fresh and strong, and Fitz kept away for a while. Bob finally landed to the mouth and set the blood running again. Rights to the mouth jarred Maher. Despite Peter's best efforts, Bob was cleverly able to elude the returns. Fitz landed three times to the mouth, but Maher landed a stinger on the jaw that caused Fitzsimmons to stagger against a ring post. However, he got himself out of trouble and was safe again, landing on the mouth.

11th round

Maher landed a solid body blow. Bob clinched his teeth and compressed his lips as if the blow had made him mad, and quickly responded with a hard left on the right side of Maher's jaw, staggering him. They exchanged a bit, but then Bob took his time, playing with his man and tapping him all over. Maher could not reach him. His face was battered and purple from Fitz's continual lefts, two of which made Maher groggy.

12th round

DP: Bob's jab continued landing. One left to Maher's bleeding mouth staggered him. Bob's left sent Maher back. Peter tried to rush in, but Fitz was too clever at avoiding him. A right sent Maher's head back. Apparently, during the round, Maher told Fitzsimmons that he had enough. Fitz landed some more jabs until the bell rang. Fitz told the referee that Maher wanted to quit, and when the referee asked him, Maher confirmed that he wanted to retire. His seconds threw in the towel signifying defeat.

TD: Fitz was fresh and strong and came up smiling. Maher was groggy and a bit unsteady on his legs. Bob landed a half-dozen blows on Maher's face in rapid succession before Maher could put up his guard to ward them off. Bob fought him to a standstill and seemed about ready to finish him. However, Maher spoke to him, and Bob stepped back and seemed puzzled. Bob appeared reluctant, but jabbed him several times to the mouth and face. The round ended with Fitz fresh and Maher groggy and bloody, his green trunks spattered with his own fluid.

During the minute of rest, Carroll, who had been speaking with Fitzsimmons, walked over to the referee and said something to him. Referee John Duffy then walked to Maher's corner, and after a few moments of speaking with Billy Madden and Gus Tuthill, the towel was thrown up. Apparently, Maher had given up the fight. Some in the crowd called him a quitter. Fitz walked over to Maher, shook hands with him, and both took a drink from Bob's pocket flask.

Maher told the reporters that during the fight, he had told Fitzsimmons that he could not hit him, that he knew Bob was the better man, and that he would give up the fight. His cornerman echoed that Maher saw that he could not win, so he stopped.

Fitzsimmons said that Maher was a rattling good man and could hit terribly hard. Regarding whether he would tackle any other heavyweights, Bob said that he would have to think about it.[209]

The Times-Democrat was very high on Fitzsimmons. It summarized that Fitz had a narrow escape early, showed wonderful pluck and coolness, and masterful ring tactics. Maher was a quick, hard hitter, but lacked generalship. "Fitzsimmons is quick and shifty with hands, feet and head and appears in his boxing to have mastered the art of producing the maximum of effect from the minimum of effort." It said that the victory was even greater than that over Jack Dempsey, "and places Fitzsimmons' name alongside that of Tom Sayers in the history of the prize ring."

Steve Brodie, who had been a Maher supporter and had wagered big money on him, said that Fitz was the greatest fighter the world had ever produced, barring Sullivan. Charley Mitchell said that Fitz was the cleverest man he had seen. "He's a wonder."

Another observer said that Maher was suffering from intense pain. "Every tap from Fitzsimmons made him wince visibly. He said after the last smash on the face, 'I'm done, don't hit me any more. I can't reach you and I'm done. Don't hit me and I'll give up.'" Some Maher supporters were upset that he had retired.[210]

---

[209] *Times-Democrat*, March 3, 1892.
[210] *Times-Democrat*, March 3, 1892.

The local *Daily Picayune* said that Fitzsimmons had outgeneraled, outfought, and punished Maher. Bob had outboxed Maher on the outside, made him lose blood by jabbing his lip, occasionally jarred his head, and kept away and dodged Maher's blows, frustrating him. Still, Maher was a strong, aggressive, hard puncher, and landed some good punches of his own. This made Bob's victory all the more creditable. Fitz had proven that he could absorb some big shots, punch hard and box cleverly, demonstrating marvelous quickness in ducking and getting away from blows. It too reported that some called Maher a quitter.[211]

The San Francisco Examiner said:

[Fitzsimmons has] demonstrated his right to a high position in the pugilistic world, and the judgment of those who have characterized him as a second edition of the Boston lad; has been more than abundantly vindicated.... The Australian has demonstrated his prowess, science and skill....

The consensus of opinion of the spectators was that Maher had made a great and game fight, but the pace was so hot that he was forced to succumb. The Australian is looked upon as a wonder, and the belief prevails that he can make it very interesting for the pugilists who are strictly first class in the top-weight class.[212]

Being compared to the Boston lad, which meant John L. Sullivan, was a high compliment indeed.

A Philadelphia paper said that Bob's cleverness with both hands was marvelous, that "there are few tricks in the ring and few hits that Fitzsimmons is unacquainted with."[213] Another said that Fitz clearly outclassed Maher, striking him hard and often, landing when and where he chose.[214]

Top heavyweight contender Frank Slavin had sparred with Charley Mitchell as part of the preliminary. Despite having predicted a Maher victory, Slavin now said that Maher had licked a bunch of nobodies, that his victory over Gus Lambert was meaningless because Lambert had only done well with Peter Jackson because Jackson had been quite sick. He said that Maher had little science, had no left, was slow on his feet, not quick to

---

[211] *Daily Picayune*, March 3, 1892. New York gamblers had lost an estimated $100,000 on Maher, which might explain why they were angry and called him a quitter. Leo N. Miletich, *Dan Stuart's Fistic Carnival* (College Station: Texas A&M University Press, 1994), 100.
[212] *San Francisco Examiner*, March 3, 1892.
[213] *Philadelphia Public Ledger*, March 3, 1892.
[214] *Philadelphia Inquirer*, March 3, 1892.

react to openings, poor with his guard, and just depended on his powerful right.

Still, Slavin called Fitzsimmons a first class fighter and a "cool, clever, shifty man." He also said, "Fitz is one of the best men I ever saw, either in boxing, on guard or ducking. He has two good hands and a head to back them up."

According to Slavin, Fitz dropped Maher in the 1st round with two body blows. He punched Peter in the face and bloodied him. However, Maher rallied and chased Bob to the ropes, where he landed two hard punches to the body and jaw. Fitz staggered against the ropes and was within one punch of being taken out when the call of time saved him and he was carried to his corner. They exchanged blows in the 2nd, but by the 3rd round, it was evident that Peter could not avoid Bob's left and right punches. Maher was weak by the 4th. After that round, Bob mostly picked him apart with his left. "Maher was badly punished and quit like a cur after the twelfth round. Fitz wasn't scratched."[215]

The New York Clipper said that Maher had quit when he still had a chance. "The Irish champion was unwilling to take more punishment. He considered that Fitzsimmons was a better man than he was, and therefore was unwilling to take the chance of knocking him out for being knocked out by the clever middleweight." Although critical of Maher's courage, it was also high on Fitzsimmons.

> [Maher] felt he had been outgeneraled; so he lost heart, and what little courage he possessed vanished as if by magic. Maher proved to the spectators that he was a hard hitter and that his schooling had been good, also that he lacked gameness and staying power. On the other hand, Fitzsimmons' victory elevates him to a prominent place among the heavyweights. His science, coolness and generalship kept his long arms in action at all times. He is a wonder. It was toward the close of each round that he put his batteries to earnest work…. [H]e always aimed to get in a good blow just when the gong would sound, so as to prevent a return.[216]

The day after the fight, Fitzsimmons spoke about the bout. Bob said that he had badly hurt his right hand in the 1st round when he knocked Maher down, landing on the ear, which was a little higher than he had intended. He thought his thumb was broken or dislocated, for his hand was

[215] *San Francisco Examiner,* March 3, 1892.
[216] *New York Clipper,* March 12, 1892.

swollen and discolored. "After that one blow I was unable to use my right on him, and had to do all the punching with my left." In the subsequent days and weeks, Bob received a great deal of credit for essentially having whipped Maher one-handed.

When asked about his narrow escape in the 1st round, Bob said, "Well, perhaps not as narrow as it looked. I may have been dazed a bit, but I was strong, and would have straightened up right off had I not been in a manner tangled up in the ropes. As it was you saw how I kept ducking out of his way."

When asked what he thought of Maher, Bob said, "He is a lot better man than many people think him. Let him go against somebody who will give and take with him and people will begin to think he can fight, for he is quick and a very hard hitter, and a tremendous in-fighter." Bob said that Maher was the best man he had fought, although Dempsey was better in his own weight class. Bob did not think Maher had shown a lack of pluck, as some were saying. "There was such a flow of blood from his nose and mouth that it almost choked him, and there are not many men who would care to keep on as long as he did after seeing that he could not hope to land a blow."

Referee Duffy said that Bob was a man of "good, sound sense as well as speed, pluck and cleverness. He is the kind of man you can put your money on and feel confident that he won't go off and burn it up." He said that during the fight, Maher had asked Bob to go ahead and knock him out. Fitzsimmons, who knew that he had him whipped, asked Maher to quit, but Peter refused and kept on fighting for a while, telling Bob all the time that he was choking on the blood from his injured lip.

Jimmy Carroll echoed that Maher had asked Bob to put him out, seeing that he could not land on Fitz and had no chance at winning. Maher began the talk in about the 9th round, telling Bob that the blood was choking him, and that his strength was going. Fitz responded, "You are good and strong, come on and hit me." In the 12th round, Maher said, "I can hardly breathe; I can't reach you; hurry up and knock me out." Fitz told him to come on and do his best, but Maher said that he was too weak. Carroll said that Maher showed sense by retiring, that he was not in it for the last four or five rounds. "Any man who took as much punishment as he did from Fitzsimmons cannot be called a cur."

Carroll said that Bob had knocked Maher down in the 1st round, but Maher almost knocked him out that same round by a chance blow. At the bell, Choynski brought Fitz over to the corner, and Carroll "placed the ammonia to his nose and revived him immediately."

Carroll wanted Fitz thereafter to fight only as a middleweight. He said that Bob would not fight Jim Hall unless it was at middleweight.

Hall's manager, Charles "Parson" Davies, said that after seeing the Maher fight, Hall was more convinced than ever that he could defeat Fitzsimmons. He questioned Bob's courage, saying that Fitz had just fought at 165 pounds. "Why should he then ask Hall to come to 156 pounds? If Fitzsimmons insists upon that weight limit, I think the conclusion is irresistible to the minds of unbiased sportsmen that Fitzsimmons is afraid of Hall." Hall was willing to meet Bob at catch weights.[217]

Almost two weeks after the bout, Fitzsimmons said,

> I think Peter Maher the best man I ever met…. He hits a hard blow, and is far more clever a fighter than many persons give him credit for. I tell you Maher is capable of making a man see stars, and I think it a downright shame for his friends to speak of him as they have done.

He also said, "There has been an attempt to belittle him, but it is a mistake. I think he will yet make his mark. He has a good reach, is very strong, and is no dub at cleverness." Bob was right. Maher would be heard from again.

Fitz said that the vicious blow that he received behind the left ear in the 1st round almost sent him through the ropes, but it was not a knockout blow, for he was well aware of what he was doing at all times.

> [Maher] hit me so hard my balance was gone, and I went over sideways. I then discovered that he was a stiff puncher. Before that I had knocked him down, and that gave me more confidence. I hurt my right hand in the first round, it is true, but that fact only makes my victory the more complete, for with my left alone, after the first round, I beat a strong two-handed man.[218]

Almost two months after the bout, Fitzsimmons "ridiculed the assertion made by critics that the Irishman was not game." He also said,

> I punched him in the mouth in the first round, and it bursted an artery…. Then when I swung my right he went down. He was groggy, and I thought the thing about over when I went back to him…. He made a desperate lunge and caught me on the ear. I fell on the ropes

---

[217] *Times-Democrat*, March 4, 1892.
[218] *New York Sun*, March 15, 1892; *New York Clipper*, March 19, 1892.

as the gong struck. Choynski was right there, and he picked me up and carried me to the corner. When I hit Peter with my right hand I broke my thumb. I never used that hand but once more in the fight, when I got in a pivot blow! [219]

Almost four years after the fight, Jim Carroll said,

In the first round…Fitz…give Maher his left and followed quick with his right and knocked Maher completely down and made him groggy, but the blow very near cost Fitzsimmons the fight, because he broke one of the bones in his right hand. … Maher was groggy but was swinging right and left hard. The swing caught Fitz hard and he would have fallen flat if the ropes hadn't caught him. … Choynski carried Fitz to his corner and restoratives were applied and when time was called for the second round he was as fresh as ever. … Fitz walked over to Maher and punched him hard in the nose [with his left] which started a stream of claret. From that time on Fitz kept Maher's nose bleeding and did all the fighting with his left until Maher give up the fight. … Maher couldn't hit Bob at all and got tired of trying. [220]

The Philadelphia Press said that Fitz had gained many admirers. "His fight was one against odds well calculated to test his skill and strength, if not his gameness, and the outcome raised him several rungs on the ladder of fame."

Heavyweight contender Jim Corbett said that he was not surprised at the result, saying that he had expected it (contradicting his pre-fight prediction). Corbett spoke highly of Fitz, saying, "He has shown himself a corking good man, and in my opinion he is now justified in fighting any of the heavyweights. … He is game, clever, and a hard hitter, and would probably make it warm for anyone."

Corbett said that he would fight Fitzsimmons if Bob challenged him. With Fitz weighing 170 pounds and he at around 180 pounds, there would not be much of a size difference between them. One reporter soon thereafter said,

---

[219] *Newark Evening News,* April 27, 1892. Over a decade later, when speaking of the fight, Fitzsimmons contradicted himself by criticizing Maher for quitting the finish fight. "He was not game – the only Irishman that I have ever seen who would not take a beating. He had fearful punching powers and was big and strong, but as soon as I began to get to him he was attacked with fright and passed out of the ring." *Louisville Courier-Journal,* March 26, 1905.
[220] *El Paso Daily Herald,* January 22, 1896.

There would be nothing unfair in a contest between Corbett and Fitzsimmons, and the marvelous science of the two men would make as spirited a contest as the world has ever seen. Such a fight would be of peculiar interest. It would be of far more importance than any contest between heavyweights. ... I believe that Corbett would best Fitz, and yet if I should be mistaken, I would not be greatly grieved.

Of course, almost immediately thereafter, Corbett arranged to fight John L. Sullivan in September for the world heavyweight championship.[221]

Regardless, after the Maher fight it was reported that Fitz was averse to again fighting as a heavyweight, wanting to return to defending his middleweight crown, "so that it is not probable that they [Corbett and Fitzsimmons] will come together, at least not for a finish battle."[222] Still, even as of March 1892, a Corbett vs. Fitzsimmons fight was on the minds of some as a potentially competitive and intriguing match-up.

[221] *Philadelphia Press,* March 4, 1892.
[222] *New York Clipper, Times-Democrat,* March 12, 1892; *Philadelphia Press,* March 4, 1892.

CHAPTER 7

Exhibition Tour

Following the victory over Peter Maher, cashing in on his star status, Fitzsimmons and his own combination of sparring partners gave money-making exhibitions across the country. Top boxers typically did this after a big fight. Fitzsimmons would easily demonstrate his vast superiority over all those he met at every performance.

Two days after the Maher fight, on March 4, 1892 at the New Orleans Olympic Club, Fitzsimmons boxed 3 amusing rounds of "the lightest and most playful sort" with Tom Casey, the local heavyweight who had once been defeated by Arthur Upham. Bob's right hand was so hurt that he did not use it, but he demonstrated wonderful cleverness with his left.[223]

Bob again boxed in New Orleans on March 10, 1892 at the St. Charles Theatre. Wearing baby pink, first Fitz sparred Alex/Alec Greggains, who was wearing purple and white, in a set-to that was "mild, scientific and interesting." After some intervening exhibitions, the event of the evening was said to be the sparring between Fitzsimmons and Joe Choynski. Joe "made a favorable impression, being very clever and strong. Neither of the men used his right hand, but sparred scientifically with the left." Choynski then sparred Greggains 4 rounds, after which Fitzsimmons sparred 4 more rounds with lightweight Jimmy Carroll, no damage being done.[224]

Fitz and Carroll arrived in New York on March 14. It was said that they would likely be seen at theatres there, "as their services are in demand." They were preparing for an extended trip throughout the country.[225]

When asked for his opinion of the now-scheduled Corbett-Sullivan contest, Fitzsimmons thought that Sullivan would win easily if he was in condition. However, he felt that John would have to some serious training, because "Corbett is a clever all-round man."

It seems to me, from what I have heard of Sullivan, that he will not do his work like a man who is going to meet a good and clever boxer.

---

[223] *Times-Democrat*, March 5, 1892.
[224] *Times-Democrat*, March 11, 1892; *New York Clipper*, March 19, 1892.
[225] *New York Clipper*, March 19, 1892; *New York Sun*, March 15, 1892.

It may be that Sullivan will underestimate Corbett. If he does that, and will not train, he will be beaten, for Corbett is a remarkably clever man, and can hit a hard blow. Sullivan has no "cinch" with him at any stage of the game.

Jim Carroll agreed, and was going to bet on Corbett. "We all know that John L. is a wonder. He has done many men in four rounds; but you must remember that this man Corbett is fast, shifty, and a puncher, and I like such odds as three to one."[226]

On March 28, 1892 in New York, Fitz had a friendly set-to with Peter Maher at a complimentary benefit for Peter. It was quite mild (too much so for the crowd). However,

[The sparring] convinced all that the New Zealander is far the cleverer and quicker man; indeed, the spectators were much surprised to see how very light on his underpinnings and how shifty was the boy with the auburn hair. He appeared to be able to get on and to avoid Maher quite as he pleased.[227]

On April 8, 1892 in Providence, Rhode Island before a crowd of 400 people, Fitzsimmons exhibited 3 friendly rounds with local boxer Jim Dolan.

In the set-to with Dolan he exhibited the style of shifty tactics and scientific movements which kept Maher at a disadvantage, and demonstrated that he could duck and dodge Dolan's attacks whenever he desired, and at the same time could land wherever and whenever he pleased. Dolan could not make a very impressive showing, and he was aware of the fact. It was a good-natured and interesting exhibition however.[228]

Starting on April 17, 1892, Fitz's specialty company gave exhibitions before crowded houses twice daily at Chicago's People's Theater for a week. A variety show which augmented the athletic exhibition included an

---

[226] *New York Sun*, March 23, 1892; *San Francisco Chronicle*, April 4, 1892; *Times-Democrat*, March 17, 1892.
[227] *New York Clipper*, April 2, 1892.
[228] *Providence Journal, Providence Evening Bulletin*, April 9, 1892. Claims that Fitz undertook to stop him or that the bout was a draw are incorrect.

acrobatic act by the Julian family. They would soon feature prominently in Bob's life.

Fitzsimmons (who claimed to weigh 156 pounds) was scheduled to spar 3 rounds with any willing local boxer at each performance. On the afternoon of the 17th, Bob boxed Jimmy Carroll. Exclamations from the audience were, "Soak him one, Fitzy," and "Bob, paralyze him." However, Bob was kind to his manager/trainer, leading to reactions such as, "Augh! Wha'did I pay me money fer?"

That night, Carroll boxed Harry Gilmore 3 rounds. "Fitzsimmons did not have as worthy an opponent in John Dalton, but he had enough against him to show his ability at hitting, stopping, ducking, and getting away."[229]

On April 18, before another big house, Bob gave a 3-round exhibition with Michigan middleweight champion Henry Baker. "So far as Baker was concerned he was not in the contest after the first half of the first inning." Fitz toyed with him and had the best of it throughout the 3 rounds.[230]

While Bob was in Chicago, a press release said that Fitzsimmons wanted to fight Corbett should Jim be successful against Sullivan. That challenge was printed at the bottom of Fitzsimmons' play bill, and was also announced during his performances. "Mr. Fitzsimmons in his programme declares with three large, effulgent exclamation points that he is ready to annihilate Mr. Corbett. In fact, just as soon as Mr. Sullivan is all through with Mr. Corbett Mr. Fitzsimmons is yearning for a whack at him."

Responding to the prospective challenge, Corbett called it ridiculous and amusing. Corbett said that he was set to box in Chicago in a few days, and if Fitz wanted to meet him there, Jim would consent to stop him in 4 rounds. If he failed to knock him out, he would give Bob the gate receipts.[231]

However, the police refused to allow any rough work there, so Bob could not have accepted Corbett's offer even if he was so inclined. This made Corbett's counter-challenge appear to be a bluff. Fitz responded,

> I always considered Corbett a gentleman…but I see now he has taken a front pew in the cur class. … Mr. Corbett and his manager, Mr. Brady, know most conclusively that no knock-out exhibition can be given in Chicago. … The Chicago public knows that a strong detail of

[229] *Chicago Times, Chicago Daily News,* April 18, 1892; *Daily Inter Ocean* (Chicago), April 17, 1892.
[230] *Chicago Herald,* April 19, 20, 1892; *Chicago Tribune,* April 19-21, 1892; *Chicago Times,* April 19, 20, 23, 1892.
[231] *Chicago Herald,* April 20, 1892; *Chicago Tribune,* April 21, 1892; *Chicago Times,* April 19, 20, 1892.

officers will be present to stop the show at the first evidence of an attempt to "hit hard." ... Mr. Corbett, or his manager, evidently thinks the Chicago public easily gulled, and is seeking to brace up his waning boom by issuing bombastic challenges to me in which he proposes what he knows can under no possible circumstances take place, a 'knockout.'

My declaration to challenge Mr. Corbett, should he by some unforeseen chain of (for him) fortunate circumstances defeat the world's champion, John L. Sullivan, is a strictly legitimate one; not "frothy vaporings." Thus far I have been found ready, willing, and able to fill all contracts undertaken by me.... I shall be on hand with both challenge and money to back the same to fight him for the championship, and flatter myself (many others hold the same opinion) that I can defeat the gentleman from California, or at least keep him quite busy to the finish.[232]

Despite the odds being strongly in Sullivan's favor, Fitz knew that a Corbett victory over John L. was not entirely out of the question. Sullivan admitted that he had weighed 276 pounds upon his return from Australia, and was 245 as of April. Sully also admitted that he still drank "at least five bottles of ale a day. That much won't hurt me. When I trained for the Kilrain fight I had just gotten up off a sick-bed, having been laid up for nine weeks with typhoid and gastric fever." Despite three years of relative inactivity and lots of hard drinking, Sullivan seemed overconfident. "Of course I will win easily. ... I look on that purse...as very easy money."[233]

At that time, there was also further talk of and negotiations for a Hall-Fitzsimmons fight. In America, Hall had been racking up a string of quick and impressive knockout victories. Therefore, a lot of experts thought that Hall would beat Fitzsimmons.

During April, Hall was giving sparring exhibitions with Joe Choynski in New York. One report said that Hall "came within an ace of 'doing' Joe Choynski in their friendly set-to.... Jim landed three light uppercuts, each catching Joe on the jaw, and the latter was dazed in no time." Because public opinion was so high on Hall, "Fitzsimmons is being harassed a good deal by the Eastern sporting Press and public, and unless he agrees to give Hall a fight he will not get much peace as he goes along the road."

If the two boxers met, it would be a good way to resolve "the question whether Hall really whipped Fitz that night in Sydney, as Hall claims, or whether Fitz 'lay down' for a paltry sum as he confesses." Fitz said that he

[232] *Chicago Times, Daily Inter Ocean*, April 21, 1892.
[233] *Chicago Daily News*, April 18, 1892.

would have no problem with making the fight winner take all. However, Bob wanted to make Hall fight at no more than 158 pounds.

Responding to Fitz's allegation that he threw their fight, Hall contemptuously said that Bob's claim was "false and absurd." He showed the *Referee's* report of the fight, which gave the impression that it was a legitimate knockout. Hall said,

> I knocked Fitzsimmons out fairly and squarely. This talk about laying down to me is very foolish. ... Fitzsimmons knows he cannot lick me. He talks about fighting Sullivan and Corbett, but he won't speak of me for less than $10,000, nor more than 158 pounds. It is amusing to hear him. Am I better than Sullivan or Corbett? Fitzsimmons must think so if he is in earnest in what he says. If not, why should he give away 30 to 40 pounds to those men and hold me down to a specified weight?

A later report said that although Fitz had wanted 158 pounds as the limit, "stung by the caustic remarks indulged in by Hall, Bob finally concluded to go a bit higher, and he announced that he was ready to make a match to fight his quondam adversary at 162 lb." This report said the fight would be held before the club offering the highest purse, likely to take place between November and December.

John L. Sullivan said that Hall would defeat Bob. "If Fitz fights Hall at catch weights his goose is cooked. Hall has a longer reach than Fitz, punches harder, and is undoubtedly gamer." He was not alone in that opinion. "Many of the eastern pugilists think Hall will whip Fitzsimmons easily." However, those who saw Bob box made the odds on the fight shift in Fitz's favor.

It was clear that this would be a grudge match.

> Two men never approached each other to do battle in the ring with more of a personal nature at stake, more old scores to wipe out, than Hall and Fitzsimmons. ... Each has denounced the other in the most vitriolic language at every opportunity.[234]

---

[234] *New York Sun*, April 11, 16, 1892; *New York Clipper*, April 16, 23, 1892; *Chicago Daily News*, April 16, 1892; *Chicago Times*, April 19, 21, 1892; *Chicago Tribune*, *Chicago Herald*, April 19, 1892; *Philadelphia Inquirer*, April 22, 1892; *Referee*, April 27, 1892.

While in Chicago, Bob said, "Is 'Smiler' in town? If he is, I'll punch the head off his shoulders, the bloody cur. I'd pay a good fine to break his jaw." Bob was "plainly disgusted when told that Mr. Hales had left Chicago." "Smiler" Hales, a *Referee* writer, had refereed the Hall-Fitzsimmons rematch which Bob claimed was fixed. Apparently, Hales had asserted that Hall's knockout victory was legitimate.[235]

Continuing his Chicago exhibitions, Fitz was scheduled to meet Paddy Brennan on the 19th, and Henry Baker again on the 20th and 21st, but there were no confirming post-exhibition reports, as was often the case for these minor exhibition bouts.

Bob last performed in Chicago on April 23. He was scheduled to meet two heavyweights, "Denny" Kelleher/Kelliher of Philadelphia in the afternoon, and Chris Vogle, "the Michigan Giant," (another paper called him "The Ohio Giant") in the evening. "This is a good card for the wind-up of a very successful week for Fitz."[236]

An out of state report the following week discussed the exhibitions that took place in Chicago that week and on the 23rd.

Fitzsimmons's tour throughout the country since his victory over Peter Maher has been a continual series of brilliant victories. Last week in Chicago he bested three men in one night. They were Denny Kelliher of Philadelphia, a heavyweight scaling 247 pounds; Baker, of Chicago, weighing 190 pounds, and Vogel, of Peoria, who tipped the beam at 200 pounds.[237]

In an interview, Fitzsimmons said that every time before he spars, the fighters all ask him to keep it light and tell him that they will not go on otherwise. He would tap them and they would get mad even from his light blows. Both middle and heavy weights squealed when he punched them. "Do you know it is harder for me to spar than it is to fight? It's a fact. When I go on to spar I try to give my opponent a little chance to hit me, and in doing so I often get a hard rap.... In a fight I won't let 'em hit me." Fitz said that he was weighing 155 pounds.[238]

During the last week of April in Newark, New Jersey, Fitzsimmons met all-comers in 4-round exhibitions. He gave two performances on April 26, 1892. In the afternoon, Bob met Charlie Puff, a young 6'4" 230-pound

[235] *Daily Inter Ocean*, April 17, 1892.
[236] *Chicago Herald*, April 19, 20, 1892; *Chicago Tribune*, April 19-21, 1892; *Chicago Times*, April 19, 20, 23, 1892; *Daily Inter Ocean*, April 23, 1892. Carroll boxed with a man named Ed Myer.
[237] *Newark Evening News*, April 27, 1892.
[238] *Newark Evening News*, April 27, 1892.

giant. The powerfully built Puff went right at Bob, who ducked and countered. Two or three "taps" had Puff on the defensive. "Fitzsimmons could strike as he pleased, and he annoyed the local man, sticking his head out at him and then dodging the lunge made."

In the 2nd round, "Fitzsimmons put a succession of light blows on Puff's face, and holding his head tantalizing near." Puff missed two uppercuts. They both landed some hard blows, but a Fitz right made Puff's knees waver. Fitz shook him with another blow, followed him, and then sent Puff to the floor with one more blow on the jaw. He was carried from the stage, taking many minutes to recover his senses. "Fitzsimmons's blows were not hard ones, but they were effective."

That evening, Fitz met Bill Farrell. Bob did not damage him much, other than giving him a bloody nose. "The champion amused the crowd by showing how easy it was to be in a fight and not get hit."[239]

On April 27, ex-policeman Malone was introduced as James Newcombe. A police officer made Fitz promise not to be too rough on him. Still, Malone/Newcombe made a sorry showing.

To begin the bout, Malone mostly pranced about and was followed by Bob, who occasionally jabbed his face and ribs. Malone winded himself with his own footwork. In the 2nd round, jabs brought blood from Newcombe's nose, and lefts to the ribs further distressed him. Bob also landed about six left swings. The round ended abruptly when Bob's glove became loosened, but then Malone quit. His nose was bleeding and he was badly winded.[240]

On April 28, Fitz boxed both Thomas Robbins and Thomas Burns, who were each attempting to win $50 offered to anyone who could last 4 rounds. Apparently, the 6'2 ½" 180-pound Robbins was an English boxer with a good record, who in the past had made a good showing with England's middleweight champion, Ted Pritchard. Robbins claimed that Jim Hall had refused to meet him two weeks earlier, feeling that Robbins was a "ringer." Fitz was willing.

Against Robbins, Fitzsimmons was very accurate with his left. Robbins backed away and countered. "Fitzsimmons got home a right-hand blow just before time was called and Robbins reeled into the scenes." In the 2nd round, a blow to the stomach made Robbins wince, and he was jabbed several times. The 3rd was short, for after Fitz twice landed his left to the jaw and neck, Robbins threw up his hands and quit.

[239] *Newark Evening News*, April 27, 1892.
[240] *Newark Evening News*, April 28, 1892.

Fitz also had an easy time with Tom Burns, who quit after 3 rounds. "Once he fell under a light punch."[241]

Still in Newark, on April 29, Bob again met William Farrell, the brawny blacksmith whom he had boxed a few days earlier. Farrell refused to go on unless Fitz promised not to knock him out, and only use taps. Bob agreed, but despite this, bloodied Farrell's nose.

> Fitzsimmons seemed to be on springs, and he "generalled" himself out of more hard punches than one could count. His left hand beat a merry tattoo throughout on his brawny adversary's face, but Farrell was stronger at the end of three rounds than any one who had met Fitzsimmons during the week.[242]

Fitzsimmons next traveled to Philadelphia to fill a sparring engagement at the Lyceum Theatre, giving both afternoon and evening exhibitions. On May 2, 1892, Fitz sparred welterweight Fred Woods. "Three exciting rounds were contested, and the curtain was rung down with the two men pummeling each other." Despite that description, Bob had been lenient, only jabbing him occasionally with lefts and rights.

On the 3rd, Fitz had the upper hand at all times in boxing 3 rounds with Richard Wiley/Wyley, a local heavyweight of some reputation.

On the 4th, Bob boxed Professor William McLean (also called Billy M. Lean).[243]

On May 5, Fitz again sparred welterweight Fred Woods. Woods frantically tried to hit Fitzsimmons with hard blows, but Bob did some very clever dodging. "The Australian did not make much attempt to hit Woods, but contented himself with avoiding his blows."[244]

On May 6, Fitzsimmons fought Joe Godfrey, who "gave way in the second round before the champion's blows." Godfrey (not to be confused with George Godfrey) had an 1886 LKOby2 to Jake Kilrain and 1892 LKOby1 to both Peter Maher and Joe Choynski. Fitz was said to be meeting Woods again on the 7th.[245]

---

[241] *Newark Evening News,* April 29, 1892.

[242] *Newark Evening News,* April 30, 1892.

[243] *Philadelphia Public Ledger,* May 3, 4, 8, 1892; *Philadelphia Press,* May 4, 5, 1892; *Philadelphia Record,* May 3, 1892; It was a year later reported that Wiley stayed 4 rounds with Joe Goddard when they had boxed. *Philadelphia Record,* April 13, 1893.

[244] *Philadelphia Inquirer, Philadelphia Press,* May 6, 1892.

[245] *Philadelphia Inquirer,* May 8, 1892.

Summarizing its observations of Fitzsimmons that week, the local *Philadelphia Inquirer* said,

[Fitzsimmons is] one of the most scientific men who ever put on the gloves, and his equal in agility has not been seen in any of the line of champions that have visited this city…. Fitzsimmons is not only a pugilistic phenomena but he is a physical wonder, and he is just entering upon a most brilliant career.[246]

That was a very high compliment indeed.

The Fitz variety company next traveled to New York City to meet all comers there. On May 10, Bob was well received at Miner's Eighth Avenue Theatre.[247]

On May 11, 1892, Fitz scored a KO2 over New York's Jerry Slattery. "It was probably the worst knockout that the middle-weight champion ever dealt any one. Slattery was unconscious fully fifteen minutes, and was badly used up." Slattery had previously been knocked out in the 2nd round by Jake Kilrain (1890), Joe Choynski (April 1892), and Jim Hall (April 1892).

It was said that Bob would meet Jim Brady of Buffalo on the 12th and Thomas Knifton, an English heavyweight, on the 13th, but there were no follow up reports.[248]

As of July, Bob was residing at Bay St. Louis, training for potential fights with either Ted Pritchard or Jim Hall that never actually materialized. Instead, Pritchard wound up fighting Hall in England on August 20, with Hall scoring a knockout in the 4th round. It was reported that Bob was going to begin a theatrical tour on September 11 with a new play.[249]

From Boston's Globe Theatre, Fitzsimmons wrote the *Referee* a letter on August 4, 1892 saying that for the past eight months he had been traveling from town to town with his theatrical group, making 200 pounds ($1,000) per week. His upcoming play was called *The Heroic Blacksmith*.

Bob said that the one man in the world who had to fight him before he retired was Jim Hall. Bob wanted to teach him a lesson. "He won't get me to go out for fifteen bob, as he did at Foley's." Referencing that former bout, Bob said,

---

[246] *Philadelphia Inquirer*, May 7, 1892.
[247] *New York World, New York Sun*, May 11, 12, 1892.
[248] *New York World*, May 12, 1892; *Referee*, July 6, 1892; Boxrec.com.
[249] *New York Clipper*, July 23, 1892.

Everyone present must know that I went out purposely just to oblige Hall and that person who was running him. Notwithstanding all these facts, "Smiler" [the bout's referee] has reported throughout the States that Hall whipped me in real earnest.

Fitzsimmons also said that Peter Jackson was the best fighter living, and that fit and well, would defeat Corbett and Sullivan. "As for Sullivan, Jackson would do him up badly inside of four rounds." Fitz differed in his predictions as to who would win the Sullivan-Corbett fight. He told Americans that he favored Sullivan. However, he told the Australian press that Corbett would defeat Sullivan. "I intend to witness the Corbett-Sullivan battle, and you can take my straight tip...Corbett will lick the 'bully' badly." During August, Bob again told the American press that he would challenge Corbett should he win.[250]

Some secondary sources report that on September 3, 1892 in Alabama, Fitz scored a KO1 over 300-pound Millard Zender or William Zuller. Without providing a date, the *Referee* said that Fitz knocked out Millard Zeubur, a 300-pound pug, in less than two minutes at Anniston, Alabama.[251]

A local New Orleans source said that Fitzsimmons would give a sparring exhibition at a benefit there on Sunday, September 4, 1892, but it is unclear whether it occurred.[252] Fitz observed Sullivan training for the Corbett fight on that date, and spoke with John.[253] On September 6, the day before the heavyweight championship fight, Bob took a swim with Sullivan.[254]

On September 7, 1892 at the New Orleans Olympic Club, Fitzsimmons observed James J. Corbett defeat John L. Sullivan in 21 rounds for the world heavyweight championship. After the fight, perturbed by Bob's challenges, Corbett would not allow Fitzsimmons into his room. Bob had also told local reporters that Sullivan would defeat Corbett, which could have factored into Corbett's decision as well.

Oddly enough, Fitzsimmons apparently told a local reporter that he had never challenged Corbett, and that it had been an advertising dodge by his former manager (Jimmy Carroll). When asked if he would challenge Corbett, Fitzsimmons replied, "No, sir, I do not intend to go out of my class any more. I will fight any man in the world from 150 to 158 pounds."

---

[250] *New York Clipper*, August 20, 1892; *Referee*, October 19, 1892.

[251] *Referee*, December 21, 1892.

[252] *Times-Democrat*, September 1, 1892.

[253] *Times-Democrat*, September 5, 1892.

[254] *Times-Democrat*, September 7, 1892.

However, a couple weeks later, Fitz said that he was willing to fight Corbett. Did he really want to fight him, or did he just say so to get some free advertising for himself? Either way, Fitzsimmons had been impressive enough to that point such that the prospect of a Fitz-Corbett fight was being discussed. Of such a match, one expert said that Fitzsimmons would have a chance with any fighter, while another said that he did not think Bob would be in it with Corbett.[255]

James J. Corbett

After the Sullivan-Corbett fight, Fitz opined,

---

[255] *Daily Picayune*, September 8, 9, 1892; *Times-Democrat*, September 14, 1892.

Sullivan's day has passed, and he met a cleverer man. Corbett is as clever as any man in the world. I think he is the white champion and Jackson is the black champion. If they ever meet I think Jackson will win, because he is bigger and stronger and just as clever. I wouldn't like to see Corbett fight him, for I feel that he would lose. However, I am not always right.[256]

Less than a week later, Bob contradicted his own opinion of a Corbett-Jackson fight, saying, "I rather think Corbett would win in the end, but it is possible that the darkey would get the best of it."[257] It is unknown whether Bob gave different opinions to different papers, or he changed his opinions, or if the reporters took liberties with their quotes.

Fitzsimmons arrived in New York on September 11. That night at Brooklyn's Novelty Theatre, Bob opened his theatrical company's play, *The Heroic Blacksmith*.[258]

In October, Fitzsimmons and Jim Hall agreed to fight in early 1893. Negotiations were still ongoing, and clubs were making their bids for the fight.[259]

Fitzsimmons toured the Southwest with his theatrical company, but eventually it was disbanded as a result of having "come to grief." Bob arrived back in New York in early November.[260]

Tensions had been mounting between Corbett and Fitzsimmons. Although Corbett had previously given Bob high compliments, after Bob's challenge, Jim generally liked to denigrate him.

Corbett had affected to ignore his (Fitzsimmons') verbal challenge to fight, and to further state that Bob was "not in his class." That was a bitter pill for Fitz to swallow, as he considers that, judged by his record, he is in anybody's class, and in so thinking the facts certainly bear him out.

It was said that should the two meet in person, "there is likely to be a right smart jawing match."[261]

---

[256] *Daily Picayune*, September 9, 1892.
[257] *Times-Democrat*, September 14, 1892.
[258] *New York Sun*, September 12, 1892.
[259] *New York Clipper*, October 22, 1892.
[260] *New York Clipper*, November 5, 1892.
[261] *New York Clipper*, November 5, 1892.

Years later, Corbett told Nat Fleischer that he had seen Fitz box an exhibition with Peter Jackson at the California Athletic Club and that "it was like a professor giving a pupil a lesson."[262] Corbett's claim was truer than he realized, because Fitzsimmons had indeed been a Jackson pupil back in Australia.[263]

At that time, it seemed that the thing to do to get one's name in the paper and get some free advertising was to challenge champion Corbett, something others had been doing as well. Australia's Joe Goddard, who had fought Peter Jackson to an 8-round draw and held knockout victories over Dooley, Choynski, and Joe McAuliffe, also made a challenge. This challenge was taken more seriously than Fitz's challenge, particularly because a monetary deposit accompanied it. In early December 1892, Goddard scored a KO3 over Peter Maher, whom Fitzsimmons had bested in 12 rounds earlier that year.

Even Fitzsimmons felt that Goddard had a legitimate chance to defeat Corbett, saying,

> The Barrier champion is not clever, and don't understand much about science, but he can fight and take more punishment than any man that ever stood in a twenty-four foot ring. And such a jaw! Why, he is the hardest man to knock out in the ring today. He would give Corbett a great fight, and while it is said that Corbett would tire him out making him hit the air, Corbett would break his hands trying to put Goddard out. He is bad medicine for the best of them.[264]

Fitz's challenge to Corbett may well have been in earnest, because arranging a fight with the heavyweight champion could mean big money in exhibitions, and to defeat him would mean even more. But first, Bob had an even bigger grudge match to take care of.

---

[262] Nat Fleischer, *Black Dynamite* (U.S.: Nat Fleischer, 1938), volume 1, 123. Whether and when this exhibition took place is unknown. Fitz arrived in San Francisco in May 1890. Jackson was out of state, had a May 19 fight in Chicago, but then returned to California and had a bout there in late July 1890 before returning to Australia for a while, having his last bout in Australia on November 19, 1890. He returned to the U.S. in late 1890 and scheduled the May 1891 Corbett fight.
[263] *Referee*, February 5, 1890.
[264] *New York Clipper*, February 11, 1893.

CHAPTER 8

Revenge

In November 1892, Bob Fitzsimmons and Jim Hall signed articles of agreement for a fight to the finish in March 1893 at the New Orleans Crescent City Athletic Club, for a $40,000 purse, the largest ever offered for any fight in any weight division, including heavyweight. The previous record was the $25,000 paid out for the Sullivan-Corbett fight. Apparently, there was also a side bet of $10,000 per side, making it a potential $50,000 payday for the winner.[265]

The newspapers had hyped this fight for almost two years. Minnesota authorities prevented their much anticipated scheduled 1891 bout. Fitz and Hall subsequently talked of fighting again, and opined about each other and their previous matches in various reports, but the bout never seemed to materialize. Meanwhile, both continued winning and impressing the press and public. All of the ink that the prospective fight had received over the past couple of years only served to advertise and build it to immense proportions.

In May 1892, Fitz had said,

> I only want to face Hall in a ring and then it will be proved conclusively who is the better man. He says that he licked me. Well, he didn't, and what is more, he cannot. We have met four times. Three times I have made him quit and the fourth time I laid down. I have no desire to belittle Hall's abilities. Far from it. On the contrary, I say that he is a very clever boxer, but he cannot take punishment.[266]

Later that year, Fitz said that Hall "is clever, but lacks both heart and staying qualities. If I ever get a chance I will do him in four rounds."[267] That was an interesting prediction.

---

[265] *New York Clipper*, November 12, 1892; *Philadelphia Inquirer*, March 5, 1893.
[266] *Philadelphia Press*, May 2, 1892.
[267] *San Francisco Chronicle*, August 22, 1892.

After the match was finally made, Hall said, "I am very much pleased the question looks like being settled between Fitzsimmons and myself, as it is pretty near time one of us was out of it. As I have neither variety company nor theatrical engagements, I prefer fighting to talking."[268]

The public was excited about the fight because there was much debate regarding who would win, and many top sportsmen picked Hall.[269] The odds were fairly even, swinging back and forth.[270] It was another gambler's dream fight.

In the meantime, Bob gave some exhibitions. On December 10, 1892 in Newark, New Jersey, Fitz took on both Jack Britton and Jack Fallon. Britton quit after only 2 rounds. Heavyweight Fallon had in 1889 scored a KO8 over Tom Lees. In 1890, Fallon boxed Peter Jackson 2 rounds in a bout stopped by the police. Jackson was superior. In 1891, Peter Maher knocked out Fallon in 2 rounds. Fallon was in Maher's corner when Peter fought Fitzsimmons. In November 1892, Joe Choynski knocked out Fallon in 4 rounds.

Jack Fallon

Against Fitzsimmons, Fallon was initially cheered, but the "cheers changed to cries of derision when he began his peculiar method of lying down to avoid punishment." Through this method, he stayed the 4 rounds. "Fitzsimmons and his sparring partner [likely Frank Bosworth] then gave a pretty exhibition, which ended the show." Thus, Bob actually boxed three times.[271]

On December 17, 1892 in New York, Fitz and Hall sparred in separate exhibitions to allow the public to size them up. First, Hall and Alex Greggains sparred 3 two-minute rounds. "The exhibition was a pretty one and Hall showed several of his clever tricks."

---

[268] *New York Clipper*, November 19, 1892.
[269] *San Francisco Chronicle*, August 21, 1892.
[270] *Los Angeles Times*, March 9, 1893.
[271] *Newark Evening News*, December 12, 1892; Boxrec.com. Bosworth was later listed as weighing about 170 pounds.

It was perhaps not so coincidental that Hall's sparring partners over the years had included Billy Woods, Joe Choynski, and now Greggains, all of whom had previously been Fitz sparring partners. Hall was probably trying to get an inside line on Fitzsimmons.

Bob's sparring with Frank Bosworth was more interesting than the Hall bout. Fitz showed his "wonderful agility" and "did some clever dodging of Bosworth's vicious blows." After mostly playing defense in the first 2 rounds, in the 3rd round Fitzsimmons drove Bosworth around the ring. One report said that Fitz made a better impression than Hall, but that the difference in their opponents prevented a true comparison.[272]

Bob continued sparring with Bosworth in early 1893 in preparation for the Hall bout. Beginning with a matinee on January 22, 1893, Fitzsimmons filled a week's engagement in Chicago with his specialty athletic and vaudeville company. These exhibitions would be the last opportunity to see Fitz before he went into training at Bay St. Louis for his fight for the largest purse ever. Bob would leave Chicago on January 30. Hall was already in training.

In Chicago, Fitzsimmons was to meet all comers in friendly 3-round set-tos, and would not object to boxing two or three different men nightly. "Bob takes this course as a part of his training for the coming fight. At each performance he will put in ten minutes' time punching the ball and will then meet the local aspirants and wind up with his trainer, Frank Bosworth." Bob was set to spar Bosworth 4 rounds at each show.[273]

During the evening show on the 22nd, Bob boxed a fellow named Wing, making "a chopping-block of him, abstaining from a knock-out a dozen times in deference to a promise the man exacted before he would put on the gloves with the Cornishman."

Bob was scheduled to meet Henry Baker, the local middleweight, on the 23rd, and wind up by sparring Bosworth. Speaking of the upcoming Hall fight, Bob said, "I have just as good legs as he has and just as good wind and he can't put me out in a week."[274]

Bob's specialty company also included Rose and Martin Julian, the "contortionists and acrobats," as well as musicians, comedians, and other entertainers. The story behind Fitz and Martin Julian is simply too interesting not to tell. While on his theatrical tour in early 1892, Bob came across an acrobatic trio called "The Julians," consisting of Martin and his

[272] *New York World, Brooklyn Daily Eagle,* December 18, 1892; *Newark Evening News,* December 19, 1892.
[273] *Daily Inter Ocean,* January 20, 22, 1893; *Chicago Herald,* January 22, 23, 1893; *New York Clipper,* January 28, 1893. Jim Corbett was in Chicago that week with *Gentleman Jack.*
[274] *Daily Inter Ocean, Chicago Daily News,* January 23, 1893.

two sisters, Rose and Theo, native-born Australians. They began traveling with Bob, and as Martin was the manager of the acrobatic act, he eventually convinced Bob that he could do a good job managing him, better than Jimmy Carroll. So, in late 1892, Carroll was out and Julian was in.

Bob likely had another reason for assenting to the suggestion – he was in love with Martin's sister, Rose. However, Bob was married to a woman named Alice Jones (whom he married in Australia). No problem. By mid-1893 (after the Hall fight), Bob and Alice divorced, Bob married Rose, and, interestingly enough, Martin Julian married Alice. So, Martin Julian was Bob's brother in law, and also married to Bob's ex-wife.[275]

The Hall fight would not be for the middleweight championship, but would be fought at heavyweight. The 170-pound Hall refused to come down to the then middleweight limit of 158 pounds. Bob said that he was weighing 156 pounds, and intended to enter the ring at 160 or 165 pounds.

> I am stronger than he is and can punch a bit harder. I will never give up the fight if it lasts a week. So far in a finish fight not a glove has touched my face. I don't believe in taking blows. ... When this match was made I wanted the winner to take everything, but Hall wanted $2,500 to go to the loser and I let him have it. This fight will be on the level too. There will be no splitting of the purse. ... I say this because there has been talk of fixing the battle. There isn't money enough to buy me off. ... I will close my theatrical season Saturday and...will leave for Bay St. Louis, where I have rented a cottage of which my wife [then Alice Jones] is already in charge. My trainers will be Frank Bosworth, my sparring partner, and my brother William, who arrived in this country a few weeks ago. My manager, Martin Julian, will also be on hand to overlook things. I am in pretty good condition now. I run every morning, am rubbed down, punch the balls at the theater in the afternoon and meet from two to three men each evening. Every morning and evening this week I will take five-mile runs and do other light work.[276]

Fitz's assurance that they would not split the purse and that the fight would be on the level was likely a response to editorials of the kind written by Pat Sheedy, a former Sullivan backer, who wrote,

---

[275] Odd at 74.
[276] *Chicago Herald*, January 23, 1893.

These two men are not, in the opinion of leading sportsmen, honest fighters. One, Fitzsimmons claims to have "laid down" to the other in their native land for the insignificant sum of 15 pounds or about $75. What guaranty have the public that this precious twain will not repeat the performance at New Orleans with such a tidy fortune as $40,000 to "split up" between them? The inducement for a "barney" is tremendous. ... The remedy for existing pugilistic abuses is very simple. First, let representative athletic clubs refrain from giving gigantic purses and insist upon each principal putting up a fair-sized wager on the outside. Ten thousand dollars, all told, purse and wager, is plenty to battle for, and the chances for a corrupt deal between the principals minimized. Second, let the public frown upon all attempts of fighters to star as actors, either in heroic, comedy or vaudeville roles; then we will have a genuine revival of honest, manly art, and breed a race of pugilists and not poseurs.[277]

Bob's Chicago show drew crowded houses that week. One man said that the nightly closing bout between Fitz and Bosworth "is the best he has ever seen upon the stage."[278]

There was some excited anticipation regarding a scheduled set-to between Fitzsimmons and George Siler, a well-known sporting writer and lightweight boxer who had recently performed well in an exhibition bout against Jack McAuliffe.

The professor is a scientific boxer, knows all the tricks, and will no doubt make it somewhat warm for the antipodean slugger. 'Fitz' has been meeting two or three men nightly, and his wind-up with Bosworth is a clever exhibition. He also gives a scientific exhibition of bag punching.[279]

The first man to go up against Fitzsimmons on January 27, 1893 was a boxer by the name of Fitzpatrick. "Fitzpatrick went against Bob in the opening bout. He was counted out in the third round." Next, George Siler boxed Fitz 4 lively rounds. "The veteran more than held his own and fully deserved the high tribute to his ability voiced by his famous opponent."[280] Years later, Siler would referee the Fitz-Maher rematch and the Corbett-Fitzsimmons fight.

---

[277] *Chicago Daily News*, January 23, 1893, reporting a January 11 New York dispatch.
[278] *Chicago Herald*, January 26, 1893.
[279] *Chicago Daily News*, January 26, 1893; *Chicago Herald, Daily Inter Ocean*, January 27, 1893.
[280] *Chicago Herald*, January 29, 1893.

On February 1, Fitz and crew arrived and set up training camp in Bay St. Louis, Mississippi to train there for a month. Bob told a reporter that he "thinks Hall will put up a rattling good fight for about four rounds, but intimates that after the fourth round it will all be Fitzsimmons." The ticket prices for the fight were set at $10, $15, and $25.[281]

Jim Hall's career had included the 1889 LKOby5 to Fitzsimmons and the 1890 KO4 victory over Fitzsimmons. Bob's assertion that the latter bout was pre-arranged had "lost Fitzsimmons a great many friends and admirers in this country."[282] Because Hall was so well-regarded, some Americans questioned whether Fitz really threw their previous fight, or whether he preferred to be thought of as a cheater rather than to admit that he had been defeated. However, Fitz had earlier easily knocked out Hall in the 5th round, and even some local Australian reports had indicated that the Fitz loss was a fake.

Later in 1890, against Owen Sullivan, Hall was by far the cleverer boxer, punishing Sullivan and even dropping him in the 8th round, but in the 9th, the game Owen began attacking and getting the better of matters. However, in the 11th round, Hall landed well and knocked Sullivan about the ring, attempting to finish him. Yet, just when it looked as if it was all over, Sullivan landed a tremendous right and knocked out Hall.[283] Jim also lost a January 1891 8-round split decision to Billy McCarthy, after Fitzsimmons had easily knocked out McCarthy in 9 rounds the year before. However, that was all in Australia.[284]

After traveling to America in 1891, Hall scored a KO1 over Alec Greggains, and sparred in exhibitions with Billy Woods, Jim Corbett, and Tommy Ryan. Hall had looked good in his 4 exhibition rounds with Corbett, showing "quickness and good straight hitting ability, but without the power characteristic of Fitzsimmons' best work."[285] Still, Corbett said that Jim was the cleverest man that he had ever boxed with and that Hall would defeat Fitzsimmons.[286]

Also in 1891 and continuing through 1892, Hall earned a slew of knockout victories over lesser-knowns, impressing the American sports experts with both his skill and power. During 1892, Hall sparred in 3-round exhibitions with Joe Choynski.

[281] *New York Clipper*, February 11, 1893; *Chicago Daily News*, January 31, 1893.
[282] *Philadelphia Inquirer*, March 9, 1893.
[283] *Referee*, August 27, 1890.
[284] *Referee*, January 21, 1891.
[285] *Chicago Tribune*, August 6, 1891.
[286] *Referee*, December 23, 1891.

Jim Hall

In August 1892, Hall stopped England's middleweight champion Ted Pritchard in 4 rounds. Pritchard had an 1891 KO8 over Jack Burke ('85 L5 Sullivan, '87 ND8 Corbett) and a KO3 win over heavyweight Jem Smith (who in '87 had fought Jake Kilrain to a 106-round 2 ½ hour bareknuckle draw). After his victory over Pritchard, Hall was described as the best middleweight seen in England for a long time.[287]

During February 1893, Fitz was training faithfully at Bay St. Louis, varying his work daily. Generally, he ran, hit the ball, and sparred Bosworth. Bosworth said that Fitzsimmons "can hit almost a heavyweight blow and that for cleverness he beats them all outside of Corbett."

---

[287] *Philadelphia Inquirer*, May 8, 1892; Boxrec.com.

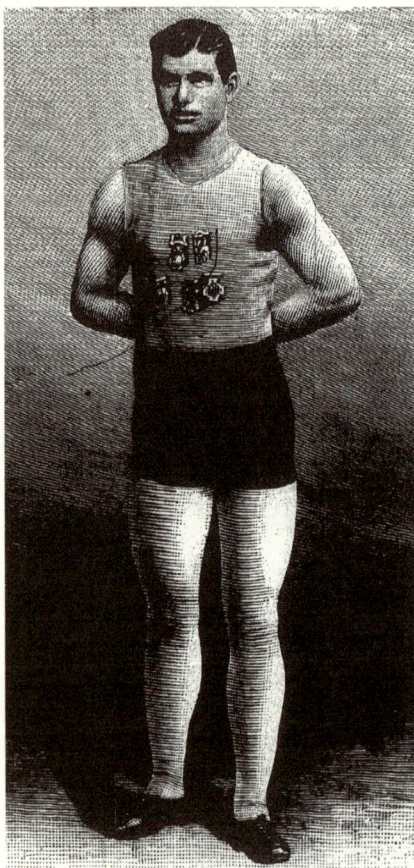

Ernst Roeber

On February 18, Bob ran and walked 20 miles with Martin Julian and Ernst/Ernest Roeber, the German-born wrestler who had just arrived that day. Roeber was 29 years old, 5'7 ½", and 178 pounds. Later that day, Fitz sparred and wrestled 8 rounds with Roeber, 8 with Bosworth, and 8 more with his brother William Fitzsimmons. "Roeber says he never saw a man with such a wind. Fitzsimmons tired out the crowd and was ready for fresh material."

Roeber preferred wrestling, but was also clever with the gloves. He said that he had sparred Hall before, and felt that Fitz was quicker and cleverer. Therefore, Ernst would bet on Bob. Still, Hall had the height, reach, and weight advantage, and a very good right.[288]

On February 20, Fitz ran 13 miles with his trainers. Roeber fell down at the end of it, "exclaiming that another such a run with the champion would kill him." That afternoon, Bob sparred 10 rounds and boxed the ball 14 rounds. While sparring the approximately 170-pound Bosworth, Bob accidentally knocked him out.

[Bosworth] was asked today how it was done, and he said it was over with so quick he thought lightning had struck him or something else very powerful. Fitzsimmons, not aware of how hard he was hitting, caught him on the left ear, which today is swollen so much that leeches will be applied tonight. Bosworth says Fitzsimmons never meant it, and that the middleweight does not know his own strength or just how hard he can hit. Bosworth said today: "You can say for me, that I believe that Fitzsimmons can hit as hard as Sullivan, and is as quick as Corbett."

288 *Times-Democrat*, February 17, 19, 1893.

Bosworth is a quiet man and not given to boasting or exaggeration, and what he says about Fitzsimmons he honestly believes. Bosworth is as heavy as Hall, but the latter is taller and would have the reach on Bosworth. Roeber thinks Fitzsimmons the greatest runner and worker he ever met.[289]

By the end of February, New Orleans was filling up with visitors wanting to see the many scheduled fights there.

Legalizing glove contests has undoubtedly made prize fighting one of the most popular of American sports, and if any one is disposed to doubt this he has only to note the immense sums of money which the clubs of this city can afford to hang up in purses for boxers, who a few years ago were wholly unknown in this country.[290]

There was an equal division of opinions as to who would win the Hall-Fitz fight. Joe Choynski, who had sparred with both men, said that the winner would be hard to pick. He was not sure. Pat Sheedy said that he would bet on Bob. Bat Masterson said,

Hall and Fitzsimmons ought to be a marvel in the way of science. I have seen both men fight, and regard them as the cleverest sort of fellows. Hall, I think, ought to win. He is a man who "likes his gruel," and rather relishes mixing matters with an opponent. He is what is termed a glutton for punishment. Fitzsimmons I know to be a clever man and the best outfighter who ever stepped in a ring, and while I believe he will stand the gaff, I have never seen him undergo the punishment which Hall or an equally good man can administer.[291]

Alec Greggains, who had sparred with both men, felt that Hall was the better of the two. He said that Hall was the harder hitter, more aggressive, and equally skillful. "Fitzsimmons though, is wonderfully quick, and while not such an aggressive fighter as his opponent, is not one to allow an opening to escape his notice, and is always on the lookout for that critical time known as the moment when a man is 'going.'"[292]

---

[289] *Times-Democrat*, February 21, 1893.
[290] *Times-Democrat*, February 27, 1893.
[291] *Times-Democrat*, February 27, 28, 1893.
[292] *Times-Democrat*, March 2, 1893.

Within a week of the Fitz-Hall fight, on March 3, 1893, another big fight also took place in New Orleans. In a back and forth grueling battle, Denver Ed Smith knocked out Joe Goddard in the 18th round.

On March 5, Bob's exercise included wood chopping and slinging the sledgehammer down at a local blacksmith shop.[293] Julian said that Fitz walked 3.5 miles, then ran the same distance back, his breathing being no harder than what an average man's might be walking up stairs. Bob later punched the ball, and then sparred five different men, including Bosworth, 22 rounds total, changing his style of fighting every second round, until his partners all had enough. Later, Bob took another run.[294]

On March 6, two days before the fight, Hall was said to be weighing about 175 pounds. Fitz weighed 166 ½ pounds in the morning. Julian examined the sets of light green gloves that were to be used for the fight, and found them satisfactory. He said that Fitz was "game as a pebble," a natural fighter, and in the best condition possible. "When a man with Fitzsimmons' skill and strength goes after a man with the determination of licking him; some one is going to get hurt." Julian said that Bob would win, "to a dead moral certainty."[295]

At that point, the betting was slightly in Hall's favor, with bets on Fitz being given at even money. By the day of the fight, the betting was about evenly divided. Most of the bets against Bob, as usual, came out of New York. Pat Sheedy, William Harding, and Ed Carney were the only well-known New Yorkers who backed Fitz. Jim Corbett bet $200 on Hall.[296]

The day before the fight, Bob Fitzsimmons became an American citizen. He went to the courthouse and filled out the naturalization papers. Fitz said, "I don't know what the Queen of England has done for me. America is my home, and I want to have it for my country." The following day's fight report several times referenced his new status as an American. Still, over the years, most reporters erroneously called him an Australian.

On March 8, 1893 at the New Orleans Crescent City Athletic Club, 29-year-old Bob Fitzsimmons once again took on then 24-year-old Jim Hall in a grudge match. According to the local *Daily Picayune*, when asked their weights, Fitzsimmons gave his as 165 pounds, and looked it. Hall claimed to be 163 ½ pounds, but appeared much heavier. The same article later said that Fitz was 162 pounds and that Hall must have weighed nearly 170.[297] The local *Times-Democrat* said, "There are different stories about the weight of the men. Reliable authority had it that Hall entered the ring weighing 167

---

[293] *Times-Democrat*, March 5, 1893.
[294] *Times-Democrat*, March 7, 1893.
[295] *Times-Democrat*, March 7, 1893.
[296] *Times-Democrat*, March 8, 9, 1893.
[297] *Daily Picayune*, March 9, 1893.

½ pounds, Fitzsimmons' weight being 163." However, it also said that Fitz's seconds gave his weight as 167 pounds, and that Charley Mitchell, a Hall trainer, gave Hall's weight as 167 pounds as well.[298] Regardless, this clearly was a heavyweight bout. Bob was listed as standing six-feet in his stockings, while Hall was 6' ¾" barefoot.

In the dressing room, the balding Bob combed his hair and asked, "How does my hair look?" Someone jokingly responded that he had missed a hair. Bob then took a drink of liquor before going out.

Hall entered the ring at 9:02 p.m. along with his seconds, Jack McAuliffe, Charley Mitchell, John Kline, Squire Abington, and Michael Lawler. Carrying an American flag, Fitz entered a minute later, wearing red trunks (which may have been trousers), a belt of American colors, red socks, and a striped overcoat that went down to his ankles. Accompanying him were Martin Julian, William Fitzsimmons, Frank Bosworth, and club representative Tom Anderson. The crowd contained between 5,000 and 6,000 people.

At ring center, the two boxers did not shake hands, although McAuliffe and Julian did. Referee John Duffy said that the men could hit when their hands were free in clinches, but barred the pivot blow. Julian objected to Mitchell "working" Hall's gloves on the knuckles, and Duffy had to intervene to bring the five-ounce gloves back to their proper proportions. They began boxing at about 9:23 p.m.[299]

1st round

Daily Picayune (DP): Fitz carried his shoulders and head well back, his arms close to his side and well forward. He was the aggressor, and landed the best punch of the round, a hard right to the side. Throughout the fight, Fitzsimmons went to the body with his right. Mostly, the round was devoted to sparring and testing each other's points. Hall generally stayed away and allowed Fitz to do the work, for at close quarters, Fitzsimmons "had a right which could be piled for mischief."

Times-Democrat (TD): Fitz feinted with his left and Hall quickly raised his guard and readied his right for a counter. Bob danced away. He came back and tapped Hall on the stomach. Rushing forward, Fitz landed his left lightly on the body and followed with his right for the head, forcing Hall to the ropes. Hall ducked and clinched. After breaking, Fitz landed a swift and heavy right half-arm blow, but Hall countered with effect to Bob's neck.

[298] *Times-Democrat*, March 9, 1893.
[299] *Times-Democrat, Philadelphia Inquirer*, March 9, 1893.

Hall quickened the pace a little. Jim's contingent cheered. Fitz feinted with his right and threw the left for the head, but fell short. Hall countered with the right and Fitz ducked under it and clinched.

The men kept tapping each other at long range for half a minute, making a pretty exhibition. Hall then assumed the offensive, shooting out a hard right, but with wonderful skill and quickness, Fitz ducked and landed a counter right to the body, following up with a clinch.

> The round was an excellent test of skill. Fitzsimmons showed remarkable quickness in his lefthanded leads and with his short half arm blows with his right. Hall exhibited great skill in warding the blows and even this early in the fight was put down by all who saw him as one of the quickest and best scienced men that Fitzsimmons had ever been pitted against. Honors were easy in the round; the followers of the respective men claimed superiority for their favorite, but it was as even a round as could well be imagined.

It later summarized, "Both showed marvelous cleverness, and though the exchanges were at times sharp and hot, the round ended before either man had received much damage."

2nd round

DP: Hall was growing more confident and had the better of it from a distance. Jim eventually attacked and brought Fitz to the ropes, where Bob clinched. The attacking Hall landed a number of blows along the ropes. At that point, Hall seemed quicker and cleverer, though Fitz fought back gamely. Eventually, Bob was forced to clinch again, for he could not get off the ropes.

TD: After some preliminary sparring, Bob went at the stomach with left and right in rapid succession, landing the second blow. Hall clinched. After breaking, Hall landed his right and left to both of Bob's temples. Fitz then ducked and ran off to the side and gave a playful smile. Bob feinted several times with the right, and then shot out his straight left to Hall's chin. Hall attempted a counter, but missed, and Fitz landed a right to the jugular. Hall responded with a right to the shoulder. Fitz dodged away from the aggressive Hall, and in his retreat, managed to land a left swing to the stomach. A hot rally followed, with both men succeeding in parrying most of the blows, until Hall drove a stinging punch onto Bob's cheek bone. Fitz clinched.

After the subsequent sparring, Fitz assumed the aggressive and chased Hall about the ring, but missed his punches. When Hall got near the ropes, he changed tactics and became aggressive, and Fitz retreated. There was a rapid interchange of ineffective blows.

Hall advanced while Bob retreated warily. Near the end of the round, Hall landed a stinging left on Bob's right ear and followed it immediately with a terrific straight right that missed because Fitz ducked and clinched.

A later summary said that the fighting was faster this round. Fitz landed a good stiff lead over the heart, but in the fast rallies at short range, Hall appeared to have a shade the better of it. Once, while Fitz ducked, he caught an uppercut on the jaw, and he hugged tightly to prevent a repetition. Although Hall was inclined to force the fighting, he did not inflict much punishment. The general feeling was that Hall had the slight edge in this round.

3rd round

DP: Fitz forced the fighting, and kept at it even when he got the worst of it. Hall landed a number of solid blows, mostly uppercuts that seemed to hurt Fitz, who clinched. However, by the end of the round, Bob was having slightly the better of it. Fitz seemed angry and continued attacking and crowding Hall. Apparently, Hall landed more, but Fitz landed the hardest blows, particularly at the end of the round.

TD: Their clever give and take continued. "Hall started to do some fighting in this round and he worried the champion considerably." Hall would both lead and counter, forcing Bob back, landing some good blows to the body and head. Fitz would duck or rush in and clinch tightly to save himself. Hall "had decidedly the better of the greater part of the round, and Fitzsimmons was at one time in a state very near approaching distress." Hall pressed his advantage. "Again and again Hall attempted to land, but Fitzsimmons was too quick for him and saved punishment by running in and clinching."

Despite the fact that Hall was in control for most of the round, Bob "rallied surprisingly and before the round was ended he landed three clear left-handers full in Hall's face, which seemed to somewhat astonish the Australian. Though the round ended in Fitzsimmons' favor, Hall had the better of it as a whole." The lefts that Bob landed at the end of the round were all strong, stiff punches.

A later summary said that the fighting was mostly at short range in this round, with Hall appearing to be the better of the two. Fitz was defensive, ducking his head and working to gain time, while Hall fought savagely. The round was in Jim's favor. "He appeared the steadier and cooler of the two, and the straighter hitter, Fitzsimmons' blows being mostly round arm swings, which Hall parried cleverly." Still, it must be remembered that "Fitzsimmons rallied very pluckily shortly before the gong sounded; and did some very effective fighting, in spite of the lead that Hall had obtained over him." In the corner, Fitz had a quiet look of determination which showed that he was far from being whipped.

4th round

DP: During the round, Fitz made an awkward feint with his left. Hall dodged and then smiled. Fitz then shot out his lightning right to the jaw. "The sound of the glove when it reached the fatal point was followed by a dull sound as Hall fell full length on the padded floor. He went down like a log, stiff, and to all appearances unconscious." Hall had hit his head on the floor and was completely out. There was some fear that he was seriously injured, as Hall recovered consciousness very slowly.

TD: "In this $40,000 round there were but two blows passed: Fitzsimmons struck Hall, and Hall struck the floor! It was a right-hand swing that Fitzsimmons landed and it caught Hall right on the point of the jaw." The blow was "swift as a flash of lightning" and dropped Hall to the floor "as if pierced to the heart by a bullet." The round only lasted about a minute.

At the start of the round, Fitz's friends were a bit uneasy. In the 3rd round, Hall had shown easy, graceful ring tactics and had little trouble landing. Those who had bet on Hall grew confident. In the corner, Mitchell told Hall, "Take your time; you have a 'cinch'."

However, Fitzsimmons had sized up Hall and called all his experience into play. He knew that he could not afford to take chances with him and watched Hall's every move. "It was in this round that the superb self-possession of Fitzsimmons and his ability to take advantage of every opportunity was shown. His manifestation of these qualities evidences his superiority as a ring general."

Hall began the round in a confident and nonchalant manner, watching for an opening. Jim "manifested a disposition to mix matters as soon as possible." Fitz led with a left half-arm blow for the stomach, but Hall stopped it. The men moved about a bit and stood poised and watchful, with guards raised.

Fitzsimmons' eyes gleamed from beneath his brows menacingly and there was an expression of intense eagerness on his face. Suddenly he made a swift feint with his left hand and then like a flash of lightning, too quick to be seen, his right arm shot out in a swing, entirely clear of Hall's guard and landed full on the left jaw with crushing force. Not a man in the vast assemblage saw exactly how it was done. The hand was quicker than the eye. It was no chance blow. It was an opportunity and Fitzsimmons took it. ... Had Fitzsimmons been a hundredth part of a second slower Hall's guard would have stopped the force of the blow. As it was, it went straight to the jaw, with the full strength of Fitzsimmons' strong right arm and the sweeping momentum of his body to give it power. Fitzsimmons was balanced on his left foot and as he struck threw himself forward, concentrating in the blow his entire strength for his supremest effort. ... It was an ideal knockout blow, calculated, determined upon and executed in the fraction of a second ...

Hall hardly moved out of his tracks, but fell like a man whose head is taken off by a cannon ball.... He fell heavily, unconsciousness having doubtless been instantaneous upon the contact of the glove with his chin. His body hit the floor first, the back of his head struck immediately afterward with a whack. He never made a motion, but lay as one dead, his limbs and body rigid, his upturned toes quivering as if he had been death struck, until counted out.

Once Hall went down, Bob knew it was over. He turned to his seconds and "made a downward motion with his hands, indicating that the fight was over." The crowd was breathless with astonishment for a few seconds, but then broke into wild cheers. Bob took the American flag and waved it above his head. The crowd cheered again.

Hall remained unconscious for quite some time, and did not show the slightest sign of returning to consciousness. His seconds and others were anxiously busy trying to revive him. Fitz walked over and knelt down to look at him, then left him. A few moments later, Hall finally came to, was given a drink of liquor, lifted up onto his chair, and ice applied to his head and neck. Bob went over and shook hands.

Another description of the end said that Fitz led for the stomach and was stopped. Fitz eyed him sharply for a few seconds, and then working into range again, shifted his feet, stepped forward with his right, and landed on the jaw.

How the blow landed was a mystery, for Hall's guard was up at the time. The blow was a terrific one, and delivered with such lighting-like swiftness that few saw the delivery. There was a muffled thud, and Hall's neck appeared twisted almost off his shoulders, and he fell backward insensible upon the canvas. ... [H]e struck the floor with such momentum that his head bounded from it nearly or quite a foot. ... Of all the prize fighting that has been done in New Orleans within the past four or five years not once has such a tremendous blow been delivered. ... Hall was literally driven furiously against the floor by the force of the blow. There was no reeling or staggering, but the terrific force of Fitzsimmons' fist literally mowed him down.

Yet another discussion of the knockout again questioned how Bob landed, given that Hall's guard seemed to be in place.

It may be that for the merest instant Hall's attention was distracted by the shifting of Fitzsimmons' feet, for just as he delivered the blow he changed his position, stepping forward so as to advance the right foot instead of the left, and it is also possible that this sudden change of distance may have made an opening for the blow which did not exist at the longer range.

The National Police Gazette said that Fitz fired out a sudden right hand that "shot out like a piston rod. Hall was not expecting it and it landed with crushing force." The blow to the jaw was "heard in the remotest part of the ring." Hall fell directly backwards, his head striking the floor. He was out cold for well over two minutes.[300]

Summarizing the fight, the *Daily Picayune* felt that Hall had seemed cleverer than Fitz at long range and a vicious fighter at close quarters, especially with the uppercut. Hall outpointed him scientifically in the first two rounds, but Fitz probably had the better of it in terms of punishment inflicted. The question as to who would win was still in the air going into the 4th round, but a moment of carelessness had cost Hall. He was "whipped by the cleanest knockout blow ever seen in the local ring, after one of the briefest and prettiest fights in the history of pugilism."

The Times-Democrat said that Fitzsimmons looked formidable, especially to the trained eye of an expert. It described his general style:

His light, cat-like motions, as he bounded away from his antagonist, his constantly bent knees, ready to spring backward or forward like a flash, and his cool, good natured manner, all indicated that he was a dangerous man to meet.

---

[300] *Daily Picayune, Times-Democrat,* March 9, 1893; *National Police Gazette,* March 25, 1893;

His style of fighting is almost as peculiar as his conformation. He will advance when his antagonist least expects it, and often when in full retreat will wheel suddenly about and meet his advancing rival with right or left just in time to borrow his momentum, and add it to the force of his own blow. Though exceedingly apt to advance and force the fighting at times, he has a wonderful faculty of doing so just when his opponent is not ready to meet him with a blow, and by the time the blow is launched in his direction he is generally in the act of getting away, so that even should it land, it reaches him deprived of a large percentage of its momentum.

The agility with which Fitzsimmons will bound about the ring must be very puzzling to his antagonist. He will leap half way across the ring at one spring, so that the average boxer never knows where or when to look for him, and with all his violent exertion he never appears to become tired.[301]

Summarizing the fight, the *Times-Democrat* said that nothing about the first 3 rounds would have led one to believe that the fight would have a speedy termination. However, the knockout blow early in the 4th round resembled a cyclone that immediately rendered Hall unconscious. It had been an excellent exhibition of scientific pugilism by both men, and Hall was the first man to make Bob exert himself.

The fight was a short and hot one, neither man having any very pronounced advantage up to the moment when the knockout blow was delivered, although in the third round Hall had obtained a sufficient lead to make his backers and seconds exceedingly jubilant, though Fitzsimmons had the better of the contest throughout with the exception of this round. …

Such clever and fast sparring has never been seen in New Orleans and it may be doubted if a more brilliant exhibition of scientific pugilism has ever been witnessed at any time.

Another summary said, "Hall showed wonderful skill and coolness from the outset, proving himself a marvelously clever two-handed fighter, a straight, clean hitter, and a master of the art of dodging and parrying. Up to the landing of the knockout blow it appeared to be anybody's fight." No one could doubt that Fitz had met and defeated a worthy opponent. "He has attained a decisive triumph over one of the cleverest pugilists that ever

---

[301] *Times-Democrat, Philadelphia Inquirer*, March 9, 1893.

entered the ring." Bob had also shown his gameness in the 3ʳᵈ round, when he stood the gaff and took some punishment.

When interviewed,

> Fitzsimmons said that he could have dealt Hall the knockout blow in the first round if he had desired. He said that he kept punching him short all the time for a purpose, and that he only delivered the knockout blow when he had fully measured the skill and strength of his antagonist. He acknowledged, however, that in the first three rounds Hall had given him a couple of good jabs on the head; but he never wavered in his confidence in being able to defeat him.[302]

An out-of-state newspaper said that Fitzsimmons recognized that he had defeated a good opponent. "Hall is the cleverest man I ever met. He clearly out-pointed me in the third round. But he thought, because some of my blows fell short, I could not reach him, and I fooled him."[303]

Hall said that Bob only landed about four meaningful blows – one on the nose, two to the stomach, and one on his side. "He evidently forgot to mention the knockout blow." Hall was so concussed that he probably did not remember it. Jim also said that he did not feel Bob's punches during the fight. After the 3ʳᵈ round, in the corner, he told Mitchell that Fitz did not put any steam in his blows. "I feel satisfied that a chance blow got me. I do not believe Fitzsimmons is a better man than I am, and I want another set-to with him." Hall still felt that he could defeat him.

Most of the debate was regarding whether Bob had merely gotten lucky with a chance blow, or whether he had set up the punch and landed it by design. Bottom line was that he threw it, meant to land, and did. It was equally clear that Hall failed to block, move, or duck.

George Siler, who had once sparred Fitz, said that Bob was looking to land a right.

> It was not a chance blow, for he meant it to land as it did. The only chance there was at all was that Hall would guard it. Fitzsimmons feinted repeatedly with his right and sent in the left on the stomach. Just before he swung the last time he again feinted with the left for the wind. Hall expected to be struck on the stomach and drew his

[302] *Times-Democrat*, March 9, 1893.
[303] *Los Angeles Times*, March 9, 1893.

body back, allowing his head to come forward. It was the chance that Fitzsimmons wanted.

Joe Choynski said that it was a rattling good fight between wonderfully clever and evenly matched men. Hall grew a trifle careless about his guard and it cost him the fight. Joe said that he would like to fight Bob.

Steve Brodie said that Fitzsimmons was the most scientific and marvelous man of the present day, and good enough to fight anybody.

Later that evening, Fitz gave a speech, saying,

> I have won the fight of my life. I can honestly say that it was the one ambition of my life to defeat Jas. Hall, and why? Simply because I could have the chance to show the American public that I told the truth when I told them that I laid down to him in Australia. It was a very bad mistake, I'll admit, but when you take into consideration that I was only an amateur and knew nothing of reputation or its meaning, I think you will forgive me.
>
> I assure you that I have wiped out the stain on my reputation tonight, and went out of my class simply to show the American public that I told the truth. Now, I suppose you will believe me.
>
> Tonight's the last time my friends and the public will have a chance to see me fighting out of my class, for I positively made up my mind that I should never fight again unless it is at the middleweight limit.[304]

Fitzsimmons had learned his lesson from his poor conduct in Australia. He said that a Hall backer had once approached him, offering that they divide the large purse evenly, regardless of outcome, but he rejected it. "I had played the sucker role once in my life, and it has taken me ever since to set myself right before the world. I determined that I would never again lay myself liable to criticism, and, therefore; refused."[305]

The following day, there were many different viewpoints regarding the contest and its details. "To one unaccustomed to the talk that is current after a great fight, it would seem impossible that men could see a short fight of four rounds from such apparently widely different standpoints." Some said the win was a fluke, while others said that Bob had worked all along to set up for the knockout blow.

---

[304] *Times-Democrat*, March 9, 1893.
[305] *Times-Democrat*, March 10, 1893.

Most said that up until the knockout, it was anybody's fight. Some felt that it was beginning to look like the fight would go to Hall. Others countered that Bob turned things around at the end of the 3rd, and had the fight at that point. Billy Madden, who won considerable money as a result of taking Joe Goddard's advice to bet on Bob, said, "Hall boxed, but Fitzsimmons fought."

Fitz said that he had waited, longed, and watched from the beginning for the opportunity to get in that blow. He landed his right to the heart often in order to make Hall believe that he was going to keep hammering away at that spot. This caused Hall to block for the body more. He kept going for the body to get Hall in the habit of guarding the body more than any other place. When he thought the proper time had come, he made a feint with his left and landed the right, not on the body where Jim would have been expecting it and consequently slightly lower his guard, but to the jaw.

Bob said that he never feared defeat during the fight. Although Hall landed some blows in the 3rd round, the only ones he felt were two pretty smart ones on the face. He was not worried though, and he "caused Hall a great deal of trouble by the blow he landed on his chin just before the gong sounded. The blow, he says, made Hall's knees come together, and then he knew that he could defeat him." After that round, in the corner, Fitz told Julian that he was going to knock him out the next round. Still, Bob said that Hall was a formidable man, the first ever to land flush on his face.[306]

Later that month, Fitzsimmons said, "People say that it was a chance blow that knocked Hall out. Well, if it was, it was well studied out. For weeks I practiced that blow with my sparring partner, Frank Bosworth. I feinted at his stomach with my left and landed my right with a short arm blow on his jaw."[307]

About a month after the bout, Fitz said,

> Hall is very clever…but I never had the least doubt that I would beat him. He had a longer reach than I, and when I found that I could not reach him I purposely left myself open in the first two rounds and allowed Hall to land on me twice. In the fourth round I landed a hard blow on Hall's ribs and it hurt him. When we came together again I made a feint to land the same blow and he dropped his left arm to protect his body. This left his face open, and I knocked him out with a half upper cut.[308]

---

[306] *Times-Democrat*, March 10, 1893.
[307] *Chicago Herald*, March 26, 1893.
[308] *Philadelphia Inquirer*, April 10, 1893.

The experts were unanimous in saying that it was the hardest punch that they had ever seen. Pat Sheedy, who had bet on Fitzsimmons, said that the knockout punch "would have knocked senseless the strongest man that ever lived." He had seen Sullivan drop Kilrain, but said that this punch was harder than Sullivan's blows. "I was afraid it had killed Hall." This was the consensus of opinion.

Sheedy also said that Hall was the better infighter and was clever with his uppercut. "His dodging and parrying were also very clever, and all around, he is an artist in the ring." Fitzsimmons too was good at infighting and a marvelously clever dodger. Although his long range work was not as pretty as Hall's, it was "wonderfully scientific and effective. As a ring general Fitzsimmons has seldom, if ever, had an equal." Sheedy said that Fitz had a "wonderful and inexplicable faculty of knowing how to fight a man" and "always seems to know just what to do and when to do it. He is a genius in that line."

Fitz insisted that he would never fight outside of the middleweight class again. Although Bob was loath to fight as a heavyweight, now saying that he would have no chance with men like Corbett, Jackson, or Slavin, most of the experts disagreed. They felt that Bob was good enough to compete with the best heavyweights. Pat Sheedy said,

This fight proves both Fitzsimmons and Hall fit to match any heavyweights in the world. Should a match be made between Fitzsimmons and Corbett I suppose the odds would be on Corbett, and in that case I would have my money on Fitzsimmons, as I think he has a good chance to knock out any man living.

English middleweight Bill Goode said,

Fitzsimmons is a wonderful general in the ring, and so shifty that one can never know where to look for him. I have seen many a prize fight, but I never saw such a terrible blow as that with which Hall was knocked out. Such phenomenal speed and marvelous power as was displayed in that blow must make a pugilist capable of delivering it very dangerous for any man to face, no matter to what class he may belong.

Ed Carney said, "Fitzsimmons is fit to fight any man in the world, no matter how much weight he may be giving away." P.J. Dwyer said, "I think

Fitzsimmons will come very near whipping any man in the world. He is good enough for any class, regardless of weight."[309]

A few days after the fight, perhaps encouraged by all the favorable press regarding his potential to defeat heavyweights, Fitzsimmons relented a bit from his edict that he would not fight heavyweights.

> Bob Fitzsimmons would not be opposed to fighting Jim Corbett. He admitted as much yesterday. He said that he did not believe that the champion heavyweight would have anything like an easy time with him, and is confident that Corbett cannot hit as hard as he can. He does not think that Corbett can hit much harder, if as hard, as Hall, and is willing to meet him. … In talking over this matter Fitzsimmons made no boast whatever, and talked as if he meant every word he said. He argues that no middleweight will meet him now, or that if one can be found who really wants to fight him, it will be hard to make the public believe that "the other" man has a chance, and the contest, therefore, would be but poorly attended.[310]

Fighting Corbett made the best business sense, and Bob knew that he had at least a reasonable a chance to win.

When asked if he was concerned that Hall was seriously hurt when he decked him, Bob said that he was just a trifle anxious. However, he had seen it before.

> But I have knocked out several men in my time and have seen them fall in much the same fashion that Hall did, so I knew how to take it. In Newark, N.J., I hit a big 250-pounder a good clip on the jaw and he went out for half an hour. At Chicago I hit another fellow and his seconds had to work all that evening to bring him to.[311]

The Crescent City Athletic Club was unable to pay Bob his full share of the purse, which was $37,500. It paid him $26,000 and agreed to pay the balance within a reasonable period of time, so that it could raise the remainder. On March 14, Bob left New Orleans and returned to Bay St. Louis.[312]

---

[309] *Times-Democrat*, March 10, 1893.
[310] *Times-Democrat*, March 12, 1893.
[311] *Times-Democrat*, March 12, 1893.
[312] *Times-Democrat*, March 14, 15, 1893.

The Hall-Fitzsimmons fight and the rise of the smaller, more skillful pugilist was said to be good for boxing. "Sullivan's appearance caused immense importance to be attached to weight and size. He was a whirlwind and he was also immense." Since then, "Big men became the fashion." However, the smaller men were lately defeating the larger, "and science is once more asserting its qualities." "As society is always pleased instinctively to see skill triumph over brute force, the aspect of the fistic profession must be regarded as much more satisfactory generally than it was a few years ago."[313] Bob Fitzsimmons had both skill and power.

Just a few months later, in late May 1893, Jim Hall knocked out the approximately 190-pound heavyweight contender Frank Slavin in the 7th round. This made Fitzsimmons' victory over Hall all the more impressive, because Slavin's career had included: 1887 KO10 Mick Dooley, D34 and KO9 Martin "Buffalo" Costello, and KO2 Bill Farnan (the only man to hold a win over Jackson); 1888 D8 Jack Burke (Slavin better) and KO1 Dooley; 1889 KO3 Jack Burke (who in 1885 went the 5-round distance with Sullivan and in 1887 boxed an 8-round no decision with Corbett); 1889 D14 Jem Smith (London rules, Slavin better but fight stopped by police); 1890 KO2 Joe McAuliffe; 1891 KO9 Jake Kilrain; and 1892 LKOby10 Peter Jackson. Clearly, both Fitzsimmons and Hall were good enough to compete with heavyweights.

313 *Times-Democrat*, March 16, 1893, quoting the *New York Sun*.

CHAPTER 9

All Comers Exhibitions Resumed

Following the Jim Hall fight, Bob Fitzsimmons remained quite active, giving exhibitions for the rest of 1893 and for the early part of 1894. Like Sullivan, he often took exhibitions seriously, stopping his opponents after offering them money to last 4 rounds. He also sometimes worked with them in a friendly manner. Despite saying that he did not want to fight as a heavyweight, quite a few of the men that Bob met in these exhibitions were heavyweights, many of whom were much larger than Bob.

Some secondary sources claim that Fitz supposedly took on seven heavyweights in one night in Chicago, stopping all of them, but the date is unknown. One source said it was a couple months prior to the opening of the World's Fair, that each man weighed over 200 pounds, one as much as 240 pounds.[314]

Just over two weeks after the Hall fight, on March 25, 1893 at Chicago's 2nd regiment armory, a packed house of 5,000–6,000 people paid $1 and $1.50 a ticket to watch Fitz box two men a scheduled 4 rounds each. Bob wore indigo-blue tights with the same American-flag-colored belt that he wore in New Orleans.

The first opponent was a tall local man named Sam Bird, who had knocked out Mike Dwyer. Bird was devoid of science, so Bob mercifully tapped and toyed with him at will, monkeying around without trying to stop him, although he could have done so at any time. "A punching bag would have served Fitzsimmons' purpose as well. ... In fact it took considerable science on the part of the champion to keep from knocking Bird out." Bob refrained from hurting him, "much to the disgust of the howling rabble." However, in the 4th round, when Fitz hit him a trifle harder with his right, Bird reeled back and nearly fell through the ropes. Bob caught and held him up, beckoned for the call of time, and led Bird back to his corner.

---

[314] Cyberboxingzone.com; Mike Attree. A.J. Drexel Biddle, Introduction to Robert Fitzsimmons, *Physical Culture and Self-Defense* (London: Drexel Biddle, 1901), 144. Because the date has not been found, the claim is as of yet unproven. However, it was not uncommon for Bob to take on two or three large men in one day or night.

The second opponent was Will Mayo, who had gained considerable experience sparring and touring with the 180-plus-pound Joe Goddard. Mayo was listed as 6'1½" and 192 pounds, and he had a formidable appearance, looking like a tanned Goliath in short black trunks. Fitz did not weigh more than 165 pounds. Mayo asserted that he did not believe anyone could knock him out. Saying that to Bob Fitzsimmons was a big mistake.

From the opening bell, the crowd cheered as Mayo went at Fitz and there was lively work. As he attacked, Mayo elevated his left shoulder to guard his chin, and Bob was not able to land squarely in the 1st round. Mayo did some good close short-arm work, and the crowd cheered every blow he landed.

In the 2nd round, there were terrific exchanges at close range. After two minutes, Mayo had "shot his bolt" and Fitz "kept him going and finally getting him near the ropes led low with his left and bringing the right up high landed on Mayo's jaw. The latter went down like an ox, completely knocked out." Even after the ten seconds were counted off, Mayo was still in dreamland, out cold.

Fitz allegedly told one paper that he would never go out of his weight class again, but would defend his middleweight title against all-comers. Another paper quoted Bob as saying that he would fight heavyweight Denver Ed Smith, Goddard's recent conqueror, if enough money was offered.[315]

Just two days later, on the 27th, Fitz arrived in Baltimore, Maryland. He was scheduled to remain there for a week, giving exhibitions of ball punching and sparring at Kernan's Monumental Theater. The management was offering $100 to anyone who lasted 4 rounds with Bob. Fitz again confirmed that he did not want to fight heavyweights.[316]

On March 30, 1893 in Baltimore, Fitzsimmons scored a KO1 over Jack Warner, who was listed as the New Jersey middleweight champion. He lasted just one minute. The local paper said,

> Warner is a fairly good middleweight, but he did not look very strong. He appeared somewhat timid. Fitzsimmons tapped his antagonist lightly on the right side of the head with his left hand and then gave a short, jabby blow on the left jaw with his right. Warner went down and while he got up in about eight seconds he walked off the stage

---

[315] *Chicago Tribune*, March 26, 1893; *Chicago Herald*, March 25, 1893, March 26, 1893; *Daily Inter Ocean*, March 25, 26, 1893.
[316] *Baltimore American*, March 28, 1893. The local paper said that Fitz had previously visited Baltimore after his victory over Dempsey.

and said he was satisfied. Fitzsimmons then sparred three rounds with his partner.[317]

His "partner" was Frank Bosworth, who was traveling with Bob.

Of a potential match with heavyweight champion Jim Corbett, Fitzsimmons said,

> That thought has not entered my mind.... Corbett is a very clever man, and if I fought him I would have to give him about thirty-five pounds or more. He is besides a very clever boxer, as clever as I am, and weight must tell in such a fight as that would be.[318]

Unlike the active Fitzsimmons, Corbett did not box seriously at all during 1893, only engaging in some short, friendly exhibitions, mostly as part of his play. Clearly though, at that point, Fitzsimmons was not overly interested in boxing champion Corbett. At best, he oscillated back and forth in his desire and willingness to do so.

Throughout April, Bob gave a number of performances in Philadelphia. On April 10, 1893 at Philly's Lyceum Theater, first Bob gave an exhibition of ball punching. Jack Hockey or Haughey (local sources differed) declined the offer of $100 if he stayed 4 rounds, admitting that Fitz could do him in a punch. He agreed to spar in a friendly way, which they did for 3 rounds. Fitz then went 3 more with Frank Bosworth.[319]

The next night, Fitz offered $500 to anyone who stayed 3 rounds with him, but no one accepted. Bob instead sparred 3 friendly rounds with Bosworth.[320]

On the evening of April 12, first Fitzsimmons punched the bag. After taking a break, he took on Dan Curry, who sprinted about the stage for a round. In the 2nd round, after "being nearly knocked over by the wind of a right-handed swing, he retired." Next up was Hank Smith, who was "forced into permanent retirement at a very early stage, the result of his chin getting mixed up in some way with Fitzsimmons' right." Smith did not last a round, and left the stage in a dazed condition.[321]

---

[317] *Baltimore American*, March 31, 1893; *Philadelphia Inquirer*, April 1, 1893.
[318] *Philadelphia Inquirer*, April 10, 1893.
[319] *Philadelphia Inquirer*, *Philadelphia Press*, *Philadelphia Record*, all April 11, 1893.
[320] *Philadelphia Inquirer*, April 12, 1893. Whitey Connors failed to appear on April 11.
[321] *Philadelphia Press*, *Philadelphia Inquirer*, *Philadelphia Public Ledger*, all April 13, 1893.

On April 13, Alexander Kilpatrick, who supposedly weighed in the neighborhood of 200 pounds, attempted to win $100 for staying 4 rounds with Fitzsimmons. For the first 2 rounds, Fitz made no effort to stop Kilpatrick, but only played with him. Alex adopted wrestling tactics, but "found Bob a master at the art, and was heavily thrown in the second round by the Australian." In the 3rd round, Bob made a clever duck and then landed a right to the jaw that badly dazed Kilpatrick, who "then wisely stopped." "His seconds took him off, being satisfied that he had no chance to get the money."[322]

On April 14, Bob only boxed sparring partner Frank Bosworth 3 rounds, because at the last minute, two local men who had agreed to meet him became too frightened to do so.

On April 15, Fitzsimmons scored a KO1 over Jack Sheridan, an ex-policeman who only lasted two minutes.[323] Called a master of the art of the knockout blow, Bob's style was admired.

> The champion's style of boxing is one peculiarly his own, and is one which has and will bother the most scientific men of the world. Combined with his skill he has great agility and can use his feet equally as quick as his hands, a quality which very few fighters possess.[324]

When asked what he thought of Fitzsimmons, former heavyweight champion John L. Sullivan said that he was a "mighty clever boxer." However, he thought that Bob would be foolish to fight as a heavyweight, because weight would tell.[325]

Still in Philadelphia, on April 21, 1893, 1,600 people paid $2 and $1.50 for tickets to watch Fitz meet three men in one night. Bob began with an exhibition of ball punching.

First up to spar was Joe Godfrey, who had met Bob once before (May 1892 LKOby2). Upon Bob's first feint, Godfrey ran away, to the hisses of the crowd. Some yelled, "Take him away." He only lasted two minutes into the 1st round; a right swing to the jaw stopping him. Another account said that an open handed push caused Godfrey to fall from fright. The spectators groaned and hissed as he was taken from the stage.

---

[322] *Philadelphia Inquirer*, April 14, 15, 19, 1893; *Philadelphia Record*, April 14, 1893.
[323] *Philadelphia Record*, April 16, 1893.
[324] *Philadelphia Inquirer*, April 16, 1893.
[325] *Philadelphia Inquirer*, April 19, 1893.

Next up was Mike Monahan or Monaghan, who Corbett had stopped in 2 rounds in a March 1892 exhibition. There was a report that Denver Ed Smith had knocked out Monahan in the 1st round just two days earlier.

One account said that Fitzsimmons knocked out Monahan in the 1st round with a similar right hand blow that took out Godfrey. Another said, "Fitzsimmons punched him three times in the stomach and after a while sent his right onto Monaghan's jaw. Mike fell, but did not appear to be badly hurt." The audience groaned and laughed as he was taken away.

Third up that evening was heavyweight Alexander Kilpatrick, whom Bob had stopped in 3 rounds earlier that week. Kilpatrick tried to wrestle, adopting the same tactics that he had previously used, and the crowd laughed. It was apparent that Fitz was just playing with him. Alex was winded in the 1st round, and in the 2nd had a bloody nose. He tried to throw Fitz in that round, but Bob instead threw him down. He did the same thing a minute later. In the 3rd round, a back-hand slap made Alex's nose bleed again. One account said that he was supposed to spar 4 rounds, but Kilpatrick refused to box the final round. Another source claimed that the police would not allow the contest to continue.[326]

From Philadelphia, Fitzsimmons and his athletic and vaudeville company headed to Boston's Howard Athenaeum, where they began performing on May 1, 1893. Fitzsimmons first boxed Matt Cunningham. "The latter, however, was easily disposed of, and his place taken by Charles Farrell. The latter gave a very interesting exhibition."[327]

On May 6, 1893 in Boston, Fitz fought heavyweight Mike Brennan, the "Port Costa Giant," an experienced veteran of the game who in early 1887 had boxed 3 exhibition rounds against Jim Corbett. The local papers said of the Corbett exhibition, "Corbett knows how to box and Brennan knows how to fight. The result was some wild-rushes on the part of Brennan and some clever getting away on the part of Corbett."[328] Also in 1887, a 219-pound Joe McAuliffe stopped Brennan in the 44th round of a fight that lasted 3 hours. In 1892, Brennan boxed 4 exhibition rounds with Joe Goddard.

Fitzsimmons contracted to knock out Brennan in 4 rounds. For over 3 rounds, Brennan was on the defensive, taking punishment from Fitz's "terrible and stunning blows." Mike did not make much of an effort to throw back. In the latter part of the 4th round, Fitz went at him ferociously and repeatedly knocked Brennan down. After the last knockdown, Fitz's manager, Martin Julian, acting as referee, counted out Brennan just as he

---

[326] *Philadelphia Inquirer, Philadelphia Record,* April 22, 1893.

[327] *Boston Daily Globe,* May 2, 1893.

[328] *San Francisco Examiner,* February 4, 1887. See also Adam J. Pollack, *In the Ring With James J. Corbett.*

rose and the bell rang. He only received $10, although some believed that he had beaten the count and lasted the 4 rounds, which would have entitled him to $100.[329]

Mike Brennan, The Port Costa Giant

The press said that Jim Hall's May 29 KO7 victory over Frank Slavin raised Fitz to third place in the championship list, behind champion Corbett and Peter Jackson.[330]

In late May and early June, Bob was back in Philadelphia. On May 29, 1893 at Philadelphia's Lyceum Theater, Fitzsimmons boxed 3 clever rounds with Al O'Brien.[331]

On May 30, Fitz "had the best of Daniel Coner at the end of the first round, and he then donned the gloves for a three-round set-to with John McVeigh."[332] 210-220-pound Jim/John McVey/McVeigh (local source spellings vary) had been one of Corbett's chief sparring partners in 1892, and was in Jim's training camp for the Sullivan fight.

---

[329] *Boston Herald,* May 7, 1893.
[330] *Philadelphia Record,* May 30, 1893.
[331] *Philadelphia Record,* May 30, 1893.
[332] *Philadelphia Public Ledger,* May 31, 1893.

Jim McVey

On May 31, Fitz again boxed 3 scientific rounds with McVey that were "clever in the extreme." In an interview, McVey said that a bout between Corbett and Fitzsimmons was worth going 1,000 miles to see. "His opinion was that Fitzsimmons was more of a heady fighter than Corbett." He would know, given his previous boxing experience with Corbett.[333]

On June 1, 1893 at the Lyceum, Fitz again sparred 3 rounds with McVeigh when Joe Donnelly pulled out of a scheduled match with fright.[334]

In July, Fitzsimmons filed a lawsuit against the Crescent City Athletic Club for $9,050 due on promissory notes, the unpaid balance from the Jim Hall fight. Unfortunately, Louisiana's Attorney General had filed a $1,000 licensing fee suit against the club which he claimed was entitled to prior consideration. The AG also argued that although gloved boxing was legal, prize fighting was illegal, that the Fitz-Hall bout had been a prize fight, and therefore the notes given for an illegal act were of no value.

When the local judge was apparently about to decide in the State's favor, Fitz applied for a trial by jury, which was denied. His lawyers applied to the State Supreme Court for a writ of mandamus to compel the judge to grant the request. Making matters worse for Bob was the fact that the Chief Justice was Francis Nicholls, the ex-governor (1888-1892) who had called out the militia to prevent the Sullivan-Kilrain fight from taking place in Louisiana. He was no friend to boxing, and the court decided that the status of glove contests was up to the local judge.[335]

On Labor Day, September 4, 1893 at a New York benefit held for Jack Dempsey, Fitzsimmons sparred in a set-to with Dempsey. Heavyweight champion Jim Corbett sparred with John Donaldson.[336]

---

[333] *Philadelphia Public Ledger, Philadelphia Press,* June 1, 1893.
[334] *Philadelphia Press, Philadelphia Record,* June 2, 1893.
[335] *New York Clipper,* August 5, 1893, October 28, 1893.
[336] *New York Clipper,* September 9, 1893.

On September 5, 1893 in Newark, New Jersey, Bob boxed middleweight Jack Hickey. One paper said that Fitz was going to try to stop him within 4 rounds.

The local *Newark Evening News* said that Hickey was the alleged Irish middleweight champion, who was heralded as the hero of sixty battles and the conqueror of Peter Maher (this has not been confirmed). However, Hickey's "ambition died a sudden and violent death in the first round. From the expression on his face when the blond-haired champion landed the first straight left it was plain that Hickey had changed his mind about being the champion." Hickey tried to hit Fitz, but Bob was gone like a flash. After landing a hard left, Bob played with him, hitting Jack whenever he wished.

At the end of the 2nd round, Hickey "was staggering and Fitzsimmons caught him in his arms and held him after the gong sounded." In the 3rd round, after Fitz landed half dozen easy blows, Hickey's seconds threw up the sponge.[337] Even experienced veterans were playthings to Bob Fitzsimmons, including some heavyweights.

---

[337] *Newark Evening News,* September 6, 1893; *Brooklyn Daily Eagle*, September 5, 6, 1893. According to Matt Donnellon, Maher and Hickey sparred as part of an exhibition tour, but Hickey never defeated him in an official battle.

CHAPTER 10

Making the Challenge

In October 1893, Bob Fitzsimmons was becoming bolder. Reversing his earlier position, he said that he indeed wanted to fight heavyweight champion Jim Corbett.[338] Corbett was scheduled to defend his title against Charley Mitchell in January 1894. Bob noted that Jim's best punch was his left jab, and predicted that Corbett would outclass Mitchell.

Fitzsimmons was not overly impressed with Corbett. He still believed that Peter Jackson was the best heavyweight in the world. Bob said that a victory over a diminished Sullivan proved nothing, feeling that on the night that Corbett beat Sullivan in 21 rounds, he would have stopped Sullivan in 3 rounds.[339] Some agreed. Just after Corbett had defeated Sullivan, Bat Masterson said, "I believe that Fitzsimmons or Jim Hall, the middle-weights, could whip him just as Corbett did."[340]

On January 25, 1894 in Jacksonville, Florida, world heavyweight champion James J. Corbett defended his crown for the first time by knocking out a 165-pound Charley Mitchell in the 3rd round. Fitzsimmons said, "Just the result I expected. ... Corbett, in my opinion, could have defeated Sullivan just as easily as he beat Mitchell, but he only played with the big fellow, while he went at the other man like a tiger." Bob claimed that he had told Corbett weeks ago that Mitchell would be easy.[341]

Although Fitz wanted to meet Corbett, one paper opined, "Corbett, however, is not given to fighting, if he can possibly avoid it; especially when it comes to such a good one as either Jackson or Fitzsimmons." Corbett responded that Bob's challenge was a "bluff," pure and simple. "Further, Bob is not in my class, being a middleweight, but, as I have said before, I am willing to meet anybody who can get the necessary backing, provided a good purse is offered for the meet."[342]

In February, "When questioned regarding Fitz's challenge, Corbett smiled and said: 'When he whips Choynski I might consider his challenge,

[338] *Brooklyn Daily Eagle*, October 15, 1893; *Los Angeles Times*, October 17, 1893.
[339] *National Police Gazette*, November 11, 1893.
[340] *Referee*, October 19, 1892.
[341] *Newark Evening News*, January 26, 1894.
[342] *Newark Daily Advertiser*, January 26, 27, 1894.

but until he does that I shall not pay any attention to him.'"[343] Later that year, Fitz would fulfill Corbett's condition.

Fitzsimmons continued giving exhibitions. On February 15, 1894 in Paterson, New Jersey, Bob "gave a display of scientific boxing" with Jim Dwyer.[344]

Owing to the interference of the local New York authorities, a scheduled February match with Dan Creedon was called off.

In March, Bob was in St. Louis, Missouri. On March 11, Fitz put in two hours of work at the Business Men's Gymnasium, sparring with local boxers. "He wore down his opponents as fast as they were brought before him. 'Fitz' wrestled with George Baptiste and succeeded in throwing the clever St. Louis wrestler after a long struggle."[345]

On March 14, 1894 at the St. Louis Armory, a crowd of 4,000 paid $.50, $.75, and $1.00 to watch Fitz spar 4 friendly rounds with Jack Stelzner, the local amateur heavyweight champion. It was said to be the largest crowd that ever turned out to a local athletic entertainment.

The locals were impressed. "Fitzsimmons fully came up to expectations in his exhibition, and clearly demonstrated that he is good enough to go up against the best of them." Still, Stelzner made a very creditable showing against his shifty opponent. In subsequent years, Stelzner would become a regular Fitzsimmons sparring partner.

In a speech to the crowd, Fitz announced that he was willing to meet any man in the world for $50,000, "barring Peter Jackson, whom he regards as the greatest living fighter."[346]

On March 21, 1894 in New York, Fitz sparred with Jimmy Handler, who was preparing for a fight scheduled for the 23rd. Handler "tapped Fitzsimmons's claret in great shape."[347]

During March, after one of his performances in the play *Gentleman Jack*, Jim Corbett again said that Fitzsimons had not gained the right to challenge him, and he would not fight him until Fitz had defeated some of the men that he had. When asked whom he meant, Corbett responded, "Joe Choynski."[348] Initially, Fitz responded to Corbett's statement by saying that

---

[343] *Philadelphia Press, Philadelphia Inquirer,* February 13, 1894.

[344] *Newark Evening News,* February 16, 1894.

[345] *St. Louis Daily Globe-Democrat,* March 12, 1894.

[346] *St. Louis Post-Dispatch,* March 12, 15, 1894; *St. Louis Daily Globe Democrat,* March 15, 1894. By comparison, the price of the local newspaper was 2 cents. Fitz left for New York on the morning of the 15th.

[347] *Newark Daily Advertiser,* March 22, 1894. This report said their boxing took place in New York.

[348] *Newark Evening News,* March 20, 1894.

Corbett was the one he wanted to fight. "I want to meet him, and if he succeeds in besting Peter Jackson, which I doubt, I will post my money and compel him to recognize me or forfeit his title."[349]

Joe Goddard believed that Joe Choynski "would kill Bob. Why, I never knew of a fellow punching as hard as he does."[350] Corbett also felt that Choynski would defeat Fitz.[351] Eventually, Bob decided to take the challenge and made a match with Choynski, scheduled for 8 rounds on June 18 at the Boston Theatre.

Back in 1888, "Jewish" Joe Choynski had exhibited 4 rounds with Peter Jackson. In 1889, Choynski put up a game effort against Jim Corbett before being stopped in the 27th round. Fitzsimmons and Choynski had been sparring partners in 1890 and again in 1892. Joe was in Bob's corner for the McCarthy and Maher bouts. In 1891, Joe had boxed 3 exhibition rounds with John L. Sullivan. Choynski's resume also included: 1890 W10 Jim Fogarty; 1891 LKOby4 Joe Goddard, KO2 Mick Dooley, KO2 Owen Sullivan, rematch LKOby4 Joe Goddard, and KO34 Billy Woods; 1892 exhibition sparring partner for Jim Hall, EX4 Denver Ed Smith (police stopped it in 4th round when Smith was decked), Peter Jackson sparring partner to assist Peter for his 1892 bout with Frank Slavin, KO15 George Godfrey, KO4 C.C. Smith, and KO4 Jack Fallon. In early 1894, Choynski had again been regularly sparring with Peter Jackson, who was anticipating a showdown with Corbett that year. Joe was a very experienced veteran.

In 1892, one San Francisco expert said of him,

> Joe Choynski is a wonder. He will fight anybody, no matter who he is or how big he is, and there is no man of his weight in the world who would stand a show with him. He hits a terrific blow. You see Choynski fights at about 168 lb., and has been meeting men twenty and thirty pounds heavier than himself, and generally defeating them, too.[352]

The local Boston press was enthusiastic about the Fitz-Choynski bout. "[Choynski] is a hard, break-up hitter, with more cleverness than he is generally given credit for. In front of Fitzsimmons it is safe to say that his ability will be tested to its utmost." Fitz trained hard, for he knew that he had a tough job on his hands.[353]

[349] *Newark Evening News,* March 21, 1894.
[350] *San Francisco Chronicle*, September 5, 1892.
[351] *Daily Picayune*, September 27, 1894.
[352] *Referee,* April 20, 1892.
[353] *Boston Post,* June 8, 1894.

A couple weeks prior to the fight, Choynski was listed as weighing 172 pounds.[354] Apparently, a mere three days later, on June 8, Joe weighed 163 pounds stripped. Choynski was training and sparring with Tom West and a Worcester heavyweight named Whalen.[355]

A couple days before the fight, Fitz had his mind on Corbett:

> I wish he would get settled one way or the other with Jackson, for I want to make a match with him…. He cannot bluff me off…. I do not believe he will ever meet Jackson, and I hope he does not, for Jackson will defeat him and I will lose all chances of getting on a go with him.[356]

That month, Jackson had said, "The fact of the matter is that Corbett will not fight. He'd rather be an actor."[357]

The scheduled 8-round Fitzsimmons-Choynski bout took place at the Boston Theatre on June 18, 1894. One local paper opined that Choynski "has proven much more clearly than Fitzsimmons that he has all the necessary qualities of a first-class ring gladiator except the one quality of superior and phenomenal cleverness." Fitz was attempting "to show that he is better entitled than any white man in the world to fight Corbett."[358]

Despite having fought almost exclusively as a heavyweight during his career, Choynski, like Fitzsimmons, was more of a middleweight. Fitzsimmons was actually the larger looking man for this bout fought with five-ounce gloves, although the men probably weighed about the same, give or take 5-10 pounds. Bob may have been a shade taller. The previous day, Fitz said that he was 158 ½ pounds, but would likely enter the ring close to 162 pounds. He said that he was told a couple days earlier that Choynski weighed 161 ½ pounds.[359]

A local paper said that Choynski weighed about 162 pounds, and that Fitz looked about 10 pounds heavier.[360] There apparently was no official weigh-in because it was a heavyweight bout, so it did not matter what they weighed. Fitzsimmons was 31 years of age to Choynski's 25.

---

[354] *Boston Post*, June 5, 1894.
[355] *Boston Post*, June 10, 1894.
[356] *Boston Daily Globe*, June 17, 1894.
[357] *Boston Post*, June 8, 1894.
[358] *Boston Post*, June 18, 1894.
[359] *Boston Herald*, June 18, 1894.
[360] *Boston Daily Globe*, June 19, 1894.

Joe Choynski

The audience "was a large one, about 1400 people being in attendance," including ex-champion John L. Sullivan. Charley White, Sam Kline and Jimmy Handler seconded Bob. Manager Parson Davies, Mick Dunn, Ned and Charlie McAvoy, and Tommy West (who had sparred Jack Sullivan in a preliminary) were in Choynski's corner. Captain William Daly, Jr. was the referee.

1st round

Boston Herald (BH): Joe forced matters, doing the most work. After ducking under Fitz, Joe stood up and lifted Bob off the ground, showing his strength.

Boston Daily Globe (BDG): There was some hot work in close, and Joe did better, landing his left to the body and head. However, at the end of the round, a Fitz right to the ear staggered Joe.

Boston Post (BP): "[T]here wasn't a good blow stuck. Fitz led many times, but it was wildly most of the time. Choynski got in a couple of punches, but they were light blows." It also said, "Choynski was very clever and avoided Fitzsimmons's leads in a very scientific way."

2nd round

BH: Joe darted in and out like an eel, doing clever work that pleased the crowd.

BDG: Bob attempted rights off feints, but Joe eluded most of them. Bob landed his long left to the nose and followed with a right over the heart.

BP: Both men fought fast. In the middle of the round, "Joe, who had been punching with a straight left on the face, snapped the left between the eyes and knocked Fitz down. He stayed down for six seconds. He was groggy when he got up, but knew enough to stay away and duck and hold till he got strong." It also said, "The blow that knocked Fitz down in the second round was a fearful left-hand punch straight on the nose. It floored Fitz completely and knocked him five feet across the stage." Although Joe won the round and Fitz was very groggy, Choynski could not finish him.

It should be noted that most newspapers (including national accounts) reported the knockdown as having occurred in the 3rd round, but the *Boston Post* consistently reported it as having taken place in the 2nd round, disagreeing with its local competitors.

3rd round

BH: Bob landed a hard right to the face, and in trying to recover, Joe slipped down. Fitz began forcing matters, landing a number of good blows until Joe got away. As Bob came after him, Choynski caught Fitzsimmons with a left on the jaw that sent him down. When Bob rose, Joe rained blows upon him, but Bob clinched to save himself. Bob was fought to the ropes, but Joe became wild and allowed Bob to escape. Joe's hard work began to fatigue him. However, a hard punch to the mouth staggered Fitz, who was again fought to the ropes. Bob began to recover and made a rally as Joe was tiring. The round ended with the crowd so loud that no one could hear the gong. A policeman entered the ring and cautioned them, which ended the round.

BDG: Joe took a right to the back of the head and at the same time slipped to the floor. Fitz was eager to get at him, but was hit by a counter left hook that sent him to the floor badly dazed. Joe attacked like a tiger, but Bob clinched. After the break, Joe went at him for about 30 seconds in the "hottest and fastest" action seen in quite some time. Fitz kept clinching. He partly recovered by the end of the round, as Joe was tiring. The crowd was so boisterous that the police captain sent the men to their corners 15 seconds before the round ended.

BP: "Fitz braced up and had the best of the argument, which was mainly of a give and take order, with several lively mix-ups." It was "furious and fast work, and told on Choynski, who was very weak at the end."

4th round

BH: The round was a reversal of fortune. Despite having been down the previous round, this round opened with Fitz stronger and more willing than Choynski. Bob was revived, and a nonstop series of punches with both hands sent Joe down. A left and right dropped him again. "It seemed odd to see the supposed conqueror of a moment before being rapidly conquered." When Bob attacked again, Joe ducked and grabbed his legs. Bob continued punching with almost no return. Joe crouched to avoid blows, but when he straightened up, a right to the heart dropped him. Twice more was Choynski decked, five times in all in the round.

BDG: Fitz was fine at the bell to begin the 4th round, but Joe was still fatigued from his hard work in trying to finish Fitz in the previous round. Bob forced matters, and Joe was unable to keep away. A right and left sent the cornered Choynski down. Another right and left caused Joe to slip to the floor. The bell saved him. This account only indicated two knockdowns.

BP: "Fitz began his hard punching. He led with a left and then scored a heavy right. Then he drove his glove towards the stomach, and Joe went down." Joe was dropped four more times, for a total of five knockdowns in the round. He stayed down nine seconds every time. The gong saved him from a knockout. "Choynski was lying helpless on the floor, and could not have arisen in ten seconds. But just as he went down the bell rang and Joe was dragged to his chair and revived."

The National Police Gazette reported that when Bob's punches landed, it sounded like "breaking sticks." In the corner, Choynski's head flopped as if his neck was broken.

BH: Fitzsimmons "was as strong as a nine-story granite building and as confident as a man with a royal flush playing poker." Bob punched him when and where he pleased, sending Joe down time and time again. Joe staggered and slipped about the ring, such that "it would have been wise for the management to stop it. That was not done, so the police did." No one objected, as everyone knew that Joe was beaten.

BDG: Coming out for the round, Joe looked defeated. Fitz dropped him in the first minute. Bob knocked him about the ring until Choynski was decked again. When Fitz was putting on the finishing touches, the police captain asked the referee to stop the bout. It was only the interference of the police that saved Joe.

BP: "Bob had Joe at his mercy. He jabbed him on the nose and floored him. He punched him on the jaw and put him to earth. And a couple of body punches also put him down. Choynski reeled around and swung his arms wildly." It also said,

> In the fifth he was still weak. He was simply a punching bag for Fitz. It got to be brutal in the fourth and fifth rounds. The fifth had gone on 1 minute 40 seconds when it was stopped. Fitzsimmons had Choynski on the ropes, and ready to give him the last punches. They weren't clinched, although Choynski was holding.
>
> Referee Daly went over and separated the men. This he shouldn't have done, in the opinion of many there. These men claim that he saved Choynski from defeat. Just after he separated the men, Sergeant Sullivan, followed by a half-dozen bluecoats, leaped on the stage, with Captain Warren outside of the ring.
>
> The edict went forth that the battle should stop, and according to the articles was declared a draw, as there was a clause calling for such a decision, in case of police interference, provided both men were on their feet.

The bout was technically declared a draw. This was because the articles of agreement required that a draw be declared if there was interference and they were both on their feet. Ironically, Fitzsimmons himself had insisted on this term, because he objected to decisions being rendered in major fights. He felt that unless a fight had a clear knockout without police interference, it should be declared a draw.

Regardless, everyone knew that Bob was the better man and would have stopped Choynski but for the police terminating the bout. Back then, it was often the case that unless a boxer took the ten-count, a referee would not stop it. The police were essentially acting as humane referees. All accounts agreed that Joe was badly defeated at the end. Because it was a draw, the men split the gate receipts.

The local accounts all summarized the fight. *The Boston Herald* said that Choynski had forced the pace too fast. Fitz was well gone for about 15 seconds in the 3rd round, but had the ring instincts to clinch. "No man not in good trim could have recovered with the rapidity of Fitzsimmons and waged such a hard battle, bringing off a virtual victory in two rounds after defeat seemed to stare him in the face."

The Boston Daily Globe felt that Choynski had exercised bad judgment in failing to take his time and measure Fitzsimmons when he was hurt. By rushing in like a wild man, Bob was able to clinch. It complimented Fitz's wonderful recuperative powers, saying that the quickness of his recovery was surprising.

The Boston Post said,

> Fitz was very stiff and awkward for the first two rounds. This may have been from his anxiety. … Choynski used a straight left-hand punch a good deal, and with effect, too. He was cleverer than Fitz. … [Although Choynski decked Bob in the 2nd round,] all of Choynski's force seemed to go out with that punch. … Both men drew blood in the second round. But constant punching on the face and nose made Choynski's face bloody. With his mass of hair and strongly-marked features, his face was a gruesome sight. … The contest was rather brutal, and blood spattered all over the ring. … It was a fast and furious battle, but all one-sided after the third round. … Joe was the victim of abuse administered by Fitz to such an extent that he was knocked down three times in the last round, and when Sergeant Sullivan and Captain Warren of Station 4 walked into the arena Choynski was helpless on the ropes. … But for police interference Bob Fitzsimmons would have signally defeated Joe Choynski last night.[361]

Bob later said that Choynski "was by far the most clever man he had ever met." The following year, Bob was quoted as saying, "Joe Choyinski

[361] *Boston Herald, Boston Daily Globe, Boston Post,* all June 19, 1894; *National Police Gazette,* June 30, 1894; Alexander Johnston, *Ten and Out!* (N.Y.: Ives Washburn, 1927), 105-106; Lardner at 104; Fleischer at 123.

came the nearest putting me out of any man I have ever gone up against. … He is a terrific hitter, and really gave me the worst punching I ever got." In another interview, Bob said that although dropped by a couple of hard blows, "I didn't lose my head, though. I knew enough to keep at close quarters till the gong gave me a chance to recover, and then as you can remember, I was all right and had matters pretty much my own way."[362]

The day after the fight, Choynski claimed that the police interfered in the 2nd round when he had decked Bob, preventing him from winning.

I do not see any newspaper mention of the interference by them at that time. When I sent Fitzsimmons to the boards full down with a lefthander on the jaw I thought the jig was all up. He probably thought so about me in the fifth round, when the police interfered again. … He thinks that he would have won, I suppose, if the officers had let him alone. Well, I think that I'd have won if they had let me alone.[363]

Both Fitzsimmons and Choynski returned to New York.

In getting decked by a well-respected hard puncher, but then coming back and quickly reversing the fortunes of the fight, Fitz had turned a negative into a positive, proving his heart, conditioning, and recuperative powers. "The supporters of Fitzsimmons are arguing that their favorite has flaxed out Choynski with much greater ease than was exhibited by Corbett when he and Choynski exchanged courtesies in the ring."[364]

Fitzsimmons said that he was confident that he could defeat Jim Corbett in a finish contest. He wanted to see Corbett fight Peter Jackson, because he felt that Jackson would win. However, from a business standpoint, he wanted to meet Corbett first. At that point, Jackson was concerned that Corbett might use Bob's challenge as an excuse for avoiding him.[365]

The New Orleans Olympic Club offered $20,000 for a Corbett-Fitzsimmons fight. It was said that although a Corbett-Jackson fight would be bigger and more of a true championship fight, "a considerable host of

---

[362] *Daily True American*, August 14, 1894; *Washington Post*, March 11, 1895; *National Police Gazette*, April 13, 1895.

[363] *Boston Post*, June 20, 1894. Many years later, Choynski claimed that the referee gave Fitz a slow count and kept telling Joe to get back or he would suspend the count, that after a long count, the bell rang, but that it had only been one minute and forty-five seconds into the round. *Winnipeg Free Press*, January 22, 1927. The primary sources did not support this claim.

[364] *Boston Post*, June 23, 1894.

[365] *National Police Gazette*, July 7, 1894, reporting on a June 23, 1894 dispatch.

ring followers who have no relish for contests in which white men contend with black ones, would most emphatically welcome" a Corbett-Fitz championship bout instead."[366] Even some in the North felt that if Jim were to lose to a colored man, it "would abruptly end his career."[367]

The Florida Athletic Club said that it would put up a purse of $35,000 for Corbett to fight Jackson there. However, if Jackson would not consent to fight in Florida, it would offer a like purse for a battle between Corbett and Fitzsimmons.[368] Jackson refused to fight in the South, fearing that the area's racial prejudice would lead to his death should he defeat Jim. Corbett could make the same amount of money for a fight with Fitzsimmons, and the South was the one region offering such massive purses.

In late July 1894, the *National Police Gazette* said, "Fitzsimmons' victory over Choyinski places him in line to fight for the championship of the world." It believed that by defeating heavyweights Peter Maher, Jim Hall and Joe Choynski, Fitz had proven himself. He had done exactly what Jim Corbett asked him to do, quoting Corbett as having said that if Fitz defeated Choynski, he would listen to his challenges, because he did not think Bob could win. "If Fitzsimmons ever beats Choynski I'll fight him." *The Police Gazette* felt that if Corbett was a man of his word, he would fight Bob if the Jackson match fell through.[369]

Next up for Fitzsimmons was heavyweight Frank Keller. They boxed in Buffalo, New York on July 28, 1894, just over one month after the Choynski bout. Bob was promised 40% of the gate receipts, with a minimum guarantee of $2,000. It was a scheduled 4-rounder with scientific points to count.

This was actually considered a good challenge for Fitz. The local *Buffalo Courier* said that Keller was "quick as Jersey lightning," and it "seems to be the unanimous opinion that 'Fitz' is meeting a far more dangerous man than either Joe Choyinski or Peter Maher." Keller would weigh close to 185 pounds and was "as finely a developed man as there is in the boxing business. He has every confidence in himself, as he has been in 37 contests without sustaining a single defeat."[370]

1,300 spectators watched the bout, including Fitz's wife. Keller weighed 180 pounds. Bob wore black tights and a belt made of an American flag.

---

[366] *Boston Post,* June 23, 1894.

[367] *Daily True American,* July 21, 1894.

[368] *New York Clipper,* July 7, 1894.

[369] *National Police Gazette,* July 28, 1894.

[370] *Buffalo Courier,* July 17, 1894, July 27, 1894. However, a secondary source disagrees, saying that Frank Kellar (different spelling – so perhaps a different fighter) had a number of losses, including: 1889 LDQby14 Joe Sheehy; 1892 LKOby24 Billy Smith; 1893 D6 William Mayo and L6 Henry Baker; and 1894 L8 Baker. Boxrec.com. Perhaps it was a different Keller/Kellar?

Bob sized him up in the 1st round, "moving with an easy grace and freedom he presented a picture just to the contrary of Keller, who was almost elephantine in his carriage." Fitz initially forced matters, but then danced around, using his left. After Bob landed a right, a series of clinches followed, for Keller held to avoid punishment. There was a claim that Keller attempted to bite in the clinch. At one point, Keller became aggressive, and Fitzsimmons "half stumbled and was half knocked down when Keller rushed him against the ropes. He smiled, however, and took his time in getting up, regarding the incident as a joke."

[The 2nd round] had hardly opened before he was next to Keller. Feinting with his left, 'Fitz' shot his right over and plump against his opponent's jaw. It was a skillful blow and skillfully delivered.... Keller dropped to the floor like a log, rolled over upon his back, and 'dreamed' for nearly a minute.

Fitz had quickly ended matters early in the 2nd round with "as pretty a crack on the jaw as was ever seen."[371] One New York paper said that it took a force of surgeons to bring Keller to life.[372]

After the bout, Fitzsimmons said that he wanted to meet Corbett. He felt that Jim was ducking him. "Corbett says I am out of his class, but that is only a dodge to get rid of meeting me, for didn't he take on Mitchell who was in fact a middleweight?"[373] One paper opined, "There is a growing impression that lanky 'Bob' will make serious trouble for the champion, that is if 'Jim' gives him a chance."[374]

Corbett said that Fitzsimmons was only looking for cheap advertising by challenging him. He said that Bob must first send an open challenge to the world, and if no one else accepted, then Corbett would take the challenge.[375]

On August 12, 1894 under the auspices of Captain Lenox, Fitz arrived in Trenton, New Jersey to give sparring exhibitions there for a week.[376] Fitz was at that time set to defend his middleweight crown against Dan Creedon in September. Bob assured his fans that Creedon would not last 5 rounds. He also said that he was anxious to meet Corbett, who he believed was

---

[371] *Buffalo Courier,* July 29, 1894.
[372] *Brooklyn Daily Eagle,* July 29, 1894.
[373] *Brooklyn Daily Eagle,* July 29, 1894.
[374] *New York Evening Telegram,* July 30, 1894.
[375] *Paterson Evening News,* August 17, 1894.
[376] *Daily True American* (Trenton, New Jersey), August 13, 1894.

afraid of him. "Fitz says the Corbett-Jackson talk is a myth originated solely for the purpose of staving him off."

On August 13 at Trenton's Cochran Park, 1,500 fans watched Fitz punch the bag and box his sparring partner, Tom Dwyer. Bob was impressive enough that "the universal expression seemed to be that Corbett would have his hands full if he ever met the Australian in the ring."

> Fitz's work with the bag was very clever and elicited rounds of applause. The three round go between the champion and his partner was really a scientific exhibition. Dwyer, who had met and defeated some very good men, put up a stiff fight, while Fitz showed the spectators how easily he could protect himself with his long arms, and occasionally he would tap Dwyer around at his will. Fitz will be at Cochran Park for the remainder of the week and meet some of our best men, including Rulon and Courtney.[377]

At that time, it was reported that Newark Police Captain Charles Giori was resigning from the force to become Bob's manager. Fitz had Giori wire back to the New Orleans Olympic Club his acceptance of their recent offer of a $25,000 purse to meet Corbett there, winner take all.[378]

Fitz drew big crowds at his nightly exhibitions that week. On August 16, 1894, 1,000 Trentonians first watched Bob give his "usual startling exhibition of bag-punching." 240-pound Bob Rulon, claiming to be the New Jersey state champion, attempted to win the $100 Fitz offered to anyone who could last 4 rounds with him. "Rulon is very clever with his fists, but somehow or other the lanky Australian's fist seemed to reach him every time, and in fifteen seconds he gave up the sponge and retired from the ring." Another source said that Rulon quit after being hit twice. Fitz then had a bout with his sparring partner, Tom Dwyer, which was heartily applauded.[379]

On the 17th, Fitz hit the bag and sparred before another crowd of 1,000 spectators. He likely boxed Dwyer, but this is unclear.

Peter Courtney, Trenton's champion, was advertised as going to attempt to win the $100 offered to anyone who could last 4 rounds with Fitz, the bout to take place on Saturday, August 18, 1894.[380] Although the local

---

[377] *Daily True American,* August 14, 1894.
[378] *Daily True American,* August 15, 1894.
[379] *Daily True American, Newark Evening News,* August 17, 1894; *Brooklyn Daily Eagle,* August 17, 1894, September 8, 1894. Non-local sources called him Bob Rutan.
[380] *Daily True American,* August 18, 1894. Unfortunately, the local paper did not have a follow-up report.

paper did not have a follow-up report, Courtney and Fitz later offered their differing accounts.

Fitzsimmons pounded on the 180-190-pound Courtney over 4 rounds. Courtney admitted that it had been a one-sided affair, but felt that he had added to his reputation by lasting the 4 rounds.[381]

Courtney claimed to be 26 years old and to have started boxing a year and a half earlier.

> There was a duck there named Ed Warner, and they said he was the champeen of Jersey. Well, Jack McNally, a boxing instructor in Trenton, give me a few lessons, and I just put this here Warner to sleep in just one round. Soon after that I did up Jim Glynn in two rounds, Jim Dwyer in three, Jack Welch in four, and recently I went agin Bob Fitzsimmons, who couldn't put me out in four rounds.[382]

However, Fitzsimmons told a different story. He said that Courtney was going to attempt to stand before him for 4 rounds to win $100, but Courtney only wanted a friendly bout, and refused to face him unless Bob promised not to punch hard. The house manager said that it would be better to have a bout than none at all, so Bob consented, and allowed him to last the 4 rounds. "I complied, and sparred lightly with him, but I could have put him out with a punch any time." Bob also related a different story regarding Courtney's experience.

> There was a big heavyweight up there. I cannot be sure about his name, but it sounded like Hulong, or Oolong [likely Bob Rulon], who put Courtney out in a round and a half. Courtney weighs about 190 pounds, and this other fellow is about fifty pounds heavier. Well, I met this Hulong, or whatever his name is, and it took me just two punches to put him out. There is a welterweight in Trenton who also knocked out Courtney, and afterward I met this same welterweight in Baltimore, and it took just one blow to settle him. ... Courtney is not a man of any class at all, and I can tell you he never will be. He does not even know how to put up his hands.[383]

---

[381] *New York Sun*, September 8, 1894; *National Police Gazette*, September 22, 1894; *Brooklyn Daily Eagle*, August 17, 1894, September 8, 1894.
[382] *New York Sun*, September 8, 1894. Spelling and grammatical errors in the original.
[383] *Times-Democrat*, September 11, 1894.

Jim Corbett vs. Peter Courtney

Just a few weeks later, on September 7, Jim Corbett would stop Courtney in the 6th round of a fight that was filmed. Because of the filming requirements, each round only lasted 1 – 1½ minutes, and the rests were 1½ - 2 minutes long.[384] After being knocked out by Corbett, Courtney said, "This Corbett is much stronger and a harder hitter than Fitzsimmons, and can lick him, sure. I've tackled both and I know what it is." Of course, Corbett had tried to knock him out, while Fitz had carried him.[385]

In late October, after watching the films of the Corbett-Courtney kinetoscopic battle, Fitz said of Courtney, "He fought just like a man who had his strength and nothing more to depend upon. Surely he is not clever. When I met him in Trenton they made me promise not to stop him, but I had all I could do to keep that promise."[386]

---

[384] *New York Sun*, September 8, 1894; *National Police Gazette*, September 22, 1894.
[385] *New York Sun, Newark Evening News, New York Herald*, all September 8, 1894; *National Police Gazette*, September 22, 1894.
[386] *New York Evening Telegram*, October 29, 1894.

Corbett had been in negotiations with Peter Jackson for a rematch. Jackson did not want to fight in the South. Corbett did not want to fight in England. This eliminated the two places that were legally offering sufficient purses for the fight. The negotiations went nowhere.

It was reported that Corbett had said that he would not fight Fitzsimmons unless he first whipped Peter Jackson. However, Jackson only wanted Corbett, saying, "I will not fight anybody again unless it is Corbett. Fitzsimmons is all right, but I made up my mind this way long ago."

The New Orleans Olympic Club had offered Corbett $25,000 to fight Fitzsimmons if the Jackson match fell through. Once the Jackson fight went nowhere and Peter left the country, Corbett changed his mind and said that he was willing to box Fitz, although Jim later oscillated. Bob said that he had been hoping for this chance for years.

Although newsmen were generally less excited about a Fitzsimmons challenge than they were for a Jackson challenge, it was still an intriguing match-up. Many felt that Bob had both the skill and the power to compete with Corbett. If Jim was not going to fight Peter Jackson, sportsmen wanted to see Corbett against Fitzsimmons.[387]

[387] *New York Sun,* August 14, 15, 1894.

CHAPTER 11

Still the Middleweight Champion

Fitzsimmons had scheduled a world middleweight championship title defense against New Zealand's Dan Creedon, set to be held at the New Orleans Olympic Athletic Club in late September. Apparently, the match was made in part because Jim Corbett allegedly said that he would not give Bob a fight until he defeated Creedon.

> The champion middleweight had made strenuous efforts to secure a match with the champion heavyweight, but again and again had he been put off with the reminder that he was not in Corbett's class. Corbett had told him to fight Choynski, and after he had proven his superiority over the plucky Californian, Creedon was next designated by Corbett as the man who stood between Fitzsimmons and a right to battle for the heavyweight championship of the world.[388]

The undefeated 5'8" 158-pound New Zealand-born Australian-trained Creedon's career results included: 1890 D30 Jimmy Ryan and W8 Jim Hall (Hall contracted to stop him in 8 rounds but failed, though Dan took a beating); 1891 KO5 Jim Watts, KO7 Starlight (for the vacant Australian middleweight crown), KO2 Jimmy Ryan, and W6/KO8 Martin "Buffalo" Costello; 1892 D23 Costello and KO6 Ryan; 1893 KO15 Alec Greggains and KO2 Jerry Slattery; 1894 W4/KO4 Frank Craig, D10 and KO9 Dick Moore, and W3/KO3 Frank Childs (police intervened).[389]

Perhaps most importantly, Creedon had in 1893 and 1894 given exhibitions with champion Jim Corbett, for he was a regular Corbett sparring partner in preparation for Jim's early 1894 fight with Charley Mitchell. Creedon even exhibited with Corbett a bit after the fight. Corbett said that Dan was the most scientific boxer he had ever sparred. He believed that Creedon would defeat Fitzsimmons. Still, Corbett also gave Fitz his due respect, saying, "He can hardly be classed strictly in the

---

[388] *Times-Democrat*, September 27, 1894.
[389] Boxrec.com; *Referee*, September 28, 1892; *Times-Democrat*, September 26, 1894.

middleweight class, for he is a wonder in this, that he can fight in either the middle or heavyweight class."[390]

Earlier in the year, *National Police Gazette* publisher Richard K. Fox predicted that Creedon would defeat Fitzsimmons.[391] The Olympic Club president did not think Bob would have an easy time with Creedon.[392]

Fitz said he knew that Creedon was a hard puncher, "and I do not hold him cheap at all."[393] Still, Bob believed that it would be a short contest, and wagered $50 that Creedon would not last 4 rounds.[394]

Dan Creedon

[390] *National Police Gazette*, September 15, 1894; *Times-Democrat*, September 14, 1894.
[391] *National Police Gazette*, March 24, 1894.
[392] *Times-Democrat*, September 14, 1894.
[393] *National Police Gazette*, October 13, 1894.
[394] *Times-Democrat*, September 17, 1894.

While training in New Orleans, on September 4, 1894, the then 157-pound Fitzsimmons sparred 146-pound Jack Dempsey, who was concluding his preparations for a rematch with Billy McCarthy. Jack's nose was still less shapely than it was before he had fought Bob back in 1891.

After Jack hit the bag for a short time, Fitz and Dempsey boxed and then wrestled in a friendly, scientific way. In an interview, Dempsey said that Fitz would defeat Creedon, and "was the one man who would test Corbett's wonderful powers to the utmost if he did not actually defeat him." Dempsey's trainer opined that Fitz would defeat Corbett.[395]

Bob was training hard at the local Young Men's Gymnastic Club, and as of September 10, was only weighing 156 pounds.[396] A little over a week prior to the fight, the betting was 3 to 5 on the favorite Fitzsimmons.[397]

Corbett sent his friend and former sparring partner Creedon a letter.

Corbett was greatly impressed with Creedon's cleverness and powers of endurance. He believes Dan has a splendid chance of downing 'Lanky Bob,' but in his letter to Creedon, the champion warns him not to be overconfident, as it will not do for him to take any liberties with 'Fitz.' In the same letter Corbett also mentions some points regarding Fitzsimmons' style of fighting which his (Corbett's) sparring partner, Steve O'Donnell, became acquainted with when he fought Bob in Australia. O'Donnell defeated the middleweight champion in the old country, and when Fitz talked recently about fighting Corbett the champion and his manager retorted with an offer to match O'Donnell against him for $10,000.[398]

Fitzsimmons vehemently denied Corbett's claim that O'Donnell had defeated Bob in Australia. Fitz said,

That was a falsehood which O'Donnell emphatically denied in my presence when I asked him about it. In fact, O'Donnell said that it was Haley who started the story. I do not believe that O'Donnell was in any way responsible for that story, for it would be altogether too ridiculous. The only time we ever had the gloves on together in Australia was one evening in the gymnasium after the pupils were all gone. I proposed it and if I remember rightly, there was no one

---

[395] *Times-Democrat*, September 5, 1894. Dempsey and McCarthy fought to a 20-round draw.
[396] *Times-Democrat*, September 11, 1894.
[397] *Times-Democrat*, September 14, 1894.
[398] *Times-Democrat*, September 17, 1894.

present but ourselves. We sparred for a short time in the lightest manner possible, neither attempting to gain any advantage or thinking of such a thing…. There was not a blow struck that would hurt a ten-year-old boy.[399]

It sounded as if Corbett was making the claim that O'Donnell had defeated Fitz in order to obtain press for O'Donnell and to create a buzz that would lead to a fight between Bob and Steve.

The general feeling during the week before the fight was that the undefeated Creedon had a chance and would put up a good fight, for he was skillful and strong, but that Fitzsimmons was special. The day of the fight, Fitz was a strong favorite at 1 to 3, while Creedon bets were being taken at 2 to 1 and by fight time, 2 ½ to 1. The majority believed that Bob would win.[400]

The day before the fight, on the 25th, Fitz did his usual work. He took a morning run, and in the afternoon sparred lightly for 8 or 10 rounds with then welterweight Kid McCoy, showing his wonderful speed and shiftiness. Bob was hardly breathing, while McCoy was panting. Fitz was weighing 153 pounds, "appears to be carrying absolutely no waste flesh, and yet appears to be as strong and healthy as if he were weighing 170 pounds."[401]

The skillful McCoy was a good sparring partner. He would later become world middleweight champion, and eventually a heavyweight contender with a number of very good victories.

On September 26, 1894 at the New Orleans Olympic Club, before a crowd of 6,000 people, 31-year-old Bob Fitzsimmons defended his world middleweight championship against 26-year-old Dan Creedon. The two fought for a $5,000 purse, which was "a handsome year's salary for a distinguished member of one of the learned professions." The fight was at the middleweight limit of 158 pounds. Both local papers agreed that Fitz weighed in at 155 ½ pounds to Creedon's 158 pounds, their weights as taken at ringside just before the fight began.

When it is considered that by today's standards, Fitzsimmons was still essentially a junior middleweight even at the age of 31, his prior and subsequent successes against heavyweights is even more remarkable, and also makes it clearer that Bob was truly a middleweight. Given that he weighed in at 155 pounds just before entering the ring, if he had weighed in the day before the fight the way most boxers do now, he quite easily could

---

[399] *Times-Democrat*, September 28, 1894.
[400] *Times-Democrat*, September 26, 27, 1894.
[401] *Times-Democrat*, September 26, 1894. McCoy's career will be further discussed in the Jeffries volume.

be boxing as a welterweight today. Very few welterweight/junior middleweight boxers today could have the same knockout record that Bob Fitzsimmons had against fighters 175, 185, and even over 200 pounds.

Fitzsimmons' seconds for the Creedon fight were Jack Dempsey, Kid McCoy, and Tom Dwyer. Before the fight, Bob told Dempsey how he wanted to be handled, telling him that if he was dazed, to pass the bottle of ammonia under his nose.

At about 9:10 p.m., Creedon entered the ring first, wearing a white breech-clout, and black stockings and shoes. Fitz wore blue trunks, an American-flag-colored belt, and a pendant of the black and gold colors of the New Orleans Young Men's Gymnastic Club, where he had trained.

When Creedon heard Fitz's weight announced as slightly less than his own, Dan seemed puzzled, "as if trying to understand how such reach and shoulder and chest development could be contained in a body that was actually a trifle lighter than his own."

1st round

Daily Picayune (DP): Creedon hit the body, which drew crowd approval, but his frequent clinches were resented. Bob's lefts slightly swelled Dan's eye. After feinting a left to the stomach, Bob followed with a right and left to the jaw that weakened Creedon. Fitz began landing more to the body and head, and Dan clinched. After Bob landed a left jab on the mouth, he followed it up with rights and lefts to the jaw. Creedon went to his corner dazed.

Times-Democrat (TD): Neither man was taking unnecessary chances. They watched cautiously, feinting, dodging and dancing away. Fitz carried his head high with his arms well extended. Creedon kept a high guard. Dan led for the ribs with his vaunted body punches, but Bob danced away laughing. Creedon tried to force matters, going for the body, but each time Bob danced backwards. Most of the punches in the early part of the round were taps. Bob was studying his man as a cat does a mouse.

One account said that it was not until time was nearly expired that the men did any effective work. Creedon landed one counter to the ear, but Fitz had the better of a two-handed rally. Dan landed a good one to the ribs, but Fitz planted three straight leads which landed with enough force that they were heard several rows of seats from the ring. Except at the finish of the round, the points were about even, and it looked as if Bob was "drawing out his man as if to study his pet style of offense and defense."

Another account said that after the preliminary feeling out, Dan missed a right for the head and was countered with a jolt on the jaw. Dan landed a good right to the body. Bob feinted a right, landed a hook to the ribs and right to the ear. Creedon clinched. After breaking, Dan feinted for the body with the left and then landed an effective right to Bob's left ear. Bob grew cautious for a moment, but then came back and landed a right to the neck and another punch to the ear.

The men had done good and hard work during the three minutes' fighting, and it was remarked that if the pace were kept up the fight would not last ten rounds. The remark was prophetic. Fitzsimmons showed little or no signs of his exertions, for he really did not let himself out at all and seemed as if he were engaged in ascertaining just what Creedon could do before him. Creedon had made the most of the three minutes and he was puffing a bit when he took his seat.

2nd round

DP: Although Creedon was more aggressive in this round, he had difficulty with Bob's clever ducks and feints, so he went to the inside. However, on the inside, a Fitz right half-arm swing caught Creedon on the jaw and sent him down. He rose and continued. Off of a left uppercut, Dan managed to land a good right. The irked Fitzsimmons responded with lefts and rights. After landing three jabs, Bob paused, shoved Creedon away, and then "hooked his right in like a lighting bolt against the side of Creedon's face about the region of the temple, which blow had scarcely landed when his left shot up, and catching Creedon under the point of the jaw, ended the fight. Creedon toppled over and fell heavily."

TD: Fitz was more aggressive at the outset. "About the first thing he did was just what Corbett had said that he himself had been unable to do, for he walked up to Creedon and struck him squarely on the jaw without any preliminaries." A left hand jolt caused Dan to break ground and throw up his guard to prevent a repetition. Fitz gave him no time to recover, but attacked with right and left. Occasionally Creedon would strike out savagely, but Bob would easily jump back and then spring forward again on the attack with cat-like agility.

Fitzsimmons kept increasing the pace as the round progressed, forcing Creedon to guard, duck and dodge. Fitz landed frequent left leads for the jaw, and the fighting was "so fast that it was impossible to keep anything like an accurate account of the blows landed."

> Finally Fitzsimmons hooked at half-arm distance with his right for Creedon's head and the St. Louis man ducked clear of it, but with lightning-like quickness Fitzsimmons met the duck with a left-hand uppercut, which took effect on the chin and Creedon went down "in a heap."

> In this rally the two blows were so nearly simultaneous that it was difficult to separate the right-hander, which missed its mark, from the left-hander, which scored a clean knockdown. The uppercut was delivered at very close range (a sort of half-arm hook) with only eight or ten inches to travel, but it was effective, for Creedon was stretched at full length from its effect, and though he quickly rolled over and rose to his knees, he took his full time before rising to resume hostilities.

Creedon smiled, and upon rising clinched often to gain time. Despite Creedon's guarding and clinching, Fitz landed multiple lefts to the jaw and ear, not giving Dan any time to recover. When Dan rushed in for a clinch, Fitz danced away out of reach, and then suddenly sprang forward with a short, quick downward right chop behind the ear. Creedon staggered forward with his head down, and immediately was met by tremendous follow-up hook which flowed off that right chop and caught Dan on or just above the mouth, knocking him backward to the ground, utterly senseless. That last punch caused an ugly gash alongside Creedon's nose. Creedon lay on the ground out cold, gasping with blood trickling from his gashed face. It was over after four minutes and forty seconds of fighting.

Another account of the first knockdown said that first Fitz landed a downward right to the head. Bob feinted a left, missed a right, but then, "in ducking the swing Creedon met a left hand uppercut and fell flat, but quickly rose-partially, and rested on one knee."

As soon as he rose, Fitz was after him, but was clinched. After breaking, Bob landed some hard jabs that sent Creedon's head back, and the blood started flowing from a cut in the mouth. Fitz landed a hard right that made Dan unsteady. A couple more hard blows to the head and mouth, which resounded with thuds that could be heard all over the amphitheatre, had

Dan staggering. Bob followed him, landed a right to the head and left to the body. Creedon was getting weak while Bob was fighting like a demon.

Two more blows ended the fight. Bob landed a staggering right to the head as Dan was ducking, and then followed with his powerful left hook on the mouth and cheek bone which in and of itself was sufficient to have knocked him senseless. Creedon fell over backwards and laid there without moving, even after being counted out by referee John Duffy. After being dragged to his chair, Creedon was dazed for over a minute, the blood gushing from his mouth. "It was some minutes before Creedon was wrapped up in his bath robe and escorted through the crowd to his dressing room." According to the *National Police Gazette*, Creedon was out for over five minutes before regaining consciousness.

In conclusion, the local *Daily Picayune* said that Bob quickly discovered that Creedon was overmatched. *The Times-Democrat* summarized that Fitz defeated Creedon with wonderful ease, studying him in the 1st round and whipping him in the 2nd. Creedon was game and clever, but outclassed.

When interviewed afterwards, Fitzsimmons said that it was an easy victory, that he had won his bet that he would stop him within 4 rounds. Bob said that he was never hurt, although he was hit with a couple stiff punches in the 1st round. He had heard a great deal about Creedon's stomach punch, "and wanted to see just what it was." He allowed Creedon to hit him with one, "a sort of experiment to see if it would hurt." Bob was also hit with a good one to the right ear. "That was a stinger…the pain was considerable, but I was foxy enough not to show it, and went right at him."

Of the knockout, Fitz said that it was with the left. He had heard that Creedon had said that Bob was just a right hand puncher and could only jab with the left, so he was determined to prove him wrong and knock him out with the left.

> The blow which gave me the opening I wanted was his stomach blow. He does not cover his jaw enough in delivering the blow, and I hit him a stiff straight-arm right hander about the ear. The blow was a good, sound one, and as he was stooping at the time would have knocked him down. Almost at the same instant I rounded my left up and around like this and caught him full on the nose and mouth. Yes, it was an awful blow, but that was what I intended it to be. He's a good man and game. I hit him some terrible blows as he was going, but he stood the gaff remarkably well.

Another paper quoted Fitz as saying of the knockout,

He came to me for a clinch, but I caught and shoved him off with my right, then I stepped in with my left foot and gave him a down clip with my right and I put him out with my left. Yes, the left was on the lower point of the right jaw.

Creedon had nothing to say on the night of the fight. His manager, Colonel Hopkins, said of Dan, "He fought as well and as long as he could, and got licked by a man who was too much for him. We have no excuses to make. Creedon was well and in condition. He just went against too much."[402]

The typical praises were again heaped upon Fitzsimmons, and many wanted to see him in the ring with Corbett. *National Police Gazette* owner Richard K. Fox sent a telegram asking Bob to challenge Corbett from the ring after the contest was over. The crowd cheered when it heard the telegram. Bob announced and confirmed his desire to meet Corbett.

The general sentiment was that Bob was one of the hardest hitters who ever stood in a ring, and would have a good chance to defeat Corbett. *The New York Sun* said that the "easy and scientific manner in which the Australian scored his victory proves what a great pugilist he is, and it is the general opinion of every one who was present that he is a worthy rival of Corbett's." *The Times-Democrat* said, "Everyone was unanimous in the expression that Fitzsimmons was little short of a wonder, and that he would keep Corbett busy." Even those who felt that Corbett would win believed that Bob would give him a hard fight, better than anyone else would. One man said, "I don't see how Corbett can refuse to give Fitzsimmons a fight."

Fitzsimmons signed articles of agreement with the Olympic to meet Corbett for a $25,000 purse and a side bet of $10,000. However, Corbett replied, "I will say nothing about Fitzsimmons at the present. He must meet Steve O'Donnell first before I will notice him."[403]

Fitz's challenges to Corbett grew bolder. He said that if Corbett "loses his head when he fights me as he did when he fought Charley Mitchell, I will guarantee to find it for him in quick time." Bob was ready and willing to meet Jim at any place and time. "He will find out when I meet him that he has got to fight. He won't have such an easy thing as he had with poor old Sullivan, who was merely a punching bag in his hands." Fitz said that Kilrain, Sullivan and Mitchell were "poor old has beens" when Jim fought

[402] *Daily Picayune, Times-Democrat*, September 27, 1894; *National Police Gazette*, October 13, 1894. Hopkins later changed his mind, the next day saying that Creedon was fouled, but no credence was given to his claim.
[403] *Times-Democrat, New York Sun*, September 27, 1894.

them. "I'll make him fight hard…and give him a thump or two he will remember for a long time." He also said, "Corbett claims that he has never yet fought a man who was able to hit him hard. I don't think he will have that opinion after I meet him." Fitz said that Corbett would have to fight him or retire. However, Bob still realized that a fight with Corbett would be tough. "Corbett will not be an easy man to whip. He is game and full of life, and will put up the battle of his life against me, but I believe I can win."[404]

The day after the Creedon fight, Fitzsimmons took the train heading for his home in Newark, New Jersey, where he was scheduled to set out with his vaudeville company beginning on the 29th.

Speaking of Creedon, Fitz said that he was a plucky, clever fighter, and a good hitter. "Leaving me out, he ought to 'do' any of the middleweights, and there are a lot of heavyweights who are rated pretty well who could not last long with him."[405]

Although Fitzsimmons had impressively taken out the previously undefeated Creedon, who was Corbett's former sparring partner, the man who Corbett had predicted would defeat Bob, Jim said,

Fitzsimmons may keep on fighting middle weights until doomsday, but I will not meet him until he gets into my class. He has been challenged time and time again by O'Donnell, and he has got to recognize him before I will fight him. The statement that I said I would meet Fitzsimmons if he defeated Creedon or Choynski is untrue. I have never talked that way to him or to any one.[406]

Corbett's last statement certainly contradicted multiple reports that said otherwise.

On September 28, Corbett wrote Fitzsimmons and told him that he needed to prove himself a champion heavyweight, not a middleweight.

I must acknowledge that as a middle weight you have no equal, but all you ever did in the heavy-weight class was to defeat Peter Maher and Joe Choynski, two second-class heavyweights, as both of the men have been defeated by Joe Goddard of Australia, another second-class heavy weight…. If I defeated you of course you would say, "He

[404] *Daily Picayune*, September 27, 1894.
[405] *Times-Democrat*, September 28, 1894; Cyberboxingzone.com; Mike Attree.
[406] *New York Sun*, September 28, 1894.

ought to beat me; I am only a middle weight." Just like the time when I beat Sullivan, when they said, "He is an old man," and Mitchell, he was "a little fellow; he was too small." …

You say that I promised to give you a match if you defeated Choynski or Creedon. When you say that you know that you lie. I never even noticed you, and don't intend to unless you prove yourself a champion heavy weight.

When asked about Corbett's edict that he should first fight Jim's sparring partner Steve O'Donnell, Bob said that he would pay no attention to it. "What is O'Donnell as far as reputation goes, that I should consent to a meeting with him?" Fitzsimmons wrote Corbett a letter (which was published in the newspapers, as these letters usually were). In that letter, Bob said to Jim,

At every opportunity when my name has been used in connection with a battle with you for the world's championship you have endeavored to belittle my claim for a fight, on the grounds, as you put it, that I am not in your class, or that you have not seen the color of my money.

I am very well aware of the fact that although I have earned more money than you at fighting since I have become middleweight champion, you could buy and sell me financially, no doubt, your faculty of saving being better than mine. Therefore, I hope that a $10,000 side bet will not stand as a barrier against securing a match with you. …

I hope you will not refuse. When you sign for a $25,000 purse, such as is offered by the Olympic Club at the present time, you will find my name attached without asking for a loser's end.[407]

Bob was willing to fight Corbett winner take all, and Corbett would have a potential $35,000 payday as an incentive.

Upon arriving at a New Jersey train station on the 28th with 4,000 fans waiting to see him, Fitzsimmons said:

I want to meet him above anybody else… I have worked hard and honestly for my reputation, and no one can say anything wrong about

---

[407] *Times-Democrat*, September 28, 1894.

me. Corbett is a great pugilist. I admire him as a boxer, and think he is worthy of being a representative champion – that is, if he will defend his title. ... The public wants to see this fight. ... I think I can beat him. I am not an actor; I am a fighter.... The Olympic Club of New Orleans tell me that if Corbett does not fight they will declare me champion of the world. ... If Corbett ignores me, I will go ahead and do the fighting and permit him to enjoy his ill-earned reputation by posing as an actor.

I will not notice Steve O'Donnell. I am after Corbett. I suppose Jim will next ask me to go and lick "Denver" Smith, if I should agree to fight O'Donnell and beat him. ... He can't fool yours truly that way, you may rest assured. ... I'm sure I can lick him, and will try to do it in a punch, if I can.[408]

Fitz was referring to the fact that Corbett was doing more acting in plays than fighting, and stalling in the making of championship matches.

Corbett's manager William Brady responded, "I don't see why you should make any objection to fighting O'Donnell, Fitzsimmons. He licked you in Australia." Fitz replied, "That's a contemptible lie! He never did." Bob also said, "Let O'Donnell whip Maher or Hall, or somebody I have defeated. Then I will fight him. I shall try to get a fight out of Corbett, and I shall put my fist in his face yet."[409]

The press did not support Corbett's edict that Bob had to fight O'Donnell first. Some were scathing, saying that it would "appear that he wishes to do some more shuffling before facing the issue fairly and squarely." It was said that it would not be long before the general public would disapprove of Corbett's constantly putting off fights.

Even Corbett's warmest friends in this city look upon his demand that Fitzsimmons shall fight Steve O'Donnell as an absurd one. Nobody thinks that Corbett should be forced to fight Fitzsimmons against his will, but they hold that he should either fight or relinquish his claim to the world's championship. A pugilist who will not accept a reasonable proposal for a fight is not favorably regarded by sporting men generally. If Corbett's business engagements are so pressing and important that he cannot afford to meet Fitzsimmons for a big purse and a liberal side bet, he has a good reason for retiring from the ring.... [A]nd above all, this suggestion of another "trial horse" for

[408] *New York Sun*, September 30, 1894.
[409] *New York Sun*, October 2, 1894; *Times-Democrat*, September 29, 1894.

the Australian is weak, childish and unsportsmanlike. ... The pugilistic world has no use for a champion who will not fight.[410]

The press felt that Corbett was just seeking to put as many obstacles in Bob's way as possible. Fitz had defeated Maher, Hall, Choynski, and Creedon, all of whom were considered legitimate tests.[411] Sportsmen saw Fitz as the hardest hitter outside of John L. Sullivan; but he also had speed and skill and was not past his prime as John L. was when he met Jim. One man who had seen Fitz in four of his big fights said, "I believe he carefully studies out these unpleasant surprises for the unfortunates who have to meet him."

John L. Sullivan called Fitzsimmons the coming man. He was positive that Bob could defeat Corbett, but "in my opinion Corbett does not want to fight anybody." Upon reading that statement, an indignant Corbett said, "Sullivan had always more mouth than courage. ... If I ever meet Fitzsimmons in the ring it will make a better fight than Sullivan did with me." Sullivan retorted,

> Whatever else may be said of me, I am sure they will give me the credit of being at all times willing to defend the championship. They cannot say the same of Corbett. ... His pretext that Fitzsimmons is out of his class is nonsense. If he is, so much the better for Corbett, for he can win the money just as easily as he did from Mitchell. The proposition made by Fitzsimmons to Corbett is fair and should be accepted in good faith. ... My opinion of Corbett is that he is afraid to meet Fitzsimmons.[412]

Some opined that Corbett was wisely refraining from taking on a tough challenge because he was "making money now and wishes to reap in the coin while the sun shines." It was in Fitz's best economic interest to make the challenge because it got him free publicity, which could enhance his value as an exhibitor as well. "Fitzsimmons wants to make money and by his challenging the champion is taking a good way to gather in the shekels."[413]

Fitzsimmons posted a $1,000 forfeit and issued a statement to Corbett:

---

[410] *Times-Democrat,* September 28, 1894.
[411] *New York Sun,* September 28, 1894.
[412] *Times-Democrat,* September 28-30, 1894.
[413] *Paterson Evening News,* October 2, 1894.

I have consulted all the best sporting authorities in America on this point, and they all agree that you are obliged to fight me or lose the championship by default. ...

I might cite numerous battles where middle weights have fought and even whipped heavy weights. I think that Peter Maher would class as a heavy weight when I defeated him in New Orleans, and also Joe Choynski and others who have suffered defeat at my hands.

Have you forgotten that Jim Hall, whom I defeated in four rounds...knocked Frank Slavin out in seven rounds after you refused to meet Slavin, because you considered him a bit too big and husky?

Corbett responded,

I am the champion heavy weight of the world. I won that title, not by defeating middle weights, but by battling with every heavy weight that stood between myself and John L. Sullivan.... I dispute your right to claim a battle with me...your record gives you no right to a place in my class. I propose to enter the prize ring once more and then retire whether I win or lose. I want my next contest to be with the best man in the world. I do not consider you that man. I do not propose to meet you, and then, after having defeated you, be told by your friends that you are only a middle weight, after all. I care nothing for the past history of the ring or its obsolete rules.[414]

Fitz replied that Corbett had not really done very much to acquire a reputation. "Corbett has only beaten broken-down stiffs like Kilrain, Sullivan and Mitchell. I am entitled to a fight with him, and it won't be all his way."[415] He had a good point. Both Sullivan and Mitchell were over the hill. Kilrain was only a 6-round points win for Jim. Corbett had taken much longer than Fitzsimmons did to defeat Choynski. His fight with Peter Jackson had essentially ended in a draw. Newspapers raised these points, amongst others.

While Corbett would undoubtedly enter the ring a favorite over Fitzsimmons, there can be no doubt that the performances of the two men in this country show the Australian the better man of the two. In Sullivan and Mitchell Corbett defeated two men who were

---

[414] *New York Sun*, October 2, 1894.
[415] *Times-Democrat*, September 30, 1894.

clearly in the "sear and yellow leaf." In Jackson (provided the colored man's ankle is all right) he made a draw with a thoroughly good man. ... Had the good fortune to meet Sullivan in his last battle come to Fitzsimmons instead of Corbett the Australian would, by the records, have had a much better right to deny a match to Corbett than Corbett now has to refuse him; but all who know "Lanky Bob" know that he would, under similar circumstances, have thrown no obstacles in the way of such a meeting.

Corbett cannot afford to hold his present attitude much longer. The sporting public, and indeed all who take an interest in pugilism, admire pluck as much as they do skill, and they cannot fail to quickly tire of a champion pugilist who will not, or dare not, fight. Two courses are open to Corbett. He may retire from the ring permanently, or he may meet Fitzsimmons, but he cannot longer remain the heavyweight champion and refuse to defend the title against the only aspirant who appears to have a chance of defeating him.

As for the cowardly subterfuge to which Corbett has resorted in causing O'Donnell to challenge Fitzsimmons, it is hardly worthy of serious consideration.[416]

Speaking of Peter Jackson, if Fitz was not the "best man in the world," Jackson was, and Corbett was not fighting him either. The fact that the Corbett-Jackson negotiations had fizzled out helped Fitzsimmons, because by putting obstacles in Fitz's way, it was beginning to seem as if Corbett did not want to fight anyone, and was just a bluffer.

However, ironically, Fitzsimmons said that if he won the heavyweight championship, he would fight against all comers, except blacks, such Peter Jackson. Fitzsimmons, like Sullivan, was open about the fact that he would draw the color line as champion. "I will fight anybody except Jackson, whom I would not meet because he is a colored man."[417] Jackson was good enough for Bob to receive instruction from, but not good enough to fight. Or perhaps he was too good. As early as March 1894, Fitz had announced in a speech that he was wiling to meet any man in the world except for Peter Jackson, "whom he regards as the greatest living fighter."[418]

Despite his color line stance, while in Australia, Fitz had exhibited with a black fighter named Bonnar and fought a black fighter named "Starlight,"

[416] *Times-Democrat,* September 30, 1894.
[417] *New York Sun,* October 2, 1894; *National Police Gazette,* October 20, 1894; *San Francisco Chronicle,* November 14, 1896.
[418] *St. Louis Post-Dispatch,* March 12, 15, 1894.

and in America, one called "The Black Pearl." Either his opposition to fighting blacks was only an opposition to meeting them in a championship bout, or Bob was essentially using the color line as a preemptive excuse not to meet a man whom he thought might defeat him. Perhaps he said it to make the American public happy. As an American, Bob had apparently taken on America's social mores.

As predicted by Fitzsimmons, Corbett and Peter Jackson never met in a championship match. This left Bob as the next logical contender.

The negative press eventually got to Corbett. Jim said that the Olympic Club had no right to declare Fitzsimmons champion of the world, but also said,

> I do not propose that a foreigner shall take my title from me by default. ... I am anxious to retire from pugilism, but the gang of queer sports who are hoping that I may be beaten shall never have the satisfaction of saying that I show the white feather.[419]

Corbett agreed to meet with the Fitzsimmons party to negotiate a match.

Fitzsimmons, who had been exhibiting in Philadelphia, traveled to New York with manager Captain Giori and Olympic Club President Scholl to meet with Corbett. Bob said, "I care nothing for Corbett's weight. I have knocked out bigger men than he, some of them weighing over 200 pounds, and I am confident that I can punch harder than he can." Bob said that Corbett could not bluff him, and if he gave him any tongue, he would run him out of the room and have it out with him there and then.[420]

The two parties met at the *New York Herald* offices on October 11. Jim did not want to fight until July 1895 because he had theatrical engagements until then. Peter Jackson had not been willing to wait that long to fight, but Fitz agreed, saying that he was willing to fight Corbett any time and anywhere, and that he would make every concession just to get Jim into the ring. "Corbett had no alternative but to put up his money and fight. In short, Fitzsimmons has the satisfaction of knowing that he compelled Corbett to accept his challenge and that the O'Donnell bluff didn't go."

The two agreed to fight sometime after July 1, 1895 before Jacksonville's Florida Athletic Club, which made the highest purse bid of $41,000. They also agreed to a stake/side bet of $10,000 each. "This arrangement is the culminating point of a series of violent ultimatums, proclamations and taunts made by the friends of both men."

---

[419] *Paterson Evening News,* October 3, 1894.
[420] *Paterson Evening News,* October 11, 1894.

The Florida Athletic Club via its representative Joe Vendig agreed to put up a $5,000 deposit, which was to be forfeited to the fighters if it was unable to bring off the fight.

> The fighters argued that they would have to give up no less than eight weeks of their theatrical tours in order to train for the event, and as they would be under great expense for training quarters, trainers, etc., it would be but fair for a deposit to recompense them for their expenditures and loss of time in event the Florida authorities should make it impossible to bring off the fight in that State.

However, they did not sign the agreement there because to do so would have been a violation of New York law, which made it illegal even to agree to a fight. The Superintendent told them that everyone would be placed under arrest if the agreement was signed.[421] But, the fight was on, at least initially.

---

[421] *New York Sun*, October 12, 1894; *National Police Gazette*, October 27, 1894; *Washington Post*, March 13, 1895.

CHAPTER 12

Death and Delay

During the time that Fitzsimmons and Corbett were engaging in their newspaper war of words in late September and early October 1894, Fitzsimmons gave theatrical exhibitions with his specialty company in New Jersey and Philadelphia. These exhibitions continued over the next couple of months, after Fitz and Corbett had agreed to fight.[422]

Starting October 22, 1894, Bob gave nightly exhibitions at New York's Miner's Bowery Theatre.[423] On October 26, 1894, Fitzsimmons hit the leather bag and sparred 3 rounds "with an energetic and clever boxer, Ike Williams." The newspapers usually did not give daily accounts for these minor exhibitions, but Fitz was said to have again sparred Williams on the 29th. Bob gave a matinee there on November 3.[424]

On the afternoon of November 8, 1894 at the New York Athletic Club, Fitzsimmons sparred Professor Mike Donovan in a friendly and interesting set-to. Donovan, the elder statesman of boxing, who had the experience of sparring both John L. Sullivan and James J. Corbett, said,

It was the first time I ever faced Fitzsimmons, and what most surprised me was the man's remarkable quickness and the apparent lack of exertion with which he delivers very hard blows. I never faced a big man who was quicker on his feet. ... I am of the opinion that no one can teach him much about the fine points of boxing. ... Corbett is a very clever and very strong man. He will no doubt get the greatest battle of his life. The encounter will be a remarkable one.[425]

---

[422] Cyberboxingzone.com; Mike Attree.

[423] *New York Evening Telegram*, October 22, 1894.

[424] *New York World*, October 27, 30, 1894, November 3, 1894. At that time, Fitz was dealing with his ex-wife in regards to alimony payments. Bob was apparently booked in Newark the following week.

[425] *New York Evening Telegram*, November 9, 1894.

Mike Donovan

Jim Hall, who had been in the ring with both, said that a Corbett-Fitzsimmons fight "ought to be a good one. Bob is a good man, and he has got a chance to win that fight. ... It ought to be an even money fight."[426]

Unfortunately, in order to prevent the fight, the Jacksonville, Florida City Council unanimously voted to repeal the ordinance that allowed boxing there. Therefore, the Florida Athletic Club would have to find another location to hold the fight.[427] Things were about to get even more complicated.

On November 16, 1894 in Syracuse, New York at the Jacobs Opera House, Bob Fitzsimmons boxed in an exhibition with his current sparring partner, Cornelius "Con" Riordan. The 5'11½" Australian native Riordan was an experienced veteran who weighed either 170-175 or 180 pounds in condition, and his reported ages were 30, 31 or 34, depending on the source. He had sparred Steve Taylor on the 1886 undercard of Sullivan vs. Ryan III. He became a boxing professor in 1887 at San Francisco's Golden Gate Club. While there, he taught and sparred with a young Joe Choynski. He fought Martin Costello to a 6- or 8-round draw. One report said that Riordan had been a Sullivan sparring partner in 1888. He had briefly trained Joe McAuliffe in 1889. Riordan was bested in a bout with Denver Ed Smith. In 1891, Riordan scored a KO18 over Max Fenner or Feurner. Australian Billy Smith stopped Riordan in the 26th round (some say 18th round).

Riordan boxed Peter Jackson 4 rounds in 1888 and again in 1892. At one point, he was listed as Jackson's trainer/sparring partner and had traveled to England with him in February 1892. Jackson said that Riordan was a good boxer.

---

426 *New York Evening Telegram*, October 30, 1894.
427 *New York World*, November 9, 1894.

In mid-1892, Jack Slavin stopped a then 29-year-old 5'11½" 161-pound Riordan in the 19th round. In late 1893, Riordan defeated 240-pound Con Coughlin in 65 seconds. In April 1894, Riordan scored a KO1 over Mike Monohan.[428]

Unfortunately, during their November 16 evening sparring session, in the 1st round, after a Fitzsimmons blow landed on Riordan's jaw, Con dropped down. At that point, Riordan retired, but soon thereafter passed out. He did not recover consciousness "despite the efforts of two physicians, who gave him hypodermic injections and applied an electric battery." The physicians applied electricity from

Con Riordan

10:30 p.m. until 12:30 a.m. Riordan died at 3:30 a.m. Apparently, the blow was a light one, but Riordan was reported to have been drinking heavily all day and just before the exhibition.

Ironically, in Bob's follow-up sparring with Joseph Dunfee, a pugilist who had killed J. Donovan a year and a half earlier, Fitzsimmons himself was knocked down in the 2nd round. Bob had boxed him after Riordan because the seriousness of Con's condition was not immediately realized.

After the exhibition, the police arrested Fitzsimmons. Riordan died later that evening. The cause of death was listed as blood clots compressing the brain. Fitz blamed it on Riordan's inebriated condition, insisting that it had been a light tap with the back of the hand. In the courtroom at his initial appearance the next morning, Fitz broke down in tears and said that he would not have killed Riordan for $100,000. Fitzsimmons' bail was set at $10,000 for a first degree manslaughter charge.[429]

Regarding the events that evening, the *New York Evening Telegram* said that Riordan appeared to have been drinking heavily. They boxed at about 10:00 p.m.

---

[428] *Times-Democrat*, February 28, 1892; *New York Clipper*, April 2, 1892, November 24, 1894; *Newark Evening News*, September 6, 1893; *Philadelphia Inquirer*, April 19, 1893; *National Police Gazette*, December 1, 1894, July 5, 1902; *Referee*, April 20, 1892, July 13, 1892; *New York Sun*, November 18, 1894; *New York World*, November 17, 1894; Boxrec.com.
[429] *New York Tribune*, November 17 and 18, 1894.

He gave evidence of his condition as he walked on the stage, but, despite this, he was allowed to enter into the bout. There were a few exchanges and then Fitzsimmons with a quick pass landed on Riordan's jaw with his right.

There are differences of opinion as to the force of the blow, but it was sufficient. Riordan reeled and fell to his knees. Then he fell over like a dead man. ... Back in the wings the unconscious man lay in his ring costume, with two physicians vainly endeavoring to bring him back to consciousness.

Fitz said,

Do you suppose I would strike my sparring partner with any force? I knew he had been drinking hard, but did not know he was in such a condition. ... I never struck him hard. ...

Last night I noticed after the fist exchange of blows that he was not right. The blow that I delivered that caused the trouble, was light as I could make it, merely slapping him with the back of my hand. He fell down, and then rose and staggered round. I put my arm around him to assist him off the stage.

When he fell headlong, I thought he was faking, and was as thoroughly disgusted because somebody in the house, thinking it was a fake, hissed me. I was never hissed before. I began to comprehend a few minutes later that something was wrong with my sparring partner and I was horrified to find him still unconscious. I attributed this to his drunken condition, and thought he would revive from the stupor in a few minutes.

I have known this man for eight years and he was always a hard drinker. Being in poor condition, I presume he had some heart difficulty that brought on the disorder.

I am not fearful of my position. Everybody in the opera house was aware that the blows which I struck Riordan were light as I could possibly make them.

Charles Giori, manager for the company, said, "He's been drinking ever since I engaged him three weeks ago in New York. ... He promised to be sober, but did not keep his promise." Regarding the series of events that evening, Giori said,

Bob punched the bag for over a minute before his round with Riordan. When the latter came on he said to Bob; - 'Don't hit me in the stomach or in the ribs.' So Bob aimed all his blows at Con's head. The boxing was the tamest I ever saw and made me disgusted.... Suddenly, Con turned to me and said, 'call time.' The next instant he sank down. I looked at my watch and found that just thirty-five seconds had passed since I had announced that it was time for the commencement of the round. The blow was so light that it would not have injured a ten-year old child. If it should have been the blow that Dunfee gave Fitzsimmons when he knocked Bob down, Con's death might have been laid to it. ...

When he was carried off the stage and placed in a chair, nothing was thought of his condition except that he was drunk, and Dunfee went on for his round. ...

Still, a doctor who examined Riordan that night said, "The man is evidently suffering from a brain hemorrhage, brought on by something more serious than drinking."

However, Dr. Fay, the first physician on the scene, said that his opinion was that Riordan's death was from apoplexy and not by a blow. The doctor said, "All who saw the blow say that it was really only a slap." Yank Sullivan said the blow was very light, and that he had seen Riordan drink a half pint of Scotch whiskey before sparring. He also said that Con had been drinking all day long. Joe Dunfee, who subsequently sparred Fitzsimmons, said that Riordan went down so easily that the audience hissed and cried "Fake."

After boxing Riordan,

Then Dunfee went on. His first round was long range sparring. The next was to have been Riordan's round, but as it was thought that he was drunk, Dunfee went on. He asked Fitz to "mix it up," meaning to fight at closer range. Fitz did so and in a moment Dunfee landed a blow on his chin which knocked the middleweight champion off his feet and numbed Dunfee's arm. Then the audience raised another cry of "Fake."[430]

Another newspaper noted, "In the second round Dunfee landed a right hand blow on Fitz's jaw, resulting in a clean knockdown. ... He was so

[430] *New York Evening Telegram,* November 17, 1894.

dazed when he regained his feet that he could not see Dunfee's hand when it was extended at the call of time."[431]

The New York Clipper's version of events said that a Fitz quick right uppercut to Riordan's jaw did the trick. The cause of death was given as hemorrhage within the cranial cavity, causing compression of the brain. The coroner said that there was an excessive hemorrhage and clot. It was his opinion that Riordan "must have been struck a terrific blow on the point of the chin."[432] Perhaps his head striking the hard floor did the real damage.

The New York World's version reported that Riordan had been traveling with the Fitzsimmons Vaudeville and Specialty Company, which opened in Syracuse on the 15th. At about 10:30 p.m. on the 16th,

> After two minutes of hot work Fitzsimmons feinted with his left and landed heavily on Riordan's jaw with his right. Riordan staggered for a moment and then toppled over. He was knocked out, and the stage hands did not know what action to take. … Fitzsimmons finally got Riordan on his feet, when the latter gave a lurch and fell prone to the floor, where he lay unconscious.

Fitzsimmons said,

> Riordan, when he came on the stage, was under the influence of liquor. In my opinion…he would have fallen behind the scenes without my striking him at all. … When he fell to his knees, I did not think that I had hurt him, and supposed he only wanted to escape.
>
> We had only been at it a few minutes, when I made a pass at him. I hit him on the right cheek with the back of my right hand. It was merely a smart tap, and could not have more than stung him. He made one or two feints at me, then I was surprised to see him put up his hands and say, 'Call time.' It was quite a while before I realized how bad he was.
>
> He drank a good deal of Bass's ale yesterday, and before he went on the stage downed a big drink of whiskey. I suppose it all went to his head.[433]

---

[431] *Paterson Evening News, New York World,* November 17, 1894.
[432] *New York Clipper,* November 24, 1894.
[433] *New York World,* November 17, 1894.

A couple weeks later, Fitz further illuminated what had happened that evening. "It was not my blow that killed Con Riordan. It was apoplexy." He claimed that his last blow was just a light touch.

> Why, after he quit sparring with me he talked to three or four people, and laughed and kidded about our go. You know that anybody I hit a knockout blow won't laugh and kid about it before he goes out. Why, I hit a fellow in Philadelphia one night and he was out three hours and a half, but he came around all right and was as good as gold. You couldn't tell he had been hit. Riordan was all right until he took a fit and fell off the chair. He was subject to fits of apoplexy. A well-known physician in Philadelphia told me that after he went on with Monahan for four rounds Riordan took two apoplectic fits in the dressing room and came within an ace of dying....
>
> Do you know the nearest I was ever knocked out? It was that night that Riordan died. Just after I finished boxing with Riordan I went on with a fellow named Dunfee. I was watching Riordan as he was sitting on his chair. I was not paying any attention to the man I was boxing with. Suddenly he caught me with a left-hander. Then he crossed me with his right and knocked me down. I was out. He picked me up and put out his hand to shake with me. I saw 50 hands, but I reached out and he took hold of it. I was dizzy for half an hour after the knock-down. It was the nearest I was ever out.[434]

Bob also told another paper that he had Riordan with him for about three weeks, and "was such a good soul I'd become very much attached to him." However, he always found him drinking and would be wobbly in the legs for their sparring.

> On this night he said to me: 'Now, Bob, go easy.' And when we came out we did a little dancing about, made a few passes, and I tapped him lightly on the chest. All at once he began to sink altogether, his knees began to shake, and he said to me, 'Tell him to call time,' and sank down to the floor as easy as a baby. We took him into the wings, sat him in a chair, and had one of the boys watch him. Then I went on with this man Dunphy. I was worried all the time about Con, and every time I could get a chance I'd look around to see how he was getting on. While I was stealing a look at him over my shoulder

---

[434] *Cincinnati Enquirer,* December 3, 1894. On May 20, 1895, Dan Creedon would knock out Dunfee in 3 rounds. Boxrec.com.

Dunphy lit into me. He gave me one under the left jaw, and before I could tell what was going on he soaked a left–hander on the other side of my neck, and I went heels over head. Oh, but he did soak it to me. I staggered up to my feet just as he reached out his hand to give me a shake. Everything was going around and I saw about fifty hands at once. They took me down to my dressing-room, and I don't remember much what happened for an hour except my wife telling me about Con. I was dazed. That side of my neck is sore now from Dunphy's blow. I asked my wife: 'Who hit me? Con or the other fellow?' And I remember she told me it was Dunphy. Poor Con, I think it was an apoplectic shock that took him off. He had a spell like it one night in Philadelphia. Any way, I know I never struck him hard enough to hurt any one.[435]

Fitzsimmons attended Riordan's funeral on November 19.[436]

Ironically, regardless of the cause of Riordan's death, it further improved Fitz's already strong reputation as a hard puncher. "If Bob can hit like that in fun, what will he do to Corbett when he meets the champion in earnest?"[437] Another report said,

Bob Fitzsimmons has never been given the credit for being able to hit as hard a blow as any pugilist that ever fought in the ring. It was only by a fortunate accident that he did not send Jim Hall to eternity…. The blow Fitzsimmons delivered on Hall's jugular sent him to sleep for fully 7 minutes. Many supposed that Hall would not recover…. At the time Fitzsimmons knocked out Dan Creedon the blow did not fairly land, or else Creedon would have been insensible even longer. Hall says he could not tell how long he was insensible, and Creedon says he thought Fitzsimmons had hit him with a club.[438]

James Corbett offered Fitzsimmons financial aid and permission to allow him to draw down some forfeit money from their fight to assist him, to be returned once he was free from legal complications.[439]

Undeterred by the death, Fitzsimmons continued giving regular exhibitions in late 1894 and early 1895.[440]

[435] *Cincinnati Commercial Gazette,* December 3, 1894.
[436] *Paterson Evening News,* November 19, 1894.
[437] *New York Tribune,* November 18, 1894.
[438] *National Police Gazette,* December 8, 1894.
[439] *National Police Gazette,* December 8, 1894.

About ten days after Riordan's death, Fitz began exhibiting for a week in Philadelphia with his All-Star Athletic and Vaudeville Company, working with his new sparring partner; 26-year-old 6' 168-pound Charles Farrell. Usually Bob would hit the bag, "an athletic feat in which he has no equal," and then spar Farrell 3 rounds.

The local report said of the November 26 exhibition, "The act is exceedingly clever and demonstrates to a nicety Fitzsimmons' quickness in striking and dodging. Undoubtedly Corbett will have to exert himself to the utmost if he expects to keep out of the way of the fists that played such a tattoo on the pigskin."

On the 29th, Fitz exhibited twice (likely afternoon and evening shows), both times giving "rattling" set-tos with Farrell.[441] Bob exhibited in Philadelphia for the last time on December 1. Fitz claimed that his exhibitions had broken all the house records.

Beginning on December 2, 1894, Fitzsimmons appeared for one week at Cincinnati, Ohio's Fountain Theater. Bob gave a bag punching exhibition, and then sparred 3 light but pleasing rounds with his new sparring partner, Tom McCarthy, who was from Philadelphia.

Fitz said that McCarthy was a dead ringer for Corbett, stood over 6-feet tall, weighed 215 pounds, and had some creditable victories on his record. "He is a stiff puncher, and it keeps Fitz busy looking out that Mac does not 'cop' him one on the point of the jaw and put him out." Bob claimed that he had actually sparred with McCarthy in Philadelphia on Thursday night (but it was probably Friday November 30 or Saturday December 1) because Farrell was too light and could not take it.

Bob said that he was weighing 162-165 pounds and would not be any larger than that for the Corbett bout. "No, I'll weigh just about what I do now. There is no use to put on a lot of flesh that will do you no good. Oh, yes, I have seen Corbett spar and fight, too. I know just what I am going against, and I wouldn't have made the match unless I thought I could win it." Fitz was measured as having a reach of 6'2 ½", a ¼" more than Corbett's. He stood 5'11 ¾" in his stockings, but 6' ½" in his shoes.[442]

Fitzsimmons noted the irony that boxing was illegal in many states, but football was popular in Ivy League schools.

---

[440] *New York Evening Telegram,* November 17, 1894. It was reported the day after Riordan's death that after being arraigned and released on bail, Fitz would return to Jacob's Opera House to appear in the afternoon and evening performances. It is unclear whether Fitz actually exhibited there that day.

[441] *Philadelphia Inquirer,* November 26, 27, 30, 1894; *Philadelphia Press,* November 25, 1894.

[442] *Cincinnati Enquirer,* December 2, 3, 1894; *Cincinnati Post,* December 1, 3, 1894. Fitz's vaudeville company consisted of 22 persons, which included comedians, musicians, singers, a ventriloquist, dancers, a juggling waiter, and an acrobat.

Talk about brutality. I went down to see the Princeton game, and every man in the lot was trying to kill somebody. It's very funny, too, how those fellows will go into a game with the chances that they'll come out crippled, and fight each other like bulls. And the minute you put a glove on a man and ask him to stand up and fight, he says: 'Oh, no!'

The Princeton boys wanted to show me a few tackles and bucks, but I said: 'Not any for me. That game's a little too rough.'[443]

Fitz sparred McCarthy on December 3 and slightly hurt the knuckles on one of his hands. He still punched the bag on the 4th. On the 6th, Bob demonstrated his smithy skills, forging two horseshoes in 15 minutes.[444]

There was further discussion and analysis of the Corbett-Fitzsimmons match. Corbett said to Colonel Hopkins, Dan Creedon's backer, "You seem to think that Fitzsimmons is the most dangerous man in the world, Colonel." The Colonel replied, "You will have reason to think so, too, if he hits you as he did Creedon." Corbett smiled and replied, "No man has ever hit me when I did not want to let him, and I don't think that Bob will succeed where Jackson failed."

Corbett was sparring with Steve O'Donnell, hoping that Steve would give him a line on Fitz. "O'Donnell has boxed with Fitzsimmons often in Australia, and thinks he knows all the tricks of the man who is expected to give Corbett the fight of his life next summer." O'Donnell might have known a few things, but "Fitzsimmons, however, is much quicker than O'Donnell and much more original in his methods. His motions in fighting are very eccentric. As Corbett says, 'He's got a lot of crazy movements that have to be watched.'" Fitz was said to have cat-like quickness, excellent punching powers, and shadow-like bounds in getting in and away. He could also miss a punch but have another to catch his opponent with when they were ducking away.[445]

Corbett said that after he whipped Bob, he would retire from the ring, "never to don the gloves again. It is my only ambition now to become an actor. ... While I do not take any pride in my profession, I take pride in the thought that I have elevated the ring. I believe I have."[446]

As if things were not bad enough, at that time, the old political and legal anti-boxing fervor was once again rearing its ugly head. The Jacksonville City Council had already repealed the ordinance which allowed boxing

[443] *Cincinnati Commercial Gazette*, December 3, 1894.
[444] *Cincinnati Commercial Gazette*, December 5, 1894; *Cincinnati Post*, December 7, 1894.
[445] *Cincinnati Enquirer*, December 4, 1894; *Chicago Times*, December 26, 1894.
[446] *Daily Picayune*, December 11, 1894.

there. On December 14, 1894 in New Orleans, in a fight to the finish, Kid Lavigne knocked out Andy Bowen in the 18th round. Bowen died soon afterwards, which once again brought out the anti-boxing hysteria from the press, public (particularly the ministerial and religious community), and politicians. "Andy Bowen is dead, and professional pugilism in New Orleans will more than likely fill the same grave." Many felt that Bowen's head coming in contact with the hard floor was the real culprit.

Louisiana's Attorney General informed the Olympic Club that he was taking the position that the fights it put on were illegal prizefights, and that they should be terminated until the courts could decide the matter. The club agreed to suspend its contests pending a legal decision about their status.[447] New Orleans was no longer an option for the Corbett-Fitzsimmons fight.

Parson Davies, backer of fighters, said,

> Well, I believe that the accident will give the sport a set-back…. But I do not believe that it will kill the sport. Not at all. It merely gives the preachers and cranks a chance to limber up their thunder machines and lubricate the wheels of wrath that are set a-turning with every accident, whether it happens on the football field or in the prize ring. Now, to be frank with you, men have been killed before, not only in the prize ring, but in all athletic games – football, baseball, jumping, wrestling, etc. What is the value of athletics if every degree of danger is removed? … Suppose two sets of fighters come to town. One pair announce that they will fight to a finish and another that their contest will be merely scientific for points. The contest that is to be fought to a finish will draw the crowd. … I want to say that the mayor of this city, and of other cities, have no backbone. They are afraid of the clamor of cranks. In one paragraph Mayor Fitzpatrick says if it was an accident that killed Bowen the sport is not fatal, but he revokes the permit to allow the fights. … There have to be reforms in everything, and there are some reforms to be made in the ring. They will be made and the sport will go on as long as there is a public to patronize it.[448]

Jim Corbett responded to the Bowen situation by saying, "It will hurt pugilism, and makes me more eager than ever to get out of the business." When asked his opinion of the future of pugilism, Corbett said,

---

[447] *Daily Picayune*, December 16, 1894. Perhaps too many finish fights contributed to Bowen's death: 1893 D110 Texas Jack Burke and KO85 Jack Everhart; and 1894 D25 Jimmy Carroll.
[448] *Daily Picayune*, December 17, 1894.

I believe it is coming to an end pretty fast. In another year it will be pretty hard to pull off a fight anywhere. For me, I'm sick and tired of it, and am getting more anxious every day to get out of the business. … I wish it understood everywhere that my next fight, the one with Fitzsimmons, whatever the result, will be absolutely my last, come what may. I shall retire at the conclusion of that match.[449]

On December 16, 1894 in Louisville, Kentucky, just before Bob went on stage at the Buckingham Theatre to spar 3 rounds with Tom McCarthy, Fitzsimmons spoke about the troubling situation.

"[T]he adverse public opinion will die out after a time and everything will go on as heretofore." When shown Corbett's statement that he was disgusted with the business and wanted to retire, Fitzsimmons replied laconically: "Well, he may have a chance after I meet him."[450]

There was some preliminary talk about Texas being a possible alternative site for the big fight. Attorneys there felt that there could be no legal objection to it, and it "is not thought probable that there will be any objections interposed by Governor Culberson."[451]

In late December, Bob was set to have a two-week engagement in Chicago.[452] However, when he found out that the police superintendent was against boxing exhibitions taking place, Fitz cut sparring out of his show and only gave bag punching exhibitions, starting on the 23rd. Bob said, "When I arrived here this morning I heard that a boxing bout had been stopped last Wednesday by the police…. That was enough for me, for I do not intend to make myself amenable to the law." Bob Fitzsimmons was a law-abiding citizen.

Responding to the political pressure against boxing, Bob said,

These fatalities coming close together and along with the talk of the big fight for the championship has made those who would bring the whole world to their way of thinking by force cry out. The result is always extreme measures. They will not be lasting.[453]

---

[449] *Daily Picayune*, December 17, 1894.
[450] *Daily Picayune*, December 17, 1894.
[451] *Daily Picayune*, December 22, 1894.
[452] *Chicago Herald*, December 23, 1894.
[453] *Chicago Herald*, December 24, 1894. On December 19, 1894, Louisiana moved for an injunction against the Olympic Club, arguing that boxing was contrary to the laws

Interestingly enough, on December 24, 1894, Fitzsimmons was invited to give a private exhibition before the Chicago stock exchange. When Fitz told them that the police chief had asked him to refrain from boxing, they informed Bob that the chief had granted special permission. So it was with boxing. In the afternoon, with the police present, Fitzsimmons boxed 3 rounds with Tom McCarthy. Fitz mostly boxed on the retreat and defended, without trying to hit McCarthy. The crowd heartily cheered him.

Afterwards, Fitz went down to the Chicago Athletic Association for a ceremony tendered to boxing instructor George Dawson. Fitzsimmons and Dawson engaged in a light tapping affair and put up "one of the cleverest exhibitions ever seen here, illustrating all the beauties of the art." Bob complimented Dawson's cleverness. "It is so seldom that I meet a really clever and fast man that it is a great pleasure to me to spar with one."[454]

Thomas Edison's Kinetoscope Company had offered Jim and Bob thousands of dollars to fight before its cameras. Fitz was interested.[455] Corbett said that the kinetoscope was not technologically advanced enough to film a Marquis of Queensberry rules bout with the proper rounds and rest lengths, and that Fitz was making a big bluff by saying that he wanted them to fight before it. Fitzsimmons responded,

Corbett is the last man who ought to say anything about using the kinetoscope or any other means for advertising purposes. A kinetoscope contest may not be much of a contest of endurance, but Corbett might find it more than he imagines if he were before one for a genuine contest instead of a mere "fake." He seems to fear a chance blow...having dodged Peter Jackson, with little credit to himself, he now seeks to get out of meeting me. Peter Jackson is not pretty. Neither am I. We are not afraid of getting hit and are willing to take our chances with "chance blows." Corbett is too pretty, and pretty men are particularly afraid of chance blows. I think I can whip Corbett.... If I am so easy I should think Corbett would have no hesitancy in meeting me.... It is far easier to pose and talk about

---

prohibiting assault and battery. Corbett did not want to fight there anyway, because the Olympic had threatened to recognize Fitzsimmons as champion if Corbett did not accept his challenge. Leo N. Miletich, *Dan Stuart's Fistic Carnival* (College Station: Texas A&M University Press, 1994), 15-16.

[454] *Chicago Times*, December 25, 1894. It is unclear whether this was the same fighter, but this was likely the Australian born lightweight George Dawson, whose record included: 1889 and 1890 D39 and KO31 Jim Burge; 1890 KO20 Billy Maber; 1891 KO17 Dummy Mace and LKOby4 Tommy Williams; 1892 KO42 Billy Gallagher, D20 Ned Burden, KO29 Danny Needham (in America), KO20 Doc O'Connell; and 1893 ND6 Tommy Ryan (in Chicago). Boxrec.com.

[455] *New York Evening Telegram*, October 30, 1894.

elevating the ring than it is to fight. I am not a reformer and I shall let the ring take care of itself. I am a fighter and want to fight Corbett.[456]

The Edison people had assured Fitzsimmons that they had been improving their technology and that the fight could be filmed with three-minute rounds and one-minute rests.[457]

At his highest weight of 214 pounds, Corbett claimed to be bigger, better, and stronger than ever before. Jim said,

> I am fully aware that Fitz will give me perhaps the most scientific battle of my career.... He is an awkward shifty fellow and a harder man to hit than the average pugilist, who doesn't depend on his awkwardness. He is a hard hitter and cool headed. I saw him fight Dempsey and posted myself on his style. He is my equal almost in height and reach, though after carefully comparing his method of boxing with mine, I can't see where he has any advantage over me, as I am younger, stronger and shiftier, hit oftener and mix my blows more. Fitzsimmons is foxy – he was cute enough to feign grogginess in several of his battles, thus throwing his opponents off their guard. He can't fool me by working the groggy dodge. I will take no chances with him.... After my fight with Fitzsimmons I will devote my entire attention to my theatrical enterprises and retire permanently from the prize ring.[458]

In January 1895, Fitz continued sparring with Tom McCarthy in Milwaukee, Wisconsin. However, the two separated under less than amicable circumstances. As Fitzsimmons told it,

> You see, this fellow McCarthy had been idle for two weeks in Chicago, where they would not let us box, and had taken on about fifteen pounds through his laziness. The first night we came together here he was as frisky as a kitten.... I was...surprised...to get a swat on the side of the head that made my teeth rattle, for he is as powerful as a young bull. I asked him what he was trying to do, in a sort of stage whisper, and a moment later got another hot one. I had not tried to hit him up to that time, but his evident intention of making a sucker of me drove me mad. He kept rushing me into the

---

456 *Chicago Herald*, December 25, 1894.
457 *Chicago Times*, December 26, 1894.
458 *Chicago Herald*, December 26, 1894.

scenery, and by way of reproval I clipped him a hook in the back and then touched him hard on the nose. He seemed surprised, but did not let up with his rough work until, in self-protection, I was obliged to daze him. Then he quit and refused to finish out his engagement. I suppose he will give it out that I tried to punch him out, but I am giving you the truth of it.[459]

Bob next arrived in St. Louis, Missouri on January 19 to exhibit there for a week. On that same date, a New York grand jury indicted Fitzsimmons with a charge of manslaughter in the first degree in relation to the death of Con Riordan. Fitz was telegraphed to come to New York to post a $10,000 bond, which he did a week later, being arraigned there on January 28.[460]

In the meantime, during that week in St. Louis, the local folks had an opportunity to size Bob up. "Fitzsimmons may be a middle-weight, but to judge the two men in their street clothes the Australian is a larger man than Corbett." Bob said,

I do not admit that Corbett is more scientific than I am, or that he knows any more about the game. He has a more graceful and taking style of boxing, it is true, and his foot-work is the acme of elegance and swift precision. All this may be pleasing to spectators at the theater, but it is not fighting. I know I am not a gazelle. ... Nevertheless, I generally manage to get there.[461]

Later that week, in assessing Fitzsimmons, the local paper said,

The consensus of opinion among local experts who have seen the lanky Antipodean in action, is that, judging from appearances and record, he has not got one chance in ten to defeat Corbett.... Close students, and they are many, of the men will admit that a strong contrast is apparent between them, both on the street and in fighting costume. Fitz's worst enemies must acknowledge that he is a jovial, talkative, agreeable sort of fellow. ... In ring costume he fails to come up to the Corbett standard of physical excellence, and lacks the symmetrical grace that distinguishes the champion - ...

---

[459] *St. Louis Post-Dispatch,* January 22, 1895 (speaking of their engagement in Milwaukee, Wisconsin).
[460] *New York Clipper,* January 26, 1895, February 2, 1895.
[461] *St. Louis Daily Globe-Democrat,* January 20, 1895.

Fitzsimmons does some pretty bag punching, but he is a mere tyro in the art at which his prospective opponent excels. ... Fitz lacks the swift double-handed precision displayed by Corbett in his exhibitions. He ducks more than the champion, and does not care to imitate Corbett's trait of incessant feinting. But it is in footwork that the tremendous difference between the two men becomes really apparent. All Fitz's foot movements are executed in a flat-footed style, and his motions bear about the same resemblance to Corbett's as the playful antics of a cow to the finished pas seul of a French ballet dancer.

Corbett is certainly a prettier and more taking exhibition boxer than his Australian rival, but the latter has proved himself to be what he claims he is, a fighter, pure and simple. ... He has the arms and shoulders of a heavy-weight, but in all other particulars he is a middle-weight, and weighed 156 pounds in sparring costume yesterday.[462]

At that time, Fitz was engaged in a contract dispute with theatrical manager Captain Charles Giori. Their agreement called for a 50/50 split after expenses had been paid. "Fitzsimmons' work consists of punching the bag and a short three-round sparring bout. Giori looks handsome at the front door and counts the tickets sold. This, Fitz thinks, is not earning his half of the money." Giori said that he had a contract that did not expire until mid-August 1895 and would hold Bob to it. He further said,

When he came to me last winter in Newark he had not money enough to buy a meal. I was Captain of the police at the time. I fed him at my house and allowed him to sleep at the police station. ... I also drew up the articles of agreement for the Corbett fight, which put Fitzsimmons in a position to do what he never did before – draw crowds to see his show. On former sparring tours he could not draw flies. Why, his last appearance in Milwaukee brought him $2,000 more than the preceding one made last year. He has got the big head. He thinks that it is Fitzsimmons that brings the crowds, and hasn't sense enough to know that he owes his present prominence solely to the fact that he is matched with Corbett.[463]

[462] St. Louis Daily Globe-Democrat, January 26, 1895.
[463] St. Louis Daily Globe-Democrat, January 26, 1895.

In late February 1895, Fitz exhibited for a week in Cleveland, Ohio. Although the locals felt that Bob looked too light to whip Corbett, he had looked too light to whip other men that he had defeated. "His power is in his extraordinary ability to land a heavy blow with a pair of arms that have the foundation of a pile driver in a mass of muscle and sinew that constitutes this boxer's torso. His legs never would win him a prize as a fighter."[464]

On February 22, 1895 in Cleveland, Fitzsimmons gave a sparring exhibition with Pat Murphy, a local heavyweight. "Although he refrained from doing more than tapping his gloves against the local man the boxing was clever and Murphy was glad it was only a friendly exhibition." The locals were impressed. "Fitzsimmons' bag punching act far excels anything in that line ever before witnessed in this city." His company was drawing full houses at every performance. Bob told the local press, "I want to meet Corbett because I can beat him. I am quicker, have as good a reach and will guarantee to stand more thumping than he can."[465]

Bob was set to meet "Doc" J.E. Paine of the Cleveland Athletic Club on the 23rd, but there was no follow up report.[466] He was there at least until the 26th.[467]

When asked whether Fitzsimmons was a very scientific fighter, Jim Corbett responded,

Where has he demonstrated that? Surely not in the battles he has fought. In a recent glove contest Choyinski nearly had him out, Fitzsimmons was groggy and I have defeated Choyinski several times. I do not say that I can defeat him in three rounds, but I am confident that the fight will not last twenty.[468]

On the afternoon of March 2, 1895 in Buffalo, New York, Fitz put in an hour or more at his old blacksmith trade, making horseshoes. In the evening, "John Donnelly, the iron worker, who was such an easy victim for Jim Daly at the Bowen benefit thought he could stay at least three rounds and earn $50." Fitz carried him for the first two rounds, but at the start of the 3rd round,

---

[464] *Cleveland Leader,* February 22, 1895.
[465] *Cleveland Plain Dealer,* February 23, 1895.
[466] *Cleveland Plain Dealer,* February 23, 1895. Paine is sometimes called James Payne.
[467] *Cleveland Leader,* February 27, 1895.
[468] *Scranton Times,* February 28, 1895.

Donnelly got one of those right hand jolts on the jaw for which the champion is so noted. The presumptuous one dropped in a jiffy, and after he had lain on the floor for several seconds, 'Fitz' walked over and helped pick him up, when the curtain was rung down. Afterwards in his dressing-room Donnelly mournfully said: "Well, he got a good one in on me, didn't he?" Indeed, he did, Mr. Donnelly, and you had better retire from the game unless you are looking for an easy way in which to quit the world.[469]

On March 4, Fitz was in Baltimore. He said that he would disband his company, get rid of Captain Giori, and thereafter appear with the Julian Specialty Company. Fitz owed a deposit towards the $10,000 stake money for the Corbett fight. On account of his financial troubles and difficulties with Giori, Bob asked Corbett to give him more time, which Jim granted, until May 1. Corbett said that he did not want to obtain Bob's stake money through default, but scored Fitz for not having the same stance.

In forcing me into this match you used every contemptible method available, even going so far as trying to take my title from me by default and it was to prevent a foreigner like yourself from having the faintest claim to the championship that I consented to meet you. You represented that you had unlimited backing; I glean from Capt. Giori's interviews that the match was made with me simply to try and boom your theatrical engagements.[470]

Fitzsimmons was less than appreciative, saying that Jim had done no more than what was justified by the circumstances. *The National Police Gazette* disagreed, saying, "Corbett's action in declining to pull down Fitzsimmons' forfeit money is unprecedented in the annals of the prize ring."[471] Typically, if a fighter was unable to make deposits or fight on the date set, he would lose his forfeit money.

Giori said that instead of saving his money to make his $2,500 deposit which was due, "as any man would do who was anxious for the fight of his life," Fitz threw away money in a reckless fashion. Giori had told Bob that if he failed to make his deposit, people would say that his Corbett challenge was really just a bluff to improve his theatrical attendance. "Then it was that he turned on me and used epithets that I could not afford to notice. He wanted me to break the agreement with him." After that, Bob made an

[469] *Buffalo Courier*, March 3, 1895.
[470] *Washington Post*, March 5, 1895.
[471] *National Police Gazette*, March 23, 1895.

arrangement with his brother-in-law, Martin Julian, to manage the company, and Julian engaged a new specialty team. Giori called Fitz an ingrate.[472]

Fitzsimmons settled matters with Giori by returning the $750 that he had put up as part of the stake money. Bob said, "The $5,000 now up is all my own money, and I will be prepared to put up the third deposit of $2,500 at the time agreed on between Corbett and myself."[473]

Speaking of the upcoming fight, Fitz said that it would not matter that Corbett was bigger, because no man could ever put him out. He had proven it against men like Maher, Hall, Choynski, and Creedon, all of whom were hard hitters and clever. He had even intentionally allowed Hall to hit him, because it gave him an opening to land. He never yet went into the ring with a man whom he could not hit, and hit hard. Bob also noted that Corbett's height advantage was not much, for Jim stood 6'1½" to Bob's 5'11¾", and that would not matter because Corbett's reach was 72 inches to Bob's 72 ½ inches.[474]

Regarding his fighting methods, Fitzsimmons said,

> I have no idea of the style of fighting which I shall adopt. ... I never fight two battles alike. I never go into the ring with any fixed purpose, except that I am going to whip the other man just as quick as I can without becoming reckless enough to give him too much of an opening. When I see Corbett before me with his hands up I will know what to do.[475]

The Julian Specialty Company got its start at Washington, D.C.'s Kernan's Lyceum Theater on March 11, 1895. During that week, Bob would hit the punching bag, "at which art he has no superior in the world," and spar anyone who took up the offer to stay 3 rounds to win $100.

On that night, after punching the bag, when Fitz "gave an imitation of a sparring match with Dan Dwyer, Sullivan's old sparring partner, the audience hissed him, and many left before the turn was finished." Dwyer simply was not up to giving a spirited effort, so Bob handled him lightly. No one took up the $100-for-lasting-3-rounds offer.[476]

---

[472] *Washington Post*, March 10, 1895. Reporting a March 9 Baltimore dispatch.
[473] *Washington Post*, March 5, 1895.
[474] *Washington Post*, March 11, 1895.
[475] *Washington Post*, March 11, 1895.
[476] *Washington Post*, March 10, 12, 13, 1895. The entertainment also included a song and dance team, descriptive vocalists, a singer and monologuist, and comedians, including a comical horizontal bar act.

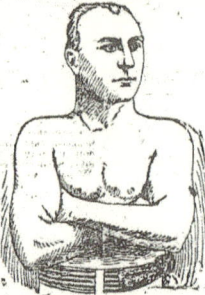

On the 12th, Fitz showed his wife Rose how to hit a bag, and "she was an apt pupil." With a look of pride on his face, Bob said that "she can handle her right in a way that would make a fellow see stars if she ever landed it." Rose said that she was going to start hitting the bag every afternoon. "I don't feel right unless I have a good deal of exercise. Every woman ought to do something of this kind."[477]

Fitzsimmons was concerned that the Florida Athletic Club would not be able to host the fight, in part because there was talk that the Florida state legislature would convene and pass a new law preventing gloved boxing in the state, which indeed eventually happened.

> I have often said that New Orleans is the only place in this country in which to pull off these big fights, though I will gladly fight Corbett anywhere. Now that the Louisiana courts have again decided that glove contests are allowed in chartered clubs in that State, I believe that it should take place there.[478]

However, that decision would eventually be overturned and boxing was once again banned in Louisiana.

On March 14, 1895 at Kernan's, Fitz sparred 3 fancy rounds with Billy McMillan, who "all things considered, made a creditable showing."[479]

One report said that Fitz's company gave exhibitions in April 1895 in Hoboken, New Jersey.[480] Another paper said that Fitz would be giving exhibitions at a New York theater for one week beginning April 15.[481]

---

[477] *Washington Post*, March 13, 1895.

[478] *Washington Post*, March 13, 1895.

[479] *Washington Post*, March 15-17, 1895. McMillan likely weighed 150-160 pounds, because earlier in the week, there was discussion of him engaging in a fight with another boxer if he could get down to 147 pounds. The previous fall, McMillan had defeated Baltimore's Charley Campbell. Campbell said that he would attempt to win the $100 against Fitz on the 16th, but at the last minute decided not to do it.

[480] *New York Herald*, April 15, 1895.

On April 16, 1895 at New York's Third Avenue Theatre, where Bob's company was showing, Fitzsimmons took on San Francisco's Alfred Allich. Although it was supposed to be a friendly 3-round bout, in the 2nd round Allich adopted foul tactics, and therefore Bob knocked him down. In the 3rd round, Allich hit Bob with a savage low blow, which dazed Fitz for a moment. When Bob recovered, he knocked Allich out.[482]

On April 19, a well built young fellow named Mike Connors accepted Bob's offer of $100 to any man in the audience who could last 3 rounds.

> Connors shaped pretty well for a little while, and when he escaped some well-directed swings the crowd applauded vociferously. However, before a minute of the first round had elapsed, "Bob" brought his left flush upon Connor's mouth and he fell to the floor, completely knocked out. He had to be carried off the stage, and it took the united efforts of several of the attendants of the theatre to bring him to.[483]

During April, Jim Corbett said that if Fitz did not soon come up with his end of the guarantee money, he would go to England to fight Peter Jackson. Some accused Corbett of being afraid of Bob, feeling that Jim wanted an easier time of it with Jackson, who was then said to be completely out of shape and working on a drinking habit. Fitz noted, "Well, I guess he will have a hard job to get away from me. ... The fact is, Corbett has got to fight or quit. No skin game will go with me. What's the matter with the man? Is he afraid, or what else ails him?"[484]

As of May, Corbett did not think that there was anywhere for the Fitz fight to take place in America anyway, owing to the recent legislation and court decisions banning boxing in Florida and Louisiana.

> I don't see one chance in a thousand of the Fitzsimmons fight coming off, now that the only two places that have allowed a fight to come off in the last three years have been knocked out. ... I don't propose to be chased over the country without a show of meeting him.[485]

---

481 *Buffalo Courier*, April 16, 1895.
482 *New York Sun, New York Evening Telegram*, April 17, 1895.
483 *New York Sun, New York Evening Telegram*, April 20, 1895.
484 *National Police Gazette*, April 27, 1895, May 25, 1895.
485 *Daily Picayune*, May 10, 1895.

Corbett's words were prophetic.

However, hope springs eternal. A May 9 dispatch said, "Since the outlawing by legislation and court decision two days ago of prize fighting in Florida and Louisiana, William A. Brady and Joe Vendig have been in wire communication with Dan A. Stuart, the wealthiest sporting man in Texas, to arrange to have the fight take place in Dallas."[486]

In late May, Corbett said that if Fitzsimmons did not put up his $5,000 guarantee money and the fight had to be called off, he would pull Fitz's nose. Bob said that if Jim did so, he would "endeavor to make it interesting for him."[487]

Fitzsimmons, his attorney, Corbett, Brady, and Joe Vendig met in New York on May 27 to iron out contract items. After verbal jousting about the details, Jim and Bob engaged in a more personal discussion.

> "You said I was afraid of you," sneered Corbett, turning to Fitzsimmons. "I did," was the pleasant rejoinder.... "Will you tell me that I am afraid of you to my face," asked Corbett, livid with rage. "I say I am not afraid of you," continued Fitz, doggedly. "Shall I prove to you right here that I am not afraid of you," asked Corbett. "As you like," retorted Fitz, who did not appear to be at all rattled by Corbett's manner.
>
> Vendig said that he had given his word that there should be no trouble in the room, and he meant to keep his word. It was then agreed that the men should settle their differences in the ring. ... Corbett will begin training at Asbury Park at once. Fitzsimmons says that he will not begin work until his Syracuse trouble is over.[488]

On June 8, 1895, both Fitzsimmons and Corbett each posted $5,000 to guarantee their appearance in the ring at the then scheduled location of Dallas, Texas, for a bout to be held on October 31. The Florida Athletic Club was still sponsoring the match.

That evening at New York's Madison Square Garden, Fitzsimmons and Corbett were both part of a grand benefit held for Jack Dempsey. Fitzsimmons sparred with Frank Bosworth, who had been his sparring partner in late 1892 and early 1893. Champion Corbett sparred with John McVey. John L. Sullivan sparred with Dempsey in the wind up.[489]

[486] *Daily Picayune*, May 10, 1895.
[487] *Daily Picayune*, May 25, 1895.
[488] *Daily Picayune*, May 28, 1895.
[489] *New York Clipper*, June 15, 1895. Other sparring sessions included Joe Choynski and Bob

In assessing their relative merits, one paper said that Corbett was graceful, active and cat-like, and merely slapped his lumbering and fat opponent. Fitzsimmons' showing was not as pretty. Bosworth "is a pretty lively sort of fellow, and he got in a few punches." As a result, many "superficial observers jumped to the conclusion that Corbett would have a walkover." However, Fitz showed his effectiveness against a better opponent than Corbett had faced. Also, unlike Corbett, "Fitz did not slap; he hit straight and he showed how easily he could have settled his man had it been necessary."[490]

Bob's next opponent was so dangerous that he could have been knocked out of the game for years had he lost. Fitzsimmons' criminal manslaughter trial began on June 24, 1895 in Syracuse, New York. They began with jury selection. "A question upon which the defence seemed to lay great stress in examining talesmen was as to whether or not the witness was prejudiced against prize fighting or prize fighters." Apparently, this was a very difficult and complicated process, for jury selection was not completed until June 28, four days later.

The first witness was a local newspaper editor who saw the blow delivered upon Riordan. He said that after they had chased each other around the stage, Fitz forced Riordan into the wings and delivered a heavy blow on the jaw and neck, knocking Riordan unconscious. On cross examination, he said that after being struck, Riordan made an effort to raise his hands to strike back, but fell from weakness. Another witness said that Riordan was the aggressor and that the blow was a light one. It was revealed that Fitzsimmons had paid all of the funeral and burial expenses. When court adjourned, "the opinion was prevalent that so far the prosecution have put up a weak case."[491]

The trial was nearing its conclusion with defense testimony on July 2 and 3. "Unprejudiced spectators who have listened to the testimony believe that the defence has far the best of the trial.... [T]here are men sitting in the box who believe in all kinds of sports." Fitz's lawyer said that a doctor would testify "that Riordan, while in the East, was affected with a stroke of apoplexy, and was advised if he did not desist from drinking and violent exercise he would die in a short time. In spite of this warning Riordan engaged with Fitzsimmons, the latter not knowing of his ailment."

The police captain, who was the first defense witness, said that he had observed the contest and did not see any hard blows struck. The police

Armstrong, a black fighter, Peter Maher and Pete Burns, as well as George Dixon and Jack Lynch and Kid McCoy and Harry Pidgeon.
[490] New York Evening Telegram, June 10, 1895.
[491] New York Herald, June 25, 29, 1895.

commissioner corroborated him. A doctor said that he heard Riordan's head strike the floor, but saw that the blows were light.

Another doctor testified that with Riordan's arteries in the poor condition that they were, a blow could cause a rupture. He felt that the part of the brain found to be ruptured was apt to be torn in the course of the autopsy. Another witness said that such a brain laceration as alleged by the prosecution would have caused immediate paralysis and death, but that Riordan had put up his hands, and had even sat in a chair afterwards, before passing out. Still another said that the head falling on the floor in a certain way might have caused the blood clot in the brain.[492]

At the conclusion of the ten-day trial, on July 3, 1895, after deliberating for three and a half hours, at 8:11 p.m., the jury found Fitzsimmons not guilty. Fitz shook hands with the jurors and the judge.[493]

That same night in Syracuse, Bob boxed with Frank Sullivan, and "Fitzsimmons was knocked down by the Syracuse man."[494] That was twice in Syracuse that Fitzsimmons had suffered a knockdown.

In June and July, Corbett had his own problems to deal with. He was in the middle of a divorce trial in which his extramarital affairs were revealed.[495]

[492] *New York Herald,* July 3, 1895; *New York Daily Tribune,* July 4, 1895; *New York Clipper,* July 6, 1895.
[493] *New York Herald,* July 4, 1895; *National Police Gazette,* July 20, 1895.
[494] *New York Herald,* July 4, 1895.
[495] *Fistic Carnival* at 22.

CHAPTER 13

Boxing Versus the Law

As of July 1895, it appeared that the scheduled October 31 Corbett-Fitzsimmons championship match was on in Texas. Lawyers submitted opinions agreeing that there was no law on the statute books to prevent the contest.[496]

However, on July 29, Texas Governor Charles Culberson announced that he would not allow the Corbett-Fitzsimmons fight to take place in his state.[497] The combatants were still hopeful that the fight could be held in Texas.

On August 3, 1895 in Philadelphia, Bob won a horseshoe-making match, forging 30 horseshoes in 27 minutes. That evening, he sparred 4 lively rounds with Tom Forrest.[498] Bob continued exhibiting in Philly that week with Forrest.

Still in Philadelphia on August 10, 1895, Fitz gave an exhibition of bag punching, "which brought down the house, and then sparred four very spirited rounds with P.J. Griffin. The wind-up was between Fitzsimmons and his boxing partner, Tom Forrest, of New York, and they gave a very clever exhibition." James J. Corbett was also in Philly, and earlier that day made money playing baseball.[499]

Late in the evening on the 10th at Philadelphia's Green Hotel, Fitzsimmons, Corbett, and Jim's crew got into a scuffle at the registration desk and in the barroom and café. Each man gave his own version.

Fitzsimmons was in the act of registering when Corbett came up to him, and remarked, "I see you have been at your old tricks again, talking about me; why don't you say such things to my face?"

Fitzsimmons looked up and said, "Hello, Jim, how are you," without answering Corbett's question.

---

[496] *New York Herald,* July 4, 1895.
[497] *Buffalo Courier,* July 30, 1895.
[498] *Philadelphia Inquirer,* August 3, 4, 1895. During that week, as part of the card, Ernest Roeber was engaging in separate wrestling bouts with various challengers.
[499] *Philadelphia Inquirer,* August 11, 1895.

"Oh, I'm all right," replied Corbett, and then he repeated his original question. "No, I have not been talking about you," replied Fitzsimmons, "but what of it if I had."

"Why then I'd pull your nose," and suiting the action of the word, the champion attempted to pull Fitz's nasal organ. Corbett says he pulled Fitz's nose, but the latter says he didn't. "I pushed his hand aside," said Fitzsimmons, "when Joe Corbett [Jim's brother] came up behind me and gave me the 'strong arm', and Brady and McVey rushed at me and held my arms, Jim Corbett was just coming at me when Proprietor John McDevitt rushed in and caught him. I turned quickly, and, being unable to free my hands, I butted Joe Corbett twice in the face, and flattened his nose. I struggled away from them and Corbett made a rush for me. The special officer of the hotel and two big reserves caught and held me and Mr. McDevitt held Corbett.

"Things got quieted down a bit," continued Fitzsimmons, "and I went to a table to sit down to eat some chops Tom Forrest had ordered for me. Joe Corbett came around to near where I was and called me a vile name and said: 'You big red-headed stiff. I can whip you myself.' 'Give me fair play,' I replied, 'and I can whip your whole gang.' Then Joe Corbett came at me and McVey came rushing towards me with an uplifted chair. I picked up a water bottle and threw it at them. Joe ducked and the bottle struck a colored waiter on the arm, and glancing off it hit Brady in the chest. Then everybody rushed and held me again, and after a great deal of loud talk Corbett and his party walked down to the desk.

"I returned to my meal, but [Jim] Corbett was determined to continue the quarrel, and he called to me; 'You big stiff, you're afraid of me.' 'Am I,' I replied, and I got up and walked towards him, when he called out: 'Look at him trying to cop a sneak on me.' 'No,' I said, 'I am not trying to cop any sneak on you, but when I get you in the ring at Dallas I'll knock your big pompadour head off.' 'You will, will you,' said Corbett, and he made another rush at me. There was another mix-up and I could not get at him. Then Corbett went into the ladies' restaurant and a friend took me outside. I returned and went to my room and here I am, all safe and sound, except a slight bruise on the lip."

Corbett gave his version of matters:

"During the day out at the ball field I had heard that he had been making a number of disparaging remarks about me, and when I saw him I said, just in a stringing way, you know:

"Well, I see you've been talking again since you got in town."

"'Oh, I don't know that I have,' says he, 'but if I have, what of it?'"

"Then I took hold of his nose and pulled it. I just wanted to pull his nose – and I did it. Then about fifteen people grabbed hold of me. My brother got hold of Fitz while Brady held me. Fitz couldn't get away from my brother and it made him mad. Joe told him, 'I don't believe you could even whip me.' This made Fitz hot and he threw a glass at my brother Joe, but never touched him. McVey got in the game and picked up a chair to hit the fellow that had hold of Brady. We all seemed to get mixed up pretty lively. But Fitz fought everybody but me. I told him 'you're a nice big cur, ain't you?'

"There wasn't any fight – no trouble between Fitz and I - but you'd have thought somebody was getting killed."

"What did he throw at your brother, Jim?" the champion was asked.

"It was a castor off the table, I think. You see he was paying attention to everybody in the room but me. Why, he butted Joe in the mouth with his head. The whole thing was just this," said Corbett, as a clincher, "I wanted to pull Fitz's nose, and I did it."[500]

On August 17, 1895 before a crowd in Buffalo, New York which paid 50 cents each, Fitzsimmons hit the bag and then sparred 4 rounds with Tom Forrest. Fitz held back and only slapped his man in the face with the open glove. This provoked Forrest, who then started attacking more. However, Tom's punches "only met the empty air, for Robert cleverly ducked out of the way. Fitzsimmons gained many admirers through his showing, and many were the remarks that 'he'll give Jim the fight of his life.'"[501]

Things were heating up in Texas. Dallas Sheriff Cabell asked Governor Culberson whether he would be justified in using deadly force to prevent the fight. The governor referred the matter to Attorney General Crane, who answered that those involved would constitute an unlawful assemblage, that those who refused to disperse would constitute a riot, and that homicide was justifiable when necessary to suppress riot and there was

[500] *Philadelphia Inquirer*, August 12, 1895.
[501] *Buffalo Courier*, August 18, 1895; *Buffalo Evening News*, August 17, 1895.

no other way to do so except by taking life. It was the sheriff's duty to suppress the riot "and let the consequences take care of themselves."[502]

In order to test the Texas law, on September 1, Jess Clark fought Tom Cavanaugh. They were arrested, but at Clark's habeas corpus hearing on September 17, Chief Justice James M. Hurt of the Court of Criminal Appeals held that although he was personally against prizefighting,

> I am not responsible for the condition of the laws of the State; am not responsible for the fact that it requires the highest intellect and most searching examination…to determine whether we have a law against prize fighting or not. I do not believe that under the provisions of our statutes…that this man has violated a law…and I shall discharge him.[503]

Dan Stuart, who was now reportedly president of the Florida Athletic Club, said that his position from the start was that the club would not violate any law, and that he had acted on the advice of his attorneys who informed him that there was no law against boxing in Texas. For the time being, they were correct.[504]

On September 22, Fitz left New York heading for his training quarters in Corpus Christi, Texas, traveling with Martin Julian, trainer Charley White (who had worked with Bob for the Choynski fight), wrestler Ernst Roeber, Jack Stelzner, and Nero, Bob's pet lion.[505] Corbett would eventually train in San Antonio, sparring with Steve O'Donnell and John Donaldson.

On September 29, 1895, a crowd of 500 met the Fitz crew at a train stop in San Antonio, Texas. Bob said that he was weighing 162 pounds, and planned to weigh between 160 and 168 when the fight came off.

Regarding his training, Bob said that he began the day with a little walk and then a swim. After breakfast, he varied his routine, either by walking five or six miles and then running home, or running out and then walking home, or sometimes running in spurts – walking a half-mile and then spurting a mile, or walking the distance between two telegraph poles and then spurting the same distance. After bathing and eating, in the afternoon he would punch the bag, spar, wrestle, throw the medicine ball, and go through other gymnastic exercises.

[502] *Austin Daily Statesman*, August 28, 1895.
[503] *Austin Daily Statesman*, September 18, 1895.
[504] *Austin Daily Statesman*, September 28, 1895.
[505] *Austin Daily Statesman*, September 23, 1895.

At that time, there was some hot discussion regarding when the referee should be selected. Bob insisted that he did not want a referee appointed any sooner than the day before the fight. He was concerned about the referee being fixed. He noted that Jack Dempsey had insisted that the referee be selected on the day of the fight, and had two men watch him to make sure that no one could try to bribe him. Bob preferred that the referee be picked at ringside right before the fight, feeling that such a method was the best way to ensure honesty. He was having difficulties negotiating with Corbett manager Brady and the Florida Athletic Club on this and other points. Fitzsimmons suspected some sort of conspiracy.

> Brady says if I don't select a referee soon he will substitute Peter Maher to fight Corbett in my place. … Vendig told me that Brady and Corbett had no more to do with the Florida Athletic Club than myself or Julian. If that is so, what right has he got to say that he will substitute Maher for me? I will bet $500 that Brady has an interest in the club. He has a 10 per cent interest in it. I know all about the bloody thing. I don't believe Stuart would do me a wrong, but the others would.

Fitz said that he liked Dan Stuart, and felt that he was an honest man, but did not feel the same about Joe Vendig. "I don't like Joe Vendig, and you can put that down, too. … Vendig has lied about me all along." Regarding the referee situation, Bob said, "They have some object in picking the referee a long time ahead of the fight. I know if the referee is picked now he'll be fixed before the fight comes off." Martin Julian echoed, "Peter Maher is matched to fight Steve O'Donnell; if Brady can substitute him to fight, doesn't it show that Brady owns an interest in the club? They are very wary about this referee business. They are afraid they won't have him fixed." [506]

That evening in San Antonio (the 29th), Fitz and his specialty company performed before the "largest audience ever in the Grand Opera House." "His exhibition of bag punching was something marvelous. The quickness and precision of his blows astonished all. He strikes a powerful blow." Fitz then sparred 2 rounds with Ernst Roeber and then 2 more with the listed 180-pound Jack Stelzner (with whom Bob had sparred back in March 1894). Fitz was impressive against both Roeber and Stelzner, who were described as "very clever." "He is agile with his legs and quick with those long arms, and inspired fresh confidence in the hearts of his backers."[507]

---

[506] *San Antonio Daily Express,* September 30, 1895.
[507] *San Antonio Daily Express,* September 30, 1895.

Unfortunately, at the request of Texas Governor Charles Culberson, the state legislature specially convened on October 2, 1895 and enacted a law making boxing a felony punishable by imprisonment from two to five years. It was obviously done to put an end to the Corbett-Fitzsimmons fight. "Thus, within three hours did the Legislature put an end to prize fighting in Texas." Even the President of Mexico said that he was opposed to allowing boxing in his country.[508]

The town of Hot Springs, Arkansas was anxious to host the event, particularly because of the financial benefits to be derived from hosting a big fight. Although prize fighting was a misdemeanor under state law, it only carried a fine. Hot Springs itself had no ordinance against boxing, and the local mayor, W.W. Waters, was in favor of hosting the fight. The Hot Springs Railroad Company said that it would provide transportation to the fight grounds.[509]

Unfortunately, Arkansas Governor James Clarke said that he would do everything in his power to prevent the fight. Joe Corbett said, "We are not confederating together for the purpose of fighting anywhere where there is a law on the statute books against prize fighting. It has never been our intention to break any laws." They were going to seek legal means to bring off the fight in Hot Springs by arguing that the anti-prize fighting statute did not cover the type of bout that they intended.[510]

On October 9 in Corpus Christi, Texas, Fitz boxed Walter Tymon, an amateur who was complimented for his bravery, but "of course Tymon was not in it."[511]

The previous day, Bob's pet lion Nero had escaped, so naturally the local folks were freaking out, hiding their children in their homes. Nero would eventually wander back to his master some days later.

Making matters worse, on October 10, Hot Springs Judge Duffie summoned local Sheriff Houpt to inform him that a fight there would be in violation of the law and would outrage the dignity of the state. Arkansas Governor Clarke agreed (Duffie was an old classmate of his), and the next day, he wrote a threatening letter to the pugilists and promoter Dan Stuart warning them not to have a fight there. Clarke told them that it would be impossible, and that "any attempt on your part to do so will subject you to penalties and to treatment that I am sure will be highly distasteful to you."

[508] *Austin Daily Statesman*, October 4, 1895; *New York Clipper*, October 12, 1895.
[509] *Daily Arkansas Gazette* (Little Rock), October 10, 1895; *Austin Daily Statesman*, October 8, 1895.
[510] *Austin Daily Statesman*, October 9, 1895.
[511] *Austin Daily Statesman*, October 10, 1895.

A concerned Martin Julian said that before taking Bob to Arkansas, he wanted a guarantee that the officers there would not molest them.[512]

Governor Clarke was even considering calling upon the state militia to prevent the fight. He estimated that he could obtain the service of 10,000 men. Clarke's "vigorous determination" was "plainly visible," and he even went so far as to say that if the fight occurred in his state, he would resign. Clarke also said that although he did not want to see blood shed, he would do everything in his power to prevent the fight.

Joe Vendig said that they had not come to Arkansas with the purpose of violating its laws, and would not do so. He said that they would make an appeal to determine whether the law would be violated under the circumstances of a soft glove contest with a limited number of rounds and officials being authorized to stop the contest if it became brutal. "The best authority at our service says this will be no violation of the State laws."[513]

Corbett did not believe that the fight would be pulled off. "I am disgusted with the business. I am losing valuable time and I don't believe we will fight in Hot Springs." Jim said that he wanted the matter settled so that he could get back to his theatrical engagements. He was not all that interested in the fight anyway. "If we fight he has everything to gain and nothing to lose, while I have everything to lose and scarcely anything to gain." Jim expected to be placed under arrest and to have the issue settled in the courts.[514]

On October 15, 1895 before a large crowd of ladies and gentlemen in Corpus Christi, Texas, Fitzsimmons sparred with Duncan C. Ross (who was also a Greco-Roman wrestler), and also boxed several rounds with other company members, including Jack Stelzner. "Fitzsimmons was breathing as easy as ever."[515]

The local Hot Springs folks were in favor of the fight and could not understand the furor being raised over it.

> The people contend that there are worse evils and greater infractions of the law going on every day of the year here than a contest with soft gloves, and cannot conceive wherein is the consistency in the authorities raising such a hue and cry about a simple athletic

---

[512] *Daily Arkansas Gazette*, October 11, 12, 1895. Interestingly enough, Governor Clarke had in April gotten into a physical confrontation with a state representative and was arrested. Seems he was not all that opposed to fighting after all. *Fistic Carnival* at 68.

[513] *Austin Daily Statesman*, October 15, 1895.

[514] *Daily Arkansas Gazette*, October 15, 16, 1895.

[515] *Daily Arkansas Gazette*, October 16, 1895.

exhibition while other and more flagrant violations of the law are never noticed.[516]

The articles of agreement were amended to make the fight one of a limited number of rounds (25) rather than to a finish, and to give the referee the power to stop the exhibition if it became too brutal. It was believed that legally, this would make the bout a boxing match rather than a prize fight.[517]

Fitzsimmons initially objected to it being scheduled for 25 rounds instead of to the finish. He did not want the referee to be able to interfere, but wanted a clean and decisive knockout either way, to determine absolutely who the better man was. Corbett accused him of looking for a way out of the fight. Fitz kicked about it for several days, but had to relent because it was believed that the rounds limitation was legally necessary. "Fitz doesn't seem to have much confidence in the Arkansas move."[518]

On the 17th, Corbett was arrested on a warrant charging him with conspiring to commit an unlawful assault on Bob Fitzsimmons. The judge ordered him to pay a $10,000 bond to keep the peace, but Corbett refused and remained in custody. His attorneys sought a writ of habeas corpus to secure his release. "This will bring the question up for judicial hearing, as to whether a glove contest, such as is now proposed, will be a violation of the laws of the state."[519]

The Governor had an 800-man militia ready, and he met with Brigadier-General Taylor to discuss its use to prevent the fight. General Taylor assured him, "The fight will not occur at Hot Springs, nor in Arkansas. There is no doubt on that score." However, Sheriff Houpt said that 95% of the local Hot Springs constituents were in favor of the fight.[520]

Promoter Dan Stuart wanted Fitzsimmons to come to Arkansas, but Bob did not want to do so until all the legal wrangling was settled. Bob wanted a guarantee that he would not be arrested. "Corbett talked very bitterly about the affair. He said that he was going through all the unpleasant features of the affair, while Fitzsimmons was in Texas enjoying life to his heart's content."[521]

---

[516] *Daily Arkansas Gazette*, October 16, 1895.
[517] *Daily Arkansas Gazette*, October 16, 1895; *New York Clipper*, October 19, 1895. They were fighting for a $40,000 purse.
[518] *National Police Gazette*, November 2, 1895; *Daily Arkansas Gazette*, October 17, 1895; *El Paso Daily Herald*, October 18, 1895. Fitz was charging 25 cents to watch him train.
[519] *Austin Daily Statesman, Daily Arkansas Gazette*, October 18, 1895.
[520] *Daily Arkansas Gazette*, October 18, 19, 1895.
[521] *Daily Arkansas Gazette*, October 19, 1895.

On October 19, Chancellor Leatherman ruled that there was no law in effect preventing prize-fights or gloved boxing contests. A proposed 1891 law had not passed. Although prize fighting was an offense at common law, the proposed bout was one with gloves and for a limited number of rounds, and therefore not a brutal prize-fight as contemplated under the common law. Corbett was released.

The state's attorney-general said that he would appeal the decision to the state supreme court. Governor Clarke said that he was "never more determined than at present to prevent the fight and I am sure beyond peradventure that I will do so." Sheriff Houpt wrote Governor Clarke a letter objecting to the governor's proposed use of the militia in his county to prevent the fight.

> As the chief peace officer of this county, I beg to assure you of my ability to cope successfully with any situation that is likely to confront our people. ... I also beg to inform you that the bringing of the militia into this county for such a purpose is entirely unnecessary and will be extremely humiliating to our people.[522]

Because the ultimate decision was undecided as a result of the appeal, Dan Stuart requested a postponement of the fight for eleven days, until November 11. Stuart also reasoned that even if the ultimate decision was resolved in their favor, it would take time to restore confidence and get the crowd to come. "Where a month ago hundreds of excursion parties were being organized for the trip to the fight, there are none today." Corbett was willing to wait, but Fitzsimmons was not. If the fight was not brought off on time, Julian and Bob intended to claim their $2,500 forfeit.

Fitz also refused to come to Arkansas until the day of the fight. He argued that the contract did not require him to train in a given location, but only to be at the designated fight site on the 31st. Fitz said, "This is a bloody bluff of Vendig's, and it won't work. If they declare the fight off because I am not on Arkansas's soil...it is clear proof that Corbett and his party have seized upon that as an excuse to keep from fighting." However, Corbett said that Fitz's refusal to be reasonable was proof that Bob did not want to fight.

At that point, Stuart called the fight off. He said that unless Bob changed his mind and agreed to a postponement, Peter Maher would be substituted as an opponent. Julian said that Bob would go stale waiting, and also felt that Corbett wanted additional time to train. Julian believed that

---

[522] *Daily Arkansas Gazette*, October 20, 24, 1895.

there was collusion between Corbett and the club to postpone the fight because Corbett was not in shape. Also, Julian quite frankly did not think the fight could be brought off in Arkansas, and wanted the forfeit money that the club would owe if the fight did not take place.

Stuart proposed a private meeting for the $10,000 side bets and an additional $10,000. Corbett manager Brady accepted, but Julian objected, wanting the full $41,000. "In all equity, in the face of the entanglements which have beset the path of Stuart and Vendig, this can not be done." Brady said that Fitzsimmons was afraid to lose. Some speculated that Fitzsimmons was in debt and unable to come up with the rest of his stake money, so he was secretly hoping the fight would not be able to happen.[523]

Corbett said that since there was at present no law against fighting, he proposed that they fight immediately, for Julian to bring Bob into the state so that they could fight before the Supreme Court could possibly overturn the lower court decision. Julian insisted on the scheduled date of the 31st. Corbett and Brady called Fitz a cur and said that he was afraid to fight.

> Corbett and Brady then went to dinner, and over the meal the champion declared that he was through with the prize ring and would never fight again. The championship belt which he holds, he said, he would put up for Maher and O'Donnell to fight for. "I am through forever. I have had enough," finished the Californian.

Obviously, Corbett had already strongly contemplated retirement. However, late that evening (the 22nd), Julian gave in somewhat, agreeing to fight on the 31st in private for the side wagers and a $10,000 purse.[524]

Fitz did have some supporters in the media.

> From first to last the Hot Springs affair seems to have been cut and dried for the purpose of preventing a conflict that would in any way jeopardize "Gentleman Jim's" title to the championship. It was Jim's friends that insisted on the fight taking place at Hot Springs. Fitzsimmons has always said the authorities would never allow the fight to occur there – and he seems to have been right. ... The governor of Arkansas announced himself on the subject from the beginning. He said no fight should occur at Hot Springs.[525]

---

[523] *Fistic Carnival* at 75. *Austin Daily Statesman*, October 21, 22, 1895.
[524] *Daily Arkansas Gazette*, October 22, 23, 1895.
[525] *El Paso Daily Herald*, October 22, 1895.

The next day, all of these issues became moot. On October 23, the Arkansas Supreme Court decided that the applicable law in effect was the 1891 law making prize fighting with or without gloves a misdemeanor punishable by a fine from $1,000 to $2,500. As boxing was indeed illegal, the newspapers said that the agony was over, that there was no prospect for the fight to take place. Technically, the governor would be within his rights to use the militia to stop the fight.

The Florida Athletic Club said that it was through with the fight and would temporarily go out of business, having lost thousands to find out "we were on 'a dead one.'" It had been planning a carnival of fights to be held in early November, but that was all over. "Maher and O'Donnell would have fought for the heavy weight title and the championship belt relinquished by Corbett."[526]

On the 24th, Bill Brady said that Corbett would go to New York and announce to the world his retirement from pugilism forever.

> The premature announcement that Corbett will tomorrow retire from the ring bears out this construction that has been slowly dawning upon the mind of the unprejudiced onlooker for three days past that there was more bluff and bluster under the surface on the Corbett side than a desire to bring off a meeting with Fitzsimmons.[527]

However, Corbett did not leave the state, perhaps fearing that he would be made to look bad. A couple days later, it was said that the fight situation was in status quo, that there was a "quiet tip" that the two would meet in private. The Corbett people insisted that Fitz would never come to Arkansas. Julian said that Fitz would be in the state to claim the forfeit money owed if the club failed to bring off the fight, which at that point, looked fairly certain.[528]

The Hot Springs Athletic Club still wanted the match to be held on its scheduled date of October 31, because violating the law would only subject the participants to a fine from $1,000 to $2,500. The Club wired Fitzsimmons in Texas and asked him to come to Hot Springs, guaranteeing him $500 for attorney's fees if he was arrested for entering the state for unlawful purposes. Fitz agreed.

On the 28th, warrants were issued for the arrest of all of the participants. The governor said that Fitz and Julian would be intercepted upon entry

---

[526] *Daily Arkansas Gazette*, October 24, 1895.
[527] *Daily Arkansas Gazette*, October 25, 1895.
[528] *Daily Arkansas Gazette*, October 27, 1895.

into the state, brought before a judge, and required to show good cause why they should not be placed under bond to abstain from violating the laws. He believed that they were going to try to hold the fight in private. "It is hardly probable though that Fitzsimmons can get into the county, inasmuch as the way is blocked by officers with warrants ready to serve on him and his backer, Julian." The governor was quite determined, and things did not look good.[529]

The El Paso Daily Herald said,

> The general opinion of the sports around town is that neither of the pugilists wants to fight and that Corbett has persisted in remaining in Hot Springs, knowing that they could not fight there and that if Fitz went to Arkansas to claim the forfeit he would be arrested and the fight would have to be declared off.[530]

As of the 29th, several sheriffs were on the hunt for the participants. The governor was exhausting every power to prevent the fight. Hot Springs' Sheriff Houpt, who was in favor of the fight, was in Marshall, Texas, where Fitz was supposed to be passing on a train. Houpt had a warrant for his arrest, but it was unclear as to whether he intended to serve it. "This is said to be a ruse of the Hot Springs people to get Fitzsimmons over there to fight." The next day it was reported that a warrant was issued for Houpt's arrest, because it was believed that he was actually helping to transport Fitz to Hot Springs so that the fight could be held.

On the 29th, Fitzsimmons said he was weighing 156 pounds and would leave for Hot Springs in the evening. His wife, Martin Julian, Jack Stelzner, Ernest Roeber, and Duncan Ross would accompany him. A telegram said that Fitz had left San Antonio at 8:00 p.m. Sheriff Dillard boarded a train coming from San Antonio and searched every car. The belief was that Bob would pass into the state either late that night or the next day. "Should he do so his arrest is certain."[531]

It was claimed that Corbett and crew were arrested that day and were either under bond to appear in court or under the charge of deputy sheriffs. However, it was unclear as to whether Corbett was actually in custody or if so, whose custody. It was later claimed that he was actually free, in hiding. Manager Brady said, "We have Corbett planted and will be ready to produce him in twenty minutes' notice prepared to fight." Still, one paper

[529] *New York Clipper*, November 2, 1895; *Daily Arkansas Gazette*, October 29, 1895.
[530] *El Paso Daily Herald*, October 29, 1895.
[531] *Austin Daily Statesman*, October 30, 1895; *New York World*, October 30, 1895.

opined, "There is not one chance in one hundred of the big fight being pulled off."[532]

On the 30th, just outside the Arkansas border, Sheriff Houpt boarded the train that Fitz and Martin Julian were taking and informed them of the warrants for their arrest. Apparently, he told them that they should take another special train that would transport them to the bout's location. Julian did not believe that the fight could be brought off and was on his way to claim the forfeit money. Fitz and his manager declined the offer, feeling that it was some sort of Corbett trick. Julian thought that Houpt was acting on behalf of the club, which did not want to pay the $2,500 forfeit money, and was therefore trying to prevent Fitz from reaching Hot Springs by the 31st so as to make it impossible for him to claim the forfeit. Basically, he did not know whom he could trust.

When the train crossed the Arkansas state line, Sheriff Dillard entered the train and arrested them. Houpt was seated next to the Fitz party, and he protested Dillard's actions, saying that he had already arrested them. Houpt was arrested too.

Brady said that Fitz and crew went joyfully with the Governor's men because that would end the prospect of a fight, which is exactly what he felt Bob and Julian wanted. He said that Fitz was afraid to fight. Everyone was spinning arguments in their favor.

The Hot Springs Railroad confirmed that there was indeed a special engine and car ready for Fitz, which would have brought him to Hot Springs without trouble. Fitz instead took his chances with the other rail, and as a result, he got arrested.[533] However, in Bob's defense, there was still the governor's militia to deal with, so the prospects for the fight to have actually taken place were not good. The Arkansas state line and Hot Springs were swarming with men waiting to prevent the fight and arrest the combatants.

Both Corbett and Fitzsimmons accused the other of not wanting the fight. Fitz got arrested, and Corbett was retiring. Corbett said, "I don't believe that ever Fitzsimmons intended to fight me and used me for his own advertising purposes." Fitz responded, "I am not going to break any laws or break into any jails. I am satisfied that it is all off for the time. But mark my word, I'll get him again and when I do get him I'll lick him."[534]

John L. Sullivan said that neither wanted to fight.

---

[532] *Daily Arkansas Gazette*, October 30, 1895; *Austin Daily Statesman*, October 31, 1895.
[533] *Daily Arkansas Gazette*, October 31, 1895; *Austin Daily Statesman*, November 1, 1895.
[534] *Daily Arkansas Gazette*, November 3, 1895.

I don't see why these fellows can not get together if they are really anxious to fight. In fact I know very well that if they are dead set on fighting they can do it, governor or no governor. It looks to me as though Corbett don't care about fighting and Fitzsimmons don't want to. When I fought Kilrain we had a worse time than this. We were chased into the woods, we had no special trains and Deputy Sheriffs to help us and there was a $1,000 fine over our heads and a prison wall before us. In spite of that Jake and I found the ring and had our little troubles out.

Of course, what Sullivan left out was the fact that he was arrested, tried, found guilty, sentenced to one year in prison, spent all the money he had made on the fight on trial and appellate lawyers, and eventually plead guilty and paid a $500 fine. Also, because Sullivan had eluded law enforcement, the governors were doubly vigilant this time to make sure that it did not happen again.

The reality was that the fight's failure to take place was not the fault of either party. The political and legal impediments were just too great. Given the governor's determination, the fight was simply not destined to occur in Arkansas.

Fitzsimmons said that he was still willing to have the fight.

I am ready and anxious to meet Corbett at whatever place a meeting can be arranged and I can knock him out beyond question. I'm in better condition than he is. In fact Corbett is dead anxious to avoid a fight. He and Brady know I can whip him, no matter how much they pretend to the contrary. Corbett is not in condition to put up a stiff fight and it wouldn't be a hard thing to do to put him out. Nobody knows that better than he does and you can depend on it that he will try to keep out of a fight.[535]

He had a point, because Corbett indeed retired soon thereafter.

On November 1, a judge enjoined the boxers from fighting with or without gloves under penalty of contempt. The judge said,

I warn you that any violation of that order would entail far more serious consequences than any criminal proceeding would cause. While the power of a criminal court is limited, that of a chancellor is

---

[535] *Daily Arkansas Gazette*, November 1, 1895.

practically unlimited in contempt cases, and I assure you that any violation of that injunction will insure your residence in the Pulaski County Jail for two years and probably five.

He was also empowered to fine them up to $10,000. This absolutely destroyed any hope for the fight to take place in Hot Springs. The governor informed the boxers that he would not pursue the conspiracy charges if they left the state.

The local press did not blame the fighters for a situation that was really beyond their control. "The big fight is off and off for good. It is easy to see now that it never was really on as far as the state of Arkansas was concerned."

There is no doubt that Corbett and Fitzsimmons individually have been willing to fight all along, but Fitzsimmons will take no chance of going to jail, and Corbett will not fight without the posting of the side bet on the part of Fitzsimmons which the latter is evidently unable to do.

Dan Stuart will tomorrow make a new proposition for the fight, but it is denied before it comes. He will offer a purse of $20,000 for a fight in Mexico, close to El Paso, Texas.[536]

Brady was fed up. "I will not go to El Paso. ... If I go down there I will have the same trouble with the courts as I have been having here, and I will be bullied in this way no longer.[537]

Some of the national press blamed Fitzsimmons for the bout's failure to take place. If he had avoided the service of the warrant by taking the special train, never gone before the judge, and never become subject to an injunction, the participants would only have had to deal with a misdemeanor fine if they had secretly pulled the fight off. Neither side could fight once they were threatened with serious jail time for contempt. However, successfully holding the fight in secret would have been an almost impossible task under the circumstances.

Corbett called Fitz a coward, saying that he voluntarily submitted to arrest so that the fight would be called off. *The National Police Gazette* backed this theory, saying, "Every step he took seemed to indicate his fear... Fitzsimmons' position is a most humiliating one. He went out of his way to

[536] *New York Clipper*, November 9, 1895; *Daily Arkansas Gazette*, November 2, 3, 1895.
[537] *Austin Daily Statesman,* November 2, 1895.

badger Corbett into making the match…and then at the last moment quit, with all the characteristics of 'yaller dog.'" Like Sullivan, Fitzsimmons had a frosty relationship with that paper.[538]

The Florida Athletic Club said it would pay Corbett the $2,500 forfeit money, but refused the same payment to Fitzsimmons "on the plea that the Australian did everything to avoid a fight."[539]

The reality was that given the governor's liberal use of the militia, Fitzsimmons did not see how the fight could be brought off. He did not want to break the law, did not want to go up against the governor and his men, and feared the repercussions. Fitzsimmons explained, "I am a law abiding citizen…. I will not break the law. I do not want to go to prison if I know myself."[540] He had already stood trial earlier that year and had to pay out massive attorney's fees for a trial that lasted longer than one week. He was well aware of all the legal difficulties that John L. Sullivan had encountered when he fought against the will of politicians.

Fitzsimmons was willing to fight only when it would not violate the law. He had been consistent. He had refrained from sparring in Chicago in late 1894 when he heard that the police were against it, then saying, "I do not intend to make myself amenable to the law."[541] It was said that Fitz "dreads the courts." Still, his reputation took a temporary blow in the national press, some calling him a coward.

Interestingly and prophetically, despite the attacks on Fitzsimmons, there were reports even before the train fiasco and Fitzsimmons' arrest that Jim Corbett no longer wanted the fight. An October 26 report said that Corbett "has no desire to meet Lanky Bob. He is afraid he would be whipped…. The latest dispatches state that Corbett has declared himself through with pugilism."[542] Corbett was in fact saying that he was retiring even before Fitz got arrested. He did not really think the fight would happen. As it turned out, as of November 6, Corbett confirmed his retirement. "I fail to see any money in the fighting business, and that is my sole reason for getting out of it." Jim was frustrated by the anti-boxing legal climate. He would instead focus on his acting career.[543]

Before leaving the state, on November 4, 1895 at the Glenwood Park Theater in Arkansas, Fitz gave an exhibition before a crowd of 200 people. "His bag punching exercises especially evoked enthusiasm and it was generally remarked that Fitz was far superior to Corbett in that respect."

[538] *National Police Gazette*, November 2, 23, 1895; Corbett at 246-247.
[539] *New York Clipper*, November 16, 1895.
[540] *Los Angeles Express, Brooklyn Daily Eagle*, November 1, 1895.
[541] *Chicago Herald*, December 24, 1894.
[542] *Los Angeles Express*, October 26, 1895.
[543] *New York World*, November 7, 1895.

Fitz then sparred 4 rounds with Jack Stelzner. Although Bob was in fine form, there were split opinions of his prowess as a boxer compared to Corbett. "A good many inclined to think that Corbett is more agile and a better ducker, but none of the champion's defenders failed to concede that Fitz controlled a very dangerous assortment of blows." The Fitz party was said to be leaving for a tour through Texas.[544]

---

[544] *Daily Arkansas Gazette*, November 5, 1895.

CHAPTER 14

The New "Champion"

Eleven days after the Corbett-Fitzsimmons fight failed to take place, on November 11, 1895 at Long Island, New York, Peter Maher scored a 1st round knockout victory over Corbett sparring partner Steve O'Donnell, knocking him down three times in 63 seconds. Even before the Fitzsimmons fight was definitively called off, Corbett had said that he would give his championship to the winner of the Maher-O'Donnell bout. True to his word, retired champion James J. Corbett named Peter Maher as his successor.

The 177-180-pound Australian native O'Donnell's bouts included: 1893 W4 Frank Craig and D6 George Godfrey; March 1895 D8 220-pound Jake Kilrain, and May 1895 KO21 Kilrain. Other than that, he was mostly known as Corbett's chief sparring partner.[545]

The 170-pound Maher had been defeated by both Fitzsimmons (March 1892 LKOby12) and Joe Goddard (December 1892 LKOby3). Maher did have an 1894 KO2or3 over Frank Craig and a KO6 win over George Godfrey, both top black fighters, but Craig had a number of losses and Godfrey was way past his prime and had already been stopped in 1892 by Choynski, whom Fitzsimmons and Goddard had bested. Some sources say that just after Peter Courtney fought Corbett, Maher stopped Courtney in 2 or 3 rounds.

Under suspicion that the fight was a fake and neither giving an effort, the referee stopped a March 1895 bout between Maher and Jim Hall in the 6th round and declared it a draw.[546] Fitz had knocked out Hall in 4 rounds. Still, in Maher's fights against lesser-known fighters, he usually scored very quick knockouts, quite often in the 1st round, his punching power impressing most experts.

Clearly though, Peter Maher's resume showed that he was not the most deserving of the title, despite his impressive 1st round knockout over O'Donnell, who himself had not done much to be a top title contender.

Of his selection, Corbett said,

---

[545] *National Police Gazette*, March 30, 1895, May 18, 1895.
[546] *National Police Gazette*, March 9, 1895.

I bestowed the championship upon Maher because he is an Irishman, and because I prefer that he should bear and defend that title, rather than place it in the custody of either an Australian or an Englishman…. I consider Peter Maher the peer of any man in the ring, and have no hesitancy in saying that he can whip Fitzsimmons.[547]

However, Maher said that he wanted to win the title in the ring.[548] He felt that he needed to defeat Fitzsimmons or Corbett to deserve the crown, showing a "disposition to repudiate Corbett's generosity in handing over the championship." Maher "declined to accept a title which Corbett, without authority, presumed to bestow upon him." So, to his credit, Peter Maher did not call himself champion.[549]

Although some newspapers recognized Maher as champion, the *National Police Gazette* said, "He has been hailed as the champion, but conservative, reasonable, thinking people, appreciate the fact that the simple act of handing a title to a man on a gold plate is not the only thing that is requisite to make him a champion."[550] Most agreed that Maher needed to defeat Corbett to be champ, but if Corbett was retired, then he needed to fight Fitz to earn the vacant crown.

The day after Maher beat O'Donnell, on November 12, promoter Dan Stuart offered Corbett and Fitzsimmons a $20,000 purse to fight in Mexico. Fitzsimmons signed the contract. Corbett's manager William Brady telegraphed back saying that Corbett had retired and given the title to Maher. Stuart replied that Corbett had no authority to do so, that the sporting law and usages had no such precedent. *The New York Clipper* opined,

If Jim ever did have a desire to fight Fitz, the way to demonstrate the fact would seem to seize this opportunity. … In case Corbett adheres to his stated determination to permanently retire, then a fight between Fitzsimmons and Maher would appear to be the proper thing, the former certainly having the better claim on the title.[551]

---

[547] *National Police Gazette*, December 14, 1895.

[548] *National Police Gazette*, December 7, 1895.

[549] *New York Clipper*, November 30, 1895; *National Police Gazette*, December 7, 1895, February 29, 1896.

[550] *National Police Gazette*, November 30, 1895.

[551] *New York Clipper*, November 23, 1895.

However, Corbett insisted that he was retired. Given all of the strong legal obstacles, Corbett simply did not believe that the fight would be allowed to take place, and did not want to bother with all the hassle, training, and expenses when he would not be able to fight, particularly when he could be making good money in the theater, his true love.

Making things more confusing was the fact that Fitzsimmons began claiming that he was the heavyweight champion, apparently because he had already defeated Maher. Bob said, "I have already claimed both the middleweight and heavyweight championships of the world, that I now stand ready to defend both titles against the world and all comers, providing they be white men."[552] A champion who had not won the title in the ring was already drawing the color line. Still, Bob was correct in saying that he had a better claim to the vacant title than did Maher.

On December 5, Fitzsimmons agreed to a February 14, 1896 rematch with Peter Maher for a $10,000 purse and the world championship. Apparently, Dan Stuart had secured a location within a couple miles of El Paso, in Mexico. Fitz signed the articles of agreement on the 17th in Houston. "It is thought Corbett intends to make a match with the winner, as he remarked that if Stuart could pull off one fight near El Paso he could engineer another." Jim was taking a wait and see approach.[553]

At that time, Corbett said that he would return to the ring if Fitzsimmons were to beat Maher. Jim would be rooting for Peter. "I hope he'll beat that Australian's brains out." If Maher won, he would leave him alone, unless he "makes cracks at me. ... I don't care to enter the ring again, but I won't allow any one to make any bluffs in my direction." However, he would return to the ring if Fitz won, saying things like "I'll make him fight.... I'll show that fellow up before I get through with him," and "I am not going to allow a flunker like Fitzsimmons to hold the championship. He flunked once with me and I am determined that he won't do it again.... I do not say that I will not fight again." Obviously, even just one month into his so-called retirement, Corbett was not definitively permanently retired.[554]

On December 25, Fitzsimmons arrived in El Paso, Texas with Jack Stelzner and Nero, Bob's pet lion. Ernest Roeber got sick, so Fitz would mostly spar with Jack Stelzner, but also William McCoy. On December 28

[552] *National Police Gazette*, December 14, 1895.
[553] *New York World*, December 5, 1895. Fitz was residing in Texas during December, giving some exhibitions.
[554] *New York World*, December 7, 1895; *Brooklyn Daily Eagle*, December 8, 1895; *New York Clipper*, December 14, 1895; *National Police Gazette*, February 1, 1896. *Fistic Carnival* at 96.

in New York, Maher exhibited with Billy Woods before heading southwest. In training, Maher would primarily spar with Jim Hall.[555]

Regarding the upcoming fight, one paper opined,

> Fitz will be the favorite, if there is a favorite … There is no denying that Maher is a much improved man since he argued with Fitzsimmons in New Orleans … Everyone knows that Maher can hit hard enough to hurt a man with one punch … The same can be said of Fitzsimmons. The latter, however, has proven to be far above Peter as regards science, and this should tell the tale.[556]

In an interview, Fitz said, "Those eastern Irish are boosting Maher up, but it will do them no good." When asked, "Are you not Irish?" Fitz responded, "Yes I'm half Irish, but I don't go on my stock. I'm banking on my own abilities and not on my nationality."[557]

Bob began active training on January 4 in the Ochoa building in Juarez, Mexico, just over the border from El Paso. He would begin the day with a long run, about 10 miles. In the afternoon, he punched the bag, wrestled and boxed with Jack Stelzner, and then rode his bike for an hour or so.[558]

On January 8, 1896, Fitzsimmons put in an intense day of training that showed his wonderful condition. First, he hit the bag for one hour and fifteen minutes without stopping. He then immediately sparred Stelzner 6 rounds. Between all of the rounds, instead of taking the one-minute rest, Fitz would punch the bag, "and did not seem the least bit winded or tired." Bob told Jack to do his best,

Jack Stelzner

---

[555] *Fistic Carnival* at 110-136; *New York World*, December 28, 1895; *El Paso Daily Herald*, December 26, 1895. In early January, Bob played in a football game in El Paso.
[556] *El Paso Daily Herald*, December 27, 1895.
[557] *El Paso Daily Herald*, December 31, 1895.
[558] *El Paso Daily Herald*, January 7, 1896.

because he was "going in for business." Despite Bob's extra work, Stelzner "was pretty well done up at the end of each round."

After their 6 rounds of sparring were completed, Bob engaged Stelzner in three Greco-Roman wrestling matches, each bout lasting until there was a fall. "Stelzner is a good wrestler and very strong." The first fall came after six minutes. "Bob jumped up while Stelzner would lie on his back to catch his breath." Their second bout lasted nine minutes until Fitz won the fall. Their third and final bout lasted fifteen minutes, until Fitz prevailed and put Jack on his back. Later, Bob went on a bike ride.[559]

Fitzsimmons sometimes even trained with his pet lion, "and if any one thinks the lion can't wrestle then all he has got to do is to try it on." Fitz "never quits until the lion is tired out and wants to stop. The lion is as gentle as a house cat, but it is strong. It never sticks out its claws or tries to take hold with its mouth."[560]

By mid-January 1896, it was said that Corbett had lost prestige with the public since he turned over the championship belt, and his show business had not been as prosperous as it had been before. "A majority of the American people believe that Corbett wilted when he had his contest on with Fitzsimmons before." Perhaps this motivated Corbett's return. Still, Jim's ability was respected. "Pugilists do not believe Corbett is a fighter, but they all admit that he is the most scientific boxer that ever entered the squared ring." In late January, Corbett confirmed that he would challenge the winner of the Maher-Fitzsimmons fight.[561]

Since Corbett was only "retired" for two or three months, much of the general public still considered him the champion. Corbett had bestowed the championship as a gift to Maher, which he declined to accept and did not deserve, which unaccepted gift Corbett shortly thereafter repudiated. That said, because Corbett had given up the title and refused to reschedule the Fitz fight, many newspapers said that he could not reclaim the crown at his whim, and that the winner of the Maher-Fitzsimmons fight would be the recognized champion.

Jimmy Carroll, who had no love for Bob Fitzsimmons since they separated, still spoke admiringly of him.

> Fitzsimmons is the greatest fighter the world ever knew. He is a wonder in the ring and no mistake. In one round he can be so badly knocked out that he has to be assisted to his corner, but when time is called for the succeeding round he is on his feet as fresh as when he

[559] *El Paso Daily Herald*, January 9, 1896.
[560] *El Paso Daily Herald*, January 14, 1896.
[561] *El Paso Daily Herald*, January 16, 1896.

entered the ring in the first round, and woe be unto his opponent in that round if he does not keep out of Fitzsimmons' way. The harder the blows he receives the harder he fights, and if he lands with either hand he will knock his opponent's head off. I do not think there is a harder hitter than Fitz in the ring. I believe he can whip Corbett inside of six rounds. Corbett can hit Fitz, but he can't hurt him, while one of Fitz's blows will lay the ex-champion low.[562]

Carroll unsuccessfully tried to convince Maher to let him train him. Upon returning from Maher's training quarters in Las Cruces, New Mexico, Jimmy said that Maher was in better condition than ever before. However, he still was not willing to pick him to win, because Fitz "is a shifty, nervy fighter and a hard hitter, and that the public are mistaken if they think Fitz cannot fight with both hands."[563]

On January 29, in the 7th round of what had been a pretty heavy sparring session, Fitz worked easy for the first minute, but then Stelzner threw a hard punch that missed.

Fitz feinted with his right and swung his left. Instead of Jack throwing up his right guard, as he usually did, he ducked and the full force of Fitz's left hand swing caught him on the nose. Jack grabbed his nose and went over to his corner and sat down. ... Jack's nose had been broken.[564]

Analyzing Fitzsimmons, the *El Paso Daily Herald* said,

Fitz has steadily improved and is now a better ring general than he ever was. .... Fitz is also a very shifty fighter and does not cover much ground while in the ring. His dodges and ducks are all body motions and he does not move his feet except when changing location. He swings his long body backwards, forward and sideways in such a fashion that he is hard to hit and always keeps himself in position to send out a driver when he perceives an opening. As to his blows there is no doubt about them having force enough to lay anybody out, if landed properly. ... Bob's short arm blows are something that are dangerous to fool with. ... It is hard to tell which hand Fitz will use, because he is very shifty and is as good with one

[562] *El Paso Daily Herald*, January 22, 1896.
[563] *El Paso Daily Herald*, January 23, 1896.
[564] *El Paso Daily Herald*, January 30, 1896.

hand as the other. He has invented more new blows than any other pugilist and this is what makes him so dangerous. His opponents don't know exactly what to expect nor how to guard to keep him away from the vital spot. If he holds his guard high Fitz will fight low; if he removes his guard from his chin Fitz will land on it with lightning speed.[565]

The anti-boxing forces feared that the fight might take place in New Mexico, which was not yet a recognized state, and therefore had no law against boxing. As a federal territory, it was subject to federal law. On February 5, New Mexico territory congressional delegate Thomas Catron introduced a federal anti-boxing bill. It quickly passed through the Congress. On February 7, 1896, U.S. President Grover Cleveland signed the Catron bill into law, making boxing in any federal territories or in the District of Columbia a felony punishable by imprisonment from one to five years. It did not affect the states, but it did not matter, because boxing was technically illegal in most states anyway.

The law was an obvious attempt to prevent the Fitzsimmons-Maher fight. There was word that even Mexico was in favor of the bill. Certain Mexican governors said that they too would attempt to prevent the fight. The law simply did not want to leave boxing alone.[566]

Fearing that the legal activity would discourage spectators, promoter Dan Stuart insisted to the press that the fight would take place, and was so certain that he made a public offer to reimburse the expenses of anyone who paid to come see the fight and did not get what they paid for. [567]

Texas Governor Culberson warned Stuart that if the fight took place in his state that he would not rest until everyone connected with it was arrested and punished. Texas Rangers arrived in El Paso to watch Fitzsimmons' movements.

The U.S. Attorney General said, "If they fight on any territory of the United States we will follow them to the ends of the earth if necessary to bring them to justice." Even Mexican President Porfirio Diaz said that he was against allowing the fight on Mexican soil. This was ironic, given that bullfighting and cockfighting were legal there.[568]

As of February 8, reports were that Fitz was in good shape and training hard. Upon waking, he would play with his pet lion Nero for about an

---

[565] *El Paso Daily Herald*, February 6, 1896.
[566] *San Antonio Daily Express*, February 8, 1896. *Fistic Carnival* at 139-140.
[567] *El Paso Daily Herald*, February 8, 1896.
[568] *New York Clipper*, February 15, 1896; *El Paso Daily Times*, February 11, 1896. *Fistic Carnival* at 154.

hour. He would next go for a run, usually covering 15 to 20 miles. In the afternoon, he would punch the bag for 20 rounds. He would then spar 4-minute rounds, up to 15 rounds with his several trainers and attendants. The medicine ball was tossed for 20 minutes, and then he would work at the wrist and chest machines. The routine work closed with wrestling bouts. Spectators were charged 25 cents each to watch Bob train.

Training in Las Cruces, New Mexico, Peter Maher was reported to be in good condition as well, and was expected to enter the ring weighing about 175 pounds to Bob's 160 pounds or more.[569] Maher was confident.

> When Fitzsimmons defeated me at our first engagement I was a big, strong fellow, to be sure, but a mere novice in the art of boxing. I was hardly more than a boy and had but the most elementary knowledge of the game of stop, hit and get away. ... Even at that I had Fitz nearly out in the first round, but I did not know enough to take advantage of points I had gained. I also made the mistake of sparring him at long range after that round instead of getting in to him and fighting at close quarters. He was clever and shiftier than I at that time and at long range wore me out. ... I make no secret of my plan of action... I will get to the Australian as quickly as I can. I do not mean to repeat my former mistake and stay away from him. I honestly believe that I will win.... Of one thing the sporting public can rest assured – the battle will be swift and hard. ... Fitz will have to knock me stone out to win ... I will be in the acme of condition.[570]

Promoter Dan Stuart continually gave assurances to the press that the fight would happen, although he did not say where. Most suspected Texas, Arizona, New Mexico or Mexico as the most likely candidates. It was unclear whether Stuart had something up his sleeve or just wanted to represent certainty so that potential spectators would show up. Bets were even being taken on whether the fight would take place.

Law enforcement agencies in the surrounding states and even internationally between Mexico and the U.S. were having discussions about how to prepare and cooperate in using their troops to prevent the fight. Even the Arizona governor prepared his militia.

General Marbry of Texas said that if they attempted to hold the fight in Texas, he would order the rangers to shoot to kill. No wonder Jim Corbett no longer wanted any part of all this. Some thought that Mabry was merely

---

[569] *San Antonio Daily Express*, February 9, 11, 1896.
[570] *El Paso Daily Herald*, February 13, 1896. Maher also said that if he won, he would be a fighter and not an actor or theatrical performer.

bluffing, but Fitzsimmons grew concerned about all of the animosity and "declared his antipathy to being shot and demanded absolute protection, without which he would not fight at all." Stuart assured him that everything would be all right.

Some wrote that Dan Stuart had apparently been negotiating with the Mexican authorities for the use of a tract of land near El Paso. Another rumor was that he had found a piece of land where they could quickly pull off the fight and hop back over the border before the Mexican troops could get there. Either way, it was looking as if the fight would take place in Mexico, but nobody knew for certain.

After a day of training, when Fitzsimmons returned to Texas from Juarez, Mexico, two rangers approached him and told Bob to consider himself under arrest. General Marbry told Fitz that he would be under surveillance as long as he was in Texas. "This made Fitz feel uncomfortable as he had never violated any law of this country." They were basically leaning on him.

An upset Fitzsimmons wrote a letter to the local El Paso editor complaining that on February 12, two officers acting under Governor Culberson's authority "subjected me to the indignity of watching my house and home as though it was the abode of a thief in the night. I am a tax payer and a citizen. I have never transgressed a law on the statute books of the state of Texas."

Even the city of El Paso was upset. Its city council objected to the governor's placement of a large force of state rangers in the city and their arresting and guarding men who had committed no crime, when the city had no difficulty enforcing the law. The council called it an outrage and insult, and a shameful attempt to gain cheap notoriety under the guise of enforcing the law. The city was said to be practically under martial law.[571]

The fight was originally set for February 14, but about four days before the fight, Maher suffered an eye affliction which required its postponement. His eyes were inflamed and swollen, with a green shade over them, called acute opthalmia, said to be the result of alkali dust. At first, it was said that it would only delay the fight for a few days, so it was thought that the fight would take place on the 17th.

Initially, Fitz and Julian did not claim the $1,000 forfeit money for Maher's failure to be ready on the designated date. Fitz was upset that Maher had not taken care of himself, but realized that the injury was legitimate. "The constant dogging of his every movement by the rangers

[571] San Antonio Daily Express, February 13, 14, 1896; El Paso Daily Times, February 14, 15, 1896.

has added another feature to the disgust which Fitzsimmons entertains of the general situation."[572]

However, Maher required more time to heal. A doctor said that he thought Maher's eyes would be well in a week. At that point, Fitz wanted to claim the $1,000 forfeit money. Bob insisted that the fight was off, that Maher did not want to fight, and that Peter and his manager were welchers. After some debate between the two fighters' managers, Fitz said that he would bet $1,000 that Julian could lick Maher's manager Buck Connelly. Connelly responded that he was not a fighter. He would not allow his man to fight until he was well, because a lot of friends had wagers on Maher. He said that Maher would be ready on Friday the 21st. He offered to give over an additional $1,000 forfeit if Maher was not ready on that date. A committee was designated to decide the issue, and it agreed that Maher could keep the $1,000 forfeit money, but would have to be ready on the new date of February 21 or forfeit $2,000, which in the meantime would be turned over to and kept by Stuart.[573]

Jim Corbett said he felt all along that there would be no fight. Mexico would not allow him and Fitz to fight there, so he did not think it would allow Bob and Peter to fight there either.

> The fight won't come off. ... If they pull the fight off every one of them will go to jail. I learned my little lesson at Hot Springs. I never thought from the first that the fight would come off. Why if I had, I would have been there fighting instead of Maher, but I'm not going to chase around the country testing law any more. ... However, if the fight is pulled off successfully I will fight the winner.[574]

Corbett had a point, because word was that Mexican President Diaz was ordering the arrest of anyone connected with the fight.

Perhaps in an attempt to ingratiate himself, on the afternoon of February 17, 1896 in Juarez, Mexico, Fitzsimmons gave an exhibition for Governor Ahumada and his staff. Bob boxed with Will McCoy and Jack Stelzner, and looked to be in magnificent form. He later wrestled with his lion.[575]

---

[572] *Daily Inter Ocean,* February 15, 1896.
[573] *New York Clipper,* February 22, 1896; *San Antonio Daily Express,* February 14, 18, 1896; *El Paso Daily Times,* February 14, 16, 18, 1896.
[574] *El Paso Daily Times, San Antonio Daily Express,* February 18, 1896.
[575] *El Paso Daily Times,* February 18, 1896.

Peter Maher

As of the 18th, Maher was back in training and it looked like he would be ready by the 21st. John L. Sullivan said that Fitz would win. "That freak is the best of them all."[576]

Jim Corbett sent Fitzsimmons a telegram saying, "Read in tonight's paper that you said I was a cur. The first time I see you I will make you take it back like I did before." Martin Julian wrote Jim back saying, "Get yourself in better condition than you was at Hot Springs and get down here. Fitz will put you out of existence the day after he puts Maher among the has-beens."[577]

Most felt that Maher's best play would be to attempt a quick knockout, which he had done with most of his opponents. "Maher will have to win in a hurry, if at all. Fitzsimmons is fit to fight a whole day and will undoubtedly make it a long fight, if necessary."

---

[576] *El Paso Daily Times*, February 19, 1896; *San Antonio Daily Express*, February 14, 1896.
[577] *El Paso Daily Times*, February 19, 1896.

Fitz and Maher were both predicting a short fight. Although Maher said he expected to win, Fitz was supremely confident. "His confidence in his ability to win is almost beyond comprehension. He does not concede Maher a chance, but says he is as sure of winning the $10,000 as though he had it in his purse already."[578]

To avoid the U.S. legal authorities, the Fitz-Maher bout was held in Mexico, not near El Paso, as had been anticipated, but in a more remote location. The fight took place on February 21, 1896, just across the border from the small town of Langtry, Texas, on the Mexican side of the Rio Grande in Coahuila. Leaving at about 11:20 p.m. (some said 11:45 or 11:50) on the 20th, they took a 389-mile train-ride southeast from El Paso to get there. Spectators had to pay $11.65 for train fare ($3 more for a sleeper car) and $20 admission to view the fight. They had to bring their own seats or be willing to stand to watch the fight. The train arrived in Langtry at about 3 p.m. (some said 3:35) on the 21st, and they walked the rest of the way.

General Marbry and 26 of his armed Texas rangers went with them to make sure that they did not fight in U.S. territory. Apparently, 200 Mexican troops were stationed at Eagle Pass, but it would have taken two days of marching to reach the scene. "No more perfect place free from interference could be devised. On the Mexican side it cannot be reached except by coming up or down the stream for a long distance."

The battle ground was a sandy outdoor flat in a rocky amphitheatre in a bend in the Rio Grande River on the Mexican side. 42 Mexicans had carried the ring material down to the river bank on the previous night. A narrow pontoon footbridge was erected across the flowing stream. The crowd also had to walk over a stony path and waded ankle deep in sand.

[578] *Daily Inter Ocean,* February 21, 1896; *Times-Democrat,* February 21, 1896.

A tall canvas fence/wall, about 200 feet in diameter, encircled the ring and immediate grounds, raised to prevent free views, but this did not stop the rangers, with their revolvers and Winchesters, and some locals, from seeing the fight from a bird's eye view across the river in the steep, nearby 200-foot tall Texas cliffs. One source said that there were exactly 189 persons who saw the fight, but this meant paying customers. Almost another 200 people watched for free from the cliffs above.

The 24-foot-ring was pitched in the sandy ground, elevated four-feet from the ground. The board floor was covered with canvas, over which rosin was sprinkled. On opposite sides of the ring were two little tents for the principals, which were their dressing rooms. At one side of the ring was the frame compartment for the kinetoscope. The weather was not good, for it was a gloomy and cloudy day. A light rain began falling just before the men entered the ring. It stopped, but came again in occasional spurts.

Accompanying Fitzsimmons into the ring was Martin Julian, William McCoy, Jack Stelzner, and lightweight Jack Everhardt. Bob wore a striped bathrobe, and underneath had on short dark blue thigh trunks with a belt showing the American colors. He sat in the corner nearest the steps leading to the platform on the west side. Owing to the fact that there was no sunshine, there was no toss up for corners (fighters usually preferred having the sun behind them rather than shining in their corner).

One minute later, Maher entered, accompanied by Jim Hall, Buck Connelly, Peter Lowry, Jack Quinn and Peter Burns. Maher wore black trunks half way to the knees, with a green belt.

Fitzsimmons was 32 years of age to Maher's 26. "No weights were announced at the ring, but Fitzsimmons weighed about 165 and Maher about 180." Those were the weights that most next-day newspapers reported. One paper listed Maher as 5'11 ¾" and weighing 176 pounds in condition. *The New York Clipper* said that Maher's weight was given as 173 pounds and Fitzsimmons' as about 162 pounds.

Martin Julian asked Referee George Siler if he had the $10,000 prize money that Stuart was supposed to give him. Fitz/Julian had earlier insisted that the money be put into the hands of referee Siler in the form of *cash* before he would fight. Siler produced certified checks. After a Julian protest, Tom O'Rourke said, "Do you think I would pack $10,000 cash down here?" Julian wanted cash. Siler said the checks were certified, and were all right. Bob said, "Oh, let it go. We have given in to everything else and we will give in to this."

Referee Siler examined the 5-ounce gloves and placed them in the center of the ring. There was no squabbling over who received which pair. Fitz chose the light green gloves, while Maher took the dark brown. The referee instructed them that when there was a clinch that they were to break away promptly, each to take one step backward before resuming. If there was a knockdown, the man had to be on his feet before he could be struck again. "Be careful about fouls. Get ready."

Each went to their corners, and Fitz removed his bathrobe. The referee then asked them to shake hands. Fitz confidently advanced and did so, and they both then retired to their corners again and took their seats.

Louis Houseman of Chicago's *Daily Inter Ocean* and Bert Sneed of the New Orleans *Times-Democrat* were two of the timekeepers. Houseman blew a warning whistle five seconds before ringing the bell, and both boxers stood up.

The following account is an amalgamation of local sources and sources which had reporters on the scene, such as the *El Paso Daily Herald*, *San Antonio Daily Express*, New Orleans *Times-Democrat*, Chicago *Daily Inter Ocean*, and *El Paso Times*.

At the opening bell, the men advanced to the center of the ring, with Fitzsimmons' "little eyes flashing like balls of burnished blue." There was no preliminary sparring. Fitz feinted a right and stepped away as Maher punched. Fitz led with his left and Maher backed away. Fitz stepped forward and landed his left, right, and left on Maher's temples. Maher countered but Bob moved away. A Fitz right uppercut headed for Peter's chin missed by about an inch. Maher countered but Fitz ducked and they clinched.

As they were breaking away, Maher hit Fitz on the right cheek. Bob asked, "Ain't that a foul?" Several cries of "foul" were heard. Referee Siler told Maher, "If you do that again I will decide the fight against you." Fitz said, "Let it go, I'll lick him any way." Queensberry rules usually allowed such a tactic, but the men had agreed before the fight not to hit in clinches and on breakaways, although Maher later claimed not to have made that agreement. Regardless, the referee had so instructed them before the fight. He wanted clean breaks after a clinch.

The men began fighting hard, exchanging so many fast blows that it was difficult to tell which were landing. After another clinch and break, Peter landed a left to the neck. Close in fighting followed and Maher landed a left to Fitz's upper lip, drawing a little blood. Fitz landed a left and right and a clinch followed. Maher again fouled Fitz over the heart. The foul was overlooked and they continued. Maher feinted and Fitz missed a right. They mixed it up and Maher landed both hands to the sides of Bob's head. Maher led with his left and they clinched again.

Fitz seemed a bit bothered or slightly distressed, breaking ground on Maher's leads. "Fitz ducked and dodged and watched for an opening, making Maher do all the fighting." Maher rushed Bob to the ropes and landed some grazing blows that would have been damaging if "Fitz's head had not been on a pivot." Bob ducked and dodged, but kept his eye on Peter. Some in the crowd began to murmur, "Maher has got him." Fitz suddenly rushed forward into a clinch. According to the *El Paso Daily Herald*, after a breakaway,

> Maher shot his arm out at Fitz's chin. Fitz caught the blow on the left arm, threw his head to one side and it passed by his neck. Quick as lightning Fitz shot out a half arm hook [with his right] and caught Maher on the left jaw. Maher's head dropped, his frame trembled and he fell to the platform, rolled back until his head struck and then rolled again with his left arm on the floor, his head and feet slightly raised from the platform, and his eyes turned white.

Of this final sequence, the other sources said that Maher followed Bob up, led with his left, but Fitz side-stepped it and swung his right on the point of the chin. Maher went down full length, his head striking the floor with great force. He vainly tried to rise, but could not do more than raise his head, until he sank back down.

As Maher was counted out, his seconds tried to throw water on him to revive him, but were stopped.

During the count, Bob retired to his corner and sat down. His seconds urged Bob to get up and be ready to fight. "Look out for him. ... He may come at you." Bob snapped, "Get away from me... It's all over, he's out."

After the count was concluded, Bob said, "There, didn't I tell you he was out." He put his bathrobe back on to protect himself from the cold, drizzling rain.

According to the *El Paso Daily Herald*, "The actual time of fighting was just one minute and twenty-five seconds." The other sources claimed that the fight had lasted one minute and thirty-five seconds.

After it was over, people jumped into the ring and shook Bob's hand, and several hurrahs for Bob were heard.

Maher was totally unconscious for fifteen seconds, and after he was carried to his corner, it was fully a minute more before he regained full consciousness. Even then, "It was several minutes before Maher realized what had happened to him."

Bob walked over and offered his gloved hand to shake. When Maher reached out, Fitz drew it back with a laugh. He then had the glove removed and offered his bare hand, and they shook. Maher kept his head down while shaking; sitting down as Bob was standing before him. After a few minutes, Maher was assisted to his dressing tent.

Except for slight bleeding from the nostrils as a result of Maher's hard jabs, Bob was unmarked and appeared fresh. Maher had a slight break in the skin just above the left point of the chin, where the "master stroke" had landed.[579]

Bob Fitzsimmons had won the $10,000 stake money, and had also won what many called the world championship. The local writer observed, "Fitzsimmons was confident, smiled all the way through the fight and only looked serious when he got ready to make his final rush."

Martin Julian announced, "Bob Fitzsimmons is now champion heavy weight of the world. He has fought his way up from the bottom. He will be ready at all times to meet any one who is worthy of his notice." The crowd cheered for Fitz and then started back to the Langtry train depot.

Maher's backers were not upset. They said that they would still back him against anyone but Fitzsimmons, whose "knock out blow was too much for any man in the world." The general opinion was that Bob's play in the fight was to lead Maher on until he left an opening, and then to take advantage of it.

Various newspapers quoted Maher as saying things such as,

---

[579] *El Paso Daily Herald*, February 21, 22, 1896; *San Antonio Daily Express, Daily Inter Ocean, Times-Democrat*, February 22, 1896; *New York Clipper*, February 29, 1896; *Los Angeles Express*, February 21, 22, 1896; *Los Angeles Times*, February 22, 1896.

I thought I had licked him until he punched me under the jaw and then it was all over. ... He got me good and hard, and that was all there was to it. I heard the referee counting and heard the men in my corner calling me to rise, but I could not rise. When I knew anything at all I was in my corner and they were rubbing my face with water. ...

He is a clever fighter, and I don't know exactly where I was hit. It seems to me it was on the jaw, and the back of my head has a big lump on it, and that's where it struck the floor. I thought I had him licked from the start, and so far as my condition is concerned, I have nothing to complain of, and I would like to get a fight with somebody else.

In an interview, Fitzsimmons said,

There never was a minute since the match was made that I have anticipated any other result than this. I was sure of him at all stages of the game. He was afraid the minute he put up his hands and I knew it. ... I got in on him with my right and caught him squarely on the jaw. I knew it was all over when I landed on him. It was dead easy from the start.[580]

Bob also said, "I told the people there would be two hits; one was for Maher and Maher's head would make the other. ... He fouled me three times, and the blow he gave me in the jaw set me dizzy. It was a hot soaker, and for a second I thought I was gone."[581] Fitzsimmons told an El Paso reporter, "Maher gained confidence from my plays and forced the end. He did daze me once though, and I had it once on a foul, but I want the crowd to see the fight they had paid for."[582] Years later, Fitz said, "I made about $12,000 in just ninety seconds, which, I guess, is laying it all over Mr. Morgan."[583]

Some said that the knockout blow was more of an uppercut. Some called it a short-arm swing, similar to the punch that knocked out Jim Hall. Another said that Maher's right was blocked with the left arm, and then Bob countered with a right.[584] An El Paso dispatch said of the knockout

[580] *San Antonio Daily Express, Daily Inter Ocean, Times-Democrat,* February 22, 1896.
[581] *Times-Democrat,* February 22, 1896.
[582] *El Paso Daily Times,* February 22, 1896.
[583] *Louisville Courier-Journal,* March 26, 1905.
[584] *New York Clipper,* February 29, 1896; *Los Angeles Express,* February 21, 22, 1896; *Los Angeles Times,* February 22, 1896.

that Fitz feinted a left, and as Maher's guard fell to stop a blow he thought was coming, a lightning swing from Fitz's right to the jaw knocked him out. Martin Julian agreed with this version. Another account of the knockout said Fitz followed his own left with a right.[585]

Fitzsimmons played the same old game he has so often played before, leading on his opponent until he had him where he wanted him, and then landing a lightning right-hand swing on the jaw – and it was over. It was the identical blow that knocked out Jim Hall in New Orleans.

The fight was sharp while it lasted. Fitzsimmons took the aggressive from the call of time. There were four clinches and no more than half a dozen exchanges. ...

For the first part of the round Maher had the better of it. He led often and forced the fighting. In his eagerness to get at Fitzsimmons he committed a palpable foul during a clinch and was warned by Referee Siler that its repetition would cost him the fight. Maher fought well, but he was no match for his red-headed opponent, who proved himself today one of the craftiest men that ever stepped into the ring. Fitzsimmons is now, by Corbett's action in presenting the championship to Maher, the champion of the world, and after the fight was over he declared through Julian his willingness to defend the championship against any and all comers.[586]

The *Times-Democrat* wrote,

Up to the time of the knock-out it was any sort of odds that victory would perch on the Irishman's banner. Fitzsimmons in the early stage of the short fight was most uncertain in his delivery, and seemed to have a very poor idea of distance, and his wild misses with his right hand caused consternation in the ranks of his advisers and backers. Three different times Maher escaped right hand swings. They were not ordinary misses, nor was it by cleverness or agility that Maher got his head out of danger. It was due to Fitz's wildness. All three of the blows were at least a foot wide of the mark. ...

The fight, though short, was full of action, and it was fight all the way through. Both men started in from the beginning to make a hot pace. Fitz, except in the rally, did not use his left, and then he only feinted

[585] *El Paso Daily Times*, February 22, 1896; *Times-Democrat*, February 25, 1896.
[586] *Daily Inter Ocean, San Antonio Daily Express*, February 22, 1896.

in the strange way so characteristic of the man. It was more of an uppercut than a straight lead, and drew Maher's head in range. Quick as a flash Fitzsimmons shot his right across square on the point of Maher's jaw and the Irishman's head hit the floor. It was a short right hand blow.[587]

After several minutes had elapsed and Maher had recovered, he called the knockout a chance blow and claimed that he was not at his best owing to his eyes. However, Bob Fitzsimmons had a way of landing those "chance" blows quite often in his career.

One reporter responded to some attempts to belittle Bob's victory by calling it an accident, saying,

> But it is strange how some people insist on refusing to give Fitzsimmons credit for anything. According to their prejudiced minds everything he accomplishes is an accident, and yet he has won all of his big victories in the same manner. There is no getting away from the fact that Fitzsimmons is a master of successful ring tactics. He undoubtedly played Maher with a loose rein for a purpose.[588]

Although some called it a chance blow, the majority gave Fitz full credit. George Siler asked, "[W]hen a man aims at the chin and lands on the chin how can it be a chance blow? … [I]n Fitzsimmons' record has he not made too many of those kind of 'lands' for them to be called 'chance blows?'"

Observers of the fight shared their thoughts, being interviewed on the train afterwards. The general feeling was that Maher was doing well, having the edge in the short fight, until Bob landed the knockout blow.

J. Quinn: "I was confident Maher would win and he had the best of it until Fitz got in that blow."

W. W. Naughton: "The most noticeable characteristic of the fight was Fitzsimmons' supreme confidence and Maher's lack of confidence. Fitz was so confident he fought slovenly. His knock-out blow was a beautiful exhibition of time and distance and proved to me that his wild misses were only a ruse."

Harry Weldon: "I thought Fitz put up a very slovenly fight, but he may have been playing for the opening he got. Fitz is a foxy fighter. It was a lucky blow for Fitz, as Maher clearly out pointed him in the start. But Fitz

[587] *Times-Democrat*, February 22, 1896.
[588] *El Paso Daily Times*, February 23, 1896.

has won so many fights in the same way I must conclude there was method in his tactics. We must acknowledge the Australian is a great fighter."

Jim Whitfield: "It has been demonstrated again that Fitz is one of the craftiest fighters that ever entered the ring and emphasizes the fact he is the hardest hitter of the present time. Maher was drawn on as was Hall and when lured into a seeming victory Fitz measured his distance and landed a fatal right hand back. Fitz can now get backing to fight Corbett or anybody."

Langdon: "Maher held his own up to the time of the final punch."

Howard Hackett: "I thought Maher had the shade the best up to the knock out. But Fitz is very tricky."[589]

Bob's stock rose immensely. One said, "Fitz's knockout blow is invincible, and men that were formerly strong Corbett men are now of the opinion that Fitz is the man that can handle him."[590] Another wrote that the "general opinion is that Fitzsimmons is capable of giving Corbett or any other man on earth a desperate, hard fight at any time."[591]

Bob was so supremely confident in the fight that it had "verged on the reckless," despite realizing that Maher "would certainly knock him out if he happened to land in the right place, yet he 'mixed' matters with the Irishman in a manner that alarmed his friends and delighted the Maher contingent." Bob said, "I risked his blows to get an opening."

Fitz was willing to take risks with a big puncher, and therefore was willing to take even more risks with Corbett, whom he considered to have much less power than Maher. That is, if they ever fought. Bob told the *El Paso Daily Herald* reporter,

Well I did just what I told you I would do, didn't I? … When he hit me over the heart he dazed me, but I never lost my head and only played him for an opening. If I ever get a chance to fight Corbett I will take more chances with him than I did with Maher, because I know Corbett cannot hit hard enough to knock me out. Corbett is quick but his blows lack steam.

Regarding his future plans, Fitzsimmons said,

[589] *El Paso Daily Times*, February 22, 1896.
[590] *San Antonio Daily Express*, February 23, 1896.
[591] *New York Clipper*, February 29, 1896; *Los Angeles Express*, February 21, 22, 1896; *Los Angeles Times*, February 22, 1896.

I don't know yet what I will do in regard to fighting Corbett, but think I will let him do some of the chasing he has given me for two years. I am now heavyweight champion of the world, and if Corbett wants that title again he will have to hunt me up.[592]

Although the kinetoscope was set up, the fight could not be filmed. The newspapers offered multiple different reasons for this: the weather was bad and the lighting poor, the storage batteries would not work, and/or the magnets would not work. The kinetoscope man, Enoch J. Rector, wanted them to fight again the next day, so he could film it. Bob said that he would do it for a purse of $5,000 and 50% of the net receipts of the film exhibitions. Apparently, Julian demanded $10,000 and 50% of the profits. Maher would have to agree as well. No deal was made.[593] It was said that Rector had a total outlay of $45,000, with the film stock alone costing $6,000 (enough to film 50 rounds).[594]

There were no subsequent legal troubles. Mexican President Diaz said that Mexican law did not cover prize fighting, and his endeavor to prevent the fight was merely out of consideration for the United States. Local Mexican officials said that the boxers had violated what was practically only a police regulation, and even if they had been caught, would have only been subject to a misdemeanor charge. It was not an extraditable offense.[595]

At that point, most newspapers recognized Fitzsimmons as the heavyweight champion. "Fitzsimmons is now, owing to Corbett's action in presenting the championship to Maher, the champion of the world."[596] Ironically, despite its previous harsh criticism of Fitzsimmons for failing to make the Corbett bout occur in Hot Springs, the *National Police Gazette* awarded Fitz its diamond belt signifying that he was the world champion.[597] It overlooked the fact that Fitz had turned down its belt back when he had won the middleweight championship.

The New York Clipper also recognized Fitzsimmons, and criticized Corbett's "presumption to attempt to reclaim the title of champion of the world, basing his absurd claim upon the assertion that when he announced his retirement it was with the express understanding that in case the championship was won by a foreigner he would reclaim it."[598] Of course, the puzzling thing was that Maher, the man to whom he had bestowed the

[592] *Times-Democrat*, February 23, 1896.
[593] *San Antonio Daily Express, El Paso Daily Times*, February 22, 1896.
[594] *Daily Inter Ocean*, February 20, 22, 1896.
[595] *El Paso Daily Times*, February 22, 1896.
[596] *San Antonio Daily Express*, February 22, 1896.
[597] *The National Police Gazette*, February 20, 1896.
[598] *New York Clipper,* February 29, 1896, March 7, 1896.

title, was a foreigner, from Ireland. Fitzsimmons was a naturalized American citizen. Because Corbett was of Irish descent, as was O'Donnell and Maher, he likely did not see them as "foreigners." Oddly enough though, Fitz was half Irish. Corbett just did not like Fitzsimmons.

The Maher victory subsequently became even more significant and impressive, given that Maher resumed his career and scored a number of impressive victories in 1896, including: KO4 Frank Slavin, KO6 Joe Choynski (after Joe had scored a KO13 Jim Hall and KO4 Joe McAuliffe), and a rematch KO1 Steve O'Donnell.

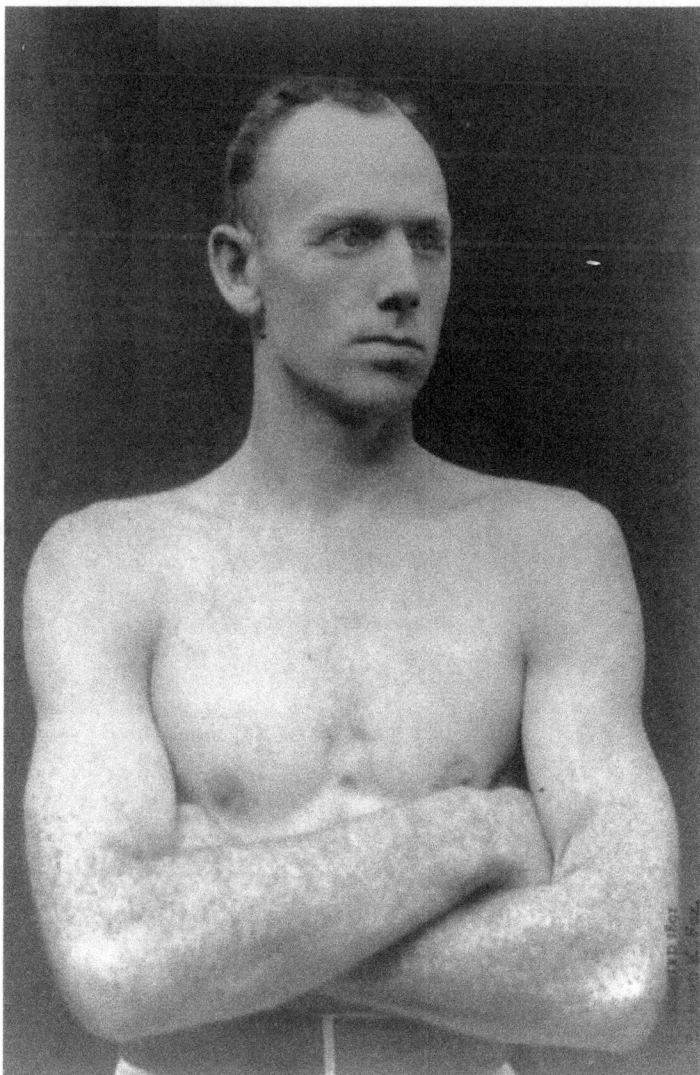

CHAPTER 15

The Championship Cloud

Immediately after Bob Fitzsimmons defeated Peter Maher, James Corbett wired Bob a challenge for the championship and posted a $1,000 forfeit, telling Fitz to come to Chicago at once to make the match. He said that the only places where they could legally fight were England, South Africa, and Australia, and he would go to any of those places for a fight.

One newspaper responded to the manner of Corbett's challenge,

> The idea that Corbett possesses the right to peremptorily send for Fitzsimmons is too funny to be real. Fitzsimmons stands today, by Corbett's own declaration, the champion of the world, and, as such, is entitled to the privileges of the position which Corbett so arrogantly claimed for himself. All the talk about getting on a train should be in regard to the man who must fight and fight quick if he ever hopes to be anything but a bad actor and a bully.[599]

Denver Ed Smith, who held an 1893 victory over Joe Goddard, posted $1,000 and said that he was willing to fight either Fitzsimmons or Corbett. "I think Fitzsimmons ought to ignore Corbett's offer to fight after the way Corbett avoided a meeting and turned the championship over to Maher."[600]

Responding to the challenges, Martin Julian said, "Fitzsimmons has done with fighting for the present. He is entitled to a rest, and he is going to take it." Bob was set to give exhibitions in cities like New York, Boston, Philadelphia, Washington, Chicago, and Pittsburg. After that, in about May, they planned to take a trip to England. Julian said that Bob "likes to fight and intends to fight, but he thinks he would like a little rest just now." He had a good point. Fitzsimmons had been almost constantly training for many months, first for the failed late October 1895 Corbett fight, and then until the late February 1896 Maher fight. And when Bob Fitzsimmons trained for a finish fight, HE TRAINED!

---

[599] *Daily Inter Ocean*, February 22, 1896.
[600] *Times-Democrat*, February 22, 1896.

Julian said that in the meantime, top contenders like Smith and Corbett and others should fight it out to determine who was superior, and then the winner could take on Bob. "We have been taking just this same kind of medicine for the past three or four years; now we will let some of the others try it a while and see how they like it. We are in a position to dictate, and we intend to have our own way." [601]

Fitzsimmons echoed that he would not accept Corbett's challenge.

> I will not pay any attention to him. I have been training now seven months or over for what I won, and I think I am entitled to some of the fruits of the victory. Corbett held me off a long time when I wanted to fight him, and then had it fixed when there was a prospect of our meeting so that I could not get to where he was. I believe if he hadn't been afraid of Maher, and thought the latter had a chance to whip me, he'd never have made that silly break of resigning the championship into Maher's keeping. Let him show he's fit and able to whip Peter Maher or Joe Choynski. He talks about England, Africa and Australia being the only countries in which men can fight. Haven't we just fought in this country? Why? Because Maher and I wanted to fight. If Corbett had been in Maher's place there would never have been a fight, and I believe if both parties to a match really want to fight there will be no difficulty in finding a place in America. [602]

At this point, it was Fitzsimmons who was not interested in a Corbett fight. He needled Corbett by essentially engaging in the same tactics that Corbett had used, saying that he would not notice him and that Corbett had to fight other men to prove that he was deserving of the right to challenge for the title, all of which Jim had previously said to him. "His idea now is that he will pay Corbett back with the same treatment he has received from Corbett." Bob said that Maher and Choynski could both defeat Corbett. "I whipped with ease the man Corbett presented the championship belt to in order to escape a match with me." [603]

Regardless, it was not entirely clear whether Fitzsimmons actually considered himself the champion. Fitz said,

[601] *Times-Democrat*, February 25, 1896.
[602] *New York Clipper*, February 29, 1896.
[603] *San Antonio Daily Express*, February 23, 1896.

To show Corbett how little weight his championship present carried, I now formally, through the Associated Press, renounce all claim to the belt and refuse to accept it. I am going to Madison Square Garden for the night of Feb 29 with a half dozen contracts I made conditionally on winning from Maher, and then, with Julian, Stelzner, Roeber, and my family, I sail for England.[604]

Corbett responded,

He is a big coward. … I predicted he would not make a match with me if he won the fight with Maher, but if he goes to England he will find me in England after him. He said after his fight with Maher was over he would fight any man in the world. He is now getting out of this country as fast as possible, bag and baggage.[605]

The Clipper said that ordinarily, a pugilist had to accept a challenge backed by a monetary deposit, but that since Corbett used insulting language in his challenge and called himself "Champion of the World," which it felt he had no right to do; Bob was justified in ignoring such a challenge.

[Corbett] has the hardihood to sign his alleged challenge "Champion of the World," a position to which he has no claim, and it is extremely doubtful if he ever will have again in case he has to win it from Fitzsimmons, who, after his quick disposal of skillful and hard hitting Peter Maher, is regarded by very many shrewd and experienced ring goers as the master of any pugilist of the present day.[606]

Still, because Corbett had repudiated his retirement before Maher had fought Fitzsimmons, and Maher had said that he did not want the title until he defeated Bob, there was a portion of the general public which disregarded any Fitz championship claim.

Just over a week after the Maher victory, on February 29, 1896 at New York's Madison Square Garden, Fitzsimmons gave a set to with "Brennan, of Buffalo, who was a mere plaything in the hands of the champion." Bob

[604] *Times-Democrat,* February 23, 1896.
[605] *San Antonio Daily Express, El Paso Daily Times, Times-Democrat,* February 23, 1896.
[606] *New York Clipper,* February 29, 1896.

then boxed 3 exhibition rounds with Peter Maher. Owing to the police warning, the Maher bout was "devoid of pepper", but was still "chock full of science and apparent vim." Even though the rounds were brief, the crowd of nearly 5,000 cheered them.[607]

Fitz went on a money-making exhibition tour. During early April, Corbett was in St. Louis set to give boxing exhibitions as part of his play. Although Fitzsimmons was also booked at one of the local theaters, he did not show up, because the local police chief was preventing any sparring from taking place. It was said that Corbett could make money whether or not he boxed, whereas if Fitz was prohibited from sparring, his "box office receipts will require medical assistance." However, Corbett boxed anyway, was arrested, but then the prosecutor dismissed the case.[608]

Soon thereafter, Corbett said, "If the American people can stand Fitzsimmons without meeting me, all right. I can stand it too, as I don't have to depend on fighting for a livelihood." Corbett was acting instead.[609]

From April 6-9 at Pittsburg, Pennsylvania's Academy of Music, Fitzsimmons "the pugilistic marvel of the age" sparred Dan Hickey in daily matinees. The Australian-born Hickey was a member of the Australian boxing crew that had sparred so often back at Larry Foley's gym. While in Australia in the 1880s, Hickey had boxed with the likes of Peter Jackson, Billy McCarthy, and Steve O'Donnell.[610]

Beginning on April 13, 1896, Fitzsimmons, the "undisputed middleweight and recognized heavyweight champion of the world," exhibited for a week at Cleveland, Ohio's Star Theater. Upon his arrival in town, Bob was surrounded by a crowd of those who were "drawn to him by that natural curiosity which the American public has for 'great' men."

That afternoon and evening, Fitzsimmons boxed with Dan Hickey. Bob was scheduled to give exhibitions of bag punching and sparring with Hickey all week, with both matinee and evening shows.

Fitz said that he would not fight Corbett until he proved himself worthy. Jim had kept him waiting, "and now I am going to give him a dose of his own medicine." Bob called Jim a coward and not capable of fighting a man that is worth anything. "He is a clever boxer in his way, but not a fighter. He never was a fighter. He gave Maher the belt to defend instead of defending it himself like a man and of course I won the belt."

[607] *New York Clipper*, March 7, 1896.
[608] *St. Louis Republic*, April 7-9, 1896.
[609] *Pittsburg Press*, April 12, 1896.
[610] *St. Louis Republic*, April 8, 10, 1896; *Pittsburg Press*, April 5, 9, 1896; *Pittsburg Post*, April 7, 8, 1896. Also with Bob was the Greco-Roman wrestler, Ernest Roeber, who gave separate wrestling exhibitions.

Bob said that he would not fight as long as there was money in show business. Besides, he did not think a championship fight to the finish could take place in America, given all the legal constraints.

> The general law in the United States is so clear that you cannot get around it, and of course I can never go to Mexico again without being arrested. And I do not believe that I would care to fight again under such conditions as I fought under in Mexico. We were in the cars fourteen or fifteen hours and during that time the cars were crowded by gangs of curious people.... It was very uncomfortable. I am going to enjoy myself now that I am the champion of the world. I will sail for England next month and remain there for some time.[611]

After the April 16th performance at Cleveland's Star Theatre, Fitz and wrestler Ernest Roeber went to see Bob's pet lion, Nero. Upon their arrival on the roof where the lion was being kept, the excited lion ran to greet them, but the chain attached to his collar contacted some electrical wires, electrocuting him. When the lion leapt out in pain, the chain contacted Bob's thighs, shocking him as well. Bob told his friends to keep away, fearing that they would be shocked also. In its pain, the lion jumped off the roof and dangled by the chain around its neck. The lion was pulled back up, but died soon thereafter. It was unclear whether it died from electrocution, suffocation, or a broken neck.

Bob's thighs and right hand were burned from the awful shock. "It felt like as if someone put three or four giant firecrackers on my insides and touched them off." Despite his injuries, Bob said that he would give his usual exhibition the following day. They gave their final two shows there on the 18th.[612]

On April 16, 1896 in San Francisco, Joe Choynski contracted to knock out "Sailor" Tom Sharkey in 8 rounds. After fighting Fitzsimmons, Joe Choynski had fought an 1895 6-round draw with Dan Creedon, and won a January 1896 KO13 over Jim Hall, significant because Hall had knocked out Frank Slavin.[613]

---

[611] *Cleveland Plain Dealer*, April 12-14, 1896; *Cleveland Leader*, April 14, 1896.
[612] *Cleveland Plain Dealer*, April 17, 1896; *Cleveland Leader*, April 18, 1896; *New York Clipper*, April 25, 1896.
[613] *Los Angeles Times*, January 21, 1896. In the 9th round, the 160-pound Hall dropped the 161-pound Choynski, but Joe managed to come back and drop Hall in the 11th and 12th rounds before knocking Hall out in the 13th round.

The 22-year-old "Sailor" Tom Sharkey had for three years been the undefeated Navy champion, and had impressed fans with his natural fighting abilities. Although unpolished, he had shown great strength, courage, and recuperative powers. Except for an early 1896 8-round draw against Alec Greggains, the 180-pound Sharkey had won all of his fights by knockout, including a July 1895 KO7 over Australian Billy Smith.[614]

Tom Sharkey

In the 1st round of the Choynski-Sharkey bout, after being pounded on and dropped by Choynski, Sharkey landed a vicious low blow. The badly hurt Choynski continued with the fight, and although he mostly pounded on Sharkey and even dropped him a few times, Tom was game and had his moments, fighting hard throughout. Choynski was clearly better, but Sharkey was awarded the official 8-round decision because Joe had failed to knock him out, as required by the contract.

Still, the local press was high on Tom's potential. Sharkey had "demonstrated that he is a perfect glutton for punishment and does not know when he is defeated. He is a fighter of the Goddard type." Sharkey was called a man "famous for stamina, recuperative powers and courage," as well as "remarkable physical development as to make him proof against the assaults of all ordinary men." Before 1896 was over, Sharkey would meet both Corbett and Fitzsimmons in two famous fights.[615]

It was during April that Fitzsimmons began taking some heat for not accepting Corbett's challenges. Jim had posted the traditional $1,000 to bind a fight with Fitzsimmons, but it was not accepted. Reversing its previous position, the *New York Clipper* said,

_____

[614] There is also an unconfirmed report that Sharkey fought a 21-round draw against an Englishman named Williams in 1894. Tom dropped him in the 21st, but fell down from the effort. Neither could rise, so they declared it a draw. *San Francisco Call*, December 26, 1896.
[615] *San Francisco Chronicle*, April 18, 1896; *San Francisco Examiner*, April 17, 1896; *San Francisco Evening Post*, June 24, 1896; *San Francisco Bulletin*, June 24, 1896; *New York Sun*, June 25, 1896.

Bob Fitzsimmons, by persisting in his refusal to accept the challenge issued by Jim Corbett, is taking the proper course to reinstate the latter in the position of Champion without a fight for the honor, as the auburn haired slugger from the Antipodes cannot decline to make a match with the Californian without forfeiting to him the title that he so easily won in Mexico.[616]

In late April, Dan Stuart offered Fitz and Corbett a $12,000 purse to fight. Corbett's manager Bill Brady signed the agreement. However, Fitz's manager Martin Julian said that Bob would not fight Jim until he had defeated one of the boxers they had named.

As a result of his refusal to defend against Corbett, the same newspapers which had recognized Bob as champion now believed that he had forfeited the championship back to Corbett. *The Clipper* opined,

> Corbett will now be justified, according to the custom in championship matters, in claiming the title which he voluntarily gave up, and which Fitzsimmons is unwilling to defend under the rules governing such matters. Bob has had warning enough, and if he and his manager are unwilling to abide by the laws made and provided in such cases they will have no one but themselves to blame for the result of their folly.[617]

This championship cloud was not anything new. Jake Kilrain had once claimed the championship when everyone knew that Sullivan was the champion, but Sullivan was slow to accept his challenge. Even before that, Jimmy Elliot, who had lost to Sullivan in a gloved match, claimed the bareknuckle championship when he posted an unaccepted challenge and forfeit for a bareknuckle fight. His claim generally went ignored. Sullivan had announced his retirement following his victory over Kilrain, but no one even bothered to claim the championship. By then everyone realized that Sullivan was the champion until someone defeated him in the ring. During Sullivan's semi-retirement years, some newspapers recognized Frank Slavin as champion, until he lost to Peter Jackson. After Corbett defeated Sullivan and did not accept Joe's challenge, Joe Goddard claimed the championship. This claim disappeared after he lost to Denver Ed Smith.

---

[616] *New York Clipper,* April 18, 1896.
[617] *New York Clipper,* May 2, 1896.

Ultimately, who really was the champion would have to be decided in the ring. James J. Corbett had won the title from Sullivan, and for Bob Fitzsimmons to be recognized as the true champion, he needed to fight and defeat Corbett. As John L. once said, "Championships won by wind are frail honors."

On May 27, 1896, Fitzsimmons set sail for England, accompanied by Ernest Roeber and Dan Hickey. Fitzsimmons was set to visit the leading cities in Great Britain and the continent and display his fistic prowess in exhibitions. *The Clipper* opined that he would not meet with a warm reception, owing to the fact that he had failed to make a match with Corbett. It believed that Bob's leaving America demonstrated that "he really dreads the result of a meeting in the ring with the Californian."[618] To a certain extent, Bob was mirroring what Corbett had done as champion, making money in exhibitions. Jim had toured the British Isles in 1894 for about four months.

As of late June, it was reported, "Fitzsimmons expects to remain in London for some time, and it is his intention to give some sparring exhibitions both in this city and in the provinces. He is using the stage of the National Sporting Club as an exercise ground." Another report said that Bob had just arrived in London, and wrote to a friend, "I am being lionized by the sports of London, and I firmly believe that I will be very successful with my show. I saw Peter Jackson the other day. Peter is not looking like his old time self, and I don't think he will be able to fight again."[619]

On June 3, 1896 in San Francisco, 182-pound Tom Sharkey knocked out undefeated 180-pound Jim Williams in the 7th round. Williams had a pretty good record, including victories over George LaBlanche, Jack Dempsey, Mexican Pete Everett, and a recent KO7 over Jack Stelzner, a Fitzsimmons sparring partner.

On June 24, 1896 at San Francisco's Mechanics Pavilion under the sponsorship of the National Athletic Club, after having trained for less than three weeks, James J. Corbett struggled with Tom Sharkey in a 4-round bout that was declared a draw. It was mostly a wrestling and clinching match. Corbett had started well for the first 2 rounds, hitting Sharkey at will, but Tom took it, threw back, clinched to avoid punishment and utilized his wrestling tactics. As Corbett grew fatigued, Sharkey continued forcing the pace, and Jim began holding on for dear life. Corbett was completely exhausted by the 4th round, and most felt that if it had been a fight to the finish that Sharkey would have won. Corbett's stock dropped and Sharkey's rose.

---

618 *New York Clipper,* May 23, 1896, June 6, 1896.
619 *San Francisco Bulletin,* June 20, 1896; *New York Sun,* June 24, 1896.

The critics were fairly hard on Jim and high on Sharkey. One writer for the *National Police Gazette* later said,

> But for Corbett's cleverness in clinching he would not have lasted a round. Sharkey uppercut him, side-wiped him, threw him down and walked on him, and made him look as cheap as possible before the big audience…. I expected to see a fight. Whenever Sharkey would make a rush Corbett would make another, to a clinch. He evidently regarded it as a hugging match. When unable to shake off the desperate man, who was clinging to him for dear life, Sharkey would simply toss him over into his corner and try another rush. Corbett repeatedly appealed to the referee, and that worthy did all he could to save the ex-champion from annihilation.[620]

The San Francisco Evening Post said that Corbett had joined the ranks of good old "has beens."

> The fast pace at which he has traveled during the past few years has sapped his vitality, and he is today a mere wreck compared to what he was…. In fact, he looked stale and weak…. Sharkey was magnificent by comparison. … Whether or not Corbett will ever regain his old form is a question. Certainly he is a poor apology for a first-class performer at present. He is clever, but has not the sprightliness of old, and is physically weak and exhausted…. For the present, however, he is out of the game, and the sooner he appreciates his humiliating condition the better. He is far from the top now, and in order to regain his lost laurels will have to go through a course of self-denial.
>
> So far as Sharkey is concerned, the path to the championship looks clear. He has only Fitzsimmons to defeat. In that "phenom," however, he will find a hard nut to crack, as all have learned who have gone against the New Zealander.[621]

Another said that Corbett's championship days were about over. "Sharkey is the coming champion of the world. If Jim ever meets Fitzsimmons, the Australian will surely win." Still another man said, "I don't think Corbett can lick that fellow [Sharkey]. … He can't keep away

---

[620] *National Police Gazette*, September 19, 1896.
[621] *San Francisco Evening Post*, June 25, 1896.

from that fellow. He is as strong as a bull and pretty lively, too. I was disappointed in Corbett, and I don't think he can lick Fitzsimmons."[622]

Most were impressed with Sharkey's durability and conditioning. One said, "[Corbett] battered like a ram, but it was hitting a stone wall." Another said,

Why that fellow would have licked Corbett if they had let him go on. He was as strong as an ox and he had blood in his eye. He actually had the best of it, and at the end Corbett was glad enough it was over. It was a rattling mill. That fellow Sharkey is a wonder.

The biggest criticism of Sharkey was that he needed to work on his skills. Corbett trainer Bill Delaney said, "Of course he is no match for Jim in science, but he held out wonderfully and proved that he could stand up to anyone in the world.... There is no bluff in him, for he is a fighter from the word go." Another paper said,

Sailor Sharkey proved himself to be a new pugilistic wonder, who, if he can be...taught to strike straight from the shoulder, will be a match for any heavy weight champion in the ring. ... Sharkey is an extraordinary man. ... He is as light on his feet as Sullivan was in his prime, but his blows are not so effective.[623]

Sharkey said that he wanted to fight Corbett either to a finish or for 10 rounds for a side bet of $10,000. If Corbett did not accept, he would take on Fitzsimmons. Corbett said that he would challenge Fitzsimmons, but if Bob did not accept, he would take on Sharkey.[624]

From England, Fitz said that he would not fight Corbett until he defeated some top boxers, which some called a ridiculous proposition and the reason why Bob had forfeited the title. Corbett and Sharkey allegedly signed articles of agreement for a fight to the finish.[625]

As of early August, according to the *London Sporting Life*, Fitzsimmons was having a run of hard luck.

[622] *San Francisco Bulletin*, June 25, 1896.
[623] *San Francisco Chronicle, San Francisco Examiner, San Francisco Bulletin, San Francisco Evening Post, New York Sun*, all June 25, 26, 1896.
[624] *San Francisco Bulletin*, June 25, 1896.
[625] *New York Clipper*, July 4, 1896.

Fitzsimmons, who concluded his two night's engagement at Birmingham, paid a visit to Wolverhampton, and held a one night's entertainment at the Exchange Hall where he gave an exhibition of punching the ball, wrestling…but so badly was the affair advertised, and so high the prices of admission, that as was fully anticipated, the affair proved a frost.

Fitz was induced to remain one more night. The prices were lowered and the show was better advertised, but despite the improvement in attendance, "it was nothing in comparison to that which assembled when John L. Sullivan visited Wolverhampton."

That evening, Fitz punched the ball, which "greatly pleased the audience, and it was acknowledged that he was by far the most brilliant ball puncher ever seen in the midlands. … The wind-up was between Dan Hickey and Fitzsimmons. After boxing three light rounds, they retired amid applause."[626]

Fitzsimmons left England, arriving back in America on August 22.

He stated that he had a most enjoyable time during his stay abroad, although it might not have been as pecuniarily profitable as he had anticipated. Bob still claims the championship and continues to insist that Corbett shall "get a reputation" before he will consent to meet him in the ring. As Jim is again the rightful champion, however, through default of Bob in accepting his challenge, as required by the rules, the Californian holds the key to the position and can afford to laugh at the Antipodean.[627]

On August 31, 1896 in New York, Tom Sharkey sparred 3 rounds with former champion John L. Sullivan. It was only a "tapping affair," but one report said that Sharkey demonstrated more science than for which he had been given credit. "He is nimble and catlike in his movements, and dances around with much agility." It also said that he was "adept at blocking and guarding against leads. His left hand may be said to be, in ring parlance, a 'corker.' He used it straight several times on Monday night and landed it easily on each occasion." Sharkey held back his right, owing to the fact that it was just a friendly exhibition. Regardless of the praise, there was still a division of opinions regarding his merits as a skillful boxer, and Tom's

[626] *New York Sun,* August 2, 1896.
[627] *New York Clipper,* August 29, 1896.

ability to counterpunch was criticized. Many New York critics felt that he was overrated.[628]

In September 1896, it was reported that even the English, who disliked Corbett, refused to accept Fitzsimmons as the legitimate champion. That report said that Fitzsimmons realized that he was not the champion in the public's opinion, and that the only way he could achieve that distinction was by fighting Corbett.[629]

The fact that reporters no longer recognized him as champion, and accused him of cowardice, probably motivated Fitzsimmons to come to the table and negotiate a fight with Corbett. Jim was probably motivated to make the match because his reputation had taken a blow from the Sharkey bout, not to mention that years of taunting back and forth between the two had made it a genuine grudge match. Both needed the fight, and it was the fight that the press as well as the sporting public most wanted to see.

The Corbett and Fitzsimmons parties met in New York on September 12, 1896. They agreed to fight to the finish for a bet of $10,000 a side, before the club offering the most money, winner take all. The match was scheduled to take place sixty days after the currently scheduled Corbett-Sharkey fight. However, if the Sharkey fight was declared off for any reason, Corbett agreed to box Fitz on or before March 1, 1897.

> [Fitz had] finally concluded that it was about time he stopped making himself appear either ridiculous or "afeard," just as people chose to look at it, by insisting upon the Californian doing something to "get a reputation" before he would agree to face him in the ring. The fact that Fitzsimmons had by his persistence in this respect, and his flat refusal to accept Corbett's challenge, forfeited the title of champion doubtless influenced him and his manager in taking this step.[630]

Because they had made this fight agreement, and the bout was not scheduled to be held at an incorporated club for a limited number of rounds, which was technically in violation of New York's recently enacted Horton law, the police arrested both men, Fitz on the 21st, and Corbett on the 23rd. The indictment charged them with conspiring to commit a crime

---

[628] *National Police Gazette*, September 12, 1896, September 19, 1896.
[629] *National Police Gazette*, September 5, 1896.
[630] *New York Clipper*, September 19, 1896. Fitz said that if he won he would not accept the *Police Gazette* diamond belt, because he did not consider it emblematic of the championship.

by assisting in arranging a prize fight. They posted bail and were released.[631] New York was sending its message that it did not want them to fight there.

Corbett had scheduled a December rematch with Sharkey in a fight to the finish for $10,000. However, after agreeing to fight Fitzsimmons, Jim pulled out of the Sharkey fight, allegedly because none of the California clubs had deposited a purse.[632] The reality was that there was plenty of money available, but that Corbett had simply used the Sharkey fight as a way to leverage Fitzsimmons into agreeing to fight him. Corbett did not really want to fight Sharkey, and he admitted that their fight had been an advertising scheme. However, this was unbeknownst to an upset Sharkey, who felt that he could defeat Corbett. One paper said that the "alleged match was a fake from its inception."[633]

However, in an interesting twist, in mid-October, Fitzsimmons showed-up Corbett by agreeing to fight Sharkey in an early December 10-round bout for $10,000, winner take all.[634] Within a week of making the match, San Francisco's National Athletic Sporting Club, promoter of the Fitzsimmons-Sharkey fight (which in June had promoted Corbett-Sharkey), deposited $5,000, half of the purse. Californians wanted to see Sharkey fight again, and if Corbett would not take him on, Fitz would.

One can speculate as to why he did this. Perhaps defeating a man who had hurt Corbett's reputation would further place Jim with the ranks of "has beens," and Bob could then further needle and taunt Corbett about needing to go out and get a reputation. Bob could make about the same amount of money for a fight with Sharkey as with Corbett, and given his dislike of Corbett, Bob was more than happy to make a lot of money against someone else and leave Jim out in the cold. It could have been Bob's way of showing up Corbett and making him look the coward for pulling out of the Sharkey match, while showing his willingness to fight Tom. Another way to look at the situation was that it was just too much money to turn down, and Fitz could earn two big paydays by taking on both Sharkey and Corbett. Bob never called off the Corbett fight, so he likely intended to fight both.

---

[631] *New York Clipper*, September 26, 1896, October 3, 1896. Although the Horton Law, signed by the governor on April 17, 1896 and effective as of September 1, 1896, legalized sparring exhibitions at incorporated clubs with a one year or greater lease or which owned the property, this only legalized limited rounds bouts for points ("sparring exhibitions"), not fights to the finish (which fell under the understood definition of an illegal prizefight). Corbett-Fitzsimmons was scheduled as a fight to the finish. NY Laws, 1896, Ch. 301, Sec. 458; *Brooklyn Daily Eagle*, August 31, 1896.

[632] *New York Clipper*, October 10, 1896.

[633] *National Police Gazette*, September 12, 1896, September 19, 1896, November 7, 1896; *New York Clipper*, October 3, 1896.

[634] *National Police Gazette*, December 6, 1896; *San Francisco Bulletin*, December 2, 1896. A San Francisco city ordinance had legalized limited-round contests.

Bob probably still intended to take on Corbett subsequent to the Sharkey match, because discussion of the Fitz-Corbett fight and its future location was ongoing, even after the Fitz-Sharkey fight was made. Even in late November, there were continued unsuccessful attempts to convince New York legal authorities to allow the Corbett bout to take place there.[635] To a certain extent, Fitzsimmons' victory over Sharkey was treated as a foregone conclusion, a mere precursor to the inevitable Corbett-Fitzsimmons championship match. However, others had something else in mind.

[635] *New York Clipper,* October 24, 31, 1896, December 5, 1896.

CHAPTER 16

The Fix

As of early November 1896, Tom Sharkey was in hard training for his upcoming early December bout against Bob Fitzsimmons. In an interview, Sharkey said that he was undefeated in 33 battles and had not stopped training or fighting for three years. "I have been training while those other people were having a good time." As of November 8, he said that he was weighing 180 ¼ pounds.

A mature Tom Sharkey

Sharkey's typical training consisted of a morning 10-mile run and a swim in the ocean. In the afternoon, he punched the bag 6 rounds, sparred Billy Smith (a former opponent) 4 rounds and George Allen 3 rounds. He then swung clubs and worked the machines. The day ended with a swim, and sometimes a 10-mile bicycle ride after dinner. Tom had run 14 miles on the 8th. "One of Sharkey's trainers was nursing a darkened eye, and the other a swollen hand that was sprained on Sharkey's face. They are even more confident than Sharkey himself that he will put up a memorable battle."[636]

"Lanky Bob" began training for the fight on November 11 in the boat-house at the Pacific Yacht Club in Sausalito, California. Fitzsimmons said, "I must knuckle down to business, as I have only three weeks in which to get ready for those awful smashes I expect to receive from the sailor champion when we meet in the ring." Bob was confident though.

---

[636] *San Francisco Call*, November 9, 1896.

I know the sailor is as strong as a lightning bull, but that don't cut any ice with me. I think I can stop him. I have had dealings with rushers during my time and I managed to stop them before they got too gay. But this sailor may be the wonder of the age for all I know. Well, we shall wait and see what kind of stuff he is made of.

That day, Fitz ran several miles in the morning. Later, he sparred 6 rounds with Dan Hickey, which "satisfied those who witnessed the set-to that 'Fitz' is as speedy as ever with his 'dukes,' and can administer an awful blow when the occasion demands a little extra force in the delivery of knockout goods." Although Hickey was a "very clever exponent of the manly art," in Bob's hands, he was "but a child." It was said that all those who came to spar with Fitzsimmons would have to take their medicine daily and would well earn their salaries. Bob's training would also consist of bag-punching, boat-rowing, and swimming.[637]

The local folks were excited about the upcoming fight.

The world has not much changed since the days of ancient Rome and Greece, when gladiators fought each other and wild beasts in the arena, and nothing but the sight of blood could bring the spectators up to the proper pitch of enthusiasm. But that was long ago. We are living in the closing years of the nineteenth century, with "reform" as our watchword and hammer and tongs as our favorite weapons for effecting reforms. But human nature remains the same and will remain the same until the end of time. [638]

As of November 19, the *San Francisco Bulletin* reported that both fighters' training was going well.

The doughty sailor is as tough as a pine knot. He fairly revels in his work, and by the vigor with which Australian Billy Smith and he slog each other in their daily six-round bout it can be seen that Sharkey will not lack for staying qualities when he faces lanky Bob in the ring. The Australian is working away as hard as ever in the Sausalito mud. He covers ten or fifteen miles daily over the hills. … [H]e punches

[637] *San Francisco Call*, November 12, 1896.
[638] *Sausalito News*, November 14, 1896.

holes in his trainers daily. He will be fit to fight for his life by December 2.[639]

On November 20, some students from the San Anselmo Theological Seminary visited Bob's training quarters. "Fitzsimmons engaged in a six round bout with one of his assistants." Bob's hard training was promising. "Fitzsimmons is doing some good work in the training line. ... [H]e has the activity and endurance necessary to make it very interesting for Mr. Sharkey."[640]

On November 22, a number of people watched Fitzsimmons punch the bag for 6 rounds and then spar 3 rounds each with Dan Hickey and Jack Stelzner. "He strikes like the sledgehammer he used to wield and he is as quick on his feet as a cat. Sharkey must move speedily if he hauls clear of those heavy lightning-like strikes." Hickey gave Bob plenty of footwork, while Stelzner "played the Sharkey trick and threw him about, or at least tried to." Afterwards, Bob had Corbett on his mind. "Corbett does not want to meet me. ... Champion fighter! He's the champion faker!"[641]

Fitzsimmons was a strong betting favorite, but it was believed that Sharkey's friends would "come to the front pretty strong on the day of the contest." Billy Jordan called Fitz a demon puncher, a terror who could whip any man on earth. However, Alec Greggains, who had sparred Fitz and fought Sharkey to a draw, said, "A whole lot of these fellows who pretend to know it all may get badly fooled in Sharkey. I am aware that Fitzsimmons is a hard man to whip, but I think he will find that Sharkey is the hardest game he has ever tackled." Another man said, "This fellow Sharkey is as strong as a bull, and although he may not be a polished fighter, he has a style of his own that will puzzle any man. They say he can't hit; but you will find that he hits hard and strong enough to put most fighters to sleep."[642]

On November 25, 1896 in Sausalito, the captains of four sailing ships, Captains McKinnon, Richardson, Moulton, and Pritchard, took on Fitzsimmons. After Bob hit the punching bag for a while, McKinnon said that a little sparring with Bob would do them good. Bob suggested that they play a game of "one down and the other come on." Basically, this meant that as soon as Bob knocked one down, another man would step up and take his place. Bob gave them 2- or 3-ounce gloves.

[639] *San Francisco Bulletin*, November 19, 1896.
[640] *Sausalito News*, November 21, 1896.
[641] *San Francisco Call*, November 21, 23, 1896; *San Francisco Bulletin*, November 23, 1896.
[642] *San Francisco Call*, November 25, 1896.

The captains were a bit nervous at first, but McKinnon kept his friends' spirits up by saying, "Why, we will do up this big fellow in less than five minutes, boys; he can't possibly hurt us much at this game."

> The captains banged away with right and left and Fitz received many hard cuffs on body and neck, but he was dropping his opponents in quick order and the contest was short and spirited and according to Mons. Julian's chronometer the battle lasted 3 ¼ minutes, when the last of the sea-faring Mohicans cried "Enough, McDuff; we came and saw, but you have conquered."

> McKinnon was the last man to face the great fighter, but when his left arm fell by his side paralyzed from a blow he acknowledged defeat. Captains Richardson, Moulton and Pritchard are now nursing many wounds.[643]

In speaking of his solid preparation for the upcoming fight, Bob said, "Corbett, Greggains and Choyński held Sharkey too cheap, and the result was that they virtually were bested when they met him. I know I have a hard game on hand."[644]

Less than a week before the fight, Bob was a 3 to 1 favorite based on his previous results against top fighters, but some felt that such odds were unfair to Sharkey. Many were impressed with Tom's ability to take heavy punishment and then to return "like a roaring lion for more medicine." The question was whether Bob could hit Tom hard enough to stop his rushes.

Fitz said that he was well aware that Sharkey would charge like a bull with his head down. However, he was prepared.

> I understand that he will hold his left arm in such a manner as to protect his chin and the right will be used as a weapon for administering punishment. This is all well and good…but you can bet dollars to doughnuts that I will bring that left arm down the first smash I give the champion sailor in the short ribs. Then you will see how he will hold his chin, the point of which I will touch gently; yes, gently enough to satisfy Sharkey that he was never born to become a champion pugilist.[645]

---

[643] *San Francisco Call*, November 26, 1896.
[644] *San Francisco Evening Post*, November 27, 1896.
[645] *San Francisco Call*, November 28, 1896.

Jim Corbett said that Fitzsimmons should whip Sharkey in short order unless Tom used his wrestling tactics.

When Sharkey was told that the betting odds were steadily rising in Bob's favor, he said that he hoped they would go to 10 to 1. When asked why, the confident Sharkey said, "My pals'll make all the more money." Tom admitted that he had never seen Fitzsimmons fight.

Sharkey at first did not want to allow a doctor named Lustig to examine him, but National Club managers Groom and Gibbs told him it was all right, and he relented. Dr. Lustig examined both boxers and found them to be in fine condition.[646]

Fitzsimmons finished hard training on the 29th. He did his usual long run, punched the bag, and sparred his trainers, working them over harder than on previous occasions. Fitz said that he expected to gain five to ten pounds over the next few days, as he would only be doing light exercise, hoping to enter the ring at about 172 pounds.[647]

As of November 30, Fitz was still a 3 to 1 betting favorite. Sharkey said that the public had always been wrong about him. Billy Smith was a 10 to 5 favorite over him, Greggains was 3 to 1, Choynski was 4 to 1, "and it was a case of make out your ticket when I went against Corbett. Yet, in spite of the odds, I won every one of those fights. Some of the decisions I was swindled out of, but that makes little difference, as the public knows I had the best of the engagements."[648]

The day before the fight, Fitz spoke about his plan of attack.

> Sharkey is a strong, aggressive fighter, but I do not think I will have any trouble in disposing of him, as I am in condition to go a long route. As I understand it, Choynski, Corbett and Greggains found no difficulty in landing on Sharkey. ... I have studied Sharkey's style of fighting and believe that I will be able to stop him with straight lefts as he plunges at me, as I hear he intends to do. If he takes the aggressive in the fight that will suit me exactly, as it will give me an opportunity to get in such a blow as I used on Peter Maher in the fight in Mexico. If on the other hand he does not force the pace, I will hurry the fight myself, as I have made up my mind to win in from one to five rounds.

---

[646] *San Francisco Bulletin, San Francisco Call,* November 30, 1896.
[647] *San Francisco Call,* November 30, 1896.
[648] *San Francisco Evening Post,* December 1, 1896.

Sharkey said that his strong suit was aggressiveness, that at long range he would be a mark for Fitz. He planned to rush in and fight at close quarters, to win through his strength and stamina. "I have got to get inside Fitz's guard and I must do it quick, as it will be dangerous to stand off and allow him to jab me while I, with my short arms, would be unable to counter effectively." Sharkey said that he had no doubt that he would win and that both he and his manager Dan Lynch had bet every dollar they had on the result, which, as it would turn out, was a very interesting fact indeed.

The interest in the fight was immense. As of the day before the fight, over $20,000 had been taken in for seats at the Mechanics' Pavilion. The "fight has for the time being taken possession of San Francisco. Nothing else is thought of or talked about."[649]

It is an understatement to say that the selection and decision of the referee became one of the most controversial aspects of the fight. Therefore, many of the facts surrounding his selection are interesting. Almost a month before the fight, it was noted that "in case the principals are unable to mutually agree upon the referee, the club will name that official."[650] As the fight approached, there had been no agreement as to whom the referee would be.

On November 27, Martin Julian met with Sharkey manager Dan Lynch to discuss who would referee. Lynch said that he would not hurry in his choice and "announced his intention of holding off until the last moment, Wednesday next at noon, when, if a referee is not chosen, the National Athletic Club will take the matter out of their hands. Finally Julian promised to draw up a list of competent men."[651]

As it turned out, all the way up to the day before the fight, despite the suggestions of several prominent sporting men, Lynch would not agree on a referee. "There has been a great deal of quibbling over the selection of a referee."[652] Lynch had expressed no preference for a referee, but simply rejected all those named by Fitz's side. Instead of finding a mutually agreeable referee, Lynch seemed to want the club to decide, which decision would bind both parties. It was reported that the referee may be a surprise, that the club managers were holding someone in reserve to referee the fight.

When Julian put forth Hiram Cook's name, Lynch said, "He won't do for us." When asked why, he offered no legitimate reason, but simply said, "No matter; he won't do." Julian suggested boxing writer Bill Naughton, but Lynch rejected him too. Julian said,

[649] *San Francisco Evening Post*, December 2, 1896.
[650] *New York Clipper*, November 14, 1896.
[651] *San Francisco Bulletin*, November 28, 1896.
[652] *San Francisco Examiner*, December 1, 1896; *San Francisco Evening Post*, December 2, 1896.

Lynch would not listen. He would not state his objections, but merely declined all my nominations. It was very unsportsmanlike of him. It looks to me as if he wanted the club to choose the referee. I will state right here that unless he is a man who knows his business Fitz will not go into the ring.

Why did Lynch obviously want to leave the referee selection up to the club managers?

Lynch later admitted that Hiram Cook had shown himself to be an honest and capable referee, but claimed that he simply did not want him because those who Lynch thought were enemies plugged Cook as the best referee.

Julian opined,

I think Sharkey and his backer have acted very peculiarly. At every point they have raised all possible objections to all fair and square propositions regarding the selection of a referee. They have refused Hiram Cook positively and, in fact, have objected strenuously to talking on the referee question. …

I do not want the club to select the referee if I can possibly help it. We are not particular about the referee so long as he understands the rules and has a reputation to lose by making a bad decision.

Julian also said,

The whole thing is a farce. When Sharkey was making his arrangements to fight Corbett he proposed the name of Hiram Cook and Corbett objected. Now, when I propose the name of Cook, Sharkey himself objects. I am not going to accept any Tom, Dick or Harry that nobody has ever heard of before…. We don't want any the best of it, but we are not going to have the fight handled by a man who doesn't know what a foul is when he sees one.

These were prophetic words.

Lynch only proposed a couple men to referee, later claiming that his team simply did not know many referees, which was preposterous. One of the men he put forth was inexperienced as a referee and unanimously thought of as much too small to handle the large men, particularly one like Sharkey. Another man Lynch mentioned was a gambler who knew about horses, but not boxing. As Lynch was a gambler who raced horses, the suggestion seemed less than neutral.

Name after name was submitted, but somehow no one was satisfactory to both. Lynch seemed to be the harder to please. He was chary about naming candidates, but was not loth in rejecting Julian's selections. Judging by the tenor of his remarks, he was glad to leave the matter to the club.

Despite Bob's favored betting odds status, the night before the fight, there was strong betting on Sharkey. Oddly enough, the day of the fight, the *San Francisco Bulletin* reported that an anonymous correspondent had informed it that the police were instructed to protect the interests of their superior, Police Commissioner Mose Gunst, who had allegedly bet on Fitzsimmons. They were to step in and stop the fight before the final round if it appeared that Sharkey would win. However, Gunst claimed that he had not bet a cent on the fight, not believing in doing so for limited-round contests. Was this rumor designed to make Sharkey an even bigger underdog?[653]

On the afternoon of December 2, 1896, the day of the fight, the National Athletic Club announced that it had chosen Wyatt Earp to be the referee, and that no one else would referee. Who was Wyatt Earp? Earp was a famous marshal, frontiersman, gunfighter, and gambler. He had fought alongside Doc Holliday in an 1879 gunfight. He apparently participated in the 1881 Gunfight at the OK Corral. He owned racehorses, a saloon, and a gambling hall, and was an occasional boxing referee. Gambling and boxing seemed to go hand in hand, but gamblers did not usually make the best referees.

Earp had never refereed a big fight. His claim to fame was his handiwork with a gun. One paper said that in the opinion of some of those with whom he had come into contact, Earp was a "bad man." "He has not heretofore been especially prominent in connection with 'peaceful' glove contests, though of his ability to assert himself in conflicts of another character there seems no good reason for holding doubt."[654]

Knowing little about him, Fitz manager Martin Julian was initially willing to accept Earp. However, according to Julian, that position changed on the evening of the fight, when "several Eastern and local sporting men

[653] *San Francisco Chronicle, San Francisco Call, San Francisco Bulletin*, all December 2, 1896.
[654] *San Francisco Evening Post*, December 2, 1896; *San Francisco Chronicle*, December 3, 1896.

came to me and stated positively that they had been informed that the 'referee was fixed,' and that we would not be allowed to win."

On the night of the fight, there was a massive crowd of 15,000 at the Mechanics' Pavilion. At 10:09 p.m., wearing a bathrobe, Fitz climbed into the ring with his seconds - manager Martin Julian and sparring partners Dan Hickey and Jack Stelzner. Fitz shook hands with Major Frank McLaughlin. Police Captain Wittman examined two pairs of gloves and threw them to the ring center.

Four minutes later, Sharkey entered the ring, also wearing a robe. Manager Dan Lynch and trainers Danny Needham, Australian Billy Smith, and George Allen accompanied Tom. Sharkey received greater applause upon his entry than did Fitzsimmons. Bob walked over and shook hands with Tom. Fitz then walked back to his own corner and laughed as he was speaking with his seconds.

Fitzsimmons weighed in at 173 ½ pounds to Sharkey's 182 pounds. One report said that Fitz weighed 172, and according to Sharkey's trainers, Tom was 175. The day before the fight, the newspapers listed both as weighing 172 pounds. Sharkey said that he was 23 years old. Fitzsimmons was 33 years of age. Bob was listed as standing 5'11 ½" to Tom's 5'8 ½". They fought in a regulation 24-foot ring, elevated three feet from the floor.

In the ring, Julian strenuously objected to Earp on the grounds that Wyatt was fixed to award the fight to Sharkey. "I have been informed by responsible gentlemen that the referee selected by the club has been fixed in the interest of Sharkey." Julian said that he would accept any referee in the house except Earp. "Take anybody in the house, we don't care whom; but spare us from Earp."

The articles of agreement stated that if the men could not agree on a referee, the club would decide, so Julian and Fitz were not in the best of positions. The club insisted on Earp. Why did the club insist on Earp even when Julian had so strenuously objected to him based on tips that the referee had been fixed? Was the club in on something?

At 10:16 p.m., Billy Jordan announced Tom Sharkey as the pride of the American navy and the champion of the Pacific Coast. Tom wore green tights with the American flag as a belt. Jordan announced Fitzsimmons as the champion of the world. The crowd cheered both men, though Tom had the better of it.

Jordan then called for Wyatt Earp, several times. What took him so long to enter the ring? Was Earp hesitant to referee, or was he delayed by something? Earp finally came forward and entered the ring. Police Captain Wittman talked with him for a few moments. Earp had illegally carried a revolver into the arena, and Wittman ordered him to hand it over.

A young Tom Sharkey

Jordan announced that the club had selected Wyatt Earp as referee. Some cheered and some hissed. Jordan continued, "But owing to remarks that are going around that there is something crooked about Earp, which Julian has heard, he refuses to accept Mr. Earp as referee." The crowd yelled and hissed.

Julian then announced to the crowd that he had offered the names of several prominent men, but that Dan Lynch, without giving reasons, had objected to every name. The club selected Earp, who was initially satisfactory, "but since 6:30 o'clock this evening several sporting men belonging to San Francisco have come and told us that the referee is fixed." As Julian was speaking, "Earp hung his head during the speech." Someone in the crowd asked Julian to name the men who had provided the information.

Dan Lynch then stepped up and said that Sharkey had always lived up to the articles of agreement for his fights, and was ready and willing to fight with the referee the club had selected. The crowd's deafening yells of approval followed for a couple of minutes. They wanted to see a fight. Jordan then announced, "Mr. Julian is willing to select any referee in the house." Some yelled for Earp. When Hiram Cook was mentioned as someone whom Julian would accept, some chanted for Cook. Lynch stuck to his guns that Earp should referee, as did the National Club. Unfortunately, the crowd was unsympathetic to Fitz. The debate led to a fifteen-minute delay, which caused the waiting crowd to jeer.

Fitz then went to ring center, raised his hand to ask for silence, and announced to the crowd that he would give in. He said that he had given in to Sharkey on all other points, and might as well surrender on this one, too. "I have given in in all my fights, and I will give in in this one." The crowd cheered. However, he insisted that Sharkey remove his hand bandages. Bob was not wearing any. The crowd cried, "Take them off, Sharkey." Tom assented.

Jordan announced that Fitz had accepted the referee, and that the fight was scheduled for 10 rounds, with the decision to be awarded to the man having the best of the contest. The club representatives handed Referee Earp the $10,000 check representing the prize money, which he was to hold for the winner.[655]

At ring center, Fitz "put his hands on Sharkey's shoulder, evidently illustrating a break-away." Jordan then announced, "The men have agreed in a clinch to break away fair and square and not do any fighting." The gong sounded for the 1st round at 10:46 p.m.

The round by round account is taken from the following newspaper reports: *San Francisco Call* (Call)(as provided by Professor Walter Watson), *San Francisco Chronicle* (SFC), *San Francisco Examiner* (SFE), *San Francisco Evening Post* (EP), and the *New York Clipper* (NYC).

1st round

At first, Sharkey pursued careful tactics and tried to fight at long range. Sharkey seemed a little nervous and jumped away at Fitz's feints. They feinted, moved in and exchanged some blows, clinched, stepped back and repeated.

---

[655] *San Francisco Chronicle*, December 3, 1896.

[Fitzsimmons was] cautious and shifty, feinting continually with his left and looking for a chance to land a hot right.... Sharkey showed immediately that he was astonishingly spry on his feet.... He also immediately displayed a very creditable ability to duck right-handed cross-counters.

Fitz forced the pace and threw his punches straight from the shoulder, while Sharkey responded with right and left swings. Sharkey ducked incessantly and mostly went for the body. Tom hit Bob on a breakaway and the crowd hissed. When Bob complained to the referee, Tom apologized.

After a number of leads and counters by both, Fitzsimmons dropped Sharkey, some saying twice, others saying just once:

Call: Fitzsimmons floored Sharkey. He rose in a groggy state, and Bob immediately floored him again. After Tom got up, Bob missed a left and the gong sounded. Sharkey went to his corner groggy, while Fitz was very cool.

SFE: Fitz dropped Sharkey twice in the 1st round with rights.

EP: "Just as time was called Bob drove in his right and sent Tom to the floor, but the blow did no material damage."

SFC: One writer said that after Sharkey threw himself off balance with a swinging punch that spun him around, Bob landed a right to the arm that brought him to the floor. Another writer said that Sharkey was knocked down with a back-handed left. And still another said that a light left from Fitz steadied Sharkey, and then a short straight jolt from the shoulder to the jaw dropped him. Like the *Call* and *Examiner*, this writer mentioned a second knockdown, saying that a left hook dropped him as well. Bob forced matters in close more, landing a hard right to the jaw.

2nd round

Fitzsimmons was even more confident in this round.

While more vicious in his attacks he was cooler, more systematic and scientific and had evidently gauged his man. He smiled grimly as he pressed the fight like a consummate general and kept the left and right in such rapid proximity to the sailor's jaws that it was only by the liveliest leg work and the most vigorous ducking that he escaped a stunner on the chin.

Tom improved in his defense, but his blows were generally wild or ineffective. When Bob landed, the punches only served to stimulate Sharkey to greater effort. Although the pace was brisk, Fitz slowed a bit. Tom came forward and attacked the body, but without any noticeable effect. The crowd usually cheered when Tom landed.

They would exchange, Sharkey would rush into a clinch, and occasionally try to hit on the break or push Bob's head back, to the crowd's hisses. Fitz would protest "unavailingly to the referee."

Sharkey backed away, with Fitz following and forcing the fighting. Bob forced Tom to the ropes and they clinched. Bob blocked some punches, and then again forced Tom around the ring. Sharkey swung wildly and they clinched. Fitz landed a right to the head and Sharkey responded with a punch to the breast as the gong sounded. Fitz went to his corner laughing.

3rd round

As he did before the previous round, Fitz rose several seconds prior to the gong. Bob feinted and fiddled, forcing Tom around the ring. Sharkey rushed in to a clinch. They exchanged some blows. After another clinch, Sharkey hit Bob on the break and the crowd hissed. Fitz laughed. The shorter Sharkey swung in a circular fashion and there were a number of exchanges.

Sharkey kept at the body and struck Bob "rather low." Fitz "shook his head and motioned to the referee as if he intended to call attention to a foul." Bob told Tom to be careful. Subsequently, the "men continued to fight in wild fashion in the center of the ring."

In the clinches, Sharkey grabbed Fitz around the hips and sometimes even around the knees. The crowd jeered these tactics. "Sharkey is putting up his usual rough and tumble fight, but has not so far landed a blow fair." Nevertheless, the crowd cheered Sharkey during the one minute rest.

4th round

There was some disagreement regarding whether Sharkey dropped Fitzsimmons in this round.

Call: "Sharkey stepped up more confident and briskly. He landed left and right on body and knocks Fitz down with a left-hand blow on the body. The crowed yelled as if it were mad. Fitz got up quickly and went at Sharkey wickedly."

SFC: One writer said that Sharkey floored Fitz with a right to the jaw, while another said that Sharkey dropped Fitzsimmons with a left. Still another writer disagreed with the other two accounts, saying that Fitz slipped to the floor when trying to avoid a left, and that many had incorrectly thought he was knocked down.

SFE: It agreed that Fitz was not knocked down, but slipped down.

NYC: Its dispatch reported that Fitz slipped and fell.

In an interview later that month, Bob claimed that he had slipped. "Why, Sharkey was not within three feet of me when I fell, and what's more, I slipped, do you understand, and was not hit at all. Why, he never hit me hard enough at any stage of the game to hurt me. It's absurd."[656]

After Bob rose, Tom focused on the body. Sharkey rushed him to the ropes and tried to hit him, but Bob jumped away laughing. Fitz began forcing Sharkey about the ring. Both hit the body. In the clinches, Sharkey was hitting while holding and Fitz's lips moved as if complaining.

There were some intense mix-ups and wild infighting, during which a Fitz right to the eye drew blood. A straight left opened up Tom's cheek, while Bob's ducking abilities saved him from punishment.

Another account said that Sharkey became very groggy, the blood flowing down his face, partially from his nose. Some cried, "Put him out, Fitz!" A Fitzsimmons right to the cheek raised a lump around Tom's left eye. Sharkey hit the body and threw Bob into a corner, where he continued hitting the stomach. After a clinch and breakaway, the bell sounded.

5th round

During the intermission, the crowd cheered louder than ever because Sharkey had lasted 4 rounds, which was one of the betting points.

In a clinch, Sharkey grabbed Fitz by the legs, lifted him up, and then dropped him. The crowd hissed and yelled "Foul." Blood streamed down Tom's face. On another Sharkey duck, Tom grabbed Bob's legs, again to the crowd's hisses. Tom might have hit a bit low as well. "The round was marked by considerable foul play from Sharkey." Fitz landed a good right to the jaw. Sharkey hit in a clinch and the crowd hissed him. "Sharkey was fighting rotten, but Earp was blind."

One account said that the crowd hissed Bob for going down voluntarily to dodge a blow. Another account said he slipped down to avoid

---

[656] *Rocky Mountain News*, December 27, 1896.

punishment when hit in a clinch. A third account said that Sharkey wrestled Fitz to the floor.

After rising, Fitzsimmons once again dropped Sharkey, each local account giving its twist:

Call: Fitz landed a hook and an effective left and right. A right made Sharkey grow very groggy. "Fitz hits him twice with his left in Sharkey's corner and Sharkey goes through the ropes to the floor."

SFC: Bob hit Tom with, a left and right to the jaw, knocking Sharkey through the ropes. The other *Chronicle* writer said that Bob knocked him to the floor with a right and left swing. Yet another said that a left and right hurt Sharkey and a left swing sent him under the ropes.

SFE: After beating Sharkey back with several lefts and rights, Bob sent him under the ropes with a left up-swing or hook.

EP: This was a disastrous round for Sharkey. A right to the chin sent Tom down.

The downed Sharkey was close to the edge of the platform and it looked like he might fall off. Bob in sportsmanlike fashion reached out and pulled him back into the ring. Tom clumsily staggered to his feet and was unsteady when he rose. Fitz went at him, but Tom clinched at every opportunity. As in prior rounds, the crowd hooted Sharkey for grabbing around the waist. Tom showed his wonderful recuperative powers and struggled on, sending in straight lefts to the body.

However, Bob landed a straight left and two left uppercuts, which had Tom going. Sharkey was "badly punished." Fitz drew blood, "taking the skin off Sharkey's left eye by sending in a brushing left hook." "The remainder of the round was a disastrous one for the mariner, and nothing but the gong saved him."

Sharkey staggered to his corner. He looked tired. Fitz was cool and laughing. It seemed that Bob had Tom sized up and would win. Fitzsimmons had the best of the encounter up to this point.

6th round

Sharkey was "outboxed completely" in the round. They exchanged, with Bob landing more often and effectively. Fitz forced Sharkey around the ring and hit him, but Tom took the blows and fought back. However, Sharkey also clinched often and would hit in the clinches, "contrary to agreement," which caused the crowd to hiss him. In between clinches and Sharkey fouls, Fitz would nail him.

Bob landed some hard rights over the heart and one on the jaw. When hurt, Tom again grabbed Bob around the hips. Sharkey also shoved Bob's head back and Fitz laughed. The crowd hissed Tom's actions. Bob began landing straight lefts at long range without being countered. Sharkey caught him by the leg and it looked for a moment as if he was about to throw Bob over his head. "Fitz lands right and left four or five times on Sharkey's face. Fitz lands left hook and Sharkey tries to trip him. Crowd hisses."

Sharkey was tired at the end of the round. His cheek was cut badly and his nose bleeding.

7th round

Sharkey came up slowly. Fitz landed a vicious swing to the head and they clinched. After a series of exchanges, on three separate occasions Sharkey hit on the breakaway, to the crowd's hisses. After another clinch, Sharkey ducked and grabbed Bob's legs. Fitz laughed.

Fitzsimmons was landing body blows, rights, and left uppercuts. Regardless of the pounding, Sharkey was persistent in this round, going at Fitz, although he was not able to land effectively. He seemed to hurt Bob worse in the clinches by the hustling he gave him than by any punch. Sharkey would not let go in the clinch and was "fighting foul," holding and hitting, which occurred more often at this point, and even pushing Bob's head back, all of which brought hisses from the crowd. Martin Julian admonished the referee regarding Sharkey's foul tactics, and Earp warned Tom. One said that Sharkey should have lost the fight on fouls "at least a dozen times."

Sharkey kept boring in, attempting to tire Bob out. Fitz was unable to keep Sharkey off of him. "Sharkey was looking badly at the end of this round, very serious and bleeding badly from a cut over the eye. Fitz looked a little tired, but smiling and confident."

8th round

Call: Sharkey was slow to rise. Fitz was "very chipper and dancing around." Bob landed a very hard straight left on the nose. After a right hit Sharkey, he held very tightly, while Bob laughed. Fitz landed a right to the body and they clinched, with Sharkey pushing his head back on the break, to the hisses. They engaged in some sparring. As Walter Watson told it,

Fitz forcing the fighting and uppercuts Sharkey. Lands straight right on chin and left swing on jaw. Uppercuts Sharkey, who is against the ropes, with his left and lands right on jaw and left on body. Sharkey falls to the floor, half rises, and then falls back again and is motionless. The noise of the crowd is deafening. Sharkey lies perfectly still on the floor and Danny Needham jumps on the platform and yells "Foul," and the referee holds up his hand and points to Sharkey. ...

It was not until after Sharkey had been carried out of the ring that the decision of the referee was made known to the great number of people, for Wyatt Earp remained only long enough to announce his decision to those in and immediately about the ring. He then with the utmost speed made his way off the raised platform which constituted the ring, out of the building and beyond the reach of the crowd.

Fitz paced about like a caged wild beast. He raised his hands above his head and shouted, "The referee has given the fight to Sharkey on a foul. It is nothing but a robbery." The audience's amazement was so great that they were silent for a few seconds. Then there were "shouts of investigation." Most were quite surprised to learn that Fitz had been disqualified.

In an interview, Bob said,

> He fouled me every time in the breakaway and several times tried to throw me by wrestling. Once he tried to throw me over his head. I never fought fairer in my life. ... I never struck a cleaner knockout blow in all my life. ...
>
> I feinted with my right for his jaw, then swung my body toward the left and with a left-hand shift landed square on his stomach and he went down. I noticed that when he fell he instinctively placed his hands over his stomach, then quickly shifted them to the groin. ...
>
> The whole plan was fixed up in advance, and Sharkey was coached just how to act in case he got knocked out so as to give the referee an excuse to give him the fight on a foul.

SFC: Its version of the 8th round said that after a hot rally in the center of the ring, "the sailor, who had previously caught it in the jaw with both hands, went down. It looked as if in the rally Fitzsimmons had hooked him on the chin, though it was impossible to tell from the reporters' position exactly how it occurred." Sharkey rolled over and grabbed his groin with an expression of intense pain. The referee decided that Fitz had hit him with a low blow and disqualified Bob, awarding the fight to Sharkey. Sharkey remained motionless on the ground, until he was eventually carried from the ring. "To a disinterested observer from the press stand the first impression last evening was that Sharkey had been stunned by an uppercut, for he had been already rattled by a couple of stiff blows on the jaw."

Another *Chronicle* writer noted that although he was game,

> [Sharkey fought] with an unfairness that earned him many a chorus of hisses…. It seemed as if he could not help fouling. Not once but a dozen times he wrestled the Australian, butted him with his shoulders and grasped his legs as he tried to hurl him over his head. None of these things was apparent to the referee, and the police pulled Julian down as often as he tried to mount the platform for a protest.

As for Fitzsimmons, "if there was any intentional fouling on his part the crowd did not know it until afterward." As of the 8th round,

> Sharkey seemed to be on his feet only by virtue of his remarkably sturdy legs and long-suffering body. His lips were swollen and bleeding, from his nose the blood trickled, and his left eye was cut, bruised and almost closed. He looked desperate and beaten, while Fitzsimmons showed not a mark of the conflict.

This writer believed that Fitzsimmons legally dropped him with a savage uppercut. Of the disqualification, some yelled, "Fraud! Job! Robbery!"

Another said of the knockout, "Sharkey walks right up to Fitz and smashes him flush on the face. Fitz comes back and knocks Sharkey cold with right and left uppercuts."

Still another said that Fitz began with stiff lefts and rights that staggered Sharkey. Tom tried to make a stand, but his blows lacked force. Tom grabbed around the waist, and the referee experienced some trouble breaking them. Sharkey staggered to the center of the ring dazed.

> Fitz stepped forward quietly close to Sharkey, and, guarding with his right, hooked his left in the pit of the sailor's stomach. He repeated the operation without moving. Sharkey's body swayed and he seemed about to fall. Fitz then stepped back a couple of feet and with a seeming rush landed a terrific punch, which apparently landed full on the pit of Sharkey's stomach. At the same time and apparently with

the same movement his right shot up and landed on the point of the sailor's falling chin, and the latter fell to the floor.

SFE: Its writer, W.W. Naughton, said that Fitz was "fast beating the sailor down." Of the knockout, he said,

> I saw a whizzing left hook go up somewhere from about Fitzsimmons' hip. It caught Sharkey on the chin or mouth and the sailor began to sink. Then I saw Fitzsimmons' right elbow come back and he delivered a body punch. I should imagine it took effect somewhere about Sharkey's stomach or short ribs on the left side. Anyhow, the next moment Sharkey was on the floor on his back.

Another description by him said that a right rocked Tom, then when Sharkey seemed to be falling, Fitz whipped up his left, connected with the chin, and then followed with the right to the body, and Sharkey went down.

Naughton noted that Fitz had fought cleanly and that Sharkey had "ignored ring etiquette entirely and commenced to strike foul blows just as soon as he began to feel the gaff." He observed Sharkey's grabbing around the hips and legs, and noted Bob's complaints to the referee. Despite all of this, Fitz had helped Tom to his feet after he had knocked Sharkey down under the ropes.

Naughton did not see any foul blow, but could not definitively say that it was not foul. He thought it would be odd though for Bob to foul when he had matters well in hand. However, he did note that many said that they had seen the foul. Some said they thought Fitz had struck him low with his knee. Others said that Sharkey had tricked the referee.

Another *Examiner* writer said that he did not see any foul blow. He saw Fitz uppercut him twice, landing on the neck and chin. This writer noted that Fitz had initially lost the sympathy of the crowd by objecting to the referee. However, that changed when the crowd saw that Sharkey was a foul fighter, grabbing the legs and striking in the clinches. Fitz clearly had the better of the fight and had fought cleanly throughout. Thus, his disqualification was ironic, given that it was against "one of the foulest fighters that ever donned the gloves." This writer criticized Earp for acting as referee after an objection to him was made "on a very fishy turn in the betting."

EP: Its version of the 8th round said that Fitz started to hurry matters.

A few lefts and rights made Sharkey groggy, and as the latter was leaning over from the effect of the blows the Australian landed a left hand uppercut which landed on the body. ... After it was delivered Sharkey straightened up, reeled half-way around, then fell flat on this back near his own corner, with his gloved hands over his groin and his features writhing from intense pain.

There was no simulation in his action. Everything was genuine. Danny Needham immediately entered a claim of foul, but he had no need of such action, as the referee had observed what he claims was a foul blow and had declared Sharkey the winner.

Summarizing the fight, it said,

The result was certainly a false one, as Fitzsimmons displayed superiority, and could not have lost were it not for the claim of foul. At the same time he did not put up the bold, dashing fight expected. He appeared over cautious, and was somewhat slower on his feet than when first seen here in his battle with Billy McCarthy.

On the other hand, Sharkey showed improvement and while he lacked punishing powers and his blows were ineffective, he recuperated so quickly and took punishment so greedily as to demonstrate that he is probably about the hardest man to knock out in the ring today. In the mill last night he adopted foul tactics and on numerous occasions in clinches grabbed Fitz below the belt. He also fought when breaking after having agreed not to. On the whole he put up an unfair fight, and it seems wrong that he should triumph through an unintentional foul.

NYC: As of the 8th, round, "Sharkey was doing nothing but wrestling." A left hook knocked out Sharkey.

It was clearly an unfair decision, as the knock out blow was a fair punch in the jaw. The crowd became boisterous, and cursed Earp loud and long. The unanimous sentiment was that Fitzsimmons had been robbed in the most cold blooded manner. ... The general opinion was that Fitz made a great fight. He never struck a foul blow, and throughout the fight he did what Corbett failed to do – he kept off the mad rushes of Sharkey, and was not injured by a single blow. It was a superb exhibition of the power of a scientific pugilist to render null and void all the brute strength of an unusually powerful man. The knockout blows were right and left upper cuts following straight lefts and rights in the face.[657]

The San Francisco Bulletin said that opinions widely differed in a most remarkable degree regarding what observers saw, "or, rather, what they thought they saw." It believed Sharkey had been fouled because he was rolling around in agony.

Sharkey told the *Bulletin* that an uppercut took him in the groin. "I fell in a faint, and that is all I remember until they brought me to the hotel." Of course, loss of consciousness is not typical for someone struck in the groin, or even the body. Perhaps a head shot had concussed him. However, Sharkey later insisted that he was not hurt by a head punch. So, how is it that he could not remember anything after the alleged low blow?

Although even those who believed that the blow was low almost unanimously agreed that it was accidental, referee Earp said, "It was the most deliberate foul I ever saw struck." Earp said that he was not surprised at the many complaints regarding his ruling, because it was the same way at the racetrack when a favorite lost money for those who had bet on it. "Won't a roar go up to the clouds, especially if the judges disqualify the favorite for fouling?"

Regardless of the outcome, another *Bulletin* writer felt that Fitzsimmons had shown himself immeasurably superior to Sharkey, and that the end would come at any moment. Sharkey had lost his temper from the beginning, and tried to wrestle at every opportunity. "Fitzsimmons played with the sailor from start to finish. Sharkey fouled him frequently, but the Cornishman never lost his temper." Sharkey made some clever ducks and counters, but mostly only landed on the neck. He generally was outclassed, and the gong twice saved Tom.

In the 8th round, Sharkey was bleeding, tired, groggy, and reeling back to the ropes. Although it looked as if no finishing blow was necessary after a vicious uppercut landed, Fitz followed up with "what looked like a straight drive in the stomach." Sharkey had technically won, but "Fitz added to, rather than lost, his reputation. He made an infinitely better showing against Sharkey than did Jim Corbett." Sharkey was branded as a rough, foul fighter.

The San Francisco Evening Post reported that the majority who witnessed the battle declared that Fitz was robbed of the decision. Earp was "scored unmercifully in sporting circles."

---

[657] *San Francisco Chronicle, San Francisco Examiner*, December 3, 1896; *New York Clipper*, December 12, 1896.

When objection was made to him by Julian he should, out of respect to himself, have refused to serve. The fact that he hung about the ring and almost insisted on acting, against the objections of Fitzsimmons, gives the part he took in the fight a suspicious look.

The change in the betting is the point upon which Fitz's friends base their cries of fraud. At the racetrack bookmakers early in the week laid 10 to 4 against Sharkey. ... Yesterday a change suddenly took place, and offers of $500 to $1000 were made that Sharkey would win. Riley Grannan thought it a good thing, and played $1300 at the above quotations. ...

Later in the day Sharkey money became so plentiful that Grannan became suspicious and when he came to town he called on Fitz and advised him not to accept Earp as referee.

M.A. Gunst and Major McLaughlin were at the track and became convinced that something was wrong, their suspicions being based on the changes in the gambling. They also warned the Australian.

It felt that Earp, as a matter of delicacy, should have declined to referee the bout after charges were lodged against him. Still, it was not so sure that Earp was not fair. "There is no doubt that [Sharkey] committed many fouls by fighting in clinches and in the break-aways, but they did not harm, and for that reason were overlooked by the referee. It is feared that the unsatisfactory result of the mill will injure boxing as a sport in this city."[658]

Fitzsimmons confirmed that the articles of agreement stated that if neither side could agree upon on a referee, the club would select one, so he was stuck with its selection of Earp. "I suspected when Sharkey's people refused to agree to any of the men that I named that something was wrong.... During all that time we couldn't get the other side to name anybody but a few unknown sporting men who couldn't get anybody to vouch for them."

The Chronicle noted that Lynch had systematically objected to every name submitted by Julian for the referee position, even though those named had the confidence of the sporting fraternity. Lynch acted as if he wanted the club to select the referee. Had the club made an error in judgment, or were they in on a sinister plan?

Explaining why he fought at all, Fitzsimmons said, "I knew I was going to be robbed before I entered the ring.... But what else could I do? If I had refused to fight the whole country would have said that I was afraid to meet the man who nearly put Corbett out." The crowd had been jeering for

[658] San Francisco Evening Post, December 3, 1896.

the fight to begin, and appearances were against Fitz, so he felt pressured to go forward despite his reservations. "I have always fought fairly...and I made no exception tonight. I never struck a foul blow in my life."

Describing the fight, Fitzsimmons said,

> I knocked him down twice in the first round for fun, and just played with him through the rest of the fight. He fouled me at every clinch. I appealed eight times.... In the fifth round Sharkey clinched and caught me round the hips. The referee deliberately stuck his fingers in my face, cutting my eyelid with his nails, and as he did so Sharkey hit me in the face.... The hit that knocked Sharkey out was a very simple one and one of my oldest moves. It was a plain left-hand shift. I first jabbed him in the stomach with my left and he staggered. In the swing I threw the same arm up to the point of his jaw and caught him fairly at the point where I aimed. Sharkey dropped like a log and was out.... Julian told me before we went into the fight that this man Earp would do us up, no matter what the real result was. But what could we do? At the beginning the audience was dead against us, and to please the audience I consented to go ahead.... It was fixed, and the whole thing was a barefaced robbery.... What would I want to foul this man for? Wasn't he at my mercy all the time?

The Bulletin quoted Fitz as saying,

> "I was robbed; that's all. I expected it and I got it. I never fouled Sharkey at any stage of the fight; whereas he fouled me from the word go. I knocked him out as clean and fair as any one ever was knocked out. In that eighth round I had him gone, and I uppercut him. He began to fall, and to finish him I let him have it here." And Fitz planted a hairy fist in the region of the dividing line between the chest and stomach of his interlocutor.[659]

Another paper quoted Fitz as saying,

> I was made the victim of one of the meanest jobs ever put through on earth. ... I never fought fairer in my life, while Sharkey fouled me deliberately at least twenty times. I appealed to the referee, but he took no notice of my protests, and told me to go on and fight. Once

---

[659] *San Francisco Bulletin,* December 3, 1896.

in a clinch Earp tried to separate us by pressing his hand against my face. His fingernails penetrated my eye and cut the flesh on the inside of the lid.

Sharkey conducted himself like a loafer in the ring. He used the foulest kind of language. I don't suppose he knows any better, however, as he is an ignorant pig. … He is a hard nut. He don't know much about fighting, however, but relies on brute strength, foul tactics and a crooked referee to win. … Sharkey knows, if he will only tell the truth, that I did not hit him foul. He was leaning over when I struck the blow of which he complains. It was a left-handed uppercut, and took effect in the pit of the stomach. He straightened up a bit after receiving the punch, and I finished him with a left on the jaw.[660]

The town of San Francisco itself was under scrutiny. Fitz said, "I will say one thing for Corbett, and that is that I don't blame him for saying that he was robbed out of the Jackson fight in this town. No pugilist can get a square deal from the thieves who handle fighting in this city." The general feeling was that such a decision was a black eye to the city and boxing itself, and might kill boxing in the town.

Fitz's manager, Martin Julian, said,

I met Mr. Earp just before the fight began and told him that I believed he had been fixed and that he would not give an honest decision…. [S]everal well-known men…had assured me late in the afternoon that they had positive knowledge of a job, and that, if we accepted Earp, we would get the worst of it.

Julian backed up his claims by naming names. Amongst the men who had earlier told him and Fitzsimmons that the fight was fixed were Riley Grannan, the racetrack plunger, Tom James, who was the bout's timekeeper, M.A. Gunst, who was one of the town's Police Commissioners, Major Frank McLaughlin, Eddie Greaney, as well as a half dozen others. Julian and his attorney said that they had proof of a conspiracy and would prove their charges in the courts.

Julian said to Mr. Groom, president of the National Athletic Club, "I warn you not to pay Mr. Sharkey that purse, because it is a ___ ___ robbery …. I tell you tonight that this referee was bought." Groom nodded

[660] *San Francisco Evening Post*, December 3, 1896.

affirmatively. Continuing, Julian said, "Mr. Groom himself had to yell to Earp half a dozen times to call his attention to fouls. Ain't that so, Mr. Groom?" Groom again nodded in the affirmative.

> I am told by responsible people that he was fixed by racetrack people. They call him Bloody Earp and say he is a dangerous man, but I will tell him to his face what I think of him and punch the stomach out of him. I ought to have knocked the stuffing out of him right there in the ring. I don't know why I didn't.

The following morning, Julian said,

> Reliable sportsmen, men behind the scenes and in the town came to me as late as 8 o'clock last evening and told me the fight was fixed for Sharkey to win, and that Earp was the man put up to do the job. I protested, therefore, at the ring side. But what was the use? Afterward I thought that the crowd would shame Earp into acting on the level, so I agreed to go ahead. The decision was a disgrace to San Francisco sports. I hold the club responsible for it all …. [T]he National Club shall never hold another contest, mind you that…. Now as to fighting. I sent a telegram to Stuart last evening, accepted his offer of $15,000 for a go with Corbett. … As for Mr. Earp, I hear a lot of talk of his being a fighting man. All I say is, let him drop his guns and I'll take him into a room and give him all the fight he wants. He'll referee no more fights, I can tell you.

Earp claimed to have no bias for or against either fighter. According to one newspaper, Earp said that he had never before met Sharkey, until that evening. However, another newspaper quoted Earp as saying that he had met Sharkey once before, when Tom had fought Corbett. Earp said that he had met Fitz several times beforehand, and that Bat Masterson had introduced him to Bob a few years ago.

However, there was some question as to the relationship between Wyatt Earp and Sharkey's manager, Dan Lynch. One paper said that Earp admitted to being Lynch's friend. However, other newspapers said that Earp claimed otherwise. Wyatt said, "I know Lynch pretty well. I have been around the tracks with him, but I never knew him well enough to make an intimate of him." Earp also said,

I wish to say that I am not in partnership with Lynch in the horse business and never have been. He does not now and never has had one of his racers in my string... My acquaintance with Lynch runs back only a year. At no time, however, have I been a close friend or confidant of his.

The Chronicle disagreed. A few days after the bout, it said, "Dan Lynch and Wyatt Earp were close friends. This was generally known, and it seems strange that Groom and Gibbs were not aware of this fact." Earp said he knew Lynch for a year, but only occasionally spoke a few words to him. Earp and Lynch said the cry about his decision was coming from those who had bet on Fitz, and the bookmakers, who had lost money on Sharkey bets.

The Call alleged that Dan Lynch had an interest in the National Club, and had on the night of the fight stood at the door and "kept a watchful eye on the tickets." "Lynch's reputation is very shady. He came here with a lot of racehorses and called them the 'Arizona Stable.' Earp was then in Arizona." The implication was that Lynch had influenced the National Club's selection of his fellow horseracer, Earp, who may or may not have been his friend from Arizona and at the racetracks.

Earp admitted that Martin Julian had approached him before the fight and told Wyatt that he had heard that he favored Sharkey. Earp regretted not leaving when Julian objected to him, but felt that he would be quitting under fire, and that he should not do so unless told to do so by the club.

Many commented on the fact that Sharkey's fouls were obvious to everyone but Earp, who did not notice them at all. Earp said, "Sharkey did not foul Fitzsimmons, although it might have seemed so.... Sharkey never once struck him below the belt."

Despite the unanimous opinion of the reporters that Fitz had fought fairly, Earp claimed,

I saw the foul blow struck as plainly as I see you, and that is all there is to the story. In the fourth or fifth round I warned Fitzsimmons that he was fouling in the wrestling. In every clinch the tall man would force himself down upon Sharkey, who was fighting low, and attempt to smash him. Fitzsimmons replied that he was not fighting foul. I answered that I wanted no more of it and demanded that he quit it and be square.

Earp saw Fitzsimmons fouls when others did not, and did not see Sharkey fouls when others plainly did.

Even his description of the final blows was different. Of the alleged foul blow, Earp said, "Fitz smashed with his right on Sharkey's shoulder and then with an uppercut with the left he struck the Sailor below the belt." Earp said that it was a "most palpable foul."

Then Earp said a curious thing, most revealing of his bias.

> There is one thing I regret. I should have given Sharkey the fight earlier in the contest. In the fourth round, I think it was, Fitz landed a left-handed blow and returned with his elbow, cutting Sharkey's eyebrow open. The Sailor should have had the fight then.

He came very near to disqualifying him then, and actually regretted not doing so at that point. No one else noticed this alleged foul.

The day after the bout, Earp modified his statements by saying,

> Sharkey did not strike a foul blow, to my mind. At the break he struck Fitzsimmons as soon as his arm was free. That is following Queensberry rules. It is true that it was stated that there was to be no fighting at the break, but my instructions from the club were not to be technical, but to give the audience a good fight for their money.

Earp said that Sharkey's fouls of grabbing the legs were not intentional, and that he did not mean anything by them. "Fitzsimmons certainly committed the most palpable fouls and that is why I decided in favor of Sharkey." Earp again reiterated,

> I sometimes regret that I didn't give the fight to Sharkey in the fourth round when Fitzsimmons gave him his elbow in the eye. It was uncalled for, and, moreover, premeditated. They are talking about Sharkey fouling. Why, he didn't fight one-half as dirty as the other fellow did.[661]

John Gibbs, one of the National Athletic Club's managers, confirmed that he had told Earp that he did not want him to pay strict attention to

---

[661] *San Francisco Bulletin*, December 4, 1896.

technical fouls that would not affect the chances of either contestant. He told Earp to overlook little unimportant fouls and not to interfere unless he absolutely had to.

> I know that Sharkey on several occasions clasped his opponent about the body and partly lifted him from the floor. He was hissed for it and, while such a procedure may have been a technical foul I conscientiously believe that had Fitz been awarded the fight upon the grounds the audience would have rebelled. ... Up to 1 o'clock on the very day of the fight [Earp] was satisfactory to Fitz and Julian. Then the latter came to me, saying that he had heard rumors that the referee had been fixed. 'Oh, that's all rubbish,' I replied.[662]

Gibbs claimed that he did not see the fatal blow, as he was looking away from the ring at the time, so he declined to render an opinion.

Sharkey's perception of the fight was wholly different from that of the reporters. He said that he was "satisfied that I had the best of it in every round." He accused Fitzsimmons of elbowing him dozens of times, claiming that was what caused the gash over his left eye. "I am certain Fitzsimmons fouled me deliberately. He did it to save himself from defeat." He felt that but for the low blow, he would have knocked Fitz out in the next round.

Sharkey had two visible bruises on the left side of his face, a slight abrasion and lump on the cheek bone, a cut which had divided the left eyebrow lengthwise, requiring three stitches, and his lips were swollen and cut.

The Examiner published some observations from those in attendance who claimed that there was a foul. A police captain said that the "foul was a palpable one." A contractor said that he sat a few feet from ringside and saw that Tom was fouled. It is unclear as to how many of these people had bet money on Sharkey. Of course, it is also unclear how many of those who insisted that there was no foul had bets on Fitz. Clearly, some on either side of the argument had a potential bias.

The Evening Post also said that there was a diversity of opinion as to the fairness of the blow. National Club Master of Ceremonies Billy Jordan said that the blow was fair. "If he had been struck where they say he was he would have doubled up and fallen forward instead of on his back."

---

[662] *San Francisco Evening Post*, December 3, 1896.

No one could confirm exactly when or how Sharkey was injured, because on the night of the fight, Dan Lynch refused to allow the club's doctors to examine Tom. Sharkey was taken from the dressing room to his hotel room. The National Club's chief physician, Dr. Lustig, said,

> Had I been admitted to Sharkey's dressing-room immediately after the fight, as I demanded, being the physician of the National Athletic Club, I would have been better able to judge of the injury, if any existed then. I cannot understand why Lynch should refuse the free services of any reputable physician in a case where his man was alleged to be so severely injured.

Dr. Lustig said that three other doctors accompanied him, and all were refused admission. Lustig was refused admission even after a request by club representative Groom. Dr. Lustig had been allowed to examine Sharkey *before* the fight.

It was certainly suspicious that Lynch would not allow the club's doctors to examine Sharkey until a day later. It was noted that on the night of the fight, one alleged doctor (Dr. Lee) sent for by Lynch did privately examine Tom at the hotel, and Sharkey was from behind closed doors heard to moan and groan as if in pain. However, he did not do so the following day when Lynch finally allowed him to be examined by other doctors. It was noted that Lee had applied leeches and hot applications to Sharkey, and had bandaged up Tom's groin.

The doctor who privately examined Sharkey at the hotel, Dr. B.B. Lee, had somewhat of a shady reputation. Lee was said to be "well known to the police, and they have been keeping an eye on him for a long time. He first attracted their attention by offering himself as a witness for Joe Fair, a notorious pickpocket." Lee had attempted to provide Fair with an alibi, saying that Fair had been in jail at the time of the crime and that he had bailed him out. However, apparently, the testimony was disproved and Fair was convicted. Furthermore, "A few months ago Lee was taken in custody while trying to dispose of some bonds stolen from a bank." Lee claimed that he did not know the bonds were stolen, but had been asked by a young man to dispose of them. Certainly though, such circumstances were more than suspicious. However, Lee agreed to assist officers in capturing the thieves and was released. It appeared that Lee was not necessarily the most savory of characters. Another report said that Lee was "an illegal practitioner."[663]

---

[663] *San Francisco Evening Post*, December 3, 1896; *San Francisco Call*, December 4, 1896.

The day after the bout, six physicians examined Sharkey, and concluded that there was a swelling. However, they could determine neither its cause nor the timing of the incident which caused it, particularly 16 hours after the fight. "All we can say at best is that there is an injury – that's all. Whether the harm is an hour or seventy-two hours old cannot be determined." Regardless, Dr. Lustig said that the injury to Sharkey was not severe and that there was not as much swelling as he would have expected from such a low blow as Fitz was said to have given him. He also said, "I know as a fact that he did not give it, as I was present at the fight and had a good view of the blow, which hit Sharkey in the stomach." Their final report said that Sharkey's injuries were not severe, and insufficient as to incapacitate him from continuing in the fight.

Still, a number of persons were quoted as saying that the blow was a little too low. A clerk for the district court said, "He was 'going,' but that does not alter the fact that his final knockout was accomplished by a blow below the belt."

However, most observers said that there was no foul whatsoever; and that it was "the worst steal ever perpetrated on the public." A detective said it was a clean blow. A bookmaker said, "Julian stated before the fight in the presence of the referee that it was fixed, and I think this alone should have caused Earp to step down. The referee's decision and the betting shows that Julian was right."

Those critical of the decision were very strong in their critiques. Words used included "outrageous," "unjust," "rank" and "disgraceful." A number of men said the knockout came from a left to the body and a right to the jaw, with some saying that there was another blow, a left that was more of a push as Sharkey was falling.

The San Francisco Call's report, written by old Corbett trainer Professor Walter Watson (hence its detail) called it a "barefaced robbery" and "the most bald-faced steal that has ever been seen." Watson said that Sharkey fought foully all through the fight, and went down from a hook on the chin and a left drive in the pit of the stomach. The house howled in derision when it learned of Earp's decision.

> Earp did not wait to see what effect the decision would have on the crowd, but sneaked from the ring, while Fitz's friends were crowding about the big Cornishman to congratulate him and was far away when the crowd understood and began to yell, 'Fake,' 'Steal' and other expressions of that character.

> It is safe to say that his fake reputation as a bad man from Arizona would not have saved his hide had the crowd been able to get hands on him.

He showed the "yellow dog" in him by going into the ring with a Colt's navy revolver in his pocket, indicated that he feared trouble over the decision that he knew he would give if opportunity offered.

When Captain Wittman saw it pushing out his coattails he demanded the gun, and it was only after repeated orders from the big police officer that Earp gave up the weapon on which he depends for a living.[664]

Earp went to the ring with a gun, and then hurried out of the ring after he had made his decision, of which very few realized until he was gone. Clearly, his quick disappearance was a sign that he was not too eager to deal with the crowd's potential wrath. Some took his carrying a gun as a sign that he felt he might need it to protect himself from the angry mob after carrying out his plan to disqualify Fitzsimmons. He left so quickly that he didn't even bother to hand over the winner's check.

Earp said that he was foolish to enter the ring with a revolver in his pocket, but that he had not been without a weapon in 17 years, and forgot all about it. He had a gun because he had been out at the races all day, and needed it for protection at night after all the races were over. Going over to the stables after everyone was gone, he did not know whom he might meet. "Now, on the night of the fight I got in very late from the races, much later than I expected, and had to go straight out to Mechanics' Pavilion." He therefore forgot to remove his gun.[665]

Although Fitz's error in judgment in not insisting on a referee change had cost him $10,000, it had not cost him "a whit of his reputation, for not a fair-minded man in the audience saw more than one man in the fight, and that man was Bob Fitzsimmons."

The crowd was with Sharkey at first, but Bob won them over with his fair fighting.

When he helped Sharkey through the ropes after knocking him in that position he had the crowd to a man. Sharkey's persistent attempts to throw Bob by catching him by the legs, and his striking in a clinch after agreeing in the ring not to do so, showed very unfavorably against the Cornishman's fair breakaways.[666]

---

[664] *San Francisco Call*, December 3, 1896.
[665] *San Francisco Bulletin*, December 4, 1896.
[666] *San Francisco Call*, December 3, 1896.

Undefeated world lightweight champion Jack McAuliffe said,

Well, I think it was a shame that Sharkey was so badly defeated. He is a good, willing fighter, but has no science whatever. When Fitzsimmons fought Jack Dempsey I said he was the greatest fighter on earth, and I adhere to that opinion still. He can conquer any man in the ring today. I lost a great deal of money on this fight, but I do not care to question the decision of the referee. This I am willing to admit, from where I sat I saw no fouling on the part of Bob. But, as I say, I never question the decision of a referee.

The very rich sugar magnates, Adolph and John Spreckels, called it a robbery. Adolph said, "It's a steal, pure and simple." He called it a disgrace for the sporting community.

I felt sure yesterday afternoon, there was such a sudden scramble to get money on Sharkey at any odds, that something was wrong. It was almost impossible late in the afternoon to get takers of bets on Fitzsimmons, and when I witnessed the fight by Fitzsimmons, which was one of the finest any man ever put up, and heard the referee's decision, I was convinced that my suspicions formed early in the afternoon were well founded. I saw the blow which they term 'foul.' I was in the box closest to the men when Sharkey was knocked out. Fitzsimmons simply hooked him in his wind, and no one who observed it could conscientiously term it a foul.

His brother John echoed his feelings.

I saw every detail of the fight, watched it from a splendid point of view, and term the decision of the referee, without hesitation, as unjust in the extreme. ... I observed it carefully. He had simply doubled the sailor up with a left-hander just below the ribs, and as his man came forward he upper-cut him with his right.

Major Frank McLaughlin said that he had spoken with Fitzsimmons before the fight, and that Fitz had told him that he was informed that he could not win on account of the referee. McLaughlin noted,

[Earp] did not, as a square man would have done, say that as he was unsatisfactory to one of the contestants he would withdraw.... Sharkey's managers had the choice of Jim Neal, Eddie Greaney and Hiram Cook, any one of whom would have given an honest decision. But no one except Earp would satisfy the sailor's friends. Another feature of the affair that looked bad was the betting. Fitzsimmons started in a 4 to 1 favorite, but before the fight began the men were at even money.

A sudden and large swing in the odds meant that a lot of large wagers were placed on Sharkey close to the fight. What had changed their minds? The inference was that there was inside information regarding the fix.

McLaughlin told another paper that the decision was "rotten" and "a rob of the worst kind." Fitz had told him before the fight that he heard that Earp would not give him a fair show. The major told Bob that he too had heard rumors of a fix on the street. "It was all over town...and then look how the betting changed." He advised Fitz, "Bob, under the circumstance, you make a mistake in fighting. If you have any reason to regard the friends who have warned you as reliable you should positively refuse to accept Wyatt Earp as referee." However, Bob had a lot of pressure to fight, given how the Corbett fight had fallen through. Fitzsimmons replied, "Major, I'll be made the laughing stock of the country if I refuse to fight now, so I am going to accept this man, because there is no way out of it."

McLaughlin also had some criticism of Earp for entering the ringside with a gun. "Then, another thing, who ever saw a referee come to the ringside before with a mountain howitzer in his pocket? What did he want that for?" The suggestion was that he feared trouble as a result of the decision he was going to make. "Finally, why did Earp insist on going on as referee when objection was made to him? Was that the action of a high-toned, honorable man?"[667]

He had advised the club managers to change the referee, and made two suggestions, "but they refused to listen to my advice. ... If they think that because they named a frontier bully that fear of him is going to stifle criticism they are mistaken."[668]

McLaughlin said that he had carefully watched the fight, and had no wagers on it. After the 1st round, there was no question in his mind as to what the result would be. In the 8th round, Fitz had Sharkey thoroughly whipped.

---

[667] *San Francisco Evening Post*, December 3, 1896.
[668] *San Francisco Evening Post*, December 5, 1896.

He had him going and was driving Sharkey towards his corner. I saw the hook which he gave him in the ribs. It was a perfectly fair blow in every respect, and had he stepped away from Sharkey at that time the sailor would have fallen. Fitzsimmons evidently wanted to finish it, and he followed the hook with a smash on the chin, which, so far as I could see, fell a little short and merely grazed the sailor's chin.

Riley Grannan confirmed that he had advised Fitz to be on his guard.

The betting operations assumed such proportions yesterday afternoon that I felt convinced something was wrong. Up to noon the odds had been in favor of Fitzsimmons at about the right price, 4 and 5 to 1, but when after that time, nothing was seen but Sharkey money, which was offered at any price, and when I could find absolutely no one who would take a bet on Fitzsimmons at even money, I felt sure something must be wrong. ... I felt so convinced that things were crooked that I immediately tried to hedge a $1300 bet on Fitzsimmons...which I was not successful in doing. I immediately hunted up Fitzsimmons and communicated to him my suspicions.

I told him I knew nothing definite, but I thought it a remarkable thing that when on Tuesday it was impossible to bet money on Sharkey at 4 to 1, it looked queer to see at least $20,000 go begging yesterday at odds of even money on the sailor.

I watched the fight from beginning to end. I cannot say too much in praise of Fitzsimmons' work and I confidently assert that the blow which Sharkey claims is a foul was above the belt, and fair in every respect.[669]

Police Commissioner M.A. Gunst disagreed with Earp's call.

The only money I had up was $20 that Fitz would win in four rounds. I lost that fair enough, of course, and I had no bet on the final result. But if there was a foul blow struck I did not see it, and I don't like the decision. The statement made, though, that I warned Fitzsimmons that Earp was programmed to decide against him is a mistake. A half dozen people, however, reputable men, all of them, warned me that this was the arrangement, and, thinking that I had been betting

[669] *San Francisco Evening Post*, December 3, 1896.

heavily, told me to get my money off Fitz and to drop in behind Sharkey. ... What first attracted my attention as being curious was the change that took place in the betting yesterday afternoon, when it began to get around that Earp was to be referee. ... [I]t looks queer.[670]

The next day, Gunst was quoted as saying,

It was an outrageous steal. Fitzsimmons was clearly the victor. ... While we were dining, a man whose name I do not care to bring into this affair came to me and asked if I was betting any money on the fight. I answered truthfully that I was not. In return, I inquired the reason for such a question at that time. He answered, 'Nothing, only if you're betting you had better shift over to the Sharkey end.' I paid little heed to this until another man came to me and the same story was told. Then again, another man, just as trustworthy as the first two, repeated the warning, and gave the same advice. My eyes began to open then.

My friends, who had been offering to bet $1000 to $800 on Fitzsimmons and who could find no takers, stepped down in the street with me, and all around us we found plenty of Sharkey money at odds of $100 to $65. That was too great a jump to be honest, and it gave us sufficient corroboration of the rumors that had reached us at dinner to risk any money on the game.

Then it was that I met Riley Grannan, the horseman. He said that he had been 'onto' the crooked work hours before. He had seen Wyatt Earp in busy conversation with Joe Harvey immediately after Earp's selection as referee. When Earp and Harvey separated, the latter asked, 'Well, I can depend on that?' Earp answered, 'Yes.' It was but a short time after this conversation that the Sharkey money began to flow like water.

After hearing this report I told the whole thing to Hickey, the trainer of Fitzsimmons.... Before going to the Pavilion I ran into Joe Harvey... I said to him: 'Here, Harvey, things do not appear to be right. I'm told that this fight is not to be on the square, and if it's so I want to hear of it positively.' ... Harvey declared he had nothing more to do with it than to bet his money on the short end, because he believed it to be a good thing.

---

[670] *San Francisco Evening Post*, December 3, 1896.

Now, I don't accuse any man of crooked work in this affair, but I insist that the surrounding circumstances look as if the whole matter had been cut and dried for Sharkey to win and that the sure-thing gamblers did not begin to plunge until they were positive that the referee was safe. ...

Sharkey was knocked out as fairly as any man ever was. He was a whipped man at any and all stages of the fight. He fought in the most outrageously foul manner.[671]

Some believed that Earp should have removed himself because of potential bias after the accusation of being fixed, even if he was not.

The mere act on Julian's part of announcing his disbelief in the fairness of the referee was sufficient to excite a prejudice on Mr. Earp's part. It would not have been consistent with human nature for him to have had anything but a feeling of enmity toward the man who raised a question about the honesty of his intentions.[672]

How did Wyatt Earp become the referee? National Athletic Club representatives Gibbs and Groom gave their versions. Gibbs told the *Examiner* that they had met Earp a week before the fight, and he told them that he had refereed at least 30 bouts. Gibbs suggested Earp as a suitable referee. Groom prepared a list of eligible referees for submission to the respective managers, but "forgot" to include Earp's name. *The Call* quoted Gibbs as saying, "Neither Mr. Groom nor myself spoke to Earp regarding the matter until noon on the day of the fight." The reality was that they were holding him in reserve as the likely referee, as they later admitted.

The Call printed a report saying that Gibbs had informed Mr. Bunker of the *San Francisco Report* a day or two in advance of the fight that Earp would be the referee. "Gibbs was supposed to not decide upon any referee until ... noon on Wednesday. Still, Gibbs was sure enough of his ground to name the man to the Report a day or more in advance." Gibbs later claimed that Bunker had suggested Earp, but Bunker denied the claim, saying that the opposite was true. Bunker said that Gibbs asked him the day before the fight what he thought of Earp, and he told Gibbs that the *Report* had already advised the club to avoid the responsibility of selecting a referee.[673]

---

[671] *San Francisco Call*, December 4, 1896.
[672] *National Police Gazette*, December 12, 1896.
[673] *San Francisco Call*, December 8, 9, 1896.

A few days later, the *San Francisco Call* printed a different story. It took the opportunity to note almost gleefully that its competitor, the *San Francisco Examiner*, had previously hired Wyatt Earp to act as a bodyguard for its managing editor, Andrew "Long Green" Lawrence. Earp had also occasionally been hired to write stories about frontier life for that paper. *The Call* was especially interested in attacking and impugning the integrity of Lawrence, and by association, the *Examiner*, which was owned by William Randolph Hearst, a man with his own credibility problems.[674]

The Call claimed that Lawrence had suggested or backed Earp for the referee position. When Gibbs was being cross-examined by reporters regarding the referee situation, Gibbs blurted out to an *Examiner* reporter, "What kick have you got coming? It was at Andy Lawrence's suggestion Wyatt Earp went in as referee." Groom said that the day before the fight, Lawrence called for Gibbs to come and see him. Lawrence had heard that the men could not agree on a referee, and suggested Earp. Groom quoted Gibbs as saying that if Earp was good enough for the press, he was good enough for them. It seemed that Gibbs and Groom were telling a lot of different stories as to how Earp came to be selected as referee.

The Call also claimed that after the fight, Lawrence went to Fitz's hotel accompanied by Earp. In the course of the conversation, Fitz asked Earp to describe the final blows and to position himself in front of another man as they were at the time of the final blow. This having been done, Fitz said, "Now, Mr. Earp, don't you see that as we are now placed I could not have struck Sharkey as you describe?" Earp "looked confused" and said, "Well, I guess the positions must have been different."[675]

Lawrence did not want to dignify the *Call*'s allegations with a response. He did confirm that Earp had written stories for the *Examiner* some time ago. "He got his pay and the connection ceased. That's all there is to it."[676]

Lawrence had seen the fight, and felt that Sharkey had quit. However, a police lieutenant told him that Sharkey was fouled. Moments later, the referee disqualified Fitz. According to Lawrence, "While there were thousands at the mill who declare they saw no foul, there are a few gentlemen of reputation and character who are willing to make affidavits that they saw the unfair blow delivered." Bill Delaney said that he saw a foul blow, as did Al Smith and some policemen.

Groom confirmed that Fitz and Julian told him the night of the fight that Earp was fixed, but nevertheless was firm that Earp would referee the bout. There was not much of an explanation as to why they were firm on

---

[674] *San Francisco Evening Post*, December 4, 1896.
[675] *San Francisco Call*, December 5, 1896.
[676] *San Francisco Evening Post*, December 5, 1896.

Earp, although they later claimed that there simply was insufficient time to find someone else, and they did not believe the rumors.

Groom claimed that Earp came to him and "begged to be allowed to retire," which was directly contradicted by Earp's statements. Earp said that he did not want to quit under fire, which is why he did not ask to be excused when Julian made his objection.

> I was put there not by him nor by Lynch, but by the club. If either Mr. Groom or Mr. Gibbs had asked me to step out of the ring I would have been only too glad to have done so. ... But I was determined not to let anybody drive me out of the ring.[677]

It is interesting to note that both Lynch and Earp were horsemen whose horses raced at the local track, and quite a few persons at the track were aware of a potential fix. It was reported that men like Dan Honig, the horseman, was advised to hedge his bet on Fitz. Riley Grannan knew of the fix before he left the local race track. Many folks at the local track either bet Sharkey or hedged their bets on Fitz. Earp had been at the racetrack on the day of the fight (seen speaking with Joe Harvey) and had spent the next day at the race track as well.

Charley Dexter, a well-known gambler, said that Joe Harvey bet $5,000 - $6,000 on the fight. "Does anybody think he would have played that amount if he did not have everything fixed? Why, he wouldn't bet $29 on anything unless he had a string to it." One paper said Harvey denied betting more than $50 on the fight. Another quoted Harvey as saying that he only bet $600 on Sharkey. However, people who were present at the race track on the day of the fight said that Harvey was in consultation with Earp on several occasions that day. Harvey did say of his decision to bet Sharkey, "I did so, to some extent, upon the impression my horse-trainer had that Sharkey was a sure winner."[678]

The day after the fight, the police arrested Earp on a charge of carrying a concealed weapon, having done so on the night of the fight when entering the arena.

Interestingly, the police did not arrest Earp on the night of the fight, although they could have done so. When asked why Earp was not arrested that night, Chief Crowley said,

---

[677] *San Francisco Evening Post, San Francisco Bulletin,* December 5, 1896.
[678] *San Francisco Evening Post,* December 4, 1896.

It would have been a very impolite action to arrest him in the presence of 12,000 spectators. They would have said that the police were trying to stop the fight for a very trivial reason. He handed the revolver to Captain Wittman when asked to do so, and it is my belief that no judge nor jury would convict him in the circumstances.

Chief Crowley sounded more like a defense attorney than a policeman. And he was wrong. Earp was later convicted of the charge. The police had word that Earp was fixed. Therefore, the concealed weapon violation would have been the most legitimate excuse to arrest and prevent him from carrying through with the plan. Did some members of the police force want Wyatt Earp to referee?

Police Commissioner Gunst said that he was told before the fight that it was fixed for Sharkey, and was advised to hedge if he had bet on Fitz. He sent word to Grannan and others, including fellow commissioner Tobin *and Chief of Police Crowley.* Although some newspapers quoted Gunst as saying that he never bet on anything but a finish fight, the *Examiner* quoted Gunst differently, saying that he was advised "to protect myself in the money I had bet on Fitzsimmons, and that I promptly did. I advised a number of my friends to do likewise, and we are all congratulating ourselves on saving our money."

Questions naturally arise from the Police Commissioner's statements. If Gunst never bet on anything but a fight to the finish, why did he have a bet on Fitz which he then had to hedge? Was he misquoted? The really important question is: Why didn't the police prevent the bout from occurring or arrest Earp on the night of the fight when they had the opportunity to do so? Why didn't they announce their knowledge and insist upon a referee change? It is likely that some members of the police force had more than hedged, but had capitalized on their knowledge.

Fitz noted that his manager

[Julian was] black and blue all over his body from the rough handling he got from the police every time he tried to jump into the ring to claim a foul for me. On the other hand, Needham [Sharkey's trainer] was allowed to crawl under the ropes whenever he wanted to, and on the knockout blow he was in the ring two seconds before the referee had given his decision.

As some members of the police force were aware of the fix before the fight, it is quite possible that they not only placed Sharkey wagers, but therefore also had reason to ensure that no one interfered with Earp, and to ensure that Fitz's protesting manager Julian was unsuccessful. *The Chronicle* confirmed that the police had grabbed Julian when he had mounted the apron to protest Sharkey's fouls. *The Examiner* quoted a number of police force members as saying that they thought it was a foul blow and that Earp's decision was correct. If they had bets on Sharkey, it would have been in their interest to put forth that version.

The day after the fight, Sharkey manager Lynch and Referee Earp appeared at a local bank seeking to cash the $10,000 check, but they were turned away. Fitzsimmons had quickly filed for a court injunction, claiming that Lynch, Earp, Sharkey, and the National Athletic Club had fixed the fight in a conspiracy. The court granted a temporary restraining order preventing the bank from making payment.

Regarding Sharkey, Fitz said, "He knows as well as I do that I never struck him a foul blow at all." Regarding Tom's capabilities, he said, "The man is nothing but a foul barroom fighter." A number of days later, Bob also said, "Sharkey has a head harder than a nigger's."[679]

Fitzsimmons again described the knockout.

> Sharkey threw his left for my head, but I countered with my right, and then, side-stepping in, jabbed him in the pit of the stomach with a long left. His arm dropped from my neck and he put both his hands on his stomach, doubling over from the effects of the blow. I then immediately advanced a step and gave him the left again on the point of the chin, knocking him out with this face blow.[680]

The Examiner printed further ringside witness statements. William Harrison, ex-President of the Olympic Club, said he was within fifty feet of the ring and saw that it was a clean blow. He said the only possible way Sharkey could have been fouled would have been from an accidental butt from the knee. An Olympic Club member said he saw the knockout; that it was with a straight left to the body and a left uppercut, both fair blows. He also said, "No fair-minded man, when once his honor had been called in question, would have accepted the position of referee." However, a champion wrestler said that he thought there was an accidental foul.

The Examiner reported that a majority of those who said there was a foul had said it was by the knee. However, Earp insisted that it was a punch. The paper was critical of Earp and felt that he had revealed his prejudice

---

[679] *San Francisco Chronicle*, December 4-6, 1896.
[680] *San Francisco Chronicle*, December 4, 5, 1896; *San Francisco Examiner*, December 4, 1896.

when he said that he should have awarded the bout to Sharkey earlier in the fight and that Sharkey had not fouled. "Earp's idea as to what constitutes a foul seems very crude indeed."

A couple days after the fight, the *Evening Post* printed a dispatch sent east by Sharkey trainer Danny Needham just before the fight, on the 2nd. It allegedly said, "Play all you can on Sharkey. Cannot explain further." This was a strange dispatch indeed.[681]

The next day, the Postal Telegraph Company Superintendent "admitted that Needham sent many dispatches off on the afternoon of the fight advising Eastern friends to bet their last dollar on the sailor, but none were worded exactly as quoted, although they were very similar in substance." Needham responded by agreeing that he had sent dispatches advising people to bet Sharkey, but that was simply because he felt Sharkey would win, and he had made no secret of his opinion.[682]

The Call said that the majority of sporting men believed that Fitz was robbed of the decision and the purse. They recalled Julian's declaration before the fight that the referee was fixed, as well as "Earp's peculiar action in not defending himself before the assembled throng and the fact that he was relieved of a gun in the arena." Also discussed was the fact that Earp was indifferent to Sharkey's incessant fouling, as well as Earp's "sudden and precipitate disappearance from the ring" after the fight. Furthermore, the incident that caused a great deal of talk was the refusal of Sharkey's trainers and backers to allow the club's doctors to see the sailor. No physician was allowed to see him until "a man named Lee, an irregular practitioner, with whom the police are well acquainted, was called and with no one but Sharkey's people present at the examination pronounced him seriously injured." The National Club managers Gibbs and Groom received much unfavorable comment for not withdrawing Earp when objection was made to him, especially since Julian said he was willing to accept any other man in the house.[683]

The day after the fight, on December 3, 1896, Fitzsimmons boxed 4 rounds with trainer Dan Hickey at the Bush-Street Theater. Bob explained how he knocked out Sharkey. "I caught Sharkey a left hook… Then a right quickly followed, and as Sharkey was falling I uppercut him in the stomach. He fell and resorted to an old dodge, in the hope of getting a decision on a foul."[684]

A lot of fuss was made about the big shift in the odds. However, although Sharkey money was initially scarce, causing the odds to move up

[681] *San Francisco Evening Post*, December 4, 1896.
[682] *San Francisco Evening Post*, *San Francisco Bulletin*, December 5, 1896.
[683] *San Francisco Call*, December 4, 1896.
[684] *San Francisco Call*, December 4, 1896.

to 10 to 4, one paper felt that the fact that a lot of Sharkey money came in on the day of the fight was not all that unusual. *The Evening Post* said,

> It is a well-known fact that the local talent never plays a fight until a day or two before the event is decided. Hence it was natural to suppose that when Sharkey's friends turned their money loose a few hours before the boxers stepped into the ring, it would affect the odds.[685]

Dan Lynch said that it was Fitzsimmons' supporters who tried to fix the fight for Bob, but failed. He said that the majority of those who were hollering fraud were mixed up in some crooked fights and were sure-thing players.

> They thought they had this fixed, but got fooled. They were going to stop the fight if Fitz got the worst of it, but they never got that chance. I am aware two wrongs do not make a right, but there was nothing wrong with our fight. ... They have been giving this man the worst of it right along, but they got fooled this time.[686]

How were they fooled?

A couple days after the fight, Sharkey's left upper lip was swollen and cut, his left cheekbone swollen and discolored, and his left eyebrow stitched together in a zigzag line. Still in bed, puffing on a cigar, he sized up Fitz and Corbett, having been in the ring with both.

> Fitzsimmons is the harder hitter of the two, but Corbett is much the cleverer. He does not take the chances Fitz does. He never goes in and mixes things up, but depends on landing at long range and getting away without a return. He is quicker on his feet than Fitz, too, but his blows lack steam. However, Fitz has only two blows that hurt. They are his right and left swings.[687]

---

[685] *San Francisco Evening Post*, December 5, 1896.
[686] *San Francisco Bulletin*, December 5, 1896.
[687] *San Francisco Call*, December 9, 1896.

The Call said that more and more sports were beginning to think that the injuries done to Sharkey's groin area "were made in his room after being taken away from the pavilion."

It was said that Fitz would punch the bag and spar 3 rounds each with Jack Stelzner and Dan Hickey in both the afternoon and evening on December 6 at the Chutes, and he would demonstrate the knockout blows.

As of December 5, three days after the fight, Sharkey was still confined to his bed; an awfully long time to bedridden from a low blow. It was reported that he would not be allowed to leave his room for *another four days*. Joe Choynski had continued to fight after Sharkey had hit him badly low in their bout, yet Tom could not even get out of bed for a week.[688]

Earp and Lynch were having their troubles at the racetracks. It was reported that some jockeys were shunning Wyatt. "Earp asked Patsy Freeman to ride a horse for him at Ingleside yesterday, but the jockey refused."[689]

A couple days later, the *Chronicle* said, "Dan Lynch, Sharkey's manager, was warned off the turf in this city some time ago, and is barred even now from running in his own name what horses he possesses."[690] Now there is a sterling reputation.

The controversy was just warming up.

---

[688] *San Francisco Examiner*, December 5, 1896; *New York Clipper*, December 26, 1896.
[689] *San Francisco Chronicle*, December 6, 1896.
[690] *San Francisco Chronicle*, December 8, 1896.

CHAPTER 17

The Fight After the Fight

In the days subsequent to the Sharkey-Fitzsimmons fight, rather than subsiding, the controversy only grew hotter. Fitz had filed for an injunction preventing the $10,000 check from being paid to the Sharkey delegation on the grounds of a conspiracy to defraud him. The court testimony was another act to the story that the newspapers closely and eagerly followed.

Although they were served subpoenas, Gibbs, Groom, Sharkey, Lynch, and Earp all failed to show up to court, much to the judge's chagrin. Judge Groezinger issued warrants for their arrest, except for Sharkey, who was reportedly still in bed on December 6, four days after the fight.

As of December 8, it was reported that the bedridden Sharkey had suffered a "relapse." Fitz playfully joked that he felt sorry for Sharkey, for Tom was missing the beautiful weather when nothing was wrong with him, commenting that "in order to carry out this 'badly injured' gag he's got to stay where he is till the gang tells him he may get up."

When Wyatt Earp finally showed up in court, the judge admonished him for ignoring the subpoena. Earp said that he had "clean forgot all about it." The judge replied, "It is a peculiar thing that you should forget the service of a subpoena."

According to the *Chronicle*, amazingly, in his testimony Earp swore more than once that Sharkey had never fouled Fitzsimmons, that the sailor had never caught his opponent by the legs, that Fitzsimmons was fouling all the time throughout the fight, and that Martin Julian never made any announcement of any kind in the ring on the night of the fight about the referee being fixed, nor did he object to his being the referee. Earp also swore that Fitz had never said a word about the bandages on Sharkey's hands. Earp said that he had ordered Sharkey to remove the bandages (although Sharkey later claimed that it was Fitz who ordered him to do so). All of this testimony was quite astounding, apparently even to Sharkey's lawyer, and completely contradicted the reports of all the local papers. According to the *Call*, Earp testified that he was poor, only leased his racehorses, and only owned the clothes on his back.

Testimony was taken from Sharkey trainer Danny Needham, whom the *Chronicle* said in "the short space of twenty minutes…succeeded in flatly contradicting his own testimony fully half a dozen times."

When Dan Lynch finally showed up, he testified that he was Sharkey's manager and an owner of a number of race horses. "I have no interest whatever in any money Sharkey wins by his fights. I get no pay or reward…. Anything I make out of my connection with Sharkey comes from my side bets on the result and nothing else." Afterwards, the *Chronicle* interviewed Sharkey, and without realizing how Lynch testified, Tom said that Lynch always received a share of his purses, contradicting his own manager's testimony.

Promoters Gibbs and Groom took the witness stand and "each man contradicted his own statements repeatedly." Gibbs said that he told Earp that he did not want the fight decided on technical fouls, such as "the fouls Sharkey committed on Fitzsimmons- picking him up round the legs and trying to throw him; clutching him round the neck and jabbing him in the breakaway. I call those technical fouls, because they were not serious and had no bad effect on Fitzsimmons." Of course, this contradicted Earp's sworn testimony that Sharkey had not done those things.

Gibbs said that both he and Groom had Earp slated for the referee position a week before the fight, but had not told anyone. However, he acknowledged that he had spoken with several persons and pumped them about Earp's qualifications. This could have tipped them off as to his being their likely referee selection if the two sides could not agree.

Gibbs also testified that until the day of the fight, he did not know that Earp owned or ran any horses, but later contradicted himself by saying that in making the referee selection, he had carefully studied Earp's whole history, including his gun fights and horse races, etc.

As of December 9, Dr. Lee, who Lynch had hired, reported that Sharkey had a fever, a fast pulse, and was in a state of general collapse. All that from a low blow? "This mournful diagnosis, however, didn't prevent the sailor from sitting up on a couch all day and smoking big cigars. For a man on the point of dissolution he appears to unprofessional observers to be in a rather healthy condition."[691]

Back in court, the bomb landed in the form of Billy Smith's testimony. It was so powerful that the headline of the December 9 *Evening Post* said, "The Fight was Fixed." 28-year-old boxer "Australian" Billy Smith, who had been living in America for seven years, was a Sharkey sparring partner and one of his seconds for the bout. Sharkey previously had an 1895 KO7

---

[691] *San Francisco Chronicle*, December 9, 1896; *San Francisco Call*, December 16, 1896.

over Smith. Billy trained Sharkey along with Dan Needham and George Allen.

Smith testified that about three weeks before the fight, Sharkey asked him to suggest potential referees. Smith said Hiram Cook was a fair and honest referee who would give a square decision. However, Dan Lynch later said that Cook would not do. Sharkey told Smith that Lynch had asked Cook, "Supposing your brother and a Chinaman were fighting, would you decide in favor of the Chinaman?" Cook responded that he would if the Chinaman had the best of it. Lynch then decided that Cook was not acceptable, saying, "We don't want that kind of a man for referee." The logical conclusion was that Lynch did not want a fair referee.

Smith further testified that Sharkey told him that Gibbs and Groom were broke, that Lynch had purchased an interest in the club and would get 20% after the purse was taken out of the receipts. Therefore, as an interest holder in the club, Lynch also had a say regarding whom the club would select as referee. Because the contract terms allowed the club to name the referee if there was no agreement between the parties, Lynch would object to every name given by Julian so that the club could name the referee that Lynch wanted.

Smith had heard Earp's name mentioned as a possible referee ten days before the fight. On one of their training walks,

> Sharkey told me Lynch knew a horseman named Earp, and if he could get him he would be all right. He said there was good money in it for the referee if he could get the decision – that there would be $2,500 in it for the referee. He said they would object to every referee proposed…and then the club would have to name the referee.

On the day of the fight, Sharkey told Smith that Earp would give him the fight on a foul in the 1st round.

> He said Earp was to be referee and the first time Fitz was to him in the body Needham was to jump into the ring and claim a foul. He said the referee was all right and understood his business. That conversation took place about 10 o'clock on the morning of the fight.

Smith believed that Sharkey, Lynch, Earp, Needham, Gibbs, and Groom were all cognizant of and part of the fraud.

Smith also said that on the night of the fight, when Fitz objected to Sharkey's bandages, Earp told him to take them off; that it would be "all right, anyhow." When later interviewed regarding Smith's testimony, Sharkey responded that Earp did not order him to remove the bandages, saying that it was one of Fitz's seconds, "who stood in my corner and growled until I took them off." However, even Earp testified that he had told Sharkey to remove the bandages.

According to Smith, after Fitz stopped Sharkey in the 8th round, when Smith went to pick him up, Tom was lying flat on his back with his arms stretched out. He did not have his hands on his body at all. He was very dazed. Initially, the semi-conscious Sharkey placed his hands on his head and over his ears, where he said he had pains. While still on the ground, Lynch came up and whispered to Tom to keep his hands down low and to pretend to be in great pain, which he eventually did.

However, some of the initial post-fight reports had said that Sharkey held his hands low while on the ground. The question was whether he did it as a natural reaction, or because he was coached to do it.

After they carried Sharkey to the dressing room, Lynch excluded most everyone, including both doctors and reporters. For an hour, Sharkey "lay there complaining of pains in his ear and head." They then took Tom to the hotel. In his room, when Sharkey was stripped, Smith saw no injury or discoloration whatsoever, nor did Sharkey complain of any injury other than on his head. Tom said that the only punches that affected him were the left and right swings to the head.

After a while, a Dr. B.B. Lee arrived and Lynch asked Smith and Allen to leave the room. Outside the door, they heard Sharkey shrieking and howling with pain, as though the doctor was hurting him. When they were again admitted to Sharkey's room, several leeches were feasting on his swollen ear and the doctor had bandaged Sharkey's body. Sharkey told Smith, "That fellow can beat Corbett in two rounds. He hits like a kick from a mule."

After the doctor left, Sharkey jumped out of bed and lit up a cigar. He did not walk at all lame and showed no symptoms of being injured. He did not require any treatment for the rest of the evening.

Smith said that Wyatt Earp showed up at the door between 12 and 3 a.m. in the morning. Earp looked at Smith and said, "Hello, Sharkey, how do you feel?" Smith replied, "I'm not Sharkey. He's in bed." Then Earp entered and spoke with Tom for about fifteen minutes.

The press said that Smith's testimony was straight-forward, never wavered or faltered, and was unshaken under cross-examination by the defendants' attorney General Barnes.

In an interview with the newspapers, referee Hiram Cook basically corroborated Smith's story about Lynch having spoken with him. He said that when Lynch asked him if he had anything against Sharkey or for Fitzsimmons, he had told Lynch that if his own brother was in a fight with a Chinaman and the Chinaman won, he would award it to the Chinaman. He said that those were his, not Lynch's words. Regardless, Lynch had objected to Cook as referee in the face of his statement of fairness, and the fact that Smith knew something of the interaction between Lynch and Cook partially corroborated his story. Perhaps Cook was too square for Lynch. The newsmen took critical note of the fact that a man with 20 years of honest experience was objected to in favor of a fellow horseracer and gambler who had never refereed a big fight.[692]

Further damning court testimony followed. Like Billy Smith, George Allen was a Sharkey trainer who had sparred with Tom every other day for five weeks before the fight, and was in his corner on the evening of the bout. He testified that he saw the 8th round, that Fitz made two feints, allowed Tom to fall short with a left, and then Fitz, "guarding his own head with his right, gave Sharkey a left shift, hitting him fairly in the pit of the stomach with a half swing. Then Tom began to double up, and as he did so Fitz brought his left round again and uppercut him on the jaw." Allen was positive that there was no foul, and that Sharkey made no complaint of a foul. Tom went down on his back insensible.

After six seconds of the count had elapsed, Allen tried to enter the ring and throw up the towel in acknowledgment that his man was fairly out, but a policeman and Danny Needham prevented him from doing so, grabbing and pulling him down from the ring. Allen said the rule was that if any of the seconds believed their man had enough, they were to throw up a towel or sponge. Lynch entered the ring and had Sharkey carried to his dressing room. Allen first learned that Sharkey had won on a foul while he was helping to carry him to the dressing room. Tom did groan a bit on the way there.

In the dressing room, Allen bathed Sharkey with water for two minutes on the allegedly injured part. Sharkey did not show him anything indicating an injury. "So far as I could see there was no inflammation or discoloration." Sharkey did however moan when water was placed over his groin. They remained there an hour. When asked if Sharkey made any complaint of being injured, Allen replied, "He made no complaint to me." Sharkey did not cry out in pain either (as he later did with Dr. Lee), only moaning a bit. Lynch and Sharkey spoke, but in a whisper. Gibbs asked to have the club doctor look at Tom, but Lynch refused. Lynch would allow no doctor's examination until Sharkey was moved to the hotel.

---

[692] *San Francisco Evening Post*, December 9, 1896; *San Francisco Examiner*, December 10, 1896; *San Francisco Call*, December 10, 11, 1896; *San Francisco Bulletin*, December 10, 1896.

At the hotel, after removing Sharkey's pants, a wet towel was placed on the groin area. When Dr. Lee arrived with Danny Needham, Lynch ordered everyone out of the room except for the doctor, Sharkey, Needham, and himself. Allen regarded this as "uncalled for and unusual in this case, seeing that he was one of Sharkey's trainers and that there was no occasion for secrecy if everything was fair and above board."

When asked if Sharkey was injured as claimed, Allen said that he was not. Sharkey hollered out for the first time when he was in the room with the doctor. The next day, Sharkey's groin was bandaged up and there was blood on the cloths (most likely from leeching). So, two Sharkey trainers had confirmed that there was no foul blow, and one of them flatly said that the fight was fixed.[693]

Why did Smith and Allen tell the truth? After all, they were Sharkey trainers, so their loyalty would naturally have been with him. Both Smith and Allen felt that Sharkey had not properly compensated them. Thus, they felt no duty to hide the truth for him. Sharkey had told them that he thought $100 was sufficient compensation for their sparring services, despite the fact that it was a $10,000 purse. Although they were paid a bit more, they felt that Tom was cheap, and as a result, had no particular love for him. Why didn't Smith simply capitalize on the information Sharkey had given him?

Naturally, someone supportive of Sharkey's side could argue that they were bought by the Fitz side to perjure themselves, or made up the stories because they felt that they had not been properly compensated. However, there were a lot of pieces to the puzzle that did not look good for the Sharkey team.

In the meantime, a judge found Wyatt Earp guilty of carrying a concealed weapon and sentenced him to a $50 fine. Earp had testified that he was obliged to be out late at night at the race track, and that it was through his negligence that he had failed to obtain a permit to carry the revolver.

Another Sharkey second, William Abbott, testified that Lynch entered the ring and ordered Sharkey to be carried to the dressing room. Lynch would not allow any reporters or doctors into the dressing room, but said that he would have a doctor of his own look at him. Abbott saw no injury. At the hotel, he was sent out of the room when Dr. Lee arrived. His testimony was similar to and corroborative of Allen's.

Dan Lynch claimed that he did not enter the ring, and said that he would produce witnesses who would back him up. However, Colonel

---

[693] *San Francisco Chronicle*, December 11, 1896; *San Francisco Evening Post*, December 10, 1896.

Kowalsky, Fitz's lawyer, said that he knew Lynch did appear in the ring. "Why, I saw him there myself."[694]

Just when things were looking good for Fitzsimmons, Judge Sanderson said that he was simply having the depositions taken of those witnesses who were not residents, and were about to leave the City. "I am not trying this case now, and I don't know whether it ever can be tried." Sanderson was essentially implying that the matter might be outside of his jurisdiction for the reason that prize-fighting was an offense under the penal code. "But this part of the code has been interpreted by some lawyers to mean a fight to a finish." The San Francisco Board of Supervisors had passed a local ordinance legalizing gloved contests for a limited number of rounds, but there was a question as to whether State law permitted such bouts. *The Bulletin* opined, "It seems strange that so much time is being wasted in the taking of depositions when a demurrer interposed to the complaint by General Barnes might wipe the whole business off the calendar for good and all." Sanderson was more than implying to the Sharkey side his inclination to rule in their favor should they make a motion for a dismissal on technical grounds. This was a harbinger of things to come.

The Call claimed that Earp had once unsuccessfully tried to get someone to throw a horserace in San Diego, and that ever since then, he had not been seen in that part of the country. It again criticized Lynch for rejecting many respectable referees with reputations for honesty and integrity, for they were not the kind that he wanted. On the other hand, Earp had a reputation for fairness which he had earned "by boring holes in persons who had made assertions to the contrary."

The Call said that people were asking why Sharkey was kept in the dressing room for an hour without any competent physician being allowed to examine him. "It is natural to suppose that if Sharkey had received a foul blow both he and Lynch would have been only too willing to have let the whole world examine the injured fighter in order that there might not be the slightest doubt or suspicion in the matter."[695]

The Bulletin criticized Earp's failure to explain why he did not stay in the ring at the fight's conclusion and to announce his decision to the howling mob. "Perhaps it was because of the howling mob that he did not do so." One opined, "Sharkey is the luckiest pugilist of the nineteenth century, for after he was out he made a home run."[696]

Fitzsimmons was scheduled to box at the Chutes again with Stelzner and Hickey on December 13.

---

[694] *San Francisco Evening Post*, December 11, 1896.
[695] *San Francisco Call*, December 11-13, 1896.
[696] *San Francisco Bulletin*, December 12, 1896.

On the 14th, the judge again said that he was not sure whether the entire proceedings were not a waste of time, "on the ground that nothing could come of the main proceeding. The law against prize-fighting, it was said, acted as a bar to any suit for money alleged to have been won or lost over such a contest." Nevertheless, the testimony proceeded.

Dr. Lustig, the National Club's medical examiner, testified substantially in accordance with what he had told the newspapers, which was that neither he nor four other doctors were allowed to examine Sharkey on the night of the fight. He had been allowed to make an examination of both boxers on the Sunday before the fight, so Sharkey and Lynch were familiar with him.

When Dr. Lustig and other doctors arrived at the hotel the next day at about 5 p.m., Dr. Lee was there. Sharkey had a slight discoloration and two little wounds, probably due to the leeching. There was no way to tell what caused Sharkey's injuries, including whether they were created via artificial means, or even when they were inflicted. Dr. Lustig additionally noted that what injuries Sharkey did have were not serious enough to have incapacitated him or kept him in bed for a week.

Fitzsimmons and Martin Julian provided their testimony, which was consistent with what they had told the newspapers. Humorously, when asked if he knew Thomas Sharkey, Fitz responded, "Well...I seen the gentleman on one occasion. I was in his company about half an hour." This answer drew laughter from the audience, including Sharkey.

Fitz said that one hour before the fight, in the dressing room, after Julian objected to Earp, Gibbs and Groom called Julian and Fitz "kickers," and said that it was a pretty late time to demand a referee change. They said they would see what they could do, but later returned and said that they could not secure another referee.

In the ring, Julian announced in front of Earp that Wyatt was crooked and that there was a job to do Bob out of the fight. Earp told them to put the gloves on. Bob initially refused, but the audience shouted at him to go on and fight. "I didn't put on the gloves at first, but finally I spoke to the audience and said I had given way to Sharkey in everything else, and I might as well give him his own referee."

Bob tried not to give Earp any excuses to disqualify him, and fought a bit differently as a result. "Knowing I had a crooked referee, I had to be cautious. I fought at long range and took no chances of committing a foul." Fitz said that he and Sharkey had agreed not to fight in the clinches or in the break-aways, but Tom had not honored that agreement. However, fearing disqualification, Bob abided by the agreement, and also tried to make sure that his blows were clean and obvious. Fighting at long distance, he awaited his opportunity for a knockout blow, and it finally came.

Describing the knockout sequence, Bob said that he delivered a left on Sharkey's face. He feinted and Tom threw his hands up, thinking it was coming again, leaving his body exposed. Bob threw his right foot forward to deliver the left-hand shift in the stomach. He delivered it and Sharkey threw his arms down, leaving his face open. Fitz then landed the left uppercut on the face. Sharkey sank back and fell.

Another paper quoting the same testimony heard it a bit differently, saying that Fitz landed two or three blows, and then a left to the face. Bob next feinted the left, and then landed a right-hand shift in the pit of the stomach and a left uppercut to the jaw.

When asked on cross-examination whether it was possible that he had made a mistake and delivered a foul blow, Fitz said it was impossible. "I never made a mistake in delivery yet." He also made the excellent point that Sharkey did not act like a man who had been hit low. "A man when injured that way bends over on his knees, gets up, falls down, rolls over and howls with pain. I've had it, so I know." However, that was not how Sharkey had acted. "I didn't fall backward as Sharkey did."

Martin Julian testified regarding Lynch's refusal to agree upon a referee. Lynch told him that Sharkey was not going to get the worst of it in this deal. "I don't intend to agree to a referee until the day of the fight." When Julian suggested Hiram Cook, as well as a number of other respected men, Lynch called them "old dubs." "He said we might as well quit, as he would not accept any of my names. I asked him to give some names. He remarked that it would be useless as he knew I would not accept any of his nominees." Lynch did mention two men, but said that he knew Julian would not accept them because they were personal race-horse friends. Thus, Lynch never made a good faith effort to name anyone who would be neutral. It was obvious that Lynch wanted the club to select the referee, which per the contract would bind Julian and Fitzsimmons.

Groom told Julian that he did not think Dan Lynch would agree to a referee, but that he knew of a fearless man who could serve. He did not reveal the name, but on the day of the fight, one of the bartenders at a local hotel told Julian that it was Earp. When Julian asked Groom whether it was true, Groom confirmed it. Julian did not know him, so he did not object initially. This was about 2 p.m. on the day of the fight.

Julian spoke of how Riley Grannan, Mose Gunst, and others came to him on the night of the fight and warned him about the referee. Grannan warned him not to accept Earp under any circumstances. Two days prior, he had been unable to place money on Fitz at any odds, because most gamblers thought Bob would win. However, on the day of the fight, at the racetrack Earp was seen speaking with Joe Harvey, the horseman. Harvey said, "It's all right, then?" Earp replied, "You can rely on me." Then,

Grannan noticed that men who never bet on anything other than sure things were backing Sharkey at the racetrack for thousands of dollars. Gunst echoed Grannan's feelings about Earp. Gunst told Julian not to fight at all if they could not get another referee.

Julian called on Groom and told him that Fitz would not fight with Earp as the referee. Groom said he would see what he could do. However, they did not come up with anyone new.

Before the fight, Julian met Earp at the Pavilion and told him what he had heard. Earp said that the club had selected him and he would appear in the ring and stay there until one of the club managers asked him to retire. Continuing his story, Julian said,

> After the men were in the ring I made another protest. I told Earp as he was climbing on the stage that I would insult and disgrace him if he got into the ring. He said he had made up his mind what he was going to do. I then spoke to the audience and said that I had learned that Earp was crooked.

Another reporter quoted Julian as saying to Earp that it would be best for him to step out and allow the club to select another man, that if he did not do so he would tell the audience what he knew about him. "He answered that he had been selected by the club and he was gong to stay, and he walked away laughing."

Unfortunately, the spectators were howling for a fight, and so Julian and Fitz felt pressured to go on. They believed that if Bob did not fight, the next morning newspapers would say that Fitz was afraid to meet Sharkey.

Julian swore that several times in the clinch, when breaking them, Earp stuck his fingers into Fitz's eyes. Wyatt also allowed Sharkey to repeatedly strike on the breakaways.

Julian was actually supportive of club promoter Groom, who had told him during the fight that the proceedings were disgraceful. Groom called upon the referee to keep Sharkey from fouling. Instead, Earp warned Fitz and told Bob that he was doing more wrestling than Sharkey. At that point, co-promoter Gibbs told Groom to mind his own business.

After the fight, fearing for the club's reputation and calling it a "barefaced robbery," Groom demanded admittance to Sharkey's room for an examination, but was refused. Julian quoted Groom as saying that the decision was an outrage, that he was through with Gibbs, and that that he "can't afford to be mixed up with a lot of thieves."

Examiner writer W.W. Naughton testified that he had not seen Fitz strike Sharkey below the belt. He saw the right land in the short ribs or stomach, then a left uppercut to the chin, and Tom went down. Fitz did not land a foul blow during the fight. Dan Hickey, a Fitz trainer, corroborated that Sharkey was knocked out fairly.[697]

In its daily attack on Earp and the *Examiner*, the *Call* claimed that Earp did not appear on the *Examiner* payroll as a bodyguard, but as a library attaché. Earp was paraded and advertised as the author of a Sunday story column, but the *Call* claimed that the stories were actually written by a man named Chambers, who Hearst imported from New York. "It was under the guise of pay for these stories that Earp figured on the payroll." Earp was really a bodyguard for *Examiner* editor Lawrence. It said that a member of the *Examiner* bet a large sum of money on Sharkey in the poolrooms three hours before the fight. "He has nothing outside of the salary he earns running errands for Long Green, and yet he bet hundreds on Sharkey."[698]

As of December 15, the *Evening Post* opined, "That the decision in the Sharkey-Fitzsimmons fight was the result of a disgraceful criminal conspiracy, there can no longer be the slightest doubt." It said that Dr. Lee was rumored to be $1,000 richer since he "happened to be in the vicinity" of the Windsor Hotel, where Sharkey was staying, and was "called in" to treat Tom. It was also rumored that Lee had offered $500 to another physician to back his story that the injury was caused by a low blow, but that the overture had been refused.

Taking the stand again, Dan Lynch testified that he had never known Earp personally. He raced his horses on the same tracks as Earp, had nodded to him half a dozen times at the track, but they had never spoken. He later said that he and Earp had not spoken more than ten words at a time. This contradicted the news reports claiming that it was generally known that Lynch and Earp were friends. Earp had gone with him to the bank to try and get the check cashed.

Lynch said that he had no interest in the National Club, that he had only watched the ticket office when Mr. Groom had asked him to do so when he went away for a while. Lynch further totally denied ever having a conversation with Hiram Cook about what he would do in case a Chinaman and his brother were in a fight. This flatly contradicted what Cook had told the newspapers. Lynch said that he did not want Cook because people who had bet on Fitz wanted him.

Lynch testified that he received no pay for his managerial duties. He simply bet on Sharkey. When asked why he managed Sharkey for no pay,

---

[697] *San Francisco Evening Post, San Francisco Bulletin,* December 14, 1896.
[698] *San Francisco Call,* December 14, 1896.

Lynch said, "I like to know what I am betting about and prefer to be on the inside track." Still, he claimed that he had bet less on this fight than any other Sharkey fight, placing $400 to $1,000 a week before the fight. This contradicted what Sharkey had told the newspapers before the fight, which was that both he and Lynch had bet every cent they had on the bout.

Lynch admitted to not allowing any of a number of willing doctors into the dressing room to examine Sharkey, even though Tom was apparently laying there in agony. He claimed that there were simply too many people in the room already, and it was hot and uncomfortable. If true, why not have some people leave? He did that at the hotel. Another excuse he gave for refusing to admit Dr. Lustig was because Lynch was incensed at the club's officers for having refused to put the prize money check into the referee's hands until the fighters had shaken hands. "This very thin excuse for barring out physicians provoked a smile of incredulity among the audience."

When Lynch was asked about his reputation as a horseman and whether any of his entries had been refused at the racetrack within the last few years, General Barnes, the Sharkey side's attorney, objected. "If we have got to try horse-racing as well as prize-fighting we will never get through with this case. We will next get down to cock-fighting." Fitz attorney Kowalsky responded, "At which you are an expert." Barnes retorted, "Yes, I have watched you many a time." The judge sustained the objection, as he did quite often for the defense when the Fitz side explored potentially embarrassing areas.

Lynch denied being acquainted with Dr. Lee. He had never seen him before and did not know that he was a physician. He claimed that he told Mr. Dowdell to bring a good physician, and that Dr. Lee later showed up. "After Mr. Lynch had denied almost everything but the fact of his own existence he was let go for the present, the hour of adjournment having arrived."

There was some discussion at the bench with the judge, and something Sharkey attorney Barnes said caused Fitz attorney Kowalsky "to retort that Mr. Barnes was going back on his agreement not to resort to technicalities; that he was claiming a foul when he was getting the worst of it, and that he had buried the hatchet with the handle sticking toward himself." Apparently, Barnes had said that he was going to bring a motion to have the whole matter discharged on a technicality. Another paper quoted Fitz's lawyer as responding,

[Sharkey's lawyer had previously said] that he wanted to throw this case wide open and to put no obstacles in the way of getting at the facts.... The handle of your hatchet is sticking out of your coat pocket right now. The moment your side begins to get the worst of it you squeal and try to get a decision on a second alleged foul.[699]

At the beginning of the case, General Barnes had said that if he so chose, he could have the proceedings annulled on a technicality, but that Lynch was anxious for the whole truth to come out. As a result, Barnes was called the "only respectable element on that side of the case." "It is evident that the veteran attorney does not intend interposing technicalities which in themselves would go to show the weakness of his clients' case." To resort to such technicalities would essentially indirectly confirm the truth of Fitz's allegations, because failure to defend on the merits would be perceived as the Sharkey side fearing the truth. Rather, Barnes initially attempted to fight it out on the merits.

However, as the testimony proceeded, the Sharkey team saw that their strategy was flawed. Given that things were not looking good, the truth was becoming less of an object and more of an obstacle for the Sharkey side. Therefore, they needed to resort to a strategy that would lead to a technical win of the kind that gave Sharkey the fight in the first place.[700]

Judge Sanderson remarked that he had expected that counsel would have by this point inquired into the character of the affair, as to whether it was an illegal prize-fight or merely a friendly boxing match. The judge also said that it was not his affair. However, he certainly acted as if it was. He had earlier tipped off the defense as to a winning strategy, and was again doing so. As a result of this new defense strategy, there would be some additional testimony as to the nature of the contest – whether it was a legal bout, and therefore a legally enforceable contract.

Thomas Sharkey testified that he was 23 years of age, having boxed for about three years. He basically denied all of Smith's testimony. He admitted that Lynch had put up a $2,500 appearance guarantee for both Sharkey and Fitzsimmons, because Bob was broke. For his training, Tom ran 12 miles a day, boxed, swam, and exercised.

On the night of the fight, Sharkey removed his hand bandages when Earp told him to do so. He denied that Earp said that things would be all right. Tom never saw Lynch in the ring after the fight. He claimed that the first time that he spoke with Lynch was in the dressing room.

Describing the final sequence of events terminating the fight, Sharkey said, "He hit me a left in the mouth. Then he feinted with his left, threw his

---

[699] *San Francisco Chronicle*, December 15, 1896.
[700] *San Francisco Call*, December 15, 1896.

right across my head and uppercut me with the right, striking me in the groin."

He said that he was not dizzy from the face blow, and was not unconscious at any time. "No, that was sort of a brush. The blow that caused me to fall was the foul one." Sharkey claimed to have been laid up in bed for a week, and was still suffering. Tom also said that the only injury he received was to the groin, which was contradicted by his appearance, for his eyes were badly damaged.

Sharkey claimed that as he was falling from his knees to his side that he told the referee that he had been fouled. However, "In response to other queries Sharkey said that he was in such pain that he did not know how he did fall." When asked if he fell on his back, Sharkey responded, "No. I don't think I was ever on my back." Sharkey's version disagreed with the newspaper accounts.

Sharkey again reiterated his skewed view of the fight, saying that if he had not been fouled, he would have knocked out Fitz in the same round, and only needed a couple more punches to do it. At this assertion, "The audience grinned, and so did Fitz." His claim flatly contradicted the impression of all ringside reporters.

Sharkey asserted that referee Cook was unacceptable because Tom had heard that Cook had visited Fitz's training quarters. However, he also said that the first time he ever saw Earp's name was in a newspaper which said that Earp had visited Fitz's training quarters. When asked why then was he not suspicious of Earp when he too had visited Fitz's training camp, Sharkey had no explanation. "The question was a staggerer and Sharkey gave no direct response." He also said that the reason Cook was unacceptable was because Fitz's friends wanted him. He admitted that Smith had told him that Cook had fairly refereed fights for him, and that Lynch had said that he would go see Cook. Tom confirmed that Lynch did not receive pay, but had the privilege of seeing him at work, know his condition, and then bet on him.

Kowalsky then moved onto another topic which demonstrated an interesting connection between the Sharkey camp and Dr. Lee. Sharkey testified that he knew that the man who was training Dan Needham went by the name of Louie. Apparently, this was Louie Matheny, a notorious burglar. Interestingly enough, Dr. Lee had been the chief witness in providing Matheny with an alibi in a criminal case. Matheny had come out to Sharkey's training quarters with Needham and had stayed there. Dan Lynch was also Needham's manager. Needham had introduced Sharkey to Lynch. So, Lee had provided an alibi for Matheny, who was Needham's trainer and had been at the camp, and Needham was managed by Lynch and was a Sharkey trainer. The players were all connected. Sharkey claimed not to know Lee. Regardless, it appears that his team had some familiarity with him. According to Tom, after the fight, Dr. Lee placed leeches on him and applied hot cloths and bandages.

Kowalsky cross-examined Sharkey about the fact that he screamed when Dr. Lee examined him, but had not yelled when Fitz hit him. When asked if the doctor had hurt him as much as Fitzsimmons did, Sharkey said, "No, sir, he did not." Yet he did not cry out in the ring as he did when the doctor examined him. Sharkey had no legitimate explanation other than to say that he groaned in the ring. "The question raised a buzz throughout the courtroom." Sharkey said that he was too game to holler loud. Kowalsky then asked, "Oh, you are, are you? Then why did you holler loud when Dr. Lee examined you?" Sharkey said that at that time he was very sore. Sharkey admitted that Lee had used iodine on him.[701]

Danny Needham testified that he had no prior arrangement with Dr. Lee, claiming that he just happened to see the doctor as he was walking through the hotel. However, "This morning Dr. Lee did not corroborate Needham, as he told a 'Post' reporter that he went to see Sharkey through curiosity. He applied at the door and was admitted."[702]

William Greer Harrison and others were called to testify that the bout was not a "prize-fight" but a legal gentlemanly glove contest for points. Harrison said that a prize-fight was a brutal exhibition governed by only a few rules, whereas a gloved contest was covered by a complete set of rules. He had witnessed the fight and was positive that Bob had committed no foul.

Lem Fulda testified. When asked by the judge whether fighters were injured in many different ways in boxing matches, Fulda admitted that such accidents often happened.

Walter Watson testified that he saw the finishing blows, and swore that Fitz did not strike a foul blow.

Wyatt Earp testified that he had never given an interview, and that any paper which quoted him was false. Earp denied being connected with any

[701] *San Francisco Chronicle, San Francisco Examiner,* December 16, 1896; *San Francisco Evening Post, San Francisco Bulletin,* December 15, 1896; *San Francisco Call,* December 15, 16, 1896.
[702] *San Francisco Evening Post,* December 16, 1896.

newspaper as a writer. He said that his present business was horseracing, but he leased the horses.

Earp had refereed a prize-fight in San Diego and fifteen or twenty bareknuckle fights in Mexico. When asked if the contest the other night was a prize-fight, Earp said, "They call it a glove contest." The judge asked, "What do you call it?" Earp replied, "I call them all prize-fights, but restricted by law. They are all amenable to law, although they are called glove contests." It was interesting that he was arguing that he had been a participant in a crime. Obviously, he knew of the latest defense strategy.

Earp claimed that no one had spoken to him about being the referee until 1 p.m. the afternoon of the fight. However, he admitted that he knew that he was a potential candidate. He had once visited Fitzsimmons' training headquarters in Sausalito. On the boat ride back from the visit, National Club master of ceremonies Billy Jordan said to a crowd of people that he had seen Earp referee 8-10 fights and that Wyatt would be a good referee for the upcoming fight.

Earp testified that on the night of the fight, Julian told him about how he had heard that he was fixed. Earp responded that he would give him a fair show. He incredulously claimed that Julian replied, "I am satisfied there is nothing in this report," and walked off. When later in the ring Julian accused him of being fixed, Earp claimed that he addressed the spectators and said that he had lived in the community for five years and thought that no one would question his honesty. However, the news reports said that Wyatt stood silently and did not respond to the accusation.

Amazingly, "Earp said that if there was any kindness in the world on his part it was toward Fitzsimmons." To this, Kowalsky asked if it was kindness when Earp put his fingers in Bob's eye and pushed him back. Earp denied doing so, claiming that he always put his hand on the breast. He denied seeing Sharkey catch Fitz by the legs, or trying to throw him. "If Sharkey had caught Fitzsimmons by the legs and wanted to throw him he could have thrown him clear off the stage." He confirmed that Groom had come to him between rounds and asked him to make Sharkey fight fair, saying that he was fouling. Earp responded that Fitz was doing the fouling. Earp then cautioned Bob, but he also cautioned Sharkey.

Earp flatly denied ever going to the Baldwin Hotel and asking Chief Clerk Clough whether Fitz was there. He said that nothing of the kind had happened. However, Clough told the newspapers that Earp had been coming there almost daily for his mail, and that the morning after the fight Wyatt asked if Fitz was around. He came around a second time asking the same thing. It was said that Clough was a man of unquestioned integrity, who had been a hotel man of favorable renown for the past 20 years.

Earp testified that Dan Lynch called on Earp's residence the morning after the fight because Wyatt had not delivered to him the certificate of deposit, but took it home with him. How did Lynch know where he lived?

As things were not going well factually, Sharkey team lawyer General Barnes announced that the following morning he would move to dismiss the complaint on the ground that the court had no jurisdiction over the matter. The motion to dissolve the injunction was not based on the merits of the case, but on a technicality. He argued that boxing was illegal, and no different from dog fighting or cock fighting. No court could enforce any contract concerning an illegal act. The judge said that he would hear legal arguments the next morning.[703]

Barnes was essentially arguing that his own clients had participated in an illegal act. Fitz said, "Barnes went into court and, so as to throw the injunction out, went ahead and declared the fight was a felony. He seemed to forget that he was being hired and paid by one of the felons if that was so." Such was the weakness of their case that they had to resort to such a tactic, actually arguing they had committed a crime, so as to avoid having to deal with the merits of the case. This argument might have given the Sharkey team the legal upper hand, but it would be a devastating public relations move. The press and public viewed the use of this tactic as an admission of their case's factual weakness.

Fitz's side countered that the Board of Supervisors had issued a permit for the contest, and it was held under police supervision. Therefore, it would be a stretch to say that the proceeding was contrary to statute and that all the principles and spectators were guilty of illegal acts. Boxing had taken place quite often in San Francisco. "If the law has been violated, the Supervisors who granted the permit are as guilty as the men who stepped into the ring and did the fighting."

On the morning of December 17, the judge heard arguments on the motion to dissolve the complaint. Barnes argued that the contest was illegal. He cited cases holding that a court should dismiss any action asking for compensation for an act prohibited by law. He quoted from the Louisiana reports, citing a case where the New Orleans Olympic Club was broken up by the authorities under the law prohibiting prizefighting, even though the contests were conducted with gloves at an incorporated club. Barnes argued,

> I submit, your Honor, that this is a proceeding that this court ought not to entertain a moment longer, and, while I consented on account of the intense public interest, to refrain from objecting to the taking

[703] *San Francisco Call*, December 16, 1896.

of testimony, I hold that your Honor has no power to adjudicate in the matter.

Kowalsky countered that there was a big difference between a prize fight and a glove contest. A prize fight was not allowed. A gloved contest was held with the consent of the Supervisors by and through the local ordinance and the permit they issued, not to mention the supervision of the police force. Kowalsky remarked that Barnes was essentially arguing that his own clients had committed a felony in order to avoid dealing with the fact that the fight was fixed.[704]

The Court quickly ruled in Sharkey's favor. "I may as well dispose of this matter now as at any other time." He held that the local authorities could not legalize boxing any more than they could legalize a duel, and the local ordinance was an attempt to violate the state law.

> There is no question in my mind that the parties to this engagement or exhibition or whatever you call it, the complaint calls it a boxing contest, are indictable under the law and that the people who witnessed it are amenable to the law as law breakers. I understand that these exhibitions are given because the people and the police wink at them. But no court will recognize any such proceeding and there is no doubt in my mind that this injunction should have been dissolved, and it would have been dissolved if the motion had been made immediately upon the heels of issuing it, as the court, in fact, expected. The order to dissolve the injunction will be granted.[705]

The judge held that fighting was illegal and there was no difference between boxing and fighting. To box was to fight, and the terms boxer and fighter were synonymous. The state legislature in 1893 had made prize fighting with or without gloves, wherein bodily injury may occur, a felony punishable by a fine from $1,000 to $5,000 and imprisonment from one to three years. The Board of Supervisors could not via a local ordinance overrule the state law. He said that everyone involved had made themselves indictable for a crime. Essentially, he had ruled that it did not matter whether or not the fight was fixed, because the whole affair was illegal. The court would not show its approval by consenting to re-referee a prize fight.

Lynch said that he did not fear an indictment because the whole police force and Board of Supervisors would have to be indicted as well. It was

---

[704] *San Francisco Evening Post, San Francisco Call*, December 17, 1896.
[705] *San Francisco Evening Post, San Francisco Bulletin*, December 17, 1896.

not likely that the grand jury would proceed against the boxers. "In the jury are a number of prominent citizens who delight in ring contests. They hold it would be unwise to proceed against the boxers, as it is certain convictions could not be obtained."

Fitzsimmons called it the foulest conspiracy ever perpetrated in the annals of pugilism. "The referee's decision was pretty raw, but this court business about equals it."

> I was induced to commence the suit in the belief that the issue of fraud which I charge would be fairly and squarely met, and I was encouraged in that belief when General Barnes openly stated in court that he wanted the doors of investigation thrown wide open, and wanted this case determined upon justice alone. Finding that the justice of the case was with me and that I had fully established the fraud which I charged had been perpetrated, he sought refuge in the weakness of the law to give me my just rights, and moved a dismissal of the case on the ground that the contest was nothing but a prize-fight and, that the court was, therefore, powerless to relieve. The utter hopelessness of the defense in this case was manifest when resort had to be made to a motion of this character, asking for a decision which might involve the liberty of the defendants as well as all those conspiring with them.[706]

The judge's decision reflected an internal inconsistency and conflict as to whether boxing was or should be considered legal. The national debate was alive and well.

Ultimately, although the $10,000 in the winner-take-all fight went to Sharkey's side, because Sharkey had to resort to such a technical win, the press and public believed that Fitz had been robbed.

On December 19, Fitzsimmons passed by Sharkey on the sidewalk. Bob said that Tom held his head down as he passed. "I always thought Sharkey held his head up in a proud manner when he passed friend or foe, but I guess he knows that the purse he won by a foul decision belonged to me and that is why he dropped his eyes when he passed."[707]

---

[706] *San Francisco Call, San Francisco Examiner, San Francisco Chronicle, San Francisco Evening Post,* all December 18, 1896.
[707] *San Francisco Call,* December 20, 1896.

CHAPTER 18

Paving the Way,
Predictions and Preparation

Although Bob Fitzsimmons had technically lost to Tom Sharkey, the sporting world considered it a Fitz victory, and agreed that he had fought much more impressively against Sharkey than had Corbett. Thus, the public still considered Fitzsimmons the top contender for the title. There had been ongoing negotiations for a Corbett-Fitzsimmons fight both before and immediately after the Fitz-Sharkey fight.

DAN A. STUART.

On December 17, 1896, the same day that the judge dismissed Bob's case against the Sharkey team, Fitzsimmons and Corbett once again agreed to fight. It was to be a Marquis of Queensberry rules fight to the finish for the heavyweight championship of the world, to be held on St. Patrick's Day, March 17, 1897. The agreed upon purse was $15,000, winner take all. Each side was to post $2,500 with a third party to guarantee his appearance in the ring at a location to be determined. Promoter Dan Stuart separately posted $5,000 to guarantee that he would bring off the fight. The remaining $10,000 was to be posted 30 days prior to the fight.

The parties agreed to name George Siler of Chicago to be the referee. Siler had once sparred with Fitz and had refereed the recent Fitzsimmons-Maher bout. Both sides agreed that he was a good referee.[708]

---

[708] *San Francisco Examiner*, December 18, 1896; *New York Clipper*, December 26, 1896.

Each of the boxers contracted to receive 1/3 of the money paid by the Kinetoscope Company to film the fight. Stuart planned to erect an arena capable of seating 20,000.[709] During February 1897, he set the ticket prices at $5, $10, $20, and $40.[710]

When they made the match, to the public, it was clear that it would be Fitzsimmons challenging for Corbett's true championship claim, and most talk of Fitz and/or Sharkey being champions mostly disappeared, although Fitz sometimes claimed to be the champion, and Sharkey sometimes claimed the same owing to his "win" over Fitzsimmons. However, even the newspapers felt that Bob had forfeited the title back to Corbett prior to fighting Sharkey.

Naturally, talk about the fight was immediate. In fact, the amount of ink devoted to this exciting and intriguing match-up on an almost daily basis was massive and unprecedented. One initial analysis may have been the most accurate: "The Cornishman, although not so shifty nor as clever as the champion, is nevertheless a most dangerous opponent, who may turn the tide of battle in his favor at any point in the game."[711]

Martin Julian said that they would head east on December 21, on the way giving exhibitions in Denver, Cripple Creek and other places over the next three weeks before arriving in New York.[712]

On December 25, 1896 before a large and enthusiastic crowd at Cripple Creek, Colorado, Bob punched the bag 3 short rounds and then boxed 4 lively rounds with Dan Hickey. Bob said that Hickey was one of the cleverest boxers in the country.[713]

That same day in New York, 177 ½-pound Peter Maher scored a rematch KO1 over 181-pound Steve O'Donnell, taking him out in just 27 seconds. Despite his early 1896 loss to Fitz, Maher was having a good mid-to-late 1896, scoring a June KO4 Frank Slavin and November KO6 Joe Choynski. These strong performances made Bob's two victories over Maher all the more impressive.[714]

Fitzsimmons was in Denver on the 26th and 27th before heading to Omaha, Nebraska.

One of the chief questions was where the fight would be held. Bob initially thought it would take place in Mexico. Corbett told Stuart that he would neither sign articles of agreement nor fight without a guarantee that

---

[709] *Salt Lake Herald*, January 31, 1897.
[710] *San Francisco Chronicle*, February 13, 1897.
[711] *San Francisco Call*, December 19, 1896.
[712] *San Francisco Call*, December 21, 1896.
[713] *Rocky Mountain News*, December 26, 27, 1896.
[714] *Rocky Mountain News*, December 26, 1896.

there would be no legal troubles or police interference. He did not want to go through the legal wrangling that he had previously encountered, to take the time to train for a fight that would not and could not take place, and to forgo all the money that he could have made in the theater instead.

Not only was boxing not legally or morally popular, but the fact that it occasionally allowed mixed race bouts did not endear it to many political authorities either. Just as an insight into how race relations impacted the sport, a January 1897 New York article stated that although the South had generally been more accepting of boxing than the North, there were indications that the South was shifting its position. It illustrated the South's departure with a discussion of a mixed race bout in Louisiana between Joe Green, colored, and "the terrible Swede." Green was about to knock out the Swede, and only one more blow was needed.

> That blow, however, was not delivered, for at the critical moment Judge Long, one of the most prominent residents of the neighborhood, jumped into the ring with a pistol in his right hand, and with a mighty oath declared that so long as he lived "no nigger should ever whip a white man in Jefferson parish." The effect was instantaneous. The judge's remark, if not heartily applauded, certainly met with the approval of the multitude, for the fight was declared off and "the terrible Swede" spared the ignominy of being defeated by a man with a black skin...
>
> Without desiring to be impertinent, however, and more as a matter of information than anything else, may we ask our Southern contemporaries to what, if any extent, Judge Long really reflected the sentiment of the white people of the South toward the colored brother? ... The question should be answered honestly. There is no occasion to beat bout the bush.... It must be admitted that the colored brother himself is largely responsible for the existing condition of affairs. But why be hypocritical about it? Why try to create false impressions in Northern communities as to the exact feeling entertained toward the negro by the white population in the Southern states? We must do Judge Long the credit of saying that he has the courage of his convictions. He is the representative of a type. But we do not especially admire the type.[715]

The state of Nevada was considering a bill legalizing boxing, which could open the way for the Fitzsimmons-Corbett bout to be held there. Many Nevada writers advocated boxing's legalization.

---

[715] *Brooklyn Daily Eagle,* January 25, 1897.

We do not see...any reason why a law should not be passed protecting this kind of athletic sport....

Many people form conclusions against this sport, gained from reading accounts of the old time affairs with bare knuckles, and when the spectators were a hundred or so tough characters... [T]oday in nearly every state in the Union, glove contests are taking place...and at which the very best people are the ones who attend and support them. There is absolutely no brutality under the Marquis of Queensberry rules.... In New York City and Brooklyn from one to three fights a week are now taking place.

Perhaps more importantly, it was noted that the big fight would have a positive economic impact upon Nevada, bringing in 8,000 to 10,000 visitors from around the country. The state had a population of only 60,000 and was in dire financial straits.

This same writer advocated finish fights when it came to world championship bouts, saying that such was the only way to truly settle the issue. Corbett-Fitzsimmons was scheduled as a finish fight, which is why it could not be held in New York, which via the 1896 Horton law had legalized limited round contests.[716]

In late January 1897, the Nevada legislature passed a bill legalizing boxing. The Nevada Assembly passed the bill by a vote of 20 to 9, and the Senate passed it by a vote of 9 to 6. Telegrams sent to the legislature and governor favoring the bill outnumbered those against it by 16 to 1. Nevada newspapers favored the bill. "THE NEWS believes that by this bill Nevada's morals will in no way be affected and that there will be no painful results." Another Nevada newspaper said the bill will "not have as demoralizing an effect on the public as a game of football."

On January 29, 1897, Governor Reinhold Sadler signed the bill legalizing boxing in Nevada. It required payment of $1,000 for a license, for doctors to examine the contestants before the fight, no liquor could be sold at the fight, and no bouts were to take place on Sunday.[717] The Corbett-Fitzsimmons fight was set for Carson City, Nevada. This began Nevada's great and long association with the sport of boxing.

Local writers supported the governor's action in signing the bill.

---

[716] *The News* (Carson), January 23, 1897; *Fistic Carnival* at 194.
[717] *The News*, January 28, 1897; *Nevada State Journal* (Reno), January 30, 1897; *National Police Gazette*, February 13, 1897; *New York Clipper*, February 6, 1897.

Squarely-conducted boxing exhibitions are not so brutal as footballing, which requires nothing but mule strength and capacity to endure kicks and the roughest kind of usage. It is the most brutalizing of all sports and should be tabooed. In comparison bare knuckle fighting is innocent pastime.[718]

Another said,

Nothing is more exciting than to see two men equally matched in a spirited boxing contest, the art of self-defense is a noble one and should be encouraged at all times. People go mad over football and criticize boxing as brutal, but it is safe to say if they saw the latter their views would be changed.[719]

Unfortunately, not everyone supported these positions. Discussions were being held at the federal level to implement legislation that would hinder the sport's progress and popularity. A report out of Washington, D.C. in late February 1897 said that the House Committee on Commerce was discussing the question of limiting newspaper publication of fight reports, as well as the right to transport and exhibit fight films.

The committee directed Representative Aldrich of Illinois to report to the House a bill prohibiting the transportation of pictures or descriptions of prize fights by mail or interstate commerce and fixing a maximum penalty of five years' imprisonment for a violation of the law. This bill applies to the transmission of reports from one State to another by telegraph, but it is not intended to interfere with announcement of the occurrence and result of the fight.[720]

Although no such bill was passed, it certainly was a harbinger of things to come, a reflection of the national debate about the sport and the ongoing attempts to legally attack and circumscribe it.

One Alabama writer criticized all the condemnation of boxing, calling fellow writers and even politicians hypocrites:

---

[718] *The News,* February 3, 1897.
[719] *Nevada State Journal,* February 12, 1897.
[720] *Reno Evening Gazette,* February 26, 1897.

If "the moral press of a great country" feels so cut up every time two pugs quit talking long enough to punch each other, why does it give so much space to the "brutality?" Why does it illustrate the thing it despises with great prints? Why is it so particular to get every blow down correctly? What is the use of serving up the matter by rounds? Why does it so carefully nurse that which so shocks and mortifies its delicate moral sensibilities? ....

It takes much pains to report prize fights for those who want them reported, and then curses them for the sake of those who want them cursed – and convention. Of course there are honest journalists, as there are freaks of nature and exceptions to most rules. But I am now dealing in generalities.

With the exception of their physiques, I am not an admirer of pugilists. They are a low set of people. But whatever they are, they are infinitely more respectable than hundreds of their critics, who are now abusing them as loudly as they will soon cheer them from the ring side at Carson City.

Now as to Governor Sadler's action [signing the bill legalizing boxing]; it deserves hearty commendation rather than censure... This Westerner has at least shown himself to be a man of moral courage.... He is a thousand times to be preferred to Culberson, the "Christian hero," of Texas, and Clarke, the Arkansas Pharisee, both of whom were simply intimidated into doing what they didn't want to do - ... It is funny how both of these men tolerate chicken fights.... Culberson's conduct is rendered particularly disgraceful by his having patronized the pugs but to turn upon them.

The greatest joke of all is the attitude of the dirty mongrels across the Rio...at the thought of a fisticuff between two scientific athletes who voluntarily step into a ring for a test of skill and endurance with four ounce gloves...while they delight in the torture of unhappy bulls for a national pastime. Truly modern morals are a strange thing....

While not objecting to foot ball in the abstract, I will say what is true, that even that game is far more brutal and dangerous than the four cornered ring.

Various Governors have been keeping the wires hot with indignant messages to the Chief Executive of Nevada. The Governor of Virginia proudly wired that his State had lately made glove contests for prizes, felonies, punishable by from four to six years imprisonment in the penitentiary. That the Virginian should be proud of such a harsh and unnatural law indicates that he is a fool.[721]

Regardless of opinion about the sport, the fight was on in Nevada, and almost daily pre-fight discussion proliferated. Not known for his credibility, Tom Sharkey made contradictory predictions. At one point, Sharkey claimed that Corbett would win; saying that he did not think Fitz was Jim's equal in all-around ring work. He said that Corbett was shiftier, quicker, craftier, and Fitz's equal in punching power:

> Corbett is very quick in all his movements, and his manner of delivering blows is very puzzling. He is a great upper-cutter, although I suppose a good many of his blows would be more properly called hooks or jolts than upper-cuts.... Corbett's most effective punches are delivered with his left. He uses a left hook much the same as Choynski does. He holds his arm partly rigid and sends it in swiftly with an upward motion. Then he has a straight left jab which carries plenty of force. It is a much more telling blow than Fitz's straight left.... Corbett is shiftier in every way, has a greater variety of blows and can hit equally as hard as Fitzsimmons.[722]

However, Sharkey had also predicted that Fitz would defeat Corbett in 2 rounds, saying, "He hits like a mule."[723]

The National Police Gazette said of the two, "All Fitz's movements are executed in a flatfooted style... Corbett is certainly a prettier and more taking exhibition boxer than his Australian rival, but the latter has proved himself to be what he claims he is, a fighter."[724] Fitzsimmons clearly had the superior knockout record.

John L. Sullivan picked Corbett, saying,

> Most sporting men think it will be a short fight. I do not. Both men have a great deal at stake, and, in my opinion, neither will take any chances of defeat by a random blow in a mixup. I think they will use up several rounds trying to draw each other out. I expect to see a slow fight. Now, as to the relative merits of the two men, I should say that Corbett is much superior to Fitzsimmons in ring generalship. He

[721] *The News*, March 13, 1897.
[722] *San Francisco Examiner*, December 8, 1896.
[723] *New York Clipper*, December 19, 1896.
[724] *National Police Gazette*, November 16, 1896.

is shiftier on his feet, and will thus be able to get away from Fitzsimmons' dangerous rushes. Then too, he has a good eye, keeps cool, and knows just when and where to strike. He doesn't waste any time in punching air.... I don't underestimate Fitzsimmons' ability. I know he is a game fighter and hard hitter, and a clever man in every way, but I think Corbett outclasses him.

Sullivan later said that Corbett had always shown great cleverness in making his matches, and felt that Fitz did not really want the fight, but the public forced him into it. He believed that Fitz could have eluded the Arkansas authorities, but purposely had himself arrested so as to have the fight stopped.

However, Bill Muldoon, Sullivan's former trainer, "thinks Fitzsimmons has something up his sleeve and should do the trick." Regardless, Corbett was the initial betting favorite at 10 to 7, and remained the favorite.[725]

Peter Maher thought Corbett would win, but would not have an easy time doing it.

Joe Choynski, who had fought both, also picked Corbett, saying,

> I believe Corbett will win sure. Accidents, of course, are always liable to happen, but I can see no chance for an accident in this fight. Corbett is too careful for that. From my experience in the ring with both men, I am convinced that Fitzsimmons is Corbett's inferior in speed and generalship.... Besides, Corbett is the stronger man, and that counts for something. I have frequently heard men say that Corbett is not a hitter. I know he can punch hard enough.... He can knock Fitzsimmons out with his left hand if he lands, and I do not insist upon a swinging blow to bring this about.[726]

It was interesting that both Choynski and Sharkey favored Corbett, especially since Jim had required 27 rounds to take out Joe, while Fitz had only required 5 (though Bob was once dropped), and Jim had struggled in a 4-rounder with Sharkey, while Bob had dominated and taken him out in the 8th round.

Since winning the heavyweight championship in late 1892, Corbett had not had a significant title defense. He had no defenses in 1893. Like Sullivan, Charley Mitchell had been inactive for quite some time before

[725] *Reno Evening Gazette,* March 17, 1897; *San Francisco Chronicle,* February 1, 1897.
[726] *Nevada State Journal,* February 12, 1897; *Salt Lake Herald,* February 17, 1897.

meeting Corbett. Mitchell was also shorter and smaller, past his prime, and lasted only 3 rounds in their early 1894 bout. The shorter and amateurish Courtney was a stiff, and Jim easily handled him in 6 short rounds with long rests in late 1894. Corbett had no title defenses in 1895. He boxed Sharkey only 4 rounds in mid-1896, and did not look good. Jim had otherwise only boxed in short exhibitions that were mostly friendly or against men with whom he was familiar or far superior. Thus, for over four years, Corbett had not been significantly challenged, and had not been in the prize ring very often or for very long. It would be another nine months after Jim's last bout with Sharkey before he would enter the ring again in a competitive bout, with Fitzsimmons.

On the other hand, Fitzsimmons had been fairly active against good fighters, and since arriving in America in 1890, had knocked out everyone he had fought in serious bouts. He was coming off 8 good rounds with the undefeated Sharkey just three and a half months prior to the Corbett fight.

Since his late June 1896 bout with Sharkey, Corbett had occasionally given sparring exhibitions with then 197-200-pound Billy Woods and 212-220-pound Jim McVey, both of whom worked with Corbett leading up to the Fitzsimmons fight. Woods' career included: 1891 LKOby34 Choynski; and 1895 LKOby15 Steve O'Donnell and LDQby9 George Godfrey. Woods had also been a Jim Hall sparring partner.

Both Woods and McVey had previously boxed in exhibitions with Fitzsimmons: Woods in 1891 and McVey in 1893. Having been in the ring with both men, Woods said that Corbett was a better general, faster, and could hit equally as hard. McVey said that Corbett was shiftier, stronger and cleverer. Of course, back when McVey had been Fitzsimmons' sparring partner, he had said that Fitz was more of a heady fighter than Corbett, so their opinions might have been influenced by their alliances at the time. Also, Fitz might have been gentle with them.[727]

In mid-October 1896, Corbett resumed his tour of the country and Canada with his play, *A Naval Cadet*, doing so until early February 1897. Corbett was enjoying acting, traveling from city to city, but he kept himself fit, doing conditioning training such as running and playing handball, as well as giving some occasional sparring exhibitions, usually with McVey.[728]

Even as of early December, it was said that because he was embarrassed by his performance against Sharkey, Corbett had been training and getting into shape. "For an alleged dead man Corbett is the liveliest corpse now prancing the earth, and if Fitzsimmons expects to meet a back number in Corbett he is destined to be disagreeably surprised. Corbett is very much

---

[727] *San Francisco Examiner*, March 10, 1897; *San Francisco Chronicle*, February 8, 1897.
[728] Fields at 99.

alive." He was not the physical wreck some believed. A mid-December report said that Corbett was "in magnificent condition and much bigger and stronger than he has been for the past few years. He has been in training over six weeks." Another said that a majority of good judges of fighting considered Corbett to be the most remarkable boxer of modern times. "It is true that he devotes a great deal of time to his stage work, but he does not neglect the exercise which has been part of his daily routine."[729]

While in Kansas City, Missouri with his play on January 31, Corbett expressed nothing but total confidence. "I am in the finest condition and do not need any training at all. I am ready for the ring now.... I never was in better condition in all my life.... Of course I shall have to get used to the altitude in Nevada." Jim said that he did not anticipate any trouble with Fitzsimmons. He would finish out his theatrical performances in Kansas City over the next week, and then travel to San Francisco for a week or so to visit his parents. "I shall be training all the time, as I am now. After my visit, I shall go into the mountains of Nevada for four week's hard training."[730]

Corbett gave his final performance of *A Naval Cadet* in Kansas City on February 6. On the 8th in Denver, Corbett said, "Well, I never felt better in my life and never more confident of winning a fight. ... I have been training for the past six weeks." He stopped in Salt Lake on the 9th to box exhibitions with Jim McVey and Billy Woods.[731]

Psychologically though, Corbett was less than enthusiastic about the fight game. When Jim was in Salt Lake, one reporter observed, "Pugilism has become something of a bore to him. He considers it of secondary importance and showed this feeling in every line of his rather forced talk." This was further confirmed a few days later when Corbett told reporters that this would be his last fight, win or lose. Regardless, Jim said that he was 180 pounds and felt first rate. "I would be ready to go into the ring tomorrow if it were not for questions of endurance and wind. After returning from San Francisco to the battle ground in Nevada I shall go into systematic training as far as wind is concerned."

Fitzsimmons was supremely confident as well, saying,

I have read where Corbett says that I am a tricky fighter. Perhaps I am, but the best trick I know is landing my fists on the jaw just hard enough to knock men out... [I]f I get my right or left to any part of

[729] *San Francisco Evening Post,* December 2, 18, 1896; *San Francisco Call,* December 28, 1896.
[730] *San Francisco Chronicle,* February 1, 1897; *Salt Lake Herald,* January 28, 31, 1897.
[731] *San Francisco Chronicle,* February 8, 1897; *Salt Lake Herald,* February 9, 1897.

his pompadour head he will hit the floor very hard. I don't think that he will get up, either. ...

I may see my opportunity in the first round, and then it may take me several to find his weakness. You may depend, however, that I will find his weak points. I am just as confident as ever that I will win.[732]

Fitzsimmons began his active conditioning training (running) in New York on January 25, 1897. "Fitzsimmons never looked more rugged than he does at the present time."[733] As of February 5, the *New York Journal* reported that Fitz was running 12 miles there each morning, and had added bag punching at the Bartholdi Hotel to his routine.[734]

The Journal reported on the morning of February 8 that it would be Fitz's first real hard day of training. He was scheduled to run 12 miles, box 8 rounds with Dan Hickey, and engage in a 15-minute bout of "pulling, hauling and mauling" with Ernest Roeber, the champion wrestler. He would follow that up with bag punching with dumbbells in each hand.[735]

Fitzsimmons left New York on February 10 via railroad, traveling with manager Martin Julian and sparring partners Dan Hickey and Ernest Roeber. They were scheduled to stop at Omaha, Salt Lake City, and Colorado locations such as Denver, Pueblo, Colorado Springs, and Leadville to give exhibitions of sparring, wrestling, and bag punching, before arriving in Nevada about February 18.[736]

They stopped in Chicago on the 11th and spoke with George Siler, the contest's referee. Siler told Fitz that Corbett wanted them to be able to hit on breakaways and in clinches if one hand was free. Bob responded, "Anything fair for one is fair for the other." Fitz said that he was weighing about 179 pounds, but might take off a few pounds if he felt too slow at that weight.[737]

Corbett arrived in San Francisco on February 11. Analyzing the upcoming fight, one paper said,

[732] *Salt Lake Herald*, February 8, 1897.
[733] Armond Fields, *James J. Corbett: A Biography of the Heavyweight Boxing Champion and Popular Theater Headliner* (Jefferson, North Carolina: McFarland & Co., 2001), 99-100, 237; *Salt Lake Herald*, January 27, 28, 1897 (reporting on Corbett's activities in Chicago and Fitz's in New York).
[734] *New York Journal*, February 5, 1897.
[735] *New York Journal*, February 8, 1897.
[736] *Salt Lake Herald*, February 11, 1897; *New York Journal*, February 2, 1897.
[737] *Salt Lake Herald*, February 12, 1897; *San Francisco Chronicle*, February 12, 14, 1897.

Local sports consider that the big fight will depend solely upon Corbett's condition. They say that if he is right he will not let Fitzsimmons ever land that heavy punch, and that he will take advantage of the many openings Fitz leaves. On the other hand, according to the "wise" ones, if Corbett is not in condition Fitzsimmons is cunning enough to wear him out.[738]

It was said that in order to win, Corbett would have to avoid training on French dinners the way he had for Sharkey. Corbett responded to those who said that he had been dissipating.

> I want to say that the public is all wrong about me. ... There seems to be a general impression that I have "gone back" by licensing my appetite. ... The fact is I was never in better condition prior to a fight than I am right now. When I enter the ring it will be after a month's faithful training.[739]

In San Francisco on February 12, 1897, just over a month before the fight, Corbett played handball, boxed and wrestled a few rounds with McVey, and also worked with the wrist machine, punching bag, pulleys, and dumbbells.

On the 13th, Corbett played five games of handball and then wrestled with McVey, as opposed to sparring. "Corbett's condition is certainly good, for in all this work, which was extremely severe, he did not appear to be distressed in the least." Corbett said,

> No doubt the rumors that have been floating around the country about my going back, and my contest with Sharkey, has made a great many people think that I am not the Corbett that fought Jackson and Sullivan.
>
> There is no doubt in the world that I did not train hard enough for my contest with Sharkey, and that was because I held him a little too cheap. Since the night I fought Sharkey I have been taking the very best of care of myself .... I am in first class condition at this present moment. All I need is a few weeks of work out in the open air, and I expect to be in as good, if not better, condition when I meet Fitzsimmons as I ever was in my life. I have been training the last

---

[738] *San Francisco Chronicle*, February 8, 1897; *Salt Lake Herald*, February 9, 10, 1897.
[739] *San Francisco Chronicle*, February 12, 1897.

four months in the different cities I have showed, and I shall keep it up to the time I enter the ring.

Tom Sharkey said, "If Corbett has improved, as his friends claim, he ought to whip Fitzsimmons. Otherwise he is a beaten man."[740]

While in Omaha on the 12th, Martin Julian said that he feared that a scheme was afoot by Corbett's friends to make the fight into another Sharkey fiasco, that he had information that such was the case and would be taking precautions to counteract it.[741]

Corbett responded to some rumors that the fight was to be a fake.

There is not enough money in all the world…to induce me to enter into such a disgraceful proceeding. … People say…that it is on the programme for me to let Fitzsimmons whip me, and that I will make plenty of money out of it by betting on my opponent. I hardly know what to say in answer to that. It would be best to say nothing. Such a charge is beneath my notice.[742]

Fitz exhibited in Pueblo, Colorado on February 13 with Dan Hickey and Ernest Roeber. He appeared to be in splendid condition at 180 pounds, and the altitude did not affect him at all.

Bob next exhibited in Denver on February 14. Wearing scarlet full-length tights and shirt, he punched the bag, and then sparred 3 rounds with Hickey, who was called the Australian middleweight champion. Fitzsimmons was reported to be weighing about 185 pounds, and he expected to take off about six pounds in training.

Fitz said that win or lose, after the fight; he would tour the country with his vaudeville company. He also said that he would not fight Sharkey again, "for I don't care to meet thieves, but if I ever do meet him I guarantee to kill him stone dead before he leaves the ring."[743]

On February 14, 15,000 people attended Corbett's final afternoon San Francisco sparring exhibition show, where he worked a few rounds with McVey. That day, Jim also ran a few miles, punched the bag, played

[740] *San Francisco Chronicle,* February 8, 12, 13, 14, 1897; *Salt Lake Herald,* February 9, 13, 1897; *New York Journal,* February 13, 1897.

[741] *Salt Lake Herald,* February 13, 1897.

[742] *San Francisco Chronicle,* February 8, 12, 13, 14, 1897; *Salt Lake Herald,* February 9, 13, 1897; *New York Journal,* February 13, 1897.

[743] *San Francisco Chronicle,* February 14, 15, 1897; *Salt Lake Herald, Rocky Mountain News,* February 15, 1897.

handball, and worked with dumbbells and the wrist machine. Jim expressed nothing but confidence, saying,

> I am fully aware that Fitzsimmons is a wonderfully clever man and a very dangerous opponent. He would be dangerous to any pugilist other than myself. I know his style of fighting thoroughly. There is not a trick in his repertoire that I cannot discount.[744]

By mid-February, Fitz was a strong favorite in the South, where many were betting that Bob would knock Jim out within 15 rounds. Some were betting that he would win within 10 or even 5 rounds. However, the betting in New York favored Corbett by odds of 100 to 70.[745]

Bob signed an agreement with William Hearst, owner of the *New York Journal* and *San Francisco Examiner*, to provide those papers with an exclusive account of his training and of the fight. Robert Davis, who years later wrote a Fitzsimmons biography, would interview him for the *Journal*. Fitzsimmons issued a written statement saying that all interviews or signed statements appearing thereafter in any other newspaper would be fabrications.[746]

Exhibiting in Colorado Springs on the 15th, Bob hit the bag and sparred with Hickey. Speaking to the audience, Fitz said of Corbett, "Many believe him invincible. I do not." He also issued a statement via the *Journal*, saying,

> I read in the papers that Mr. Corbett intends to give me the worst licking I ever got in my life, but, notwithstanding his enormous output of braggadocio, I will be in the ring…to receive all he can give me, including the vituperation that flows so readily from his colossal jaw. He has surrounded himself with my old boxing partners and trainers, which gives evidence that he is seeking to fortify himself with an intimate knowledge of my tactics, and fears that I know some tricks still beyond him. I consider most of those worthies an assortment of fossils, whom I was compelled to dismiss owing to their antiquated methods and total incapacity to go beyond printed instructions concerning the manly art. I am working hard to reach the best results, and weigh 168 pounds today. When I step into the ring, I

---

[744] *Salt Lake Herald, New York Journal,* February 15, 1897.

[745] *Salt Lake Herald,* February 16, 1897; *Rocky Mountain News,* February 14, 1897.

[746] *Salt Lake Herald,* February 16, 1897; *New York Journal,* February 15, 1897. According to a secondary source, Hearst paid Fitz $10,000. Tobin at 26.

expect to weigh 175 pounds, and I think at the end of the contest that I will still be Robert Fitzsimmons, Champion of the World. [747]

On February 16, Corbett arrived at Shaw's Hot Springs, Nevada, a couple miles outside of Carson City, the fight's location. Kid Eagan and Jim's brother Joe Corbett also joined them in camp. Jim began training there the next day, on February 17, exactly one month before the fight. In the handball court, he boxed 17 minutes with Billy Woods, wrestled with McVey for 35 minutes, and then sparred Woods again for 10 minutes. Another report said that Corbett also sparred with his brother Joe.[748]

Noting their contrasting styles, Corbett said, "Fitzsimmons and I have different methods in fighting. He goes at it in a whirlwind style and that is not my way at all. I like to commence carefully and feel my man."[749]

On the 16th at Leadville, Colorado, Fitzsimmons again exhibited with Dan Hickey. He also made horseshoes. Although the *New York Journal* reported that he received an ovation from the miners, the local *Leadville Herald Democrat* told a different story. It called the entertainment a fake. Bob punched the bag for only two minutes. He then sparred very tame and short rounds with Hickey, which only lasted two minutes and forty seconds owing to his acclimation to the altitude. There was no further act, and the audience moaned. Bob ran a mile afterwards.[750]

In Glenwood Springs on the 17th, in the afternoon Bob twice wrestled for 10 minutes with Roeber. He also took a bath in the hot springs, despite the fact that there was a snowstorm outside. That evening, they exhibited to a small house.[751]

On the 18th at the Grand Opera House in Salt Lake City, Utah, reportedly weighing 180 pounds, Fitz punched the bag for a few minutes, engaged in a 10-minute Greco-Roman wrestling match with the much heavier Roeber, and then boxed Hickey 3 rounds. Spectators were very impressed, and Bob's stock rose. "Bob was very shifty on his legs and can

[747] *New York Journal*, February 16, 1897.

[748] *Salt Lake Herald*, February 10, 17, 1897. Corbett said that exhibitions would be given at Virginia City, Reno, and Carson (although they were cancelled as a result of anti-boxing protests).

[749] *San Francisco Chronicle*, February 18, 1897; *New York Clipper*, February 13, 20, 27, 1897; *New York Journal*, February 17, 1897. Jim said that he would not exhibit until the fight, but would only spar at his training quarters.

[750] *Salt Lake Herald*, February 17, 18, 1897; *New York Journal*, February 16, 17, 1897; *Leadville Herald Democrat*, February 17, 1897.

[751] *New York Journal*, February 18, 1897.

dodge a blow as quickly as a cat. He can hit equally quick and Corbett will have his hands full when he faces the former in the arena."[752]

That same day, at his training quarters at Shaw's Hot Springs, Corbett boxed and wrestled with Woods, McVey, and Joe Corbett for 30 minutes (another report said 1 hour), and was looking good.

The daily reports of Corbett's training regimen varied from paper to paper, but all agreed that Jim was training hard and looking good.

Fitzsimmons criticized Jim's sparring partners and said that Corbett's appearance was all an illusion, that the men with whom Jim was sparring were not really giving him a challenge.

> I note in today's dispatches that Corbett boxed with Woods seventeen minutes and wrestled with McVey thirty five minutes. He must be in pretty good condition to tire out such dubs as they are. I would like Mr. Corbett to have a go with my wrestler Ernest Roeber, for about five minutes, to see how his condition would hold out. The fact of the matter is, Corbett is wrestling and boxing with men who don't know the first thing about their business and he tires them out rehearsing the part.[753]

On the 19th, Corbett sparred 10 minutes with Woods, wrestled and boxed with McVey, worked on his defense against his brother Joe Corbett, and then sparred again with Woods. Each bout ended when the other man said that he had enough. It was concluded after 54 minutes, and Corbett was still not exhausted.

Tom Sharkey insinuated that Corbett was a faker, and said that Jim had something up his sleeve in order to ensure his victory over Bob. When asked what he meant, Tom said,

> I mean that I have a letter from Corbett, over his own signature, that would brand him as a faker all over the world. … I received this letter previous to my four-round go with Corbett, and its publication would create a sensation. I was too honest to enter into this scheme, and our contest was on its merits.

---

[752] *Salt Lake Herald*, February 19, 1897.
[753] *New York Journal*, February 20, 1897.

When asked his opinion of the upcoming fight, Sharkey said, "If it is on the square, why, Fitzsimmons will put Corbett out of business." Corbett responded to Sharkey's allegations by challenging Tom to publish the letter.[754]

On February 20, half the Carson population met Fitz's train at the station. Bob gave Governor Sadler a finely polished horseshoe as a gift. Fitz set up training quarters at Cook's ranch, three miles south of Carson, arriving at the snow-filled training grounds that day. The ranch had a dwelling house with eight rooms, and Fitz would do his training at a pavilion 50 yards away. Bob said that he expected to enter the ring weighing about 178 pounds.

Sparring partner Dan Hickey told reporters that he was under instructions to hit Bob as hard as he could. "That is the way I train him to look out for himself. ... Now Corbett trains directly opposite. He instructs McVey not to hit hard. Corbett is a soft man and cannot take the punishment Fitz is capable of undergoing."[755]

Ernest Roeber said that when Bob threw him in their wrestling, it was legitimate and impressive, given that he weighed 217 pounds to Bob's 168.

> Fitz and I both concede that Corbett is clever and quick, but our man is by far the hardest hitter. He can afford to take two or three of Corbett's blows in order to land one of his own.... Corbett's game will probably be to spar off at long range...but...as soon as he begins to fight in real earnest Bob will keep him moving, and it will only be a matter of time before he is put out.[756]

That day, Fitz ran 3 miles in 20 minutes. He anticipated that he would run 8 to 10 miles a day and hit the heavy bag for about 2 hours.[757]

That same day (the 20th), Corbett boxed and wrestled with his trainers before invited guests, including Governor Sadler and several members of the legislature.[758] Corbett punished his partners. Woods was bleeding and stopped after 10 minutes. McVey was pounded so badly that Jim said he would give him a week off in order to get into better shape.[759]

---

[754] *San Francisco Chronicle*, February 20, 1897; *Salt Lake Herald*, February 19, 1897; *Rocky Mountain News*, February 21, 1897; *New York Journal*, February 22, 1897.
[755] *Salt Lake Herald*, February 20, 1897; *Rocky Mountain News*, February 19, 1897.
[756] *San Francisco Chronicle*, February 22, 1897.
[757] *San Francisco Chronicle*, February 22, 1897.
[758] *Nevada State Journal*, February 21, 1897.
[759] *San Francisco Chronicle*, *Salt Lake Herald*, *Rocky Mountain News*, February 21, 1897. Other reports said that Corbett worked with them for 50-52 minutes in the morning, and after

On the 21st, Corbett allowed Woods to wear a pneumatic suit of armor, consisting of a leather head protector heavily stuffed with hair, which surrounded his face and covered his ears (the first headgear), and a padded body shield. Despite the added protection, in the 2nd round, when Woods led at Jim, a counter left knocked Billy back 12 feet until he fell dazed and stunned. Jim was said to be weighing 178 ¼ pounds.[760]

There was a report claiming that a man named James Kelly was making a $100,000 bet on Fitzsimmons. "Mr. Kelly is said to have some information which leads him to believe that Fitzsimmons cannot lose." Again, a potential fix was being implied.[761]

The daily analysis proliferated. William Muldoon said that the gladiators should be careful to avoid overworking themselves and become trained too fine, that overtraining could be as detrimental as undertraining.

Tom Sharkey, who had boxed both, gave his latest analysis:

I would say Fitzsimmons is the harder hitter, but Corbett is the cleverer man. The great question is, Will Corbett last? In my opinion, I do not believe that Corbett is the same man who fought John L. Sullivan in New Orleans. I witnessed the fight and I think I know what I am talking about. The condition of the men will make a great difference in the result. ... Corbett, in the first place, has never taken care of himself, and Fitzsimmons, as everybody knows, has taken the utmost care of himself and is as hard as nails. Fitzsimmons can stand more hardship than Corbett, and unless the so-called "champ" can get himself in prime condition he will be beaten. ...

Corbett is not a great puncher, although he can hit much faster than Fitzsimmons. ... In regard to Fitzsimmons, all I have to say is that he is a cooler man than Corbett. It has been said that in certain stages of his fights he gets rattled, but in my ten-round go with him at the pavilion he seemed to me to be as cool as a cucumber. In my opinion he uses much better judgment than Corbett.[762]

---

lunch played handball for half an hour.
[760] *San Francisco Chronicle*, February 22, 1897.
[761] *New York Journal*, February 22, 1897.
[762] *New York Journal*, February 22, 1897.

Jim Corbett certainly was working hard. On the 22nd, he played handball for 30 minutes and then boxed 4 four-minute rounds with Woods. Later, Jim hit the bag for an hour, played handball again, boxed Joe Corbett 3 rounds, and then sparred again for 10 minutes with Woods.[763]

Jim was wearing out his trainers. On the 23rd, he sparred with Joe Corbett and Billy Woods, and wrestled with Jim McVey, for 43 minutes total without rest. Woods' face was taking such a battering that he was going to start wearing the face mask and breast guard on a regular basis.[764]

The Fitz camp felt that Corbett was actually working too hard, and was overtraining. "They all consider that if Corbett keeps up his present gait from now until the fight he will be as stale as a third rater." However, Harry Corbett said that such talk was all nonsense, that Jim was 182 pounds, and had weighed 176 when he fought Sullivan (although in reality Jim was probably in the mid- to high-180s when he fought John L.). Fitzsimmons was listed as weighing 172 pounds as of the 22nd, but some said that he was down to about 165 pounds on the 25th.[765]

On February 23, Fitz ran about five miles in the morning. In the afternoon, he worked the wrist and pulley machines. He then boxed with Dan Hickey in spirited fashion, "Hickey having to back all over the gymnasium to avoid the big fellow's onslaught. They kept at it in ding-dong style for seven minutes, when Hickey reeled away completely exhausted." Fitz then engaged in stand-up wrestling with Roeber. Afterwards, Bob said,

I have knocked out 300 men in my time. When I was on the road offering so much to men who could stand before me four rounds, I put to sleep four to seven a week. In my fights nearly every man I defeated was clean knocked out.[766]

Although John L. Sullivan was picking Corbett in part because Jim was more experienced, William Muldoon, who had trained John for the Kilrain fight, disagreed with Sully's reasoning. Muldoon said,

If experience is all that is necessary to win the fight, it should be Fitzsimmons's, hands down. Why, all you have to do is to read the papers to find that where Corbett has been fighting one battle Fitz

[763] *San Francisco Chronicle*, February 23, 1897.
[764] *Rocky Mountain News,* February 24, 1897.
[765] *San Francisco Chronicle, New York Journal,* February 23, 1897; *Salt Lake Herald,* February 26, 1897.
[766] *New York Journal,* February 24, 1897.

has been engaged in a dozen. The Australian has been fighting regularly and certainly nobody can say that he is a novice.[767]

The Denver analysts said that the general impression there favored Corbett. He looked active and fit when he had visited, whereas Fitz was "careless and overconfident." The consensus of opinion was that Corbett was "the shiftiest and most resourceful fighter that ever stepped in to the ring. He has no settled way of fighting, but watches his opponent and accepts what chances are left open for him." However, Fitz was well-respected too.

> The supposition that Corbett will whip him with one strong blow does not receive great favor. If whipped at all, it will be by hard and persistent jabbing away until he has no wind left and then a knockout. How long this will take is a question never yet determined, for no American audience has ever seen Mr. Fitzsimmons leave the ring a beaten man. His awkward position and seeming countrified way of getting about have probably made many an antagonist wonder where he got his reputation, until a fatal opening was left and there was no further awkwardness visible in the grinning Australian. His fights have been won by a knockout. ... If Corbett leaves the coveted spot bare for a short second of time the fight will pass into history in ten seconds. But friends of Fitz must remember that Corbett does not leave openings, Fitz must make them. [768]

Dominick McCaffrey picked Fitzsimmons. "It is a great boxer against a great fighter. ... The fighter generally brings the money home, all things being considered." McCaffrey said that although Corbett was cleverer, "there is no man alive that Fitzsimmons cannot hit, and when he lands he makes the desired impression. Corbett never got hurt up to date, and when he does he will forget his cleverness."[769]

On February 24, Corbett's trainer Bill Delaney arrived in Carson with a new sparring partner, up and coming heavyweight James J. Jeffries. After seeing Corbett spar Woods that day, Delaney said,

---

[767] New York Journal, February 23, 1897.
[768] Rocky Mountain News, February 23, 1897.
[769] New York Journal, February 24, 1897.

I am completely surprised at Corbett's condition. I firmly believe him to be as good as ever he was. It will do no harm now to confess that after the Sharkey fight I thought that my old favorite was done with ring work forever, but he has recovered himself wonderfully.[770]

Welterweight George Green also arrived at Corbett's camp to spar with the champ. Green, later known as Young Corbett, was preparing for a match against Mysterious Billy Smith to take place on the Corbett-Fitz undercard.[771]

On that same date, Jack Stelzner joined the Fitzsimmons camp as a sparring partner. Stelzner had previously trained Fitz for the Maher rematch and the Sharkey fight. Hickey and Roeber were joyous to see that another man would lighten their load and absorb the battering. Stelzner noted all the black eyes. "You must be having lively times around here," Jack remarked, asking, "Where did all the black eyes come from?" Bob replied, "Hickey gave me mine." "And I got mine from Bob," chimed in Roeber.

Stelzner suggested that he should get one of those protective suits that Woods was wearing with Corbett, but Bob advised him not to do so. "It wouldn't protect you much, for I could knock a man out just as quickly with one of these things on. I'd hit all my might, and you know, Jack, I never do that now when we are boxing." Stelzner replied, "You hit pretty hard at that," rubbing the bridge of his nose as he spoke, perhaps recalling a blow that he received in the past.[772]

That day (the 24th), Fitz did a 10-mile run in the morning. Later, he punched the bag for a round, boxed Roeber, Hickey, and Stelzner 1 round each, and then went through that rotation twice more, boxing each man 3 rounds apiece (9 rounds of sparring total for Bob).[773]

George Siler, the fight's designated referee, took a look at Fitz in training on the 25th. He said that Bob looked just as good as he did before the Hall and Maher II fights. "His weight has been given out as being between 170 and 175 pounds, but I will say if he weighs 165 pounds he is big." Siler said that Bob was in great shape, sailing through his work for an hour or so without showing any effects. He could run 3.5 miles to town and return without any effort. Although he did not "show up so clever and tricky in his boxing bouts as does Corbett," Bob was "known to be

[770] *San Francisco Chronicle*, February 25, 1897.
[771] *The News* (Carson), February 24, 26, 1897.
[772] *New York Journal*, February 25, 1897.
[773] *San Francisco Chronicle, New York Journal*, February 25, 1897.

awkwardly clever," delivering "effective blows in a manner which causes everybody to say they are 'flukes' or lucky hits."[774]

Speaking of effective punching power, Fitzsimmons said that he did not think Corbett could knock him out.

> Corbett can't be such a terrible puncher. ... I can't recollect a man that he dropped with a single punch. He certainly did not knock Choynski out that way, and he put Sullivan out an inch at a time. It required about twenty of his thumps to send the big fellow to the floor. ... I believe I could have settled any of these men with one crack. I also believe that I can stand as hard a punch as any fighter living. I have been soaked good and hard by some of the hardest hitters in the business, yet none of them have laid me out cold.[775]

On February 25, for the first time, Corbett sparred with the 210-pound James J. Jeffries, for 12 minutes (4 rounds). Afterwards, trainer Bill Delaney said that Corbett was looking so good, demonstrating his superior judgment and old-time speed, that he did not see how Jim could lose to Fitzsimmons. Jeffries said,

> Corbett is a wonder. I thought I could land on him effectively in view of his poor fight with Sharkey, but I must confess that I was very much mistaken. I never laid a glove on him and I tell you frankly I tried very hard to do so. He is the quickest boxer with his hands I ever sparred with, and it is my candid opinion that Fitz will hit the air instead of Corbett when they meet on March 17th.

Later that day, Jim also played handball, boxed for a short time with George Green, then Woods for about 30 minutes, punched the bag, and exercised with the wrist machine.[776]

On the 26th, Bill Brady watched Corbett and Jeffries spar again. "Jim is stronger than I ever knew him to be. That man Jeffries is a young giant, and Jim threw him about like a cork when they clinched." Corbett sparred with Jeff and Woods for half an hour. He then played handball, hit the punching bag, and finished off with the wrist machine.[777]

---

[774] *New York Journal*, February 26, 1897.
[775] *New York Journal*, February 26, 1897.
[776] *San Francisco Chronicle, Salt Lake Herald*, February 26, 1897.
[777] *Salt Lake Herald*, February 27, 1897.

That same day, Fitz went for a 10-mile morning run. Bob began charging $1 admission to his training gymnasium, which kept too many from visiting. In the afternoon, he hit the punching bag, and then sparred with Roeber, Hickey, and Stelzner, boxing 3 rounds with each man. A Roeber jab drew some blood from Bob's mouth.[778]

James J. Jeffries

On February 27, 1897, Corbett dropped and badly dazed Jeffries with a short right. Billy Woods replaced him, and despite the fact that he was wearing the pneumatic armor, even Woods was knocked groggy and dropped by body blows.[779]

Corbett co-trainer Charley White said, "I was amazed by Corbett's speed, cleverness, and hitting power. ... He never missed a chance, and his feints completely dazzled the Los Angeles pugilist [Jeffries]. Tell the boys to put their money on Jim, for Fitz has not got a chance." He was also quoted as saying, "He dropped Jeffries this morning with the shortest of short arm punches, and he doubled Woods up and floored him with the left body blow."[780]

Although Charley White had previously trained Fitzsimmons for the Choynski fight and the failed late 1895 Corbett fight, he and Delaney were both training Corbett. Perhaps Jim wanted an inside line on Fitz.

One observer of the sparring said,

I saw Corbett box yesterday and was surprised at his strength, activity and wonderful endurance. If he can't hit hard I never saw a pile-driver at work. McDonald of Helena, an old trainer of Corbett's, told me he was sure Corbett would win. Barring a chance blow I think it will be quite an even match.[781]

---

[778] Salt Lake Herald, Rocky Mountain News, February 27, 1897.
[779] The News, March 1, 1897; San Francisco Examiner, February 28, 1897; March 15, 1897; San Francisco Chronicle, February 28, 1897. The Corbett-Jeffries sparring sessions will be discussed in great detail in the Jeffries volume.
[780] San Francisco Chronicle, New York Journal, February 28, 1897.
[781] The News, March 1, 1897.

W.W. Naughton had also observed Corbett's improved punching power. "I saw him send big Van Buskirk down with a half-speed right at the Olympic Club a few months ago, and I saw him drop Jeffreys with a right jolt not many days since."[782]

According to the *Journal*, on the 27th, Bob skipped his morning roadwork and instead chopped wood for an hour and juggled the head of a sledgehammer. He also boxed with Hickey and Stelzner. In total, his morning work lasted 2 hours. In the afternoon, Bob hit the bag for 12 rounds, sparred 3 rounds each with Hickey, Roeber, and Stelzner, and then wound up with a wrestling bout with Roeber.[783]

Roeber split Fitzsimmons' lower lip that day, and it was looking cut and swollen. Bob's face was showing the marks of his daily hard sparring, including a blackened eye. Some felt that Bob was trying to shift the odds even further in Corbett's favor (10 to 8 at that point), while others felt that Bob was accustoming himself to receive punishment, so that he would be able to land one of his own deadly short-arm hooks. "On form Fitzsimmons should control the long end. On class Corbett easily leads."

Bob said that it was "not his style to restrain his sparring partners and make monkeys out of them that the public might think nobody could hit him." Further explaining his training methods in preparing mentally and physically for a tough fight, Fitz said,

> A man must learn to take blows as well as to give them. ... Corbett won't allow any of his men to lay a glove on him, for fear people might think he was not the marvel he believes himself. I'll show him that he can be hit just like the rest of us when we get together.[784]

Fitzsimmons claimed that he would weigh 158 pounds when he entered the ring with Corbett, that as of the end of February, he was weighing 162 pounds. He said that he wanted to show Jim that even as a middleweight, he could knock him out, despite a 30-pound disadvantage. Bob insisted that he had never been knocked out in his life.[785]

---

[782] *San Francisco Examiner*, March 15, 1897.

[783] *New York Journal*, February 28, 1897. There are other reports that said that on the morning of the 27th, Fitz ran a couple hours over the snow-covered hills. In the afternoon, Bob punched the bag for several rounds before boxing with Roeber, Hickey and Stelzner. He then wound up by wrestling with Roeber for almost ten minutes.

[784] *San Francisco Chronicle*, February 29, 1897; *Salt Lake Herald*, February 28, 1897, March 1, 1897.

[785] *San Francisco Examiner*, February 28, 1897.

Corbett too said that he was way down in weight, claiming that he was weighing 165 pounds as of February 28, and planned to weigh that amount on the day of the fight.[786] Perhaps this was his way of saying that Bob was not that much smaller, so that he would receive full credit for his victory.

Corbett said that Fitz was claiming that his weight was low so that he could affect the betting odds, or so that he would have an excuse if he lost.

> His dropping back into the middleweight class for this occasion looks to me like looking for a soft place to fall. He scents defeat, and wants to be prepared to say when the fight is over, 'Oh, Corbett only licked a middleweight. I am still champion of my class.'[787]

The claims about their weights were questionable and unproven. "Each believes the other to be much heavier than supposed, and both verge on the mysterious and secretive." Most believed Corbett to be at least 180 pounds. Even Fitz was thought to be exaggerating, and "shies whenever he encounters a pair of scales," not wanting to prove his claims.[788]

Speaking of his condition and attitude, Fitz said,

> I am thirty-four years of age now…and I think I will be able to hold my own until I am forty. I confess I do not feel as ambitious as I did ten years ago, but I am stronger, bigger and more skillful. I am in better condition today than I ever was before, but I don't think I am as vicious as I used to be. I don't have the same thrill now, when I see a man sinking to the floor, and I hate to smash a man and see him bleed. My only desire is to put it on his chin and knock him hard enough to lay him out for a little more than ten seconds.

Assessing punching power, excluding himself, Fitz said that Maher stood ahead of the class, followed by Choynski and Hall. "Any one of them can hit harder than Corbett."[789]

Peter Maher picked Corbett to win in about 8 rounds. Joe Choynski said that Corbett was too clever and strong and would win easily. "I found no trouble in hitting Fitzsimmons."

---

[786] *Salt Lake Herald*, March 1, 1897; *New York Journal*, February 28, March 1, 1897; *Rocky Mountain News*, March 2, 1897.
[787] *Rocky Mountain News*, March 1, 1897.
[788] *Salt Lake Herald*, March 2, 1897.
[789] *San Francisco Examiner*, March 1, 1897.

However, Frank Slavin said that Fitz should win in about 15 rounds. He said that Bob had a much better record and the only contest to Corbett's credit was the draw with Jackson.[790]

There were some rumors that the fight would be a hippodrome, that it was fixed for Fitz to win, but they were denied. *The Journal* said that the rumor was generated because it was learned that promoter Dan Stuart was backing Fitz for $5,000. However, he had done so before, for the Maher fight as well as the Hot Springs fiasco, so it was nothing new.

> This is the purest kind of rot, as it takes two to make a deal, and it is $1,000,000 to a bad apple that Jim Corbett would not be a party to any such work, for three reasons – first, that he believes he can defeat Fitzsimmons; second, that in so doing his theatrical tour next year will easily net him $100,000, and third, that were he and Fitzsimmons to attempt a fake, they would both be in danger of harm from the spectators.[791]

Fitz took Sunday the 28th off as a day of rest.

On the other hand, Corbett still trained. First, he played handball for one hour with Joe Corbett. He then sparred Woods, who was wearing his pneumatic armor. "Jim laid on heavily with Woods this morning, but did not manage to make him dizzy as he did on the preceding days." Although the armor protected Billy, Jim still slipped his gloves into the circular hole in the middle of his face, where he was unprotected. Jim also sparred with his brother Joe. In total, the sparring lasted an hour. Then Jim hit the bag. The morning's work occupied 2 hours and 20 minutes.

Bill Delaney said that Jim looked perfect, but warned Corbett not to do too much.

> A man's vitality is like a piece of rubber. You can stretch it so far and no further. If you subject it to too much of a strain something is going to give way. Jim is in wonderful condition just now. Almost

---

[790] *New York Journal,* February 28, 1897.
[791] *New York Journal,* February 28, 1897.

looks as if he is incapable of fatigue. That is no reason, though, why he should give proofs of his endurance every day of his training.[792]

John L. Sullivan said that all the talk about the supposed new blows invented by these boxers "makes me sick." He said that they had not invented anything new, that the punches have existed all along. "Of course it makes good reading, but it is all bombastic talk and nothing more."[793]

On March 1, Fitzsimmons ran 21 minutes out to Carson (3 miles), took a dip in the warm springs, and then ran 20 minutes back (another 3 miles). Following that, he wrestled with Roeber, punched the bag for 20 minutes, and then sparred a few rounds with Hickey and Stelzner. "Fitzsimmons showed that he knew a trick or two in feet work and danced about like an excited Plute, while his trainers flailed the atmosphere." Another report said that Fitz punched the bag for 50 minutes and sparred and wrestled 12 rounds, that his work lasted two hours.

That same day, Corbett sparred 2 or 3 rounds each (depending on the source) with Jeffries, Woods, McVey, Joe Corbett and hammer throwing champion Bob Edgren, "who is a giant of strength." Jim seemed fresh at the end of it all. In the afternoon, Corbett played three games of handball (although some said he skipped it that day), and then hit the punching bag for 15 minutes.[794] One observer opined,

[Corbett] never allows one of the men with whom he boxes to score off him. The instant they make a point that causes the onlookers to whisper, the champion sends in a swift return. He is so jealous of his reputation that he won't for an instant allow the idea to get out that he is not invincible.

Another observer explained why he thought Corbett was training so hard.

---

[792] *Rocky Mountain News*, March 1, 1897. Woods said that Sullivan made his reputation by offering money to anyone who could last 4 rounds with him. Woods wanted to do the opposite – offer $100 to anyone who could knock him out within 4 rounds while he was wearing the armor.

[793] *Rocky Mountain News*, March 1, 1897.

[794] *Salt Lake Herald*, March 2, 1897; *Rocky Mountain News*, March 2, 4, 1897; *New York Journal*, March 2, 1897. The RMN said Jim sparred 2 rounds with each man except for Jeffries, with whom he sparred 3 rounds.

You see, Corbett can't be champion any more unless he goes in and punches Fitzsimmons, for that gentleman unpunched, can stay in the ring just as long as Corbett. Also, Corbett cannot punch without going into Fitzsimmons' range, and when he is there he may receive a blow that will end his career. This may seem too obvious, but it is just the thing that people do not see when they figure it out that Corbett cannot lose. It is one of the things that Corbett thinks of, and that is why he has four men to punch at him.

One writer felt that Corbett might be too finely trained, that he should take some time off. The next day indeed was a day of rest for Jim, for his wife was visiting.[795]

When asked his opinion of who would win, Peter Jackson said that he was not sure, because they were evenly matched. He wanted to meet the winner.[796]

On March 2, Bob did some running in the morning. In the afternoon, he hit the bag for 14 rounds. He then wrestled with Roeber and sparred with Hickey and Stelzner, wearing out all three. Bob was showing improved speed.[797]

Martin Julian said that Bob would reduce his sparring and increase his bag work. There was no need for Bob to prove how much punishment he could take, for he was certain that Jim could not knock him out.

Peter Maher is the hardest hitter in the business outside of Bob, and he hit Bob a couple of times at Langtry with two blows that seemed to be hard enough to bring anyone down, but Bob stood them both and they were foul smashes at that. With dozens of instances of this kind to guide my opinion, I don't think that Corbett will hurt Bob very much before he gets a crack himself that will bring him down to our man's weight.[798]

Speaking of Corbett's training, in a teasing manner, Bob said,

---

[795] *Rocky Mountain News,* March 2, 4, 1897. Also using a dispatch from the *New York Journal.*
[796] *Salt Lake Herald,* March 2, 1897; *Rocky Mountain News,* March 8, 1897.
[797] *Salt Lake Herald,* March 3, 1897.
[798] *Rocky Mountain News,* March 3, 1897.

Corbett is now executing a move that I cannot understand. One day he comes out…and says he is ready to go into the ring at once. Then, right on the heels of that he sends for another trainer…. I can't quite see the reason for such anxiety, particularly after he has said so frequently that he cannot be improved in condition.[799]

On the morning of March 3, Bob took a 4-mile run at a good, stiff pace. In the afternoon, instead of sparring or hitting the bag, he took another run, which included the local hills.

Bob responded to those who said that he won by accident. "Three hundred accidents are a great many, I take it. I shall have another one of them in my next fight." Fitzsimmons said that he was a knockout artist and was not about to stop. However, he also said that win or lose, he would retire after the Corbett fight.[800]

That same day, Corbett covered 12 miles of walking, jogging, hill climbing, and sprinting. In the afternoon, he worked the wrist machine, punched the bag, played handball, and wrestled with McVey.[801]

As of the 4th, Corbett said that if he was whipped by Bob, "I will say that it is because Fitzsimmons is a better man than I ever was in my life." Corbett punished McVey that day in their work together, clinching, wrestling, and working on his breakaway blows.

That morning, Fitzsimmons ran between 8 and 10 miles. In the afternoon, he hit the swinging ball for 10 rounds, using a different form of hitting each round. He then worked with his three sparring partners, wearing large gloves and with his forearms padded to prevent injury. Each round lasted four minutes, and Bob was only given 30 seconds rest between rounds. "The work was fast and it appears evident that Fitz prefers vigorous punching at close quarters to the fancy touches of feinting." The afternoon's work lasted an hour and a half.[802]

On the morning of the 5th, Corbett ran and jogged for one hour and twenty minutes (about 10 miles). After taking a break, he ran for another fifty minutes over six miles. In the afternoon, Corbett hit the punching bag for 20 minutes. He then sparred 16 rounds, 4 rounds with each of his four sparring partners, alternating 1 round with each man: Jeffries, Edgren, McVey, and Woods, repeating the circuit four times.

---

[799] *San Francisco Examiner*, March 3, 1897.
[800] *New York Journal, San Francisco Examiner, Salt Lake Herald*, all March 4, 1897.
[801] *New York Journal*, March 4, 1897.
[802] *New York Journal*, March 5, 1897.

That day, Fitz ran alongside Hickey, who was in a buggy pulled by a horse. After one mile, they passed a "colored" man who was leading a large hog. While Fitz momentarily spoke with the man, the buggy horse took a dislike to the hog and danced about. The hog squealed and bolted off. Fitz and the black man gave pursuit. The latter gave up, but Fitz continued. "For about two miles back and forth through the brush the hog sprinted as fast as a hog ever does sprint, with Fitzsimmons close at his heels." Bob finally sprang onto his back, bore the hog down, returned it, and continued on his way, totaling about 6 miles.

In the afternoon, Fitz wrestled with his trainers; going 3 rounds with each, for 9 rounds total. Bob padded his wrists and hands with chamois skins and cotton, and wore big 7-ounce gloves so as to diminish the chance of injuring his hands. He then punched the bag for 10 rounds.[803]

On March 6, according to Corbett, in the morning he worked the wrist machine, punched the bag for 25 minutes, boxed 4 rounds each with Jeffries, Woods, and Joe Corbett, and wrestled 4 rounds (likely with McVey), for a total of 16 rounds. He then played a couple games of handball. He repeated the same work again in the afternoon.

Fitzsimmons that day did his morning run, despite the new carpet of snow. He also played a few games of handball. He took a rest from sparring, although he punched the bag a little. "Hickey, Roeber and Stelzner have been swinging at me pretty hard lately, and I am a little sore from guarding their smashes." Bob said that the next day he would likely only hit the bag and wrestle with Roeber, but do no sparring.

In assessing Corbett, Bob said, "I honestly believe him to be one of the cleverest men that ever entered the ring, but I am absolutely sure of beating him. I know I can hit harder than he can and I know I can stay with him when it comes to speed and generalship."[804]

Fitz's trainers claimed that Bob had arrived in camp on February 20th weighing 166 pounds, but had reduced his weight to 161 pounds. All three of his sparring partners said,

> None of us have ever known a fighter to hit with the violence and skill of Fitzsimmons, and if any one of his unrestricted blows should land anywhere on Corbett from the waist up the fight will end right

---

[803] *New York Journal, Rocky Mountain News*, March 6, 1897.
[804] *New York Journal, Rocky Mountain News*, March 7, 1897. Another source said that Jim did not spar in the morning, but in the afternoon boxed a little with Jeffries and Woods, and wrestled with McVey.

there and Fitzsimmons will be dressed in street attire before Corbett comes to.[805]

On Sunday the 7th, Bob "loafed around the hills," worked the bag for a few rounds and played handball for about an hour. He usually took it easier on Sundays. He still had a black eye from his last sparring with Roeber, who had landed a left on Bob's right eye.

Responding to the criticisms of some newspapers unhappy about his exclusive contract with the Hearst papers (*New York Journal/San Francisco Examiner*), Bob asked, "Why should I give you fellows for nothing what I could sell for a good price?"[806]

That day, Corbett punched the bag for 20 minutes, spent 45 minutes on the handball court, and then sparred alternating rounds with Jeffries, Edgren, McVey (wrestling), and Woods, 4 rounds with each, for 16 total rounds. Jim then played more handball with Joe Corbett and another man. Afterwards, Jim said, "I never was better in my life." He also said, "[I]t is certain that Fitzsimmons and myself are the two best men in the fighting business today. There is no man who can beat either one of us."[807]

The local Carson newspaper sized up the bout by saying,

> All agree that Corbett should be the best but say that two such men never before met in the ring and that both are so scienced and quick that the result may possibly be a matter of luck. It is certainly conceded that the first to make a mistake, no matter how trifling will be very liable to lose the fight.[808]

Bob once again did not spar on the 8th. Instead, he played handball for an hour, hit the bag for 12 rounds, wrestled for an hour with Hickey and Roeber, and ran 6 miles. He said that he would begin sparring again the next day.

Fitz noted that the almost 220-pound Roeber generally came at him "with a vigor that would make a faint-hearted man reluctant about going up against him." Although Roeber had cut Bob's lip, Fitz was not bothered or worried.

---

[805] *San Francisco Examiner*, March 7, 1897.
[806] *New York Journal, Rocky Mountain News*, March 8, 1897.
[807] *Rocky Mountain News*, March 8, 1897. *Salt Lake Herald*, March 8, 1897, said Jim sparred 3 rounds with each man.
[808] *The News*, March 9, 1897.

I find the best way to get familiar with punishment is to take some of it. I have not as many trainers around me as Corbett, but I will put them against any three men in the country for keeping anybody awake. I am feeling in top shape and weigh very little more than 160. I am as hard as a rock.[809]

An expert described Bob's style as "peculiar" but effective.

Nobody can imitate him. With his arms rigid and his head well back, he crouches low and watches for an opening. ... Bob requires less latitude in which to hit than any man living... [H]e can hit a terrific jolt or bat at any distance. Everybody knows what a hook he is capable of landing. Do I think he will get in on Jim? That's hard to say. If he does he will win the championship.[810]

As for Corbett's training on the 8th, first he played handball for an hour. He then boxed Jeffries, wrestled with McVey, and sparred with Edgren and Woods. He repeated the circuit as usual. In the afternoon, he again repeated the routine, working the pulleys before boxing and wrestling 16 rounds. Corbett was masterful in making his sparring partners miss.[811]

On the 9th, Corbett worked the wrist machine, did at least 10 miles of road work with Jeffries (over two and a half hours), plodding through the slushy snow, and did the usual afternoon work, including handball, 10 or 20 minutes (depending on the source) of bag punching, and sparring and wrestling with Jeffries, McVey, Edgren, and Woods. *The New York World*, which had a correspondent on the scene, reported that on the 9th, Corbett dropped both Jeffries and Woods.[812]

Having worked with Corbett for a couple weeks, James Jeffries said,

I was quite convinced before I came here that Corbett was a kingpin boxer so far as cleverness went, and I have discovered since I arrived

---

[809] *New York Journal,* March 9, 1897. However, another source said that Fitz indeed sparred and worked hard on the 8th. It said that Fitz played handball for two hours. He sparred Hickey, Roeber, and Stelzner for three rounds each. He then wrestled with Roeber for almost an hour. *Rocky Mountain News,* March 9, 1897.
[810] *Salt Lake Herald,* March 8, 1897.
[811] *Rocky Mountain News, Salt Lake Herald,* March 9, 1897.
[812] *Rocky Mountain News, Salt Lake Herald, New York World,* March 10, 1897.

that he is a terrific puncher. I cannot figure out how Fitz can hope to discount Corbett's cleverness and punching power combined.[813]

Jim would lessen his load from this point on until the fight, alternating between hard and easy days. Trainer Charley White said, 'Now Corbett is so fond of work, if we did not hold him back at times, he would do too much and might make himself stale." Assessing the men, White said,

> Corbett is the fastest big man on his feet that I ever have seen. ... I have seen Fitzsimmons in all his work and I do not think that he is as fast on his feet as Corbett, although Fitzsimmons has a side step that is as quick as lightning. Anybody who thinks that Fitzsimmons is not fast on his feet is making a large mistake, but at the same time he is not as fast as Corbett.[814]

Fitz's training on the 9th included three hours of hill climbing in the morning. He later played some handball, hit the bag for 40 minutes, wrestled with Roeber, and then boxed 8 rounds each with Hickey and Stelzner.[815]

One writer opined,

> I think the fight is any one's guess. It is foolish to say that Fitzsimmons can never reach Corbett. In a rally one man is as liable to be hit as the other. I think Fitzsimmons is too strong and game a man to be kept long at arm's length. When he decides on infighting at short range he is a knocker-out. I believe he could knock down any man in the world with a blow delivered at a distance of six inches. ... No matter what the distance that he strikes from, every muscle on one side of him is in motion from the ball of the feet to the top of his shoulder.[816]

William Muldoon felt that the fight would be lost through a mistake or error of judgment rather than physical superiority. He felt that there was

---

[813] *San Francisco Examiner*, March 10, 1897. Jim Jeffries would eventually become heavyweight champion.
[814] *Rocky Mountain News, Salt Lake Herald*, March 10, 1897.
[815] *Salt Lake Herald*, March 10, 1897. Another source disagreed, saying that it was a light day for Fitz, because his wife arrived and his heavy work was over. He only ran 8 miles in the morning, finishing with some 100 yard sprints. *Rocky Mountain News*, March 10, 1897.
[816] *Rocky Mountain News*, March 10, 1897; *San Francisco Examiner*, March 7, 1897.

little to choose between the two, and that "each will be so keenly on the alert that the slightest blunder will be taken advantage of and prove fatal."

Corbett protested that the ring floor would be covered with canvas, saying that it made a fighter leg-weary much sooner than did smooth boards. However, this was a safety precaution designed to ensure that a man would not be killed when his head hit the hard boards.[817]

A week prior to the fight, on March 10, 1897, Corbett and Fitzsimmons crossed paths while doing their roadwork. Corbett was with Jeffries and Jim Ryan. Fitz was running with Hickey, and saw Corbett ahead. "Get a move on you, Hickey, and we'll show them what road work is." Just as they caught up to Corbett, the opposing teams' dogs got into it for a moment. They pulled their dogs back. Hickey began the pleasantries, saying good morning, as did Fitz.

However, when Bob walked over to shake Jim's hand, Corbett said, "No, Fitz, after all that has been said between us there can be no hand shaking except in the ring." Jim said that he would shake his hand only if Bob licked him. Fitz did not understand this stance and eventually, "the two men had their faces as close as they could get without touching and every one in both parties were getting pretty anxious." Fitzsimmons told Jim, "Well, you will find there is a live man in the ring on the 17th." Corbett replied, "Well, that is what I want… You thought I was far from a live man or you would never have gone as far as you have." Bob responded, "You are nearly dead as it is." They separated with each trying to get in the last word. As they were leaving, Jim said to his comrades, "Look at him. Why he looks like a lightweight. The fellow is worrying himself to the bone."

Bob later that day wrote that Corbett was running on the road that Fitz typically ran on, perhaps intentionally. Nevertheless, Bob observed the custom of shaking hands, but Jim refused. "I recall without effort the readiness with which he has always posed as 'Gentleman Jim,' and I ask the public whether or not he is entitled to such distinction."[818]

As a result of this encounter, Fitz manager Martin Julian told Bob not to shake Jim's hand before the bout, and he did not.[819]

Interestingly enough, the *New York World* reported an entirely different story in a same day special from a staff correspondent who was allegedly there.

[817] *Salt Lake Herald*, March 10, 1897.
[818] *The News, New York Journal*, March 11, 1897.
[819] *Reno Evening Gazette*, March 17, 1897.

Corbett took a jaunt of about nine miles all told, deviating from his former route and turning off near Fitz's quarters. As Fitzsimmons came over the same road at nearly the same time, it was odd the rivals did not meet.

The Evening World's correspondent followed Corbett on horseback during his long jaunt. At no time did the champion breathe hard, although Jeffries was done up before they were within a mile of Shaw's Springs on the return trip.[820]

So, did they meet that day or not?

Two days later, the *World* reported that there were queer rumors circulating about the fight, and asked, "How much long green does it cost to buy a winner or loser in a fight?" One of the rumors was that the boxers had contracted with the photographic reproduction folks to stay in the ring for at least 10 rounds.

The little incident which caused this commotion is the fact that under circumstances which indicate pre-arrangement, Corbett and Fitz were induced to cross each other's path, meet and indulge in windy and illogical asinine persiflage like two knock-about comedians in a variety show. Part of the agreement, as both admit, was that they should lie about it if questioned, and both did so vigorously. Last night Corbett admitted that he had lied, and acknowledged that he had accepted money for lying about his clown turn with the other end of the show. Fitz admitted the soft impeachment, too.[821]

So, was the alleged meeting on the road a fabrication, was it a set up, or was it legitimate? Was the report of their meeting designed to sell newspapers and hype the fight? *The World* said,

The honesty of the men has been submitted to a test and found wanting, and it is now a toss-up in the estimation of many whether the affair of next Wednesday is to be on the level or a hippodrome. … "There's too much fake in this," declared a well-known sport. [822]

[820] *New York World*, March 10, 1897.
[821] *New York World*, March 12, 1897.
[822] *New York World*, March 12, 1897.

Charley White said that he knew that Corbett meant to fight for all he was worth, and would end the battle at the first opportunity. He said that both fighters were on the level in their desire to win.

After his 10-mile morning run, later on the 10th, one source said Bob sparred only 4 rounds with Hickey, punched the bag, and tossed a handball for 30 minutes. Another source said he boxed with Hickey and Stelzner and punched the bag for a short time, but it was a short day.[823]

That day, after his morning run with Jeffries and Ryan, Corbett hit the bag, worked the wrist machine, and then sparred 4 rounds each with Jeffries and Woods, followed by two games of handball.[824]

So that there would be no fuss on the day of the fight, a week in advance, referee George Siler published his interpretation of the rules governing the bout. One rule which would later prove relevant was that when a man was knocked down, the other man was to return to his corner until the other man was up. Of course, a man might go down in his opponent's corner, but Siler accounted for that. He said, "This, of course, was intended to prevent a man from standing over his fallen opponent. ... To avoid all disputes on this score, I will simply instruct you in case of a knock-down to retire at least ten feet from your fallen opponent, to give him an opportunity to arise." No one objected to this ruling.

Siler had customarily asked the combatants whether hitting in the clinches and breakaways would be allowed, but felt that more often than not, they hit each other anyway even when agreeing not to do so, causing cries of foul, criticism of the referee, and leading to fights being decided on technical fouls, something generally unsatisfactory to everyone. Therefore, he authorized the boxers to hit in the clinches and on the breakaways when one arm was free.

Siler noted that clinching and hugging were illegal, such that if done to an unreasonable extent, it could cause him to disqualify the offender. (A lot of referees today should keep this in mind!) He argued that since clinching was illegal, allowing the other man to hit in the clinch would discourage such action (another excellent point).

Do you suppose that a man is going to hug and keep at it when he knows that the other man has the right to hit him when his own hands are occupied? Well, I think not. That is why I say that permitting the men to strike with one hand free is the surest preventive of all clinching and hugging.

---

[823] *Salt Lake Herald, Rocky Mountain News*, March 11, 1897.
[824] *Salt Lake Herald*, March 11, 1897.

Coaching during the rounds was also barred.[825]

Although it was said that Siler's ruling regarding hitting in the clinches would favor Fitzsimmons and hurt Corbett, ironically Bob was the one who objected, saying that he wanted clean breaks and no punching in the clinch. Corbett said Bob was only bluffing to act as if he was conceding a point, but that Fitz really wanted to hit on the break. Siler made the valid point that when he met Fitz in Chicago, Bob had no objection to such a construction of the rules. Siler said that he was not firm in his ruling, that if the men came to an agreement otherwise, he would abide by it. Ultimately, Siler's ruling stood.[826]

Writing about his training on the 11th, Fitz said that he ran 10 miles in the morning at a good clip. Afterwards, he hit the bag for 10 rounds and sparred 4 hard-fought rounds with Hickey, putting it on him "good and hard." In the afternoon, he ran to Carson beside his wife's carriage and returned the same way.[827]

Corbett jogged 8 miles, sprinting the final quarter of a mile, and then engaged in his usual exercises of handball, bag punching, and sparring.[828] Jeffries, Woods, and Joe Corbett "gave the big fellow three hot rounds each, while McVey did his share of the wrestling." Corbett worked on hitting in the clinches and breakaways.

After that, Corbett retired to the dressing room and emerged with the 5-ounce gloves that would be used in the fight. He wanted to test them, as opposed to the 8-ounce gloves he had been using in sparring. He went at Woods for 1 round. Despite Billy's wearing the pneumatic armor, Jim managed to drop him several times, including once by a stomach blow.[829]

On the 12th, one source said that Corbett did three hours of road work, played some handball, and boxed Woods and Robert Edgren.[830] Another said that Jim's work consisted of his usual routine. Jim ran 10 miles over the fast drying roads. In the afternoon, he worked the wrist machine and punched the bag in a fast and furious manner for a bit longer than usual. He then played five games of handball with Joe Corbett. This was followed by 1 round of wrestling with McVey, and then single rounds of sparring with Jeffries, Woods, and Joe Corbett. The circuit was repeated twice more,

[825] *Salt Lake Herald, Rocky Mountain News,* March 11, 1897.
[826] *New York Journal, Rocky Mountain News,* March 12, 1897.
[827] *New York Journal,* March 12, 1897. According to one source, Bob began work punching the bag. He then wrestled Roeber, and boxed Hickey and Stelzner, punching them on the breaks. Another source said that he ran 10 miles, sparred 10 rounds with Hickey and Stelzner, wrestled with Roeber, and hit the bag.
[828] *Salt Lake Herald, Rocky Mountain News,* March 12, 1897.
[829] *Rocky Mountain News, New York World,* March 12, 1897.
[830] *Salt Lake Herald,* March 13, 1897.

so that Corbett worked 3 rounds with each sparring partner, for a total of 12 rounds.[831]

The experts were saying that Corbett was as fit as he was when he fought Sullivan. Corbett and his trainers were all saying that he was physically and mentally at his very best, that if Fitz won, he could have won at any stage in Jim's career. Corbett's wind and capacity for work was called "simply phenomenal."[832]

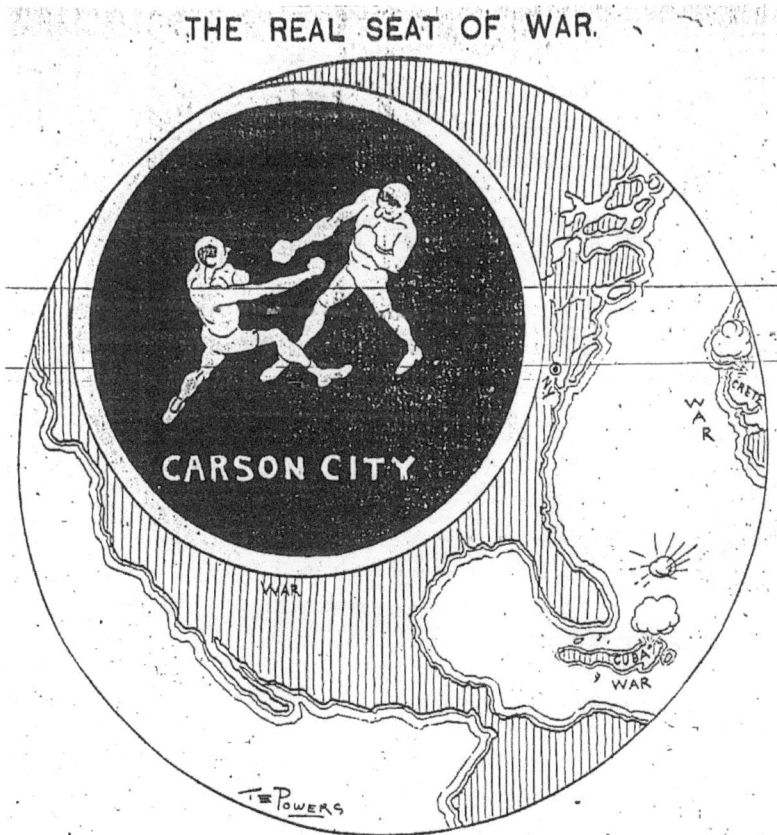

THE REAL SEAT OF WAR.

Carson City Compared to Cuba, Crete and the Rest of the World.

What's the little spat in Cuba?
What's the little snarl in Crete?
Beat the drum and sound the tuba,
For we're all at fever heat
At a real war cloud that o'er our country lowers,
And which overshadows fights of foreign powers.

What care we for foreign troubles?
We have our own fighting show;
Other war scares are but bubbles,
What this country wants to know
Is, who will get the champion persimmons?
Will Corbett win, or will it be Fitzsimmons?

---

[831] *Rocky Mountain News*, March 13, 1897.
[832] *New York Journal*, March 13, 1897.

On the morning of the 12th, Fitzsimmons biked 14 miles. Sparring Hickey, Roeber, and Stelzner, Bob worked short punches in the clinches. "His method of getting in on a break is totally different from Corbett's. Instead of swinging on his opponent's jaw with a downward and half circular motion like Jim, he slips up under the guard with a swift and strong uppercut on the chin." Bob said that he ran 10 miles in the afternoon.[833]

Fitzsimmons again denigrated Corbett's sparring partners.

McVey was engaged by Martin Julian to spar a week with me in Philadelphia, but at the end of the third night, even though the rounds were half time, he quit the stage and refused to go on with me. The fourth night Martin put Roeber, my wrestler, up against McVey with the gloves, and the German knocked him groggy in the second punch, yet he claims to have sparred with me a full week, and boasted that he knew all about me. I was obliged to handle him with the gentleness of a woman to get him to go on at all.[834]

On the 13th, in his sparring, Bob did considerable work in the clinches and in-fighting, specifically preparing this way because of Siler's ruling that hitting in the clinches would be allowed.

The result was that Hickey's right temple is split open and Roeber's ear was badly cut. Fitzsimmons also amused himself by letting the men corner him, and ducking out of their reach. Twice Roeber was knocked down with smashes that would finish an ordinary man, and which were delivered from a short distance. Fitzsimmons finished his work by fourteen rounds of bag punching, playing handball and walking into town.[835]

Fitz said that he would not throw the fight for all the money in the world. "To win is worth more money to me than anybody could possibly afford to offer. I expect to make $250,000 by licking Corbett."[836]

---

[833] *Salt Lake Herald, Rocky Mountain News*, March 13, 1897.
[834] *New York Journal*, March 13, 1897.
[835] *New York Journal*, March 14, 1897. Bob sparred both Hickey and Roeber, hit the bag, and played three games of handball. The sources disagree on the details of what he did that day – sparring either 3 or 4 rounds with each man, bag punching for either 10 or 14 rounds, and then running 12 miles or two separate runs of 5 and 6 miles, or simply just walking into town. *Salt Lake Herald, Rocky Mountain News*, March 14, 1897.
[836] *New York Journal*, March 14, 1897.

Offering his observations about Fitzsimmons, W.W. Naughton said,

> Fitzsimmons is not a stylish boxer. ... [H]e has adopted a system of his own. It is ungainly, but judging from general results it is wonderfully effective. His tactics from start to finish suggest that he is not seeking to wear a man down by constant jabbing, but rather to create an opening for one decisive smash that will end the whole business. ... He courts rather than avoids a rally. I should say he was exceedingly tricky.[837]

That day (the 13th), in the morning Jim Corbett walked and ran 10-12 miles with Jeffries. One source said that Corbett did almost continuous sprinting on his morning run, including 100 yard sprints in 11 seconds. Later, he worked with the dumb bells and the wrist machine for a half hour, punched the bag, and played 3-5 games of handball.

In the afternoon sparring, Corbett wrestled McVey for 1 round, then took on Jeffries for "three minutes of hot sparring," then Joe Corbett, and then Woods. Each man went 4 rounds total in the round-robin circuit, while Corbett went round after round without any additional rest, as usual, for a total of 16 rounds. Jim puffed up Jeffries' lip with a straight left, and did the same with Woods, who was wearing the armor. Joe Corbett was more cautious and kept at a distance.[838]

Jim would taper in subsequent days. "The change will be a relief to the big fighter and none the less so to McVey, Jeffries and Woods, who have been punched and hammered to the limit of endurance in the vigorous work."[839] Corbett said, "I am fit in every way to fight for my life, and if I should lose the battle fairly and squarely no one will hear of me offering any sort of an excuse." Fitzsimmons would also reduce his work from that point on until the fight.[840]

Stakeholder Al Smith said that never in his life had he seen a man as well conditioned as Corbett. "For nearly three hours this afternoon I stood in his handball court and I watched him spar and wrestle with his trainers and his work was nothing short of marvelous." Jim's trainers said that he was better than he was when he whipped Sullivan. It was reported that the fever of the battle was pervading all social classes.[841]

---

[837] *New York Journal,* March 14, 1897.
[838] *Salt Lake Herald, Rocky Mountain News,* March 14, 1897.
[839] *Rocky Mountain News,* March 14, 1897.
[840] *New York Journal,* March 14, 1897.
[841] *Rocky Mountain News,* March 14, 1897.

Approaching the fight, the odds still favored Corbett by 10 to 8. Jem Mace said that he was backing Corbett up to $500. Although he felt that Fitz was a great fighter, Corbett was cleverer.[842]

W.W. Naughton said that Corbett had been practicing his system of clinching.

> He has made a specialty of this clinching business ever since he fought Jackson, and he can let go, hit and clinch again so rapidly that the other fellow will need to be a quick-thinking, quick-acting piece of human machinery to avoid being worsted in this particular kind of fighting.

He also said that although Fitz was the more dangerous puncher, Corbett had improved his punching power three-fold. He noted how he saw Corbett drop Van Buskirk and Jeffries.[843]

Ernest Roeber maintained that Fitzsimmons could fight 30 rounds at a rapid gait.[844] Jack Stelzner picked Fitz, saying that Bob was stronger and could deliver the blows that count.

> People say that he cannot hit Corbett. They must not forget that, in order to hit Fitzsimmons, Corbett has to come close enough to do it, and when Fitzsimmons is in reach of Corbett, Corbett is in reach of Fitzsimmons, and he will get hit, and once is enough.[845]

Corbett was well aware of Fitzsimmons' reputation as a puncher. "Fitzsimmons has repeatedly shown that he can punch hard with both hands…. I will convince him, as I convinced my predecessor in the championship, that being a hard hitter is one thing; landing is quite another."[846]

Corbett's training on the 14th consisted of a 15-minute morning walk, working the wrist machine for 15 minutes, 20 minutes punching the bag, three games of handball, and sparring. Jim wrestled McVey for five minutes, then sparred a round each with Joe Corbett, Jeffries, and Woods.

---

[842] *Salt Lake Herald*, March 15, 1897.
[843] *San Francisco Examiner, New York Journal*, March 15, 1897.
[844] *San Francisco Examiner*, March 15, 1897.
[845] *San Francisco Examiner*, March 10, 1897.
[846] *San Francisco Examiner*, March 15, 1897.

The circuit was repeated once more, each of the four sparring partners going 2 rounds.[847]

William Muldoon saw Corbett train that day, boxing without intermission in his typical round robin fashion. "I saw for myself that he is practically tireless. His wind is superb, and more than two hours constant work did not distress him in the least."[848]

Ultimately, though, Muldoon felt that Fitzsimmons had as good a chance to win as Corbett. He believed that Corbett had the superior skills, but that Bob had the deadly punch that could end the bout at any time. Both seemed to be in superb condition.

Bob's trainers told Muldoon that he planned to enter the ring at about 162 pounds, and weighed 160 pounds the previous evening. Corbett's trainers told him that Jim was 183 pounds and would enter the ring at about 185. Muldoon said,

> There is a great difference in the men's weight, to be sure, but as you stand behind the two men, if you are asked to make a guess, you would say that there was not more than five pounds difference between them. That, perhaps, is on account of Fitz's round back and broad shoulders. Fitz loses weight in the waist, hips, head and neck, and of course being an inch and a half shorter, would make a great difference in the weight.[849]

Fitzsimmons' training on the 14th was very light. He only went for a short morning run of about 4 miles. He was scheduled to take a short run the next day and hit the bag a little, and do practically nothing the day before the fight.[850]

Corbett said that for the fight, he would be wearing a trunk of elastic material, red in color. Around his waist would be a belt of red, white and blue silk. His ring post would have the colors of the Irish and American flags.[851]

Corbett and Fitz again passed one another on the road on the 15th, but this time they exchanged no words.[852] Fitz wrote,

[847] *Rocky Mountain News,* March 15, 1897.
[848] *San Francisco Examiner,* March 15, 1897.
[849] *San Francisco Examiner, Salt Lake Herald,* March 17, 1897.
[850] *Rocky Mountain News,* March 15, 1897.
[851] *New York Journal,* March 16, 1897.
[852] *New York Journal,* March 16, 1897.

Tomorrow, barring a short jog, will be a day of rest. ... I trust Mr. Corbett can contain himself and treat his trainers kindly until the 17th. It is said of him that during the last week he has been in a very cantankerous and almost unbearable mood. He ought to know by this time that good humor saves vitality, and should be cultivated above all things by such a distinguished personage as, "Gentleman Jim." Keep cool, my boy. The day is not a great way off, and I shall be on hand to participate. ... I consider that Corbett heretofore has fought men who are my inferiors as fighters, and I believe no one knows it better than Corbett himself.[853]

Corbett did his last sparring on the 15th, working with Woods and Jeffries.[854] Another source said that he did a little light work with dumb bells, and then ate breakfast. He went at the wrist machine for a short time, then punched the bag, "but did very little with it." He then sparred several light rounds, and took some short runs and walks on the road. Later in the afternoon, he played a few games of handball.[855]

Neither Corbett nor any of his trainers will give any idea of what the champion will weigh when he enters the ring, but it is certain that he will weigh over 175 pounds, as he is above that weight now. The chances are that he will tip the scales close to the 180 mark.[856]

Fitz's exact weight was also unknown. "Fitzsimmons has kept his weight a close secret. That he is several pounds lighter than the champion is evident at a glance, but he doesn't weigh under 170 today according to the opinion of experts who have looked him over."[857] Another source said,

The stories of the weight of Fitzsimmons at the ring side have been very conflicting, but the probabilities are now that he will weigh not far from 160 pounds, and according to the assertions of the men in his camp he will be rather over than under that figure. ... [F]rom this time on he will allow himself to take on three or four pounds more than he now weighs.[858]

[853] New York Journal, March 16, 1897.
[854] Salt Lake Herald, March 16, 1897.
[855] Rocky Mountain News, March 16, 1897.
[856] Rocky Mountain News, March 16, 1897.
[857] New York World, March 16, 1897.
[858] Rocky Mountain News, March 16, 1897.

On that day (the 15th), some sources claimed that Fitz ran with his dog for 30 minutes, hit the punching bag a little, and sparred with Roeber, Hickey, and Stelzner, giving them some hard hits.[859] He did nothing in the afternoon. [860]

Bob said that for the fight, he would wear a belt of red, white and blue silk, having in the center an eagle. He had fought with the national colors around his waist ever since the Hall fight, when he had submitted his application to become an American citizen.[861]

Tom Sharkey's latest pick was Corbett. He said that Jim had a 15 pound weight advantage, was taller and stronger, and had superior generalship, science and activity. Jim also had wonderful defense, whereas Tom said that he had no difficulty in landing on Fitz. He also felt that Jim hit just as hard as Bob. W.W. Naughton also picked Corbett.[862]

William Muldoon in the end gave the edge to Fitzsimmons. He said that he had seen Bob punching the bag on the 15th, and, "His bag punching was more vigorous, harder hitting and effective than Corbett." Like Corbett, Bob was a tireless worker, but he had a better attitude. "When he made a miss it did not seem to annoy or upset him, as it does Corbett. He appeared to be in much better humor and had more patience both with himself and the men with whom he exercises than his opponent." After sparring for 30 minutes with his men one after the other, Bob was cheerful and happy. Muldoon estimated Bob's weight to be about 162 pounds. "Of course, neither of the contestants will tell you what he weighs, but I should say that Corbett is at least fifteen pounds heavier."[863]

The New York World's analysis said,

With the wary, awkward, yet tricky and cunning Fitzsimmons before him, Corbett will need to call into play all his remarkable judgment of distance, all his swiftness of foot and the delusive tactics that have made him the boxing man he is. That terrible right has knocked clever men out before, but none so clever as Corbett. If it lands with all its crushing force on the proper point on the jaw a new champion will probably step out of the ring. On the other hand it is considered, even by Fitzsimmons, that the champion will be able to hit. In fact Fitz has expressed a willingness to take a bit of the medicine in order to get in his coup. If he underestimates the champion's hitting

[859] *Salt Lake Herald, Rocky Mountain News*, March 16, 1897.
[860] *Rocky Mountain News*, March 16, 1897.
[861] *Rocky Mountain News*, March 16, 1897.
[862] *New York Journal*, March 17, 1897.
[863] *New York Journal*, March 17, 1897.

powers, and many think he does, his glimpse of the championship will simply be a wink. ... Of the staying qualities of both men none has any doubt. Corbett's long battle with Jackson and Fitz's wonderful recuperative ability after dire distress are matters of record. Neither man can be considered a winner while the other is on his feet.[864]

The day before the fight, one source said that Fitz did no work at all other than taking a short two-mile run. Another source said that Fitz wrestled with Roeber for a bit, then hit the bag and sprinted around the yard a few times, and followed with a little road work.[865]

Corbett played three games of handball and hit the bag. Another source said he only played handball.[866]

Both men expressed nothing but supreme confidence. Bob said that if he lost, he would leave the country.

Martin Julian said, "I think that Fitzsimmons can whip any man in the world, no matter what his weight may be. I know that Corbett will be much heavier than Bob, but it will not do him any good. Fitz will win the fight as sure as the men enter the ring." Jack McAuliffe picked Fitzsimmons.[867]

On the day of the fight, the entire Fitz crew expressed nothing but supreme confidence in Bob. Julian said, "He can strike a 50 per cent heavier blow than Corbett, and one good punch from him will punch Corbett down and out." Stelzner said, "He is as strong as an ox and can tire out a horse on the road." Hickey said,

Fitzsimmons will win. I don't see how he can lose. No man was ever in better condition ... He has purposely let me hit him in our bouts, and I have put in some good ones, but he did not mind them at all. Corbett may punch him a dozen times, but I don't think he can hit hard enough to make much of an impression, as Fitzsimmons' condition is so perfect that he will be able to recover quickly. Corbett cannot wear him out. All Fitzsimmons has to do is to land one stiff jab, long or short, and Corbett will not get on his feet. The blows of the two men are a feather to a ton.

Roeber said,

[864] *New York World*, March 16, 1897.
[865] *Rocky Mountain News, Salt Lake Herald*, March 17, 1897.
[866] *Salt Lake Herald, Rocky Mountain News*, March 17, 1897.
[867] *Rocky Mountain News*, March 17, 1897.

My money is on Fitzsimmons. ... He strikes like a mule kicks. No punishment Corbett can give him can knock him out. If Fitzsimmons hits Corbett once, and he is clever enough to do it before many rounds have been fought, you will see Corbett drop and be carried to his quarters.[868]

Still, the morning of the fight news report said that Corbett was the betting favorite by about 10 to 6.[869] Most experts thought that both men were at their best and that ultimately the fight would be decided by who was the better fighter. The two boxers and their trainers all agreed on this point.

Dan Stuart had this outdoor fight arena built for the Corbett-Fitzsimmons fight.

---

[868] *Rocky Mountain News,* March 18, 1897.
[869] *Reno Evening Gazette,* March 17, 1897.

CHAPTER 19

The Real Championship

On the afternoon of March 17, 1897 in Carson City, Nevada, Bob Fitzsimmons fought James J. Corbett for the world heavyweight championship. It was the culmination of a three-year wordy battle. At age 33 (then listed as 34), Fitzsimmons was actually older than the 30-year-old Corbett, and had fought longer than he had. At the time of the fight, the odds were 10 to 6 and 10 to 7 in Corbett's favor.

No one knows exactly what the men weighed because there was no official weigh-in. A day-before-the-fight report said Corbett was 183 pounds and planned to enter the ring at 185. Fitz's trainers said Bob was about 160 pounds and planned to enter the ring at 162.[870] Another paper said, "Fitzsimmons' weight is estimated at 165 pounds, although Julian said today that he will be heavier than that, 'or between 170 and 180.'"[871]

The day of the fight, a Reno newspaper said, "Corbett will enter the ring today close to 180 pounds while Fitz will tip the scales at 168."[872] Referee Siler said that Fitz weighed 157 ½ pounds to Corbett's 188. Bob claimed that he weighed 156 ½ to Corbett's 187 pounds.[873] Another paper reported Siler as saying that Corbett was 183 or more.[874] "Referee Siler gave Fitzsimmons' weight as 158, but the general belief is it was nearer 165. Corbett's weight is said to have been 185."[875] The local Carson newspaper said, "Fitzsimmons looks light but is a bunch of muscles. Corbett looks easily 15 pounds heavier."[876] *The Salt Lake Herald* said that although Fitz's weight was given at 158, he looked to be 163-165, while Corbett looked at least 180 pounds.[877]

---

[870] An album called "Fight of the Century," published by H.S. Crocker Co., San Francisco on June 1, 1897, included a March 16 report by William Muldoon providing this information.
[871] *Rocky Mountain News*, March 17, 1897.
[872] *Reno Evening Gazette,* March 17, 1897. The same article was also published in the *Nevada State Journal,* March 18, 1897.
[873] *San Francisco Examiner*, March 18, 1897.
[874] "Fight of the Century," published a March 17, 1897 statement by Referee Siler.
[875] *Rocky Mountain News*, March 21, 1897.
[876] *The News,* March 17, 1897.
[877] *Salt Lake Herald*, March 19, 1897.

Secondary sources sometimes say Fitzsimmons weighed 167-172 pounds to Corbett's 180-183 pounds.[878] Corbett claimed in his autobiography that Fitz was 172 and that he was 180.[879] Recall that even as of mid-February, Bob claimed to weigh around 180 pounds, and told reporters that he did not intend to enter the ring much less than that. However, as the fight approached, reports indicated that Fitz was weighing in the low 160s. With all the training that he was doing, this was possible.

Years later, Corbett's trainer Bill Delaney and sparring partner James Jeffries questioned the accuracy of Bob's weight, feeling that he appeared about as big as Corbett did.[880] No official weigh-in was required, so it is difficult to know. Fitz always looked bigger than he was because he had a large upper body, but he also had thin legs. Corbett could have had as much as a 30 pound weight advantage, or as little as 10 pounds. Either way, he was fighting a man who had fought the majority of his career as a middleweight. Still, Fitzsimmons had proven that he could take and administer a heavyweight's punch.

This was the first fight to the finish in which ladies' presence was encouraged. Promoter Dan Stuart set up a special ladies section. He said, "Especial care will be taken to protect them…. I have every reason in the world to believe that these contests will be creditable to a calling now under an embargo of hypocrisy and double-facedness in America." Women were allowed to watch the bout "under proper escort." However, "Lady reporters will not be admitted to the big fight under any consideration."[881]

Before the fight, John L. Sullivan, Joe Goddard, and Tom Sharkey all announced to the crowd that they wanted to fight the winner, and had financial backers ready to make a deposit on their behalves. Probably owing to the Fitz fiasco, "Sharkey did not appear to be popular." T.T. Williams, writing for the *New York Journal*, said of the three challengers,

> Of course, no one believes the ex-champion has any intention of fighting anybody. His enormous girth, flabby face and rolling walk settled that. The general impression seemed to be that Goddard had done nothing to justify his meeting a champion, that Sharkey would not be accommodated, and that we were going to see the last championship fight that would take place for many a year.

---

[878] One secondary account confirmed that at a private weigh-in before the bout, Fitzsimmons weighed 156 ½ pounds. Robert H. Davis, *Ruby Robert* (N.Y.: George H. Doran Co., 1926), 50. However, Gilbert Odd says of this biography that it is "not to be trusted factually." Odd at 15.

[879] Corbett at 261-262.

[880] *San Francisco Examiner*, May 28, 1899.

[881] *The News*, March 1, 1897; *New York World*, March 17, 1897; *The News*, March 16, 1897.

Fitzsimmons confided to me before the fight that if he won he would never fight again – that it was his wife's wish.[882]

The men entered the outdoor ring at around 12:00 noon wearing bathrobes. Bob's was blue and pink. His training team, as well as his wife (who wildly shouted instructions and encouragement to him during the fight) accompanied Bob. Corbett had his trainers and sparring partners as well. A crowd of 5,000 - 8,000 (reports widely varied, some saying only 3,000 were present) included everything from miners, merchants, farmers, cowboys, and lawyers. They sat in the arena Dan Stuart had specially built for the occasion.

The sky was clear, which was good for the kinetoscope filming. The fight was scheduled for that time of day in order to accommodate the lighting conditions necessary for filming. Although the ring was supposed to be 24 square feet, it was cut down to 22 feet in order to accommodate the camera. E.J. Rector had obtained the right to film the fight for $11,000, outbidding the Edison and Vitascope companies. Although Corbett and Fitz were originally to receive a percentage of the film profits, Rector purchased their interests for $13,000 each.

The Reno Evening Gazette said that Fitz wore light pea green gloves. He wore dark blue trunks and a belt covered with small American flags. Corbett wore a red, white and blue belt with a green buckle and rosette. His trunks were green, and his white socks were rolled down over the top of his shoes. Another source said that Jim's gloves were tan colored.

Referee Siler told them to shake hands, but Julian prevented it, saying, "No, you refused it once." The fight began between 12:05 and 12:08 p.m.[883]

1st round

"From the start it was a plain case of caution. The two sprinted around the ring, smiling at one another as though they were indulging in a little boxing work for points, and never getting close enough to be hurt." Fitz winked and Corbett laughed.

---

[882] *New York Journal,* March 18, 1897.

[883] The following account is an amalgamation of multiple reports from newspapers with writers at the fight. *The New York World* (NYW) and *The News* (Carson) had almost identical accounts. Those two papers along with the *Reno Evening Gazette* (Reno) issued same day reports. *The San Francisco Chronicle* (SFC), *San Francisco Examiner* (SFE), and *New York Journal* (NYJ) all issued next day reports. Discrepancies are noted when significant.

Bob began aggressively forcing the fight, but failed to land effectively. Jim eluded and smiled throughout the round. Corbett fought cautiously, carefully selecting his moments to punch, landing several times.

There were a number of clinches and clean breaks, and for the most part, neither attempted breakaway blows. However, in one clinch, Bob landed a heavy right to the temple that made Jim say "Oh." It was the only solid punch Bob landed in the round. Corbett had what honors there were.

Bob later told reporters that he badly hurt his right thumb in the 1st round.

2nd round

Jim was cautious and looking for openings. "The fight is of a rapid character and both men very lively on feet." Corbett began landing to the head and had the better of it, but the hits were not very hard and did not distress Fitz, who smiled. Fitzsimmons forced the issue and they clinched a number of times. Jim landed two strong lefts to the stomach that seemed to hurt Bob. Corbett feinted repeatedly with the left, and was in control of matters, but there was not a great deal of action.

<u>3rd round</u>

Jim seemed confident, but clinched often. There were a number of exchanges and clinches. When Fitz landed two strong jabs, Jim responded with hard left hooks to the body which distressed Bob, who was still forcing the pace. Both continued smiling. Corbett was wary, avoiding most blows. "Fitz mixes it up and puts the heel of his glove in Corbett's face. In the clinch Jim keeps his right working like a piston rod on Fitz's body. They clinch and Fitz roughs it in the breakaway." Bob was forcing the pace as the gong sounded, and seemed anxious to continue. After the bell, with Bob close to Corbett, Jim playfully touched Bob's face, and both smiled and returned to their corners.

<u>4th round</u>

The round was a series of exchanges and clinches by both. "They are fighting at a terrific rate and it's a beautiful contest." Fitz would rush in, and hit and rough it in the breakaways.

Although Bob remained competitive, it was clearly Corbett's round. Corbett began forcing matters more, landing hard blows up and down, his best punches being a hook to the body, left to the jaw and right to the heart. "Corbett by long odds making the cleverer fight. He's playing systematically with right and left on the body." The crowd, which was on Corbett's side, grew enthusiastic about his connections.

> They were not knockout blows, but blows at about half strength delivered with the arm stiff, and meant to hurt and not to kill. Fitz soon showed the effects of them. His face began to swell, and he would lay on Corbett's shoulder as though in hope of obtaining some respite from the punching, which was annoying. Corbett grew confident as this round progressed.

Fitz seemed a bit tired, but landed a couple lefts to the body. Corbett went to his corner "as happy as a boy."

To that point, Corbett undoubtedly had the best of the fight, landing more often. However, "when Fitz got in his terrible right on the head or body it counted heavily."

This was another clear Corbett round. He consistently landed his left to the jaw. Bob's blows had plenty of steam behind them, but were not as frequent as Jim's punches, and did not land as often. "Corbett's beautiful boxing play stood him in good stead here. Twice he saved himself by clever ducking, catching his opponent several head blows after each successful avoidance." Corbett "seemed able to land whenever he wished while Fitz was unable to hurt him." Whenever Bob rushed and attacked, Jim side-stepped in lively fashion.

Corbett's stiff "half-round" left (or both left and right in succession) drew first blood, from either Bob's lip or nose, or both (sources varied). Delaney and White called, "First blood for Corbett," which the referee acknowledged.

Jim landed some lefts before and after clinches. His seconds called out, "Take your time, Jim; you've got him." "Corbett landed three blows in succession, two lefts and a right on Fitz's face. Right took effect in the chin, and jarred Fitz." Bob seemed distressed. Corbett looked like a winner, landing two to one.

6th round

Because this was a significant round, each source's version will be presented.

NYW/Carson:

> They clinch and Fitz tries to wrestle Corbett down. ... Corbett uppercut Fitz fiercely with right, and has Fitz going. Fitz is literally covered with blood, but is fighting like a demon. Corbett is showing the signs of fast work. Fitz is down on one knee and takes the time limit. He is full of fight on arising. Corbett is slaughtering him with uppercuts. Corbett's leads are a bit wild and he misses many well intended blows. Time called with Fitz looking very much the worse for wear and Corbett puffing.

Reno: Jim tried to finish Bob. Fitz slipped down. He was a horrible looking sight as his mouth and nose were bleeding, the blood covering both men. "The clinches were frequent and owing to the interpretation of the rules both men were extremely careful on the break-aways." Corbett landed two to one in the 6th and 7th rounds.

SFC: By this time, the "blood flowed and spurted from Fitzsimmons' nose, covering his body and gloves and bespattering his opponent over the arms and shoulders." Rights and lefts to the jaw hurt Bob. "A right-hander on the jaw staggered Fitz, and in order to avoid further punishment he dropped to his knees." Bob was down for a count of 9, but upon rising battled right back and was thoroughly recovered by the end of the round. It was clearly Corbett's round.

SFE/NYJ: Corbett landed an uppercut on a breakaway that sent Bob's head back. Another right "brought the blood in showers" from Bob's nose. A distressed Fitz clung to Corbett as his blood flowed over Jim's chest. Corbett's seconds grew excited.

> Corbett smashed Fitz right and left on the face. Fitz was powerless. A succession of lefts and rights from Corbett made him dizzy and he clinched on every available occasion. Corbett worked him toward the ropes, holding him with his left and smashing him in the face with his right. Fitz was a dilapidated man. Once he swung at Jim, but his feet went from under him and he fell to the floor. He rested on his knees, and Corbett walked away from him, the referee standing between them.

After taking the count, Bob rose, only to suffer more punishment. When Fitz held, Jim pumped in right uppercuts, one sending his head back. Jim was doing all the scoring, landing often, while Bob missed. However, once, "Fitz caught Corbett on the face, and Jim came back to the corner with a little blood in his nostrils and on his lip." Still, it looked like the end was near for Fitzsimmons when the gong sounded. Bob looked weak in the corner, blood flowing from his lips despite the best efforts of his seconds.

Some sources said the knockdown was from a right behind the ear, rather than a slip or Bob's voluntarily going down:

NYJ (T.T. Williams' version):

> The blood seemed to arouse Corbett's temper, and he went at Fitz with more determination than he had shown before. He hit him time and again, and I could see Mrs. Fitzsimmons wince right across the

ring. There were words of sympathy, too, for her in the sixth round, when after the clinch, Corbett landed a tremendous smash that brought Fitz to his knees, sent the blood spurting from his nose and distorted his face almost beyond recognition. Everybody wondered whether Fitz would recover, but the ninth second found him on his feet and fighting. Again and again Corbett hit him till his own gloves were covered with blood from Fitz's face, and his own body was smeared a glaring crimson from the same source.

Corbett told reporters after the fight that he hurt his hands in this round, which affected his punching ability in subsequent rounds.

The Rocky Mountain News said that after this round, Fitz's wife became more vocal in her advice during and in between rounds. She chastised Bob's cornermen, saying, "Make him keep punching Corbett's wind and he will win. You idiots, you don't know how to second a man, you have lost your senses. Do you want to defeat my husband? Do as I tell you now, or I'll make you wish you had." During the rounds, she shouted encouragement and advice, continually telling Bob to go for the body.

7th round

A Corbett right to Bob's nose started the blood flowing again. A left increased the flow. A counter left squirted blood all over Bob's face. "Everything seemed going Corbett's way. He was taking his time and punching Fitz alternately in the face and body with his left."

Still, Fitz was "fighting like a lion. They are both looking for a knock-out blow. Jim lands a light left on Fitz's sore mouth. Fitz misses right and left swings. Fitz tries a left swing, which is ducked by Corbett and countered with heavy right over heart." Fitz continued rushing wildly, but Corbett "found no difficulty in keeping out of range. Corbett's generalship was superb and elicited rousing applause."

Another writer said of Fitzsimmons in this round,

When he came up he immediately began hard hitting, and the spectators thought he had determined to finish the fight right there or go on the floor. But no, when he found his punches did not reach the clever man in front of him he changed his tactics and waited, taking the punishment that came to him as gamely and as doggedly as a bulldog would take a beating.

Still, some writers noted a change in Corbett in this round. One said, "Corbett is very tired. Fitz looks like a stuck bullock, but is as strong as the other man." Another said that despite his superiority to that point, Corbett seemed unable or unwilling to follow up his opportunities. Fitz did most of the forcing and had more steam than Corbett.

8th round

Although Fitzsimmons was doing all the forcing, Corbett was doing the landing, ducking and countering with his left to the head or right to the body. A Corbett right on a break drew blood from Bob's lower lip and/or nose. A left jolted Bob's head back. Jim would move, duck, and clinch to avoid Bob's blows. Fitz landed a left on the body and missed some wild right swings. Jim eluded a left for the head and twice landed his left on the body. Fitz landed a left to the heart, but Jim drew back away enough to avoid the full force. After Jim landed a stiff left, Bob was covered in blood.

Corbett was fighting with "wonderful carefulness" and doing all the scoring. "Fitz had the worst of this round when gong sounded." One said,

> The eighth round was sickening. Face smashes and body blows, punches in the neck and punches under the heart were Fitz's portion. It was all over but for his gameness. The betting men almost got ready to cash their Corbett tickets.

Although the majority of accounts were very pro-Corbett, there were some who still felt that Fitz had a good chance to win. One said that Bob was "aggressive and smiling." Another said, "However, the Australian seemed to be getting stronger as the fight progressed, and the enthusiasts who were offering 5 to 3 on Corbett found a good many takers among Bob's adherents."

9th round

Early on, Fitz rushed, but did little damage. Corbett was jabbing and clinching, uppercutting with his right on the breakaway. "Fitz realized his only show was at close quarters, for he kept boring in." As the round progressed, Fitzsimmons seemed to be growing stronger, scoring more often and landing some good punches, while Corbett clinched more. Eventually, Bob landed a hard left hook to the chin that momentarily staggered Jim, which got the crowd going. Fitz had the best of the round. "He is landing more often than Corbett now."

Although the majority of accounts of this round were pro-Fitzsimmons, two writers said that Corbett still landed more often than Bob, particularly with the left hook to the body and jab to the head, which brought the blood.

10th round

The sources provided a diversity of opinions and analysis regarding this round.

NYW/Carson:

> Fitz spits the blood out of his mouth. ... Fitz comes back with stiff left and right on Jim's head and body. He's very much cooler and stronger than Corbett at this stage. Corbett stops a left swing with straight left on mouth. Fitz is bleeding rapidly, but forces Corbett back, apparently being the stronger man. They mix it up and honors are about even. Both are fighting hard. Fitz catches Corbett around the neck and drags him to the ropes. Corbett lands light left on mouth. Corbett's blows are lacking in force, but he is fighting very cautiously, when time is called.

Reno: A Fitz right to the body and left to Corbett's chin again brought cheers. At the end of the round, "Corbett lost his good nature and went at Bob savagely." Bob's face was a bloody mess. Corbett sometimes smiled, but "as the battle grew hotter and hotter and his numerous blows failed to badly injure his antagonist, he grew savage in every motion."

SFC: Although Jim won the round, Fitz was the aggressor and seemed confident. Corbett brought out a fresh supply of blood with his left to the mouth. Bob's blows did not concern Jim too much, and Corbett continued hitting the mouth, landing a right and left.

SFE: In between clinches, they exchanged a number of blows to the head and body. Fitz began landing some good punches. Corbett appeared tired and clinched more.

NYJ: Corbett was still landing good punches, but Fitz landed too, and appeared stronger and very confident as he went to his corner at the end of the round. "Corbett did not seem to be weak, but his face had a grayish pallor and his eyes shifted nervously as he sat in his chair. He had lost the confident smile with which he opened the battle."

NYJ (Williams):

> [S]omehow Fitz didn't look quite so bad when his face was washed and sponged and his wind was cleared, and Corbett wondered at the change that came over him. The man was getting stronger under the terrific beating and, incredible as it may seem, he was the stiffest puncher in this round, not that he hurt Corbett, but he worried him and made him doubtful and wonder why it was. And it was then that the doubt came into Corbett's heart and the grave look into his face, but he was game.

11th round

Fitzsimmons started Corbett on a downward journey, landing frequently in the round. Although Bob was still a "receiver-general for Corbett's left jabs," he was "like a bear in strength," while Corbett's blows lacked steam. Fitz "was growing stronger, and Corbett's wind was none too good." Clinches were frequent. Although Fitz did not land quite as often, he had a good deal more force behind his punches. Some felt that Fitzsimmons "was attempting to get in a finish blow, but his actions were so peculiar in voluntarily taking punishment and seemingly throwing himself right into danger." Corbett made Bob's face bleed again.

Corbett countered less frequently than he had before, a sign of fatigue. On the other hand, the aggressive Fitz's voluntarily taking punishment could have been done to get into range and to force Corbett to wear himself out trying to punch Fitz off of him.

Bob forced matters with hard rights to the body and head, rushing Jim about the ring. "Fitz's adherents grew wild with excitement as their man rushed in with a hard left on the jaw, a right on the body and another left on the jaw." Corbett clinched, while Fit uppercut him hard. Corbett rallied and hit back, "and I saw the hardest and fastest fighting I have ever seen in the ring." Bob kept up his attack and landed a couple straight left jolts on the chin. Corbett clinched and Fitz crossed with his right. "They mix it up and Fitz has decidedly the better of the roughing." Fitz fought Corbett to the corner and had him weak and clinching desperately as the gong sounded. "The bell was a welcome relief to the Californian." The "Corbett men looked grave and the crowd, who saw the coming change of championships, began to yell for Fitz. Even then it was anything but all over."

One writer said that at this point in the fight, Bob had the advantage in the number and importance of the blows struck. Another account said that Fitz repeatedly rushed Jim, with varying success.

12th round

Corbett rallied in this round. "There was no denying Corbett's courage, and when the twelfth round began he was full of fight." Corbett still kept away, but as Fitz stepped towards him, Jim would lead often, landing on the sore nose and body. Jim landed multiple lefts to the head and body. In the clinches, Bob's jolts "seemed to shake Corbett's whole frame." Jim rocked Bob's head with a couple rights before they broke. Corbett attacked and forced Fitz to the ropes, smashing him hard on the ribs. "Fitz spits copious wads of blood." Both landed some solid shots. Corbett rushed and hit him with left and right on the face, and again on the face and body. Jim just missed a big right uppercut. Fitz was bleeding freely at the bell. It was Corbett's round.

13th round

Corbett sparred carefully and ducked some very dangerous blows. Bob rushed him into corners, but Corbett escaped without harm, ducking, blocking, side-stepping and slipping away. "Bob seemed to be willing to take all sorts of punishment if he could only land a blow." Jim's jabs set the blood flowing from the nose and lip, which were bleeding "harder than ever." Corbett was careful, but eventually Fitz landed a hard straight left. Delaney told Jim to be cautious and to fight him to a finish in his own way.

Another writer said that despite Corbett's fancy sparring and ducking, Fitz landed a right to the body and left to the face, catching Corbett flush on the mouth and loosening one of his gold-filled teeth. Vicious in-fighting followed, with both exchanging hard lefts on the body. In follow-up sparring, Corbett spit out the loosened tooth. Bob landed a hard right to the ribs that sent Jim back a foot. Corbett jolted Bob's head back with a left to the chin and followed with a left to the body. Fitz countered with a right uppercut. Jim poked the left on the nose, which bled freely again, but it did Bob no harm. "Corbett was standing the battle fairly well, but his color was not as fresh as the Cornishman's. It was easy to see that Jim was tired."

NYW/Carson:

> Corbett lands that left jab again on Fitz's head. Fitz counters with right swing on Corbett's neck, and he has Corbett going back for a few moments. Fitz lands a terrible left jab on Corbett's stomach and Corbett goes to his knees with a frightful look of agony on his face. … The blow that did the business landed over Corbett's heart and he collapsed. The last round lasted just 1 minute and 45 seconds.

Reno: The "blow that did the business was a left hand blow over the heart. Jim staggered and Fitz struck a right on the jaw."

Corbett later said, "I can lick him, I know I can…. I don't know how I happened to let him get in that heart blow. How it hurt! It felt as if I should die for the first few moments after I went down on my knees."

SFC: Jim made a jab with his left, "when, quick as lightning, the Australian, with a terrible uppercut from his own left, caught Corbett in the stomach. This blow was followed up a second after by a right swing that landed just below the heart and threw Jim completely off his feet."

Some cried foul, including Corbett's seconds (reminiscent of the Sharkey fight), but the blow was perfectly legal, as confirmed by the referee, and later Corbett. Jim could not beat the count. One estimated that he was down for about 20 seconds. Another called his effort to rise "pitiful in the extreme."

SFE: Fitz was getting to Jim more, landing to the body and head. As Corbett stepped in towards Fitz with a left, Bob "straightened up and drove his left in at the body, catching Corbett at a point directly under the heart. Corbett fell to his knees and as he went down Fitzsimmons swung his left on the jaw." This account confirmed that there were some cries of foul, but the punch was in the body.

NYJ: Bob landed a right and left on the jaw, which jarred Jim. He followed with a left uppercut. "Fitz seemed to have more power than ever behind his blows." Jim landed a left hook to the jaw, but Bob countered with a right to the jaw and they clinched. After breaking, Fitz led with his right, which fell short. However, in eluding the blow, Corbett leaned back instead of stepping back. This allowed Fitz to instantly rip his left up into the pit of Jim's stomach a little under the heart. As Jim fell forward, Bob hit him with a right on the jaw. Corbett was down for about 15 seconds. There were some cries of "Foul!" but Corbett was knocked out fairly.

NYJ (Williams): Bill Delaney "looked anxious. He could see that Fitz was anything but whipped. His eye and ear told him that Corbett was becoming slightly tired." Bill felt that Jim could win if he saved his strength, and advised Jim accordingly.

> It was clear he was the cleverest man and unhurt while Fitzsimmons' face was battered to a pulp, but no man can fight another's battle. It was Corbett who had to do the fighting. There were a few exchanges and then I saw what I don't want to see again.

> I saw Fitz's left hand go smashing into Corbett's stomach just as though it might have gone into butter, and I saw Fitz's right reach the point of Corbett's jaw. Then Corbett sank to his knees…his eyes absolutely turned up until none of the pupil was visible.[884]

Shortly after being counted out, Jim finally rose, and then frantically rushed at Fitz on the opposite side of the ring and tried to hit him in a vain effort to continue the fight. Corbett was hysterical. It was "a pitiful exhibition of impotent rage. His seconds tried in vain to control him, but he struck viciously at them as well as at others." Bob only ducked Corbett's blows with head movement. Jim clinched and landed a right to the ear, but Fitz took no notice of it, as Bill Brady and others pulled Corbett away.

Corbett eventually calmed down, came back over and shook Fitz's hand. Jim told Bob that he was the best man he had ever met, and that Bob had won fair and square. However, Corbett wanted another go at him. Fitzsimmons told him that he would never fight again. Jim responded by telling Fitz that he would meet him on the street and force him to fight. Bob replied, "If you do, Jim, I will kill you!"[885]

Bob Fitzsimmons was simultaneously the world middleweight and heavyweight champion. He had won the $15,000 purse in the winner take all fight. There were varying accounts of whether there was a side bet or what it was. Some said it was $10,000, others $5,000 or $2,500 each, while others said that there was no side bet. By comparison, the Nevada governor's annual salary was $8,000, although the Justices of the Nevada Supreme Court earned a massive salary of $27,000 per year.[886]

The estimated expenses of newspapers, the fighters, public, and promoters were placed at over one million dollars. Corbett's estimated

---

[884] *The News, Reno Evening Gazette, New York World,* March 17, 1897; *San Francisco Chronicle, San Francisco Examiner, New York Journal, Rocky Mountain News,* March 18, 1897.
[885] Fitzsimmons at 170-171.
[886] *The News,* March 13, 1897.

expenses, including the cost of living, travel, trainers and handlers, and sacrifice of theatrical engagements, was placed at around $20,000. Fitz's were placed at $7,500. Cost to spectators, including tickets and transportation to Carson, was estimated at over $500,000, which seemed a bit high. The arena cost $10,000 for Dan Stuart to build. Stuart's additional expenses were said to be yet another $20,000, excluding the purse. Newspapers across the country had put in about $450,000.[887]

Jim Corbett was upset. He felt that he had been winning, and his victory snatched away by a moment of carelessness that allowed him to be hit with a chance blow. He claimed that he had been unhurt and unmarked. However, he was debilitated for ten seconds, and that was all that Fitzsimmons needed. On the way back to his quarters, Jim said, "To think that this fellow should have beaten me," before "the defeated champion burst into tears." Bob Fitzsimmons was not a man with whom it was wise to be careless.

Speaking of chance blows, in February 1894, Jim Corbett talked about what were called "chance blows." He said,

> A great many followers of the old system complain that under modern rules the inferior fighter may win with a "chance blow." It seems to me that there is nothing haphazard about it when two trained athletes meet in the ring. Each knows what the other is trying to do to him, and it is his business to take care of himself. It is folly to talk about "chance blows."[888]

Fitzsimmons claimed to have broken his right thumb in the 1st round. He confirmed that in the 6th, the blood was interfering with his breathing and that he was in pretty bad shape for a little while. He also said that he was badly winded from the 4th to the 6th rounds. Although Bob confirmed that Corbett's punches in the 6th round were "corkers," he claimed that he was not knocked down, but slipped when trying to get away from a punch, and that Jim stepped on his foot. While on the canvas, he let Julian know that he was all right and winked at friends. "There was no time during the fight when I was not confident of winning." He also said,

> I would have beaten him at any game he had tried, and was prepared to fool him in more ways than one. ... Why, while he was tugging at me in the clinches and trying to hammer away at my body, I was

[887] *New York World*, March 17, 1897.
[888] *St. Louis Daily Globe-Democrat*, March 11, 1894.

winking at my trainers and my wife. I knew he couldn't do any damage. I don't think any more of his hitting power than I did before... A fighter must be ready to take some knocks as well as to give them, and I was certain he could not knock me out before giving me a chance to do the trick in one way or another.

Martin Julian said,

[I]t did not look particularly bright for us at the end of the sixth round. But Bob wasn't as bad off as he appeared, and when he made the remark at the close of that round that he had him licked already I was sure he knew what he was talking about. ... That talk about Corbett being so clever that Fitz couldn't hit him was the rankest kind of nonsense.

Fitzsimmons said that after the 7th round he kept getting stronger, while Corbett was getting weaker, and he knew that he would outlast Jim when it came to endurance. He tried for the head, but was unsuccessful, for Jim "kept it out of the way in mighty good style," so he shifted to the body. "He was so clever in guarding his jaw that it meant too much waste effort on my part to keep on trying to hit him there." Bob felt that he had proven his generalship by changing his tactics and going for the body. He also said that his wife was a great coach, for her words of encouragement and advice spurred him on.

Bob admitted that Jim gave him a hard fight and that he received considerable punishment. Yet, he also said, "Corbett's hits did not have anything back of them, and I frequently let him hit me so that I could get back with some good ones." An *Examiner* writer noted that Corbett was unmarked and was able to touch Fitz almost at will, but his blows had little effect on the tough and durable Fitz.

Over the course of the fight, Fitzsimmons had observed that Corbett's blows were growing slower and had lost their force, and that Jim struck less frequently and seemed to be killing the clock to recover. Conversely, Fitz felt fine and strong. However, he also noted that Corbett did not lose his cleverness, and managed to avoid him well up until the 11th round. [889]

Speaking of the color of Corbett's face in the 10th round, Fitzsimmons said, "It was never rosy at its best, and when it turned ashen gray and the lips became set I winked at Martin Julian and nodded my head with an 'I've

[889] *Rocky Mountain News*, March 18, 19, 1897; *Brooklyn Daily Eagle*, March 19, 1897.

got him air.'" Corbett tried to rally in the 12th, but his face grew paler and paler. "His respiration was shorter than mine, and twice when I exposed myself to invite him in I found that his most violent smashes were without force." In a clinch, Bob whispered, "Well, Jim, I am going to lick you now." Jim was cautious then. At the gong, Bob said, "Pretty soon, now."

Eventually, Fitz caught up with him. Bob believed that he knocked out one or two of Jim's gold teeth in the 13th round. There were no mouthpieces then.

Of the 14th round knockout, Fitzsimmons said, "I ended Corbett with the same blow that I used on Sharkey - a left-hand swing on the body under the heart." The only difference was that "this time I got the credit for what I did." He said that Corbett had his body bent back and strained, and Bob knew that a man in that position, when hit on the side of the stomach, would "wish he was home in bed." "I don't think I will ever forget the expression on Corbett's face as he sank slowly to the floor. ... I never saw so much agony in a face before." In one account, Fitz said that when he saw Jim sinking to the ground, he threw the same left hand to the jaw, giving him the identical blows that had stopped Sharkey. In another, he said that after the body shot landed, he restrained himself and did not hit him again.[890]

Fitz further said,

> I was a bit fearful at the outset, because the first right hand lead I made at him, landed on the back of his head, wrenching my thumb. Thereafter I was at a disadvantage, and you may have noticed that my right swings were short but they were delivered with the purpose of deceiving Corbett into the belief that the thumb was not injured. That accounts for my missing so many right hand swings. I discovered at the outset that his punishment did not affect me. If his jabs had landed any place other than on my lips, where susceptible to bleeding, I would have escaped without a scratch.

> Corbett talks about a return fight and says that he will follow us from town to town until I give him a return battle. I am 36 [sic] years of age, have fought more championship battles than any two men in ancient or modern ring annals, and shall retire. I will never fight again. ...

> I have been confident all along of my ability to whip Corbett. My roasting him was prompted solely by my desire to get him into the ring. I did not think I could ever get him to face me, unless I made

---

[890] *Rocky Mountain News, New York World,* March 18, 1897; *New York Journal,* March 19, 1897.

him believe that I was a bit chary of meeting him. He gave me a hard fight and I got considerable punishment. I waited for the time and finally, as I could not get at his head, played for his body and finished him. I ended Corbett with the same blow that I used on Sharkey – a left hand swing on the body, under the heart.[891]

After the fight, Corbett came over and attacked him, losing "his head and his manners the third time" with Bob (the first being the ruckus in the hotel, the second being when he refused to shake on the road). Bob did not punch back and Jim was restrained. After Corbett calmed down, he came back over and wanted to shake hands. "I decided to show him that I had still the qualities of a man of courtesy, and offered him my hand in return."[892]

At the time, Corbett told the press that he was defeated fair and square, but still felt that he was Fitz's master. He believed that Bob's blows had no more force than his own, and that it was an easy matter for him to win the fight, but for his carelessness. He said that he had the wind knocked out of him by a left hook and did not have the strength to rise, feeling completely paralyzed.

Corbett admitted that a Fitz left in a clinch broke off one of his teeth. Yet, he also said that Fitz's head blows had no effect. He did not realize that Bob was capable of such a formidable punch to the stomach. Jim also said that overall, it was the fastest fight he had ever fought. Perhaps the pace wore on him.

The Jackson fight was faster in spots, but in this one we kept up a greater rate of speed throughout. We did not take as much advantage of the free arm and breakaway hitting as people thought we would. I do not know why Fitzsimmons did not avail himself of it, but I can tell you my reasons. This wrestling and maneuvering for a punch at one and the same time is very tiring.

Fitz was stronger in the clinches than Jim thought he would be, but Corbett still felt that he landed two to Bob's one on the inside.

Jim said that the only blows that hurt him were the left hooks to the body, which landed three or four times in the fight. The first time it landed was in the 3rd round, and it "shook me up considerably and I felt the effects of it." He was again hurt by it in the 9th. "I felt the pain of the blow and it

---

[891] *Rocky Mountain News*, March 18, 1897.
[892] Fitzsimmons at 170-171.

affected my breath. I have been told that I acted as if tired in the ninth round and the two following rounds."

However, Corbett was certain that he was not tired when he was taken out in the 14th round. He felt he that was winning throughout, cutting Bob to pieces, and that overconfidence had lost him the fight. Sparring partner Jeffries told him afterwards, "You outpointed him at every stage of the game." Yes, but this was not a points game. The real issue was whether the damage that Corbett inflicted was merely external, and also at what price to his own conditioning it came. The other issue was how long Corbett could avoid Fitz's knockout blows. Jim had to take out Bob before Bob could take him out.

Despite his continued feelings of superiority in defeat, Corbett did give Fitz credit, calling him "infernally clever. He is decidedly the best man I ever fought. His style is different from Jackson's. He will take more chances and he can punch harder." He thought that he had hurt Bob multiple times, but the "way he recuperates, though, is something marvelous. His condition must have been perfect.... I thought I had him when I knocked him down with the right hand punch in one of the early rounds, but he surprised me by getting to his feet within the ten seconds."

Corbett trainer Charley White said,

I advised him to fight a generalship fight, keeping away from Fitz, but he was so confident he would whip Fitzsimmons that he would mix up. Even up to the round he went down he was confident. He is much the better man. The chance blow did it.[893]

John L. Sullivan wrote,

I am not in favor of having ladies at fights. I make an exception in the case of Mrs. Fitzsimmons. I cannot say too much for the good it did Fitzsimmons to have his wife there.

It is no pleasure to fight a man with your thumb out of joint, to keep punching and punching with a broken hand, and realize that you are not doing yourself full justice. Many a man would lose patience under such circumstances, but Fitzsimmons never did, and he couldn't.

Whenever he would look down there was his wife, ready with cheering words and comforting advice. "Hit him in the ribs," she would say. "Keep at him in the ribs; leave his jaw alone; you can

893 *Rocky Mountain News*, March 18, 1897.

never hurt his jaw." Her advice was the best, and she cheered her husband by every word.

As to the other details, I can only say that everything was conducted with a desire to be as square as possible, and no man can complain of unfairness anywhere. It was a perfect occasion, and the scene was worthy of it.

For the Governor of this State, who has the manhood to appreciate fights and the courage to indorse them, I cannot say too much. The monument that will be built to him some day will be deserved, and I think he has set an example that the civilized world will gladly follow.[894]

Sullivan felt that Corbett "could have kept away and done a little better, but he never could have won." He derisively called Corbett's punches "love taps."

Corbett is not the man today that he was when I met him… Today I saw that his blows had less force than ever. They lacked even the steam that they formerly had. What is more, Corbett is not as quick and as shifty as he was. He showed little of that shifty quality that he had six years ago. …

Corbett put up a weak fight. He lacked steam, and although he hit Fitzsimmons when and where he pleased, he did not have force enough to land a knockout blow. He jabbed and poked away as though he was on exhibition. … Fitzsimmons had it all his own way. I challenged the winner at the ringside and if Fitzsimmons can be induced to fight me I will defeat him.[895]

Of Fitzsimmons, Sullivan said that Corbett had "met a fellow who was his equal in his tricks, could hit as hard and could recover better. Fitzsimmons is a man who recovers from punishment wonderfully well. He is one of the best I ever saw at that." He noted that Corbett punched Fitz, but his punches did not do much actual damage. True, he drew blood, but "blood don't win a fight." Sullivan said that like himself, Corbett had gone into the ring once too often. Yet, John L. also said that he wanted to have a go at Fitzsimmons.

[894] *New York World*, March 18, 1897.
[895] *San Francisco Examiner*, March 19, 1897; *Salt Lake Herald*, March 18, 19, 1897.

A week or so after the fight, Corbett trainer Bill Delaney said that Jim lost because he worked too hard in the days leading up to the fight, and would not take his advice to back off and rest up. He said that three days before the fight, Jim was in perfect condition, but when Muldoon, Al Smith, Billy Madden and other prominent sporting men showed up to his training camp, "Jim was anxious to show how much work he could do. In accomplishing this he virtually killed himself." He felt that overtraining had sapped his vitality. However, he still gave Fitzsimmons his well deserved accolades.

> As regards the result, I want to say that Fitzsimmons did not win on any fluke. Jim can't fight any better than he did, and Fitzsimmons is entitled to all the credit in the world. Jim shouldn't have melted away in the manner he did after the sixth round, and it was due to the shape he was in. He was hitting Fitzsimmons often enough, but not hard enough. I have seen him with a pair of eight-ounce gloves bring Jeffries to his knees with a blow, and I don't think Fitzsimmons can stand a harder punch than Jeffries, who is a veritable young giant.
>
> The difference between Fitzsimmons and Corbett is that Fitz never loses his hitting powers. He can always hit at the right time and in the right place. Fitz displayed more generalship than I have ever seen in the ring. I don't think the two men will ever fight again. What Corbett should do is to fight everyone who wants to meet him from four to ten rounds, and I want to say that if he can't lick those other fellows – Maher, Choynski, Goddard and Sharkey – he can't whip Fitzsimmons.[896]

Billy Madden echoed Delaney's sentiments about Corbett's training too hard as the fight approached. "He should have laid off long before he did. He was stale, too, perhaps, although he may not have known it himself. ... Corbett did not look as fast in the ring as he did in his training work."[897]

William Muldoon said that Corbett should have finished Bob when he had him hurt, but "was not quick or fresh enough." Unlike Delaney and Madden, he felt that Corbett had actually not challenged himself enough in training. Although he had sparred often, his sparring partners did not sufficiently test him.

---

[896] *Salt Lake Herald, Rocky Mountain News*, March 25, 1897.
[897] *New York World*, March 18, 1897.

My former criticism of Corbett's training methods still holds good. He practiced boxing with slow, poor boxers, while Fitzsimmons had the cleverest men to be obtained. Corbett is a beautiful boxer, but Fitzsimmons is a great fighter. He is the best man of the two.[898]

The day after the fight, Corbett showed his swollen hands to a reporter and said, "That swelling was all caused in the sixth round.... If they had not gone back on me I would have finished him in the seventh. That is why I had no steam."[899] He disagreed with assertions that he was fatiguing. Jim had hand problems throughout his career.

According to Referee George Siler, before the fight, at ring center, Bob seemed willing to shake hands, but Martin Julian interfered by stepping between them and told him not to shake. Regarding the fight, Siler said,

It looked for the first five rounds as if it was Corbett's fight. He had Fitz wobbling in the fourth and fifth, and in the fifth I was forced for the first time to go in between them to make Fitzsimmons break away. After that it appeared to me that Corbett's blows were not as effective as before, and Fitzsimmons seemed to be getting stronger all the time, and barring a knockout by Fitzsimmons I considered the only show Corbett had was to punch, worry him by degrees and follow him up until he was dead. But the knockout blow came.[900]

Siler was also quoted as saying,

Fitzsimmons today ranks head and shoulders above all living pugilists. It is a question whether the world will ever see his equal. I know that he weighed 157 ½ pounds and that Corbett scaled 185 or more. ... This weight matter is no guess. It is founded upon actual fact gathered from unimpeachable sources.

While Bob found it difficult to land on his opponent at times, the latter cleverly evading the hammer-like leads of the lanky one, he worked with a confidence and reserve which evidenced his ultimate desire to land just one.

There were stages in the contest in which Bob, with his blood-bespattered face, looked as though he was having a hard time of it.

---

[898] *Rocky Mountain News,* March 18, 1897.
[899] *Reno Evening Gazette,* March 19, 1897.
[900] *Rocky Mountain News,* March 18, 1897.

He kept up his good-natured grin throughout, however. Every time that Corbett landed on him his face expanded into a broad grin and then, gritting his teeth, he would press in and on.

The notion that Robert Fitzsimmons is not game suffered a serious setback this afternoon. He took the cleverly delivered leads of Corbett and went in after more. He acted as though he liked it. ...

Corbett boxed cleverly. He landed and landed at will, and had Fitz on what to the layman appeared like "Queer street." As a matter of fact, however, Julian's man was miles removed from this thoroughfare. He appeared to be worse than he really was. But he was as strong as an ox, and made up his mind to land that one punch even though it took all day to get there.

A left hand blow delivered under the heart won the heavyweight championship of the world for Bob Fitzsimmons in the fourteenth round.

Siler said that Jim was down for about 15 seconds. While he was counting him out, Bob reached over the ropes and shook hands with his wife. When the count was concluded, Stelzner started to enter the ring. Not realizing that the count had finished, fearing disqualification, Bob hit Jack in the stomach and sent Stelzner flying back through the ropes.

He too noted that after Jim recovered, he rushed across the ring and attacked Bob, who did not swing back, but only protected himself. Jim's seconds grabbed him and brought Corbett to his corner to calm him down. Jim then walked back over to Bob and begged for another fight, which Fitz refused.[901]

Other experts gave their views of the fight. One said that Corbett wore himself out. Fitz's trainers said he used the same double left combination as on Sharkey. A doctor said that Jim had been hit in the solar plexus. Fitz later called the final blow his "solar plexus" punch. Some said that no one could have taken that body shot. "Fitzsimmons has been putting people out for sixteen years, and that fourteenth round of his today just shows how much of a general the man is." Fitz was a marvel, essentially winning the heavyweight championship as a large middleweight.[902]

The Salt Lake Herald said that Fitz's superior hitting power offset Corbett's speed and science. It did not feel that Corbett had retrograded over the years. Quite the contrary, it believed that Jim was even better than

---

[901] *San Francisco Chronicle, San Francisco Examiner*, March 18, 1897; *Rocky Mountain News,* March 20, 1897, quoting the *New York Journal.*
[902] *San Francisco Examiner*, March 19, 1897.

when he faced Sullivan, and put up a great fight. However, he simply met a man who was an all-round athlete like himself, and who had the punching power to go with it.[903]

The consensus was that "the fight demonstrated that a scientific boxer has no chance with a scientific fighter."[904] Reddy Gallagher echoed that Corbett demonstrated little punching power.

Corbett did not work well at all. He is recorded to have hit Fitzsimmons 194 times, and yet the only mark that the latter had when the fight was over was that split lip. That might occur to anyone in the best of condition by a very light blow. ... There was not a clean punch in the fight. When Corbett tried a hook, instead of having his arm crooked properly he would have it out full length and swing in. There was no steam in those blows. Corbett kept away. Many and many a time he would punch straight at Fitzsimmons, but a long way off and with his hand half open. When the blow got to Fitzsimmons' head his hand would be open and it would barely reach. Then he would let the tips of his fingers rest a second or two on the other's head before drawing back his arm. ... Fitzsimmons rushed Corbett into his corner several times, and the latter dodged about and distressed himself more to get away. Why, he wore himself out trying to get away from Fitzsimmons in those times. When he made a lead for Fitzsimmons he would jump back and thus lose most of the force. ... Fitzsimmons missed Corbett.... But he was swinging some awful blows, taking chances in order to knock Corbett's head off. He hit Corbett about sixty times, but only twice effectively. Corbett says one of the blows that hurt was in the seventh round and the other was that last one in the fourteenth round.... But just think of two men fighting a championship contest and neither having a black eye at the close. ... Corbett wore a distressed look when he stepped into the ring. He had not slept for two nights, worrying over the fight. He worked better at the Tabor opera house when he went on for an exhibition with me. ... Two or three times it looked to the audience as though Corbett was winning, but he wasn't. ... Say, if I should put those two men into the Central Theater, with no one knowing who they were, and they should put up a fight like that at Carson, the next morning the papers would devote two columns to roasting me and trying to drive me out of town for giving a fake fight. That's what I think of the fight.[905]

[903] *Salt Lake Herald*, March 18, 1897.
[904] *Salt Lake Herald*, March 19, 1897.
[905] *Rocky Mountain News*, March 20, 1897.

John Considine agreed with Gallagher's assessment of Corbett's punching power, saying, "Fitzsimmons had a snap. Corbett could not hit hard enough to hurt, and it was only his ability to get away that saved him long before the end came. Corbett did not hurt Fitzsimmons at all." He thought that a Sullivan-Fitzsimmons contest would be an entertaining slugging match.[906]

John Ingalls, a writer for the *New York Journal*, gave his interesting and somewhat amusing fight report.

> The blows fell muffled and the contestants seemed to be on good terms and frequently united, even in the most violent encounter.... The men seemed to be fatigued early, perspired profusely and breathed with their mouths open.
>
> During some of the rounds Corbett hit Fitzsimmons on the face.... And so it went on for nearly an hour, the audience sitting quietly...with occasional cries of applause at some agile movement or some resounding blow.
>
> And then, without warning, the most surprising, unexpected and inexplicable event occurred – the first, the last and the only dramatic incident of the occasion, like the catastrophe of a tragedy that falls before the climax has been reached. ...
>
> [Corbett] was not marked by the attacks of his adversary, whom he seemed to touch almost at will. But it was observed that his blows had little effect upon the tough, obdurate trunk of Fitz. They lacked steam and force. ...
>
> Corbett advanced rapidly from his corner, with agile step and confident smile. There was the customary display of gymnastics, feinting and prancing forward and backward, ducking and dodging, followed by a repetition of the apparently harmless exchange of futile blows that had become fatiguing by their previous monotony.
>
> Suddenly Fitzsimmons was seen to deliver a savage body blow near the pit of Corbett's stomach. He then sprang away and Corbett did not follow him. Fitzsimmons was the only man beside his antagonist who recognized the awful character of the blow. He knew the fight was over, as his conduct showed. ... When Corbett, who was still erect, suddenly tottered, a swift spasm shuddered through his limbs, he sank slowly upon his left knee, his head fell forward upon his knotted chest, a deadly pallor overspread his features, he leaned for an instant upon his right hand in a precise attitude of the dying

---

[906] *Salt Lake Herald*, March 19, 1897.

gladiator.... For an instant the audience seemed quite as much dazed as the defeated pugilist, and was uncertain what had happened or how it was done.[907]

T.T. Williams described Fitzsimmons' look of determination.

I saw a face that will haunt me until time has defaced it from my memory. It was a mixture of pathos and tragedy. There was no savagery in it, and some intelligence. There was a leer and a grin and a look of patient suffering and dogged courage. It was the face of a brave man fighting an uphill fight with lip torn and bleeding, nostrils plugged with coagulated blood, ears torn and swollen, eyes half closed and blinking in the sunlight, with every line and muscle drawn to the angle of suffering, but withal watchful, intent, and set.

Fitzsimmons's face was not cruel nor passionate. It was clear and never once did he lose his hope of success, his watchfulness over his opponent, his waiting for an opening. It was one face from the time that first blood was claimed and allowed, in the fifth round, till the victory was in his hands. You can't compare it with anything, for there is not any human countenance like Fitzsimmons's when fighting against odds.[908]

Nevada Governor Sadler, who had signed the bill legalizing boxing, said that it was a great contest and the better man won. He had no regrets about legalizing boxing, despite the criticisms from other states. The fight had brought many people into the state, the management had been ideal, and the crowd was well-behaved. "It was a hard fight, but I do not hesitate to say that it was far from being as brutal and revolting as football."

Sadler's opinion of the fight was that "Corbett is by far the quicker man, there is no doubt of that, and he lands his blows much oftener than Fitz; but Fitz is much the harder hitter, and, although he landed seldom, his blows were terrific for force." He saw the left land in the pit of the stomach.[909]

Tom Sharkey said, "Jim Corbett's weak stomach, Fitzsimmons's wonderful recuperative powers and the immense force of his punches are responsible for the passing of the championship of the world from one to

---

[907] *New York Journal*, March 18, 1897.
[908] *New York Journal*, March 18, 1897.
[909] *New York Journal*, March 18, 1897. Governor Sadler deserves to be in the boxing hall of fame if he is not already there.

the other today." Jim outpointed Bob and landed when and where he pleased. The blood interfered with Bob's breathing. Jim fought viciously and was trying his best to win, but Bob withstood the punishment and recovered well when hurt.

Regarding the knockout, Tom's opinion was that it was no chance blow, but that Bob had been looking for an opening the entire fight, and found it. "Jim probably was so intent on guarding his head that for a moment in that break away he forgot the lower part of his body altogether. At any rate, he was not quick enough in jumping back, and the Australian caught him."

Years later, Joe Choynski said that although Corbett did not have the power of a Sullivan, Fitz, or Maher, Jim had plenty of effective punishing power. However, Jim was always extremely cautious and unwilling to take a chance, tear in, and risk things. "It was this extreme caution that lost him his memorable battle with Fitzsimmons. … [W]hen Fitz found that Corbett's blows, delivered on the run, did not hurt him very badly, he decided to tear in and take a chance."[910]

In the final analysis, those who supported Corbett said it was a chance blow that could not be repeated, that the fight was won through carelessness rather than superiority. Those who supported Fitz said that Bob had worn Jim down, that it was a marvelous contest in which Jim was able to hit Bob but unable to finish him, and Fitz's superior condition, recuperative powers, and punching power eventually won out. He had the punching power of Sullivan and the skill and cleverness required to land the right punch on a shifty man like Corbett. Bob Fitzsimmons did what he always did - land the knockout blow. He had become the world's fistic idol, handing James J. Corbett his first professional defeat, having knocked out the man who beat John L. Sullivan and fought Peter Jackson to a draw.

---

[910] Joe Choynski, *I Fought 'Em All*, published in *Fight Stories*, v3 #5, October 1930, (Fiction House, 1930), 128+.

CHAPTER 20

The Films and the Controversy

The March 17, 1897 Corbett-Fitzsimmons heavyweight championship was the first fight to the finish ever filmed. Although the Corbett-Courtney bout was filmed, the rounds were truncated, the rests were longer, and spectators had to watch each round in peep show devices. This time, E.J. Rector's veriscope pictures captured the entire fight with three minute rounds and one minute rests. Two months later, in late May 1897, the films were projected onto a canvas stretched across a theater stage, for many people to watch all at once.

Despite the popularity of the fight game, there was still a very strong anti-boxing contingent. After the fight, the Woman's Christian Temperance Union forwarded an appeal to U.S. President William McKinley asking him to call upon Congress to pass a law prohibiting the exhibition of the championship fight films, or of any other fight.[911]

In early April, there was further talk of legislation to prevent the business of exhibiting the fight films. However, one of the men with partial film rights said that it was unnecessary, because the films were poorly developed. This statement was a ruse, because Corbett's trainer shortly thereafter said that the kinetoscope photographs had been successful, which they in fact were.[912] Nothing came of the legal proposition, but such talk would rear its ugly head again years later.

Three different camera angles were used to film the fight, and over 11,000 feet of film were shot, a record at the time for a single event. The finished film lasted 70 minutes, the longest ever shown in a theater to that point, although a few weeks after the initial screenings it was cut down to 20 minutes to allow for more showings.[913]

A caveat to watching old films is that they are not the definitive word on fights that you might think. Even films have issues; given the potential for improper projection speed, editing, framing, and film deterioration problems. It is difficult to tell which round is which because only some

---

[911] *Rocky Mountain News*, March 22, 1897.
[912] *San Francisco Examiner*, April 4, 1897, April 9, 1897; *Reno Evening Gazette*, March 19, 1897, discussing proposed legislation in Illinois.
[913] Myler at 119; Fields at 107.

have been preserved and there are no intertitles indicating the round number. As a result of these issues, written accounts for most bouts still remain very important, including the written accounts of what was seen on the films. This is clear for the discussion of the Corbett-Fitzsimmons fight.

Watching what exists of the films today; both men entered the ring wearing bathrobes. They wore short shorts, Corbett wearing his extremely short ones that were not really even shorts, but what they called a breech clout, revealing part of Jim's buttocks. Corbett looked just a bit taller and thicker, but he was probably not bigger by a whole lot.

The footage shows that each would use feints and subtle footwork, with occasional quick offensive attacks of one or two punches to the body or head. Defensively, they would lift their arms and clinch once they drew close, or would quickly step back to elude the attack. They kept their hands down, but were very alert, lifting them up to block, clinch, or punch at the right moment when they were in range.

This fight demonstrates the style of the era's two most skilled fighters in a fight to the finish. The cautious, calmly paced, economic, clinching style was necessary given that the championship bout could be quite lengthy and would continue until someone was knocked out. Also, given that the gloves were small, even lighter punches packed good power. This meant that the fighters had to carefully select their moments to attack, but would not have too lengthy an attack, lest they wear themselves out or leave themselves open to a counter. The issue was not who was the better boxer in a points sense, but who could inflict enough damage to knock out his opponent or make him quit. The boxers would grab both to rest and to ensure that the opponent could not do much damage.

They quickly launched their attacks, clinched, and usually would then break themselves cleanly by pushing (which Fitz liked to do) or stepping back and setting up again. Corbett was quite an effective clincher, doing so more often than Fitz, lifting his hands up to block incoming punches, then placing his hands on Fitzsimmons' arms to suppress and neutralize them. Fitzsimmons would often place his left behind Corbett's neck. Neither really did much infighting except for the occasional right over the top, something Corbett especially liked to do. Corbett also threw some right uppercuts. The general lack of infighting was mostly due to the fact that both were skilled at clinching and suppressing on the inside. It could also have been due to their intelligent desire not to waste energy trying to wrestle with another good clincher. Because hitting in the clinches and breakaways was legal, both were careful on the inside and in the manner that they broke away.

Both could move back, but Corbett was more of a mover, carefully choosing his moments to step in. Fitz was overall more of an aggressor.

However, neither moved a great deal, being efficient with their footwork. Corbett usually slid back until he decided to step forward, but also occasionally danced about. He stepped in with jabs and rights to both the body and head, and sometimes long lead hooks that had an arm swing quality to them.

Fitzsimmons slid forward standing fairly erect, leaning back slightly with weight on his right leg. He moved forward, apparently looking for a big punch, but more often than not, was met by a punch and/or clinch, or Jim would slide away. However, Fitz was patiently aggressive, not often throwing from an improper range, and seeming alert to the need to defend or clinch when Corbett attacked.

Corbett appeared to have better height, reach, and command of the range. He had more of a loose, relaxed, quick in and out quality to his boxing. However, Fitzsimmons seemed undeterred, calmly stepping in with snappy jabs, a quick right, sometimes thrown overhand, and an occasional short hook. At times, Bob even countered well, waiting for Jim to throw first, and attacking at that moment. Fitzsimmons' punch form was much more compact, crisp and powerful, setting up to throw just at the right moment where he could have his body weight behind his blows. Sometimes, Fitz would miss with a right but follow with a powerful left jab that would jolt Jim's head.

To hear Corbett tell it in his autobiography, Fitzsimmons mostly missed, and he cut Bob's face to ribbons.[914] However, from the existing footage, although Corbett may have been winning on points and accomplishing what he claimed, Fitz nevertheless appeared to be putting up a competitive fight, looking strong and determined. While the boxers were in their corners, their seconds would cool them off by waiving towels or large fans.

The 6th round was the most exciting to that point. Corbett landed some solid rights. He went on the attack, throwing his punches in rapid succession. Jim landed a long hook and right over the top, and missed a right uppercut. Fitz threw some feeble punches in return that Corbett quickly blocked with his arms amidst his own fast combinations. Corbett blocked a right and/or simultaneously led with his left arm, then threw an overhand right that came over the top and landed as Fitz was slightly leaning over to the right. Corbett appeared to miss a follow up hook because Bob's right leg slipped from underneath him as a result of the force of the right (or as a result of his legs momentarily going out). Perhaps trying to prevent himself from going down, Fitz grabbed around Corbett's waist on the way down, falling to the canvas onto one knee. The referee was initially behind the men at some distance, with Jim's back to him, with

---

[914] Corbett at 262.

Bob in front of Jim. Siler quickly rushed in as Jim stepped back away from Bob, who was grabbing his waist.

The written accounts mostly seemed to indicate that Fitz's 6th round knockdown was either a slip or a voluntary action to avoid further punishment. The footage gives more of the appearance that he was knocked down, but the way his leg went out from underneath him could give the impression that he slipped. Some reporters did say that Bob was knocked down.

This is where the first controversial issue arose. In his autobiography, Corbett claimed, and it appears to be, a long count, lasting about 14 - 15 seconds. The caveat here though is that one cannot be certain that the films are being projected in real time (they might be projected too slowly). Depending on the version you watch, the count might have been almost right on time (although some versions are projected too quickly). Regardless, Corbett claimed that Bob was down more than 10 seconds in the 6th round.

Corbett said that the referee did not begin counting when Fitz hit the ground, clutching his leg. Rather, Jim asked Referee Siler to make Bob let go of his leg. Fitz released him, and then the referee began his count. Corbett told the referee that he was counting too slowly. According to Jim, the ref pushed him and ordered him to step back. Corbett claimed Bob was down for 15 seconds, rising at the count of 9. However, he noted that he did not make a public complaint about it at the time.[915]

Actually, a primary source noted that Corbett did after the fight declare "that Fitz was down more than twelve seconds when he fell in the sixth round, but added 'There was no use kicking.'" Jim was also quoted as saying, "You can bet all you have got that he was out more than ten seconds. Scores of men will back me up, but the decision is in, and there is no use kicking."[916] After the fight, Fitzsimmons confirmed that he had heard Corbett ask the referee to count faster.[917]

The footage shows that the referee did not begin counting until after Fitz let go of Jim's waist and Corbett stepped back. Referee Siler apparently did not pick up the count but rather started counting from 'one' at that point. This gave Fitz an extra two or three seconds. Corbett stood directly over him and the referee did indeed extend his left arm out to create room as he was counting with his right arm. Siler pushed Jim back just a bit with his left. His concern with Corbett's position and attempt to look over at the ringside official conducting a count seemed to make him count a bit more

915 Corbett at 263.
916 *Reno Evening Gazette,* March 19, 1897; *Rocky Mountain News,* March 20, 1897.
917 *San Francisco Examiner,* March 20, 1897.

slowly than he should have. This also seemed to give Fitz a couple more seconds.

That said, this may not be as much of a controversy as it seems (and it was not much of one at the time), because throughout the count, Fitzsimmons appeared to be all right, kneeling on one knee, ready to rise. So, long count or not, it did not appear to matter or have an impact on the ultimate determination of the contest, because it looks as if Bob could have risen quickly if he had desired.

Another reason the slightly long count was not a big deal was that Bob recovered quickly and fought well during the remainder of the round. It did not seem that he was all that hurt. Fitzsimmons' legs appeared sturdy after rising from the knockdown. He alternated between fighting back and clinching the now more aggressive Corbett. Fitz snapped in some good jabs and straight rights, such that it was clear that he was not going anywhere anytime soon.

Perhaps most importantly, the published rules for the fight stated that if a boxer went down, he had ten seconds to rise, "the other man meanwhile to return to his corner," or at least ten feet away, which Corbett clearly did not do.[918] Corbett's failure to retire at least ten feet away would have justified a slower count or for it to have been suspended entirely if the referee had so chosen.

Years later, one referee commented on the fact that Corbett did not step back far enough, saying, "If one or two seconds were lost it was largely Jim Corbett's own fault for he kept crowding forward and the referee had to divide his time between counting Fitzsimmons and pushing Jim back."[919]

This was the first time that a rule requiring a fighter to retire to a corner or away from a downed fighter, and a potential long count, had at least some play in the discussion of a heavyweight championship bout. It would not be the last.

In his autobiography, Corbett claimed to have hit Bob at will for the rest of the fight, feeling quite confident, although he granted that Fitz was "dead game."[920]

From the existing footage, Corbett was not all that busy with his punches, usually throwing only one at a time, being more concerned with defense. He may well have been tiring. Fitz had difficulty landing because Jim would move or lean back and clinch. However, Bob's punches still appeared very quick and strong, and he was the aggressor. Although Corbett may have generally out-landed Fitz for most of the fight, Bob took

---

[918] *San Francisco Examiner*, March 11, 1897, March 12, 1897.
[919] *San Francisco Examiner*, November 11, 1901.
[920] Corbett at 263.

the punches well and continued to throw hard blows in return, never seeming out of it. At one point, Jim playfully tapped Bob on the chin after the bell.

The punch that did it.

During the 14th round, Corbett jabbed and Fitzsimmons eluded it by dipping to the side, and immediately if not simultaneously landed a quick, very short counter left hook to the body that dropped Corbett. It looked somewhat odd, like a short shift across the body from left to right. The footage at that point has mostly disintegrated, but some frames have been put together to show the punch. However, its incompleteness may in part be why the punch looks odd and is difficult to read. It goes by very quickly, but a body blow can be seen to put Corbett down.

Although there were reports of a follow-up blow, (varying from a right or left to the head or a right to the body) the footage does not reveal much of any follow-up blow. To the extent that it does, Bob can be seen to throw his left arm forward just as Corbett hits the canvas. It is not clear whether or not it landed, and even if it did, it does not look to be significant.

There was some controversy when the films were released as to whether Bob had fouled Jim. Based on the films, it appears that Jim went down slowly, first crouching over low, but not actually touching the canvas. Bob started the low left, which might have landed on the head just as Jim's right hand touched the canvas. It really was not a big punch at all, and Bob might have actually held it back a bit. The motion was started before Jim was down. It is practically imperceptible on the films.

Corbett said of the knockdown that Fitz had begun a right handed head blow and Jim pulled his head back in an attempt to make it fall short so that he could counter with his own right. However, Bob pulled his blow as Jim leaned back, and then "let his idle left try something, just started it haphazard and landed on the pit of the stomach. Quicker than all this takes to tell, I sank to my knees."

The existing footage does not support Corbett's version. Corbett throws a jab which Fitz eluded and simultaneously countered with his body punch. However, because much of the film is disintegrated at this point, some parts to the sequence might be missing. We must rely on the live fight reports and primary source written accounts of what the films showed.

The punch was so devastating that Corbett felt paralyzed and was unable to rise despite his best efforts. He said that he tried to reach for the rope to pull himself up, but could not grab it. The footage reveals him crawling on one hand and one knee towards the ropes, the other side of him raised off the canvas. He did not beat the count. A burly James J. Jeffries can be seen entering the ring to come to Corbett's aid.

The New York Journal attempted to make a big deal about the last little punch that Fitz let out as Corbett went down. Never shy about posting a sensational headline in order to sell more newspapers, the *Journal* advertised that the veriscope pictures revealed a foul blow. Of course, no one, not even Corbett, claimed a late punch on the day of the fight. The only attempted foul claim at that time was a low blow, which the referee disallowed, and Corbett later admitted was a legitimate punch.

Regardless, when the *Journal* printed the May 1897 headline about the alleged foul blow, even it admitted that Corbett would have been knocked out anyway. "It does not seem to do much harm." Martin Julian said that any foul Bob committed would not have harmed a fly, and that if it had been serious somebody would have seen it. Corbett had a slew of trainers and backers at ringside, yet no one claimed such a foul. From Baltimore, when Bob read the article claiming a foul, he said that he would bet $1,000 that there was no foul. He and Julian claimed that he held back his punch and never touched Corbett. Most agreed that the punch was begun before Corbett was down anyway. The majority called it a technical foul that had no bearing on the final result. It was the blow in the stomach that settled Corbett.[921]

The New York World echoed the *Journal's* claim of a technical foul. However, it too said "it was delivered without intent to do wrong" and "it had no material effect upon the issue." The blow was so subtle that neither the referee nor the spectators noticed it on the day of the fight.

> In the knockout it will be seen that he is swinging every atom of his weight into the blow [to the stomach]. In the punch while Corbett is down he appears not to be swinging so hard. One is inclined to believe that while the blow was in midair Fitzsimmons saw that he was hitting a fallen man and that he did all in his power to hold it back.

As for the fight itself, the *World* said that the films showed that Corbett had everything his own way through the first 6 rounds. Still, "Bob fought back gamely, never ceasing the grins and winks to his wife, by which he signaled that he really didn't mind the grueling he got." However, it felt that Corbett's blows were weakening Bob from the 4th to 6th rounds. Bob's nose and mouth were bleeding so badly that his front was smeared with blood from chest to waist. Although his lip was split, Fitz continued smiling. Bob was in distress in the 6th and clinched often to save himself. His legs seemed wobbly and his head flew about from the blows.

Interestingly enough, neither the *Journal* nor the *World* mentioned anything about there being a long count in the 6th round. *The World* said,

> Before Siler had counted nine seconds Fitzsimmons had arisen and had his fists up ready for fight. ... The plain, simple, hard-working blacksmith had regained much of his strength while resting, say, eight seconds on one knee, and he was able to clinch once more and still once more and so last out the round.

> Corbett seemed tired from this point onward. He was no longer on tiptoe sprinting after his adversary. He appeared to have worn himself out punishing Fitzsimmons, who was now improving every minute and constantly taking a more prominent part in the fighting.

---

[921] *New York Journal*, May 13, 14, 1897.

The 14th round had progressed for about a minute and a half, when Corbett tried a left lead for the head, but Fitz avoided it and hurled in a long, heavy, swinging left uppercut into the solar plexus, with all of his body behind it. "Corbett is seen to be shattered by its destructive effects." His head fell forward, his eyes rolled, and slowly his knees bent forward and down. "His left hand clutches at his side, and his right arm hangs swinging helplessly." "On his face was the most awful look of agony the writer has ever witnessed."[922]

Owing to the fact that the theater was having electrical issues, the first public exhibition of the fight films was delayed over a week after the publication of the original *Journal* article. The general public was able to see the fight films starting May 22, 1897 at New York's Academy of Music. The crowd included 100 women.

After viewing the veriscope films, Corbett said, "I think I clearly showed my superiority, forcing things right up to the time I was declared out." Regarding the alleged foul, Jim said, "I do not remember that blow when Fitzsimmons struck it, but that he actually struck me when my glove was on the floor cannot be doubted for a moment." However, he also said, "I don't think it had any material effect on the result, and I never have claimed so." Corbett's bigger issue was his allegation of a long count.

Describing the fight details, Corbett said,

> First, I tried my man and studied his tactics, just as I suppose Fitz did with me. I was careful and left no openings for my antagonist. He ducked my swings several times, but his bloody mouth shows that I landed blow after blow, and those blows told, too.
>
> That sixth round must have opened the eyes of a good many people who weren't at Carson. Fitz was lucky there. I'll bet he couldn't tell how many uppercuts he got just about that time, but these pictures show I had him going, and he knew it. ... He clinched to save himself and I knocked him down. Then he hung on to me. I hollered at Siler to make him quit, but then I had to break away from him. People who see that round photographed can't be deceived. They can tell that Muldoon began to count in a jiffy, and he had got to ten before Fitz was on his feet again. Fitz was groggy. Anybody can tell that. It must have been several more than ten seconds before he got up again. ... I ask anybody who sees the photographs to find an excuse for him to say whether I am not justified in demanding another chance. ... All I want is another fight, and then it can be settled beyond a doubt whether he's my master.

---

[922] *New York World*, May 22, 1897.

Really, Corbett was simply looking for a reason to support an argument for a rematch. He was also quoted as saying,

> Let the people judge for themselves. Let them look at the pictures and see if I am not entitled to another fight. ... I think that even my bitterest enemies ...will admit...that I had much the better of it up to the time of that stomach punch...
>
> You will find that it is not the foul blow that the people who see these pictures will be chiefly interested in. The sixth round, when Fitzsimmons held me by the knees, will be the thing that will cause the arguments.
>
> Let those who see the pictures count off the seconds as Muldoon does. Let them note when he begins to count. Watch the time Fitzsimmons is on the floor before the referee begins to count. In short, let the spectators see for themselves just how the fight went, and who did most of the punishing.

The *Journal* writer said, "As to the foul – well, it wasn't much of a transgression. It came and went so quickly that you could not really say it was there." Regarding the 6th round, when Fitz went down,

> Mr. Muldoon swings his arm pump handle fashion nine times. This saves Fitzsimmons from much obloquy. It is true that Muldoon might have begun to swing his arm a fraction earlier, and Mr. Siler might have responded more promptly, and this fact will doubtless raise much discussion in the future.

Responding to the foul blow discussion, Fitzsimmons (who had not yet seen the films) said,

> It needed no Veriscope in the Corbett-Mitchell fight to show that Mitchell was fouled, yet Charley Mitchell did not go around for months after that fight wearying everybody he could reach by telling how he had been fouled. These are things Mr. Corbett should remember. Notwithstanding all Corbett's advantages, I whipped him fairly. ... Before the fight at Carson City Harry Corbett bought up four hundred seats near the ring side. These he filled with his toughs from the hardest section of San Francisco. ... Had there been a foul, all hell couldn't have controlled that mob. There was no foul, or those people would have seen it.

Timekeeper William Muldoon responded to the claims of a foul blow and a long count. He said that Fitz's last blow was "delivered just as Corbett was sinking after receiving the blow in the stomach."

> The blow was delivered as Corbett was going, not after his knee had reached the floor. ... This is only one of a hundred excuses that have been faked up to palliate Corbett's defeat. I regard it as an insult to the intelligence of his friends for him to claim that he was fouled, and that they saw it done and made no protest. Eighty per cent of the crowd was in favor of Corbett.
>
> Another thing, if Corbett, Brady or any one else claims that Fitzsimmons was down over ten seconds or even nine in the sixth round, they lie. ... The trouble is that men like Brady, who is a schemer instead of a sport, get into the business and keep up this chatter for advertising purposes and disgust the public. Corbett whipped Sullivan when he was worn out and in condition when a woman could have licked him. He licked Mitchell, a broken-down welter weight, and now, he has been licked by a middleweight. That's his record of fighting since '92, and he'd better give us a rest.

Regarding the long count and the fight, one man who was very pro-Corbett in his commentary said,

> The veriscope pictures reveal another point in the fight when Corbett was given the worst of it. This is in the sixth round, when Fitz goes down. He clings to Corbett's legs, and seems several seconds in sliding to the ground. Siler, the referee, steps forward and motions Corbett away. I say that Siler should have begun to count the time from the moment Fitzsimmons's knee touched the floor and think several seconds elapsed before the count began. The pictures show, too, that in the tenth, eleventh, twelfth and thirteenth rounds, Corbett was in good shape instead of being greatly distressed in these rounds as the newspapers have told us.[923]

Interestingly enough, at that time, no one noted or addressed the fact that Corbett failed to return to his corner or step back ten feet away, as required by the rules published before the fight. The debate simply focused on whether or not the count was long.

---

[923] *New York Journal*, May 23, 1897.

During the film exhibition, one of the spectators watching the fight in the theater exclaimed, "P'shaw! That ain't fighting!" Still, "the crowd was satisfied." The men were liberally applauded at times, and Fitz's victory received the greatest ovation.

The New York Herald relied on the report of "Honest" John Kelly, a noted referee, for its account of the films. The Academy of Music was crowded from the gallery to the floor. Kelly said,

> The first round indicated nothing as to the result. In the second round Corbett does all the leading, and in the third, also. Fitzsimmons does not appear to have anything in his favor.
>
> In the fourth round Corbett jabs his left repeatedly and gets away without a return. At the end of this round it looks as if it should be 100 to 40 that Corbett would win.
>
> It also appears as if Fitzsimmons had started with the idea of tiring out Mr. Corbett by hanging on to him. Even now Corbett shows himself to be one of the cleverest fighters ever seen.
>
> In the next round – the fifth – Corbett goes at it. See how Fitzsimmons hangs on to his opponent!
>
> The sixth round is the one in which there is a dispute about the time. Fitzsimmons was down. ... I held my watch ready for this emergency. ... The moment he touched the ground I snapped the watch. The moment Fitzsimmons struck the ground he was ready to get up. But he took the full limit. He was on one knee and was looking intently at Corbett. He was ready to rise when the referee counted "nine." He did not seem to be dazed, and I should say was fully conscious.
>
> The blood on his face was apparent to all. After he had risen and resumed the fighting the picture showed that he got in his first best blow. At the beginning of the seventh round both men were fresh, as far as I could see. That left hand jab of Corbett's is a hard thing for a man to get away from. His left is going all the time, and it is always on Fitzsimmons' face.
>
> In the eighth round, Fitzsimmons is doing the forcing, and is met with several left hand jabs. In the tenth round there is a mix-up and Fitzsimmons gets in a good body blow. It is now clear that Corbett has not the stamina and lung power of Fitzsimmons....
>
> [I]t looks to me as if Corbett had the best of the fight, for although Fitzsimmons is forcing it, yet Corbett is doing the leading. Fitzsimmons is getting enough punching from the left jabs of the

Californian to knock out any ordinary man. But it is evident that Fitzsimmons is in the very best of condition; better than his opponent.

In the twelfth round it is more and more evident that Corbett is wonderfully quick – the quickest man in the world. But at the end of this round he begins to show signs of fatigue. In the next round Corbett is after his man all the time. He cannot keep away from Fitzsimmons. Fitzsimmons is on top of him all the time, compelling Corbett to keep up his aggressive tactics. In this round I notice for the first time that Corbett's legs weaken.

So far there had not been a round in the contest where Fitzsimmons seemed to have had the best of the other man. Indeed, it looked to me as if Corbett were the best man in every round. As to cleverness, Fitzsimmons is not in it with Corbett. Corbett's left hand jabs it was impossible for Fitzsimmons to avoid.

In the thirteenth round Corbett shows for the first time in a most unmistakable manner that he is growing weak in his legs.

Now comes the fourteenth and last round. As far as I could see from the picture Corbett started in to do all the leading, but his body blows do not seem to have any effect upon Fitzsimmons, who, although bleeding, was apparently strong.

There is a mix-up. All of a sudden Corbett goes down. As far as a foul is concerned, I couldn't see anything of the kind. ... If they fight again I will bet that Corbett beats Fitzsimmons.

Various other spectators offered their opinions: Dan Smith said that while Corbett was down,

Fitz hit Corbett with the left, hook swing fashion, while the latter's knee was touching the floor. ... I do not however, believe that the blow in question had any bearing on the result of the fight. ... It was delivered like a flash, Fitz evidently realizing that he was in error, drew his hand back quickly. The pictures, however, show that Fitzsimmons won on his merits.

Dave Gideon said,

Fitzsimmons won on his merits. Fitz seemed to grow stronger and Corbett weaker after the sixth round. I think Corbett is entitled to another fight if he is willing to put up the necessary stake. I believe Fitz will defeat him if they ever meet again.[924]

The New York Clipper's analysis was very pro-Fitzsimmons.

The presentation…settled two important matters that had been in dispute, owing to the assertions made by irresponsible people, which were emphasized by alleged veriscope reproductions in certain sensational newspapers, to the effect that in the sixth round Referee Siler did not begin counting soon enough when Fitzsimmons was down on one hand and one knee, that he was on the floor more than ten seconds, and that Fitz delivered a foul blow in the closing round, after he had knocked Corbett down. The "can't tell a lie" veriscope pictures prove conclusively that these assertions are utterly false, as every intelligent, thinking person already knew they were; for each principal had an alert timekeeper at the ring side, to act as a check on the official timekeeper and on the referee, while, had any foul been committed at any time, the seconds and backers of the man fouled would have been quick and persistent in claiming it, whereas nothing of the sort occurred on the day of the fight. Common sense alone, without the aid of the veriscope, is sufficient to disprove these sensational stories, given utterance to after the lapse of two months by parties who have no regard for the truth. … Fitzsimmons won the battle fairly, and…Siler performed his whole duty. It is to be regretted that Corbett, after repeatedly acknowledging himself beaten honorably, should allow his disappointment to so sour his temper as to induce him to appear in print in a whining letter in support of the proposition that he was the recipient of a foul blow. This will certainly act as a boomerang wherever the Stuart veriscope pictures are shown, and will as surely not assist in inducing Fitz to give him another match.[925]

On May 24, 1897, two days after the first public exhibitions, Fitzsimmons saw the fight on film for the first time, watching it amongst a crowded theater.

---

[924] *New York Herald*, May 23, 1897.
[925] *New York Clipper*, May 29, 1897.

[Fitz] applauded the shadowy figure of himself that moved about the canvas, urged himself to be cool, warned himself to avoid impending uppercuts, and at the close, when his dynamic left had crashed against Corbett's solar plexus region, the Cornishman rewarded himself with the exclamation: "Well done, Bob!"

A small boy wearing a new pair of red top boots and occupying a front seat at the circus, could not have exhibited more genuine pleasure than did Fitz as round after round of the famous contest was depicted on the canvas. ...

The first few rounds showed Fitz rushing and Corbett dancing away from the Cornishman's attack. "Who is forcing the fighting?" inquired Fitz as he looked admiringly at his aggressive picture.

When the sixth round was shown, Fitz became intensely interested, and when he went to his knee in the corner he yelled: "Did you see him push me down? That's what he did at Carson, and Siler began to count just as soon as my knee touched the floor."

As the figure of Fitz arose and began to fight again, the flesh and blood Fitzsimmons fairly shrieked: "That shows whether I was groggy or not. See me fight, will you? See how strong I am. What? Had me whipped in the sixth round? Not in a thousand years. ..."

After the sixth round, when Fitzsimmons grew steadily stronger and Corbett seemed to weaken, the champion remarked in a sarcastic tone: "Why, what's the matter with this strong man Corbett? He's losing his speed and his steam. He doesn't seem to be as lively as in the first few rounds. Why should he get tired so quickly? He boxed sixty-one rounds with Peter Jackson when Jackson had a lame foot, but he can't box six rounds with me without getting tired. How do you explain that, and especially as he says he never was in better shape in his life than when he faced me? It must be that I box faster and hit harder than the other men Corbett has faced. That's the only reasonable explanation."

When the eleventh round was reached Fitz howled: "See him spitting out the tooth I knocked out!"

In the thirteenth round the pictures showed Fitz apparently whispering in Corbett's ear. "I told him I would whip him pretty quick. You see, I could feel he was getting weak as a wet dishrag, and I knew he was easy meat for me." ...

As the knockout blow was shown, Fitz said: "That's where I hit him in the stomach with a left shift, and I hooked the left under his chin just as his knees began to bend. Don't you see that I never touch him after his knee reaches the floor. There, see me step back? ... But why doesn't he get up? He's strong enough to work along the floor like a caterpillar, but he doesn't get up. He's quit, sure enough." …

When Corbett had regained his breath and is shown on the canvas rushing like a mad bull at Fitz, the latter arose and said: "Ladies and gentlemen, please take note at what a perfect gentleman Mr. Corbett is. That's how he got his title of 'Gentleman Jim.'" This caused a laugh…

"I was the aggressor from start to finish. … Yes, indeed, those pictures suit me, and Corbett's fake stories won't stand much of a show when the people can see the photographs."[926]

And now, for those who like a bit of sensationalism, here is something to ponder and discuss. No one has ever questioned the legitimacy of the knockout, and it is difficult to do so unless you were hit by the punch and felt what Jim did, but from the position he was in, it did not seem that it would have taken a great deal of effort to have risen. He had one side of his body off the canvas, his foot flat on the ground with his leg bent, and was using that in conjunction with the other side's hand and knee on the canvas to crawl towards the rope. If he could rise that far, and crawl forward, then

[926] New York Journal, May 25, 1897.

it seems that he could also have pushed upwards with his leg and risen. Again, this is speculation, but perhaps something that historians should discuss. Could Corbett have risen? Fitzsimmons suggested that he could have done so. "But why doesn't he get up? He's strong enough to work along the floor like a caterpillar, but he doesn't get up. He's quit, sure enough."

Corbett's show of bravado and anger after the fight may have been his face-saving way of covering up either that he was done for, that he had quit, or, if you want to be a cynic, that he had thrown the fight. Recall that his fight with Duncan McDonald had in part been suspected as a hippodrome/fake because neither combatant demonstrated anger over the draw decision. Perhaps Corbett had learned that the best way to cover up the fact that he had quit or thrown the fight was to put on a show and seem really upset afterward. Perhaps he regretted what he had done. Or, it could have been his way of securing a rematch, feeling that he could win (regardless of whether or not he had quit or thrown the fight).

Maybe Corbett really was just caught by a big punch which he thought was a fluke, and he was quite upset that he had lost what he thought was going to be a win. After all the acrimonious big talk the two had done, there was a lot on the line psychologically, as well as economically. Jim was emotionally invested in a big way. A knockout loss to Fitzsimmons cut Jim's pride to the core.

Still, there were those who had previously called Corbett a faker, including former opponents Dave Campbell and Tom Sharkey, so the theory that Corbett threw the fight or quit at least has to be considered. Fitzsimmons again made the suggestion at year-end 1897, saying, "Why, that Yellow won't fight. He got a little punch in the stomach at Carson City and then laid down. He wasn't knocked out. He knew he was whipped and took that opportunity to quit."[927]

Although less likely, a fix was not entirely out of the question either. Fitzsimmons claimed that he had received two separate offers to throw the fight, one out of San Francisco for $500,000, and one out of New York for $250,000.[928] Years later, he again confirmed that two bankers had offered him $700,000 to throw the fight.[929] If Fitz had not agreed, those same persons could have easily offered the same money to Corbett to throw the fight. And that was serious money in those days, more than Corbett was likely ever to earn as a boxer at that late stage of his career. Besides, Jim was tired of the game anyway. Jim Corbett was an actor, after all (and could therefore also fake it better). Also, it would have made more sense to get Jim to throw it anyway, because the payoff on Bob, the underdog, would have been bigger.

Recall that there were rumors before the fight that it was to be fixed, some saying that it was fixed for Bob to win; others saying that it was fixed for Jim. Both men denied it in the newspapers. Of course, such speculation often surrounded many legitimate fights. Fixed-fight speculation was often what followed in the wake of a suspicious bout, particularly one like the Fitzsimmons-Sharkey fight, so it did not necessarily mean anything. It is interesting though to read some accounts of Corbett's attempt to rise, calling it "pitiful in the extreme." Reddy Gallagher's comment, that some might call the fight a fake if they did not know who was in the ring, also resonates. Even John Ingalls, reporter for the *Examiner/Journal* papers, said that he felt that the contest "lacked earnestness and sincerity and left the impression of a duel on the stage." However, boxing history has shown that two really great fighters can often neutralize each other and lead to a tactical bout. Many had predicted such a contest.[930]

I realize this is sheer speculation, and I have been one to roll my eyes every time someone wants to say some fight has been thrown. I am not saying this is what happened. It is just a thought that popped into my head based on what I saw in the film, based on the fact that both Corbett and Fitz had admittedly engaged in fixed or semi-fixed fights in their lifetimes, there was some discussion of a potential fix even before the fight, and the fact that one of the combatants confirmed that there were attempts to create a fix.

However, ultimately, I do not believe (or want to believe) that Corbett threw the fight or quit. The most likely scenario is that a fatiguing Corbett

---

[927] *Chicago Tribune*, December 20, 1897.
[928] "Fight of the Century" reproduced a March 17, 1897 Fitzsimmons statement.
[929] *National Police Gazette*, September 8, 1900.
[930] *New York Journal*, March 18, 1897.

was gradually worn down and hit well by a devastating punch, and simply could not rise. The fight meant so much to Corbett's ego that it is very difficult to believe that he would have thrown it. Bob Fitzsimmons had a habit of suddenly landing the knockout punch, so it is not all that surprising that he did so against Corbett.

Really, the fight went according to both men's career strengths and weaknesses. Corbett demonstrated his excellent defense and ability to outpoint anyone, landing many more blows than Fitzsimmons. However, despite Corbett's good boxing, he really had not deterred Fitz, who calmly and consistently forced the pace. Jim was perhaps discouraged and fatigued from trying to knock him out, vulnerable to a big shot. Perhaps Jim simply did not believe that Fitz could hurt him, and grew careless, as many of Bob's opponents had done. Fitz finally landed a good one, as he always did at some point against all of his opponents. Despite being hit a lot and missing many punches, despite the bleeding, Fitzsimmons was still strong, moving forward, throwing hard, crisp punches, harder than Corbett's, while Jim was throwing less and being more defensive, a sign of fatigue. Fitz had trained for this type of fight, to pressure, to keep the pace fast so that he could eventually wear out Jim's defense, and to take a few so that he could find an opportunity.

Recall that Jim Corbett had been fairly inactive in serious bouts for a number of years and had rarely gone more than a few rounds. The last time that he had fought so many rounds in a competitive fight was in 1892 when he had won the crown, over four years earlier. As champion, he had not taken on any real tests either. Even Tom Sharkey gave him trouble in only 4 rounds. Jim was likely not at his best, despite all the great training he had done. He may well have been sufficiently fatigued by the 14th round such that a big sneaky fast body shot would have a devastating effect. Years later, Jim's sparring partner, James Jeffries, echoed this position, saying that he believed that Corbett had worn himself out, and was done for even before Bob landed the body punch. Or, Jim could have been fine, but given enough time, the law of probability held that Bob Fitzsimmons was going to land a big one somewhere, and he finally did. Even fresh fighters were usually taken out by Bob's devastating power. [931]

Fitzsimmons had been much more active against top opposition, had been a more active fighter in general, and had recently fought 8 hard rounds with Sharkey. He always recovered and came back well when hurt, and had been knocking out everyone, often only needing to land a single shot to take his opponents out or badly daze them. The knockout may have been inevitable at some point and was consistent with Bob's power-punching career results.

[931] *San Francisco Examiner, National Police Gazette*, May 27, 1899.

Jim Corbett was never really known as a big puncher. He was unable to stop Peter Jackson. He had required over 20 rounds to stop a young Joe Choynski and an old Sullivan, basically wearing them down gradually, and also allowing them to wear themselves out. Fitz was in such phenomenal shape and knew how to pace himself such that he was not going to defeat himself. Despite spotting Corbett some weight, Fitz was not going against a champion known for his power. Bob had absorbed punches from Peter Maher and Tom Sharkey, and they were considered bigger punchers than Corbett. He could afford to take a few against Jim, and Fitz trained accordingly.

Also, recall the Choynski fight, when Corbett briefly hit the wall between the 14th to 16th rounds, and it was said that if Joe could have landed at that point he would have won. One comment regarding that fight was that Corbett's rather loose guard of his body could become a detriment. However, he had managed to ward off Peter Jackson's body punches, and Peter was a famed body puncher. Still, Fitz was said to be more of a puncher than Jackson was, and took more chances.

Finally, remember that Jake Kilrain said that a past his prime Sullivan had fought the wrong fight against Jim by rushing him and wearing himself out. He said that the better plan of attack would be to consistently, but calmly pressure him, which is what Fitz had done. Bob had seen Corbett fight Sullivan, had watched him on film against Courtney, and had seen him in exhibitions. He knew about Jim's tactics.

Bob Fitzsimmons had fought a tactically brilliant fight, the one necessary to defeat Corbett. Corbett's weaknesses had finally caught up with him against an intelligent, experienced, well conditioned devastating puncher.

CHAPTER 21

Another Semi-Retired Champion

Immediately after defeating Corbett on March 17, 1897, Bob Fitzsimmons told the press that owing to a promise made to his wife, he was retiring and would not fight again. Corbett told him that he would force him to fight again. However, Bob had no intention of doing so., saying, "I don't believe I'll ever fight again."

> I am content to stand upon my record as it exists today and let others do battle for the honors I relinquish. The satisfaction of having defeated James Corbett is sufficient for me, and I prefer to be known hereafter as the retired, undefeated middleweight and heavyweight champion of the world.[932]

However, like Sullivan and Corbett before him, there were question marks regarding just how retired he was. Fitzsimmons was still going to capitalize upon his victory by performing in money-making exhibitions. Bob just meant that he was retired from competitive fights to the finish…at least for the time being. He was also quoted as saying,

> I have not decided just what I will do, but one thing is certain, and that is I will not fight any more for at least two years. It has been at least three years since Corbett fought anybody for the championship, and I am not going into any finish contests for two years myself. During that time I may decide to fight again and I may not. It all depends upon how I feel. I am getting along in years. …. However, I will not say now what I will do. I may fight again and I may not. I shall pay no attention to the challenges made by Goddard, Mitchell and Sharkey. They are all bluff challenges and are not worth my consideration.[933]

---

[932] *New York Journal,* March 19, 1897.
[933] *Rocky Mountain News, Brooklyn Daily Eagle,* March 19, 1897.

He kept his word. The public still considered Fitzsimmons the champion, and there remained uncertainty regarding whether he really was retired.

For all intensive purposes, Fitzsimmons had indeed retired from competitive bouts against top contenders for a couple years. Bob would only engage in some friendly money-making sparring exhibitions, or he would box a bit with local nobodies who tried, but were of no threat. Fitzsimmons was not above cashing in on his new status. He later became an actor and made money in that line, just as Corbett and Sullivan had done during their inactive periods.

The day after the Corbett fight, Fitzsimmons did not look too bad.

> He looked in excellent shape, and the terrific pounding that he received in the ring yesterday from Corbett did not show to any such extent as might have been expected. His lower lip was cut quite badly, and Fitzsimmons had covered it liberally with court plaster, but this was the only thing about him that gave an indication of the ordeal he had gone through on the preceding day. One thumb was tied up.[934]

Dan Stuart offered a $10,000 purse for a fight between Fitz and Joe Goddard, who had scored a November 1896 KO4 rematch victory over Ed Smith, but Bob was not interested.[935] After Fitz refused to rematch him, Corbett said that he would revive his *Naval Cadet* show and tour again.

A couple days after the fight, Tom Sharkey claimed that he was the champion because he had defeated Fitzsimmons.[936] No one took him seriously.

Four days after the championship fight, on the afternoon of March 21, 1897 in San Francisco, before a crowd of about 2,000 which paid 50 cents each, Fitz sparred 4 rounds with Jack Stelzner, showing them how he knocked out Corbett. In the evening, he sparred with Dan Hickey.[937]

Despite his exhibitions, Fitz kept telling Corbett that he was retired and would never enter the ring again.[938] He basically meant that he planned to have no competitive bouts.

Regarding the championship fight, Jack Stelzner said, "Corbett made a game fight, but when it comes to hitting he is not in it for a minute.

---

[934] *Rocky Mountain News,* March 19, 1897.
[935] *New York Journal,* March 19, 1897.
[936] *San Francisco Chronicle,* March 18, 1897; *San Francisco Examiner,* March 18, 20, 1897; *Mountain News,* March 21, 1897.
[937] *San Francisco Examiner, Rocky Mountain News,* March 22, 1897.
[938] *San Francisco Examiner,* March 24, 1897.

Fitzsimmons hits harder than any other man on earth." When asked what Bob's plans were, Jack said, "He is going out with his company, and will give exhibitions all along the line, but as to a decisive fight, I think he is through."[939] It was said that Bob would remain in San Francisco for a few days to give exhibitions before heading to New York.[940]

The Fitz party left San Francisco for the east on March 28, planning to give exhibitions on the way to New York, including Ogden and Salt Lake City, Utah, and Denver, Colorado. A purse of $50 was being offered to anyone who would stand before Fitz for 4 rounds.[941]

Upon his arrival in Salt Lake on March 31, 1897, 400 people met his train at the station. Speaking of Corbett, Bob said, "His talk about bringing the championship back to this country is all rot. I am a naturalized American citizen." Bob said that he wore the American flag into the ring, while Corbett had the Irish flag in his corner.

Regarding Corbett's boxing, Fitzsimmons said, "I think he is a clever boxer, but there it stops. He is not a fighter." Bob said that he took a lot of punishment in order to land the knockout blow. He was the aggressor all the way, and "it is vastly easier for a man to get in a good many punches when he is acting on the defense, because he can coolly wait for every lead and the opening that must follow it." Corbett landed a lot, but Bob's aggression eventually paid off for him.

That evening, Bob hit the bag, wrestled with Roeber, and then sparred Hickey 3 rounds. It was a "very pretty exhibition," because Hickey was "no slouch." Both were quick on their feet, agile, and very scientific. Bob would duck Hickey's blows with ease, and counter handily.

Corbett was in Salt Lake too. He said that he was in excellent condition for the fight, the best he had ever been. He felt that his arm was blocking his stomach in the 14th round, but somehow Bob's blow got under it. "It took the wind out of me, that was all." He said that he had leaned back before he got hit there, and something had to give.

Martin Julian sent a telegram back west that said, "Fitzsimmons' house packed to the doors. Corbett's house very bad."[942]

On April 2, 1897, Fitz was in Denver, Colorado. When asked if he would fight again, Bob said, "Well, I don't know. I promised my wife that I would retire. … Haven't I earned a rest? What I say to Corbett is this: You go and lick Maher, Goddard, Sharkey and a few others and then you can talk with me."

---

[939] *Salt Lake Herald*, March 21, 1897.
[940] *Salt Lake Herald*, March 22, 1897.
[941] *Salt Lake Herald*, March 30, 1897; *Rocky Mountain News*, March 29, 1897.
[942] *Salt Lake Herald, Rocky Mountain News*, April 1, 1897.

Bob planned to become an actor, to go out on the road the following year with a theatrical company to perform in a play especially written for him. "We are going to New York now, giving exhibitions at various places along the road, and then I'll settle down for a while."

That evening, the Lyceum Theater was filled for Fitz's show. Bob boxed 4 lively rounds with Dan Hickey, and he also gave a clever exhibition of bag punching.[943]

On April 3, 1897, Bob's athletic and vaudeville company exhibited in Omaha, Nebraska. The theater was pretty well filled, and there was a fair sprinkling of women present. Martin Julian gave a speech to the audience wherein he said that over the past five years, Corbett kept putting up obstacles to their fight, continually demanding that Bob defeat different men before he could get a title shot. Now he was requiring Corbett to start at the bottom too.

Fitzsimmons first gave a bag punching exhibition, which brought a hearty round of applause. He then boxed Hickey 3 rounds. The local paper's assessment of Bob was, "Not a particularly brilliant boxer, though by no means a novice, he makes comparatively little effort to avoid blows, his controlling idea being an effort to land on his opponent, taking what comes in pursuit of that opportunity." They closed by giving an illustration of the final blows at Carson.[944]

On April 13, 1897, a crowd of 5,000 greeted Fitzsimmons upon his return to New York. At that point, manager Martin Julian said that Fitz would consider a fight if a sufficient purse was offered.[945]

In late April, Fitz announced that he had reconsidered his retirement and said that he was prepared to receive challenges. Corbett issued a formal challenge and deposited a forfeit. Needling Corbett, Bob said that Jim would first have to go out and make a reputation for himself as a fighter rather than as just a boxer.[946] However, Corbett did not return to the ring, saying that he wanted no one but Bob. Tom Sharkey, Joe Goddard, Peter Maher, and Joe Choynski, amongst others, were also seeking title shots.

John L. Sullivan announced that he was quite serious about his challenge to Fitzsimmons. "I want the public to know that I never laid down or quit in my life, which is more than Fitzsimmons can say."[947]

---

[943] *Rocky Mountain News*, April 3, 1897. Jack Dooley, who had said that he wanted to attempt to win $50 for standing before Bob for 4 rounds, did not appear.
[944] *Omaha Daily Bee,* April 3, 4, 1897.
[945] *Salt Lake Herald*, April 14, 1897.
[946] *Salt Lake Herald*, April 21, 1897.
[947] *San Francisco Examiner*, April 22, 1897.

On May 3 at New York's Palace Athletic Club, Fitz took part in a benefit show. Bob was also fulfilling an engagement at a Brooklyn theater that week, sparring with Hickey and giving bag punching exhibitions.[948]

Fitz said that in the play that was being specially written for him, he would play Bob the blacksmith and make horseshoes, get a pretty girl, and knock out a villain, who would wear a pompadour wig.[949]

On May 10, Joe Choynski got the better of Denver Ed Smith, dropping him in the 1st round and cutting his cheek. When Smith began intentionally butting Joe in the 4th round, even knocking a tooth out, the referee disqualified Smith.[950]

It was in mid-to-late May that the Corbett-Fitzsimmons fight films were exhibited for the first time in New York, and all the discussion about them took place.

On May 24, 1897, Fitzsimmons and his vaudeville show appeared at New York's Columbus Theater. After the vaudeville bill, Fitz came on and received a warm reception, although there was a sprinkling of hoots and shouts from Corbett's friends. First, Fitz punched the bag. Then he sparred 3 rounds with Hickey. At the end of each round, Fitz would show how he knocked out a different opponent – first Maher, then Sharkey in the 2nd, and then Corbett in the 3rd round. Hickey even reproduced Corbett's attack on Fitzsimmons after the fight. "This piece of Carson City realism, which was intended as a slap at the defeated champion, caused much dissatisfaction in the audience, and there were disapproving signs heard all over the house."[951]

Tom Sharkey continued claiming that he was the champion, but neither the press nor the public recognized him.[952] In June 1897 in New York, a 175-pound Sharkey fought a 7-round "draw" against 176-pound Peter Maher. It was another Sharkey bout that ended under less than satisfactory circumstances.

After a fairly tame first 5 rounds, in the 6th, Sharkey dropped Maher with a right. However, Maher came back in the 7th, landing well and dropping Sharkey with a right to the jaw. Sharkey was worked into a corner and hit with uppercuts, but then Tom began his foul work, hugging, clinching, butting and attacking like a madman. After the bell rang, in a clinch, they kept fighting, and when Maher's seconds pulled Peter away

[948] *New York Journal*, May 3, 4, 1897; *Brooklyn Daily Eagle*, May 2-4, 1897. At that time, Fitz was weighing 164 pounds. Also present were Kid McCoy, Kid Lavigne, George Dixon, Peter Maher, and Tom Sharkey.
[949] *New York Journal*, May 5, 1897.
[950] *New York Journal*, May 11, 1897.
[951] *New York Herald*, May 25, 1897.
[952] *San Francisco Examiner*, June 8, 1897.

from Sharkey's grasp, Tom hit them. Another report said that Tom even punched at his own seconds when they tried to stop him. The police stopped it and declared the bout a draw.

The general sentiment was that Sharkey was whipped and engaged in his foul tactics in order to cause the bout to be terminated. However, ex-champion Corbett witnessed the fight and felt that it was not settled.[953]

John L. Sullivan continued making challenges, but was 39 years old and had been fairly inactive, only occasionally boxing in some tame 3-round exhibitions, usually with fellow aged fighter Paddy Ryan.

Despite his age and inactivity, Sullivan and Fitzsimmons did schedule a 6-round bout to be held July 5, 1897 in Brooklyn, New York. However, it was clear that the authorities were determined to prevent any such match. The Police Superintendent said that it could only be a lecture with a physical demonstration at the same time, as opposed to a lecture followed by sparring. This would essentially kill it as a real bout. The superintendent insisted, "There will be no subterfuge." This was a reaction to the rumors that the boxers would try to get around the law. The newsmen noticed the authorities' "remarkable zeal."

The superintendent said that the boxers had not met the requirements of the Horton law, because an athletic club with a lease for the place where the boxing was to occur had not backed them, nor was a license granted. Therefore, when Sullivan and Fitzsimmons were present to spar on the date set, along with 2,000 spectators, the police prevented it, informing the two that if they put on the gloves and attempted to spar, they would be arrested. Instead, Fitz engaged in a wrestling bout with Ernest Roeber.[954] The Sullivan-Fitzsimmons match never did happen and its genuineness has to be questioned. Why didn't they secure an athletic club?

A couple months later, Fitz went on an exhibition tour, but did not take part in any serious bouts. According to Bob, he had been taking it easy all summer, and was weighing 180 pounds. He was starting his annual swing around the vaudeville circuit.

Coming from New York, on September 14, 1897, Bob's train arrived in Wilmington, Delaware with Martin Julian and James Murphy, his current sparring partner. Bob said that he did not think Corbett was even in Sharkey or Maher's class, and until he proved himself, Corbett would not get a title shot.

That afternoon, before a crowd of 1,500-1,800 people, Bob gave an exhibition in connection with a baseball game. He hit the bag and sparred 3

[953] *San Francisco Examiner*, June 10, 1897; June 11, 1897.
[954] *Brooklyn Daily Eagle,* June 29, 30, 1897; July 6, 1897.

rounds with Murphy. "His sparring bouts with Murphy simply showed the agility of two big men in dancing about, ducking and dodging, and striking quicker than they could wink." When some called for more ginger and for Murphy to knock him out, Bob responded, "Put up your purse!"

Afterwards, Bob got in his "customary crack" at Corbett, saying, "Corbett couldn't make it interesting for my sparring partner." Fitz was "the ham in the sandwich," and when he left, fully 1,000 people also left the grounds, before the baseball game was over.[955] Bob traveled around giving short bag punching and sparring exhibitions like this one.

On October 10, 1897, Fitzsimmons began a week's engagement in Cincinnati, Ohio. Jim or Mike Dempsey (the two local papers gave him different first names) had signed a contract to act as Bob's sparring partner. Only two or three exchanges made Dempsey stagger. "A mixture of three or four kinds of whisky and a slow push from Fitz's left hand caused Prof. Jim Dempsey's head to hit the boards of the stage with a whack that could be heard all over the theater." Another local paper said that Bob gently laid his left glove on Professor Mike Dempsey, but "The Professor's heels flew up and he went down dead to the world." It only lasted two minutes.

Fitz gave a speech to the audience, saying,

> This man's fall is no fault of mine. I didn't strike him. The truth of the matter is that he was frightened. He was afraid that he was going to get hurt. He went out and took on board a dose of courage. That is what is the matter with him – he has been drinking too much.

To help matters, Ernest Roeber sparred 3 rounds with Fitzsimmons, who was looking much heavier than he did in Carson. Bob continued exhibiting that week in Cincinnati.

Fitzsimmons said that he had the right to retire upon past honors. However, when asked if he would turn over the championship, he replied, "No.... The man that gets the title from me will have to fight for it. That is, I will not give up the championship until it is won by some one of the present heavy-weight aspirants and in a fight to a finish." When asked about Corbett, Fitz said, "Why, he's a cur.... He quit at Carson City, and that's all there is to it."[956]

---

[955] *Every Evening Wilmington Daily Commercial, Wilmington Evening Journal,* September 14, 15, 1897.
[956] *Cincinnati Enquirer, Cincinnati Post,* October 11, 1897. The following day, Jim Dempsey had his foot run over by a passing wagon. *Cincinnati Enquirer,* October 12, 1897.

Corbett agreed that Fitzsimmons was the champion and would be until someone defeated him in the ring. He did not think that anyone could defeat Bob except himself. Corbett said,

> Robert Fitzsimmons is the champion pugilist of the world.... and until some one defeats him in the prize ring he holds it by every right. I must whip him fairly and squarely, or never claim the championship again. Coming into the title by forfeiture does not go with the public and certainly does not go with me. Whoever considered Kilrain or Maher the champion?[957]

GRAND OPERA HOUSE { TO-MORROW MATINEE AND ALL THE WEEK
THE PUGILISTIC MARVEL.
BOB FITZSIMMONS!
CHAMPION OF THE WORLD.
... And His Big ...
Vaudeville and Athletic Comp'y,
DIRECTION MARTIN JULIAN.
NELSON GLNSERETI AND DEMONIO.
BEAUTIFUL THEO. RYAN AND RICHFIELD.
CRANE BROS.
AMERICAN MACS,
MULVEY & INMAN.
WHITMAN & DAVIS.
CHAS. B. LAWLOR.
LAVERNE SISTERS.
ERNEST ROEBER.
CARL BECK & MIKE CONLEY,
THE ITHACA GIANT.
Next Week—Ward & Vokes.

While Bob was still in Cincinnati, Mike Conley, the Ithaca Giant, signed a contract to act as Fitz's sparring partner. He would box with Bob during his Cincinnati engagement and would go on the road with him.[958] Ernest Roeber, the Greco-Roman world champion, was also under contract to the Fitzsimmons show for 40 weeks.[959]

On October 18, 1897, Fitzsimmons, along with a variety and athletic company, began a four-night engagement at the Indianapolis Grand Opera House. The vaudeville talent included comedians, song and dance artists, trapeze performers, and Greco-Roman wrestling between Roeber and a man named Beck.

The performance concluded with a Fitzsimmons bag-punching exhibition "in which he shows remarkable hitting powers. As a wind up there is a scientific boxing bout between Fitzsimmons and Conley, the Ithaca giant." The performance was to be repeated every night, and there would also be a Wednesday matinee.[960]

---

[957] *Cincinnati Enquirer,* October 13, 1897.
[958] *Cincinnati Enquirer,* October 14, 1897.
[959] *Cincinnati Enquirer,* October 15, 1897.
[960] *Indianapolis News,* October 18, 19, 1897.

The specialty vaudeville and athletic company continued touring around, making money. In early November, they were in Louisville, Kentucky.

Beginning on November 14, 1897, Fitz began giving exhibitions in Kansas City, Missouri for a week. There were good crowds at both the afternoon and evening performances. Bob vigorously hit the bag and sparred with Conley, hitting him in a comparatively gentle manner.[961]

They were in Topeka, Kansas for a two-night performance beginning on November 22, 1897. Bob was scheduled to hit the bag, demonstrate and explain the knockout blows used to win his big fights, and box 4 scientific rounds with Conley.[962]

At the close of the 2nd round of their exhibition on the 22nd, "Connely" staggered Fitz back to his corner. Bob's face was pallid and showed anguish. He sat in his chair and held his hand on his head. Bob groaned, "It's gone! Gone! Broken! Smashed!" Bob spit out a tooth.

> The bout had cost him one of his teeth. One of the fierce fistic onslaughts of the 'Ithacan Giant' had connected with the upper maxillary of the champion, and removed a handsome incisor from his collection of dental organs. Fitzsimmons was mortified. … But he bravely withstood the sorrow. He arose to his feet calmly just before the call of time.

Such was the potential consequence of boxing at a time when there were no mouthpieces and big gloves were a mere 8 ounces.

At the start of the 3rd round, Bob "went after the overgrown Ithacan with horrible ferocity. He boxed his ears, he punched his nose, he roasted his ribs and he lambasted his jaw. The audience howled with delight." It was quite evident that Bob was by far the better man. "He seemed able to swat his opponent whenever he chose, and wherever he chose." Fitzsimmons "demonstrated to the satisfaction of everybody that he was all he has been cracked up to be. He smote the unoffending punching bag with frightful cruelty." Bob's punches made a popping sound when they landed.[963]

---

[961] *Kansas City Star,* November 14-16, 1897.
[962] *Topeka Daily Capital,* November 21, 1897.
[963] *Topeka Daily Capital,* November 23, 1897.

Mike Conley, The Ithaca Giant

Undeterred by the loss of his tooth, the performance was repeated the next night, on the 23rd, and there was another large house. "Fitz left the town considerably richer than when he came."[964]

In November 1897, Tom Sharkey scored a KO6 over Joe Goddard, which was a significant win. Goddard had an 1890 D8 Peter Jackson, two 1891 KO4 victories over Joe Choynski, 1892 KO3 Peter Maher, 1893 LKOby18 Ed Smith, but an 1896 KO4 rematch win over Smith, and an 1897 KO2 Mick Dooley and D20 James "Tut" Ryan.

James J. Jeffries fought both Gus Ruhlin and Joe Choynski to 20-round draws in July and November 1897 respectively.

Since Fitz had the two knockout victories over Maher, and had beaten up and actually stopped Choynski and Sharkey, none of these contenders particularly stood out as real threats to the crown.

By late December 1897 in Chicago, Fitz again claimed that he was going to retire.

> As soon as there is a regular battle for the championship...I shall yield the title to the winner. I am not going to try to hold the title indefinitely, even though I think I won more battles against good men in order to earn it than most fighters have done who have received the honor.

---

[964] *Topeka Daily Capital*, November 24, 1897.

The same day of his declaration, on December 19, Fitzsimmons boxed 3 rounds with sparring partner George Lawler. Fitz afterwards said, "I have retired absolutely. No kind of talk or no amount of money will persuade me to fight again. I have retired. Isn't it funny, people will not take me seriously when I say that?" His own manager was not so sure though. He said that Bob had retired "temporarily, at least.... Well, you know how Bob is; I cannot say when he may change his mind."[965] He was right.

Just over a week later, on December 29, Julian was announcing on behalf of Fitzsimmons that Bob was willing to defend the title. However, Bob would only grant Corbett a shot if he first met and defeated a good man. Corbett responded by saying, "Fitzsimmons only wants to appear to acquiesce to quiet public clamor. He has no intention of again meeting me. I certainly will not comply with his conditions."[966] However, eventually, in late 1898, Corbett took on Tom Sharkey, but lost.

Fitz had also said that he was willing to take on Kid McCoy if he first beat Choynski. McCoy and Choynski did not meet until 1899, and in the interim, the Kid lost to Sharkey.

Fitzsimmons did not enter the ring at all in 1898. That year, he began performing with his wife Rose in the play called *The Honest Blacksmith*. Fitzsimmons was doing what Sullivan and Corbett had done – capitalizing on his fame without having to box, living the good life.

In March 1898, Choynski and Sharkey fought a rematch that was declared a draw when the police intervened and stopped it in the 8th round, owing to, surprise: a Sharkey foul.

That year, James J. Jeffries scored a February KO4 over Joe Goddard, March KO3 over Peter Jackson, and perhaps most importantly, a May W20 over Tom Sharkey. Jeff also had an August W10 against Bob Armstrong.

After losing a close decision to Jeffries, Sharkey subsequently scored a June 1898 KO1 over Gus Ruhlin and a November WDQ9 over former champion James J. Corbett. In his rematch against Corbett, Sharkey scored an early knockdown and was winning prior to Corbett's second entering the ring to protest Sharkey's roughhouse tactics, causing Jim to be disqualified.

Kid McCoy in May 1898 scored a W20 over Ruhlin but Sharkey scored his KO1 over Ruhlin one month later. Sharkey in January 1899 knocked out McCoy in the 10th round. Two months later, McCoy won a 20-round decision over Choynski.[967]

---

[965] *Chicago Tribune*, December 20, 1897.
[966] *Brooklyn Daily Eagle*, December 29, 1897.
[967] The above-referenced bouts will be discussed in greater detail in the Jeffries volume.

As promised, Fitzsimmons did not defend the title for over two years after winning it. Although this is a blemish on his championship reign, both Sullivan and Corbett had their own lengthy periods of inactivity during their reigns. These champions had all become more interested in cashing in without having to train and fight. After defeating Corbett in 1897, Fitz was happy to step away from the game until a big fight came along, and chose to make easy money in the interim, as his predecessors had done.

This period of inactivity, like those of Sullivan and Corbett, probably helped cost Fitzsimmons his title. When Fitz won the championship in 1897, James J. Jeffries was still a relative novice. However, the two years time that Fitz took off from serious competition gave Jeffries time to gain boxing knowledge and experience, and was time for the already aging Fitzsimmons to get older, and more importantly, lose his sharpness.

Eventually, the 36-year-old Fitzsimmons did defend his title in June 1899 against 24-year-old former Corbett sparring partner James J. Jeffries, who by that time had emerged and established himself as a legitimate contender with his victory over Sharkey. Many boxing experts of the day were not impressed with Jeffries' boxing skills. Corbett felt that Fitz was trying to take on "something soft."[968] However, at around 220 pounds, the undefeated Jeffries was known for his strong punch, good conditioning, and ability to absorb punishment. In a long fight, those were great attributes. Jeffries was much too strong for Bob, and knocked out Fitzsimmons in the 11th round.

Bob Fitzsimmons had been a dominant middleweight champion, who, although smaller than many of his opponents, had the strength, skill, and conditioning to take on and knock out heavyweights. As such, he was the first truly great pound for pound fighter. He had been a bareknuckle and gloved fighter, a middleweight who could fight as a heavyweight, an attacking puncher, a jabbing boxer, and an awkward counterpuncher. He was a tough and intelligent finish fighter. He truly was a phenomenon, a fighter with the skill and amazing punching power that would make him dangerous no matter in what era he fought.

In the years to come, Fitzsimmons would further prove his mettle, and defy not only the rules regarding size, but also of age. His victories included 1900 KO1 Jim Daly, KO6 Gus Ruhlin, and KO2 Tom Sharkey. In 1902, Jeffries would again stop a then 39-year-old Fitz, this time in 8 rounds. However, in 1903, at age 40, Bob won the world lightheavyweight championship with a W20 over George Gardner. In doing so, he became the first man to win world titles in three separate weight divisions over the course of his career. This was at a time when there were very few weight classes. He did not defend that title until 1905, when Philadelphia Jack O'

---

[968] James J. Corbett, *The Roar of the Crowd*, (N.Y.: G.P. Putnam's Sons, 1925), 271.

432

Brien stopped the 42-year-old Fitz in the 13th round. Even as a mere shell of himself, he continued fighting competitively until 1909, and continued exhibiting all the way until 1916. But the details of those stories are for another volume: *In the Ring with James J. Jeffries: A King Amongst Kings*.

Appendix:
Bob Fitzsimmons' Record

BORN : May 26, 1863; Helston, Cornwall, England. During most of his career, Bob was said to have been born, June 4, 1862.
DIED : October 22, 1917 at age 54.

1873+?

In Timaru, New Zealand, Bob often engaged in friendly scraps with gloves with his pals. He also learned a bit about boxing from his brothers.

1878?

Fitzsimmons claimed to have fought his first bareknuckle fights under London Prize Ring Rules at around the age of 15.

1881?

At one point, Dan Lea gave Bob some boxing lessons.

1882?

| ? | Tom Baines | Timaru, New Zealand | KO 1 |

1882

June 13	? (a local amateur)	Timaru, New Zealand	EX W
June 14	? (local amateur)	Timaru, New Zealand	EX W
June 14	? (same opponent as on the 13th)	Timaru, New Zealand	EX W
Sep 13	? (local amateur) (possibly Herbert Slade's younger brother)	Timaru, New Zealand	EX W
Sep 14	?(local amateur)	Timaru, New Zealand	EX W

There are claims that the 140-150 pound Fitzsimmons knocked out four men in one night at Timaru's Theatre Royal to win the New Zealand lightweight amateur championship tournament. Some say this tournament was held in 1880 when Bob was 17 years old, while others say it was held in 1882, when he was 19 years old. Allegedly, the amateur tournament was held again about one year later. The story told is that Bob knocked out five men to win the tournament for the second year in a row. Some claim that Bob boxed Herbert Slade and either stopped him in 2 rounds, or it was stopped after 2 rounds. These claims are unproven. Fitz probably never boxed Herbert Slade.

1883-1885?

?	Arthur Cooper	Timaru, New Zealand	KO 3 (LPR)
?	Jack Murphy	Timaru, New Zealand	KO 4 (LPR)
?	Jim Crawford	Timaru, New Zealand	KO 3 (LPR)
?	Pat McCarney	Timaru, New Zealand	?

1885?

| ? | Alf Brinsmead/Brawsmead | Sydney, Australia | KO 2 |

Brinsmead allegedly weighed 170 pounds to Fitz's 148 pounds.

| ? | Jack Greentree | Sydney, Australia | KO 3 |

| ? | Dick Sandal | Sydney, Australia | KO 4 |

| ? | Joe Riddle | Sydney, Australia | EX W 4? |

Some later sources say Riddle weighed about 168 pounds.

It should be noted that because they were merely exhibitions, the majority of Fitzsimmons' Australian bouts below had no official decisions. The decisions listed here are based on newspaper opinions, unless there was a knockout or retirement.

1886

| Feb? | Pablo Frank/Fanque | Sydney, Australia | KO 2 |

| May 8 | Brinsley | Sydney, Australia | EX (likely 3 or 4) |

| May 15 | Mick Dooley | Sydney, Australia | EX LKO by 3 |

Fitz retired after being decked. Dooley likely weighed 170-175 pounds.

| May? | Steve O'Donnell | Sydney, Australia | 3rds, private friendly sparring |

Some claim they boxed on May 22, but this is not confirmed by the local reports.

| June 2 | Mick Dooley | Sydney, Australia | EX L 4 |

| June 5 | Mick Dooley | Sydney, Australia | EX L 4 |

| Aug 7 | McArdell/M'Ardill | Sydney, Australia | EX W 4 |

| Aug 25 | Tom Lees | Sydney, Australia | EX L 4 |

Lees probably weighed around 180 pounds.

| Oct 7? | Billy Smith? | Sydney, Australia | EX 4? |

Bout not confirmed by local primary sources.

| Oct 9 | M'Cardell/McCardell | Sydney, Australia | EX 4 |

| Dec 4 | Jack Molloy/Malloy | Sydney, Australia | EX 4? |

1887

| Jan 1 | Frank Slavin/Slaven | Sydney, Australia | EX L 4 |

Slavin likely weighed 180-190 pounds.

| Jan 8 | "a friend" | Sydney, Australia | EX L 4 |

This was a friendly and tame exhibition, though one local report said that the friend had the best of it.

| Feb 12 | Jack Bonnar | Sydney, Australia | EX W 4 |

This was another friendly and tame exhibition, though one report felt that Fitz had the edge.

| Feb 15? | George Seale? | Sydney, Australia | EX 4? |

This bout was advertised, but not mentioned by the local follow-up reports.

| Feb 24 | "a friend" | Sydney, Australia | EX 4? |

| Mar 1 | Dick Sandall | Sydney, Australia | EX W? 4 |

Bout unconfirmed by local sources.

| Mar 20? | Bill Slavin? | Sydney, Australia | KO 5? |

This bout is not confirmed by local sources, and likely did not take place until the following year.

| Apr 4? | George Enger/Eager? | Sydney, Australia | KO 2 or 3? |

This bout is not confirmed by a local source.

| May 28 | Jim Hall? | Sydney, Australia | EX L 4? |

This may not have been Fitzsimmons, or if it was, he may have been hippodroming.

| Sep 24 | Dave? Travers | Sydney, Australia | KO 3 |

Fight to the finish.

1888

| Jan 23? | Dan Hickey | Sydney, Australia | EX? |

The local sources do not confirm this bout.

| Jan 26 | Tom Taylor | Sydney, Australia | EX 4 |

| Feb 11 | Billy McCarthy/McCarty | Sydney, Australia | EX W 4 |

| Mar 5 | Bill Slavin | Sydney, Australia | KO 5 or 6 |

| Mar 17? | Bill Slavin? | Sydney, Australia | EX 4? |

They were advertised to box, but the follow-up reports made no mention of their having boxed.

| Apr 17 | Bill Slavin | Sydney, Australia | EX 4 |

| May 1? | Mick Dooley? | Sydney, Australia | EX 4? |

The local sources do not confirm this bout.

| Nov 10 | Jim Hall | Sydney, Australia | EX W 4 |

| Nov 24 | Jim Hall | Sydney, Australia | EX 4 |

| Dec 1 | M'Ewen/McEwan | Sydney, Australia | EX W 3 |

1889

| Jan 19 | Jim Hall | Sydney, Australia | KO 5 |

Advertised as being for the Australian Middleweight Championship, but not generally recognized as such. Bout scheduled for 8 rounds.

Fitz might have defeated Hall again in a private rematch.

| Nov 26 | Pat Kiely | Sydney, Australia | EX 4? |

| Nov 30 | Professor West | Sydney, Australia | KO 1 |

Fitz contracted to stop him within 8 rounds.

| Dec 16 | Dick Ellis | Sydney, Australia | KO 3 |

Scheduled for 20 rounds. Some later sources claim Ellis weighed 176 pounds to Fitz's 148 pounds.

1890

| Feb 1 | Dave Conway | Sydney, Australia | EX W 4/ KO? 4 |

| Feb 10 | Edward "Starlight" Rollins | Sydney, Australia | EX 4 |

| Feb 11 | Jim Hall | Sydney, Australia | LKO by 4 |

Australia Middleweight Championship. Fight may very well have been fixed.

| Feb 22 | Edward "Starlight" Rollins | Sydney, Australia | KO 7 or 9 |

Fight to the finish.

| Mar 1? | Professor West? | Sydney, Australia | KO 1? |

This fight is not confirmed by local sources.

On April 16, Fitzsimmons sailed from Australia, heading for America. He arrived in San Francisco on May 10.

| May 14 | Frank Allen | San Francisco, CA | EX 3 |

That week, Fitz also sparred with Joe Choynski. Both were preparing for late-May fights.

| May 29 | Billy McCarthy | San Francisco, CA | KO 9 |

Fight to the finish. Weights: McCarthy 160 pounds, Fitz 154 pounds.
Police order sponge to be thrown up at the end of the 9th because of the hopeless brutal beating McCarthy was suffering.

| Jul 9 | Joe Choynski | San Francisco, CA | EX 4 |

| Jul 9 | Neil Merritt | San Francisco, CA | wrestling EX |
| | | | Fitz threw him |

Fitz left for New Orleans on July 10 with Joe Choynski and manager Jimmy Carroll.

| Jul 28 | Arthur Upham | New Orleans, LA | KO 5 |

Fight to the finish. Weights: Upham 153 ½, Fitz 153 or 155 pounds.

Late in the year, Fitz trained at Bay St. Louis, MS for his upcoming bout with Jack Dempsey.

1891

| Jan 14 | Jack Dempsey | New Orleans, LA | KO 13 |

World Middleweight Championship. Fight to the finish. Weights: Dempsey 147 ½, Fitz 150 ½, as taken before ring entry.

Fitz briefly returned to Bay St. Louis, MS, where he had trained for the Dempsey fight. He then set out on a sparring tour.

Feb 16   Fitz sparred that week in New York with heavyweight Billy Woods, twice a day at variety theaters. Fitz and Woods were traveling sparring partners pursuant to an 8-week theatrical contract.

| Apr 5 | Billy Woods | Chicago, IL | EX 3 |

Woods and Fitz exhibited that week as part of a play called *Fashions*.

| Apr 13 | Billy Woods | Pittsburg, PA | EX 4 |

Fitz and Woods were in Pittsburg for a week. The sparring company then disbanded.

| Apr 27 | Abe Cougle | Chicago, IL | EX KO 2 |

Cougle was a heavyweight.

| Apr 27 | Billy Woods | Chicago, IL | EX 3 |

| May 1 | Harris "Black Pearl" Martin | Minneapolis, MN | W 4 |

Martin usually weighed 145-150 pounds.

It was reported that Fitz was traveling with Tommy Ryan.

Fitz trained with Jim Carroll for a scheduled late July fight against Jim Hall. Although scheduled for St. Paul, Minnesota on July 22, the governor prevented the bout.

Negotiations with Ted Pritchard, Martin Costello, and others fell through.

Dec   Fitz was in Bay St. Louis, MS sparring with lightweights Jimmy Carroll and Austin Gibbons, assisting their preparations for upcoming bouts.

Dec 12   Fitz sparred with Jimmy Carroll.

Dec 13	Austin Gibbons	Bay St. Louis, MS	EX 4

Dec 15   Fitz sparred 5 rounds with Jimmy Carroll.

1892

Fitz trained in Bay St. Louis, MS for the scheduled March fight against Peter Maher. Bob sparred with trainers Joe Choynski and Alec Greggains.

Feb 14	Felix Vanquelin/Vaquelin	Bay St. Louis, MS	EX

Heavyweight Vaquelin may have become a Fitz sparring partner. Fitz generally took on all-comers at his training camp. Bob hurt his knuckles on a black fighter who wanted to have a go with him.

Feb 27	Felix Vanquelin	New Orleans, LA	EX

Feb 28   Fitz ran 4 miles, hit the ball for 4 hard rounds in different styles, then sparred 4 rounds with Joe Choynski, and 4 more with Alec Greggains.
Feb 29   Fitz went for a 7-mile walk and had "rattling bouts with Choynski and Greggains."

Mar 2	Peter Maher	New Orleans, LA	KO 12

Fight to the finish. Weights: Maher 178-185, Fitz 165-167 ¼.

Mar 4	Tom Casey	New Orleans, LA	EX 3

Casey was a heavyweight.

Mar 10	Alec Greggains	New Orleans, LA	EX
Mar 10	Joe Choynski	New Orleans, LA	EX
Mar 10	Jimmy Carroll	New Orleans, LA	EX 4

Mar 14   Fitz and Carroll arrived in New York to exhibit there.

Mar 28	Peter Maher	New York, NY	EX

Fitz traveled around giving exhibitions.

Apr 8	Jim Dolan	Providence, RI	EX W 3

In Chicago, Bob gave afternoon and evening exhibitions with local boxers for a week. They were mostly of a friendly nature because the police would not allow rough work or knockouts.

Apr 17	Jimmy Carroll	Chicago, IL	EX 3?
Apr 17	John Dalton	Chicago, IL	EX W 3?
Apr 18	Henry Baker	Chicago, IL	EX W 3

Baker was called the Michigan middleweight champion.

Apr 19   Fitz was scheduled to meet Paddy Brennan in Chicago, but it is unclear whether it took place. Another report said that Bob would box Baker again, on the 20th and 21st, but there were no confirming post-exhibition reports.

Apr 23	Denny Kelleher/Kelliher	Chicago, IL	EX W

Kelleher allegedly weighed 247 pounds.

Apr 23	Henry Baker	Chicago, IL	EX W

Baker allegedly weighed 190 pounds.

Apr 23	Chris Vogle	Chicago, IL	EX W

Vogle allegedly weighed 200 pounds.

That evening, Bob took a train to Newark, NJ.

Apr 26	Charlie Puff	Newark, NJ	KO 2

Afternoon exhibition. Puff weighed 230 pounds.

Apr 26	Bill Farrell	Newark, NJ	EX

Evening exhibition.

Apr 27	James Newcombe/Malone	Newark, NJ	KO 2

Apr 28	Thomas Robbins	Newark, NJ	KO 3

180-pound Robbins attempting to last 4 rounds to win $50, but quits in the 3rd round.

Apr 28	Thomas Burns	Newark, NJ	KO 3

Burns also attempts to last 4 rounds, but quits in the 3rd as well.

Apr 29	Bill Farrell	Newark, NJ	EX W 3

Fitz next gave afternoon and evening exhibitions in Philadelphia.

May 2	Fred Woods	Philadelphia, PA	EX 3

Woods was a welterweight.

May 3	Richard Wiley/Wyley	Philadelphia, PA	EX W 3

Wiley was a heavyweight.

May 4	William McLean/Billy M. Lean	Philadelphia, PA	EX

May 5	Fred Woods	Philadelphia, PA	EX

May 6	Joe Godfrey	Philadelphia, PA	KO 2

Fitz was said to be meeting Woods again on the 7th.

The Fitz variety company then went to New York to meet all comers there. Bob was well received at Miner's Eighth Avenue Theatre on May 10.

May 11	Jerry Slattery	New York, NY	KO 2

Slattery was unconscious for 15 minutes.

It was said that Bob would meet Jim Brady of Buffalo on the 12th and Thomas Knifton, an English heavyweight, on the 13th, but there were no follow up reports.

Fitz went to Bay St. Louis to train for potential matches with either Ted Pritchard or Jim Hall. However, Hall and Pritchard fought each other in late August.

Aug   Fitz was in Boston.

Sep 3?   Millard Zender/Zeubur   Anniston, AL   KO 1
           or William Zuller
Opponent weighed 300-pounds.

A local source said that Fitzsimmons would give a sparring exhibition at a benefit in New Orleans on September 4, 1892. It is unclear whether it took place.

Sep 11   Fitzsimmons began performing in the play, *The Heroic Blacksmith*, at Brooklyn's Novelty Theatre.

Oct   Fitz and Jim Hall tentatively agree to fight in early 1893.

Fitz's theatrical company traveled in the Southwest, but eventually disbanded. Bob returned to New York in early November.

Dec 10   Jack Britton   Newark, NJ   KO 2

Dec 10   Jack Fallon   Newark, NJ   EX 4
Fallon was a heavyweight.

Dec 10   Frank Bosworth?   Newark, NJ   EX

Dec 17   Frank Bosworth   New York, NY   EX 3
Bosworth was later listed as weighing about 170 pounds.

1893

Bob continued sparring with Bosworth in early 1893 in preparation for the Hall bout. Starting January 22, Fitzsimmons filled a week's engagement in Chicago with his specialty athletic and vaudeville company. Each night, Bob hit the bag for 10 minutes, sparred with any locals who desired to box him, and wound up with 4 rounds sparring with Bosworth. Bob usually boxed two or three times a night.

Jan 22   Wing   Chicago, IL   EX 3?

Bob was scheduled to box Henry Baker, the local middleweight, on the 23rd, and spar Bosworth. There was no follow-up report.

Jan 27   Fitzpatrick   Chicago, IL   EX KO 3

Jan 27   George Siler   Chicago, IL   EX 4

Feb 1   Fitz set up training camp in Bay St. Louis, MS. Bosworth was his chief sparring partner.

Feb 18   Bob ran and walked 20 miles with Martin Julian and Ernest Roeber, who just arrived that day. Fitz later that day sparred and wrestled 8 rounds with Roeber, 8 with Bosworth, and 8 more with his brother William Fitzsimmons. Roeber was listed as weighing 178 pounds.

Feb 20   Fitz ran 13 miles with his trainers. That afternoon, Bob sparred 10 rounds and boxed the ball 14 rounds. While sparring the approximately 170-pound Bosworth, Bob accidentally knocked him out.

Mar 5   According to Martin Julian, Fitz walked 3.5 miles, then ran the same distance back. He boxed the ball, and then sparred 22 rounds, changing his style of fighting every second round. He boxed five different men, including Bosworth, until they all had enough. Later, Bob took another run.

Mar 7   Fitzsimmons filled out the papers to become a naturalized American citizen.

Mar 8   Jim Hall   New Orleans, LA   KO 4
Fight to the finish. Weights: Hall 167 ½, Fitz 162-165 pounds.

Mar 14	Fitz returned to Bay St. Louis.		

Mar 25	Sam Bird	Chicago, IL	EX W 4

Mar 25	Will Mayo	Chicago, IL	KO 2

Mayo weighed 192 pounds.

Mar 27 Fitz arrives in Baltimore, MD to give exhibitions there for a week. Bob would hit the bag and spar with Frank Bosworth.

Mar 30	Jack Warner	Baltimore, MD	KO 1
Mar 30	Frank Bosworth	Baltimore, MD	EX 3
Apr 10	Jack Hockey/Haughey	Philadelphia, PA	EX 3
Apr 10	Frank Bosworth	Philadelphia, PA	EX 3
Apr 11	Frank Bosworth	Philadelphia, PA	EX 3
Apr 12	Dan Curry	Philadelphia, PA	KO 2
Apr 12	Hank Smith	Philadelphia, PA	KO 1
Apr 13	Alexander Kilpatrick	Philadelphia, PA	KO 3

200-pound Kilpatrick attempted to win $100 if he could last 4 rounds.

Apr 14	Frank Bosworth	Philadelphia, PA	EX 3
Apr 15	Jack Sheridan	Philadelphia, PA	KO 1
Apr 21	Joe Godfrey	Philadelphia, PA	KO 1
Apr 21	Mike Monahan/Monaghan	Philadelphia, PA	KO 1
Apr 21	Alexander Kilpatrick	Philadelphia, PA	EX 3/ KO 4

Either Kilpatrick refused to box the 4th round, or the police refused to allow it to continue.

May 1	Matt Cunningham	Boston, MA	EX KO
May 1	Charles Farrell	Boston, MA	EX
May 6	Mike Brennan	Boston, MA	KO 4

Some thought Brennan beat the count and was saved by the bell, but Martin Julian counted him out. Brennan was a heavyweight attempting to last 4 rounds.

May 29	Al O'Brien	Philadelphia, PA	EX 3
May 30	Daniel Coner	Philadelphia, PA	KO 1
May 30	John McVeigh/McVey	Philadelphia, PA	EX 3

McVey was generally listed as weighing 210-220 pounds.

May 31	John McVeigh/McVey	Philadelphia, PA	EX 3
Jun 1	John McVeigh/McVey	Philadelphia, PA	EX 3
Sep 4	Jack Dempsey	New York, NY	EX
Sep 5	Jack Hickey	Newark, NJ	KO 3

Hickey was allegedly the Irish middleweight champion.

1894

| Feb 15 | Jim Dwyer | Paterson, NJ | EX |

Mar   Bob was training in St. Louis, MO.

Mar 11   Fitz trained for two hours at a local gym, sparring with a number of local boxers. Fitz wrestled with George Baptiste and succeeded in throwing the clever St. Louis wrestler after a long struggle.

| Mar 14 | Jack Stelzner | St. Louis, MO | EX 4 |

Later reports list Stelzner as weighing 180 pounds.

Mar 15   Bob went to New York.

| Mar 21 | Jimmy Handler | New York, NY | EX |

| Jun 18 | Joe Choynski | Boston, MA | D 5/KO 5 |

Scheduled for 8 rounds, both weighed about 160-162 pounds.
In reality, Choynski was helpless and about to be knocked out, so the police entered the ring and stopped it, not wanting the brutality to continue. However, a clause in the contract said that if the fight was terminated by the police prior to the end of the 8 rounds, and both men were on their feet, that it would be declared a draw.
Jun 19   Bob returned to New York.

| Jul 28 | Frank Keller | Buffalo, NY | KO 2 |

Keller weighed 180 pounds.

Aug 12   Fitz arrived in Trenton, NJ to give exhibitions there that week. Captain Charles Giori became Bob's manager.

| Aug 13 | Tom Dwyer | Trenton, NJ | EX 3 |

| Aug 16 | Bob Rulon | Trenton, NJ | KO 1 |

Rulon was 240 pounds.

| Aug 16 | Tom Dwyer | Trenton, NJ | EX |

| Aug 17 | Tom Dwyer? | Trenton, NJ | EX |

| Aug 18 | Peter Courtney | Trenton, NJ | EX 4 |

Courtney weighed about 190 pounds.

| Sep 4 | Jack Dempsey | New Orleans, LA | EX |

Sep 25   Fitz did his usual training in preparation for the Creedon fight. He took a morning run, and in the afternoon sparred lightly for 8 or 10 rounds with then-welterweight Kid McCoy, who was one of his sparring partners.

| Sep 26 | Dan Creedon | New Orleans, LA | KO 2 |

Middleweight Championship fight to the finish. Weights: Creedon, 158, Fitz 155 ½ pounds.

Sep 27   Fitz headed back to Newark, NJ, where he was set to begin touring with his theatrical company on the 29th. They likely performed in Paterson, NJ, Philadelphia, and New York. The company was managed by Charles Giori.

| Sep 29 | Ernest Roeber | San Antonio, TX | EX 2 |

| Sep 29 | Jack Stelzner | San Antonio, TX | EX 2 |

Stelzner weighed 180 pounds.

| Oct 11 | Corbett, Fitzsimmons, and their representatives met in New York to negotiate a match. | | |

Oct 11   Corbett, Fitzsimmons, and their representatives met in New York to negotiate a match.

Oct 22   Fitz began giving nightly exhibitions at New York's Miner's Bowery Theatre.

| Oct 26 | Ike Williams | New York, NY | EX 3 |
| Oct 29 | Ike Williams | New York, NY | EX |

Fitz also exhibited there on November 3rd. He may have exhibited in Newark, NJ.

In late October, Con Riordan was engaged to be Fitz's sparring partner, and worked with Bob through mid-November.

| Nov 8 | Mike Donovan | New York, NY | EX |

Nov 15   Fitz began sparring in Syracuse with Con Riordan.

| Nov 16 | Con Riordan | Syracuse, NY | EX KO 1 |

Riordan likely weighed 170-180 pounds. Riordan died later that evening. Fitzsimmons was arrested and charged with manslaughter.

| Nov 16 | Joe Dunfee | Syracuse, NY | EX 2 |

Dunfee decked Fitzsimmons and had him badly dazed.

It was reported the day after Riordan's death that Fitz would return to Jacob's Opera House in Syracuse to appear in the afternoon and evening performances, but it is unclear whether this happened.

Fitz arrived in Philadelphia with his new sparring partner, 168-pound Charles Farrell, set to give 3-round exhibitions there for a week.

| Nov 26 | Charles Farrell | Philadelphia, PA | EX |
| Nov 29 | Charles Farrell | Philadelphia, PA | EX |

They boxed in both the afternoon and evening.

Nov 30   Fitz may have sparred 215-pound heavyweight Tom McCarthy in Philadelphia on this date, and possibly on Dec. 1.

Dec 1   This was the last day that Fitz exhibited in Philadelphia.

Fitzsimmons appeared for one week at the Fountain Theater in Cincinnati, Ohio.

| Dec 2 | Tom McCarthy | Cincinnati, Ohio | EX 3 |
| Dec 3 | Tom McCarthy | Cincinnati, Ohio | EX |

In mid-December, Fitzsimmons was exhibiting in Louisville, KY.

| Dec 16 | Tom McCarthy | Louisville, KY | EX 3 |

Dec 23   Upon arriving in Chicago, after learning that the police superintendent was against boxing exhibitions, Bob only gave a bag punching exhibition.

| Dec 24 | Tom McCarthy | Chicago, IL | EX 3 |

The police granted Fitz special permission.

| Dec 24 | George Dawson | Chicago, IL | EX |

These two exhibitions were held at separate locations.

Jan   Fitz continued sparring with Tom McCarthy in Milwaukee, Wisconsin. However, when Fitz dazed him, McCarthy quit and did not finish the engagement.

Jan 19   Fitz arrived in St. Louis, MO to exhibit there for a week, giving 3-round sparring exhibitions.

Jan 28   Fitz was arraigned in New York on the first-degree manslaughter charge.

In late February, Fitz exhibited for a week in Cleveland, Ohio.

Feb 22   Pat Murphy   Cleveland, OH   EX
Murphy was a heavyweight.

Bob was set to meet "Doc" J.E. Paine/Payne of the Cleveland Athletic club on the 23rd, but there was no follow up report. Bob was there at least until the 26th.

Mar 2   John Donnelly   Buffalo, NY   KO 3
Donnelly attempted to last 3 rounds to win $50.

Bob went to Baltimore.

Mar 11   Dan Dwyer   Washington, D.C.   EX
Fitz exhibited for a week in Washington, D.C.

Mar 14   Billy McMillan   Washington, D.C.   EX 3

Apr   Fitz's company gave exhibitions in Hoboken, New Jersey.

Apr 15   Fitz gave exhibitions at a New York theater for one week.

Apr 16   Alfred Allich   New York, NY   KO 3

Apr 19   Mike Connors   New York, NY   KO 1
Connors attempting to last 3 rounds.

Jun 8   Frank Bosworth   New York, NY   EX

Jun 24   Fitz's criminal manslaughter trial began.

Jul 3   The jury acquits Fitzsimmons.

Jul 3   Frank Sullivan   Syracuse, NY   EX
Fitz was knocked down.

Aug 3   Tom Forrest   Philadelphia, PA   EX 4

Bob exhibited in Philadelphia that week with Forrest.

Aug 10   P.J. Griffin   Philadelphia, PA   EX 4

Aug 10   Tom Forrest   Philadelphia, PA   EX

Later that night, Fitz and Corbett got into a scuffle at a local hotel.

Aug 17   Tom Forrest   Buffalo, NY   EX 4

Sep 22   Fitz left NY heading for his training camp in Corpus Christi, TX. His chief sparring partners were Jack Stelzner, Ernest Roeber, and Duncan C. Ross.

Oct 4	Fitz gave an exhibition at his training quarters in Corpus Christi, TX.		

Oct 9	Walter Tymon	Corpus Christi, TX	EX
Oct 15	Duncan C. Ross	Corpus Christi, TX	EX
Oct 15	Jack Stelzner	Corpus Christi, TX	EX

Fitz likely sparred with other company members.

Oct 31	Scheduled Fitz-Corbett fight called off owing to legal restraints.		

Nov 4	Jack Stelzner	Glenwood Park, AR	EX 4

The Fitz party was said to be leaving for a tour through Texas. Bob resided in Texas during December, giving some exhibitions there.

In late December, Fitzsimmons traveled to El Paso, Texas with Jack Stelzner. He exhibited there on Dec 25.

1896

Jan 4   Fitz began active training in the Ochoa building in Juarez, Mexico, just across the border from El Paso. His sparring partners included Jack Stelzner and later William McCoy.

Jan 8   Fitzsimmons hit the bag for one hour and fifteen minutes without stopping. He then immediately sparred Stelzner 6 rounds, hitting the bag between rounds. They then engaged in three Greco-Roman wrestling bouts lasting six minutes (draw), nine minutes (Fitz won the fall) and fifteen minutes (Fitz). Later, Bob went on a bike ride.

Jan 29   Fitz broke Stelzner's nose in the 7th round of their sparring.

Feb 8   Reports were that upon waking, Fitz would play with his pet lion Nero for about an hour. He would next go for a run, usually covering 15 to 20 miles. In the afternoon, he would punch the bag for 20 rounds. He would then spar 4-minute rounds, up to 15 rounds with his several trainers and attendants. The medicine ball was tossed for 20 minutes, and then he would work at the wrist and chest machines. The routine work closed with wrestling bouts.

Feb 17	Will McCoy	Juarez, Mexico	EX
Feb 17	Jack Stelzner	Juarez, Mexico	EX
Feb 21	Peter Maher	Coahuila, Mexico	KO 1

Fight to the finish for World Heavyweight Championship. Weights: Maher 176-180, Fitz 162-165 pounds.

Bob returned to El Paso, and then went to New Orleans for a few days until heading to New York for an engagement there.

Feb 29	Brennan (not Mike)	New York, NY	EX W
Feb 29	Peter Maher	New York, NY	EX 3

Fitz was scheduled to give exhibitions throughout the country, set to exhibit in places like New York, Boston, Philadelphia, Washington, Chicago, and Pittsburg.

April 6-9   Fitz exhibited with middleweight Dan Hickey in Pittsburg, PA.

April 13	Dan Hickey	Cleveland, OH	EX

They exhibited in both the afternoon and evening.

Fitz and Hickey exhibited for six days in Cleveland, OH. Their final two matinee and evening exhibitions took place on the 18th.

May 27   Accompanied by sparring partners Ernest Roeber and Dan Hickey, Fitzsimmons set sail for England. He was set to tour Great Britain giving exhibitions. Bob would punch the ball or bag, and spar and/or wrestle a few rounds with Hickey and/or Roeber.

Aug 22   Fitzsimmons arrived back in America.

Sep 12   Corbett and Fitz agree to fight in March 1897.

Nov 11   Fitz begins training in Sausalito, CA for his upcoming match against Tom Sharkey. On that day, Bob ran in the morning, and later sparred Dan Hickey 6 rounds. He generally ran 10-15 miles, hit the bags, sparred, and swam. He sometimes rowed a boat.

Nov 20   Bob boxed 6 rounds with one of his sparring partners.

Nov 22   Bob punched the bag for 6 rounds and then sparred 3 rounds with Dan Hickey and 3 more with Jack Stelzner.
Nov 25   At his training quarters in Sausalito, CA, Fitz took on Captains McKinnon, Richardson, Moulton, and Pritchard, one stepping in to replace the other after a knockdown. Bob made them all quit in 3 minutes and 15 seconds.

Dec 2   Tom Sharkey   San Francisco, CA   LDQ by 8
Scheduled 10 rounds. Weights: Sharkey 175-182, Fitz 172-173 ½ pounds.
Fight may well have been fixed. Earp disqualified Fitz for a low blow which most claimed was legal.

Dec 3   Dan Hickey   San Francisco, CA   EX 4

It was said that Fitz would punch the bag and spar 3 rounds each with Jack Stelzner and Dan Hickey in both the afternoon and evening on December 6 at the Chutes, and would demonstrate the knockout blows.

Fitz was scheduled to box at the Chutes with Stelzner and Hickey again on December 13.

Dec 17   Fitz and Corbett agree to fight on March 17.

Fitz was scheduled to head east on the 21st, on the way giving exhibitions in Denver, Cripple Creek and other places over the next three weeks before arriving in New York.

Dec 25   Dan Hickey   Cripple Creek, CO   EX 4

Fitzsimmons was in Denver on the 26th and 27th before heading to Omaha, NE.

1897

Jan 25   Fitz began active conditioning training in New York for the upcoming Corbett fight.

Feb 5   It was reported that Bob had been running 12 miles a day, and just added bag punching to his routine.

Feb 8   This would be the first real hard day of training for Fitz. He was scheduled to run 12 miles, box 8 rounds with middleweight Dan Hickey, wrestle 15 minutes with then 217-pound Ernest Roeber, and punch the bag with dumbbells in each hand.

Feb 10   Fitzsimmons left New York via railroad, traveling with manager Martin Julian, and sparring partners Dan Hickey and Ernest Roeber. They were to stop at Omaha, Denver, Salt Lake City, and Colorado locations such as Pueblo, Colorado Springs, and Leadville to give exhibitions of sparring, wrestling, and bag punching, before arriving in Nevada about February 18.

They stopped in Chicago on the 11th. They were in Omaha on February 12.

Feb 13	Dan Hickey	Pueblo, CO	EX
Feb 13	Ernest Roeber	Pueblo, CO	EX
Feb 14	Dan Hickey	Denver, CO	EX 3
Feb 15	Dan Hickey	Colorado Springs, CO	EX
Feb 16	Dan Hickey	Leadville, CO	EX
Feb 17	Dan Hickey	Glenwood Springs, CO	EX

Fitz also wrestled twice that day with Ernest Roeber.

Feb 18	Ernest Roeber	Salt Lake City, UT	EX

10 min. Greco-Roman wrestling.

Feb 18	Dan Hickey	Salt Lake City, UT	EX 3

Feb 20   Fitz arrived at his training camp at Cook's Ranch, three miles south of Carson City, NV. He ran three miles.

Feb 23   Fitz ran about five miles in the morning. In the afternoon, he worked the wrist and pulley machines. He then boxed with Hickey in spirited fashion for seven minutes. He then engaged in stand-up wrestling with Roeber.

Feb 24   Fitz did a 10-mile run in the morning. Later, he punched the bag for a round, boxed Roeber, Hickey, and Jack Stelzner 1 round each, and then went through that rotation twice more, boxing each man 3 rounds apiece.

Feb 25   Fitz continued his daily training regimen. He ran about 7 miles and sparred with his trainers for about an hour.

Feb 26   Fitz went for a 10-mile morning run. In the afternoon, he hit the punching bag, and then sparred with Roeber, Hickey, and Stelzner, boxing 3 rounds with each man.

Feb 27   Bob chopped wood for an hour and juggled the head of a sledgehammer. He also boxed with Hickey and Stelzner in the morning. In total, his morning work lasted 2 hours. In the afternoon, Bob hit the bag for 12 rounds, and then sparred 3 rounds each with Hickey, Roeber, and Stelzner, winding up with a wrestling bout with Roeber.

Feb 28   Fitz did no training, for it was a day of rest.

Mar 1   Bob first ran 6 miles - 21 minutes out to Carson (3 miles), took a dip in the warm springs, and then ran 20 minutes back (another 3 miles). Following that, he wrestled with Roeber, punched the bag for 20 minutes, and then sparred a few rounds with Hickey and Stelzner. Another report said that Fitz punched the bag for 50 minutes and sparred and wrestled 12 rounds, that his work lasted two hours.

Mar 2   Bob did some running in the morning. In the afternoon, he hit the bag for 14 rounds. He then wrestled with Roeber and sparred with Hickey and Stelzner.

Mar 3   In the morning, Bob took a 4-mile run. In the afternoon, instead of sparring or hitting the bag, he took another run, which included the local hills.

Mar 4   In the morning, Fitzsimmons ran between 8 and 10 miles. In the afternoon, he hit the swinging ball for 10 rounds, using a different form of hitting each round. Working with his three sparring partners, Bob boxed four-minute rounds with only 30 seconds rest between rounds. The afternoon's work lasted an hour and a half.

Mar 5   In the morning, Fitz ran about 6 miles. In the afternoon, Fitz wrestled with his trainers; going 3 rounds with each, for 9 rounds total. He then punched the bag for 10 rounds.

Mar 6   In the morning, Fitzsimmons ran and played a few games of handball. He took a rest from sparring, although he punched the bag a little.

Mar 7   Bob "loafed around the hills," worked the bag for a few rounds and played handball for about an hour. He usually took it easier on Sundays.

Mar 8   Bob played handball for an hour, hit the bag for 12 rounds, wrestled for an hour with Hickey and Roeber, and ran 6 miles.

Mar 9   Fitz's training included three hours of hill climbing in the morning. He played some handball, then devoted 40 minutes to bag punching, wrestled with Roeber, and then boxed 8 rounds each with Hickey and Stelzner.

Mar 10   Corbett and Fitzsimmons allegedly crossed paths while doing their roadwork. Bob ran 10 miles. One source said Bob sparred only 4 rounds with Hickey, punched the bag, and tossed a handball for 30 minutes. Another source said he boxed with Hickey and Stelzner and punched the bag for a short time, but it was a short day.

Mar 11   Fitz said that he ran 10 miles in the morning. Afterwards, he hit the bag for 10 rounds and sparred 4 rounds with Hickey. In the afternoon, he ran into Carson and returned the same way.

Mar 12   One source said that Fitzsimmons biked 14 miles in the morning. He boxed with Hickey, Roeber, and Stelzner, and Bob worked short punches in the clinches. Another source said Bob ran 8 miles and boxed with Hickey and Stelzner. Bob said he ran 10 miles in the afternoon.

Mar 13   Bob sparred both Hickey and Roeber, hit the bag, and played a few games of handball. The sources disagree on the details of what he did that day – sparring either 3 or 4 rounds with each man, bag punching for either 10 or 14 rounds, and then running 12 miles, or two separate runs of 5 and 6 miles, or simply just walking into town.

Mar 14   Fitzsimmons' training was very light. He only went for a short run in the morning of about 4 miles. He was scheduled to take a short run the next day and hit the bag a little, and do practically nothing the day before the fight.

Mar 15   Corbett and Fitz passed one another again during their roadwork, but did not speak. Bob said he would rest on the 16th, except for a short jog. One source said that Fitz ran with his dog for 30 minutes, hit the punching bag, and sparred with Roeber, Hickey, and Stelzner for about 30 minutes, giving them some hard hits. He did nothing in the afternoon.

Mar 16   One source said that Fitz did no work at all other than taking a short two-mile run. Another source said that Fitz wrestled with Roeber for a bit, then hit the bag and sprinted around the yard a few times, and followed with a little road work.

Mar 17   James J. Corbett   Carson City, NV   KO 14
World Heavyweight Championship fight to the finish. Weights: Corbett 183-188, Fitz 157 ½ - 170. Reported weights for Fitzsimmons widely vary.

Mar 21   Jack Stelzner   San Francisco, CA   EX 4

Mar 21   Dan Hickey   San Francisco, CA   EX

It was said that Bob would remain in San Francisco for a few days to give exhibitions before heading to New York.

The Fitz party left San Francisco for the east on March 28, planning to give exhibitions on the way. Bob was set to exhibit with Roeber at Ogden and Salt Lake City, Utah. Another report said that he would make three stops on the way to New York, including one in Denver.

Mar 31   Ernest Roeber   Salt Lake City, UT   wrestling ex

Mar 31	Dan Hickey	Salt Lake City, UT	EX 3
Apr 2	Dan Hickey	Denver, CO	EX 4
Apr 3	Dan Hickey	Omaha, NE	EX 3

Apr 13   Fitz arrived back in New York.

May 3   Fitz took part in a benefit held in New York. Fitz was fulfilling an engagement at a Brooklyn theater that week.

Fitz was seen in Baltimore, MD.

May 24	Dan Hickey	New York, NY	EX 3

Some secondary sources report that on June 5, 1897 in Colorado, Fitz knocked out in the 2nd round an unknown named Leadville Blacksmith. However, the local *Leadville Herald Democrat* does not confirm this. Bob likely remained on the east coast.

Jul 5   The Brooklyn, NY police prevented the scheduled 6-round bout with John L. Sullivan. Instead, Fitz engaged in a wrestling bout with Ernest Roeber.

Sep 14	James Murphy	Wilmington, DE	EX 3
Oct 10	Jim or Mike Dempsey	Cincinnati, OH	EX KO 1
Oct 10	Ernest Roeber	Cincinnati, OH	EX 3

Bob continued exhibiting that week in Cincinnati. While Bob was still in Cincinnati, heavyweight Mike Conley, the Ithaca Giant, signed a contract to act as Fitz's sparring partner. It was said that he would box with Bob during his Cincinnati engagement and would go on the road with him.

Oct 18	Mike Conley	Indianapolis, IN	EX

Fitzsimmons, along with a variety and athletic company, began a four-night engagement at the Indianapolis Grand Opera House. The performance was to be repeated every night, and there would also be a Wednesday matinee.

The specialty company continued touring around. In early November, they were in Louisville, KY.

Nov 14	Mike Conley	Kansas City, MO	EX

They sparred in the afternoon and evening that week in Kansas City.

Nov 22	Mike Conley	Topeka, KS	EX 3 or 4

Conley knocked a tooth out of Bob's mouth.

They were in Topeka for a two-night engagement.

Dec 19	Charles Lawler	Chicago, IL	EX 3

1898

Fitzsimmons began performing in the play, *The Honest Blacksmith*.

Significant subsequent bouts included:

1899

FItz trained for the Jeffries fight with Yank Kenny, Dan Hickey, and Jack Everhardt.

| Jun 9 | James J. Jeffries | Coney Island, NY | LKO by 11 |

World Heavyweight Championship. Fitz age 36.

| Oct 28 | Geoff/Jeff Thorne | Chicago, IL | KO 1 |

1900

| Mar 27 | Jim Daly | Philadelphia, PA | KO 1 |

| Apr 30 | Ed Dunkhorst | Brooklyn, NY | KO 2 |

Fitz trained for the Ruhlin and Sharkey fights with Bob Armstrong, Jeff Thorne, Dan Hickey, and George Dawson.

| Aug 10 | Gus Ruhlin | New York, NY | KO 6 |

| Aug 24 | Tom Sharkey | Brooklyn, NY | KO 2 |

1901

Jun?   In Boston, Fitz did some sparring with the 220-pound heavyweight, Sandy Ferguson, who quit as a result of the punishment.

Jul 9   Fitz lost a Greco-Roman wrestling match to Gus Ruhlin in New York.

Dec 14?   Fitz and Tom Sharkey boxed 5 friendly rounds wearing 8-ounce gloves in a 15-foot ring at the Theatrical Business Men's Athletic Club at 139 West Forty-First Street (in New York?).

1902

Mar   Bob sparred with Gus Ruhlin.

May   Bob sparred 3 rounds with Jim Corbett in New York.

May-Jul   Bob sparred with Hank Griffin, Soldier Tom Wilson, and George Dawson in preparation for the Jeffries bout.

| Jul 25 | James J. Jeffries | San Francisco, CA | LKO by 8 |

World Heavyweight Championship. Fitz was 39 years old.

| Aug 9 | Hank Griffin | Los Angeles, CA | EX 3 |
| Aug 9 | unnamed opponent | Los Angeles, CA | EX 3 |

Dec   Fitz toured the country with James J. Jeffries, giving sparring exhibitions together.

| Dec 14 | James Jeffries | Spokane, WA | EX |

| Dec 20 | Jack Stewart | Butte, MT | KO 1 |

| Dec 22 | James Jeffries | Anaconda, MT | EX |

| Dec 27 | Mike Ranke | Bozeman, MT | KO 2 |

| Dec 30 | James Jeffries | Pocatello, ID | EX |

1903

Jan   Fitz and Jeffries exhibited in places like St. Joseph and Kansas City, Missouri.

Feb   Fitz and Jeffries exhibited Springfield and St. Louis, Indianapolis, Louisville, and other places on their way east.

Feb 6	James J. Jeffries	Paducah, KY	EX
Feb 12	George Weikel	Evansville, IN	EX 3
Feb 12	James Jeffries	Evansville, IN	EX
Mar 2	James Jeffries	Philadelphia, PA	EX 3
Mar 3	James Jeffries	Chester, PA	EX 3
Mar 4	James Jeffries	Philadelphia, PA	EX

Jul 31   Fitzsimmons began training and sparring with Jeffries, preparing James for his upcoming fight with Jim Corbett.

| Sep 30 | Con Coughlin | Philadelphia, PA | KO 1 |
| Oct 14 | Joe Grim | Philadelphia, PA | ND 6 |

Fitz dropped Grim nine times.

Fitz trained and sparred with Joe Kennedy and Sam Berger to prepare for the Gardner fight.

| Nov 25 | George Gardner | San Francisco, CA | W 20 |

World Light Heavyweight Championship. Fitz age 40.

1904

| Feb 27 | George Dawson | Chicago, IL | EX 4 |
| Jul 23 | "Philadelphia" Jack O'Brien | Philadelphia, PA | ND 6 |

1905

| Dec 20 | "Philadelphia" Jack O'Brien | San Francisco, CA | LKO by 13 |

Fitz 42 years old.

1906

| Jan 31 | Charles Haghey | Webster, MA | KO 4 |

1907

| Mar 7 | Tony Ross | New Castle, PA | EX 4 |
| Jul 17 | Jack Johnson | Philadelphia, PA | LKO by 2 |

Fitz age 44.

| Sep 21 | Jim/Jean Paul | NY | KO 1? |

1909

Bob gave a series of exhibitions in Nov and Dec in Australia.

| Dec 18 | Tommy Burns | Sydney, Australia | EX 4 |
| Dec 27 | Bill Lang | Sydney, Australia | LKO by 12 |

Fitz age 46.

1914

Jan 29	Bob KO Sweeney	Williamsport, PA	ND 6
Feb 20	Jersey Bellew	Bethlehem, PA	ND 6

Bibliography

Primary sources

Austin Daily Statesman
Baltimore American
Boston Daily Globe
Boston Herald
Boston Post
Brooklyn Daily Eagle
Buffalo Courier
Buffalo Evening News
Carson News
Chicago Daily Inter Ocean
Chicago Daily News
Chicago Herald
Chicago Times
Chicago Tribune
Cincinnati Commercial Gazette
Cincinnati Enquirer
Cincinnati Post
Cleveland Leader
Cleveland Plain Dealer
Daily Alta California (San Francisco)
Daily Arkansas Gazette (Little Rock)
Daily True American (Trenton, New Jersey)
El Paso Daily Herald
El Paso Daily Times
Every Evening Wilmington Daily Commercial
Freeman's Journal (Dublin)
Indianapolis News
Kansas City Star
Leadville Herald Democrat
Los Angeles Express
Los Angeles Times
Louisville Courier-Journal
Minneapolis Tribune
Morning Oregonian
National Police Gazette
Nevada State Journal (Reno)
Newark Daily Advertiser
Newark Evening News

New Orleans Daily Picayune
New Orleans Times-Democrat
New York Clipper
New York Evening Telegram
New York Herald
New York Journal
New York Sun
New York Tribune
New York World
Omaha Daily Bee
Paterson Evening News
Philadelphia Inquirer
Philadelphia Press
Philadelphia Public Ledger
Philadelphia Record
Pittsburg Press
Pittsburgh Post
Providence Evening Bulletin
Providence Journal
Reno Evening Gazette
Rocky Mountain News
St. Louis Daily Globe-Democrat
St. Louis Post-Dispatch
St. Louis Republic
St. Paul Pioneer Press
Salt Lake Herald
San Antonio Daily Express
San Francisco Bulletin
San Francisco Chronicle
San Francisco Evening Post
San Francisco Examiner
San Francisco Morning Call
Sausalito News
Scranton Times
Sydney Bulletin
Sydney Daily Telegraph
Sydney Morning Herald
Sydney Referee
Sydney Tribune
Timaru Herald
Topeka Daily Capital
Washington Post
Wilmington Evening Journal
Winnipeg Free Press

Secondary sources

Mike Attree, http://www.fitzsimmons.co.nz/html/facts.html.

Boxrec.com.

Joe Choynski, *I Fought 'Em All*, published in *Fight Stories*, v3 #5, October 1930, (Fiction House, 1930).

James J. Corbett, *The Roar of the Crowd*, (N.Y.: G.P. Putnam's Sons, 1925).

Cyberboxingzone.com.

Robert H. Davis, *Ruby Robert* (N.Y.: George H. Doran Co., 1926).

Armond Fields, *James J. Corbett: A Biography of the Heavyweight Boxing Champion and Popular Theater Headliner* (Jefferson, North Carolina: McFarland & Co., 2001).

Robert Fitzsimmons, *Physical Culture and Self-Defense* (London: Drexel Biddle, 1901). Introduction by A.J. Drexel Biddle.

Alexander Johnston, *Ten and Out!* (N.Y.: Ives Washburn, 1927).

Gilbert Odd, *The Fighting Blacksmith* (London: Pelham Books Ltd., 1976).

Christopher Tobin, *Fitzsimmons: Boxing's first triple world champion* (Timaru, NZ: David A. Jack and C.P. Tobin, 1983, 2000).

"Fight of the Century," published by H.S. Crocker Co., San Francisco in 1897.

Nat Fleischer, *Black Dynamite* (U.S.: Nat Fleischer, 1938), volume 1.

Nat Fleischer, *The Heavyweight Championship* (N.Y.: G.P. Putnam's Sons, 1949, 1961).

Rex Lardner, *The Legendary Champions* (N.Y.: American Heritage Press, 1972).

Leo N. Miletich, *Dan Stuart's Fistic Carnival* (College Station: Texas A&M University Press, 1994).

Adam J. Pollack, *In the Ring With James J. Corbett* (Iowa City: Win By KO Publications, 2007).

Adam J. Pollack, *John L. Sullivan: The Career of the First Gloved Heavyweight Champion* (North Carolina: McFarland & Co., 2006).

Acknowledgments

I want to thank all those who were instrumental in assisting me with research, photographs, or promotion:

Randy Essing

Clay Moyle

Cheryl Huyck

Christine Klein

Tracy Callis

Wilmer Fernandez

Nick McBride

Matt Donnellon

Margaret Leask

Daniel Middleton

Alister Scott Ottesen

Stephen Gordon

Jason Simons

Dean Vios

HE Grant

Zachary Daniels

Sergei Yurchenko

McGrain

Marty Mulcahey

Kevin Smith

Dan Cuoco

Michael Hunnicut

Ron Marshall

Tom Gerbasi

Mike DeLisa

Todd Hodgson

Thomas Hauser

Steve Farhood

Pam Barta-Kacena

Amish Trivedi

Mike Attree

Christopher John LaForce

Emily Klinefelter

Cindy Parsons

Joan Parsons

Prizefightingbooks.com

Library of Congress, Prints and Photographs Division

State Library of New South Wales

Cyberboxingzone.com

Boxrec.com

Pugilibri

Eastsideboxing.com

Boxingscene.com

Maxboxing.com

Boxing Digest

Pugilistica.com

Antekeprizering.com

Our-ireland.com

Thesweetscience.com

Boxinginsider.com

Ringsidereport.com

Boxingbiographies.com

University of Iowa Interlibrary Loan Services

University of Iowa Media Services

Prairie Lights bookstore

Michael Pascoe of W & F Pascoe Pty Ltd. (www.pascoe.com.au)

Robert Archer of Gosford Micrographics Pty Ltd. (www.gosmicro.com.au)

Index

www.ingramcontent.com/pod-product-compliance
Lightning Source LLC
Chambersburg PA
CBHW020407100426
42812CB00001B/235